MEDICINAL PLANTS FROM THE EAST

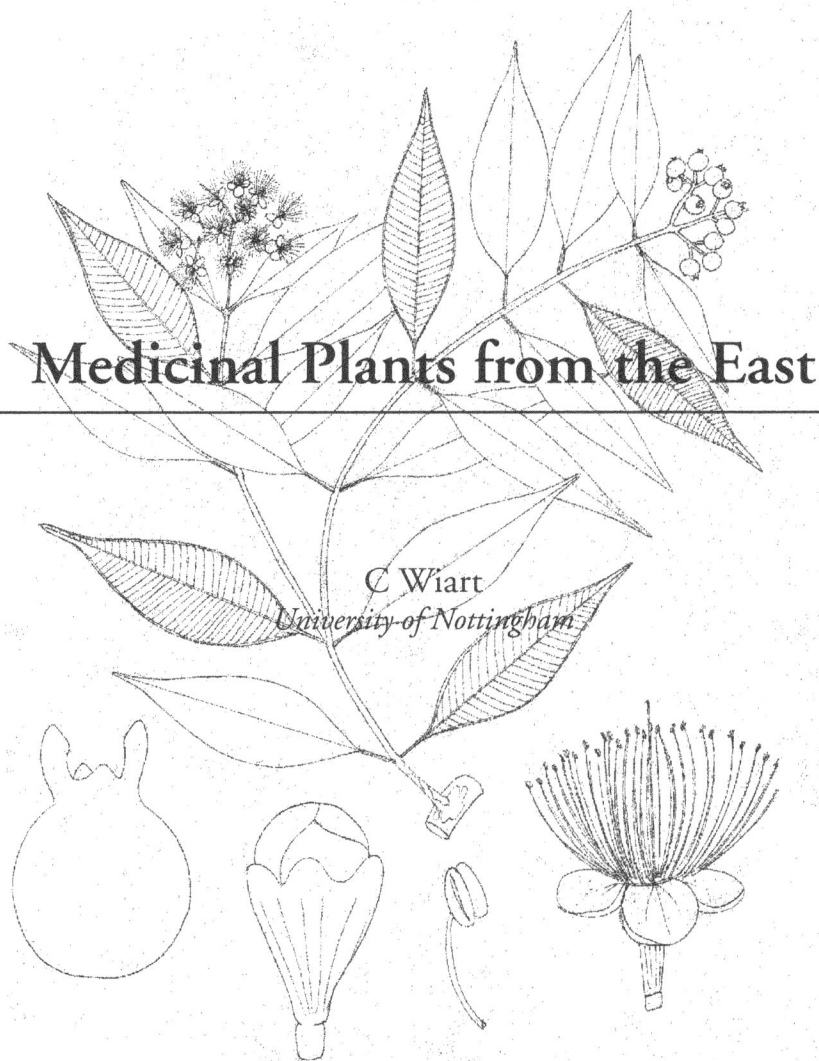

Medicinal Plants from the East

C Wiart
University of Nottingham

Nottingham
University Press

First published by Nottingham University Press

This reissued original edition published 2023 by 5m Books Ltd www.5mbooks.com

British Library Cataloguing in Publication Data
Medicinal Plants from the East
Wiart, Christophe

ISBN 9781789182910

Disclaimer

Every reasonable effort has been made to ensure that the material in this book is true, correct, complete and appropriate at the time of writing. Nevertheless the publishers, the editors and the authors do not accept responsibility for any omission or error, or for any injury, damage, loss or financial consequences arising from the use of the book.

Typeset by Nottingham University Press, Nottingham
EU GPSR Authorised Representative
LOGOS EUROPE, 9 rue Nicolas Poussin, 17000, LA ROCHELLE, France
E-mail: Contact@logoseurope.eu

Foreword

In this magnificent volume Christophe Wiart has both characterized and classified medicinal plants from the East from a drug discovery perspective. In so doing he has created a comprehensive reference source that provides cross-disciplinary researchers with a novel blueprint for the discovery of chemical entities for the ultimate creation of much needed new medicines.

This specialist volume details 290 medicinal plant species from areas as diverse as East Africa to Western USA; importantly it comprehensively correlates their botany, ethnomedicine, natural product chemistry and biosynthesis, pharmacological properties and pharmaceutical potential. From this work of scholarship it is clear that the forests of the East provide a unique natural resource for the investigation of new drug molecules. This treatise is of course most timely; the future of this delicate environment is not guaranteed and concerted action is required to preserve it for future generations. Ralph Waldo Emerson said that "the Earth laughs in flowers", let's hope that it retains its sense of humour.

The University of Nottingham's School of Pharmacy has a longstanding interest in the study of drugs from plants. This dates back originally to George Trease who was the Head of School and Professor of Pharmacognosy from 1943-1967. Our tradition, of course, embraces the work of Barrie Bycroft, Paul Dewick and many other academic colleagues. This strategic focus has been redoubled through the establishment of the School at the University's campus at Semenyih, providing us with a direct presence in the East and importantly a co-location with the actual forests that hold such untapped potential. It is an area that we have targeted to invest in the future and we look forward to the significant benefits to humanity that will arise from this important work.

Professor Saul J B Tendler
Head of School
School of Pharmacy
The University of Nottingham
Nottingham NG7 2RD
United Kingdom

Contents

To my mother Flora Monllor, my father Patrice Wiart, to my wife Mazdida Sulaiman-Wiart, and to my little fellows: Adam, Pierre and Camilla

Introduction

Today, most scientists looking for drugs from plants walk in the dark and ask themselves several questions such as "What plant shall I study and why? Where should I go into? If I am looking for a drug for AIDS or cancer what plant, or plant group should I investigate? Where can I find it? Why is a plant medicinal or poisonous?" To find drugs from plants so far, some massive screening programs have been undertaken, thousands of plants have been tested randomly and, by luck, sometimes a couple of drugs have been found. But this was enormously time consuming and has wasted billions of US dollars. The purpose of this book is to provide to the readers a comprehensive and complete compendium of medicinal plants from the East which will provide them with a logical concept to be used as a compass for the discovery of drugs. After reading this book the reader will be able to go straight to the plant or plant family to find the type of drug he or she is looking for. The aim of the book is to demonstrate that the discovery of a drug from a plant does not depend on luck but can be logically explained, achieved and even foreseen by knowing its botanical and ethnomedicinal background. The plants are introduced in the book according to their subclass, family, and order, with reference to the general pharmacological and chemical profiles in these botanical groups. This allows the reader to understand and even predict the pharmaceutical potentials of the plant mentioned, and to some extent of any flowering plants. This type of presentation gives a logical overview demonstrating that pharmacological properties depend on botanical classification. The coverage of the book is quite broad and opens doors of consciousness in the discovery of drugs from plants by logically correlating botany, ethnomedicine, natural product chemistry, pharmacological properties and pharmaceutical potentials of 290 medicinal plant species from the East. Most of these plants have not been studied for pharmacology and the book offers to the reader a wealth of plant material waiting to be investigated for their active principles. Note that some of these plants might disappear within the next few decades hence the urge to bring attention to these specimens. The book is illustrated with original botanical plates made by myself, and several chemical structures. It is an asset of research opportunities that names, classifies, identifies and even locates some plants most of which have not been studied for pharmacology. The geographical area covered ranges from East Africa, India, Sri Lanka, Bangladesh, Nepal, Burma, Laos, Vietnam, Cambodia, Thailand, Korea, Malaysia, Indonesia, China, Japan, Taiwan, the Philippines, Papua New Guinea, Australia, the Pacific Islands, and Hawaii to the US. The scientific names are provided for each plant, with complete synonym, occasionally basionym, and vernacular names (English and numerous local languages), providing the reader with a strong, reliable and accurate set of data to identify the plant (in most books, synonyms are missing, which misleads academicians in their research activities and compromises their research credibility). The etymology of the scientific name of each plant is provided. Many of these plants have not been studied and the readers may use the plants listed in the book as a reference material to start new research projects or to apply for grants or to start international research collaborative programs. The book may even be used as a field guide for plant collection. The book provides clear and precise, professionally and personally made, botanical plates for each plant, most of them illustrated for the first time and perhaps the last. Details on flowers, fruits, leaves, even anthers are given. Each plate has been made carefully and provides all possible details. None of these plates have ever been published before. Each botanical plate is provided with a set of information including the origin of the herbarium, the location of the plant, the name of the plant collector and the date of collection plus some field notes including ecological data. A reader may travel and use the book to find a plant as the location is often very accurate. The book provides exhaustive information on the medicinal use of each plant, country by country with lists of diseases which are cured by these plants (no claims are made). The paragraph on medicinal uses is followed by a section on pharmacological activity which has three purposes:

- First showing if the plant has been studied for chemistry or pharmacology or not, and quite often, nothing has been done on it. The chemical structure of the active constituent is provided. If nothing has been published on the pharmacology or chemistry of the plant, the section can provide some hypothesis on the pharmacological basis of ethnomedical activity based on chemotaxonomy and pharmacology of neighboring species, genus or order.

- Second, explaining the "why" of the medicinal uses or toxicity of the plant. This section explains the pharmacological mechanisms responsible for the medicinal properties of each plant.

- Third, advising the reader on what type of research would be worth being done on the plant. In several instances the plant has not been studied and some tips are given to the reader to go into further research activity (potential candidate for the isolation of active principles: cytotoxic, antiviral, antioxidant, etc....

In summary, this book has to be seen as a tool meant to contribute to the discovery of drugs from medicinal plants from the East.

I thank the many people who have helped me along the way. My wife Mazdida, my colleagues and friends Professor Stephen Doughty, Dr Ting Kang Nee and Mr. Khoo Teng Jin. I wish to thank as well Mrs. Galoh Munawwarah Osman, Mrs. Judy Wong, Mrs. Dian Hafini Yusoff, and Mrs. Siti Zaleha Nasir for scanning the botanical plates of this book.

Christophe Wiart Pharm.D.
The University of Nottingham (Malaysia Campus)

I. Subclass HAMAMELIDAE Takhtajan 1966

The subclass Hamamelidae consists of 11 orders and 24 families and about 3,400 species of plants which are thought to have originated early in the Upper Cretaceous. These are mostly trees, the flowers of which are tiny, packed in spikes, unisexual, with distinct carpels, and adapted to wind pollination. Common secondary metabolites found in the Subclass are tannins and flavonoids.

A.Order DAPHNIPHYLLALES Pull 1951

The order consists of the single family Daphniphyllaceae

1. Family Daphniphyllaceae Muell-Arg. In A. DC. Prodr. 16 (1): 1. 1869 nom conserv., the Daphniphyllum Family

The Family Daphniphyllaceae comprises the single genus Daphniphyllum with about 35 species of euphorbiaceous-like shrubs native to East Asia. The family produces a unique type of triterpenoid alkaloids referred to as the daphniphylline group, as well as tannin. The leaves are simple, alternate and without stipules. The inflorescences are axillary racemes. The calyx is made of 2-6 sepals. The corolla is non-existent. The androecium comprises 5-12 stamens. The gynaecium is made of 2 carpels united to form a compound ovary with 2 locules, each locule containing 2 ovules. The fruits are drupaceous.

An example of ornamental Daphiphyllaceae is *Daphniphyllum macropodum* Miq. In terms of pharmacological potential one could see the alkaloids from the family Daphniphyllaceae as a precious source of complex alkaloids (Kobayashi *et al.*, 2003) the properties of which remain surprisingly unexplored.

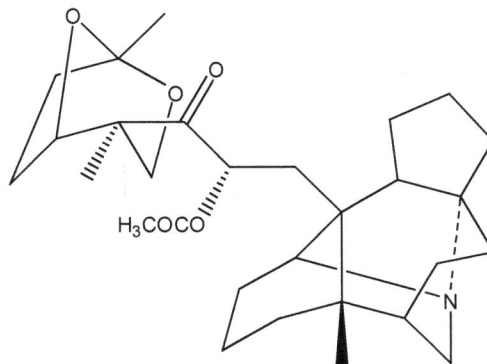

Daphniphylline

Reference: Kobayashi J, Morita H, 2003, The *Daphniphyllum* alkaloids. Alkaloids Chem. Biol.; 60:165-205

Daphniphyllum glaucescens Bl.

[From Greek *daphne* = laurel and *phullon* = leaf and from Latin *glaucescens* = glaucous]

Synonyms: *Daphniphyllum lancifolium* Hk.f., *Daphniphyllum scortechinii* Hk.f.

Description: It is a tree which grows in a geographical area covering Sri Lanka, Southeast Asia, Taiwan and Japan. The stem is terete, glabrous and marked with prominent leaf scars. The leaves are simple, spiral, and without stipules. The petiole is slender, and about 2.5 -5 cm long. The leaf-blade is elliptic, 2.5-8 x 4-18 cm, acute at the apex, leathery, and with about 10 pairs of secondary nerves. The inflorescence is an axillary raceme which is about 3 cm long. The fruits are ovoid, about 1 cm long, the surface uneven with a few knobs, seated on a persistent calyx and topped by prominent twin recurved styles. The fruit is a drupe (Figure 1)

Medicinal uses: In Taiwan, the plant is used to heal ulcers.

Pharmacology: The plant abounds with daphniphylline group alkaloids known as daphniglaucins (Arthur *et al*, 1965, Morita *et al*, 2004, Takatsu *et al.*, 2004). Kobayashi *et al*, (2003) isolated cytotoxic daphniglaucins A and B from the plant

References: Arthur HR, Rosalind PK. Chan, SN, Loo SN, 1965, Alkaloids of *Daphniphyllum calycinum* and *D. glaucescens* of Hong Kong. Phytochemistry; 4: 627-629.

Kobayashi J, Takatsu H, Shen YC, Morita H., 2003, Daphniglaucins A and B, novel polycyclic quaternary alkaloids from *Daphniphyllum glaucescens*. Org Lett.; 15;5:1733-6.

Morita H, Takatsu H, Shen YC, Kobayashi J, 2004, Daphniglaucin C, a novel tetracyclic alkaloid from *Daphniphyllum glaucescens*. Tetrahedron Lett; 45: 901-04.

Takatsu H, Morita H, Shen YC, Kobayashi J, 2004, Daphniglaucins D-H, J, and K, new alkaloids from *Daphniphyllum glaucescens*. Tetrahedron; 60:6279-84.

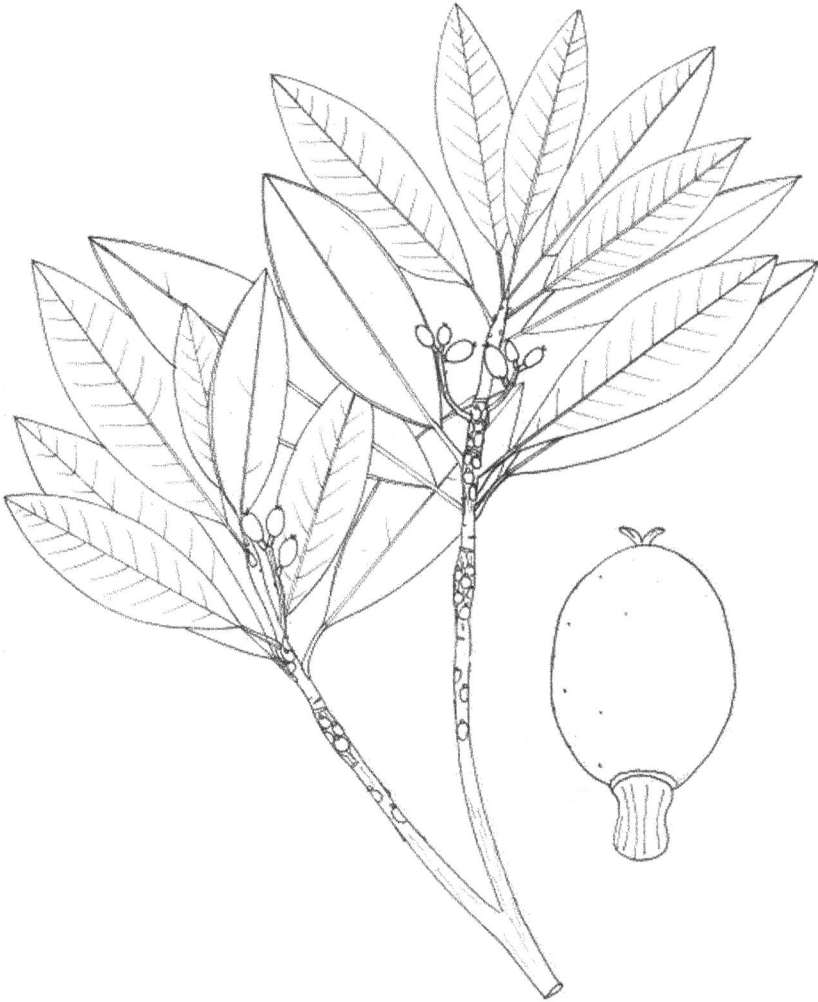

Figure 1: *Daphniphyllum glaucescens* Bl.

B. Order JUGLANDALES Engler 1892

The order Juglandales comprises 2 families of trees: Juglandaceae and Rhoipteleaceae and 60 species.

1.Family JUGLANDACEAE A. Richard ex Kunth 1824 nom. conserv., the Walnut Family

The Family Juglandaceae consists of 8 genera and 60 species of tanniferous trees known to elaborate series of naphthoquinones such as juglone, used as a dye. The leaves are pinnate, and alternate. The inflorescence is a spike of tiny flowers with 4 sepals, 5-40 stamens, with tetrasporangiate and dithecal anthers. The ovary consists of 2 carpels forming a compound ovary partially bilocular with a solitary ovule per locules. The fruit is a winged samaroid nut or drupaceous.

An example of Juglandaceae is *Juglans regia* L. or common walnut. Of recent pharmaceutical interest is pterocarnin A, extracted from the bark of *Pterocarya stenoptera* which inhibits herpes simplex virus type 2 (HSV-2) from attaching and penetrating into cells (Cheng *et al*, 2004). Taxifolin from *Juglans mandshurica* inhibited HIV-induced cytopathic activity against MT-4 cells (Min *et al*, 2002). Traditionally Juglone and other naphthoquinones are known for antibacterial, antifungal, antiviral, insecticidal, anti-inflammatory, and antipyretic properties (Babula *et al*, 2007). *Engelhardtia roxburghiana* Wall. is medicinal in the East and is treated in this section.

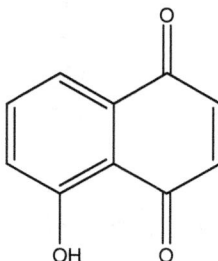

Juglone

References:

Babula P, Adam V, Havel L, Kizek R, 2007, Naphthoquinones and their pharmacological properties. Ceska Slov Farm; 56(3):114-20. Review.

Cheng HY, Lin TC, Yang CM, Wang KC, Lin CC., 2004, Mechanism of action of the suppression of herpes simplex virus type 2 replication by pterocarnin A. Microb. Infect; 6:738-44

Min BS, Lee HK, Lee SM, Kim YH, Bae KH, Otake T, Nakamura N, Hattori M., 2002, Anti-human immunodeficiency virus-type 1 activity of constituents from *Juglans mandshurica*. Arch Pharm Res; 25:441-5.

Engelhardtia roxburghiana Wall.

[After collector Georg Ludwig Engelhard Krebs (1792-1844) and William Roxburgh (1751-1815), Botanist]

Local names: Golden Malay beam, pa'ar (Malaysia)

Synonyms: *Engelhardtia wallichiana* Lindl., *Engelhardtia chrysolepis* Hance

Description: It is a timber tree which grows to 10 m in India, Burma, Cambodia, Laos, Vietnam, Thailand, Malaysia, South China and Taiwan. The bark is brown and fissured. The leaves are compound, and alternate. The rachis is 7-40 cm and bears 2 - 5 pairs of folioles. The petiolule is 0.5-1 cm long. The foliole is 5-20 x 2-5.5 cm, lanceolate, asymmetrical, and acuminate at the apex with 7-15 pairs of secondary nerves. The inflorescence is a panicle of spikes . The flower is minute. The calyx comprises 4 sepals. Male flowers have 10 -12 stamens. The fruit is a globose nut which is 0.3 cm in diameter with 3 lobes which are about 1-2.5 cm long (Figure 2).

Medicinal Uses: The bark is used to stupefy fish in Vietnam and China. In Japan, the plant is used to make a tea.

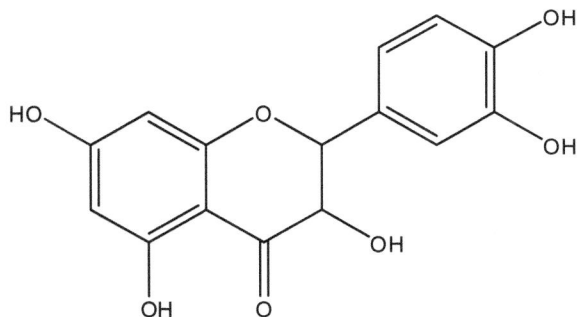

Taxifolin

Pharmacology: The plant contains dihydroflavonol taxifolin and its glycoside, astilbin, which decreased liver cholesterol of rats fed on a cholesterol-free diet and decreased liver phospholipid (Igarashi *et al.*, 1996). These flavonoids inhibited superoxide anion production in the xanthine/xanthine oxidase system, as well as the microsomal lipid peroxidation induced by NADPH-cytochrome P-450 reductase. Taxifolin inhibited mitochondrial lipid peroxidation and protected peroxy radical-damaged mitochondria (Haraguchi *et al*, 1996). Astilbin showed potent inhibition of lens aldose reductase (Haraguchi *et al*, 1996a). It also inhibits lymphocyte functions via reducing matrix metalloproteinase and nitric oxide production (Cai *et al.*, 2003).

Figure 2: *Engelhardtia roxburghiana* **Wall.**

From: Botanical Inventory of Taiwan
Taiwan, Taipei city, Neihu, on the mountain road from Chinlungshih to Vaishuanghsi, in secondary broad leaf forest, 121° 34' 01" North - 25° 06' 04" East. Elevation: 260 m on exposed side beside forest. Collection and identification: Yi-Chung Chen. 22 September 1994.

References: Cai Y, Chen T, Xu Q, 2003, Astilbin suppresses collagen-induced arthritis via the dysfunction of lymphocytes. Inflammation Res; 52: 334-40.

Haraguchi H, Mochida Y, Sakai S, Masuda H, Tamura Y, Mizutani K, Tanaka O, Chou WH, 1996,Protection against oxidative damage by dihydroflavonols in *Engelhardtia chrysolepis*. Biosci Biotechnol Biochem; 60:945-8.

Haraguchi H, Ohmi I, Masuda H, Tamura Y, Mizutani K, Tanaka O, Chou WH, 1996a, Inhibition of aldose reductase by dihydroflavonols in *Engelhardtia chrysolepis* and effects on other enzymes. Experientia; 52:564-7.

Igarashi K, Uchida Y, Murakami N, Mizutani K, Masuda H, 1996, Effect of astilbin in tea processed from leaves of *Engelhardtia chrysolepis* on the serum and liver lipid concentrations and on the erythrocyte and liver antioxidative enzyme activities of rats. Biosci Biotechnol Biochem; 60:513-5.

C.Order Fagales Engler 1892

The order Fagales consists of 3 families and more than 900 species of trees, half of which belonging to the genus *Quercus* (oak). Fagales are mostly North Temperate trees, the tannins of some of which are of pharmaceutical value.

Family FAGACEAE Dumortier 1829 nom. conserv., the Beech Family

The family Fagaceae consists of about 7 genera and 800 species of trees, the main secondary metabolites of which are tannins and flavonoids. *Quercus* (oak), *Castanea* (chestnut) and *Fagus* (beech) are common in the north hemisphere. The wood is hard, dense and valuable as timber. The leaves are simple, alternate, coriaceous, often glossy and serrate or lobate and stipulate. The inflorescences are spikes of tiny unisexual, anemophilous flowers. The male flowers comprise a calyx of 6, small, often reduced sepals and 4 - 40 stamens, the anthers of which are tetrasporangiate, dithecal and opening by longitudinal slits. The female flowers comprises 2 -12 carpels united to form a compound, and inferior ovary containing a pair of axial and pendulous ovules in each locule. The styles are free and numerous. The fruits are acorns or cupules.

A classical example of Fagaceae is *Quercus robur* L., the common European oak. The nuts of *Fagus sylvatica* L. (common beech) are expressed to yield oil. *Castanea sativa* Mill. (sweet or Spanish chestnut) yields timber and a bark used for tanning. The cupules and unripe acorns of *Quercus aegelops* (valonia) are used in tanning. *Quercus suber* yields the commonly used cork, in an industry worth £120 million to Portugal's economy. Galls of *Quercus infectoria*, or Turkish galls, are an important source of tannic acid used in pharmacy. An extract of *Quercus stenophylla* has been marketed for the acceleration of the elimination of renal and urethral calculi. The dried bark from the stems of *Quercus robur* L or *Quercus petraea* (durmast oak) has astringent properties and was formerly used in the form of a decoction as a rectal injection for hemorrhoids and as a gargle, Oak bark (British Pharmaceutical Codex, 1934). Most medicinal Fagaceae are astringent. Of pharmacological interest, is the isolation of a xylan from *Castanea sativa* which inhibited the proliferation of A431 human epidermoid carcinoma cells and inhibited A431 cell migration and invasion (Moine *et al.*, 2007). A crude extract of seeds of *Quercus lusitanica* inhibited the replication of dengue virus type 2 *in vitro* in C6/36 cells (Muliawan *et al.*, 2006).

References: Moine C, Krausz P, Chaleix V, Sainte-Catherine O, Kraemer M, Gloaguen V., 2007, Structural characterization and cytotoxic properties of a 4-O-methylglucuronoxylan from *Castanea sativa*. J Nat Prod; 70:60-6.

Muliawan SY, Kit LS, Devi S, Hashim O, Yusof R, 2006, Inhibitory potential of *Quercus lusitanica* extract on dengue virus type 2 replication. Southeast Asian J Trop Med Public Health; 37 Suppl 3:132-5.

Castanopsis megacarpa Gamble

[From Latin *castanopsis* = chestnut - like and from Greek *megacarpa* = large fruit]

Local name: Malayan chestnut, gertek tangga, berangan berduri (Malaysia)

Description: It is a timber tree which grows to 50 m in the forest of Malaysia. The bark is fissured. The stem is terete, with conspicuous lenticels, hairy at the apex and angled and about 0.4 cm with internodes which are 2-3 cm long. The leaves are simple, spiral and stipulate. The stipules are linear and deciduous. The petiole is rugose with a knob at the base, about 0.7-1.5 cm long, flat above, and hairy when young. The leaf-blade is elliptic, acute at the apex, thinly coriaceous, glossy above, , 9-17 x 5.5-6 cm, recurved at margin, hairy underneath, with 11 to 15 pairs of secondary nerves conspicuous underneath. The midrib is sharply raised underneath. The inflorescences are terminal or axillary slender spikes. The flowers are about 0.2 cm in diameter, and green-yellow. The cupules are large, dark brown, and about 6 x 4 cm and covered with branching thorns which are 1 cm long and 0.2 cm in diameter and covered with a few hairs (Figure 3)

Medicinal Uses: In Malaysia, the nut is eaten as a purgative.

Pharmacology:	The plant has not been studied for pharmacology. Note that a protein isolated from the fruit of *Castanopsis chinensis* exhibited antifungal property against *Botrytis cinerea, Fusarium oxysporum, Mycosphaerella arachidicola,* and *Physalospora piricola* (Chu *et al.,* 2003).
References:	Chu KT, T. B. Ng TB, 2003, Isolation of a large thaumatin-like antifungal protein from seeds of the Kweilin chestnut *Castanopsis chinensis.* Biochem. Biophys. Res. Commun.; 301: 364-70.

Figure 3: *Castanopsis megacarpa* **Gamble**

From: Flora of Malaya No 01426
Malaysia, Negeri Sembilan state, Kolam Sungai Beringin. Collection and identification: Mohd. Kassim. Date of collection: 27 August 1973.

D. Order Casuarinales Lindley 1833

The order Casuarinales consists of the single family Casuarinaceae

Family Casuarinaceae R. Brown in Flinders 1814 nom. conserv., the She-oak Family

The family Casuarinaceae consists of the genus *Casuarina* with about 50 species of pine tree-like trees or shrubs. The main secondary metabolites found in this family are proanthocyanidins, ellagitannins, ellagic acid and other phenolic substances. Note that pyrrolizidine alkaloids have been found in the family. The leaves are small and scale-like. The flowers are small, without perianth, male or female in aments or head-like inflorescences. The androecium consists of a single stamen, the anther of which is tetrasporangiate and dithecal. The gynaecium consist of a bi-carpelled pistil with 2 styles, each with a long decurrent stigma. The fruit is 1-seeded, winged in a woody syncarp.

To date the pharmacological potential of this family is unexplored. Note that ellagitannins such as casuarinin are known to be cytotoxic (Kashiwada *et al.*, 1992), apoptotic (Kuo *et al*, 2005), anti-oxidant (Chen *et al*, 2004), antiviral (Cheng *et al*, 2002), *Casuarina equisetifolia* L and *Casuarina sumatrana* Jungh. Ex de Vriese are medicinal in the East.

References: Cheng HY, Lin CC, Lin TC., 2002, Antiherpes simplex virus type 2 activity of casuarinin from the bark of *Terminalia arjuna* Linn. Antiviral Res; 55(3):447-55.

Chen CH, Liu TZ, Kuo TC, Lu FJ, Chen YC, Chang-Chien YW, Lin CC., 2004, Casuarinin protects cultured MDCK cells from hydrogen peroxide-induced oxidative stress and DNA oxidative damage. Planta Med; 70:1022-6.

Kashiwada Y, Nonaka G, Nishioka I, Chang JJ, Lee KH, 1992, Antitumor agents, 129. Tannins and related compounds as selective cytotoxic agents. J Nat Prod; 55:1033-43.

Kuo PL, Hsu YL, Lin TC, Chang JK, Lin CC., 2005, Induction of cell cycle arrest and apoptosis in human non-small cell lung cancer A549 cells by casuarinin from the bark of Terminalia arjuna Linn. Anticancer Drugs;16:409-15.

Casuarina equisetifolia L.

[From Malay *kesuari* = *Casuarina* species and Latin *equisetum* = horsetail]

Local names:	Beach sheoak, Australian oak; tinyu (Burma), sohn talay (Thailand), agoho (Philippines), pokok ru (Malaysia), kasa (Sri Lanka), savukku (India)
Synonym:	*Casuarina litorea* ex Forsberg & Sachet
Description:	It is a buttressed tree which grows to 20 m in sandy areas and along the seashore of East Africa, Madagascar, India, Malaysia, Indonesia, the Philippines, Australia and Polynesia. The plant is often cultivated as a coastal ornamental. The bark is thick, cracked, flaky and brownish-grayish. The wood is hard and makes an excellent timber. The stem is terete, about 0.3 cm in diameter, with series of 3 bracts, lenticelled, from which develop linear organs which are articulated, with inflated nodes and made of oblong, angled articles which are in fact the leaves. The lenticels of older stems are coffee-bean-like. Each article is about 0.5-0.8 cm long, green and ribbed. The inflorescence of male flowers is a spike which is terminal, and 1-3 cm long with several tiny bracts which are dull green with whitish margin. The stamen is about 0.8 cm long, the anther light brown and the filament white. The inflorescence of female flower is a head which is 2-4 cm long and ellipsoid. The fruit is a syncarp which about 5 x 3 cm, woody, spiny and presents several holes from which drop little winged seeds (Figure 4).
Medicinal Uses:	In India the plant yields an astringent remedy for diarrhoea, dysentery and fatigue. In Malaysia, the plant is used as an astringent and anti-inflammatory, and to heal pimples. In Burma it is used for dysentery. In Indonesia, the plant is used to treat beriberi, colic and dysentery. In the Philippines, the plant is used to promote menses and check mouth bleeding, the wood for tanning.

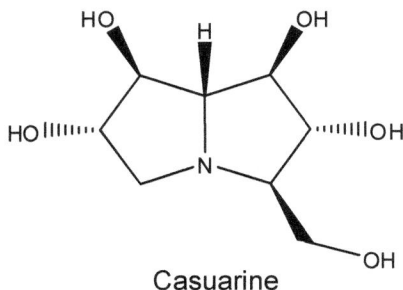

Casuarine

Pharmacology:	The medicinal uses are owed to tannins which abound in the plant such as *d*-gallocatechin, casuarine, probably casuarinin and ellagic acid (Rox *et al*, 1957). The plant contains also a

series of oleanane-type triterpenes (Takahashi *et al.*, 1999) and a pyrrolizidine alkaloid known as casuarine (Nash *et al.*, 1994). Note that Parekh *et al* (2007) measured a broad spectrum of antibacterial activity from the plant. It seems that some pharmacological testing has been done but the data are quite preliminary and the plant needs further investigation for its cytotoxic and antiviral activity.

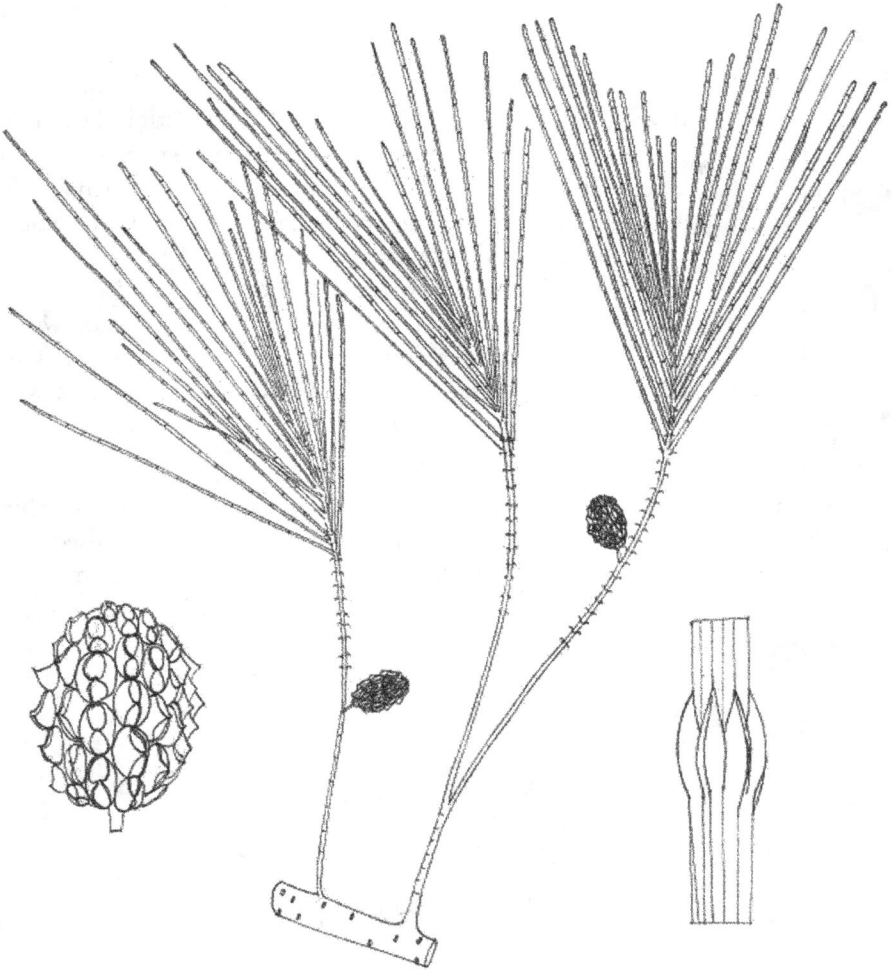

Figure 4: *Casuarina equisetifolia* **L.**

From: Flora of Thailand, Chiang Mai University Herbarium
Thailand, Ranong province, Kaper district, Laem Sohn national park, headquarters, Bahn Bain village area, Muang Gluang subdistrict. Elevation: sea level. Date of collection: 30 November 1996. In open sandy area behind the beach. Collection and identification: JF Maxwell.

References: Nash RJ, Thomas PI, Waigh RD, Fleet GWJ, Wormald MR, de Q. Lilley PM, David J. Watkin DJ, 1994, Casuarine: a very highly oxygenated pyrrolizidine alkaloid. Tetrahedron Lett; 35 2: 7849-7852.

Parekh J, Chanda SV, 2007, *In vitro* Antimicrobial activity and phytochemical analysis of some Indian medicinal plants. Turk J Biol; 31:53-8.

Roux DG, 1957, *d*-Gallocatechin from the Bark of *Casuarina equisetifolia* Linn. Nature; 179:158 - 59

Takahashi H, Iuchi M, Fujita Y, Minami H, Fukuyama Y, 1999, Coumaroyl triterpenes from *Casuarina equisetifolia*. Phytochemistry; 51:543-50.

Casuarina sumatrana Jungh. ex de Vriese

[From Malay *kesuari* = *Casuarina* species and Latin *sumatrana* = from Sumatra]

Local names: Sumatran ru; silinggaun (Malaysia, Sabah), cemara (Indonesia), maribuhok (Philippines), son-pattawia (Thailand).

Synonym: *Gymnostoma sumatranum* (Jungh. ex de Vriese) L.A.S. Johnson, 1982

Description: It is a tree which grows in South-East Asia either wild or cultivated for ornament. The plant can reach 10 m tall. The stem is slender, terete, articulated and consists of articles which are the leaves. Each article is about 0.5 x 0.1 cm, pointed at both ends and grooved. Twigs are needle-like, pale green, 5-40 cm long, articulate, articles 2-6 mm. Leaves reduced, in whorls of 4 tiny scales. Fruit a compound cone-like structure, 2-3 cm in diameter. The inflorescence of male flowers is a spike which is terminal, with several tiny bracts. The inflorescence of the female flower is a head. The fruit is a syncarp which about 6 x 4 cm, woody, spiny and presents several woody beaks which open to release little winged seeds (Figure 5).

Medicinal Uses: In Malaysia, Indonesia and the Philippines the plant is used as astringent remedy for dysentery.

Pharmacology: The plant has not yet been studied for pharmacology.

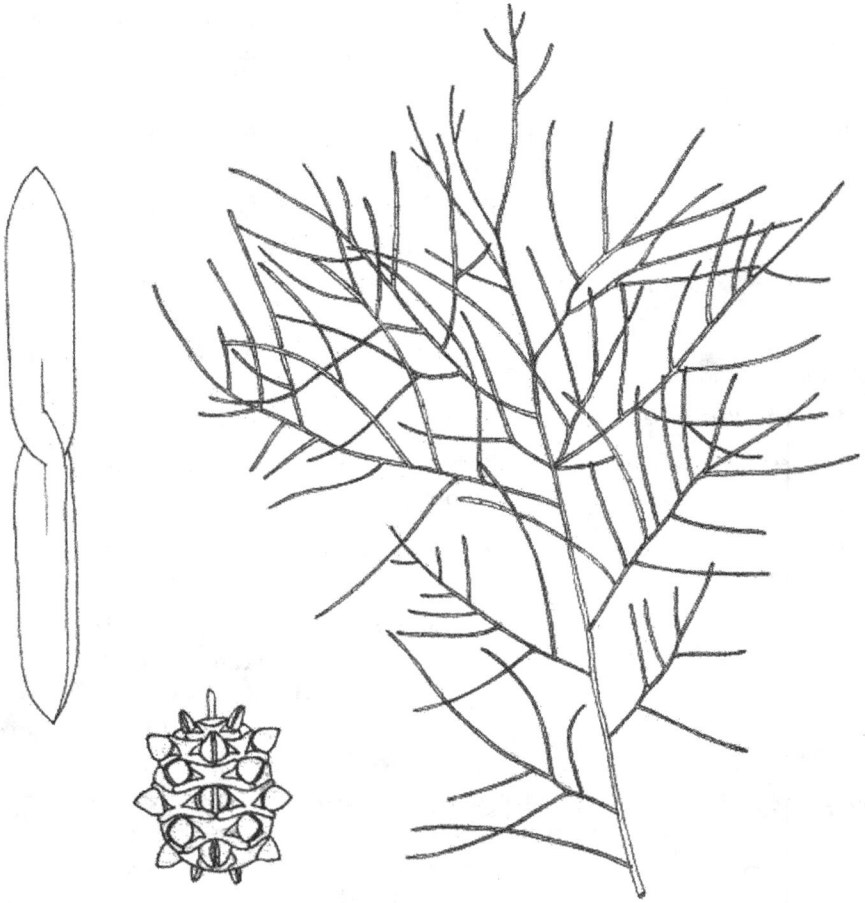

Figure 5: *Casuarina sumatrana* **Jungh. ex de Vriese**

From: Herbarium of Michigan State University. Plants of Borneo
Malaysia, Sabah state, side of bukit Hampuan at Southeast base of Mount Kinabalu, 6° North -
116° 40' East. Elevation: 800 m - 1000m. In dipterocarp forest, ultrabasic geology. Collection
and identification: JH Beaman 7401. Date of collection: 12 November 1972.

II.Subclass ROSIDAE Takhtajan 1966

The Subclass Rosidae regroups 18 orders, 114 families, and about 58,000 species of trees, shrubs, herbs and climbers thought to have originated by development from the subclass Magnoliidae early in the Upper Cretaceous. Several groups of secondary metabolites are known to occur in this family, particularly phenolic and terpenoidic substances including hydrolysable tannins cyanogenetic glycosides, triterpenes, alkaloids and iridoids. The general morphological tendency observed in Rosidae are stipulate leaves, sepals and petals free and inserted on a nectary disc from which develop several stamens initiated in centripetal sequence. The ovary in Rosidae comprises 2 - several locules containing 1 or 2 ovules per locule. Countless plant species from the Rosidae are useful agricultural and pharmaceutical products. The order Rosales is the most archaic order of Rosidae and a common ancestor for all other orders in this Subclass.

A.Order ROSALES Lindley 1833

The order Rosales consists of 24 families and about 6,600 species of herbs, climbers, shrubs and trees which are cosmopolitan which are tanniferous and saponiferous. The family Rosaceae with about 3,000 species, is by far the largest family of this order.

1.Family Pittosporaceae R. Brown in Flinders 1814 nom. conserv., the Pittosporum Family

The family Pittosporaceae consists of 9 genera and about 200 species of tropical bushy trees, best developed in Australia and Tasmania, known to produce triterpenoid saponins, proanthocyanins, and other phenolic compounds. Most species belong to the genus *Pittosporum*. The leaves are simple, alternate, and without stipules. The flowers are solitary or on short cymose inflorescences. The calyx comprises 5 imbricate sepals. The corolla comprises 5 petals which are imbricate, merged at the base, and the androecium shows 5 stamens, alternate with the petals. The gynaecium consists of 2 carpels fused into a compound unilocular ovary containing several ovules attached to parietal placenta. The fruits are berries or dehiscent capsules containing several seeds immersed in a pulp.

A classic example of Pittosporaceae is *Pittosporum tobira* (Thunb.) Ait. (Australia laurel) which is a common ornamental plant in warm temperate region. Another ornamental Pittosporaceae is *Pittosporum viridiflorum* Sims (Cape pittosporum). Of pharmaceutical interest in this are a number of cytotoxic principles including a glycolipid from *Pittosporum tobira* (Thunb.) Ait. which dose-dependently prolonged the survival of mice inoculated with SA 180 and LLC models (Barone *et al.*, 1995). Farnesyl monoglycosides, pancherins A and B from *Pittosporum pancheri* Brongn. and Gris exhibited cytotoxic property against KB cancer cell line cultured *in vitro* (Éparvier *et al.*, 2007).

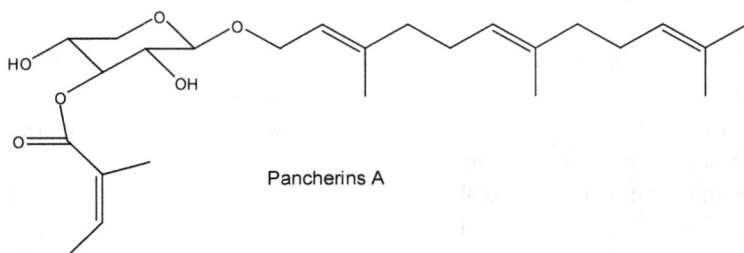

Pancherins A

Reference	Barone B, Salvetti L, Guarnieri D, D'Arrigo C, 1995, *In vivo* antitumor activity of CIDI, a glycolipide from *pittosporum tobira*. Pharmacol Res; 31, Suppl. 1: 137.
	Éparvier V, Thoison O, Bousserouel H, Guéritte F, Sévenet T, Litaudon M, 2007, Cytotoxic farnesyl glycosides from *Pittosporum pancheri*. Phytochemistry; 68: 604-608

Pittosporum ferrugineum Dryand. ex Aiton

[From Greek *pitta* = resin and *sporos* = seeds and from Latin *ferruginea* = rusty red]

Local name:	Pittosporum
Description:	It is a shrub or treelet up to 4 m tall, 4 cm in diameter at the base, and is common near the coast, especially on rocky and sandy shores of Malaysia. The plant has ornamental value. The stem is terete, minutely fissured, and lenticelled, and hairy by the apex. The leaves are simple, subopposite, and exstipulate. The petiole is 2 cm long, slender, channeled and glabrous when mature. The leaf blade is papery, glossy, broadly lanceolate, dark green above, elliptic, 9 x 3.5 cm, the margin is wavy, and the blade shows about 5 to 6 pairs of secondary nerves visible underneath. The inflorescences are axillary and terminal umbel - like clusters which are yellow. The flower pedicels are hairy. The calyx is hairy with 5 sepals which are about 0.1 cm long. The sepals are yellowish green. The petals are whitish cream. The corolla is tubular, yellowish white, 0.5 cm long and develops 5 lobes. The filaments are 0.4 cm long, flattish and whitish, and the anthers are 0.4 x 0.1 cm, and brown. The ovary is greenish and hairy and the stigma is glabrous. The fruits are capsules ripening orange, warty, flattened, 1 cm in diameter, apiculate, splitting into 2 valves to show bright red pulp in which are immersed several little seeds (Figure 6).
Medicinal uses:	The plant is used in Malaysia to break malarial fever. The plant is used to stupefy fish.

Pharmacology: Unknown. The fish poison property mentioned above is quite
                  probably owed to saponins.

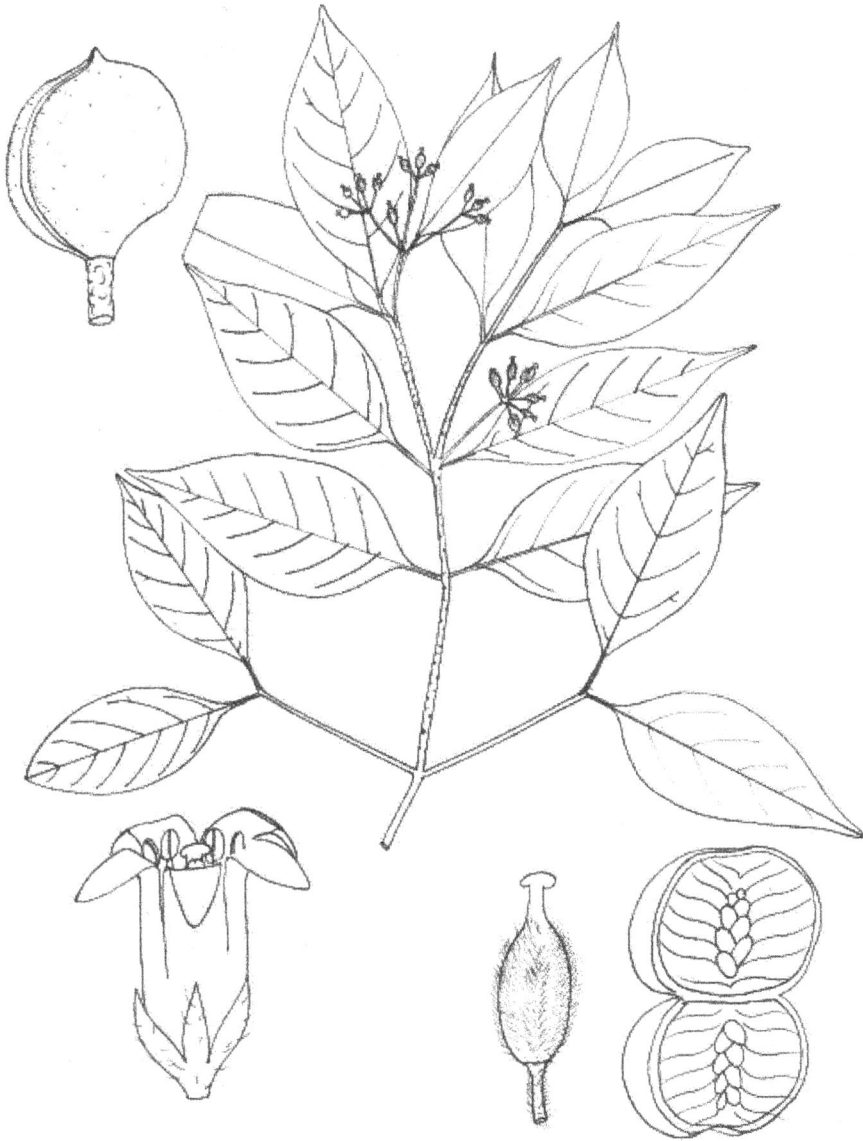

Figure 6: *Pittosporum ferrugineum* **Dryand. ex Aiton**

From: Flora of Thailand, Prince of Songkla University Herbarium
Thailand, Songkla province, Haad Yai district, Klaong Hoy Kong, West of Toong Loong.
Elevation: sea level. Date of collection: 2 October 1985. In shaded thicket on a termite mound
in savannah. Collection and identification: JF Maxwell, Nº 85-932.

2.Family Hydrangeaceae Dumortier 1829 nom. conserv., the Hydrangea Family.

The family Hydrangeaceae consists of 17 genera and 170 species of herbs, climbers, shrubs and treelets widespread in temperate and sub-temperate countries. Common secondary metabolites of this family are tannins, iridoid glycosides, interesting series of quinazoline alkaloids and saponins. The leaves are simple, opposite and without stipules. The leaf blade is often serrate. The inflorescences are cymose. The calyx consists of 4- 5 sepals. The corolla is made of 4 -5 petals which are free. The androecium consists of 2-several times as many stamens as there are petals. The gynaecium consists of 3 -5 carpels united to form a compound plurilocular ovary containing 1-several ovules attached to axile or parietal placenta. The fruit is a dehiscent capsule.

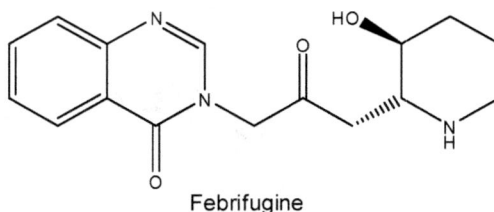
Febrifugine

A common example of Hydrangeaceae is *Hydrangea macrophylla* (big leaf hydrangea) which is a common garden ornamental plant in Europe; note that several varieties exist. Febrifugine and isofebrifugine mixture from *Hydrangea macrophylla* var. Otaksa showed some levels of antiplasmodial activity in mice (Ishih *et al.*, 2003). Thunberginols A, B, and F from *Hydrangea macrophylla* var. *thunbergii* substantially inhibited degranulation by antigen and calcium ionophore A23187, and the release of TNF-alpha and IL-4 by antigen in RBL-2H3 cells (Wang *et al.*, 2007). Hydrangenol from *Hydrangea macrophylla* var. *thunbergii* significantly lowered blood glucose in rodent (Zhang *et al.*, 2007).

References: Ishih A, Miyase T, Ohori K, Terada M., 2003, Different responses of three rodent *Plasmodia* species, *Plasmodium yoelii* 17XL, P. berghei NK65 and *P. chabaudi* AS on treatment with febrifugine and isofebrifugine mixture from *Hydrangea macrophylla* var. Otaksa leaf in ICR mice. Phytother Res; 17:650-6.

Wang Q, Matsuda H, Matsuhira K, Nakamura S, Yuan D, Yoshikawa M., 2007, Inhibitory effects of thunberginols A, B, and F on degranulations and releases of TNF-alpha and IL-4 in RBL-2H3 cells. Biol Pharm Bull; 30:388-92.

Zhang H, Matsuda H, Kumahara A, Ito Y, Nakamura S, Yoshikawa M., 2007, New type of anti-diabetic compounds from the processed leaves of *Hydrangea macrophylla* var. *thunbergii* (Hydrangeae Dulcis Folium). Bioorg Med Chem Lett; 17:4972-6.

Dichroa febrifuga Lour.

[From Latin *dichroa* = two colors and *febrifuga* = that reduce fever]

Local name:	Chang shan (China), gigil (Indonesia), phuck mon (Cambodia), nah come (Thailand), cham chan (Vietnam), baak (India), aseru (Nepal)
Synonyms:	*Adamia chinensis* Gardner & Champ., *Cyanitis sylvatica* Reinw., *Dichroa cyanea* (Wall.) Schltr., *Dichroa sylvatica* (Reinw.) Merr., *Dichroa versicolor* (Fort.) D.R. Hunt
Description:	It is a shrub that grows in a geographical area covering India, Nepal, and the Himalayas to Bhutan, Burma, Thailand, Cambodia, Laos, Vietnam, Malaysia, Indonesia, China, the Philippines and Papua New Guinea. The shrub is somewhat scandent , 2-4 m tall, with a basal diameter of 2-3 cm. the bark is smooth and brown. The stem is terete, fibrous, striated longitudinally, lenticelled, about 0.4 cm in diameter and hairy at the apex. The nodes are marked with a sort of scale or ring which is ciliate. The leaves are simple, opposite and without stipule. The petiole is flattish at the base and clasping, with a few tiny lenticels, channeled, 2-5.5 cm and slender. The leaf blade is elliptic lanceolate, papery, 6-25 cm × 2.5-10 cm, acuminate to caudate at the apex, tapering at the base, margin serrate. The leaf blade shows 8-11 pairs of secondary nerves prominent on both surfaces. The inflorescence is a corymbose panicle with hairy pedicels. The calyx comprises 5-6 lobes. The corolla shows 5 - 6 petals which are blue or white, and oblong-elliptic. The androecium comprises several conspicuous stamens. The fruits are deep blue glossy turning black purple with a sort of ring at the apex. The seeds are minute 0.7 x 0.4 cm (Figure 7).
Medicinal Uses:	In Nepal, Malaysia, Cambodia, Laos, Vietnam, and China the plant is used to treat fever.
Pharmacology:	The plant produces quinazoline alkaloids febrifugine and isofebrifugine which have antimalarial properties (Takaya *et al.*, 1998). Note that febrifugine potentiates host defense in mice against *Plasmodium berghei* NK65 (Murata *et al.*, 1999). Also, it elaborates halofuginone which has been shown to be a potent inhibitor of tissue fibrosis, and has inhibitory effect on fibroblast contractile activity (Tacheau *et al.*, 2007) and inhibition of collagen type I synthesis (Halevy *et al.*, 1996). The plant contains another quinazoline alkaloid which is anti-arrhythmic (Li *et al.*, 1979; Lu *et al.*, 1995, Lu 1999)

Figure 7: *Dichroa febrifuga* Lour.

From: Flora of Thailand, Chiang Mai University Herbarium.
Thailand, Jae Sawn national park, below the summit of Doi Lahn Gah, West side, upper water catchment valley, by 18° 5' North - 99° East. Elevation: 1875 m - 1950 m. Date of collection: 17 December 1996. In shaded to partly open wet primary, evergreen forest. Collection and identification: JF Maxwell N° 96-1659

References:

Halevy, O., Nagler, A., Levi-Schaffer, F., Genina, O. & Pines, M., 1996. Inhibition of collagen type I synthesis by skin fibroblasts of graft versus host disease and scleroderma patients: effect of halofuginone. Biochem Pharmacol; 52: 1057-1063.

Li LQ, Qu ZX, Wang ZM, Zeng YL, Ding GS, Hu GJ,Yang XY, 1979,Studies on a new anti arrhythmic drug changrolin 4-3' 5' bis-n pyrrolidinyl methyl-4'-hydroxyanilino quinazoline. Scientia Sinica; 22: 1220-28.

Lu, LL, Habuchi Y, Tanaka H, Morikawa J, 1995. Electrophysiological effects of changrolin, an anti-arrhythmic agent derived from *Dichroa febrifuga*, on guinea-pig and rabbit heart cells. Clin Expl Pharmacol Physiol; 22: 337-341.

Lu LL., 1999, Effects of changrolin on potassium currents in guinea pig and rabbit single heart cells. Zhongguo Yao Li Xue Bao; 20:1015-8.

Murata K, Takano F, Fushiya S, Oshima Y, 1999, Potentiation by febrifugine of host defense in mice against *plasmodium berghei* NK65. Biochem Pharmacol; 58: 1593-1601.

Tacheau C, Michel L, Farge D, Mauviel A, Verrecchia F, 2007, Involvement of ERK signaling in halofuginone-driven inhibition of fibroblast ability to contract collagen lattices. Eur J Pharmacol; 573(1-3):65-9.

Takaya Y, Chiba T, Tanitsu M, Murata K, Kim H-S, Wataya Y, Oshima Y, 1998, Antimalarial 4-quinazolinone alkaloids from *Dichroa febrifuga* (JOH-ZAN) Parasitol. Int.; 47,Suppl.1:380.

Hydrangea scandens (L.f.) Ser. ssp *chinensis* (Maxim) McClintock

[From Greek *hudor* = water and *angeion* = *vessel* and from Latin *scandens* = climbing]

Local names:	Chinese hydrangea; zhong guo xiu qiu (China), yaeyana konterigi (Japan)
Synonyms:	*Hydrangea chinensis* Maxim., *Hydrangea glabrifolia* Hay., *Hydrangea macrosepala* Hay, *Hydrangea obovatifolia* Hay., *Hydrangea umbellata* Rehd.)
Description:	It is a shrub which grows in the forests of China, Taiwan and Japan. The stem is terete, hairy and reddish at the apex, somewhat covered with minute angled patterns on older parts and lenticelled. The leaves are simple, opposite and without stipules. The petiole is about 1 cm long, flattish, lenticelled and subglabrous. The leaf blade is lanceolate, elliptic, papery, serrate at margin and recurved, the midrib filled with hair above, with 4-5 pairs of secondary nerves, 4-12 cm × 1.5- 4 cm, cuneate at the base, and caudate at the apex. The inflorescences are terminal on about 2 cm long pedicels. The calyx of sterile flowers comprises 3 or 4, broadly lanceolate, sepals which are about 2 x 1.5 cm, bluish and show some nervations. The calyx of fertile flowers is about 0.2 cm long with tiny teeth. The corolla comprises 4 to 5 petals which are yellow, elliptic about 0.2 cm long, clawed at the base. The fruits are fusiform capsules which are about 0.5 cm long (Figure 8).
Medicinal Uses:	In China, the plant is used for fever, headache, rheumatism, and vaginal infection.

Pharmacology: The plant contains a series of quinazoline alkaloids including hydrachine A (Patman *et al.*, 2001), febrifugine and isofebrifugine, coumarin derivatives (Khalil *et al.*, 2003) and secoiridoid glycosides (Chang *et al.*, 2003). Febrifugine and isofebrifugine may account for the antipyretic property mentioned above.

References: Chang FR, Lee YH, Yang YL, Hsieh PW, Khalil AT, Chen CY, Wu YC., 2003, Secoiridoid glycoside and alkaloid constituents of *Hydrangea chinensis*. J Nat Prod;66:1245-8.

                     Khalil AT, Chang FR, Lee YH, Chen CY, Liaw CC, Ramesh P, Yuan SS, Wu YC., 2003, Chemical constituents from the *Hydrangea chinensis*. Arch Pharm Res.; 26:15-20.

                     Patnam R, Chang FR, Chen CY, Kuo RY, Lee YH, Wu YC., 2001, Hydrachine A, a novel alkaloid from the roots of *Hydrangea chinensis*. J Nat Prod; 64:948-9.

Figure 8: *Hydrangea scandens* (L.f.) Ser. ssp *chinensis* (Maxim) McClintock

From: Herbarium of the University of the Ryukyus.

Japan, Ryukyus, along Yutum river, Iriotome Island, Okinawa. Altitude 50 m/ Date of collection: 3 July 1984. Collection: Yasukazu Miyagi No 10298. Determination: Miyagi Y.

3.Family ROSACEAE A.L. de Jussieu 1789 nom. Conserv., the Rose Family

The Family Rosaceae as mentioned above is a large group of flowering plants which is particularly well represented in temperate and subtropical parts of the world. Members of this family produce proanthocyanins, ellagic acid, gallic acid, triterpenoid saponins, some cyanogenetic glycosides, but lack alkaloids. The leaves are mostly compound, alternate and stipulate, the folioles or leaf-blade often serrate. The flowers are solitary or cymose with a prominent flower receptacle around which is inserted 5 sepals and 5 petals (or more) which are free. The stamens are numerous with dithecal and tetrasporangiate anthers. The gynaecia are numerous, made of a single carpel and covering the flower receptacle. The fruits are separate follicles, or drupelets, or berries, or pomes.

The Family Rosaceae is important in terms of commercial value as many genera are cultivated for ornament *Crataegus, Kerria, Pyracantha, Rosa, Sorbus, Spiracea* or for their edible fruits: *Fragaria, Prunus, Pyrus, Rubus* and *Malus*. In terms of pharmaceutical value, Rosaceae are the source of aromatic, flavoring, cyanogenetic and mild astringent remedies. The volatile oil of *Rosa damascena* (Rose Oil, *British Pharmaceutical Codex*, 1949) has been employed in perfumery. The petals of *Rosa gallica* (Red-Rose Petal, *British Pharmaceutical Codex*, 1949) has been used as mild astringent. The fresh ripe fruits of various species of *Rosa* is a rich source of vitamin C and as been used in the form of syrup for children. The dried fruits of *Crataegus oxyacantha* (Crataegus *French Pharmacopoea*, 1965) has been used in the form of a tincture for heart diseases. The fresh ripe fruits of *Rubus idaeus* (Raspberry, *French Pharmacopoeia* 1965) have been used as a coloring and flavoring agent. Bitter almond (*British Pharmaceutical Codex*, 1934) or the dried ripe seeds of *Prunus amygdalus* var *amara* are used for skin lotion. The fresh leaves of *Prunus laurocerasus* (Cherry-laurel, *British Pharmaceutical Codex*, 1949) has been used for the preparation of Cherry-Laurel water, which was used as flavoring agent and sedative in nausea and vomiting. Persic Oil (*British Pharmaceutical Codex*, 1934) or the fixed oil from the seeds of *Prunus persica* (peach) or *Prunus armenianca* (apricot) has been used as external ointments. The fresh ripe fruits of *Prunus cerasus* (Red Cherry, *French Pharmacopoeia* 1965) have been used as coloring and flavoring agent. The dried bark of wild or black cherry, *Prunus serotina* (Wild Cherry Bark, *British Pharmaceutical Codex*, 1963) has been used in the treatment of cough and favoring agent. The rhizome of *Potentilla tormentilla* Neck. and the rhizome of *Fragaria vesca* L (strawberry) are astringent and were used in Europe to treat diarrhoea.

The phenolic contents of Rosaceae including tannins, anthocyanins, and flavonoids are of pharmacological interest. Hydrolysable tannins from *Cowania mexicana* have anti-tumor promoting activity: casuarinin, stenophyllanin A, stachyurin, alienanin B and casuglaunin A exhibited remarkable inhibitory effects on Epstein-Barr virus early antigen activation induced by 12-O-tetradecanoylphorbol-13-acetate (Miyake *et al.*, 1999).Strawberry and raspberry extracts exhibited high cytotoxic activity against sensitive leukemia HL60 cell line (Skupień *et al.*, 2006). Extract of *Prunus domestica*

L induced nucleosomal DNA fragmentation typical of apoptosis in Caco-2 after 24 h of treatment (Fujii *et al.*, 2006). Procyanidin C-1 from *Crataegus sinaica* exhibited significant inhibitory activity against herpes simplex virus type 1 and showed antioxidant activity (Shahat *et al.*, 2002). Other principles of interest in this family are triterpenes such as 2alpha,3beta-dihydroxy-28-norurs-12,17,19(20),21-tetraen-23-oic acid which inhibit the growth of human stomach tumor cells SGC (Liu *et al.*, 2005). Most Rosaceae used for medicinal purpose in Asia are found in temperate and subtropical regions, especially in China and Japan were they are often used for their mild astringency.

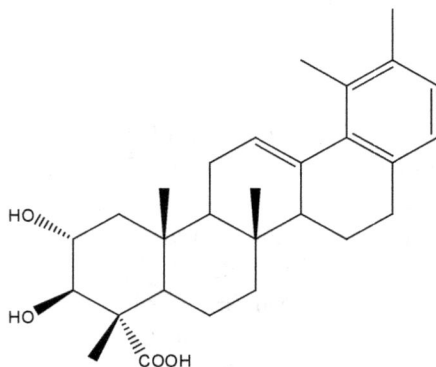

2α,3β-dihydroxy-28-norurs-12,17,19(20),21-tetraen-23-oic acid

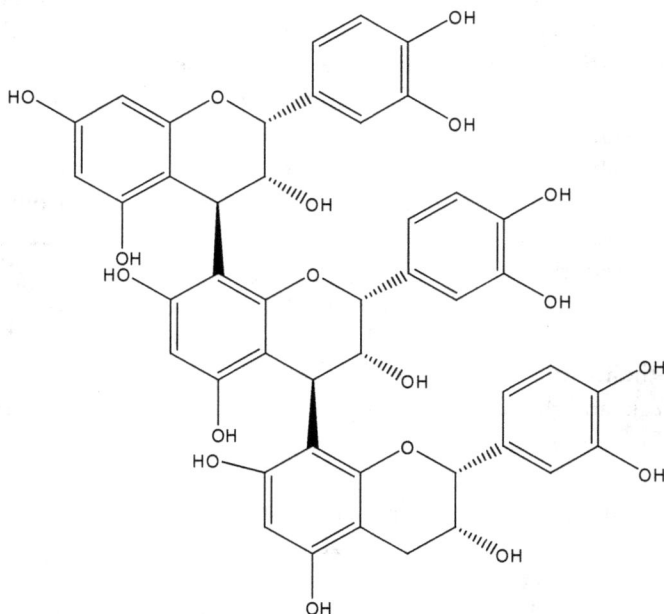

Procyanidin C1

References:	Fujii T, Ikami T, Xu JW, Ikeda K., 2006, Prune extract (*Prunus domestica* L.) suppresses the proliferation and induces the apoptosis of human colon carcinoma Caco-2. J Nutr Sci Vitaminol (Tokyo), 52:389-91
	Miyake M, Nishitani E, Mori K, Hatano T, Okuda T, Konoshima T, Takasaki M, Kozuka M, Mukainaka T, Tokuda H, Nishino H, Yoshida T, 1999, Anti-tumor promoting activity of polyphenols from *Cowania mexicana* and *Coleogyne ramosissima*. Cancer Lett; 143: 5-13.
	Liu X, Cui Y, Yu Q, Yu B, 2005, Triterpenoids from *Sanguisorba officinalis*. Phytochemistry; 66: 1671-1679.
	Shahat AA, Cos P, De Bruyne T, Apers S, Hammouda FM, Ismail SI, Azzam S, Claeys M, Goovaerts E, Pieters L, Vanden Berghe D, Vlietinck AJ, 2002, Antiviral and antioxidant activity of flavonoids and proanthocyanidins from *Crataegus sinaica*. Planta Med.;68:539-41.
	Skupień K, Oszmiański J, Kostrzewa-Nowak D, Tarasiuk J., 2006, *In vitro* antileukaemic activity of extracts from berry plant leaves against sensitive and multidrug resistant HL60 cells. Cancer Lett; 236:282-91.
	Wolniak M, Tomczyk M, Gudej J, Wawer I, 2006, Structural studies of methyl brevifolincarboxylate in solid state by means of NMR spectroscopy and DFT calculations. J. Mol. Struct.; 825: 26-31.

Duchesnea indica (Andr.) Focke

[After French botanist Antoine Nicholas Duchesne (1747-1827) and Latin *indica* = from India]

Local name:	Indian strawberry; yellow-flowered strawberry; she mei (China), saladren (Indonesia), nha ho khay (Laos), stroboeri pa (Thailand), dau dat (Vietnam), winn (Parish)
Basionym:	*Fragaria indica* Andrews, Botanist's Repository, for new, and rare plants 7: pl. 479. 1807.
Synonyms:	*Fragraria indica* Andrews; *Potentilla indica* (Andrews) Th. Wolf
Description:	It is a perennial herb which grows in moist grassy spots of Bhutan, India, Nepal, China, Afghanistan, Indonesia, Japan, Korea, Malaysia and the Philippines. The plant has been introduced in several temperate countries. The stem is prostate, pilose, angled,

rooting at nodes, with internodes which are about 5 cm long. The leaves are spiral, compound and stipulate. The stipules are membranaceous, lanceolate, 0.6 x 0.2 cm by pairs and pilose. The petioles are stem like, slender and 1 - 7 cm long. The leaf blade comprises 3 folioles which are broadly lanceolate, pilose, crenate, with 6 to 7 pairs of secondary nerves discrete on both faces, and 1.2 - 5 x 1 - 2.5 cm. The inflorescences are simple and axillary. The flower peduncle is slender and about 6 cm long and hairy and produces 5 bracts which are pilose and trifid at the apex. The calyx comprises 5 sepals which are lanceolate. The corolla comprises 5 petals which are yellow and retuse at the apex. The androecium comprises 20 - 30 filamentous stamens. The fruit is a pseudocarp which is soft, fleshy, ripening red, glossy about 1.5 cm in diameter, and spongy and contains several tiny seeds (Figure 9).

Medicinal Uses: The plant is principally used in China for the treatment of skin diseases, coughs, physical weakness, inflammation, fever, boils, burns and bites. It has also been used for the treatment of cancer. In Laos, the plant is used as a tonic for blood circulation.

Pharmacology: The medicinal properties mentioned above are most probably due to tannins. The anticancer property has been confirmed. An aqueous extract of the plant showed mild antimutagenic activity in the Salmonella/microsomal system in the presence of benzo[a]pyrene (Lee et al., 1988) and some levels of anticancer activity (Shoemaker et al., 2005). Peng et al. (2008) reported that a phenolic fraction of the plant abrogates the survival of human ovarian cancer SKOV-3 cells through induction of apoptosis .

References: Lee H, Lin JY., 1988, Antimutagenic activity of extracts from anticancer drugs in Chinese medicine. Mutat Res; 204:229-34.

Peng B, Chang Q, Wang L, Hu Q, Wang Y, Tang J, Liu X., 2008, Suppression of human ovarian SKOV-3 cancer cell growth by Duchesnea phenolic fraction is associated with cell cycle arrest and apoptosis. Gynecol Oncol; 108:173-81.

Shoemaker M, Hamilton B, Dairkee SH, Cohen I, Campbell MJ., 2005, *In vitro* anticancer activity of twelve Chinese medicinal herbs. Phytother Res;19:649-51.

Figure 9: *Duchesnea indica* (Andr.) Focke

From: Herbarium of Northeast Louisiana University, Monroe.
USA, roadside and open area between homes in St. Maurice. General area between La. 477 and US 71. Collection and identification: Keith H. Kessler No 2282. Date of collection: 11 April 1982.

Eriobotrya deflexa (Hemsl.) Nakai

[From Greek *erion* = wool, and *botrys* = cluster and Latin *deflexa* = bent]

Local name:	Bronze loquat; tai wan pi ba (China)
Basionym:	*Photinia deflexa* Hemsl. *Ann. Bot.* 9:153. 1895.
Synonym:	*Eriobotrya buisanensis* Hemsl., *Photinia deflexa* Hemsl.
Description:	It is a tree which grows to a height of about 10 m in the forests of Vietnam, China, and Taiwan. The plant is often cultivated as ornamental. The stem is finely fissured, hairy at the apex, terete, with conspicuous leaf-scars which are crescent shaped. The leaves are simple, mostly at the apex of stems, spirally arranged and stipulate. The stipules are caducous. The petioles are straight, woody, about 3 cm long, flattish above, angled, clasping the stem. The leaf-blade is oblong to elliptic, acute both at the base and the apex, the margin conspicuously toothed with tiny glands, 10 - 20 cm × 3 - 7 cm, leathery, with 10-12 pairs of secondary nerves prominent on both surfaces. The inflorescences are axillary and hairy. The flower receptacle is cupular. The calyx comprises 5 sepals which are lanceolate. The corolla consists of 5 petals which are white, orbicular, retuse, nerved and about 1 cm long. The androecium comprises about 20 filamentous stamens. The fruit is a pome yellowish red, warty, subglobose, 1.2 - 2 x 0.5 cm, glabrous; open at the apex with mixture of vestigial calyx and androecium (Figure 10).
Medicinal Uses:	The fruit of *Eriobotrya deflexa* (Hemsl.) Nak. are eaten to cool the body in China.
Pharmacology:	The plant contains a series of monoterpene glycosides, (3S)-O-alpha-L-rhamnopyranosyl-(1-->3)-[4-O-(E)-coumaroyl]-alpha-L-rhamnopyranosyl-(1-->6)-beta-D-glucopyranosyl-linalool, and (3S)-O-alpha-L-rhamnopyranosyl-(1-->3)-[4-O-(Z)-coumaroyl]-alpha-L-rhamnopyranosyl-(1-->6)-beta-D-glucopyranosyl-linalool, and triterpene glycosides of the ursane type such as, 1beta,2alpha,19alpha-trihydroxy-3-oxo-12-ursen-28-oic acid and 2alpha,3alpha,19alpha-trihydroxy-12-oleanen-28-oic acid (Lee TH *et al.*, 2001).
Reference:	Lee TH, Lee SS, Kuo YC, Chou CH., 2001, Monoterpene glycosides and triterpene acids from *Eriobotrya deflexa*. J Nat Prod; 64:865-9

Figure 10: *Eriobotrya deflexa* (Hemsl.) Nakai

From: Botanical Inventory of Taiwan. Herbarium, Institute of Botany, Academia Sinica, Taipei. Taiwan, Kaohsiung Hsien, Taoyuan Hsiang: southern Cross, island Hwy between Meishan and Likuan, in broadleaf forest, 120° 50' 58" East - 23° 15' 46" North. Altitude: 1120 m, on slope below the road. Collection and identification: Tsui-Ya Lui 501 *et al*. Date of collection: 12 May 1994.

Rubus glomeratus Bl.

[From Latin *rubus* = blackberry and *glomeratus* = clustered]

Local names:　Molucca raspberry, dum molucca (Vietnam), welbute (Sri Lanka), lintagu, kalataguk (Borneo), berete (Indonesia), auiteteya (Papua New Guinea), sapinit (Philippines).

Synonym:　*Rubus moluccanus* L.

Description:　It is a climber that reaches 10 m long which grows in open lands in a geographical area covering India, Himalaya, Nepal, Burma, Sri Lanka, Malaysia, Indonesia and Papua New Guinea, Australia, and Pacific Islands. The stem is terete, smooth, hairy at the apex, thorny, the thorns minute and about 0.75 cm long. The internodes are 4.5 - 5.5 cm long. The leaves are simple, spiral and stipulate. The petiole is 3 - 5 cm long, thorny, slender and hairy. The leaf-blade is cordate to 3 lobed, 8 - 11 x 6 - 8 cm, glabrous above, velvety below, and serrate at margin, with about 4 secondary nerves and a midrib sunken above and filled with hairs. The inflorescences are lax racemes which are velvety. The calyx comprises 5 sepals which are deeply incised and velvety. The corolla comprises 5 petals which are glabrous. The stamens are numerous. The fruit is pale green ripening red with tiny hairs (Figure 11).

Medicinal Uses:　In Malaysia, the plant is used to treat dysentery and cardiovascular ailments. In Papua New Guinea, the plant is used to assuage painful abdomen. In North Borneo the plant is used to heal mouth ulcers. In Indonesia, the plant is used to treat bedwetting in children, to induce menses and abortion. In Thailand, the roots and leaves are used for cough treatments and as a blood tonic.

Pharmacology:　The uses mentioned above most probably depend on tannins. Netzel *et al.*, (2006) reported antioxidant property in anthocyanins from the fruit. The plant contains a triterpene, rubonic acid (Shaw AK *et al.*, 1987).

References:　Netzel M, Netzel G, Tian Q, Schwartz S, Konczak I., 2006, Sources of antioxidant activity in Australian native fruits. Identification and quantification of anthocyanins. J Agric Food Chem; 54:9820-6.

Shaw, A. K., S. Antoulas, *et al.*, 1987, Rubonic acid, a new triterpene acid from *Rubus moluccanus*. Ind J Chem Section B Organic Chemistry Including Medicinal Chemistry; 26: 896-97.

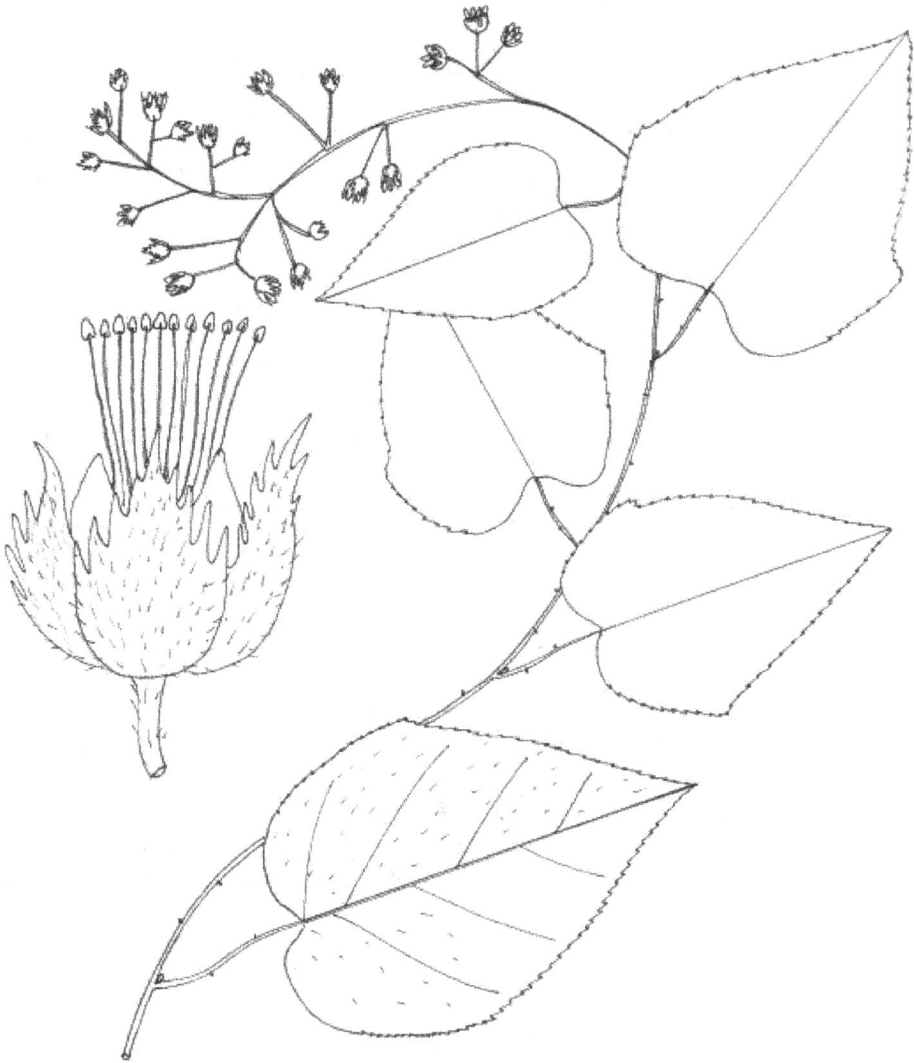

Figure 11: *Rubus glomerulatus* Bl.

From: Flora of Sabah, Herbarium of the Forest Department Sandakan, No SAN 99208. Malaysia, Sabah, Sungai Kibiribi, Labuk Sugut district. Collection: Aban Gibot. Date of collection: 13 July 1983. in old tractor path just above Sungai Kibiribi.

Rubus rosifolius Sm.

[From Latin *rubus* = blackberry and *rosifolius* = rose-like leaves]

Local name: Thimbleberry; kong xin pao (China), ola'a (Hawaii), beberetean (Indonesia), momitl (Papua New Guinea), sapinit (Philippines).

Synonyms: *Rubus comintanus* Blco., *Rubus commersonii* Poir., *Rubus coronarius* (Sims) sweet, *Rubus jamaicensis* Blco., *Rubus pinnatus* Willd., *Rubus rosaefolius* Smith, *Rubus taiwanensis* Matsum.

Description: It is a spiny shrub which grows in grassy spots in a geographical area covering East Africa, India, Nepal, Burma, Cambodia, Laos, Thailand, Vietnam, Malaysia, Indonesia, Philippines, China, Japan, Taiwan, Papua New Guinea and southern Australia. The plant can reach 2m tall and is often cultivated for its fruits which are edible. The stem is terete, hairy at the apex, thorny, the thorns about 0.3 cm long, with internodes which are about 3 cm long. The leaves are compound or simple, spiral and stipulate. The stipules are linear, at the base of rachis, hairy and about 0.4 cm long. The rachis is grooved at first with few thorns. The petiolule is minute and hairy. The folioles are membranaceous, serrate and hairy and show about 10 pairs of secondary nerves. The leaf blade shows 1 - 5 folioles which are elliptic to lanceolate, serrate,1.8 - 4 x 1.5 - 2 cm. The flowers are solitary on a 3 cm pedicel. The calyx comprises 5 linear triangular lobes which are 0.6 - 1.5 cm × 0.4 - 0.6 cm. the corolla consists of 5 petals which are white, membranaceous, nerved, obovate, 0.8 -1.5 cm × 0.8 - 1.2 cm and clawed at the base. The androecium consists of numerous filamentous stamens. The gynaecium comprises numerous follicles fixed on a prominent receptacle The fruits are globose berries which are about 1.1 cm in diameter, on persistent calyx, with 5 lobes which are 0.5 x 0.3 cm, velvety plus a vestigial androecium (Figure 12).

Medicinal Uses: In the Philippines, the plant is used in the treatment of coughs. In Cambodia, Laos and Vietnam, the plant is given to children to prevent bedwetting. In Papua New Guinea, the plant is used to calm itches. In Indonesia, the plant is used as an astringent and a vegetable.

Pharmacology: The fruits contain cyanidin 3-(6"-O-*-rhamnopyranosyl-beta-glucopyranoside) and cyanidin-3-O-beta-glucopyranoside (Byamukama *et al.*, 2005). Hydroalcoholic extract of the plant and 28-methoxytormentic acid exhibited analgesic effects in mice: writhing and formalin induced-pain. 28-Methoxytormentic acid exhibited analgesic effects several times more potent than aspirin and paracetamol (Kanegusuku *et al.*, 2007). Pharmacological studies on Rubus species have demonstrated antibacterial, anxiolytic, analgesic and anti-inflammatory activity (Patel *et al.*, 2004).

References: Byamukama R, Kiremire BT, Andersen OM, Steigen A, 2005, Anthocyanins from fruits of *Rubus pinnatus* and *Rubus rigidus*. J. Food Compos. Anal.; 18: 599-605

Kanegusuku M, Sbors D, Bastos ES, de Souza MM, Cechinel-Filho V, Yunes RA, Delle Monache F, Niero R, 2007, Phytochemical and analgesic activity of extract, fractions and a 19-hydroxyursane-type triterpenoid obtained from *Rubus rosaefolius* (Rosaceae). Biol Pharm Bull.;30:999-1002.

Patel AV, Rojas-Vera J, Dacke CG, 2004, Therapeutic constituents and actions of *Rubus* species. Curr Med Chem; 11:1501-12.

Figure 12: *Rubus rosifolius* Sm.

From: Flora of Sarawak, University Kebangsaan Malaysia Herbarium
Malaysia, Sarawak, Kelabit Highland, Bario, roadside from base camp to Pa Umor, Highland Kerengas. Altitude 1115 m. Collection: Abdul Latiff, 4215. Date of collection: 11 April 1995. Identification: A. Zainuddin. Date of identification: 17 October 1995.

B. Order FABALES Bromhead 1838

The order Fabales consists of 3 families and about 14,000 species of trees, shrubs, herbs or climbers which makes the larger group in the Rosidae. The main classes of secondary metabolites found in this order are Fabales are tannins, gums, several sorts of phenolic compounds, and several series of pyridine, pyrrolizidine, indole and quinozilidine alkaloids. The most obvious botanical feature of Fabales is the fruit: a pod.

1. Family MIMOSACEAE R.Brown in Flinders 1814 nom. conserv., the Mimosa Family

The family Mimosaceae consists of 40 genera and about 2,000 species of tanniferous and mucilaginous trees or shrubs, and herbs. Mimosaceae are often toxic owed to series of unusual amino acids. The leaves of Mimosaceae are bipinnate. Stipules are present. The flowers are actinomorphic and endowed with a showy androecium. The calyx is tubular, valvate, and 5 - lobed. The petals are valvate, and often small.. The anthers are 2 - celled and open lengthwise. The gynaecium consists of a single carpel folding into a superior and single - locular ovary which encloses 2 - several ovaries attached to a marginal placenta. The fruits are pods.

Examples of Mimosaceae are *Acacia melanoxylon* R. Br. (Australian blackwood) and *Xylia dolabriformis* Benth. (ironwood) the wood of which is of commercial value. *Mimosa pudica* L. is a common tropical herb and a botanical curiosity with leaves that will fold when being touched. The dried exudation from the stem of *Acacia senegal* Willd. (Acacia, British Pharmacopoeia, 1963) is used in pharmaceutical technology as an emulsifying and suspending agent. The dried bark of *Acacia arabica* (Lam.) Willd. or *Acacia decurrens* Willd. (Acacia Bark, British Pharmaceutical Codex, 1934) has been used to make astringent gargles. The seeds of *Entada gigas* (L.) Fawc. and Rendle (cacoon) are ornamental items. Few pharmaceutical studies have been undertaken on this large family. spermine alkaloids were isolated from the alkaloidal fraction. Rukunga *et al* (2007) isolated spermine alkaloids from *Albizia gummifera* (J.F. Gmel.) C.A. Sm. which abrogated the survival of chloroquine sensitive (NF54) and resistant (ENT30) strains of *Plasmodium falciparum*. The saponins gummiferaosides A-C showed cytotoxicity against the A2780 human ovarian cancer cell line (Cao *et al.*, 2007). Triterpene saponins pithelucosides from *Pithecellobium lucidum* Benth. showed some levels of cytotoxicity against human tumoral cell lines HCT-8, Bel-7402, BGC-823, A549, and A2780 (Ma *et al*, 2008).

References: Cao S, Norris A, Miller JS, Ratovoson F, Razafitsalama J, Andriantsiferana R, Rasamison VE, TenDyke K, Suh T, Kingston DG., 2007, Cytotoxic triterpenoid saponins of *Albizia gummifera* from the Madagascar rain forest. J Nat Prod; 70:361-6.

Ma SG, Hu YC, Yu SS, Zhang Y, Chen XG, Liu J, Liu YX., 2008, Cytotoxic triterpenoid saponins acylated with monoterpenic acid from *Pithecellobium lucidum*. J Nat Prod; 71(1):41-6.

Rukunga GM, Muregi FW, Tolo FM, Omar SA, Mwitari P, Muthaura CN, Omlin F, Lwande W, Hassanali A, Githure J, Iraqi FW, Mungai GM, Kraus W, Kofi-Tsekpo WM., 2007, The antiplasmodial activity of spermine alkaloids isolated from *Albizia gummifera*.Fitoterapia; 78:455-9.

Albizia chinensis (Osbeck) Merr.

[After Italian Filippo degli Albizzi and Latin *chinensis* = from China]

Local names:	Chinese Albizia, silk tree, bnumeza (Burma), kang luang (Thailand), jeungjing (Indonesia), khang (Laos), kool (Cambodia), cham (Vietnam), silai (India), hulanmara (Sri Lanka)
Basionym:	*Mimosa chinensis* Osbeck *Dagbok ofwer en Ostindisk Resa* 233. 1757
Synonyms:	*Acacia stipulata* DC., *Albizia marginata* (Lamk) Merr.
	Albizia stipulata (DC.) Boivin, *Mimosa chinensis* Osbeck,
Description:	It is a tree which grows in the forests of India, Burma, Thailand, Cambodia, Laos, Vietnam, China, and Indonesia. The bark is dark grey, roughly cracked. The stem is hairy, terete, 0.6 cm in diameter at the base, lenticelled, hairy at the apex and with 3.5 - 15 cm long internodes. The leaves are bipinnate, spiral and stipulated. The stipule is conspicuous, heart-shaped, deciduous and up to 2.5 cm long. The rachis is 15 - 40 cm long, hairy, with 7 - 20 pairs of pinnae, and glands near the base and between the uppermost 2 - 9 pairs of pinnae. The gland is 0.2 - 0.4 x 0.15 cm. The pinnae are 5 - 15 cm long, minutely channeled, and bear 17 - 24 pairs of folioles which are dark green above, 0.15 - 0.25 x 0.6 - 0.8 cm, falcate, glaucous below. The inflorescence is a small light green panicle of flower heads, the axis 2 - 3.5 cm. The flower pedicel is about 0.1 cm long. The calyx is yellowish green, 0.25 - 0.4 cm long, tubular, hairy, with 5 1 mm long lobes. The corolla is tubular about 0.4 - 1 cm long, yellowish green, hairy with 5 0.2 cm long triangular lobes. The stamens are 1 - 2 cm long. The pod is thin, flat, oblong, 12.5 - 20 x 2 - 3 cm, dark brown with 8 -12-seeds which are ellipsoid, about 0.5 cm in diameter, and dark brown (Figure 13).

Medicinal Uses: In India, the plant is used to heal wounds and to treat skin
                       diseases. In Indonesia, the plant is used as a fish poison.

Pharmacology;   The pharmacological property of the plant is yet to be
                       explored.

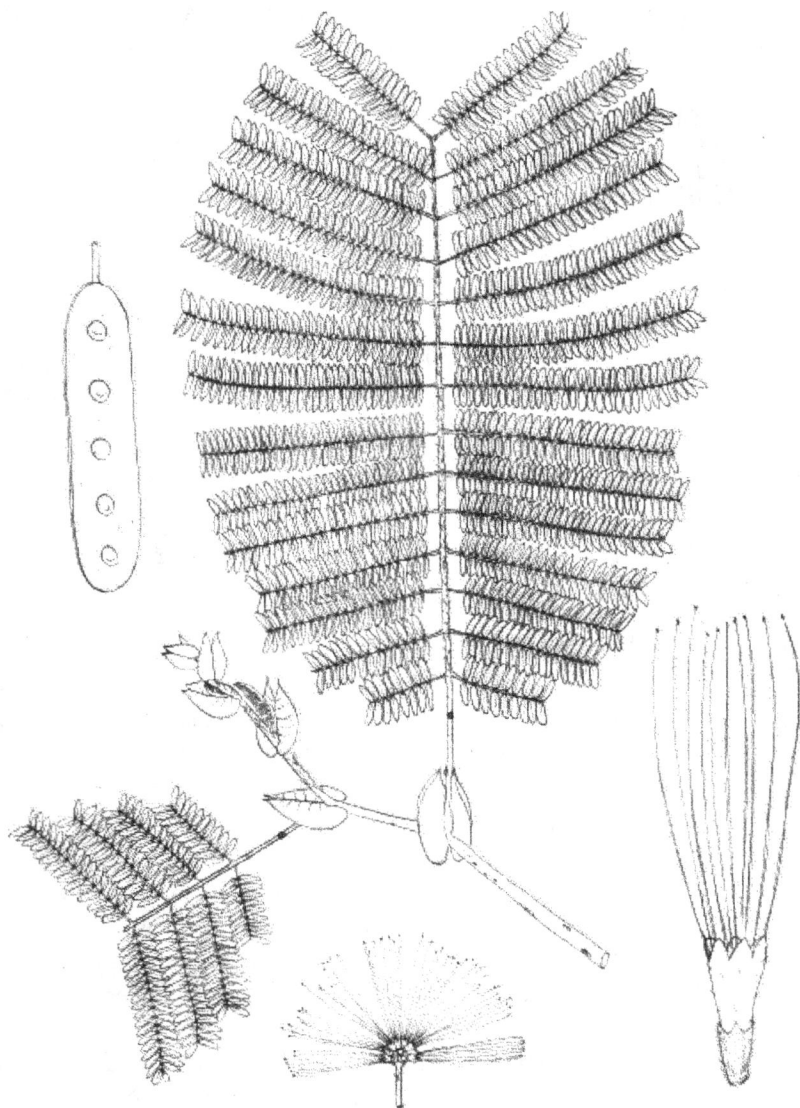

Figure 13: *Albizia chinensis* (Osbeck) Merr.
From: Flora of Thailand. Chiang Mai University Herbarium
Thailand, Chiang Mai province, Chiang Dao district, Doi Chiang Dao animal sanctuary, Huay
Mae station. By 18° 05' North - 98° East. Elevation: 1450 m. Date of collection: 4 March
1995. In open, disturbed, deciduous secondary growth in seasonal pine and evergreen
hardwood forest. Collection and identification: JF Maxwell № 95-197.

Albizia lebbeck (L.) Benth.

[After Italian Filippo degli Albizzi and Arabic *lebbeck* = name of an Arabian plant]

Local names:	Parrot tree, kokko (Burma), chang riek (Cambodia), bois noir (France), dohn doot (Thailand), harrasiris (Nepal), bhandi (Sanskrit), mara (Sri Lanka), aninapla (Philippines)
Basionym:	*Mimosa lebbeck L. Species Plantarum* 1: 516. 1753
Synonyms:	*Acacia lebbeck* (L.) Willd., *Feuilleea lebbeck* (L.) Kuntze, *Mimosa lebbeck* L., *Mimosa lebbeck* Forsk., *Mimosa speciosa* Jacq.
Description:	It is a big tree which grows on the sandy soil of tropical and subtropical Africa, India, Thailand, Malaysia, Indonesia and Australia. The plant grows to 20 m. The bark is pale to grey, thick, roughly cracked. The stem is hairy, with few lenticels and longitudinally striated. The leaves are bipinnate, spiral and stipulated. The stipule is triangular, hairy, 0.13 x 0.1 cm. The rachis is hairy, with a 0.3 x 0.15 cm gland near the stem, and bears 2 - 3 pairs of pinnae. The pinnae are 10 - 15 cm long, swollen at the base, hairy, angled, and channeled above, with 5-9 pairs of folioles. The petiolule is 0.1 cm and velvety. The foliole is dark green above, 2.5 - 4.5 x 1.5 - 2 cm, asymmetrical, oblong spathulate, with 5 - 7 pairs of secondary nerves, and hairy underneath. The inflorescence is a tassel-like head of white fragrant flowers which is 2 - 3.5 cm in diameter not including the stamens. The inflorescence axis is green and 4 - 9 cm long. The flower pedicel is 0.25 - 0.3 cm long and hairy. The calyx is hairy, light green, and 0.3 - 0.4 cm long, with 5 lobes. The corolla is 1 cm long, pale light green, with 5 pointed lobes which are 0.25 cm long. The stamens are 4 cm long and form conspicuous bunches. The pod is large, 10 - 30 x 2 - 5 cm, brown, thin, papery and marked with elliptical lumps by the 4 - 12 seeds. The seed has a horse-shoe appearance (Figure 14).
Medicinal Uses:	In India, the plant is used for headache, ophtalmia, inflammation, syphilis, gonorrhea, worms, piles, leprosy and as a tonic and aphrodisiac. In Burma, the plant is used to treat ophtalmia, and boils. In Cambodia, Laos and Vietnam, the plant is used for piles, boils and dysentery.
Pharmacology:	An extract of leaves exhibited nootropic and anxiolytic activity in albino mice by a mechanism involving gamma-aminobutyric acid (Une *et al.*, 2001). An extract of seeds elicited antidiarrhoeal activity in rodents by a mechanism involving the opioid system (Besra *et al.*, 2002). The plant may be

interesting for its neuroactive principles. The plant is probably not an aphrodisiac as an extract lowered testosterone levels and inhibited spermatogenesis in male rats (Gupta *et al*, 2006). The anti-inflammatory use of the plant might involve an antioxidant effect as an extract of the plant abrogated the oxidative stress in alloxan-induced diabetic rats (Resmi *et al.*, 2006). Stabilization of mast cells comparable to disodium cromoglicate (Shashidhara *et al.*, 2008). El Garhy *et al*, (2002) validated the anthelminthic property of the plant.

References: Besra SE, Gomes A, Chaudhury L, Vedasiromoni JR, Ganguly DK, 2002, Antidiarrhoeal activity of seed extract of *Albizia lebbeck* Benth. Phytother Res; 16:529-33.

El Garhy MF, Mahmoud LH, 2002, Anthelminthic efficacy of traditional herbs on *Ascaris lumbricoides*. J Egypt Soc Parasitol; 32:893-900.

Gupta RS, Kachhawa JB, Chaudhary R, 2006, Antispermatogenic, antiandrogenic activities of *Albizia lebbeck* (L.) Benth bark extract in male albino rats. Phytomedicine; 13:277-83

Resmi CR, Venukumar MR, Latha MS, 2006, Antioxidant activity of *Albizia lebbeck* (Linn.) Benth. in alloxan diabetic rats. Indian J Physiol Pharmacol; 50:297-302.

Shashidhara S, Bhandarkar AV, Deepak M., 2008, Comparative evaluation of successive extracts of leaf and stem bark of *Albizia lebbeck* for mast cell stabilization activity. Fitoterapia; 79:301-2.

Une HD, Sarveiya VP, Pal SC, Kasture VS, Kasture SB, 2001, Nootropic and anxiolytic activity of saponins of *Albizia lebbeck* leaves. Pharmacol Biochem Behav; 69:439-44.

Albizia myriophylla Benth.

[After Italian Filippo degli Albizzi and Greek *myrios* = numberless and *phyllon* = leaf]

Local names: Little-Leaf Sensitive-Briars, nwe-cho (Burma), cha em (Thailand), cay song ran (Vietnam)

Synonyms: *Albizia microphylla* J.F. Macbr., *Mimosa microphylla* Roxb., *Albizia thorelii* Pierre, *Albizia vialeana* var. *thorelii* (Pierre) P.H.Ho, *Feuillea macrophylla* Kuntze.

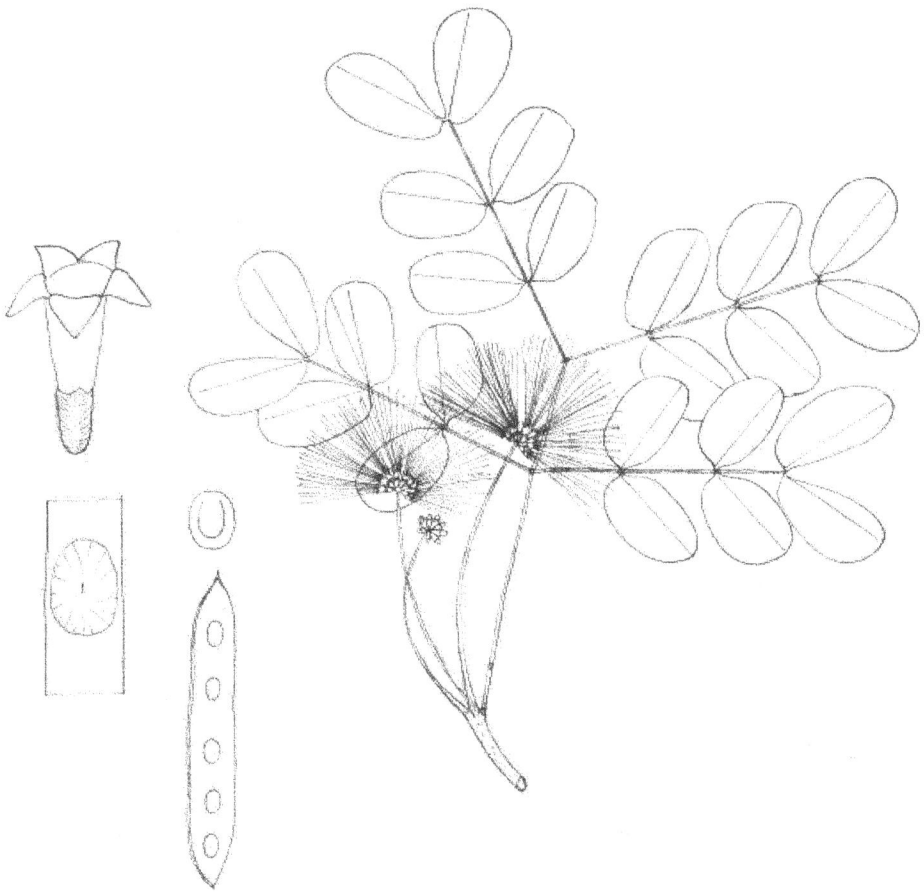

Figure 14: *Albizia lebbeck* (L.) Benth.
From: Flora of Thailand, Chiang Mai University Herbarium
Thailand, Lampoon province, Doi Kuhn Dahn national park, trail from park headquarters to
Daht Muey falls, by 18° North - 99° 05' East. Elevation: 800 m. In open, fire prone, seasonal,
much degraded deciduous forest with much bamboo on granite bedrock. Collection and
identification: JF Maxwell N° 95-238.

Description: It is a woody scrambling climber which grows in the forest of Thailand. The bark is blackish. The stem is glossy, longitudinally striated, lenticelled, zigzag-shaped, with internodes of variable length and hairy by the apex. The leaves are bipinnate, spiral and stipulate. The stipule is minute, hairy and 0.1 cm long. Velvety axillary buds are present at leaf axil. The rachis is velvety, flattish at the base and shows 0.15 cm long glands between each pair of pinnae. The pinnae is about 10 cm long and bears 21 - 30 pairs of folioles. The petiolule is 0.05 cm long. The foliole is dull green above, elliptical, 0.5 - 0.4 x 0.6 - 0.7 cm. Inflorescence is an axillary raceme of globose heads. The calyx is cup-shaped, 0.1 cm long with triangular lobes. The corolla is 0.4 cm long and hairy and develops 5 triangular lobes. The androecium and style is conspicuous up to 2 cm long. The pod is elliptical, light green, glossy, membranaceous, about 9.7 x 1.5 - 14 x 2.7 cm with about 7 seeds which are visible on the pod surface where they form like a series of buttons. The seeds are discoid, and 0.5 - 0.8 cm in diameter (Figure 15).

Medicinal Uses: In Malaysia, the plant is used to treat fever.

Pharmacology: The plant produces a series of oleanane saponins, known as albizia saponins of which albiziasaponin B which has a sweet taste (Yoshikawa *et al.*, 2002). Mouth wash preparation containing the plant lowered the number of *Streptococci* in the mouth of humans (Amornchat *et al.*, 2006). An extract of the plant elicited strong antifungal property against *Candida albicans, Candida glabrata, Candida guilliermondii, Candida krusei, Candida parapsilosis* and *Candida tropicalis in vitro* (Rukayadi *et al.*, 2008). The antimicrobial results obtained might account for the medicinal use of the plant, if the fever was due to bacteria or fungi.

References: Amornchat C, Kraivaphan P, Dhanabhumi C, Tandhachoon K, Trirattana T, Choonhareongdej S., 2006, Effect of Cha-em Thai mouthwash on salivary levels of mutans streptococci and total IgA. Southeast Asian J Trop Med Public Health;37:528-31

Rukayadi Y, Shim JS, Hwang JK., 2008, Screening of Thai medicinal plants for anticandidal activity. Mycoses. (In Press).

Yoshikawa M, Morikawa T, Nakano K, Pongpiriyadacha Y, Murakami T, Matsuda H., 2002,Characterization of new sweet triterpene saponins from *Albizia myriophylla*. J Nat Prod; 65:1638-42

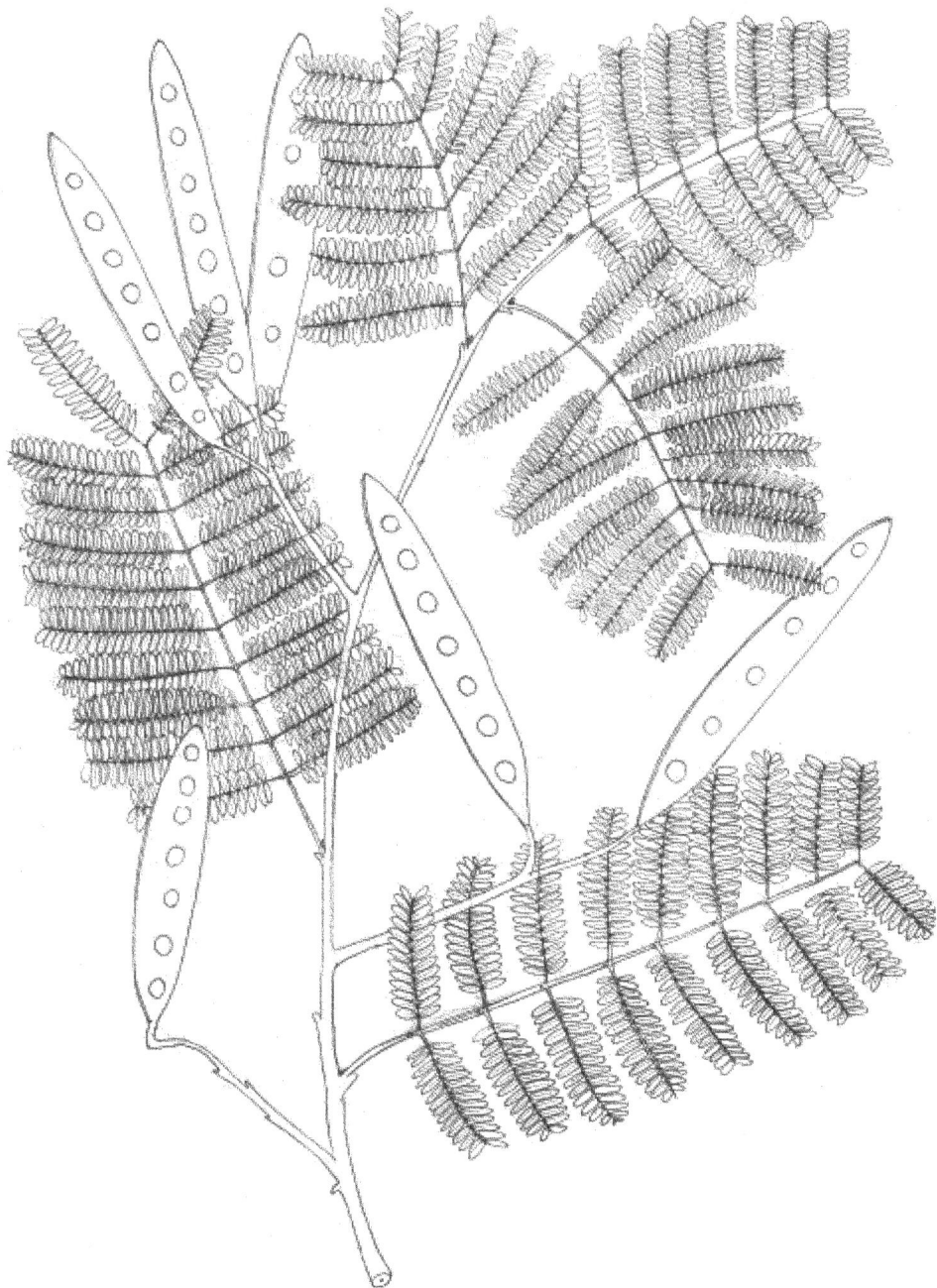

Figure 15: *Albizia myriophylla* Benth.
From: Flora of Thailand, Prince of Songkla University Herbarium
Thailand, Songkla province, Haad Yai district, Choom Sak Hill, Ko Hong Mountain. Elevation:
75 m. Date of collection: 8 February 1986. In open thicket, margins of the secondary forest.
Collection: JF Maxwell N° 86-58

Albizia odoratissima (L. f.) Benth.

[After Italian Filippo degli Albizzi and Latin *odoratissima* = strongly fragrant]

Local names:	fragrant Albizia, thitpyu (Burma), karkursiris (Nepal), favas de Lazaro (Portugal), sirisha (India, Sanskrit), huriyi (Sri Lanka), malatoco (Philippines), ma kham pa (Thailand), duks (Laos), sosng raj thowm (Vietnam)
Basionym:	*Mimosa odoratissima* L. f. *Supplementum Plantarum* 437. 1781
Synonyms:	*Acacia odoratissima* (L.f.) Willd., *Feuilleea odoratissima* (L.f.) Kuntze, *Mimosa odoratissima* L.f.,
Description:	It is a tall tree which grows in a geographical area including India, Sri Lanka, Vietnam and South China. The plant has been introduced in other tropical regions including east Africa. The plant can reach 40 m tall. The bark is grayish. The stem is terete and glabrous. The leaves are bipinnate, spiral and stipulated. The stipule is caducous. The rachis is 15 - 30 cm long with a gland at the base and at the base of the 1-2 upper pinnae. The rachis bears 4 - 5 pairs of pinnae, each pinna 7.5 - 15 cm long and bearing 8 - 15 pairs of folioles which are sessile, 2 - 3 x 1 - 1.5 cm, oblong and without apparent secondary nerves. The inflorescence is a terminal raceme, up to 20 cm long with globose heads which are 2 - 2.5 cm across. The flower pedicel is 0.6 cm long. The calyx is 0.15 cm long and pubescent. The corolla is white and 0.4 cm long with triangular lobes. The stamens are about 1 - 1.5 cm long and showy. The pod is 10 - 20 x 2.5 - 3.8 cm, thin, oblong with 8 - 12 seeds which are prominent. The seeds are ovate, 0.8 x 0.6 cm and yellow (Figure 16).
Medicinal Uses:	In India the plant is used to treat leprosy, coughs and infested wounds.
Pharmacology:	The plant is known to contain saponins (Varshney *et al.*, 1961). It has been studied for hypoglycemic activity (Singh *et al.*, 1976).
References:	Singh KN, Mittal RK, Barthwal KC., 1976, Hypoglycemic activity of *Acacia catechu, Acacia suma*, and *Albizia odoratissima* seed diets in normal albino rats. Indian J Med Res; 64:754-7.
	Varshney IP, Khan MS, 1961, Saponins and sapogenins. VII. Acid sapogenins isolated from Maharashtrian *Albizia odoratissima* seeds. J Pharm Sci; 50:923-5.

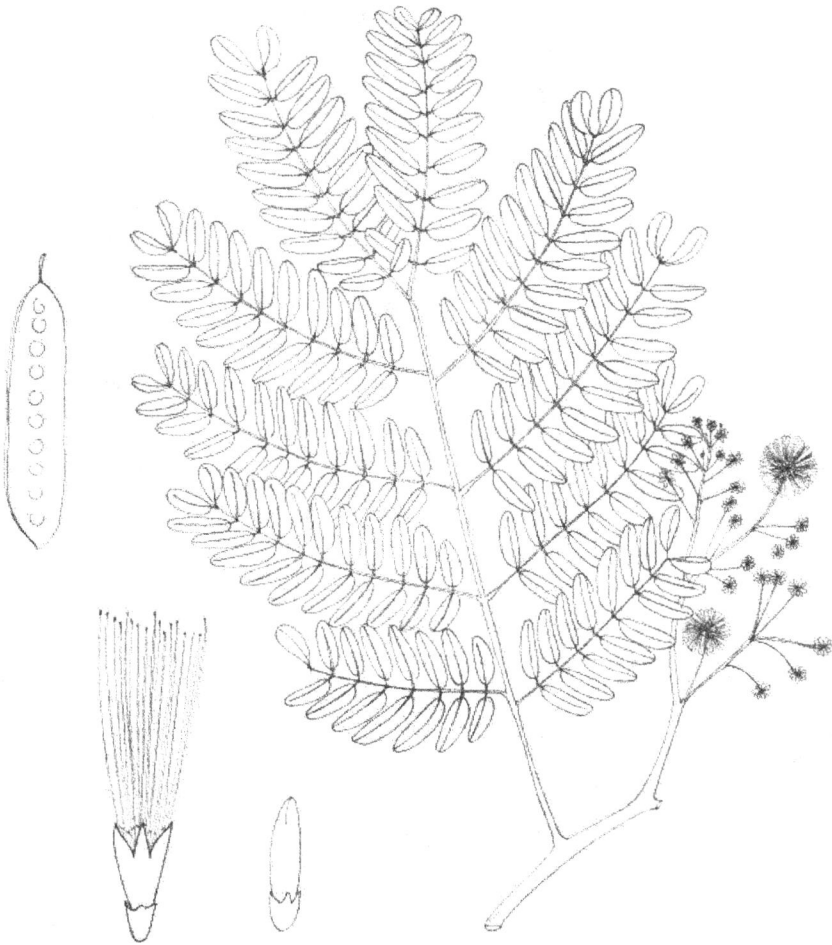

Figure 16: *Albizia odoratissima* (L. f.) Benth.
From: Flora of Thailand, Chiang Mai University Herbarium
Thailand, Lampang province.

Enterolobium saman (Jacq.) Prain ex King

[From Greek *enteron* = intestine, and *lobos* = lobes and *samana* = American name of the plant]

Local names:
Rain tree, monkey pod, pukul lima (Malaysia), arbor de lluvia (Spain), regenbaum (German), arbre a pluie (France), vilaiti siris (India), ampil barang (Vietnam), mara (Sri Lanka), tamalini, tamaligi (Samoa), trongkonmames (Guam), sirsa (Fiji)

Synonyms:
Acacia propinqua A. Rich., *Albizia saman* (Jacq.) F. Muell., *Calliandra saman* (Jacq.) Griseb., *Fueilléea saman* (Jacq.) Kuntze, *Inga cinerea* Humb. & Bonpl. ex Willd. *Inga salutaris* Kunth., *Inga saman* (Jacq.) Willd., *Mimosa saman* Jacq. *Pithecellobium saman* (Jacq.) Benth., *Zygia saman* (Jacq.) Lyons

Description:
It is a tree indigenous to central America which has spread in the tropics as an ornamental tree. The plant grows up to 50 m tall. The bark is dark grey and fissured. The stem is terete, hairy and lenticelled. The leaves are bipinnate, spiral, and stipulated. The rachis is velvety, with glands, and 9 - 15 cm long and holds 4 - 6 pairs of pinnae which are 5 - 8 cm long. Each pinna holds 3 - 6 pairs of folioles which are sessile, strongly asymmetrical, glossy above, oblong, and hairy below and 1.5 - 6 x 1 - 3 cm. The inflorescence is an axillary or terminal head which is 1.1 cm in diameter before blooming, on an axis which is 2 - 10 cm long. The calyx is 5 lobed, 0.6 cm long, and greenish. The corolla is yellow or red, and about 1 cm long. The androecium is conspicuous and comprises numerous stamens which are whitish - pink. The pod is, woody, glossy, to 25 cm long, slightly curved, and thick (Figure 17).

Medicinal Uses:
In the Philippines the plant is used to treat diarrhoea and stomach ache.

Pharmacology:
The medicinal uses are probably due to the astringent property of tannins. Note that the plant contains an alkaloid, pithecelobine (Wiesner *et al.*, 1952). The plant has molluscicidal activity (Lim *et al.*, 2001).

References:
Wiesner K, MacDonald DM, Valenta Z, Armstrong R, 1952, Pithecelobine, the alkaloid of *Pithecelobium saman* Benth. Can J Chem; 30: 761-72.

Lim NF, Abuan BT, Tauro LV, 2001, Molluscicidal activity of *Samanae saman*, *Hyptis suaveolens* and *Croton tiglium*. Phillip Women Univ Res J; 6:1-9.

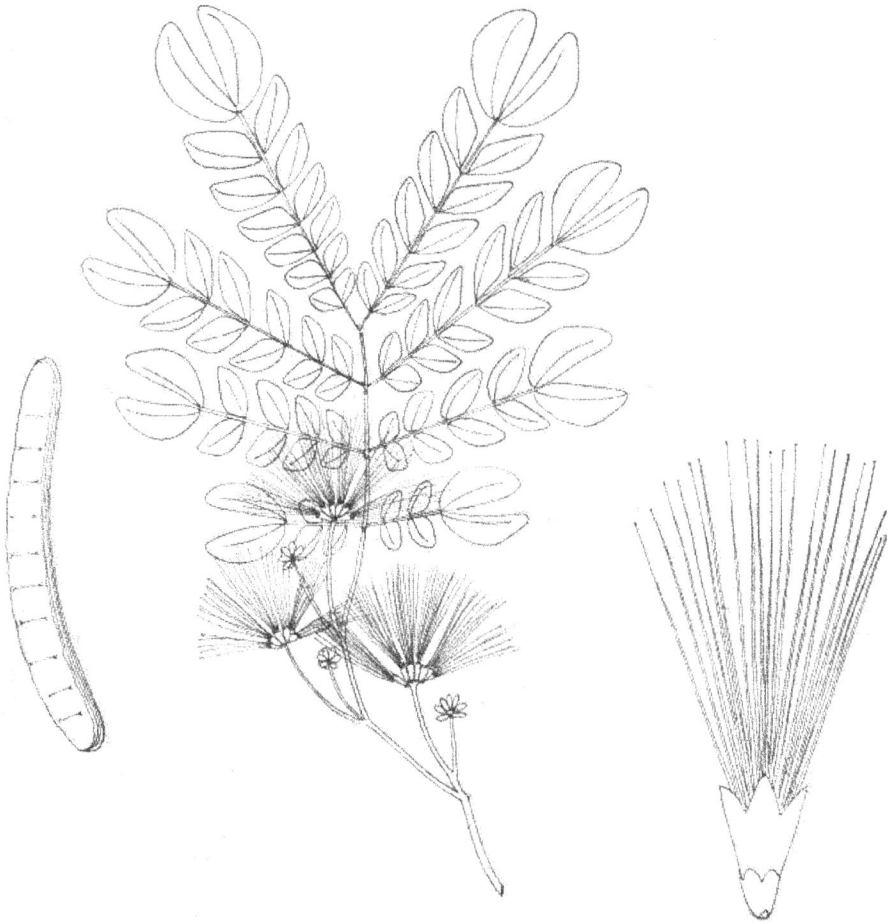

Figure 17: *Enterolobium saman* (Jacq.) Prain ex King
From: Herbarium of University Kebangsaan Malaysia N° 09709.
Malaysia, Tanjung Malim, Perak. Elevation 120 m. Collection and identification: Azuyah
Hassan. Date of collection: 1 February 1981.

Parkia javanica (Lam.) Merr.

[After Mungo Park , Scottish African explorer (1771-1806) and Latin *javanica* = from Java]

Local names:	Petai kerayong (Malaysia), kupang (Philippines)
Basionym:	*Gleditschia javanica* Lam. *Encyclopédie Méthodique, Botanique* 2: 466. 1788
Synonym:	*Parkia roxburghii* G.Don
Description:	It is a big tree which grows to 60 m wild or cultivated from India to Indonesia. The stem is terete, lenticelled, the lenticels irregular and elliptic, 0.6 cm in diameter, and velvety. The leaves are bipinnate, spiral and stipulate. The rachis is velvety, angled by end and up to 50 cm long and bears 20 -30 pairs of pinnae which are 5 - 10 x 1.5 cm with a velvety and angled axis. The pinnae bear 40 - 80 pairs of folioles, which are sessile, 0.7 x 0.2 cm, ciliate at the margin, hooked at the base, linear lanceolate, pointed and curved forward at the apex. The flower is small, cream-white and crowded on a big knob-like head on a long hanging stalk. The pod is woody, glossy, glabrous, 32.5 x 4.4 cm scarcely swollen, seeds with a thick hard wall. The pedicel of the pod is 10 - 14 x 0.4 cm (Figure 18).
Medicinal Uses:	In Malaysia, the plant is used to promote digestion, to invigorate, to heal boils and ulcers. In Indonesia, the plant is used to treat cholera. In the Philippines, the plant is used to heal wounds and ulcers.
Pharmacology:	The plant contains a lectin which inhibits the proliferation of 388DI and J774 macrophage cancer cell lines and HB98 (65.47%), a B-cell hybridoma cell line (Kaur *et al.*, 2005). The plant is nematocidal against *Meloidogyne incognita* (Joymati *et al.*, 2004).
References:	Joymati, L., Romoni, H., Dhanachand, C., 2004, Effect of *Parkia javanica* Merr. against root-knot nematodes *Meloidogyne incognita* on Vicia faba Linn. Indian J. Nematol.;34 102-104 .
	Kaur N, Singh J, Kamboj SS, Agrewala JN, Kaur M., 2005, Two novel lectins from *Parkia biglandulosa* and *Parkia roxburghii*: isolation, physicochemical characterization, mitogenicity and anti-proliferative activity. Protein Peptide Lett; 12:585-95.

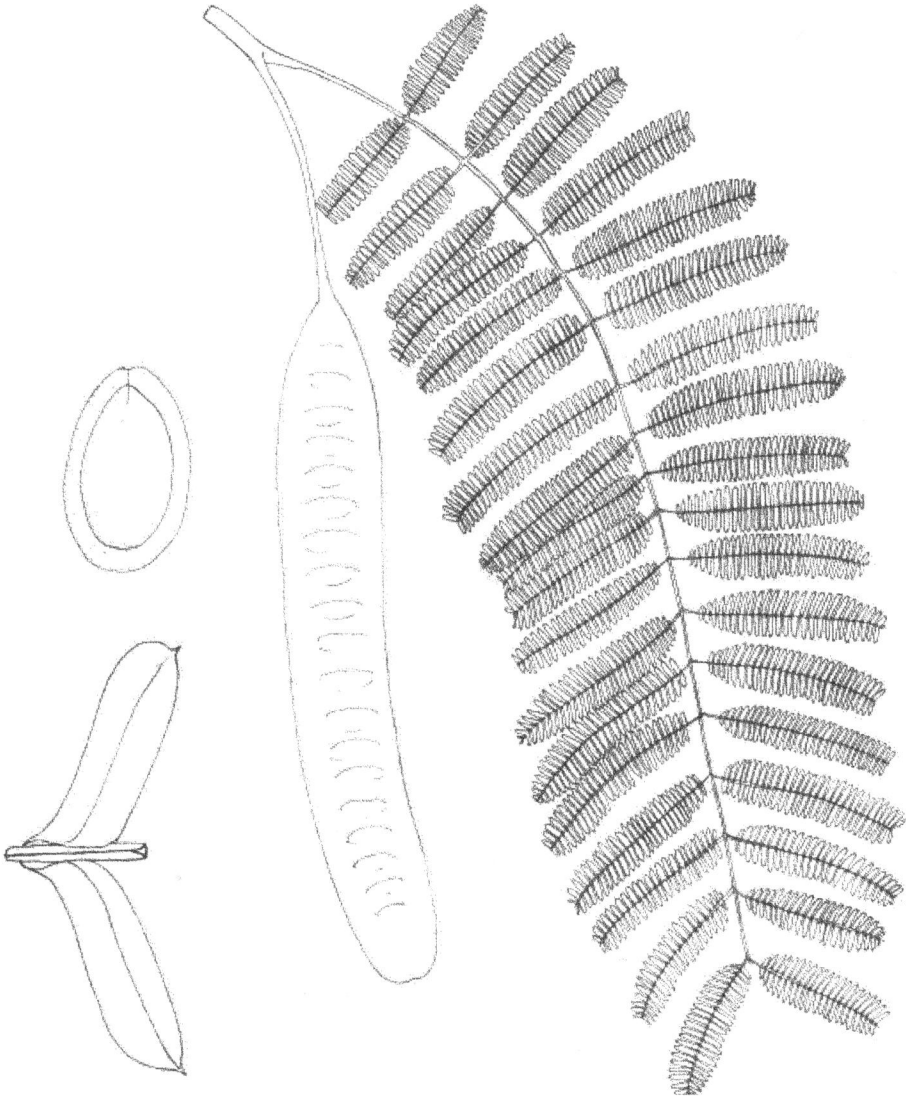

Figure 18: *Parkia javanica* **(Lam.) Merr.**
From: Flora of Malaysia. Herbarium of University Kebangsaan Malaysia N° 03800
Malaysia, Kelantan state, Kuala Krai. Collection and identification: Abdul Latiff and A
Zainuddin. Date of Collection: 29 February 1995. In dipterocarp forest.

Pithecellobium clypearia (Jack) Benth.

[From Greek *pithekos* = an ape, *lobos* = a lobe and Latin *clypeus* = a shield]

Local names: Petai belalang (Malaysia), kamanigum (Philippines)

Basionym: *Inga clypearia* Jack. *Malayan Miscellanies* 2(7): 78. 1822.

Synonyms: *Abarema angulata* (Benth.) Kosterm., *Abarema clypearia* (Jack) Kosterm., *Archidendron clypearia* (Jack) I.C. Nielsen, *Feuilleea clypearia* (Jack) Kuntze, *Inga clypearia* Jack, *Pithecellobium angulatum* Benth.

Description: It is a tree which grows in India, Burma, Cambodia, Laos, Vietnam, Thailand, Malaysia, Indonesia, and China. The plant grows to 10 m. The bark is reddish-brown and smooth. The stem is terete to angled or winged at the apex, subglabrous, lenticelled and with 2 - 5 cm long internodes. The leaf-scars are discrete. The lenticels are globose. The leaves are bipinnate, spiral and stipulated. The rachis is enlarged at the base, 10.5 - 21 x 0.3 cm, with 3 - 10 pairs of pinnae, angled, velvety, with minute trumpet-like glands below each pair of pinnae. The pinna is 10.5 - 13.5 cm long, velvety, angled and 0.1 cm in diameter with 3 - 12 pairs of folioles. The inflorescence is an axillary or terminal raceme which is 6 cm long, angled, hairy, with globose heads of flowers. The petiolule is 0.1 cm and velvety. The foliole is 2 x 1 - 4.2 x 1.8 cm, coriaceous, strongly asymmetrical at the base, with a minute tip at the apex, velvety underneath, with 6 - 9 pairs of secondary nerves looping at the margin. The flower pedicel is 0.1 - 0.3 cm long. The calyx is 0.2 x 0.1 cm, velvety with triangular lobes. The corolla bud is globose and velvety. The pod is 20 cm long, reddish green, contains 3 - 8 seeds with series of septae joined into a sort of worm - shaped structure. The seeds are black and glossy (Figure 19).

Medicinal Uses: The plant is used to treat coughs, viral infection and ulcers in Malaysia. In Indonesia, the plant is used to treat itchiness.

Pharmacology: Li *et al* (2006) isolated 7-O-galloyltricetifavan and 7,4'-di-O-galloyltricetifavan which both exhibited antiviral activity against the respiratory syncytial virus, the influenza A (H1N1) virus, the Coxsackie B3 (Cox B3) virus, and the Herpes simplex virus type 1 (HSV-1) *in vitro*.

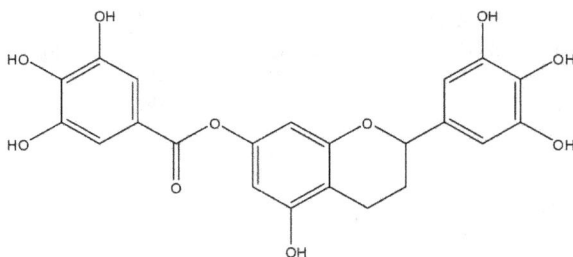

7-O-galloyltricetifavan

Figure 19: *Pithecellobium clypearia* **(Jack) Benth.**
From: Flora of Malaya. Herbarium of University Kebangsaan Malaysia No 0998
Malaysia, Kampung Padang Rumbia Pekan.

Reference: Li Y, Leung KT, Yao F, Ooi LS, Ooi VE.,2006, Antiviral
                    flavans from the leaves of *Pithecellobium clypearia*. J Nat Prod;
                    69(5):833-5

Pithecellobium dulce (Roxb.) Benth.

[From Greek *pithekos* = an ape, *lobos* = a lobe and Latin *dulce* = sweet]

Local names:	Madras thorn, manila tamarind, karkapilli (India), kwaytanyeng (Burma), duri Madras (Malaysia)
Basionym:	*Mimosa dulcis* Roxb. *Plants of the Coast of Coromandel* 1: 67, pl. 99. 1795
Synonyms:	*Acacia obliquifolia* M. Martens & Galeotti, *Feuilleea dulcis* (Roxb.) Kuntze, *Inga dulcis* (Roxb.) Willd., *Inga javana* DC, *Inga leucantha* C. Presl., *Inga pungens* Humb. & Bonpl. ex Willd., *Mimosa dulcis* Roxb., *Mimosa pungens* (Humb. & Bompl. ex Willd.) Poir., *Mimosa unguis-cati* Blco., *Pithecellobium littorale* Britton & Rose ex Rec., *Zygia dulcis* (Roxb.) Lyons
Description:	It is a tree native to tropical America which is found cultivated as an ornamental throughout the tropics. The plant grows to 20 m. The stem is terete, zigzag-shaped, 0.3 cm in diameter, striated, and lenticelled, the lenticels 0.03 - 0.05 cm long, elliptic and numerous. The internodes are 1.2 - 2.5 cm long and the nodes are swollen. The leaves are bipinnate, spiral and stipulate. The stipules are 0.3 - 0.8 cm long straight and woody thorns. The rachis is 0.8 - 1.8 x 0.1 - 0.5 cm channeled, subglabrous, shows a discoid gland which is 0.03 - 0.05 cm in diameter at the apex, and bears a pair of pinnae. The pinnae is 0.6 cm long and bears a pair of folioles. The foliole is spathulate, asymmetrical at the base, round at the apex to discretely notched, membranaceous with 5 - 8 pairs of secondary nerves. The inflorescence is an axillary or terminal zigzag-shaped raceme which is 7 - 16 cm long and bears several globose heads of flowers which are 2 - 4 cm in diameter. The pod is spiral, 10 - 18 x 1 cm, pale greenish flushing red, and containing 6 - 8 seeds which are black glossy which are embedded in a palatable white pulp (Figure 20).
Medicinal Uses:	The plant is used as an astringent. In the Philippines the plant is used to stupefy fish.
Pharmacology:	The plant abounds with oleananes triterpene saponins, some of which are anti-inflammatory, which might account for the fish poison property mentioned above (Nigam *et al.*, 1997, Sahu *et al.*, 1994). A polyphenolic extract of the plant inhibited the toxicity of *Naja kaouthia* venom *in vitro* (Pithayanukul *et al.*, 2005).
References:	Nigam SK, Gopal M, Uddin R, Yoshikawa K, Kawamoto M, Arihara S, 1997, Pithedulosides A-G, oleanane glycosides from *Pithecellobium dulce*. Phytochemistry; 44: 1329-34.

Pithayanukul P, Ruenraroengsak P, Bavovada R, Pakmanee N, Suttisri R, Saen-oon S, 2005, Inhibition of *Naja kaouthia* venom activities by plant polyphenols. J Ethnopharmacol; 97:527-33.

Sahu NP, Mahato SB., 1994, Anti-inflammatory triterpene saponins of *Pithecellobium dulce*: characterization of an echinocystic acid bisdesmoside. Phytochemistry; 37: 1425-7.

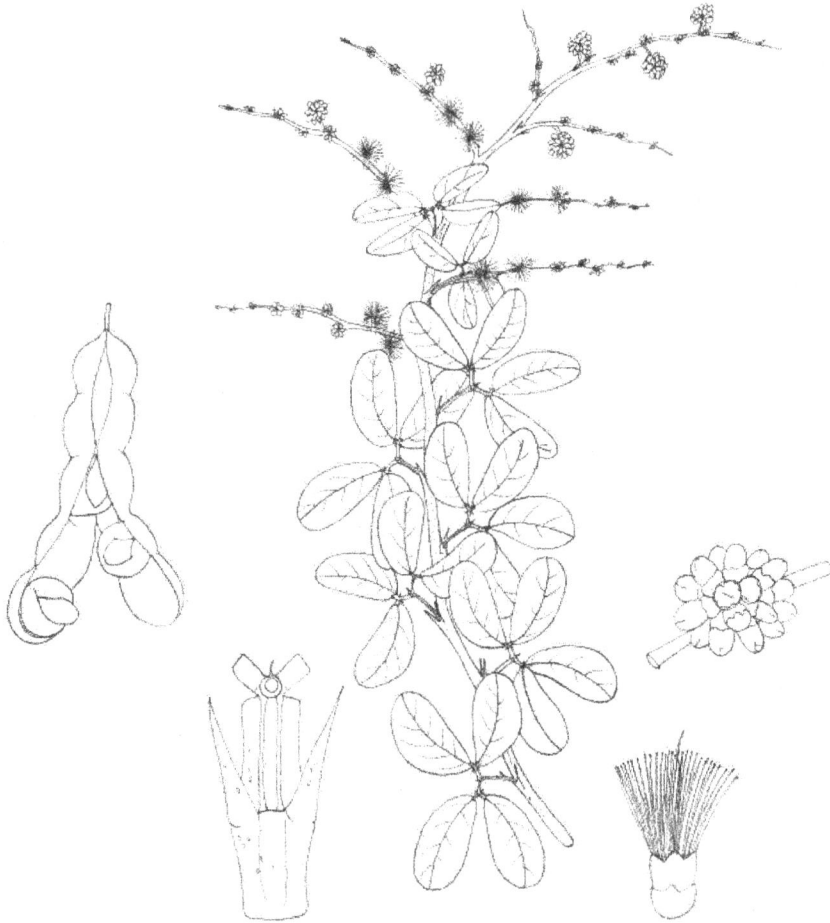

Figure 20: *Pithecellobium dulce* (Roxb.) Benth.
From: Herbarium of University Kebangsaan Malaysia No 00439.
Malaysia, Klang. Cultivated by roadside. Collection: Mohd Kassim. Date of collection: 21 July 1972.

Pithecellobium ellipticum Hassk.

[From Greek *pithekos* = an ape, *lobos* = a lobe and Latin *ellipticum* = elliptic]

Local names:	Saga gajah (Malaysia), langir (Borneo), jengkol utan (Indonesia)
Synonyms:	*Abarema elliptica* (Bl.) Kosterm, *Archidendron ellipticum* (Bl.) I.C. Nielsen, *Pithecellobium waitzii* Kosterm.
Description:	It is a tree which grows in the forests of Malaysia, Indonesia and Philippines. The stem is terete, glabrous, longitudinally striated, with globose lenticels which are 0.01 cm in diameter. The leaves are pinnate, spiral and stipulate. The leaf scars are conspicuous. The stipule is deciduous. The rachis is glabrous, 16 - 19 cm long and bears 2 - 3 pairs of folioles. The petiolule is 0.5 cm long, 0.2 cm in diameter and fissured. The folioles are broadly elliptic, 14 - 22 x 6 - 9 cm, leathery, glabrous, and show 5 - 7 pairs of secondary nerves raised underneath. The inflorescence is axillary, and 10 - 20 cm long. The pod is spiral, forming a doughnut-like structure which is 9 cm in diameter. The pod is 3 cm in diameter, woody, wavy at the margin, dark red inside with 0.8 cm long linear bodies attached to the margin and the seeds. The seeds are black, glossy, ovoid, 1.6 x 0.9 cm (Figure 21).
Medicinal Uses:	The plant is used as an astringent remedy and fish poison in Indonesia.
Pharmacology:	The plant produces a series of saponins or elliptosides which are cytotoxic against renal and melanoma cancer cell lines in the NCI's 60-cell line human tumor screen. Elliptoside A showed *in vivo* antitumor activity against the LOX melanoma cell line (Beutler *et al*, 1997).
Reference:	Beutler JA, Kashman Y, Pannell LK, Cardellina JH, Alexander MR, Balaschak MS, Prather TR, Shoemaker RH, Boyd MR, 1997, Isolation and characterization of novel cytotoxic saponins from *Archidendron ellipticum*. Bioorg Med Chem; 5:1509-17.

Figure 21: *Pithecellobium ellipticum* Hassk.
From: Flora of Malaya. Herbarium of University Kebangsaan Malaysia
Malaysia, Templer Park, Collection and identification: Mohd Kassim. Date of collection: 23
November 1973.

Pithecellobium jiringa (Jack) Prain

[From Greek *pithekos* = an ape, *lobos* = a lobe and Malay *jering* = the Malay name of the plant]

Local name:	Blackbead, jering, jering hutan, jengkol (Malaysia)
Synonyms:	*Albizia jiringa* (Jack) Kurz, *Feuilleea jiringa* (Jack)Kuntze, *Inga jiringa* (Jack) DC., *Inga kaeringa* (Roxb.)Voigt, *Mimosa jiringa* Jack, *Mimosa kaeringa* Roxb., *Pithecellobium lobatum* Benth., *Zygia jiringa* (Jack) Kosterm.
Description:	It is a tree which grows wild in secondary forest or cultivated in Burma, Thailand, Malaysia and Indonesia. The bark is smooth and pale grey. The stem is terete, longitudinally striated, lenticelled, 0.3 cm in diameter, and angled by the apex. The internodes are 2 - 4 cm. The nodes are marked with a sort of lower lip. The leaves are compound, spiral and stipulate. The rachis is yellowish green, glabrous, lenticelled, 2 - 3 cm long, with a pair of pinnae. Each pinna is 5.2 - 5.5 cm long, angled, and bears 2- 3 pairs of folioles. The petiolule is glabrous, wrinkled and 0.4 x 0.12 cm. The folioles are purple when young and shorter at the base, 5 - 14.5 x 2.7 - 5.5 cm, lanceolate, papery, discretely acuminate at the apex, acute to asymmetrical at the base and with 4 - 5 pairs of secondary nerves. The inflorescence is a velvety panicle on older leaf axils with small heads of 3 - 6 flowers which are 0.3 x 0.4 cm. The flower pedicel is 0.5 cm long. The calyx is conical, hairy, with 5 tiny triangular lobes which are 0.15 x 0.1 cm. The petals lobes are lanceolate and 0.2 x 0.1 cm. The androecium consists of numerous stamens with are about 1 cm long. The fruit pedicel is woody and 2.5 x 0.4 cm. The pod is about 20 cm long, coiled into 2 circles, strongly lobed at each seed, dull purplish brown, thickly leathery, each lobe 4 cm in diameter. The seeds are large, reddish brown and smelling of garlic and edible. The pod is a source of dye for silk (Figure 22).
Medicinal Uses:	The plant is used against itch in Malaysia.
Pharmacology:	The pod contains methyl gallate (Lajis *et al.*, 1994). An extract of the plant showed strong toxicity against brine shrimps (Mackeen *et al.* 2000). The plant needs to be studied further for pharmacology.
References	Lajis NH, Khan MN, 1994, Extraction, identification and spectrophotometric determination of second ionization constant

of methyl gallate, a constituent present in the fruit shells of Pithecellobium jiringa. Indian J Chem. Sect B; 33: 609-12.

Mackeen MM, Khan MN, Samadi Z, Lajis NH, 2000, Brine Shrimp Toxicity of Fractionated Extracts of Malaysian Medicinal Plants. Nat Prod Sc; 6(3): 131-34.

Figure 22: *Pithecellobium jiringa* **(Jack) Prain**
From: Herbarium of University Kebangsaan Malaysia № 07385
Malaysia, Kedah. Collection: Kalsom Omar. Date of collection: 28 January 1980.

Pithecellobium splendens (Miq.) Prain

[From Greek *pithekos* = an ape, *lobos* = a lobe and Latin *splendens* = splendid]

Local names:	Kungkur (Malaysia), kerek putih (Borneo)
Synonyms:	*Albizia splendens* Miq., *Pithecellobium confertum* Benth., *Pithecellobium splendens* Merr., *Serialbizia splendens* (Miq.) Kosterm.
Description:	It is a tree which can reach 50 m tall. It grows in the forests of Thailand, Malaysia, Borneo, Indonesia, Philippines, and Papua New Guinea. The bark is blackish grey and wavy fissured. The wood is of economical value. The stem is glabrous, somewhat articulated angled at the apex, lenticelled with 1.1 - 2 cm long internodes. The leaves are bipinnate, spiral and stipulate. The rachis is glabrous, 1.5 - 1.7 cm long with a 0.4 x 0.01 cm saucer-shaped gland. The pinnae are about 4 cm long. The petiolule is 0.2 - 0.5 cm long. The folioles are 2 - 4 x 4.5 - 10 cm, glossy above, elliptic, asymmetrical at the base, acuminate at the apex, with 3 - 4 pairs of secondary nerves raised underneath. The inflorescence is an axillary and terminal panicle which is about 5 cm long and bears globose heads of flowers. The corolla is about 0.6 cm long, 0.4 cm in diameter, with numerous stamens spreading showily from the corolla. The pod is massive, slightly curved, dark chocolate brown, glossy, 30 x 5 - 5.8 cm x 0.3 - 0.4 cm, with 13 - 15 articles which are 3 - 5 cm long. The fruit pedicel is stout, glabrous 2 x 0.4 cm (Figure 23).
Medicinal Uses:	In Malaysia, the plant is used as an astringent remedy for diarrhoea.
Pharmacology:	To date the plant is unexplored in regards to its pharmacological properties. One could expect the isolation of interesting principles from this tree.

Figure 23: *Pithecellobium splendens* **(Miq.) Prain**
From: Herbarium of University Kebangsaan Malaysia
Singapore, Timah hill. Collection: A Zainuddin *et al*. (AZ 1922) Date of collection: 12 February 1985. Identification: A Zainuddin

2.Family CAESALPINIACEAE R. Brown in Flinders 1814 nom. conserv., the Caesalpinia Family

The family Caesalpiniaceae consists of about 150 genera and 2,200 species of trees, shrubs or herbs which are tanniferous. The leaves are pinnate, bipinnate or seldom simple, and stipulate. The flowers are zygomorphic. The calyx consists of 5 sepals which are imbricate and free. The corolla consists of 5 petals, the adaxial petal overlapped by a pair of lateral petals. The androecium comprises 10 stamens. The anthers are tetrasporangiate, dithecal, and open lengthwise or by a terminal or basal pore. The gynaecium consists of a single carpel folded into a unilocular ovary containing 2 - many ovules attached to a marginal placenta. The fruits are pods.

Erythrophloeum guineense G. Don (*sassy* bark) is a common ornamental street tree which produces large bunches of yellow flowers. *Hymenaea courbaril* L. (locust) and *Copaifera pubiflora* Benth. (purple heart wood) provide a strong wood of economic value. Of pharmaceutical importance are the dried ripe fruits of *Cassia senna* L., *Cassia acutifolia* Delile and *Cassia angustifolia* Vahl (Senna Fruit, *British Pharmacopoeia*, 1963) which have been used as a laxative. They contain the anthraquinones sennoside A and sennoside B which irritate the bowels. Tamarind (British Pharmaceutical Codex, 1959) or the acrid paste of the pods of *Tamarindus indica* L. has been used for the same purpose but contain organic acids. A gum obtained from the seeds of *Cassia tora* has properties similar to *Acacia senegal* Willd. (Acacia, British Pharmacopoeia, 1963). Caroub flour, obtained from the seeds of *Ceratonia siliqua* L., is an effective absorbent to stop diarrhoea in the infant (Ceratonia, *British Pharmaceutical Codex*, 1949). The seeds of *Trigonella foenum graecum* L. (fenugreek) are of dietetic value as they contain abundant galactomannans which lower glycemia, cholesterolemia and lipidemia. In addition it has been used as an aromatic in veterinary medicine (Fenugreek, *British Pharmaceutical Codex*, 1949).

Of particular interest in this family is the occurrence of a unique group of diterpenoids called cassanes which are pharmacologically active. Cassane furanoditerpenoids from *Caesalpinia bonduc* (L.) Roxb. exhibited antimalarial activity against the multidrug-resistant K1 strain of *Plasmodium falciparum* (Pudhom *et al*, 2007). Cassane-furanoditerpenoids from *Caesalpinia pulcherrima* (L.) Sw. showed good antitubercular activity (Promsawan *et al.*, 2003). Macrocaesalmin from the seeds of *Caesalpinia minax* Hance. showed antiviral activity against the respiratory syncytial virus (Jiang *et al.*, 2002). Cassane-furanoditerpenoids from the genus *Cassia* represent an interesting source of pharmacologically active principles. Peptides and proteins of seeds of Fabaceae are of pharmacological interest. One such compound is cesalin, a protein characterized from *Caesalpinia gilliesi* which has been scheduled for pharmacology as a chemotherapeutic agent (Elting *et al*, 1976).

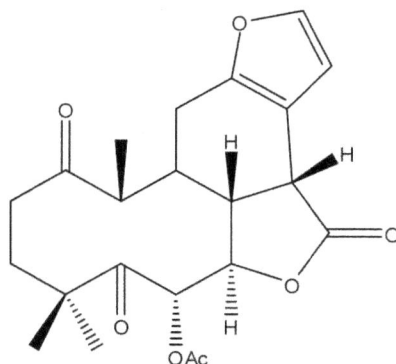

Macrocaesalmin

Bauhinia acuminata Bruce, *Bauhinia bassacensis* Pierre ex Gagnepain, *Bauhinia flammifera* Ridl., *Bauhinia glauca* (Wall. ex Benth.) Wall., *Bauhinia integrifolia* Roxb., *Bauhinia scandens* Sessé & Moc., *Bauhinia variegata* L., *Caesalpinia major* (Medik.) Dandy & Exell, *Caesalpinia pulcherrima* G. Don, *Cassia fistula* L., *Cassia mimosoides* L., *Cassia siamea* Lam., *Cynometra ramiflora* Miq., *Delonix regia* (Bojer ex Hook.) Raf., *Intsia bijuga* (Colebr.) Kuntze, and *Saraca indica* L. are treated in this section.

References: Elting J, Montgomery R, 1976, Mechanism of action of cesalin, an antitumor protein. Biochem Biophys Res Commun; 71: 871-876.

Jiang RW, Paul, But PPH, Ma SC, Ye WC, Chan SP, Mak TCW, 2002, Structure and antiviral properties of macrocaesalmin, a novel cassane furanoditerpenoid lactone from the seeds of *Caesalpinia minax* Hance. Tetrahedron Lett; 43: 2415-2418.

Promsawan N, Kittakoop P, Boonphong S, Nongkunsarn P, 2003, Antitubercular cassane furanoditerpenoids from the roots of *Caesalpinia pulcherrima*. Planta Med;69:776-7.

Pudhom K, Sommit D, Suwankitti N, Petsom A, 2007, Cassane furanoditerpenoids from the seed kernels of *Caesalpinia bonduc* from Thailand. J Nat Prod;70:1542-4.

Bauhinia acuminata Bruce

[After the French botanist Gaspard Bauhin (1560-1624) and Latin *acuminata* = having a long tapering point]

Local names: Dwarf white bauhinia, white dwarf orchid tree

Synonyms: *Alvesia bauhinioides* Welw, *Alvesia tomentosa* (L.) Britton & Rose, *Bauhinia acuminata* L., *Bauhinia acuminata* Vel.. *Bauhinia linnaei* Ali, *Bauhinia pubescens* DC., *Bauhinia volkensii* Taub., *Bauhinia wituensis* Harms, *Pauletia tomentosa* (L.) A. Schmitz

Description: It is a treelet which grows to 3 m high, native to tropical Asia and has now spread into the tropical region of the globe for its ornamental value. The stem is hairy, zigzag-shaped, terete or angled. The leaves are simple, spiral and stipulate. The stipule is 0.7 x 0.1 cm, hairy, and striated longitudinally, swollen at the base, channel or flat above. The petiole is straight. The swollen portion of the petiole is 0.5 cm long. The leaf-blade is broadly bifid, light green, 6 - 15 cm long, each apex lobe acuminate, with 4 - 11 nerves, hairy below with scalariform tertiary nerves. The flower bud is lanceolate, smooth, with 5 little hairy tips at the apex. The flower is truly magnificent, pure, white, with 5 lobes, and up to 10 cm in diameter. The 5 petals are membranaceous and broadly lanceolate. The anthers are yellow. The style is green with a globose stigma. The pod is curved, 7.5 - 15 x 1.5 - 1.8 cm, flat and acuminate at the apex and with about 15 slightly swollen pseudo-septa. The seeds are 0.8 x 0.5 cm and minutely pointed at the apex (Figure 24).

Medicinal Uses: In Malaysia, the plant is used to treat syphilitic ulceration of the nose. In Indonesia, the plant is used to treat coughs.

Pharmacology: The plant seems to have not been studied for pharmacology. It could be of interest to investigate the plant for cytotoxic or antimicrobial leads.

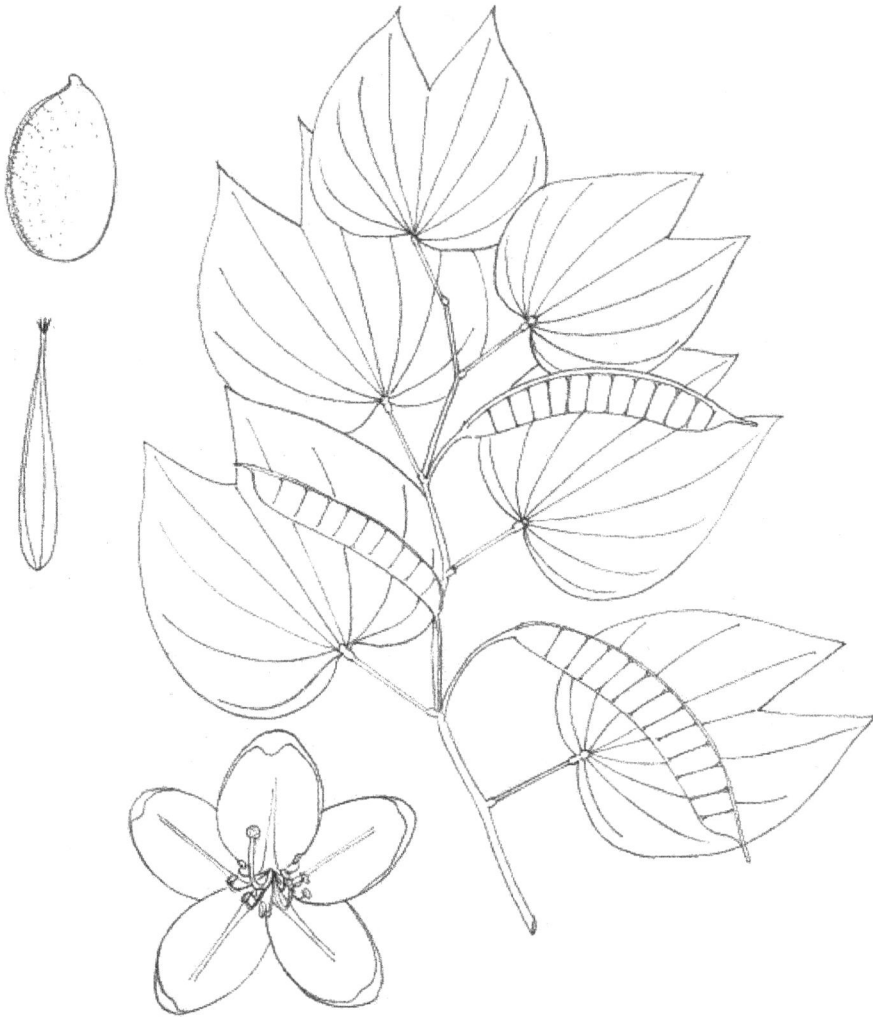

Figure 24: *Bauhinia acuminata* Bruce
From: Flora of Malaya. Herbarium of University Kebangsaan Malaysia, No 4592.
Malaysia, Petaling Jaya, Selangor. Collection and identification: Repiah Singh

Bauhinia bassacensis Pierre ex Gagnep.

[After the French botanist Gaspard Bauhin (1560-1624) and Latin *bassacensis* = from Bassac in the Mekong Delta]

Local name:	Orchid tree
Description:	It is a woody climber which grows 30 m on the canopy of the forests of Cambodia, Vietnam, Laos, Thailand and Malaysia. The basal part of the stem is about 10 cm in diameter, flattened, blackish, and very finely roughened. The bark is thin. The stem is green, velvety, angled, lenticelled, and 0.1 cm in diameter by the apex. The leaves are simple, spiral and stipulate. The stipule is deciduous. The petiole is velvety, 3 - 5 cm long, non-channeled, inflated near the leaf-blade and cracked horizontally, velvety. The leaf-blade is broad, light green, 8 - 11 x 7 - 11 cm, velvety underneath, marked at the apex by an ovoid darkish, glossy and leathery body from which originate 11 nerves and deeply bifid, each lobe slightly curved inward. The inflorescence is terminal or axillary raceme on a 15 cm long axis which with is covered with a brown indumentum. The raceme is many flowered, conspicuous, green and presents a pair of spiral tendrils by the middle of the axis. The coiled tendril is about 2.5 cm long. The flower pedicel is light green, and of variable length: 3 - 8 cm long. The flower bud is bullet-shaped, hairy and about 1 cm long. The calyx consists of a pair of sepals which are velvety, lanceolate, and 0.8 x 0.4 cm. The corolla is white or brown -violet, and comprises 5 petals on a 1.5 cm claw and a blade which is 1.5 x 1.1 cm, nerved, and trapezoidal. The stamens are 0. 4 cm long. The filaments of the stamens are glabrous and like the stigma whitish. The fruit is a flat and woody pod (Figure 25).
Medicinal Uses:	In Cambodia, the plant is used as an antidote for vegetal poisons and is used to treat diarrhea.
Pharmacology:	Unexplored. It would be of interest to validate the antidotal property of the plant. This may well involve some flavonoids and other phenolic compounds which might display interesting pharmacological properties.

Figure 25: *Bauhinia bassacensis* Pierre ex Gagnep.
From: Flora of Thailand, Chiang Mai University Herbarium
Thailand, Surattani province, Ban Takun district, Klong Saeng wildlife reserve, Chiaw Lan reservoir. In Canopy of the primary evergreen hardwood forest with much bamboo, shale and limestone bedrocks. By 8° 05' North - 99° East. Collection and identification: JF Maxwell, N° 94-246

Bauhinia flammifera Ridl.

[After the French botanist Gaspard Bauhin (1560-1624) and Latin *flammifera* = bearing flames]

Local name:	Kempaga (Malaysia)
Description:	It is a large climber that grows in Thailand and Malaysia. The stem is glabrous, slender, 0.5 cm in diameter at the base, angled and covered with beautiful red hairs at the apex. The leaves are simple, spiral, arising from a 0.5 cm stem with a tendril, and stipulate. The stipule is deciduous. The petiole is straight and 1.5 - 3.5 cm long. The tendril is coiled and about 2.5 cm long. The blade is 3.5 - 6 x 2.5 - 5.5 cm deeply bifid, thinly coriaceous, marked at the base by a 0.2 cm round body from which arise 5 nerves. The inflorescence is a large panicle of red flowers (Figure 26)
Medicinal Uses:	In Malaysia, the plant is used to treat syphilitic ulceration of the nose. In Indonesia, the plant is used to treat coughs.
Pharmacology:	The plant seems to have not been studied for pharmacology but may offer cytotoxic or antimicrobial leads.

Bauhinia glauca Bth.

[After the French botanist Gaspard Bauhin (1560-1624) and Latin *glauca* = glaucous]

Local name:	Pink climbing Bauhinia
Description:	It is a woody climber which grows to 20 m long in the forest of India, Burma, Cambodia; Laos; Thailand Indonesia; Malaysia and China. The basal diameter of the main stem is about 6 cm. The bark is thin, finely pustular, and brown. The stem is glossy, terete or angled, zigzag-shaped, longitudinally striated, with a few hairs. The leaves are simple, spiral and stipulate. The stipule is deciduous and the scar left forms a crescent bending downward. The leaf buds are velvety. The petiole is swollen at stem, hairy, channeled and straight and 2 - 3 cm long. The leaf blade is broad and bifid, glossy, leathery, with 9 nerves originating from the base and 6 - 8 x 8.5 - 6.5 cm. A 0.3 - 0.9 cm tip is present between the 2 lobes of the leaf-blade. The inflorescence is a terminal raceme the apex of which is covered with golden hairs. The axis is about 6 cm long. The flower pedicel is hairy and angled and about 5 cm long. The flower buds are hairy.

Figure 26: *Bauhinia flammifera* Ridl.
From: Herbarium of University Kebangsaan Malaysia, No 07188
Malaysia, Pahang state, Fraser's Hill. Collection: Noraini Tam

The sepals are 0.2 x 0.7 cm, velvety outside and broadly lanceolate. The corolla consists of 5 petals which are membranaceous, spatulate, conspicuously nerved, hairy and 1.2 x 1.8 cm. The anthers are 0.15 x 0.3 cm. The filament is 1 - 1.5 cm long. The style is 1.7 cm long. The fruit is a flat and woody pod (Figure 27).

Medicinal Use: The plant is used to treat dysentery.

Pharmacology: Unknown. The medicinal use is probably related to the astringency of the plant.

Bauhinia integrifolia Roxb.

[After the French botanist Gaspard Bauhin (1560-1624) and Latin *integrifolia* = with entire margin]

Synonym: *Phanera integrifolia* (Roxb.) Benth.

Description: It is a woody climber which grows in the forest of Thailand, Malaysia, Indonesia and the Philippines. The stem is terete, lenticelled and smooth. The stem presents pairs of tendrils on 1 - 4 cm long axes. The leaves are simple, spiral and stipulated. The petiole is angled and inflated at the base, and 1 - 5 cm long. The blade is ovate, coriaceous, smooth, 14 - 3.5 x 2.5 - 14 cm, bifid at the apex and with 7 nerves originating from a 0.5 x 0.2 cm patch at the base. The inflorescence is velvety terminal panicle which is yellowish. The flower bud is 0.3 x 0.2 cm and velvety The calyx is yellowish, hairy with 5 triangular lobes. The corolla comprises 5 petals which are yellow orange, hairy at the base, nerved, 1.5 x 0.7 cm, and spathulate. The androecium comprises 10 stamens which are 1.8 cm long with 0.2 cm long anthers and red filaments. The ovary is velvety and the style is 1.2 cm long and red. The pod is woody and flat. The seeds are globose (Figure 28).

Medicinal Uses: In Malaysia, the plant is used for stomach disorders.

Pharmacology: Unknown.

Figure 27: *Bauhinia glauca* **Bth.**
From: Flora of Thailand, Chiang Mai University Herbarium
Thailand, Lampang province, Muang Bahn district, Jae Sawn national park, park headquarters near the hot spring. Elevation: 525 m. Date of collection: 23 September 1995. In partly open slightly disturbed area along a small stream in mixed degraded deciduous forest with many bamboos, shale bedrock. Collection and identification: JF Maxwell N° 95-724.

Figure 28: *Bauhinia integrifolia* **Roxb.**
From: Flora of Thailand. Prince of Songkla University.
Thailand, Nakornsitammarat province, Lansagah district, Gahrome falls, Khao Luang national park. Elevation: 300 m. Date of collection: 6 July 1985. In margin of the river, primary rain forest. Collection and identification: W. Ramsi

Bauhinia scandens Sessé & Moc.
[After the French botanist Gaspard Bauhin (1560-1624) and Latin *scandens* = climbing]

Local name:	Snake climber
Synonyms:	*Bauhinia scandens* Blco., *Bauhinia scandens* Burm.f., *Bauhinia scandens* L., *Bauhinia scandens* Roxb.
Description:	It is a woody climber that grows in the forests of India, Cambodia, Laos, Vietnam, Malaysia, Indonesia, and Sri Lanka. The main stem can reach 30 m long. The stem is subglabrous, minutely fissured, terete, zigzag, pitted, angled at the apex and bears forked tendrils. The leaves are simple, spiral and stipulate. The stipule is small, linear -ovate, mucronate and caducous. The petiole is hairy, swollen at the base and about 1.5 cm long. The leaf-blade is 12 - 15 x 5 - 10 cm, bifid at the apex, cordate at the base, 7 nerved, the nerves inconspicuous. The inflorescence is racemosa paniculate and many flowered. The calyx is campanulate and about 0.2 cm long with 5 triangular lobes. The petals are yellowish white, and pubescent. The fruit is a bottle-shaped pod which is glossy, 4 - 5 x 1.5 - 2 cm and contains 4 seeds which are flat (Figure 29).
Medicinal Uses:	The plant is used to treat severe coughs in Indonesia.
Pharmacology:	Ghosh (1995) reported antitumor activity in rodents.1-*O*-alkyl-glycerol, isolated from the leaves showed a positive response in the brine shrimp toxicity test (Hazra and Chatterjee, 2008).
References:	Ghosh HA, 1995, Experimental antitumor activity of fraction of *Bauhinia scandens* L. leaf extract against a transplantable mouse tumor cell line. Environ and Ecol; 13: 853-56.
	Hazra AG, Chatterjee P, 2008, A nontoxic antitumor compound from the leaves of *Bauhinia scandens* characterized as 1-O-alkyl glycerol by gas-liquid chromatography and evaluation of its antitumor property by brine shrimp bioassay. Ind Crops Prod; 27:39-43.

Figure 29: *Bauhinia scandens* Sessé & Moc.
Flora of Thailand. From Chang Mai University Herbarium N⁰ 38722
Thailand, Chang Mai province, Muang district, Biology Department, Faculty of Science.
Elevation 350 m. By 18° 05' North - 99° East. Date of collection: 17 January 1996. Collection and identification: JF Maxwell N⁰ 96

Bauhinia variegata L.

[After the French botanist Gaspard Bauhin (1560-1624) and Latin *variegata* = variegated]

Local names:	Purple orchid tree, bwechin (Burma), taki (Nepal), mandarai (India), arbre de Saint Thomas (France).
Synonyms:	*Bauhinia chinensis* (DC) Vogel, *Bauhinia decoda* Uribe, *Phanera variegata* (L.) Benth.
Description:	It is a deciduous tree which is about 8 m tall and 33 cm in diameter at the base. The plant grows in open areas in most tropical regions where it has been introduced as ornamental. The plant is native to tropical Asia. The bark is thickened, roughly cracked, grey. The stem is green, turning brown, zigzag-shaped, and with few lenticels. The leaves are simple, spiral and stipulate. The stipule is deciduous. The petiole is inflated at the base, straight, 2.5 - 3.8 cm long, angled and channeled above. The blade is bilobed, 10 - 15 x 10 cm- 15 cm, hairy underneath, dark green above, showing at the base a round mark which is 0.7 x 0.4 cm and a pair of 0.1 cm diameter round glands, and shows. 9 - 15 nerves. The inflorescence is a pubescent raceme. The calyx is 1.3 - 2.5 cm long and 5 - lobed. The corolla comprises 5 petals which are about 6 cm long, clawed, white or purple. The stamens are showy and curved. The pod is flat, 15 - 30 x 1.8 - 2.5 cm, flat, and contains 10 - 15 seeds which are discoid (Figure 30).
Medicinal Uses:	In India the plant is used to heal ulcers, to treat leprosy, bronchitis, asthma, piles, and to check bleeding. In Burma, the plant is used as a carminative, and tonic. In Malaysia, the plant is used as post-partum remedy. In the Philippines, the leaves are used to treat headache.
Pharmacology:	5,7,3',4'-tetrahydroxy-3-methoxy-7-O-alpha-L-rhamnopyranosyl(1-->3)-O-beta-galactopyranoside from the roots showed anti-inflammatory activity (Yadava *et al.*, 2001). An extract of the plant showed some activity against Dalton's ascitic lymphoma in Swiss albino mice (Rajkapoor *et al.*, 2003), and N-nitrosodiethylamine induced experimental liver tumor in rodents (Rajkapoor *et al.*, 2006). An extract of the pant inhibited the growth of *Bacillus subtilis*, *Pseudomonas aeruginosa*, *Salmonella typhi*, *Shigella dysenteriae*, *Staphylococcus aureus* and *Vibrio cholerae* (Pokhrel *et al.*, 2004).

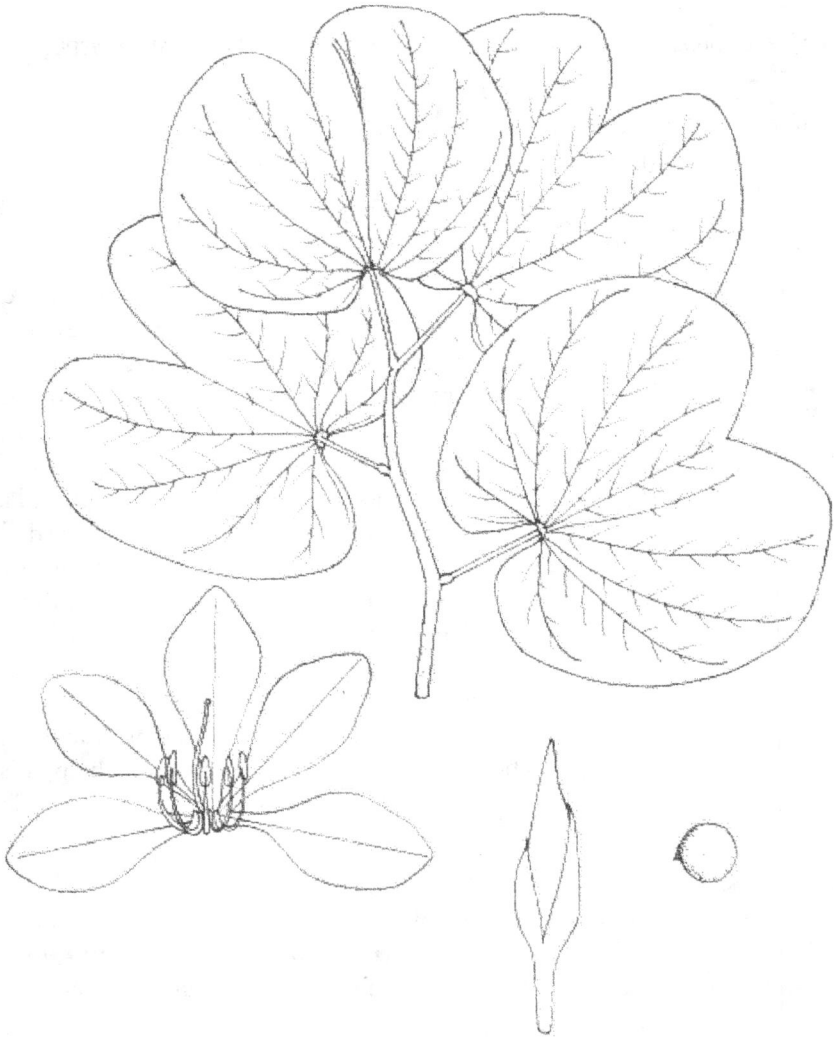

Figure 30: *Bauhinia variegata* L.
From: Flora of Thailand, Chiang Mai University Herbarium
Thailand, Chiang Mai province, Chiang Dao district, Doi Chiang Dao animal sanctuary, West side of Doi Luang and East of Huay Mae Gawk station. Elevation: 1450 m. Date of collection: 14 September 1995. In open disturbed , fired damaged deciduous secondary forest on limestone. Collection and identification: JF Maxwell № 95-715.

References: Pokhrel NR, Adhikari RP, Baral MP, 2004, *In-vitro* evaluation of the antimicrobial activity of *Bauhinia variegata*, locally known as koiralo. World J Microbiol Biotechnol; 18: 69-71

Rajkapoor B, Jayakar B, Murugesh N, 2003, Antitumor

activity of *Bauhinia variegata* on Dalton's ascitic lymphoma. J Ethnopharmacol; 89:107-9.

Rajkapoor B, Jayakar B, Murugesh N, Sakthisekaran D, 2006,Chemoprevention and cytotoxic effect of *Bauhinia variegata* against N-nitrosodiethylamine induced liver tumors and human cancer cell lines. J Ethnopharmacol;104:407-9.

Yadava RN, Reddy VM, 2001, A new flavones glycoside, 5-hydroxy 7,3',4',5'-tetra-methoxyflavone 5-O-beta-D-xylopyranosyl-(1-->2)-alpha-L-rhamnopyranoside from *Bauhinia variegata* Linn. J Asian Nat Prod Res; 3:341-6.

Caesalpinia major (Medik.) Dandy & Exell

[After Italian naturalist Andrea Cesalpino (1519-1603) and Latin *major* = larger]

Local names:	Brown nickerbean, yellow nicker, waat (Thailand), kuat (Cambodia), areuy mata hiyang (Indonesia)
Synonyms:	*Caesalpinia bonduc* auct. non (L.) Roxb., *Caesalpinia jayabo* Maza, *Caesalpinia macrantha* Delile, *Erythrostemon gilliesii* (Hook.)Link & al., *Poinciana gilliesii* Hook.
Description:	It is a woody climber which grows to 10 m in tropical America, India Southeast Asia, Ryukyu Islands, Australia and Pacific Islands. The stem is green, longitudinally striated, thorny, the thorns 0.3 cm long, from a 0.5 x 0.2 - 0.3 cm pimple. The leaves are compound, spiral and exstipulate. The stipule is subulata. The rachis is 1 cm in diameter at the base and 45 - 75 cm long, thorny with 3-8 pairs of pinnae and with a dull reddish hue. The pinnae is slightly angled, hairy, straight, thorny, 10 - 25 cm long and bears 3-4 pairs of folioles which are sub-opposite. The petiolule is horizontally striated, cracked with a few hairs. The folioles are ovate, thinly coriaceous, acuminate at the apex, pilose underneath, 3 - 8 x 1.5 - 4.3 cm., with 6 - 8 pairs of secondary nerves. The inflorescence is an axillary raceme which can reach 50 cm long. There are many fragrant flowers. The flower pedicel is 0.6 cm long and velvety. The flower bud is velvety and 0.3 x 0.6 cm. The calyx is greenish-brownish, about 0.5 cm long. The corolla comprises 5 petals which are yellow, clawed and about 1 cm long, the middle one marked with reddish crescent-shaped patterns. The anthers are dull - yellowish. The pod is 5 -14 x 4 - 5 cm, hairy, and containing 2-4 seeds which are globose, yellow, and marked at the apex by a tiny disk (Figure 31).

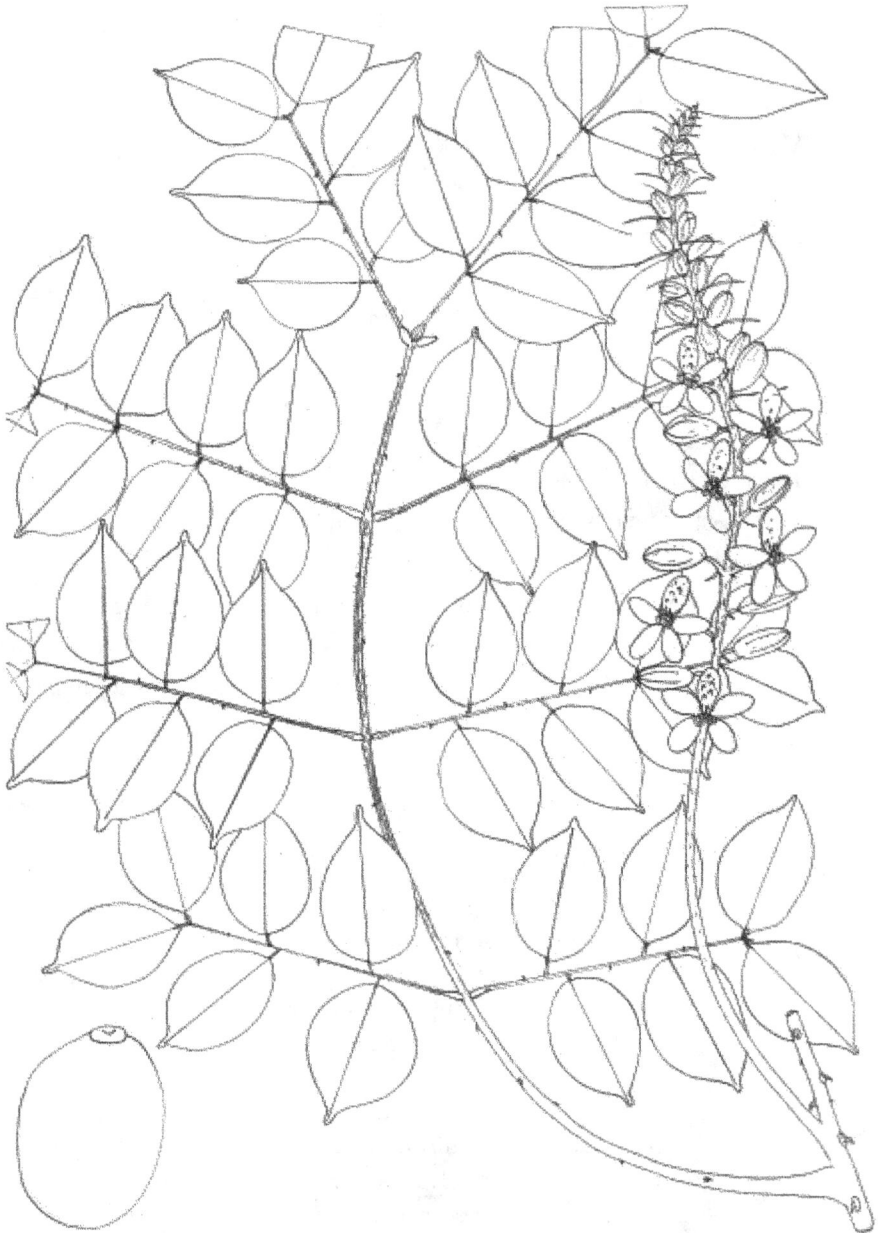

Figure 31: *Caesalpinia major* **(Medik.) Dandy & Exell**
From: Flora of Thailand, Prince of Songkla University
Thailand, Songkla province, Muang district, Sum Dtoon falls, by 99° East 9° North. Elevation: 75 m. Date of collection: 5 October 1984. In open disturbed area along the stream, secondary forest. Collection: JF Maxwell № 84-286

Medicinal Uses:	In Malaysia the plant is used to expel worms from the intestines. In Cambodia, the plant is used to treat respiratory illnesses. In Indonesia, the plant is used to treat dysentery, coughs, rheumatism and to expel worms. In the Philippines, the plant is used to break fever and is used as a purgative. In the Pacific Islands, the plant is used to invigorate.
Pharmacology:	The pod contains series of cassanes (Roengsumran *et al.*, 2000). The cassane diterpenoid, caesaldekarin a, inhibited mitogen responses of mouse spleen cells and interleukin-1 production (Kitagawa *et al.*, 1994).
References:	Kitagawa I, Simanjuntak P, Watano T, Shibuya H, Fujii S, Yamagata Y, Kobayashi M, 1994, Indonesian Medicinal Plants. XI. Chemical structures of caesaldekarins a and b, two new cassane-type furanoditerpenes from the roots of *Caesalpinia major* (Fabaceae). Chem Pharm Bull 42: 1798-1802
	Roengsumran S, Limsuwankesorn S, Ngamrojnavanich N, Petsom A, Chaichantipyuth C, Ishikawa T, 2000,Cassane diterpenoid from *Caesalpinia major*. Phytochemistry; 53:841-4.

Caesalpinia pulcherrima G. Don

[After Italian naturalist Andrea Cesalpino (1519-1603) and Latin *pulcherrima* = very beautiful]

Local names:	Spain carnation, daunts (Burma), semarah api (Malaysia), diep ta (Vietnam), fleur de paradi (France), caballero (Philippines), nalal (India)
Basionym:	*Poinciana pulcherrima* L. *Species Plantarum* 1: 380. 1753
Synonyms:	*Poinciana bijuga* Lour., *Poinciana elata* Lour., *Poinciana pulcherrima* L.
Description:	It is a magnificent shrub native to tropical America which is widespread in the tropics as an ornamental plant. The plant grows to 2 m and is armed with prickles. The stem is smooth, glabrous, lenticelled, zigzag - shaped and about 0.4 cm in diameter. The leaves are bipinnate, spiral and stipulate. The rachis is slightly constricted at the base and bears 12 - 18 pairs of pinnae. Some woody bracts are present between each pair of pinnae. The pinnae is glabrous, angled and bears 20 - 25 pairs of folioles which are membranaceous, 1.1 - 2.1 x 0.7 - 0.8 cm, sessile about and marked 7 pairs of secondary nerves, and a polyhedral net of tertiary nerves

underneath. The raceme is on a 7.5 - 10 cm long axe. The flower buds are globose, 0.4 x 0.6 cm with spoon-like lobes. The calyx is about 1.5 cm long. The corolla shows 5 petals which are 1.2 x 0.5 cm reddish yellow, clawed, and crisped. The stamens are much exerted, the filament hairy at the base. The fruit pedicel is straight and slender. The pod is flat, woody, glabrous with 6 - 8 seeds and pointed at the apex (Figure 32).

Medicinal Uses: In India, the plant is used to break fever, and to treat ulcers and tumours. In Cambodia, Laos and Vietnam, the plant is used to invigorate, to treat cholera, to abort, to induce menses, and to relieve constipation. In the Philippines, the plant is used to induce menses, to treat constipation and to invigorate. It is also used there to treat asthma, bronchitis and to break fever. In Taiwan, the plant is used to break fever, and to promote digestion and urination. In Indonesia, the plant is used to treat diarrhoea and convulsions.

Pharmacology: The plant has antibacterial, antimycobacterial and antiviral properties which may account for some of the medicinal uses mentioned above. An extract of pods exhibited a broad spectrum of antimicrobial activity, particularly against Gram negative *Escherichia coli*, *Pseudomonas aeruginosa* and Gram positive *Staphylococcus aureus* (Sudhakar *et al.*, 2006). The plant produces a series of cassane diterpenoids of which 6 beta-cinnamoyl-7beta-hydroxyvouacapen-5 alpha-ol showed strong antitubercular activity *in vitro* (Promsawan N *et al.*, 2003). Extracts of the plant exhibited strong activity against adenovirus ADV-8 *in vitro* (Chiang *et al.*, 2003). Note that 5,7-dimethoxyflavanone, 5,7-dimethoxy-3',4'-methylenedioxyflavanone, isobonducellin, 2'-hydroxy-2,3,4',6'-tetramethoxychalcone and bonducellin inhibited the inflammatory mediators nitric oxide tumour necrosis factor (TNF)-alpha and interleukin (IL)-12 *in vitro*, indicating an anti-inflammatory property (Rao *et al.*, 2005). The antitumor property is not validated yet but note that a cassane from the plant, pulcherrimin A, was found to be active in DNA repair-deficient yeast mutant (Patil *et al.*, 1997) .

References: Chiang LC, Chiang W, Liu MC, Lin CC, 2003, *In vitro* antiviral activities of *Caesalpinia pulcherrima* and its related flavonoids. J Antimicrob Chemother; 52:194-8.

Patil AD, Alan J Freyer AJ, R Lee Webb RL, Gary Zuber G, Rex Reichwein R, Mark F Bean MF, Leo Faucette L, Randall K. Johnson RK, 1997, Pulcherrimins A - D, novel diterpene dibenzoates from *Caesalpinia pulcherrima* with selective activity

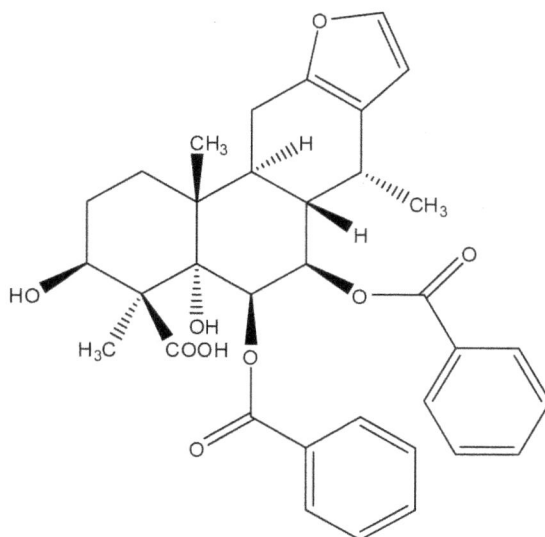

Pulcherrimin A

against DNA repair-deficient yeast mutants. Tetrahedron; 53: 1583-92.

Promsawan N, Kittakoop P, Boonphong S, Nongkunsarn P, 2003, Antitubercular cassane furanoditerpenoids from the roots of *Caesalpinia pulcherrima*. Planta Med; 69: 776-7

Rao YK, Fang SH, Tzeng YM, 2005, Anti-inflammatory activities of flavonoids isolated from *Caesalpinia pulcherrima*. J Ethnopharmacol;100 :249-53.

Sudhakar M, Rao ChV, Rao PM, Raju DB, Venkateswarlu Y, 2006,Antimicrobial activity of *Caesalpinia pulcherrima*, *Euphorbia hirta* and *Asystasia gangeticum*. Fitoterapia; 77: 378-80.

Figure 32a: *Caesalpinia pulcherrima* **G. Don (flower)**

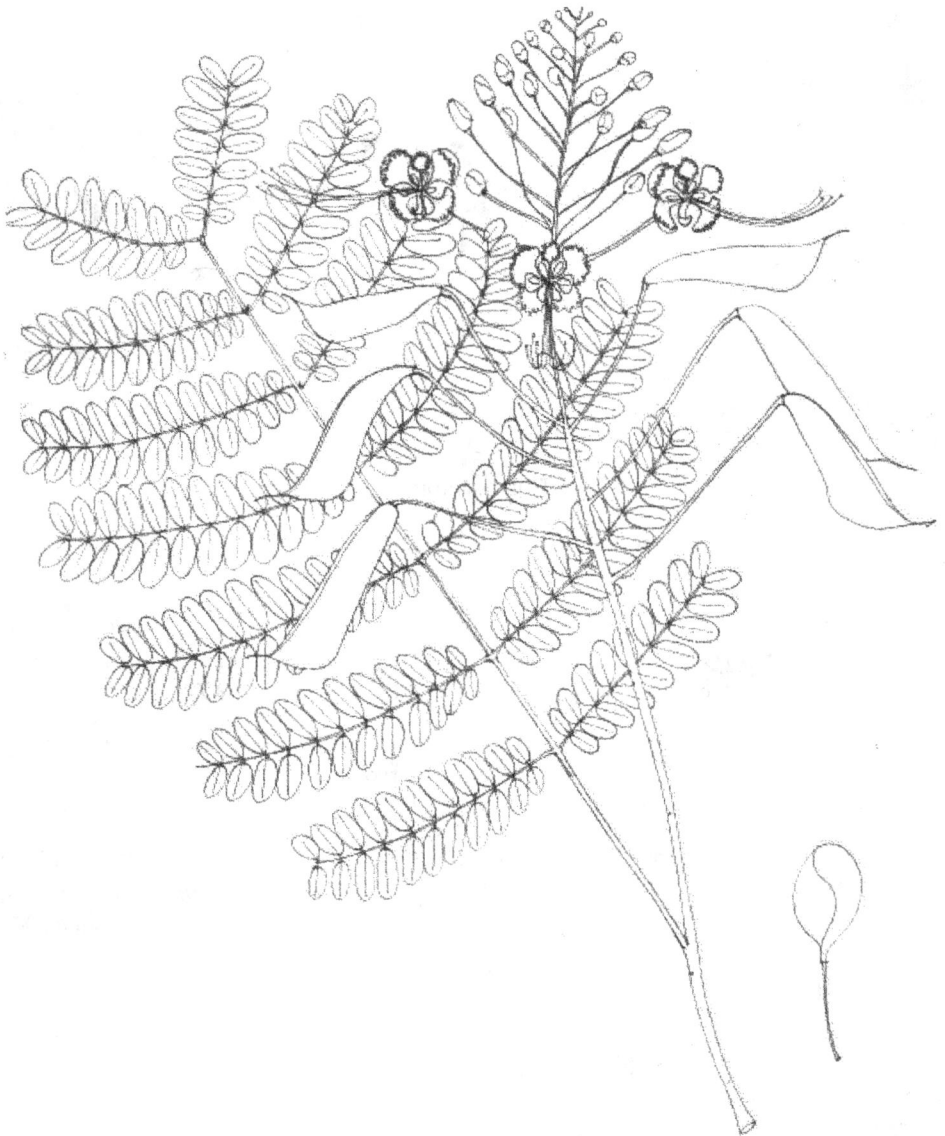

Figure 32b: *Caesalpinia pulcherrima* **G. Don**
From: Herbarium of University Kebangsaan Malaysia N° 12569
Malaysia, on the road from Kuala Lumpur to Genting Highland, Bukit Janda. Collection and
identification: Umi Kalsom Yusof. Date of collection: 17 July 1981.

Cassia fistula L.

[From Greek *kassia* and from Latin *fistulosus* = tubular]

Local names:	Golden shower, a po le (China), ngu (Burma), reach chhpus (Cambodia), kavani (Sri Lanka), bereksa (Malaysia), klobop (Indonesia), khoun (Laos), casse officinale (France), amaha (India, Sanskrit), cana fistula (Spain), ancherhan (Philippines), bo cap muoc (Vietnam), khuun (Thailand).
Synonyms:	*Bactyrilobium fistula* (L.) Willd., *Cassia bonplandiana* DC., *Cassia excelsa* Kunth., *Cassia fistuloides* Collad., *Cassia rhombifolia* Roxb., *Cathartocarpus excelsus* G.Don, *Cathartocarpus fistula* (L.) Pers., *Cathartocarpus fistuloides* (Collad.) G.Don, *Cathartocarpus rhombifolius* G Don
Description:	It is a tree which grows to 10 m tall all over the tropical world. The bark is dark brown. The wood is durable and of economic value. The stem is terete, striated longitudinally, lenticelled, 0.4 cm in diameter, angled and hairy at the apex and with 2 - 4 cm long internodes. The leaves are pinnate, spiral and stipulate. The stipule is deltoid, acute, and 0.1 - 0.2 cm long The rachis is enlarged at the base and 12 - 25 cm long with 3 - 8 pairs of folioles. The petiolule is 0.5 x 0.1 cm, channeled above, wrinkled and covered with minute hairs. The folioles are sub-opposite, ovate, papery, round at the apex, recurved at the margin, light green, glossy, with 12 - 15 pairs of secondary nerves. The inflorescence is a pendulous axillary raceme which is many flowered, showy and up to 50 cm long. The flower pedicel is 3.7 - 5.8 cm long, slender, and slightly hairy. The calyx is 5 lobed, green, hairy, and about 1 cm long. The corolla shows 5 petals which are obovate, blunt, orbicular, membranaceous and conspicuously veined. The stamens and the style are curled and conspicuous. The pod is terete, glabrous, indehiscent, to 60 cm long, black glossy brown, and contains up to 100 seeds, each one in an individual lodge in a pulp (Figure 33).
Medicinal Uses:	The aqueous percolate of crushed ripe fruits of *Cassia fistula* L. is a laxative (Cassia Pulp, British Pharmaceutical Codex, 1959). In India, the plant is used to treat leprosy, tuberculosis, constipation, fever, chest and liver ailments. In Thailand, the plant is used to remove worms from the intestines. In Cambodia, the plant is used to treat dysentery. In Indonesia, the plant is used to remove stones from kidneys and to heal infected wounds. In Papua New Guinea, the plant is used for broken bones.

Pharmacology: The antiseptic property of the plant has been confirmed: extracts of the plant exhibited a broad spectrum of antibacterial activity (Duraipandiyan *et al.*, 2007), and promoted the healing of experimentally infected wounds in rats (Kumar *et al*, 2006). An extract protected Wistar rats against diethylnitrosamine liver injuries (Pradeep *et al*, 2007), and also improved the enzymatic activity of superoxide dismutase, catalase, glutathione peroxidase, glutathione reductase and glutathione in alloxan diabetic rats (Manonmani *et al.*, 2005). The plant showed some level of inhibition against acetylcholinesterase (Ingkaninan *et al.*, 2003). Of particular interest is that an extract of seeds inhibited the growth of Ehrlich ascites carcinoma cells, increased life span and decreased the tumour volume in the tumour hosts (Gupta *et al.*, 2000). Possible active compounds could be proanthocyanidin, flavonoids or anthraquinones. Note that the pods have the highest total phenolic, proanthocyanidins, and flavonoids content and antioxidant potentials (Luximon-Ramma *et al.*, 2002).

References: Duraipandiyan V, Ignacimuthu S, 2007, Antibacterial and antifungal activity of *Cassia fistula* L.: An ethnomedicinal plant. J Ethnopharmacol:112:590-94.

Gupta M, Mazumder UK,Rath N, Mukhopadhyay DK, 2000, Antitumor activity of methanolic extract of *Cassia fistula* L. seed against Ehrlich Ascites Carcinoma. J Ethnopharmacol;72: 151-156.

Ingkaninan K, Temkitthawon P, Chuenchom K, Yuyaem T, Thongnoi W, 2003, Screening for acetylcholinesterase inhibitory activity in plants used in Thai traditional rejuvenating and neurotonic remedies. J Ethnopharmacol; 89:261-264

Kumar MS, Sripriya R, Raghavan HV, Sehgal PK, 2006, Wound healing potential of *Cassia fistula* on infected albino rat model. J Surg Res;131:283-289.

Luximon-Ramma A, Bahorun T, Soobrattee MA, Aruoma OI, 2002, Antioxidant activities of phenolic, proanthocyanidin, and flavonoid components in extracts of *Cassia fistula*. J. Agric. Food Chem., 50: 5042 -5047

Manonmani G, Bhavapriya V, Kalpana S, Govindasamy S, Apparanantham T, 2005, Antioxidant activity of Cassia fistula (Linn.) flowers in alloxan induced diabetic rats. J Ethnopharmacol; 97: 39-42.

Pradeep K, Mohan CVR, Gobianand K, Karthikeyan S, 2007, Effect of *Cassia fistula* Linn. leaf extract on diethylnitrosamine induced hepatic injury in rats. Chem-Biol Interact; 167: 12-18.

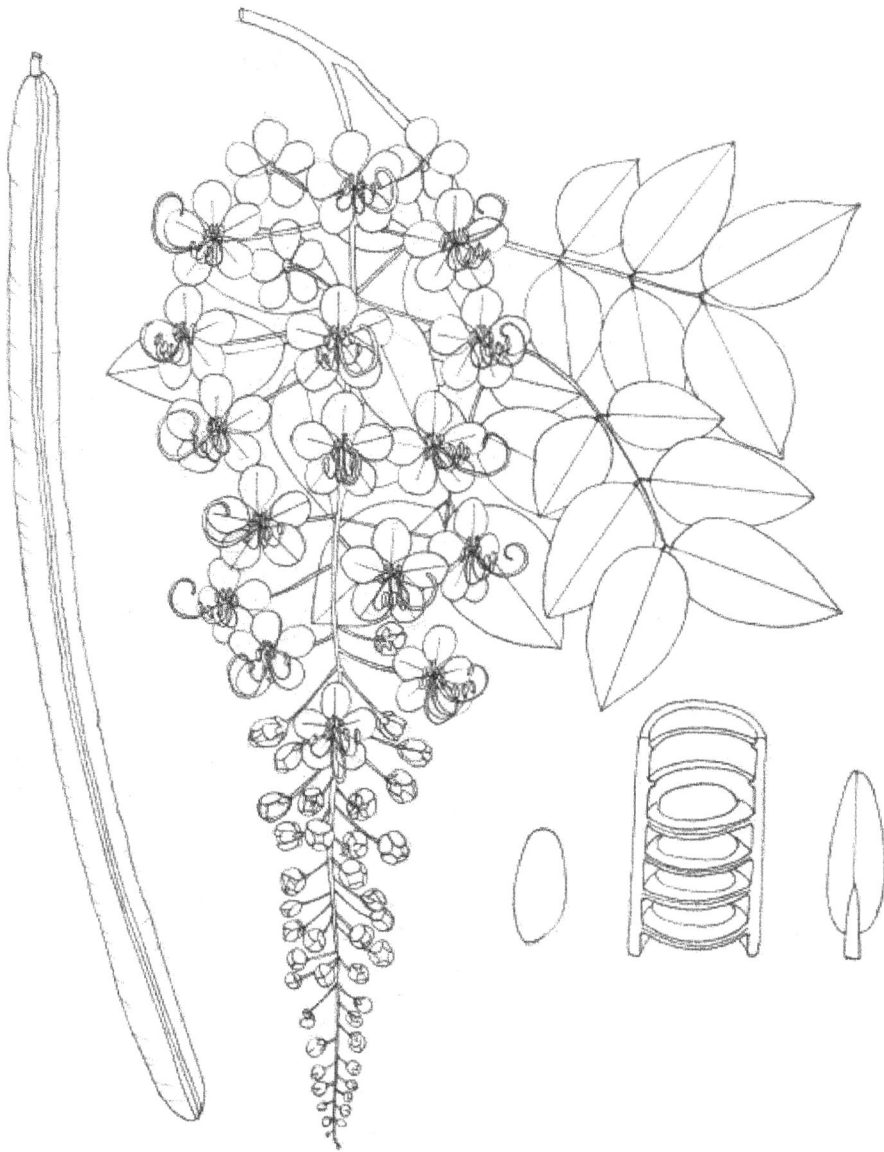

Figure 33: *Cassia fistula* **L.**
From: Flora of Malaya, Herbarium of University Kebangsaan Malaysia
Malaysia, Kuala Lumpur. Collection: Utong

Cassia mimosoides L.

[From Greek *kassia* and from Latin *mimosoides* = mimosa-like]

Local names:	Artillery plant, chiang mang (China), karagain (Philippines)
Synonym:	*Chamaecrista mimosoides* (L.) Greene
Description:	It is a herb which grows to a height of 75 cm on open lands and sandy soil in the tropical and sub-tropical regions of Africa and Asia. The stem is brown, arching, erect, hairy, and terete, about 0.3 cm in diameter, with 0.5 - 1 cm long internodes. The leaves are compound, spiral and stipulate. The stipule is deciduous, triangular, glabrous, 0.7 - 1 x 0.1 cm. The rachis is 7 - 10 cm long, hairy, channeled above, with a nectary gland at the base which is discoid and 0.3 cm in diameter. The rachis bears 20 - 50 pairs of folioles which are sessile. The foliole is 0.5 x 0.1 cm, oblong, and glabrous. The inflorescence is axillary, and bears 1 - 3 flowers. The flower pedicel is 0.5 cm long and hairy. The flower bud is 0.3 x 0.7 cm and hairy. The sepals are triangular, hairy outside and 0.5 x 0.1 cm. The petals are 0.4 x 0.8 cm, and bright yellow. The pod pedicel is 1.3 - 1.7 cm long. The pod is 5 - 6 x 0.4 cm, straight, flat, pointed at the apex, with few hairs and containing about 10 seeds which are rhomboid, dark green and about 0.3 cm long (Figure 34).
Medicinal Uses:	In Korea, Japan and Taiwan, the plant is used to promote urination and digestion. In the Philippines, the plant is used to treat diarrhoea. In India, the plant is used against vomiting. In Cambodia, Laos and Vietnam, the plant is used to heal infected abscesses. In Africa the plant is a valued medicinal material.
Pharmacology:	The plant abounds with a series of flavan dimers which are astringent and account for the anti-diarrhoea and healing uses mentioned above. (2S)-3',4',7-Trihydroxyflavan-(4 → 8)-catechin inhibited the enzymatic activity of lipase (Shimura *et al*, 1994; Hatano *et al.*, 1997) and showed effective activity in preventing and ameliorating obesity, fatty liver and hypertriglyceridemia in rats fed a high-fat diet (Yamamoto *et al.*, 2000). An extract showed some levels of antibacterial and antiviral activity *in vitro* (Sindambiwe *et al.*, 1999) which accounts for the healing property.
References:	HatanoT, YamashitaA, HashimotoT, ItoH, KuboN, YoshiyamaM, ShimuraS, ItohY, OkudaT, Yoshida T, 1997, Flavan dimers with lipase inhibitory activity from *Cassia nomame*. Phytochemistry; 46: 893-900.

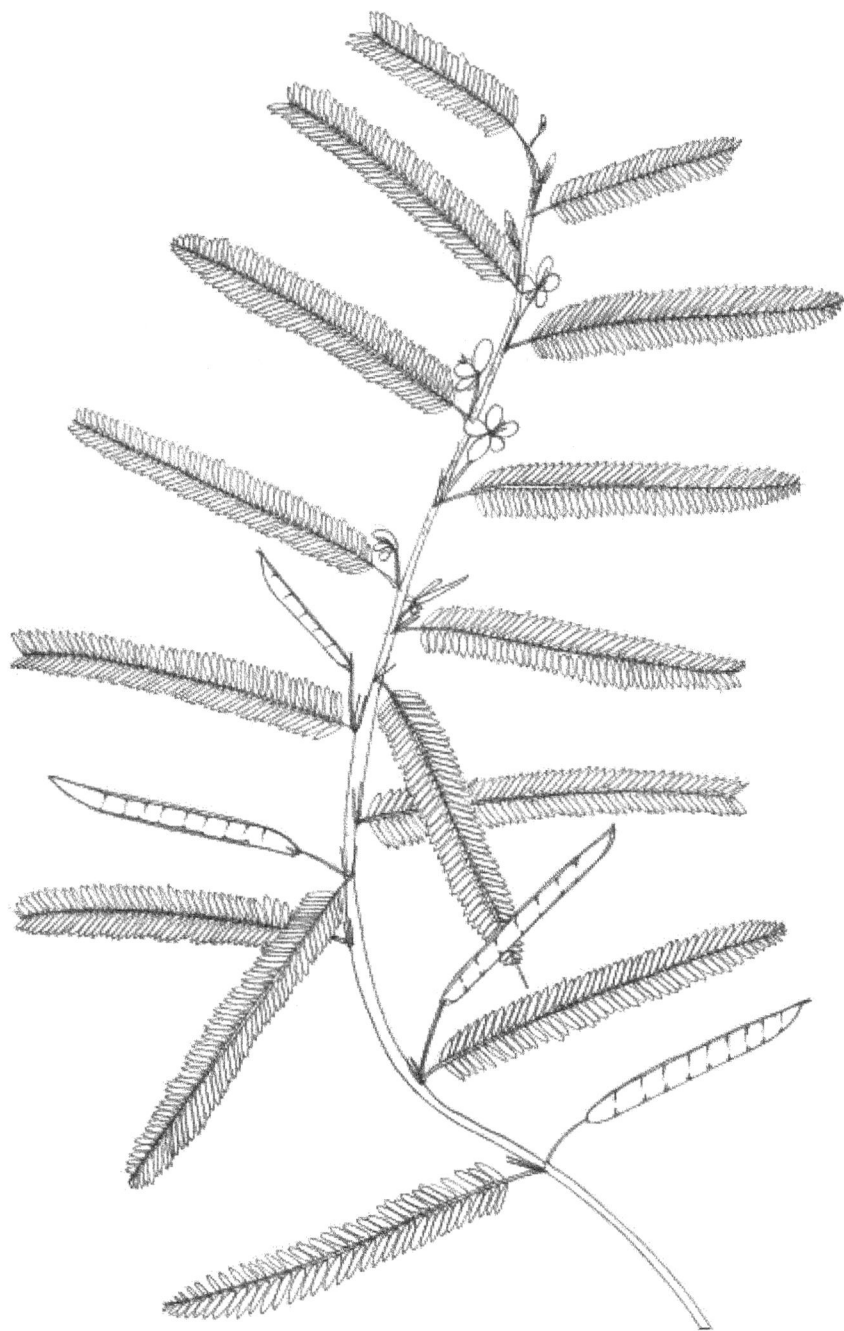

Figure 34: _Cassia mimosoides_ L.
From: Herbarium of University Kebangsaan Malaysia
Malaysia, Selangor state, near UKM campus, in cleared weedy margin of old rubber
plantation. Elevation: 100 m. Collection and identification: Benjamin C Stone № 15316.

Shimura S, Tsuzuki W, Itoh Y, Kobayashi S, 1994, Inhibitory effect of tannin fraction from *Cassia mimosoides* L. var. *nomame* Makino on lipase activity. J. Jap Soc Food Sci Technol; 4: 561

Sindambiwe JB, Calomme M, Cos P, Totté J, Pieters L, Vlietinck A, Vanden Berghe D, 1999, Screening of seven selected Rwandan medicinal plants for antimicrobial and antiviral activities. J Ethnopharmacol.65: 71-77

Yamamoto M, Shimura S, Itoh Y, Ohsaka T, Egawa M, Inoue S, 2000, Anti-obesity effects of lipase inhibitor CT-II, an extract from edible herbs, Nomame Herba, on rats fed a high-fat diet. Int J Obesity; 24: 758-64.

Cassia siamea Lam.

[From Greek *kassia* and from Latin *siamea* = from Siam, Thailand]

Local name:	Johar (Malaysia)
Synonyms:	*Cassia arborea* Macfad., *Cassia florida* Vahl., *Cassia gigantea* Bertero ex DC, *Cassia sumatrana* Roxb., *Chamaefistula gigantea* G.Don, *Sciacassia siamea* (Lam.) Britton, *Senna siamea* (Lam.) H.S. Irwin & Barn., *Senna sumatrana* Roxb.
Description:	It is a tree which grows to 20 m tall in India, Thailand, Malaysia, and Indonesia. The tree is often found by roadsides and in villages. The stem is terete, straight, 0.3 cm in diameter, lenticelled, and velvety at the apex. The internode is 4 - 5 cm long. The leaves are compound, spiral and stipulated. The rachis is flattish at the base, triangular, and presents series of glands and 7 - 11 pairs of folioles. The petiolule is 0.3 cm long. The foliole is dark above, coriaceous, glossy above, recurved at the margin with 8 - 10 pairs of secondary nerves, oblong with a tiny hair-like tip and 5 - 10 x 1.5 - 2.5 cm. The inflorescence is a terminal panicle which is hairy. The flower pedicel is 0.5 cm long. The flowers are 2.5 - 3 cm wide and bright yellow. The corolla lobes are 0.5 x 5 cm, orbicular to spoon-shaped. The anthers are brownish. The pod is flat curved, glossy, with a few hairs, pseudo-septae, brown and 14 - 20 x 2 cm (Figure 35).
Medicinal Uses:	In Burma, the plant is used to invigorate and to relieve stomach-ache. In Indonesia, the plant is used to treat malaria. In the Philippines, the plant is known to be toxic
Pharmacology:	The antimalarial use of the plant has been confirmed as it contains antiplasmodial compounds (Ajaiyeoba *et al.*, 2008)

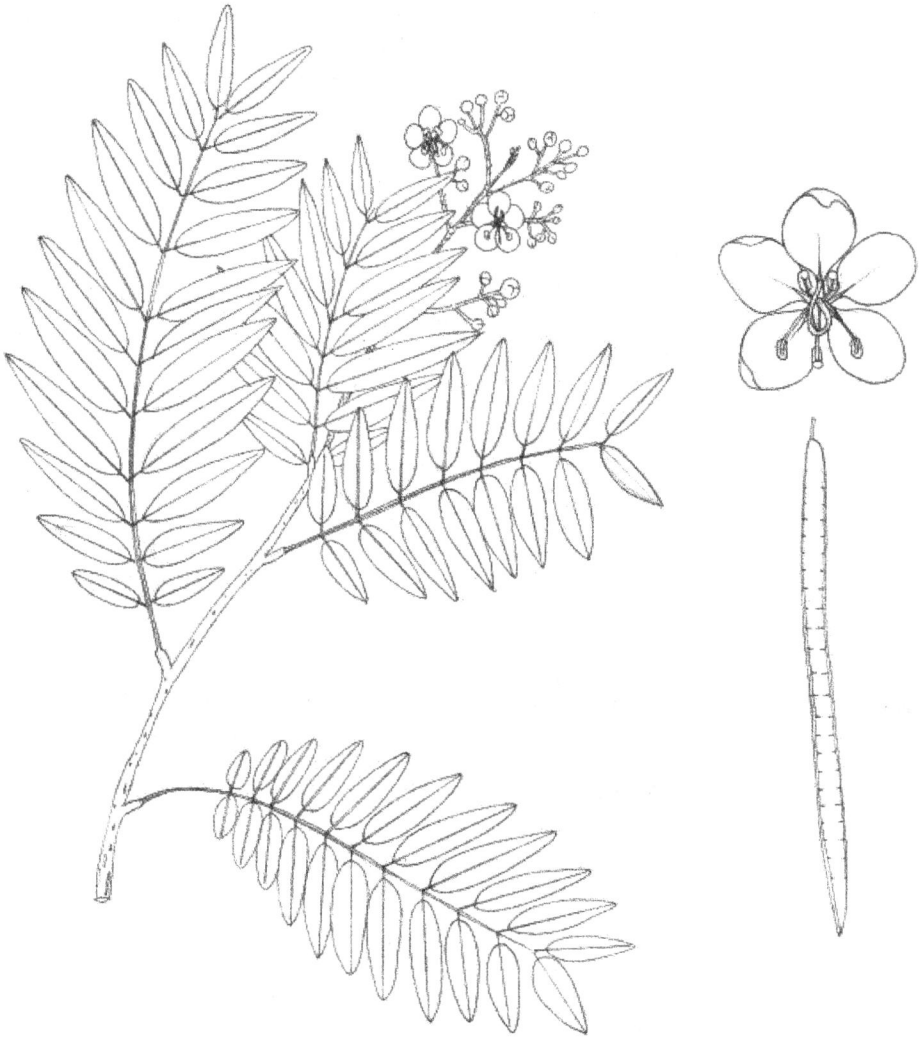

Figure 35: *Cassia siamea* **Lam.**
From: Flora of Thailand, Prince of Songkla University Herbarium
Thailand, Songkla province, foothills of Klong Raang Hill. In open area, secondary forest.

Pharmacology (Contd.)	one of which, an alkaloid, cassiarin A, showed a potent antiplasmodial activity (Morita *et al.*, 2007). Kaur *et al.*, (2006) reported potent antioxidant activity against free radicals, and prevention of oxidative damage in the liver by an extract of the flower. This activity may explain the invigorating property of the plant. However, a fraction of the plant reduced spontaneous locomotor activity, increased the number of sleeping animals and prolonged the thiopental-induced sleeping time, indicating a sedative effect (Sukma *et al.*, 2002).

References: Ajaiyeoba EO, Ashidi JS, Okpako LC, Houghton PJ, Wright CW, 2008, Antiplasmodial compounds from Cassia siamea stem bark extract. Phytother Res;22:254-5.

Kaur G, Alam MS, Jabbar Z, Javed K, Athar M, 2006, Evaluation of antioxidant activity of *Cassia siamea* flowers. J Ethnopharmacol; 108:340-8.

Morita H, Oshimi S, Hirasawa Y, Koyama K, Honda T, Ekasari W, Indrayanto G, Zaini NC, 2007, Cassiarins A and B, novel antiplasmodial alkaloids from *Cassia siamea*.Org Lett;9:3691-3.

Sukma M, Chaichantipyuth C, Murakami Y, Tohda M, Matsumoto K, Watanabe H, 2002,CNS inhibitory effects of barakol, a constituent of *Cassia siamia* Lamk. J Ethnopharmacol;83:87-94.

Cynometra ramiflora L.

[From the Greek *kynos* =a dog and *metra* = uterus and Latin *ramosus* = branched and *flora* = flower]

Local name: Cynometra, katong laut (Malaysia), oringen (Philippines), shingra (India)

Synonyms: *Cynometra bijuga* Miq., *Cynometra carolinensis* Kaneh., *Cynometra hosinoi* Kaneh, *Cynometra ramiflora* Miq., *Cynometra ramiflora* subsp. *bijuga* (Miq.)Prain, *Maniltoa carolinensis* (Kaneh.)Hosok.

Description: It is a tree which grows to15 m tall on sandy coasts, mangroves, and tidal rivers of a geographical area which ranges from India to the Pacific Islands. The bark is dark grayish. The stem is terete, with numerous pimply lenticels which are ovoid to linear and 0.01 cm long. The leaves are compound, spiral and stipulate. The stipule is deciduous. The rachis is straight, lenticelled, 3 - 8 cm long, channeled, and enlarged and fissured transversally at the base. The rachis bears 2 pairs of folioles. The petiolule is short, less than 0.01 cm long and 0.2 cm diameter. The foliole is coriaceous, glabrous, asymmetrical, 2.5 - 4 x 1 - 1.5 cm, smooth and glossy above, asymmetrical elliptic and with 6 - 7 pairs of secondary nerves. The upper pair is larger than the lower one. The flowers are small, yellowish white, and corymbiform pseudoracemes, and subtended by large bracts.

The calyx consists of 4-5 sepals which are 0.3 - 0.4 cm long. The corolla consists of 4 - 5 petals which are white and 0.4 - 0.5 cm long. The pod is globose, brown, somewhat potato-shaped, 2 - 4 x 2cm, rough, on a 0.5 cm long pedicel (Figure 36).

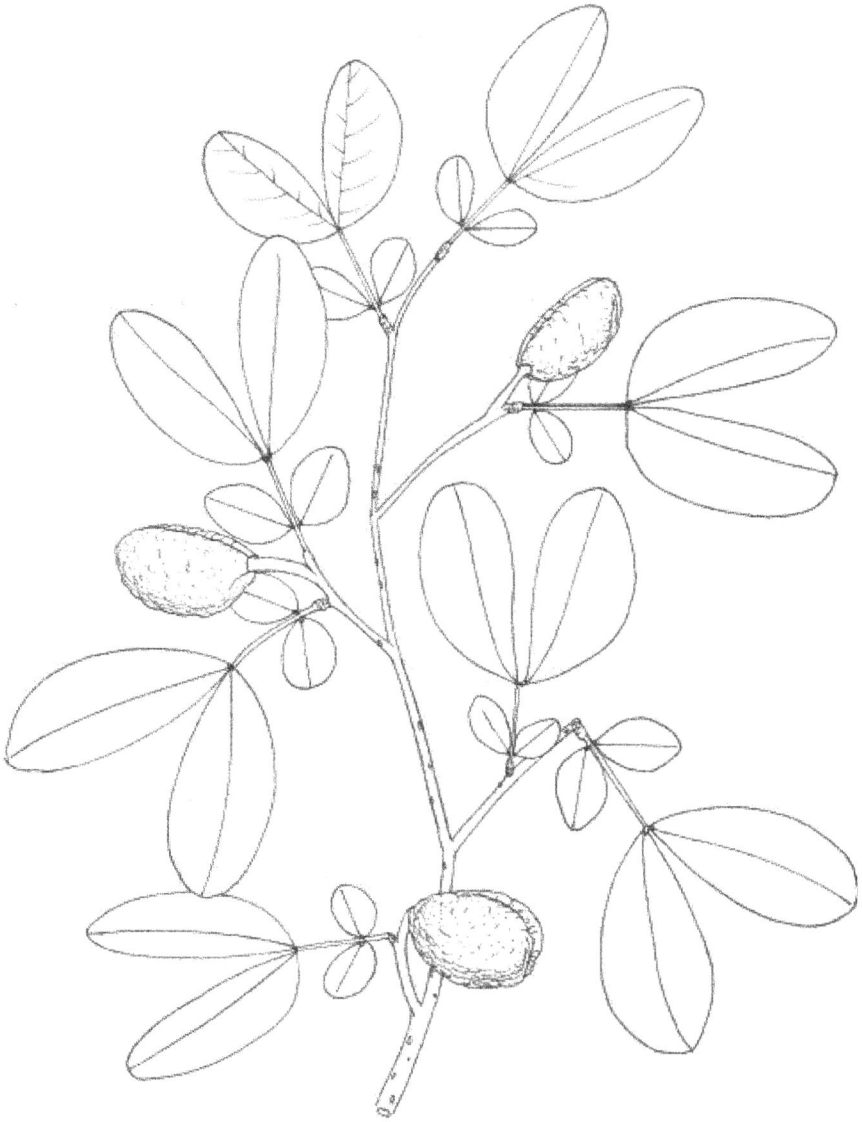

Figure 36: *Cynometra ramiflora* L.
From: Flora of Malaya, Herbarium of University Kebangsaan Malaysia No 06936
Malaysia, Pulau Langka, South of Kua near country club on rocky coastline. Tree on beach
rock. Collection and identification: Benjamin C Stone No 14337. Date of collection: 14
November 1979.

Medicinal Uses:	In Burma, the plant is used as a laxative. In the Philippines, the plant is used against herpes.
Pharmacology:	The pharmacological properties of the plant are unexplored. Note that extracts of *Cynometra cloiselii* and *Cynometra*

madagascariensis showed some levels of antiviral activity against herpes simplex virus (Hudson *et al,* 2000). These results warrant the pharmacological study of *Cynometra ramiflora* L. Imidazole alkaloids possible account for the antiviral properties of *Cynometra species.* (Waterman *et al.*, 1981, Tchissambou *et al,* 1982)

References: Hudson JB, Lee MK; Rasoanaivo P, 2000, Antiviral Activities In Plants Endemic To Madagascar. Pharm Biol; 38: 36-39.

Tchissambou L, Benechie M, Khuong-Huu F, 1982, Alcaloides imidazoliques-VI : Alcaloides du *cynometra lujae* isolement, structures, synthese. Tetrahedron; 38: 2687-95.

Waterman PG, Faulkner DF, 1981, Imidazole alkaloids from *Cynometra hankei.* Phytochemistry;20: 2765-67.

Delonix regia (Bojer ex Hook.) Raf.

[From the Greek *delo* = evident and *onux* = a claw and Latin *regia* = royal]

Local names: Royal Poinciana, klrishnachura, gul mohr (India), samarak, api (Malaysia), seinban (Burma), royal poinciana (France), hang nok yung farang (Thailand), phuong (Vietnam)

Basionym: *Poinciana regia* Bojer ex Hook. *Botanical Magazine* 56: pl. 2884. 1829

Synonym: *Poinciana regia* Bojer ex Hook.

Description: It is a magnificent tree native to Madagascar which is grown in several tropical countries as a street ornament. The stem is smooth, terete, lenticelled, about 0.4 cm in diameter, somewhat angled and minutely striated and releases a gum similar to gum Arabic. The leaves are bipinnate, ovoid, spiral and stipulate. The rachis is about 25 x 0.2 cm, smooth, subglabrous, and angled at the apex and presents 11 - 14 pairs of pinnae. The base of the rachis is inflated, hairy and flattish. The pinnae are 5 - 10.5 cm long with 12 - 24 pairs of folioles which are coriaceous, light green, ovoid, hairy underneath, asymmetrical at the base, roundish at the apex and about 1 x 0.3 cm. The inflorescence is an axillary raceme which is 10 - 18 cm long, terete at the base and angled at the apex. The flower pedicel is slender and 2.6 - 6 cm long. The flower buds are smooth, glabrous, about 2 x 1 cm, and obovoid. The calyx comprise 5 sepals which are 3.5 - 3.8 cm long and linear. The corolla consists of 5 conspicuously clawed petals which are crimson red, and about 3.5 cm long.

The stamens are hairy at the base and about 3 cm long. The anthers are 0.4 x 0.15 cm. The stigma is bifid. The fruit is a green turning dark brown, hard, woody cylindrical pod, which can reach 80 cm long with many horizontally partitioned lodges each of them containing one seed (Figure 37).

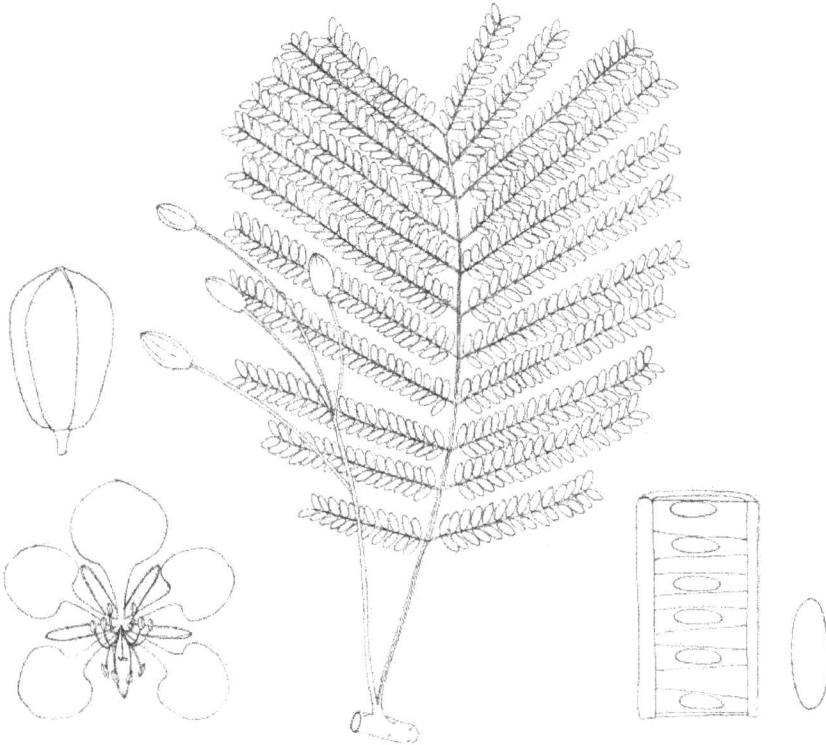

Figure 37: *Delonix regia* (Bojer ex Hook.) Raf.
From: Flora of Malaya No 00825
Malaysia, Kuala Lumpur, Jinjang. Collection and identification: Mohd Kassim

Medicinal Uses:	In Cambodia, Laos and Vietnam, the plant is used to break fever.
Pharmacology:	The pharmacological evidences obtained so far from this plant demonstrate strong antimicrobial properties which may explain the medicinal use of the plant against a fever due to bacterial infection. Extracts of the plant inhibited the growth

of clinical isolates of beta-lactamase producing methicillin-resistant *Staphylococcus aureus* (MRSA) and methicillin-sensitive *Staphylococcus aureus* (Aqil *et al.*, 2005) as well as multidrug-resistant enteric bacteria (Aqil *et al.*, 2005) and dermatophytes (Dutta *et al.*, 1998). The flowers contain cyanidin-3-glucoside cyanidin-3-gentiobioside (Saleh *et al*, 1976) as well as carotenoids (Jungalwala *et al.*, 1962). The active principle of this plant is unknown.

References:

Ahmad I, Aqila F, 2007, *In vitro* efficacy of bioactive extracts of 15 medicinal plants against ESbetaL-producing multidrug-resistant enteric bacteria. Microbiol Res;162:264-275.

Aqil F, Khan MS, Owais M, Ahmad I, 2005, Effect of certain bioactive plant extracts on clinical isolates of beta-lactamase producing methicillin resistant *Staphylococcus aureus*. J Basic Microbiol;45:106-14.

Dutta BK, Rahman I, Das TK, 1998, Antifungal activity of Indian plant extracts. Mycoses;41:535-6.

Jungalwala FB, HR Cama HR, 1962, Carotenoids in *Delonix regia* (Gul Mohr) Flower. Biochem. J; 85: 1-8.

Saleh NAM, Ishak MS, 1976, Anthocyanins of some Leguminosae flowers and their effect on colour variation. Phytochemistry;15:835-836.

Intsia bijuga (Colebr.) Kuntze

[From Indian plant name *Intsia* and Latin *bis* = twice and *jugum* = yoke]

Local names: Merbau ipil, merbau (Malaysia)

Basionym: *Macrolobium bijugum* Colebr. *Transactions of the Linnean Society of London* 12: 359, pl. 17. 1819

Synonyms: *Afzelia bijuga* (Colebr.) A. Gray., *Afzelia retusa* Kurz, *Intsia madagascariensis* DC, *Intsia retusa* (Kurz) O.K., *Macrolobium bijugum* Colebr.

Description: It is a medium sized tree of the sea coasts and the tidal reaches of rivers of the Indo-Pacific. The plant grows to 25 m and develops buttresses. The bark is brown. The stem is terete, pitted, lenticelled, fissured and about 0.5 cm in diameter. The leaves are pinnate, spiral and stipulate. The rachis is hairy, about 4 - 5 cm long, lenticelled, and bears 2 pairs of folioles. The petiolule is wrinkled and hairy. The foliole is thinly coriaceous, asymmetrical, broadly elliptic, glabrous, with 4 -5 pairs of secondary nerves and 4.2 - 7 x 3 - 5 cm. The flowers are arranged in terminal panicles . The calyx presents 4 sepals. The corolla comprises a single petal which is white with a prominent claw. The pod is large, 16 x 6 cm, flattish, woody and splits to release several oval seeds which are elliptic and 3.5 x 2.3 cm, spread by sea, and poisonous (Figure 38).

Figure 38: *Intsia bijuga* (Colebr.) Kuntze
From: Herbarium of University Kebangsaan Malaysia
Malaysia, Sedili Besar. Collection: R.Y. 63. Determination: Ramli Yusof. Date of collection: 23 January 1981.

Medicinal Uses: In Cambodia, Laos and Vietnam, the plant is used as a laxative. In Indonesia, the plant is used to treat diarrhoea.

Pharmacology: The plant seems unexplored for pharmacology.

Saraca indica L.

[*Saraca* a word derived from Sanskrit *ashoka* = *Saraca indica* L. and Latin *indica* = from India]

Local names:	Ashoka tree, thakwa (Burma), gapis (Malaysia), ashoka (India, Sanskrit), diyaratmal (Sri Lanka)
Synonyms:	*Saraca bijuga* Prain, *Saraca kunstleri* Prain
Description:	It is a tree which grows to 10 m in a geographical area covering India, Sri Lanka, Burma, Thailand, Cambodia, Malaysia, and Indonesia. The stem is smooth, fissured longitudinally, lenticelled, terete, and about 0.3 cm in diameter. The nodes are slightly enlarged. The leaves are compound, spiral and stipulate. The stipules are deciduous, 1 - 1.3 x -0.6 cm, and oblong. The rachis is angled, smooth, glabrous, straight, and enlarged at the base and bears 3 - 6 pairs of folioles. The petiolule is 0.3 - 0.4 x 0.2 cm. The folioles are coriaceous, 10 - 20 x 3 - 6 cm, oblong-lanceolate with 4 - 6 pairs of secondary nerves. The inflorescence is a stalked, slender cluster which is 10 cm across. The flower pedicel is 1.7 - 2 cm long with a pair of 0.4 x 0.2 cm bracts in the middle. The calyx is orange turning red, purplish to crimson at throat, tubular, the tube 1.3 - 2 cm long and develops 4 lobes which are oblong and 1 cm long. The androecium is much exerted with 5-10 stamens the filaments of which are filiform and 3 cm long. The anthers are purple. The pod is black, 10 - 25 x 4.5 - 5 cm, compressed , glabrous, veined horizontally, and containing 4 - 8 seeds which are ellipsoid and up to 4 cm long (Figure 39).
Medicinal Uses:	In India, the plant is used to treat tumors, to check bleeding of the vagina, to treat dysentery, to expel worms from intestines and to facilitate digestion. Note that the dried stem has been used as an astringent and uterine sedative (Ashok, Indian *Pharmacopoeia* 1955).In Burma, the plant is used to treat menorrhagia. In China, the plant is used for gynecological ailments.
Pharmacology:	The seed of the plant contains a lectin saracin, which induces apoptosis in activated T-lymphocytes (Ghosh *et al.*, 1999). The plant needs to be studied further for pharmacology.
Reference:	Ghosh S, Majumder M, Majumder S, Ganguly NK, Chatterjee BP, 1999, Saracin: a lectin from Saraca indica seed integument induces apoptosis in human T-lymphocytes. Arch Biochem Biophys;371:163-8.

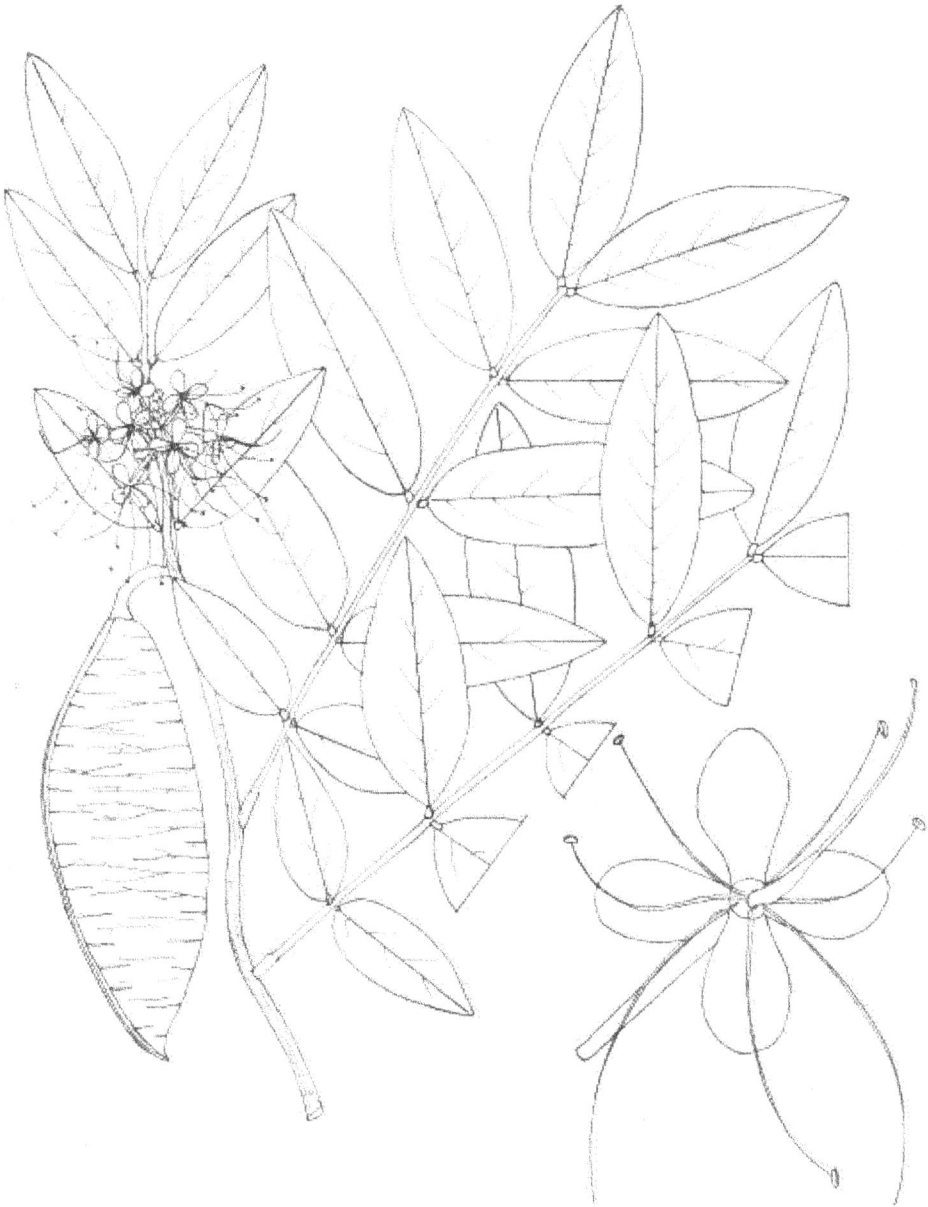

Figure 39: *Saraca indica* L.
From: Flora of Malaya, Herbarium of University Kebangsaan Malaysia
Malaysia, Johor state, Mersing, Tg Balang, Pulau Tinggi. Track to Semudu Besar. Elevation: 100 m. In volcanic lowland dipterocarp forest. Date of collection: 4th November 1995

3.Family FABACEAE Lindley 1836 nom. conserv., the Pea or Bean Family

The family Fabaceae consists of 400 genera and 10,000 species of herbs, shrubs or trees producing tannins, isoflavonoids, triterpenoid saponins, cyanogen glycosides, quinolizidine, pyrrolizidine, indole and simple tetrahydroisoquinoline alkaloids. The leaves are simple or compound, and stipulate. The flowers are zygomorphic, variously colored, with 5 petals, with the adaxial petal overlapping the lateral petals. The androecium comprises 10 stamens. The gynaecium consists of a single carpel forming a unilocular ovary. The fruits are pods. The seeds are very much enriched in proteins and peptides with potential pharmacological properties.

Examples of vegetables from this family are *Pisum sativum* L. (peas), *Phaseolus vulgaris* L., *Arachis hypogaea* L. (ground nuts), *Vicia faba* L., and *Glycine max* (L.) Merr. (soya beans). *Indigofera tinctoria* L. is a source of the dye indigo. Members of the genera *Cytisus*, *Laburnum*, *Lupinus* and *Crotalaria* produce quinolizidine alkaloids which are strong agonists of nicotinic receptors and are poisonous. *Cytisus scoparius* Link. (Scotch broom) contains sparteine (Sparteine, British Pharmaceutical Codex, 1949) which has been used as an oxytocic agent intramuscularly. .The plant has also been used as mild diuretic (Scoparium, *British Pharmaceutical Codex*, 1949). A number of plants species from the genus *Lupinus* are responsible for untimely delivery in cattle on account of anagyrine, an alkaloid which contracts the uterus. *Melilotus officinalis* (yellow sweet clover), *Psoralea argophylla* (scurf pea), *Dipterix odorata* Willd. (Tonka bean) cause lethal hemorrhages by inhibition of blood clotting. The ripe fruits of *Psoralea corylifolia* (Psoralea Fruits, *Indian Pharmacopoeia*, 1955) have been used for the treatment of skin diseases. *Dolichos lablab* (hyacinth bean), *Lotus corniculatus* (birdsfoot trefoil), *Phaseolus lunatus* (Lima bean), *Trifolium repens* (white clover) and *Vicia* contain cyanogen glycosides which are toxic. Phytohaemagglutinin from *Phaseolus vulgaris* L. is used in tissue culture to stimulate mitotic division and growth of lymphocytes. Individuals genetically deficient in glucose - 6 - phosphate dehydrogenase develop severe hemolytic anemia (favism) after ingesting the beans of *Vicia faba* L.. Classical examples of pharmaceutical products are *Physostigma venenosum* Balf (Calabar bean), which contains an alkaloid, physostigmine (*British Pharmaceutical Codex*, 1963) used to treat myasthenia gravis and primary glaucoma. *Myroxylon pereirae* (Peru Basalm, *British Pharmaceutical Codex*, 1963) has been used for healing and antiseptic properties, *Myroxylon balsamum* (L.) Harms (Tolu Basalm, *British Pharmacopoeia*, 1963) is an ingredient for cough remedy and the roots of *Glycyrrhiza glabra* L. (Liquorice, British Pharmacopoeia 1963) are used as demulcent, expectorant and flavoring agent. Isoflavonoids of Fabaceae are known to have estrogenic effects or insecticidal and cytotoxic properties (rotenoids such as rotenone in the genus *Derris*). Of recent pharmacological interest are saponins from *Pithecellobium lucidum* which elicited cytotoxic effects against human tumoral cell lines (HCT-8, Bel-7402, BGC-823, A549, and A2780 (Ma *et al.*, 2008). The prenylated flavanone 2'-4'-dihydroxy-5'-(1'''-dimethylallyl)-6-prenylpinocembrin, isolated from the roots of *Dalea elegans* Gillies ex Hook. & Arn., displayed antioxidant, antibacterial and mitochondrial toxicity (Elingold *et al.*, 2008). The compound 7,9,2',4'-tetrahydroxy-8-isopentenyl-5-methoxychalcone, from *Sophora flavescens* Aiton abrogated the survival of acute promyelocytic (HL60), mouse lymphocytic (L1210) and human histiocytic (U937) leukemia cells cultured *in vitro* (Lee *et al.*, 2007). Li *et al* (2007) Isolated a lupane acid, 2beta-carboxyl,3beta-hydroxyl-norlup (1)-20 (29)-en-28-oic acid with strong anti-HIV activity from *Gleditsia sinensis* Lam.

References: Elingold I, Isollabella MP, Casanova MB, Celentano AM, Pérez C, Cabrera JL, Diez RA, Dubin M, 2008, Mitochondrial toxicity and antioxidant activity of a prenylated flavonoid isolated from *Dalea elegans*. Chem-Biol Interact;171:294-305.

Lee JH, Baek NI, Kim SH, Park HW, Yang JH, Lee JJ, Kim SJ, Jeong S, Oh CH, Lee KH, Kim DK, 2007, A new cytotoxic prenylated chalcone from *Sophora flavescens*. Arch Pharm Res; 30:408-11.

Li WH, Zhang XM, Tian RR, Zheng YT, Zhao WM, Qiu MH, 2007, A new anti-HIV lupane acid from *Gleditsia sinensis* Lam. J Asian Nat Prod Res;9:551-5.

Ma SG, Hu YC, Yu SS, Zhang Y, Chen XG, Liu J, Liu YX, 2008,Cytotoxic triterpenoid saponins acylated with monoterpenic acid from *Pithecellobium lucidum*. J Nat Prod; 71:41-6.

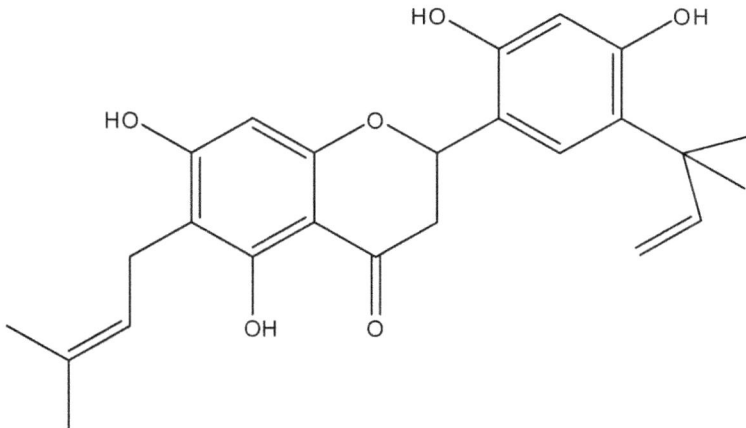

2'-4'-Dihydroxy-5'-(1'''-dimethylallyl)-6-prenylpinocembrin

Abrus pulchellus Wall. ex Thwaites

[From Greek *habros* = graceful and Latin *pulchellus* = beautiful]

Synonyms:	*Abrus melanospermus* Hassk., *Abrus strictospermus* Berhaut, *Abrus tenuifolius* Spruce ex Benth.
Description:	It is a slender climber which grows to 6 m long. The plant is ornamental and grows throughout the tropics. The stem is dull light green, terete, 0.1 cm in diameter, sub-glabrous, with internodes which are about 5 cm long. The leaves are compound, spiral and stipulate. The stipule is deciduous. The rachis is 10 - 12 cm long, slender, hairy and bears 8 to 10 pairs of folioles. The petiolule is tiny and hairy. The foliole is dull light green, 3.2 - 3.5 x 1.1 - 1.3 cm, membranaceous, with a few hairs, glabrous, translucent, oblong, asymmetrical at the base, round at the apex with a tiny tip and with about 6 pairs of secondary nerves which are inconspicuous. The inflorescence is an axillary, dull light green and slender raceme. The flowers are about 1 cm long. The calyx is cup-shaped without lobes, membranaceous, 0.2 cm long and sub-glabrous. The corolla is 0.55 cm long. The pod is velvety, woody, 4.9 - 3.4 x 0.9 - 0.2 cm, and acuminate at the apex. The seeds are glossy, reniform and 0.3 x 0.6 cm (Figure 40).
Medicinal Uses:	The plant is used as a substitute for liquorice and to clear the voice in Malaysia.
Pharmacology:	The seeds are toxic on account of lectins. The pharmacological property of the plant has not been fully explored yet.
Reference:	Márcio V. Ramos MV, Daniel M. Mota DM, Clarissa R. Teixeira CR, Benildo S, Cavada BS, Renato A, Moreira RA, 1998, Isolation and partial characterization of highly toxic lectins from *Abrus pulchellus* seeds. Toxicon; 36: 477-484.

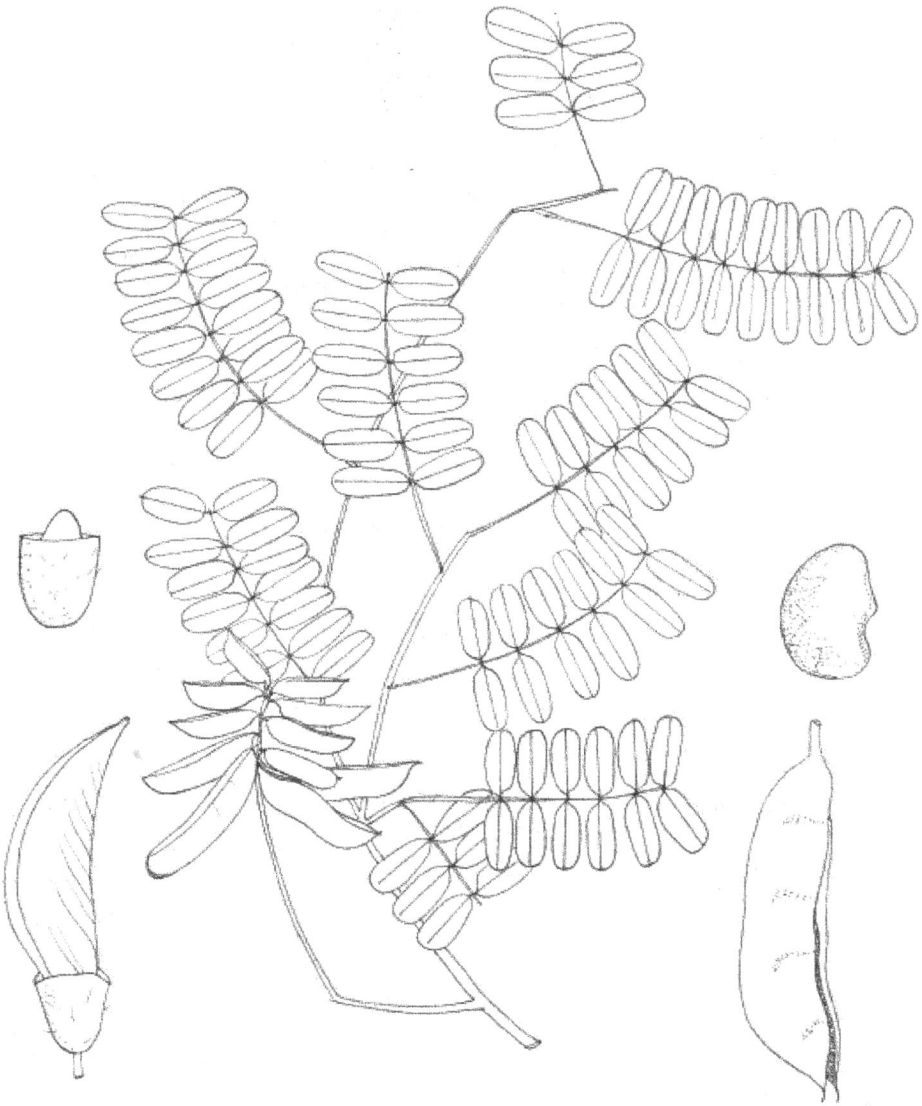

Figure 40: *Abrus pulchellus* Wall. ex Thwaites
From: Flora of Thailand. Chiang Mai University Herbarium.
Thailand, Lampang province, Muang Bahn district, Jae Sawn national park, along Mae Mawn stream, below Jae Sawn falls. Elevation: 475 m. Date of collection: 8 January 1986. By 18° 05'; North - 99° East. In open disturbed, overgrown, fire-damaged area in very degraded deciduous forest with much bamboo, on granite bedrock. Collection and identification: JF Maxwell, N° 95-951

Arachis hypogaea L.

[From Greek *arakos* = a leguminous plant and Greek *hypo* = beneath *geo* = earth]

Local names:	Groundnut, peanut, kacang Cina (Malaysia), kacang tanah (Indonesia), mani (Philippines), sandak dey (Cambodia), thwaks ho (Laos), thua din (Thailand), lac (Vietnam).
Description:	It is an annual, erect or prostrate herb, to 30 cm long, which is native to South America (first found in Peru), and has been spread by the Portuguese, Spaniards, Dutch and British in most tropical regions of the world for its seeds: peanut and peanut oil which are of economic value. The plant is a common ornamental in tropical gardens and streets. It is annual herb that grows to abut 30 cm long in open and waste land fully exposed to sun. The stem is terete, pilose, smooth, light green and somewhat stout. The leaves are pinnate, spiral and stipulate. The stipule is conspicuous, 1 - 4 cm and bifid at the apex. The rachis is 2 - 10 cm long, stout, finely grooved above and bears 2 pairs of folioles. The petiolule is about 0.15 cm long. The folioles are light green, 1 - 8 x 0.5-3.5 cm, tapering at the base, round at the apex and slightly emarginated, with 8 - 10 pairs of secondary nerves. The inflorescence is axillary, with a single flower, aerial at first and subterranean when fruiting. The flower pedicel and calyx are pilose. The corolla is golden yellow, with reddish nerves, a broad standard, and up to 1.5 cm long. The pod is 2 -6 cm long, with 1 or 2 seeds which are irregularly ovoid and oily (Figure 41).
Medicinal Uses:	In China, the plant is used to invigorate, and to treat stomach and lung diseases.
Pharmacology:	Patel *et al* (2005) isolated a prenylated resveratrol: 4-(3-methyl-but-1-enyl)-3,5,3',4'-tetrahydroxystilbene which inhibited lipopolysaccharide-induced expression of cyclo-oxygenase-2 protein and cyclo-oxygenase-2 mRNA in mouse. The seeds are antibacterial (Bonnier C *et al.*, 1952). The seed skin contains flavonoids and alkaloids (Lou H *et al.*, 2001). Some of these flavonoids are antioxidants and free radicals scavengers (Wang J *et al.*, 2007). One of these, procyanidin A1, inhibits the synthesis of immunoglobulin during allergic reaction by regulating T helper cytokine production (Takano F *et al.*, 2007).
References:	Bonnier C., 1952, The antibacterial properties of the seed of Arachis hypogaea L. C R Seances Soc Biol Fil;146(3-4): 309-10.
	Lou H, Yuan H, Yamazaki Y, Sasaki T, Oka S, 2001, Alkaloids and flavonoids from peanut skins. Planta Med;67(4):345-9
	Patel B, Patel S, Hoffman R, 2005,Inhibition of cyclo-oxygenase-2 expression in mouse macrophages by 4-(3-methyl-

Figure 41: *Arachis hypogaea* L.

From: Flora of Malaya
In Hevea plantation, Bedong estate, Kedah. Collection: Haton Din

but-1-enyl)-3,5,3',4'-tetrahydroxystilbene, a resveratrol derivative from peanuts. Phytother Res;19: 552-5.

Takano F, Takata T, Yoshihara A, Nakamura Y, Arima Y, Ohta T. Aqueous extract of peanut skin and its main constituent procyanidin A1 suppress serum IgE and IgG1 levels in mice-immunized with ovalbumin. Biol Pharm Bull; 30: 922-7.

Wang J, Yuan X, Jin Z, Tian Y, Song H, 2007,Free radical and reactive oxygen species scavenging activities of peanut skins extract. Food Chem; 104: 242-50.

Atylosia scarabaeoides (Baill.) Benth.

[From Latin *scarabaeoides* = scarab-like]

Local names:	Pigeon pea; kulthia (India), walkollu (Sri Lanka), kacang gude (Indonesia), mangkitbagin (Philippines), thuapi (Thailand)
Basionym:	*Cantharospermum scarabaeoides* (L.) Baill. *Bulletin Mensuel de la Société Linnéenne de Paris* 1(48): 384. 1883.
Synonyms:	*Atylosia pauciflora* (Wight & Arn.) Druce, *Cajanus scarabaeoides* (L.) Thou. ex R. Grah., *Cantharospermum pauciflorum* Wight & Arn., *Cantharospermum scarabaeoides* (L.) Baill., *Cantharospermum scarabaeoideum* (L.) Baill., *Dolichos medicagineus* Roxb.*, Dolichos minutus* Wight & Arn., *Dolichos scarabaeoides* L., *Rhynchosia biflora* DC, *Rhynchosia scarabaeoides* (L.) DC., *Stizolobium scarabaeoides* (L.) Spreng.
Description:	It is a climber which grows in Africa, India, south-east Asia, China, Taiwan, Papua New Guinea, and Australia. The stem is hairy, twinning, undulating, slender, hairy, 0.1 cm in diameter and with 6 - 8 cm long internodes. The leaves are trifoliolate, spiral and stipulate. The stipule is deciduous. The rachis is 2 - 4 cm long. The petiolule is about 1.3 cm long. The foliole is obovate-oblong, papery, with 3-5 pairs of secondary nerves and hairy underneath. The inflorescence is an axillary raceme which is hairy and 2-6 flowered. The calyx is hairy with linear lobes. The corolla is yellow, 0.8 - 1 cm long, the keel abruptly incurved at the apex. The pod is 1.5 - 2 x 0.5 cm, 4 - 6 seeded, hairy and with distinct septae which are 0.3 x 0.5 cm. The seeds are reddish, mottled brown or black, oblong, and 0.3 x 0.2 cm (Figure 42).
Medicinal Uses:	In Taiwan, the plant is used for sore throat.
Pharmacology:	Unknown.

Figure 42: *Atylosia scarabaeoides* **(Baill.) Benth.**
From: Botanical Inventory of Taiwan. Herbarium, institute of Botany, Academia Sinica, Taipei
(HAST)
Taiwan, Miaoli Hsien, Taian Hsiang, on the way to Taian mineral spring and Hushan mineral
spring. Elevation: 400 m. Collection and identification: Chi-Hsien Lin 536. date of collection 29
September 1990.

Cajanus cajan (L.) Millsp.

[From Malay *kacan* = the Malay name of the plant]

Local names:	pigeon pea, dhal (India), pesigon (Burma), shan tou ken (China), pois cajan (France), dau sang (Vietnam), cagyos (Philippines), tantaraga (Portugual), supya (Sanskrit), ratatora (Sri Lanka)
Basionym:	*Cytisus cajan* L. *Species Plantarum* 2: 739. 1753
Synonyms:	*Cajan cajan* (L.) Huth., *Cajan inodorum* Medik., *Cajanum thora* Raf., *Cajanus bicolor* DC., *Cajanus flavus* DC., *Cajanus indicus* Spreng., *Cajanus luteus* Bello, *Cajanus obcordifolia* Singh, *Cajanus pseudocajan* (Jacq.) Schinz & Guillaumin, *Cajanus striatus* Bojer, *Cytisus cajan* L., *Cytisus guineensis* Schum. & Thonn., *Cytisus pseudocajan* Jacq.
Description:	It is a shrubby herb which grows to 1.5 m. The plant is native to Southeast Asia and is now pantropical. It is cultivated for food, particularly in India and Africa. The stem is terete, velvety, ribbed, 0.4 cm in diameter, with 6 - 8 cm long internodes. The leaves are trifoliolate, spiral and stipulate. The stipule is velvety outside and about 0.4 cm long. The rachis is 2.2 - 2.5 cm, angled, channeled, velvety, and swollen at the base. The petiolule is velvety and about 0.2 cm long. The folioles are spathulate-oblong, dark green, glabrous above, velvety underneath, with 4 - 5 pairs of secondary nerves, 1.7 - 3.5 x 4.5 - 8.9 cm. The inflorescence is an axillary, velvety, 3 - 5 cm long raceme. The flower pedicel is 1.5 cm long. The calyx is 0.6 cm long, green, with dark maroon patches and velvety. The corolla is about 2 cm long with a bright yellow standard with crimson patches, crimson underneath, broadly lanceolate and about 1.5 cm in diameter. The wings and keel are yellowish-green. The pod is dark green with maroon blots and streaks, to 10 cm long, with purplish streaks, hairy containing 3-5 seeds and developing a long apical tail. The seed is oblong globose, about 0.5 cm in diameter and marked with an elliptic mark at one side (Figure 43).
Medicinal Uses:	In India, the plant is used to treat leprosy, tumours, weakness, piles, heart diseases, diabetes, liver diseases and inflammation. In Cambodia, Laos and Vietnam the plant is used to promote urination. In Malaysia, the plant is used to treat coughs, diarrhoea, and abdominal troubles. In Indonesia, the plant is used to treat skin diseases including herpes.

Figure 43: *Cajanus cajan* (L.) Millsp.
From: Flora of Thailand, Prince of Songkla University Herbarium
Thailand, Songkla province, Haad Yai district, in agricultural test plot, open area with poor soil. By 8° 05' North - 99° East. Elevation: sea level. Date of collection: 19 January 1985. Collection and identification: JF Maxwell.

Pharmacology: The plant has been the topic of cohorts of pharmacological and nutritional studies. The seeds contain a significant amount of phenylalanine (Ekeke *et al.*, 1990) and hydroxybenzoic acid (Akojie *et al.*, 1992) which account for most of the antisickling property reported by Iwu *et al*, 1986, suggesting some potential for the treatment of sickle cell anemia. The seeds contain proteins which are hepatoprotective in rodents including protein CI-1(Datta *et al*, 1998, 1999). Duker-Eshun *et al* (2004) isolated the stilbenes longistylin A and C, and the triterpene betulinic acid which showed some levels of antiplasmodial activity against the chloroquine-sensitive *Plasmodium falciparum* strain 3D7. An extract of the plant exhibited a strong antifungal effect against *Candida albicans*. Cajanine (longistylin A-2-carboxylic acid) has an oestrogen-like action on osteoblast and osteoclast and appears as a possible candidate for osteoporosis treatment (Zheng *et al.*, 2007). A fraction of the plant containing stilbene lowered cholesterol and triglyceride levels in diet-induced hyperlipidemic Kunming mice (Luo *et al.*, 2008). The seeds lowered glucose levels on alloxanized mice, confirming thereby the antidiabetic property of the plant

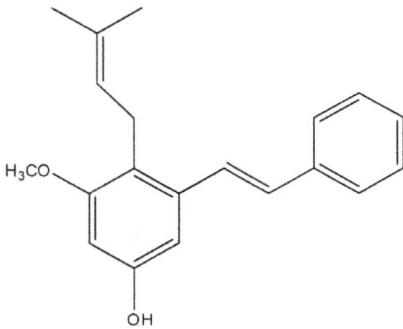

Longistiylin C

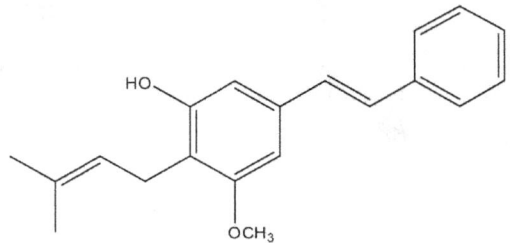

Longistiylin A

References:`

Akojie FO, Fung LW, 1992, Antisickling activity of hydroxybenzoic acids in *Cajanus cajan*. Planta Med;58:317-20.

Amalraj T, Ignacimuthu S, 1998, Hypoglycemic activity of *Cajanus cajan* (seeds) in mice. Indian J Exp Biol;36:1032-3.

Braga FG, Bouzada ML, Fabri RL, de O Matos M, Moreira FO, Scio E, Coimbra ES, 2007, Antileishmanial and antifungal activity of plants used in traditional medicine in Brazil. J Ethnopharmacol;111:396-402.

Datta S, Basu K, Sinha S, Bhattacharyya P, 1998, Hepatoprotective effect of a protein isolated from *Cajanus indicus* (Spreng) on carbon tetrachloride induced hepatotoxicity in mice. Indian J Exp Biol;36:175-81

Datta S, Sinha S, Bhattacharyya P, 1999, Hepatoprotective activity of a herbal protein CI-1, purified from *Cajanus indicus* against beta-galactosamine HCl toxicity in isolated rat hepatocytes. Phytother Res. 1999 13:508-12

Duker-Eshun G, Jaroszewski JW, Asomaning WA, Oppong-Boachie F, Brøgger Christensen S, 2004, Antiplasmodial constituents of *Cajanus cajan*. Phytother Res;18:128-30.

Ekeke GI, Shode FO, 1990, Phenylalanine is the predominant antisickling agent in *Cajanus cajan* seed extract. Planta Med; 56:41-3.

Iwu MM, Igboko OA, Onwubiko H, Ndu UE, 1986, Anti-sickling properties of *Cajanus cajan*: effect on haemoglobin gelation and oxygen affinity. Planta Med;52:431.

Luo QF, Sun L, Si JY, Chen DH, Du GH,2008, Hypocholesterolemic effect of stilbene extract from *Cajanus cajan* L. on serum and hepatic lipid in diet-induced hyperlipidemic mice. Yao Xue Xue Bao; 43:145-9.

Zheng YY, Yang J, Chen DH, Sun L, 2007, Effects of the extracts of *Cajanus cajan* L. on cell functions in human osteoblast-like TE85 cells and the derivation of osteoclast-like cells Yao Xue Xue Bao;42:386-91.

Clitoria ternatea L.

[From Greek *kleitoris* = clitoris and Latin *ternatea* = of the island of Ternate in the Moluccas]

Local names:	Blue pea, kachang telang (Malaysia), kowa (India), bukiyu (Burma), diep dau (Vietnam), fula criqua (Portuguese), asphota (India), katarolu (Sri Lanka), pukingang (Philippines),
Synonyms:	*Clitoria bracteata* Poir., *Ternatea ternatea* (L.) Kuntze, *Ternatea vulgaris* Kunth
Description:	It is a perennial slender climber which grows in the tropics native to Africa. The stem is terete, smooth, glabrous and pitted. The leaves are pinnate, spiral and stipulate. The stipule is linear and about 0.4 cm long. The rachis is slender, pilose by the apex, 3 - 5 cm long with 3 pairs of folioles and a terminal one. The petiolule is minute. The foliole is lanceolate, 2.5 - 5 x 2 - 3.5 cm, with a few hairs and apparently without secondary nerves. The inflorescence is solitary and axillary. The flower pedicel is 0.8 - 0.15 cm long. The calyx is 1.3 - 2 cm long with a few

hairs. The corolla is 3.5 - 5 cm long, intensely blue with several nervations. The pod is flattened, almost straight, beaked and contain 6 - 10 seeds which are oblong, angular and present a sort of little tube in their middles (Figure 44).

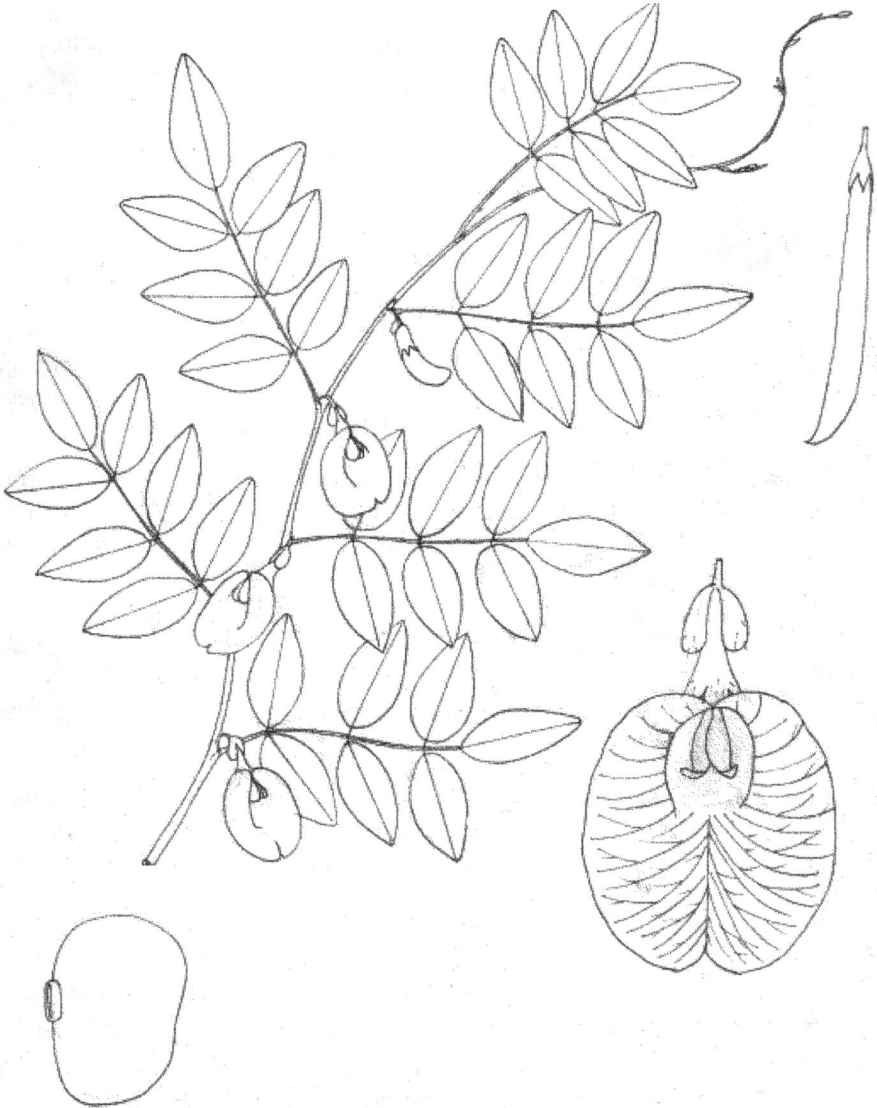

Figure 44: *Clitoria ternatea* L.
From: Flora of Malaya No 10914
Malaysia, Malacca, Bukit Baru. Collection and identification: Noraini Mansur 038

Medicinal uses:

In India the plant is used as a laxative, diuretic, for diseases of the lungs, skin diseases and impotence. In Cambodia, Laos and Vietnam, the plant is used as laxative. In Malaysia, the seeds are used to stimulate appetite. In Indonesia, the plant is used to heal boils and inflamed eyes.

Pharmacology:

The plant improved retention and spatial learning performance at both time points of behavioral tests, indicating a memory enhancing property in rodents (Rai *et al.*, 2001) by increasing acetylcholine content in their hippocampi (Rai *et al.*, 2002). An extract was found to possess nootropic, anxiolytic, antidepressant, anticonvulsant and antistress activity . The anti-inflammatory property of the plant is confirmed: an extract of the plant inhibits the rat paw oedema caused by carrageenan. The plant also has antipyretic and analgesic properties as it lowered yeast-induced pyrexia and markedly reduced the number of writhings in the acetic acid-induced writhing test in rodents (Devi *et al.*, 2003). It would be of interest to identify the active principle responsible for the CNS property of the plant.

References:

Devi BP, Boominathan R, Mandal SC, 2003, Anti-inflammatory, analgesic and antipyretic properties of *Clitoria ternatea* root. Fitoterapia;74:345-9.

Jain NN, Ohal CC, Shroff SK, Bhutada RH, Somani RS, Kasture VS, Kasture SB, 2003, *Clitoria ternatea* and the CNS. Pharmacol Biochem Behav; 75:529-36.

Rai KS, Murthy KD, Karanth KS, Rao MS, 2001,*Clitoria ternatea* (Linn) root extract treatment during growth spurt period enhances learning and memory in rats. Indian J Physiol Pharmacol; 45:305-13.

Rai KS, Murthy KD, Karanth KS, Nalini K, Rao MS, Srinivasan KK, 2002, *Clitoria ternatea* root extract enhances acetylcholine content in rat hippocampus. Fitoterapia; 73:685-9.

Crotalaria albida Heyne ex Roth

[From Greek *krotalon* = castanet and Latin *albida* = white]

Local names:	Banmethi (India), pokok gigelin jatan (Malaysia)
Synonyms:	*Crotalaria albida* Heyne ex Wall, *Crotalaria formosana* Matsum. ex Ito & Matsum., *Crotalaria montana* Roxb.
Description:	It is a perennial shrub which grows to 0.6 m tall in India, Sri Lanka, Pakistan, Nepal, Burma, Malaysia, Cambodia, Laos, Vietnam, Indonesia, the Philippines, Taiwan, China and Papua New Guinea. The stem is terete, glossy, hairy, 0.2 cm in diameter and with 0.8 - 2.3 cm long internodes. The leaves are spiral and stipulated. The stipules are hairy and 0.1 cm long. The petiole is 0.1 cm long and hairy. The blade is papery, dull dark green above, linear spatulate, dotted above, golden hairy below, tapering at the base, round and minutely apiculate at the apex, 0.3 - 0.5 x 2.5 - 3.4 cm. The inflorescence is a terminal raceme which is green, covered with golden hairs and 7 - 8.5 cm long. The flower pedicel is velvety and 0.4 cm long. The calyx is green with reddish, brownish hue. The sepals are velvety, membranaceous, translucent and 0.8 x 0.2 cm. The corolla is 0.8 cm long, pale yellow, the standard orbicular with a few hairs, dull light yellowish inside, and dull light reddish outside. The wings are yellow and the keel light green. The pod is glabrous, sessile about 1.5 cm long and contains 6 - 12 seeds (Figure 45).
Medicinal Uses:	In the Philippines the plant is used to wash inflamed eyes. In India it is used as a purgative.
Pharmacology:	Cyclophosphamide and extracts of *Crotalaria albida*, *Senecio chrysanthemoides*, *Senecio densiflorus* and *Senecio jacquemontianus* increased the life span of S180 (ascitic) tumour bearing mice (Indap *et al.*, 1986) probably due to pyrrolizidine alkaloids. The plant needs further pharmacological studies.
Reference:	Indap MA, Gokhale SV, 1986, Combined effect of cyclophosphamide and extracts of *Crotalaria* and *Senecio* plants on experimental tumors. Indian J Physiol Pharmacol;30:182-6.

Figure 45: *Crotalaria albida* Heyne ex Roth
From: Flora of Thailand, Chiang Mai University Herbarium.
Thailand, Lampang province, Muang Bahn district, Jae Sawn national park, hill behind park headquarters. Elevation: 750 m. date of collection: 20 October 1995. In open, fire damaged, seasonal area in deciduous dipterocarp-oak forest on granite bedrock, cliff area.

Crotalaria bracteata Roxb.

[From Greek *krotalon* = castanet and Latin *bracteata* = with bracts]

Local name:	Mao guo zhu shi dou (China)
Synonyms:	*Crotalaria bracteata* Roxb. ex DC., *Crotalaria bracteata* Schltdl. & Cham., *Crotalaria indobracteata* Bennet
Description:	It is a branching herb which grows to 1.5 m tall in open waste lands of India, Bangladesh; Bhutan, Burma, Cambodia; Laos; Thailand; Vietnam and China. The stem is light green, terete, somewhat fleshy, velvety, 0.4 cm in diameter with 4.5 - 6.5 cm long internodes. The leaves are trifoliolate, spiral and stipulated. The stipules are about 0.5 cm long and deciduous. The rachis is light green, straight, 2.2 - 6 cm long, constricted at the base, and angled. The petiolule is velvety and 0.2 cm long. The foliole is elliptic, glabrous above, wavy at margin, hairy underneath, membranaceous, 4.5 - 10 x 1.7 - 4 cm, with a midrib sunken above and 7 - 10 pairs of secondary nerves. The inflorescence is an axillary raceme which is light green, and 3.3 - 4.4 cm long. The flower pedicel is 0.5 cm long. The calyx is light green, 5-lobed and about 0.5 cm long. The flower is 0.9 - 1.5 cm long, all petals rapidly fading to reddish-orangish. The standard is 1 cm long and yellow. The wings are 0.7 cm long and yellow. The keel is yellowish-green. The pod is oblong, 2 x 0.5 cm-1 cm, pilose, puffy, with 7-8-seeds and an apical tail (Figure 46).
Medicinal Uses:	In Cambodia, Laos and Vietnam, the plant is used to treat herpes and fever.
Pharmacology:	The plant has apparently not yet been studied for pharmacology. The anti-herpes property of the plant might be due to pyrrolizidine alkaloids, which are yet to be identified.
Reference:	Singh B, Sahu P, Jain SC, Singh S, 2002, Antineoplastic and antiviral screening of pyrrolizidine alkaloids from *Heliotropium subulatum*. Pharmaceut Biol; 40: 581-86.

Figure 46: *Crotalaria bracteata* Roxb.
From: Flora of Thailand, Chiang Mai University Herbarium
Thailand, Lampang province, Muang Bahn district, Jae Sawn national park, Mae Mawn falls, stream area. Elevation: 875 m. Date of collection: 24 October 1995. In open, fired damaged, seasonal very degraded deciduous forest with much bamboo on granite bedrock.

Crotalaria ferruginea Graham ex Benth

[From Greek *krotalon* = castanet and Latin *ferruginea* = rusty red]

Local names:	Luc lac set (Vietnam), jia di lan (China)
Synonyms:	*Crotalaria bodinieri* H. Lév, *Crotalaria lonchophylla* Handel-Mazzetti, *Crotalaria pilosissima* Miq., *Crotalaria rufescens* Franchet.
Description:	It is a shrub which grows in open lands of India Nepal; Sri Lanka Bangladesh; Bhutan; Laos; Burma; Thailand; Vietnam, Malaysia, China, Taiwan, the Philippines, Indonesia, and Papua New Guinea. The plant can reach 1 m tall. The stem is sprawling, yellowish, and pilose. The leaves are sessile simple, spiral and stipulated. The stipule is linear, lanceolate, and about 1 cm long. The leaf blade is lanceolate, dull dark green above, pilose on both surface, membranaceous, dotted above, slightly asymmetrical at the base and 2 - 6 x 1 --3 cm. The inflorescence is pilose, axillary or terminal. The flower pedicel is about 0.4 cm long. The calyx is pilose, persistent in fruit, 2-lipped, and about 1 cm long. The standard is yellow outside, inside and wings bright yellow, the keel is pale light green. The corolla is about 1 cm long. The anthers are light yellow, the filaments very pale light greenish yellow. The pod is oblong, somewhat puffy, 2 - 3 cm, glabrous, with a tiny tail at the apex and containing numerous seeds (Figure 47).
Medicinal Uses:	In the Philippines the plant is used to heal inflamed eyes.
Pharmacology:	The plant contains pyrrolizidine alkaloids which are poisonous. Such alkaloids might account for the anti-inflammatory property mentioned above (Ghosh *et al*, 1974). *Crotalaria ferruginea* Graham ex Benth awaits pharmacological investigation; interesting results should be obtained, particularly in the search for cytotoxic agents.
Reference:	Ghosh MN, Singh H, 1974, Inhibitory effect of a pyrrolizidine alkaloid, crotalaburnine, on rat paw oedema and cotton pellet granuloma. Br J Pharmacol;51:503-8.

Figure 47: *Crotalaria ferruginea* Graham ex Benth
From: Flora of Thailand.
Thailand, Chiang Dao district, Doi Chiang Dao wildlife sanctuary, south side, along the dirt road to Bhang Hahng village, near the hydro-electric plant. By 18° 05' North - 98° East. Elevation 900 m. Date of collection: November 1996. In open, disturbed roadside thicket in seasonal evergreen, deciduous hardwood forest with much bamboo. Collection and identification: JF Maxwell, N° 96-1526

Dalbergia parviflora Roxb.

[After Swedish planter Carl Gustav Dahlberg and Latin *parviflora* = with small flower]

Local names: Kayu laka (Malaysia, Indonesia), kree (Thailand), tahid labuyo (Philippines)

Synonyms: *Dalbergia cumingiana* Benth., *Dalbergia zollingeriana* Miq.

Description: It is a woody climber which grows in river bank and sea shore forests in a geographical area which covers Burma, Thailand, Malaysia, Indonesia and the Philippines. The main stem is thorny, and to 30 m long. The bark is rough and peeling. The wood is dark red and of commercial value as a source of incense and essential oil. The stem is terete, lenticelled, 0.3 cm in diameter, longitudinally striated and marked by stipule scars. The leave is compound, spiral and stipulate. The rachis is 15 - 20 cm long, hairy, flattish, swollen at the base, and bears 5-9 folioles which are alternate. The petiolule is 0.2 cm long and angled. The foliole is glossy above, elliptic, irregular at the margin, 5 - 10 x 2 - 5 cm, with a prominent primary nerve and few hairs underneath. The secondary nerves are inconspicuous. The inflorescence is an axillary, many flowered panicle which can reach 10 cm in length. The calyx is campanulate with 5 lobes and minute. The corolla is minute. The pod is 2 - 5 x 1.5 cm, flat, round, glabrous, minutely apiculate and contains 1 - 2 seeds which are reniform (Figure 48).

Medicinal Uses: In Malaysia, the plant is used to invigorate and used as medicine for new born infants. In Indonesia, the plant is used as post-partum protective remedy. The oil distilled from the wood is used to heal infected wounds.

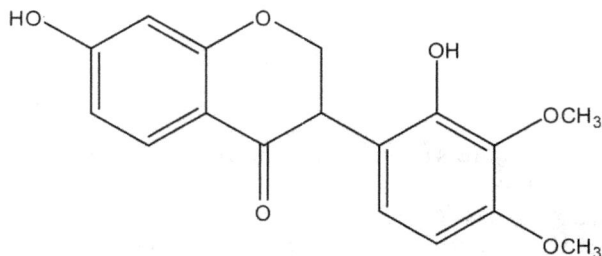

Dalparvin B

Pharmacology: The main components of the heartwood essential oil are nerolidol, farnesol and furfurol. The plant abounds with arylbenzofurans and neoflavonoids (Muangnoicharoen *et al*, 1981, 1982). Umehara *et al* (2008) isolated oestrogenic dalparvin B and C which stimulated the proliferation of MCF-7 andT-47D human breast cancer cells and kenusanone G which had activity only against MCF-7 cells.

Figure 48: *Dalbergia parviflora* Roxb.
From: Flora of Thailand. Prince of Songkla University.
Thailand, Songkla province, Satingpra district, Bantom Island, Lake Songkla. Elevation: sea level. Date of collection: 22 September 1984. In open thicket next to the lake. Collection: JF Maxwell N° 84-238. Identification: B. Sunarno, 8 February 1991.

References:

Muangnoicharoen M, Frahm AW, 1981, Arylbenzofurans from *Dalbergia parviflora*. Phytochemistry; 20: 291-93.

Muangnoicharoen M, Frahm AW, 1982. Neoflavonoids *of Dalbergia parviflora*. Phytochemistry; 21: 767-72.

Umehara K, Nemoto K, Kimijima K, Matsushita A, Terada E, Monthakantirat O, De-Eknamkul W, Miyase T, Warashina T, Degawa M, Noguchi H, 2008, Estrogenic constituents of the heartwood of *Dalbergia parviflora*. Phytochemistry;69:546-52.

Dalbergia pinnata (Lour.) Prain
[After Swedish planter Carl Gustav Dahlberg and Latin *pinnata* = pinnate]

Local names:	Damar (Nepal), cham bia ab trau (Cambodia, Laos, Vietnam)
Basionym:	*Derris pinnata* Lour. *Flora Cochinchinensis* 2: 432-433. 1790
Synonyms:	*Dalbergia dubia* Elmer, *Dalbergia livida* Wall., *Dalbergia pinatubensis* Elmer, *Dalbergia rufa* Graham, *Dalbergia tamarindifolia* Roxb., *Derris pinnata* Lour., *Endespermum scandens* Bl.
Description:	It is a shrub which grows in tropical Africa, India, Southeast Asia, China, and the Pacific Islands. The stem is velvety, lenticelled, zigzag shaped, 0.4 cm in diameter, and with 2.5 - 3 cm long internodes. The leaves are compound, spiral and stipulate. The stipule is lanceolate and 0.5 cm long. The rachis is velvety, 10 -15 cm long, straight and holds about 25 - 41 pairs of folioles which are sub-opposite to alternate, one pair every 0.5 cm. The petiolule is velvety and minute. The foliole is oblong, 1.5 x 0.5 cm, the apex round with a minute tip, round at the base, the midrib hairy below and the secondary nerves obscure. The inflorescence is an axillary raceme which is velvety and 1.5 - 2.5 cm long. The flowers are minute on a 0.01 cm pedicel which is minute. The calyx is campanulate, 0.2 cm long with triangular lobes. The corolla is 1 cm long, white with a broad standard. The pods are flat, glabrous, dull, covered with a pattern of nerves, greenish drying reddish-brown and 3.8 - 7.5 x 0.8 - 1.3 cm (Figure 49).
Medicinal Uses:	In Malaysia, the leaves are uses to treat nervous disorders. In Indonesia, the plant is used to assuage itchiness and fever. In Cambodia, Laos and Vietnam, the plant is used to expel worms from intestines.
Pharmacology:	Unknown.

Derris malaccensis (Benth.) Prain
[From Greek *derris* = a leather coat and Latin *malaccensis* = from Malacca]

Local name:	Tuba merah (Malaysia)
Basionym:	*Derris cuneifolia* var. *malaccensis* Benth.
Synonyms:	*Deguelia malaccensis* (Benth.) Blake, *Derris montana* Benth., *Paraderris montana* (Benth.) Adema

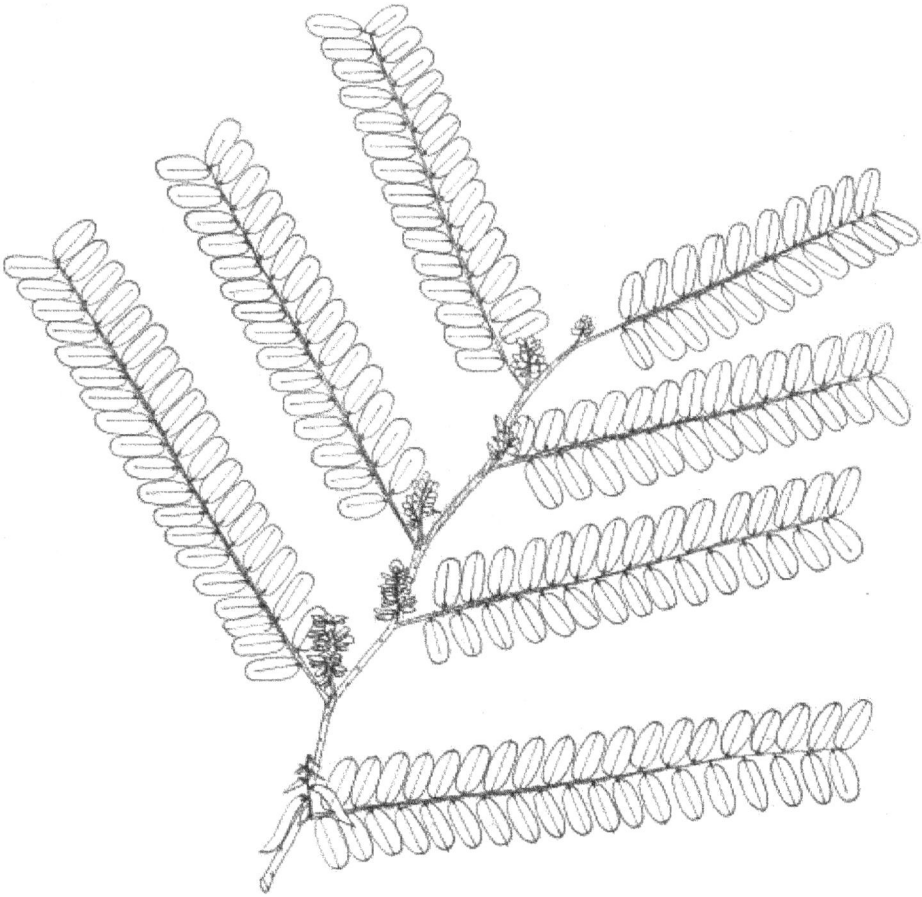

Figure 49: *Dalbergia pinnata* (Lour.) Prain
From: Flora of Sabah, Herbarium of University Kebangsaan Malaysia Nº 12077
Malaysia, Sabah, Kota Kinabalu, Jalan Bukit Signal. Collection and identification: A Zainuddin.

Description: It is a woody climber which grows, often by rivers, in the forests of India, Burma, Cambodia, Laos, Malaysia, Thailand, Vietnam, Indonesia, China, and Papua New Guinea. The main stem can reach 15 m long. The stem is terete, curved in a snake-like manner, striated longitudinally with lenticels which are ovoid and about 0.01 cm in diameter. The leaves are compound, spiral, stipulated and originate from woody formation from the stem. The stipule is broadly lanceolate and 0.2 x 0.15 cm. The rachis is inflated and cracked at the base, about 10 cm long, terete, smooth, subglabrous, slender and holds 3 pairs of folioles plus a terminal one. The petiolule is subglabrous, angled, channeled and minute. The folioles are elliptic lanceolate, red-brown at first, thinly coriaceous, acute or round at the base, acuminate at the apex, 7 - 10.9 x 3 - 5.7 cm, recurved at the margin and with 6 - 7 pairs of secondary nerves. The inflorescence is axillary, angled, glabrous, lenticelled and about 9 cm long. The calyx is cup-shaped, sub-glabrous, dark maroon, and 0.4 x 0.6 cm. The corolla is 1 cm long with a standard which is pale pinkish yellow greenish pink wings, an a pink keel with whitish the apex. The style is pink, 1.4 cm long. The fruit pedicel is 0.5 cm long. The pod is woody, glossy, subglabrous, one-seeded and with a little apical beak (Figure 50).

Medicinal Uses: The roots of *Derris malaccensis* (Benth.) Prain are used as an insecticide and fish poison. The dried root of the plant Derris (British Pharmaceutical Codex, 1949) containing not less than 3 % of rotenone has been used as an agricultural and horticultural insecticide and for external treatment of animals.

Pharmacology: The plant abound with rotenoids derivatives which showed antibacterial activity against *Helicobacter pylori* (Takashima *et al.*, 2002).

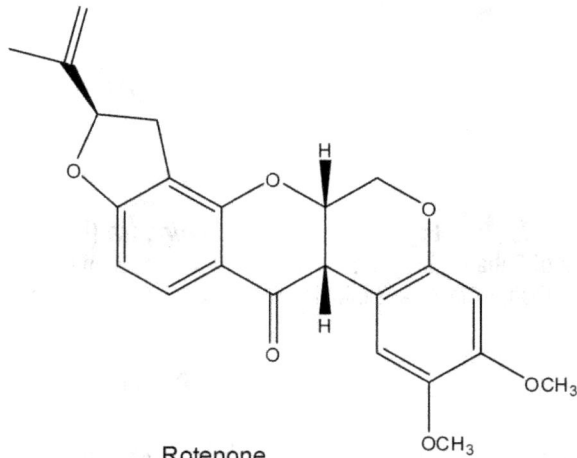

Rotenone

Reference: Takashima J, Chiba N, Yoneda K, Ohsaki A, 2002, Derrisin, a new rotenoid from *Derris malaccensis* plain and anti-*Helicobacter pylori* activity of its related constituents. J Nat Prod.; 65(4):611-3

Figure 50: *Derris malaccensis* (Benth.) Prain
From: Flora of Thailand. Prince of Songkla University
Thailand, Songkla province, Rattapoon district, Boripat fall park. By 8° 5' North - 99° East.
Elevation: 50 m. Date of collection: 4 July 1986. In partly open and canopy area of the primary evergreen forest along a stream on granite bedrock. Collection and identification: JF Maxwell, No 86-445

Derris scandens (Aubl.) Pittier

[From Greek *derris* = a leather coat and Latin *scandens* = climbing]

Local names:	Hogcreeper, thaowan prieng (Thailand), tupail (Malaysia), meekyoungnway (Burma), bendan (Indonesia), malasaga (Philippines), kalawel (Sri Lanka), takil (India)
Basionym:	*Deguelia scandens* Aubl. *Histoire des plantes de la Guiane Françoise* 2: 750-753, pl. 300. 1775.
Synonyms:	*Brachypterum scandens* (Roxb.) Benth., *Dalbergia scandens* Roxb., *Deguelia scandens* Aubl.
Description:	It is a climber which grows in the forests of a geographical zone ranging from India to Australia, including Sri Lanka and Southeast Asia. The main stem can reach 20 m long. The stem is pitted, terete, lenticelled, and hairy. The internodes are 2.5 - 4.7 cm long. The lenticels are globose and about 0.05 cm in diameter. The leaves are compound, spiral and stipulate. The stipules are minute, triangular and hairy. The rachis is deeply channeled, hairy and 4 - 9 x 0.1 - 0.2 cm and present 5 pairs of folioles plus a terminal one. The folioles are dark green glossy above, lanceolate, coriaceous, round at the base, acute at the apex, with a midrib sunken above and 7 - 12 pairs of secondary nerves. The foliole is 2.5 - 5 x 1.2 - 1.5 cm, hairy underneath. The inflorescence is an axillary raceme, the axis of which is 10 - 18 cm long. The calyx is purple conical and 0.2 x 0.3 cm. The corolla is 0.8 cm long, white, the standard light yellowish at the base. The stigma is white. The anthers are very light yellow. The pods are blade-like, smooth, with a few nerves, 4 - 6.1 - 1 - 1.3 cm on a 0.4 - 0.8 cm long pedicel (Figure 51).
Medicinal Uses:	The plant is used as a fish poison. In Thailand, the plant is used to promote urination, emptying of the bowels, menses and is used to treat colds and to assuage backache.
Pharmacology:	The plant contains series of pharmacologically active isoflavonoids including genistein which inhibited eicosanoid production and antioxidant properties *in vitro* (Laupattarakasem *et al.*, 2004). Other isoflavonoids are isoscandinone, scandenin A and scandenin B scandinone and 4', 5', 7-trihydroxybiprenylisoflavone which displayed some levels of alpha-glucosidase enzyme inhibitory and free radical scavenging properties (Rao *et al.*, 2007). Another isoflavonoid, warangalone inhibited the enzymatic activity of rat liver cyclic AMP-dependent protein kinase (Wang *et al.*, 1997). Note that

Figure 51: *Derris scandens* (Aubl.) Pittier
From: Flora of Thailand, Prince of Songkla University.
Thailand, Songkla province, Satingpra district, Bantom Island, Lake Songkla. By 9o North - 99o East. Elevation: sea level. Date of collection: 21 October 1983. In open thicket, shores of the lake. Collection: P. Sirirugsa No 646 and JF Maxwell No 84-240.

an extract of the plant increased the NK cell activity of HIV-infected individuals (Sriwanthana *et al.*, 2001). Rotenoids are probably responsible for the use of the plant has a fish poison.

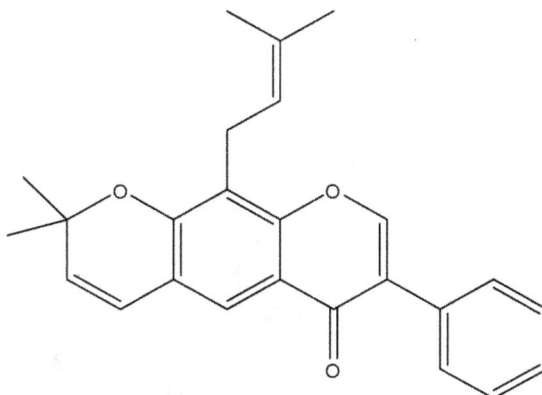

Warangalone

References:

Laupattarakasem P, Houghton PJ, Hoult JR, 2004, Anti-inflammatory isoflavonoids from the stems of *Derris scandens*. Planta Med; 70:496-501.

Rao SA, Srinivas PV, Tiwari AK, Vanka UM, Rao RV, Dasari KR, Rao MJ, 2007, Isolation, characterization and chemobiological quantification of alpha-glucosidase enzyme inhibitory and free radical scavenging constituents from *Derris scandens* Benth. J Chromatogr B; 855:166-72

Sriwanthana B, Chavalittumrong P, 2001, *In vitro* effect of *Derris scandens* on normal lymphocyte proliferation and its activities on natural killer cells in normal and HIV-1 infected patients. J Ethnopharmacol; 76:125-9.

Wang BH, Ternai B, Polya G, 1997, Specific inhibition of cyclic AMP-dependent protein kinase by warangalone and robustic acid. Phytochemistry; 44:787-96.

Derris trifoliata Lour.

[From Greek *derris* = a leather coat and Latin *trifoliata* = with 3 folioles]

Local name:	Kirtana (India), akar ketuil (Malaysia), gadel (Indonesia), phak thaep (Thailand), longkesn (Vietnam), silasila (Philippines), gamo (Papua New Guinea).
Synonyms:	*Deguelia trifoliata* (Lour.) Taub., *Deguelia uliginosa* (Willd.) Baill., *Deguelia uliginosa* (Willd.) Benth., *Galedupa uliginosa* (Willd.) Roxb., *Pongamia madagascariensis* Bojer ex Oliver, *Pongamia uliginosa* Willd.
Description:	It is a large woody climber which grows along the muddy shores of a geographical area including East Africa, Madagascar, Mascarene Islands, Southeast Asia, China, Australia and the Pacific Islands. The stem is smooth, terete, angled at the apex, longitudinally striated, glabrous, 0.5 cm in diameter, with 0.1 cm in diameter lenticels, and with 2.5 - 6 cm long internodes. The leaves are compound, spiral and without stipules. The rachis is longitudinally striated and 11 - 13 cm long and holds 3 pairs of folioles plus a terminal one. The petiolule is 0.5 cm long and channeled. The folioles are papery, broadly lanceolate, 5 - 10.5 x 2 - 6 cm, round at the apex, acuminate at the apex, with little dots underneath. The inflorescence is an axillary raceme which is about 10 - 12 cm long. The calyx is cup - shaped and 0.25 x 0.3 cm. The corolla is about 0.5 - 0.8 cm long, pinkish or pale lavender, the standard 1.3 cm broad. The pod is flat, globose, with a discrete net of nervations, minutely apiculate at the apex, 3 - 3.5 x 2.2 - 2.5 cm and containing a single seed which is compressed and reniform. The fruits are dispersed by the sea (Figure 52).
Medicinal Uses:	The plant is poisonous to fish. In India, the plant is used for rheumatism, to normalize menses and to invigorate. In Thailand the plant is used to empty the bowels, to promote digestion and for painful joints. In Papua New Guinea, the plant is used for fever and sores. Thai traditional doctors use roots or stems as a laxative, carminative and anti-arthritis treatment.
Pharmacology:	An extract of the plant inhibited the growth of a broad spectrum of bacteria (Khan *et al*, 2006). Rotenoids are probably responsible for the use of the plant as a fish poison. Note that rotenoids deguelin and alpha-toxicarol exhibited a marked inhibitory effect on mouse skin tumour promotion in an *in vivo* two-stage carcinogenesis test (Ito *et al.*, 2004). Note that deguelin inhibited invasion of human fibrosarcoma HT1080 cells through Matrigel-coated filters and showed differentiation-inducing activity in human promyelocytic leukemia HL-60 cells (Matsuda, *et al.*, 2007).

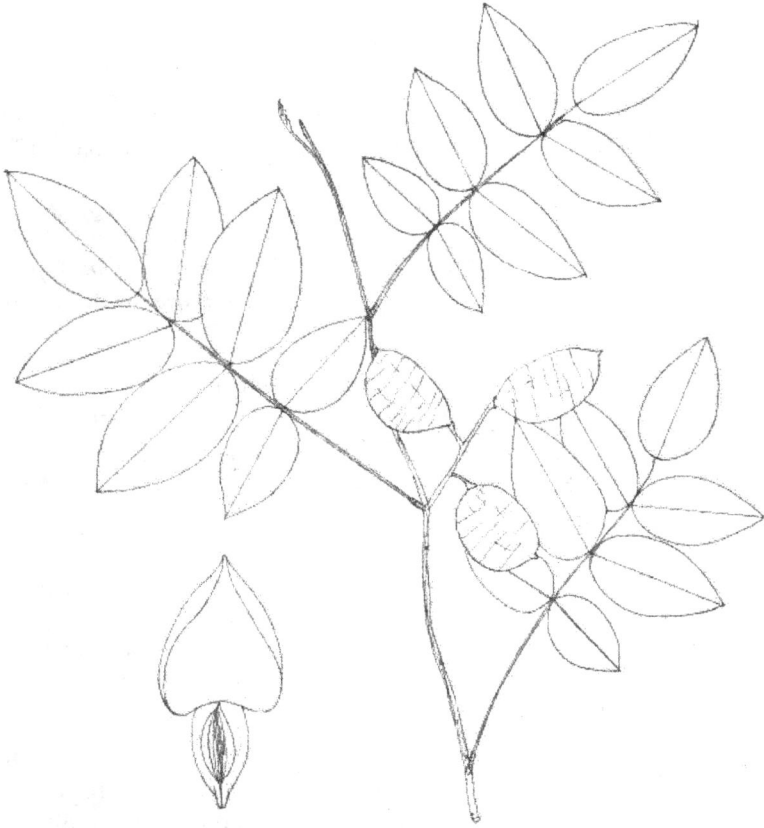

Figure 52: *Derris trifoliata* Lour.
From: Plants of Borneo. Herbaria of Michigan State University.
Malaysia, Sabah, Kuala Penyu, Pulau Tiga. 5° 39' North - 115° 43' East. Elevation: 1 m. Beach vegetation. Collection and identification: John H Beaman 9730. Date of collection: 15 May 1984.

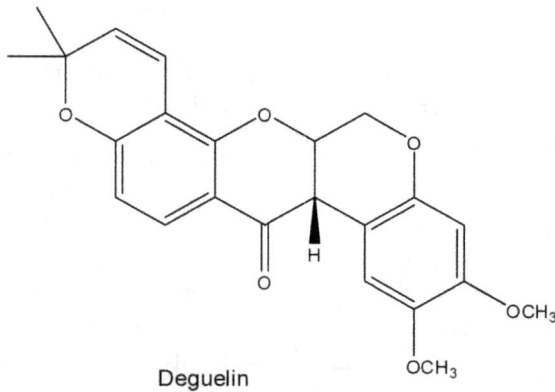

Deguelin

References: Ito C, Itoigawa M, Kojima N, Tan HT, Takayasu J, Tokuda H, Nishino H, Furukawa H., 2004, Cancer chemopreventive activity of rotenoids from *Derris trifoliata*. Planta Med;70:585-8

Khan MR, Omoloso AD, Barewai Y, 2006, Antimicrobial activity of the *Derris elliptica, Derris indica* and *Derris trifoliata* extractives. Fitoterapia;77:327-30.

Matsuda H, Yoshida K, Miyagawa K, Asao Y, Takayama S, Nakashima S, Xu F, Yoshikawa M, 2007, Rotenoids and flavonoids with anti-invasion of HT1080, anti-proliferation of U937, and differentiation-inducing activity in HL-60 from *Erycibe expansa*. Bioorg Med Chem; 15:1539-1546.

Xu LR, Li S, Wu J, Zhang S, 2007, Rotenoids from *Derris trifoliata*. Zhong Yao Cai; 30:660-2.

Desmodium gangeticum (L.) DC.
[From the Greek *desmos* = chain and Latin *gangeticum* = from the river Ganga (Ganges)]

Local names: Devi (Sanskrit), pulladi (India), paiang-paiang (Philippines), daun bulu ayam (Indonesia), tuk hma (Laos), yaa tuet maeo, baw berchai (Thailand)

Basionym: *Hedysarum gangeticum* L. *Species Plantarum* 2: 746. 1753.

Synonyms: *Aeschynomene gangetica* (L.) Poir., *Aeschynomene maculata* (L.) Poir., *Desmodium cavaleriei* H. Lev., *Desmodium lanceolatum* (Schum & Thonn.) Walp., *Desmodium polygonoides* Welw. ex Baker, *Hedysarum collinum* Roxb., *Hedysarum gangeticum* L., *Hedysarum lanceolatum* Schum. & Thonn., *Hedysarum maculatum* L., *Hedysarum ochroleucum* Moench, *Meibomia gangetica* (L.) O. Kuntze., *Meibomia polygonodes* (Welw. Ex Baker) Kuntze, *Pleurolobus gangeticus* (L.) J. St. Hil., *Pleurolobus maculatus* J St. Hil.

Description: It is a shrub widespread in the tropical regions of the globe. The plant is probably native to tropical Asia. It grows in savannahs and open areas. The plant grows to about 1 m tall. The stem is terete or angled, somewhat glossy, subglabrous and 0.2 cm in diameter. The internodes are 1.5 - 3 cm long. The leaves are simple, spiral and stipulate. The stipules are persistent, lanceolate - linear and about 1 x 0.2 cm. The petiole is hairy, flat above and 0.8 - 1.7 cm long. The blade is dull dark green above, membranaceous, translucent, acute at the apex, 10.5 - 3 x 1.7 - 5 cm, glossy above, minutely hairy with 6 to 8 pairs of secondary nerves. The inflorescence is a terminal, green axillary raceme with an angled and hairy axis. The flower pedicel is reddish. The calyx is 0.2 cm long, light green and reddish, hairy, with triangular lobes. The corolla is 0.4 cm long, the standard is 0.3 cm broad cuneate at the base and with violet wings .The fruit is pod which is 1.2 - 2 cm long. comprising 5 - 7 septae which are hemiglobose, membranaceous, hairy and about 0.2 cm long. The calyx is persistent (Figure 53).

Medicinal Uses: In India, the plant is used to break fever, to invigorate, to treat coughs, to promote urination and to treat diarrhoea. It also used as an Ayurvedic remedy for sexual anorexia, mental disorders, piles, and to prevent abortion. Malays use the plant to calm fretful children. The plant is also used to treat diarrhoea, toothaches and headaches. In Indonesia the plant is used as diuretic. In Vietnam, the plant is used as diuretic and to heal infected wounds. In Thailand the plant is used as a diuretic and anthelminthic.

Pharmacology: The plant has been the subject of several pharmacological and chemical studies which do not fully validate the medicinal uses. The plant is known to produce indole alkaloids, pterocarpanoids such as gangetin, gangetinin, desmodin, and desmocarpin (Purushothaman et al, 1975), flavone and isoflavonoid glycosides (Yadava et al, 1998). The sedative property of the plant has been validated as an extract of the plant exhibited a mild central nervous system depressant activity in rodents (Jabbar et al., 2001). This is probably the effect of alkaloids such as tryptamines, phenethylamines, and their N-oxides (Ghosal et al., 1969). These alkaloids may also account for the invigorating property mentioned above (Ghosal et al., 1972) and for the anti-amnesic effect in both scopolamine-induced amnesia and ageing-induced amnesia in rodents (Joshi et al., 2006). The plant possess strong antioxidant properties (Govindarajan et al., 1992) and possesses the ability to scavenge free radicals (Kurian et al., 2008). The analgesic property of the plant is confirmed as an extract exhibited analgesic property in rodents (Rathi et al., 2004). In addition, the plant showed anti gastric ulcer activity (Dharmani et al., 2005), hypoglycemic effects (Govindarajan et al, 2007) and antileishmanial property (Wu et al., 1992). The antileishmanial property is mediated by glycolipids which are also immunomodulatory (Mishra et al, 2005). One could have some interest in evaluating the pterocarpanoids such as gangetin for cytotoxic and or antiviral properties. Indole alkaloids of Desmodium are of neuropharmacological interest.

Figure 53: *Desmodium gangeticum* (L.) DC.
From: Flora of Thailand, Chiang Mai University Herbarium
Thailand, Lampang province, Muang Bahn district, Jae Sawn national park, off the dirt road to Bahn Miang village. Elevation: 1075 m. Date of collection: 22 October 1995. In open disturbed area in primary evergreen, seasonal, hardwood forest on granite area.

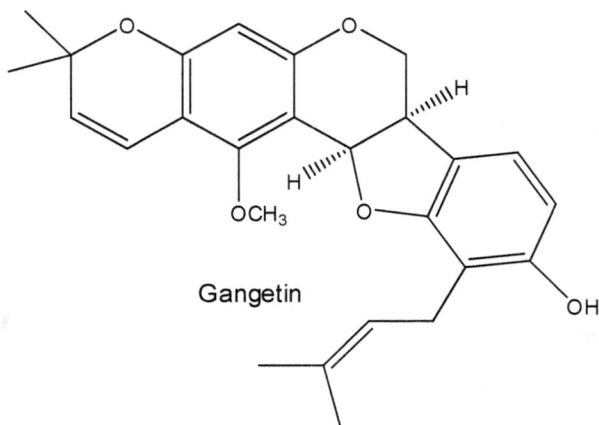

Gangetin

References: Dharmani P, Mishra PK, Maurya R, Chauhan VS, Palit G, 2005,
                      Desmodium gangeticum: a potent anti-ulcer agent. Indian J Exp
                      Biol;43:517-21.

                      Ghosal S, Banerjee PK, 1969, Alkaloids of the roots of *Desmodium
                      gangeticum* Aust. J. Chem. 22: 2029.

                      Ghosal S, Bhattacharya, SK, 1972, *Desmodium* alkaloids. II.
                      Chemical and pharmacological evaluation of D. gangeticum. Planta
                      Med; 22: 434-40.

                      Govindarajan R, Rastogi S, Vijayakumar M, Shirwaikar A, Rawat
                      AK, Mehrotra S, Pushpangadan P, 2003, Studies on the antioxidant
                      activities of *Desmodium gangeticum*. Biol Pharm Bull; 26:1424-7.

                      Govindarajan R, Vijayakumar M, Rao ChV, Shirwaikar A,
                      Kumar S, Rawat AK, Pushpangadan P, 2007, Anti-inflammatory
                      and antioxidant activities of *Desmodium gangeticum* fractions in
                      carrageenan-induced inflamed rats. Phytother Res; 21:975-9.

                      Govindarajan R, Asare-Anane H, Persaud S, Jones P, Houghton PJ,
                      2007, Effect of *Desmodium gangeticum* extract on blood glucose in
                      rats and on insulin secretion *in vitro*. Planta Med; 73:427-32.

                      Iwu MM, Jackson JE, Tally JD, Klayman DL, 1992, Evaluation
                      of plant extracts for antileishmanial activity using a mechanism-
                      the based radiorespirometric microtechnique (RAM). Planta Med;
                      58:436-41.

                      Jabbar S, Khan MT, Choudhuri MS, 2001,The effects of aqueous
                      extracts of *Desmodium gangeticum* DC. (Leguminosae) on the
                      central nervous system. Pharmazie; 56:506-8.

                      Joshi H, Parle M, 2006, Antiamnesic effects of *Desmodium
                      gangeticum* in mice. Yakugaku Zasshi; 126:795-804.

Kurian GA, Yagnesh N, Kishan RS, Paddikkala J, 2008, Methanol extract of *Desmodium gangeticum* roots preserves mitochondrial respiratory enzymes, protecting rat heart against oxidative stress induced by reperfusion injury. J Pharm Pharmacol; 60:523-30.

Mishra PK, Singh N, Ahmad G, Dubeb A, Maurya R, 2005, Glycolipids and other constituents from *Desmodium gangeticum* with antileishmanial and immunomodulatory activities. Bioorg Med Chem Lett;15: 4543-46.

Purushothaman KK, Chandrasekharan S, Balakrishna K, 1975, Gangetinin and desmodin, two minor pterocarpanoids of *Desmodium gangeticum*. Phytochemistry; 14:1129-1130

Rathi A, Rao ChV, Ravishankar B, De S, Mehrotra S, 2004, Anti-inflammatory and anti-nociceptive activity of the water decoction *Desmodium gangeticum*. J Ethnopharmacol;95:259-63.

Yadava RN, Tripathi P, 1998, A novel flavone glycoside from the stem of *Desmodium gangeticum*. Fitoterapia; 69:443-44.

Desmodium heterocarpon (L.) DC.

[From the Greek *desmos* = chain and *heterocarpon* = with various fruits]

Local names:	Asian ticktrefoil, khonthi din (Thailand), okula beluu (Palau Island), patah kemudi (Malaysia)
Basionym:	*Hedysarum heterocarpon* L. *Species Plantarum* 2: 747. 1753
Synonyms:	*Desmodium buergeri* Miq., *Desmodium ovalifolium* (Prain) Wall. ex Ridl., *Hedysarum canum* J.F. Gmel., *Hedysarum heterocarpon* L., *Meibomia heterocarpa* (L.) Kuntze
Description:	It is an erect herb which is native to tropical Asia and widespread throughout the tropics. The stem is terete, light greenish to dull dark red, pilose, and 0.2 cm in diameter. The leaves are trifoliolate, spiral and stipulate. The stipule is persistent, membranaceous, longitudinally striated, triangular, glabrous, and 0.7 x 0.2 cm. The rachis is angled, pilose, 0.9 - 3.2 cm long, flat above and somewhat articulated. The petiolule is 0.1 - 0.15 cm long and hairy. The terminal foliole shows a pair of bracts which are linear and 0.2 cm long. The foliole is membranaceous, dull dark green above, obovate to spatulate, round to minutely cordate at the base, minutely tipped at the apex, glabrous and glossy above, with 7 - 8 pairs of secondary nerves visible underneath and looping at the apex, the margin is

recurved. The inflorescence is a terminal raceme which is about 7 cm long and red. The flower pedicel is 0.4 cm long and hairy. The flower is 0.5 cm long. The calyx is very pale light greenish-whitish. The corolla is blue with white claws. The anthers are dark purple, the filaments white. The fruit is a pod which is pilose, membranaceous, with 6 hemiglobose septae, hairy, 1.5 x 0.2 cm. Each septae is 0.2 cm long (Figure 54).

Medicinal Uses: In Taiwan the plant is used to treat rickets. In Malaysia the plant is used to invigorate and to heal sores and broken bones. In Indonesia, the plant is used for gynecologic ailments.

Pharmacology: The plant has not been yet studied for pharmacology.

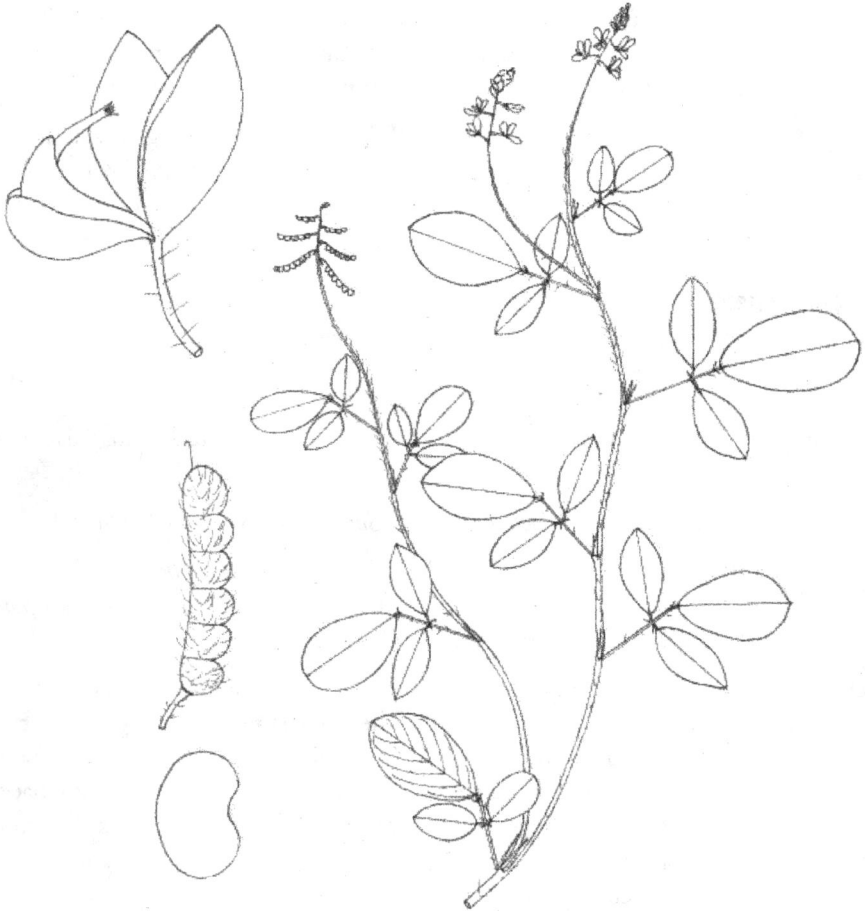

Figure 54: *Desmodium heterocarpon* (L.) DC.
From: Flora of Thailand, Chiang Mai University Herbarium.
Thailand, Chiang Mai province, Chiang Dao district, animal sanctuary, East of Huay Mae Gawk station. Elevation: 1500 m. Date of collection: 10 September 1995. In partly open disturbed fired damaged area in seasonal, mixed evergreen hardwood and pine forest on granite bedrock. Collection and identification: JF Maxwell N° 95632.

Desmodium pulchellum (L.) Benth.

[From the Greek *desmos* = chain and Latin *pulchellum* = beautiful]

Local names:	Toungtamin (Burma), payang payang (Philippines), hampilla (Sri Lanka), jatsalpan (India)
Basionym:	*Hedysarum pulchellum* L. Species Plantarum 2: 747. 1753
Synonyms:	*Dicerna pulchellum* Benth. ex Baker, *Phyllodium pulchellum* (L.) Desv., *Zornia pulchella* (L.) Pers.
Distribution:	It is a shrub which grows to 1.5 m high in East Africa, India, Sri Lanka, and Southeast Asia to the Pacific Islands. The stem is terete to angled, hairy, lenticelled at the base and about 0.15 cm in diameter. The leaves are 3 - foliolate, spiral and stipulated. The stipules are 0.5 cm long, caducous, hairy, triangular, 0.6 x 0.2 cm with numerous longitudinal nerves. The rachis is velvety, 1.8 - 2.5 cm long. The petiolule is 0.1 - 0.3 cm long and shows a pair of linear bracts which are 0.15 cm long. The folioles are ovate to elliptic, lanceolate, wavy at margin, minutely notched at the apex, thinly coriaceous, with few hairs, 2.5 - 12.5 x 1.6 - 6.3 cm and shows 6 to 11 pairs of secondary nerves and scalariform tertiary nerves visible underneath. The inflorescence is an axillary or terminal raceme which is 7.5 - 25 cm long and carries every 0.5 cm several umbellate flowers in the axils of leafy dark green bracts which are 1.3 cm across and globose and marked with 3 to 4 pairs of secondary nerves. The flower pedicel is 0.3 cm long. The calyx is yellow green, hairy, with 5 lanceolate lobes which are 0.2 x 0.1 cm. The corolla is whitish cream, 0.5 - 0.6 cm long and yellow. The pods are 0.3 - 0.6 cm long, hairy, with a 0.5 cm long apical tail, 2 septae, each about 0.2 cm long and pubescent. The calyx is persistent (Figure 55).
Medicinal Uses:	In India, the plant is used to treat diarrhoea. In China, the plant is used for fever, to assuage toothache and as a carminative. In Malaysia, it is used as post partum remedy. In the Philippines and Indonesia, the plant is used to heal wounds and sores.
Pharmacology:	The plant contains some indole alkaloids (Ghosal *et al.*, 1965) such as 5 methoxytryptamine which is a serotonin agonist as well as gramine, an indole alkaloid which binds to alpha 1 and alpha 2 receptors (Rahman, 2000). Cinnamylphenols or pulchelstyrenes (Shen *et al.*, 2005) with mild cytotoxic activity as well as physcion 1-glycosyl rhamnoside (Tiwari *et al*, 1971) have been isolated from the plant.

Figure 55: *Desmodium pulchellum* (L.) Benth.
From: Flora of Thailand. Prince of Songkla University Herbarium.
Thailand, Songkla province, Haad Yai district, Prince of Songkla University Campus at the base of Ko Hong hill. By 8° 05' North - 99° East. Elevation: sea level. Date of collection: 27 October 1984. In open field, waste area. Collection and identification: JF Maxwell, № 84-354

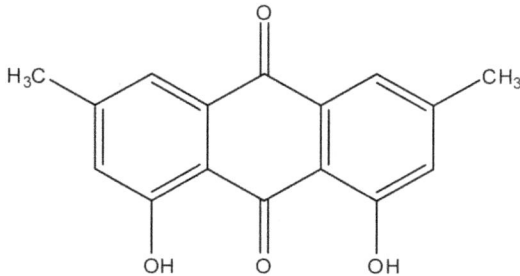

Physcion

References: Ghosal S, Mukherjee B, 1965, Occurrence of 5-methoxy-N,N-dimethyltryptamine oxide and other tryptamines in *Desmodium pulchellum* Benth ex Baker. Chem Ind;19:793-4.

Atta-ur Rahman, 2000, Studies in Natural Products Chemistry, Vol. 21. Elsevier Science

Shen CC, Wang ST, Tsai SY, Yang HC, Shieh BJ, Chen CC, 2005, Cinnamylphenols from *Phyllodium pulchellum*. J Nat Prod.;68:791-3.

Tiwari RD, Bansal RK, 1971, Physcion 1-glycosyl rhamnoside from seeds of *Desmodium pulchellum*. Phytochemistry; 10:1921-22.

Desmodium renifolium (L.) Schindl.
[From the Greek *desmos* =chain and Latin *renifolium* = with kidney-shaped leaves]

Local name: Shen ye shan ma huang (China)

Basionym: *Hedysarum renifolium* L. Systema Naturae, Editio Decima 2: 1169. 1759

Synonyms: *Desmodium oblatum* Baker ex Kurz., *Desmodium reniforme* (L.) DC., *Hedysarum renifolium* L., *Hedysarum reniforme* L., *Meibomia oblata* (Baker ex Kurz) Kuntze, *Meibomia reniformis* (L.) Kuntze

Description: It is a treelet which grows on waste land and open areas of India, Nepal, Laos, Burma, Thailand, Malaysia, Indonesia, China, Taiwan and Australia. The plant grows to 2 m tall. The stem is terete at the base, microscopically peeling longitudinally, smooth, glabrous and 0.2 cm in diameter. The leaves are simple, spiral and stipulated. The stipule is deciduous, linear, glabrous, 1 x 0.7 cm and longitudinally striated. The petiole is 0.7 - 1,7 cm long, slender, and channeled above. The blade is reniform, dull dark green, above, minutely notched at the apex, membranaceous, 3.7 - 4.1 x x 2.1 - 3 cm, and with a pair of linear bracts at the base, 5 - 6 pairs of secondary nerves. The inflorescence is a dull green slender axillary raceme which about 8 cm long. The flower pedicel is 0.2 cm. The flower bud is 0.2 cm. The calyx is whitish with a pale light green hue. The flowers are 1 cm long with a membranaceous corolla. The standard and wings are lilac, the standard obovate with 2 light blue vertical streaks inside above the claw. The keel is whitish. The filaments and the style are white. The anthers are cream. The pod is oblong 2 - 3 cm × 0.25 - 0.4 cm, subglabrous, and with 2 to 5 septae (Figure 56).

Medicinal Uses:	In Taiwan, the plant is used to break fever.
Pharmacology:	Unknown.

Desmodium scalpe DC.

[From the Greek *desmos* = chain]

Local names:	Pagagoh (North Borneo), waliketupa sapi (Indonesia), kuasathwa (Laos)
Synonyms:	*Desmodium repandum* (Vahl) DC., *Hedysarum repandum* Vahl., *Meibomia repanda* (Vahl.) O. Kuntze.
Description:	It is a herb which grows to 1 m tall in a geographical area ranging from tropical Africa, Madagascar, Mauritius, Yemen, India, Bhutan, Thailand, Laos, Vietnam, Malaysia, Indonesia, China, the Philippines, Papua New Guinea and the Pacific Islands. The plant grows in open lands and thickets. The stem is about 0.25 cm in diameter, terete, angled and hairy at the apex, with 0.7 - 1.5 cm long internodes. The leaves are trifoliolate, spiral and stipulated. The stipule is triangular, linear, with longitudinal nervations, 0.8 x 0.2 cm, hairy at the apex and deciduous. The rachis is hairy, straight, flat above, with winged edges, inflated at the base, and 1 - 3.5 cm long. The petiolule is hairy and 0.2 - 0.3 cm long. A hairy bract which is 0.3 cm long is present at the base of the petiolule. The folioles are 2.3 - 6.5 x 1.2 - 4 cm, broadly lanceolate, present 5 - 6 pairs of secondary nerves, the margin is wavy, the apex minutely acuminate and the base acute. The inflorescence is a terminal spike on an axis which is 13 - 17 cm long, angled and hairy. The flower pedicel is 0.5 cm

Figure 56: *Desmodium renifolium* (L.) Schindl.
From: Flora of Sabah. Herbarium of University Kebangsaan Malaysia № 42437
Malaysia, Sabah, Sunsuron Tabunan, near Berbatu river. Collection and identification: Joseph Pounis Guntavid.

and hairy. The calyx is pilose, 0.25 - 0.35 cm with 5 lobes which are 0.1 x 0.2 cm. The corolla is scarlet, 0.5 cm long, 0.8 - 1 x 0.7 - 0.8 cm with narrowly elliptic wings and a standard which is clawed and 1 x 0.3 cm. The pod is ovate, 0.6 - 0.3 x 0.3 cm, hairy, comprises 3 to 4 septae, and shows at the apex a 0.5 cm long tail (Figure 57).

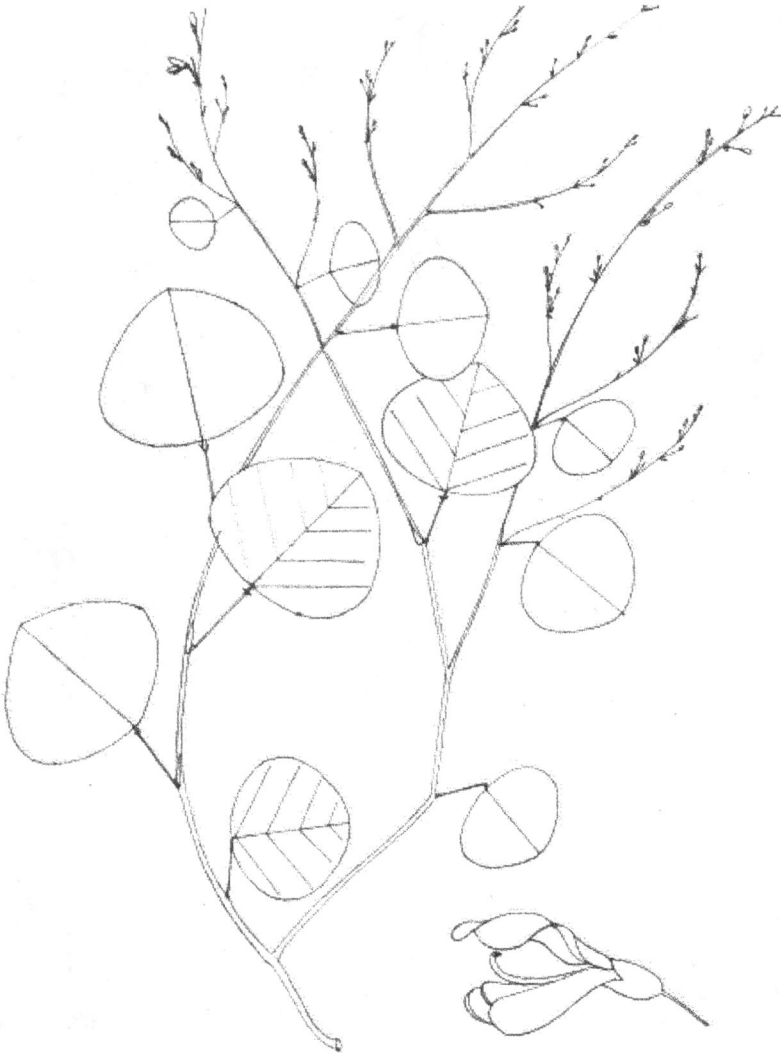

Figure 57: *Desmodium scalpe* **DC.**
From: Flora of Thailand, Chiang Mai university Herbarium.
Thailand, Lampang province, Muang Bahn (Pan) district, Jae Sawn national park off the dirt road east of Mae Jam village. By 18° 5' North - 99° East. Elevation: 1100 m. Date of collection: 3 December 1995. In partly shaded, slightly disturbed area in seasonal, primary evergreen hardwood forest on granite bedrock. Collection and identification: JF Maxwell N° 95-1266

Medicinal Uses: The plant is considered as healing in Indonesia.

Pharmacology: This common herb has not been yet studied for pharmacology.

Desmodium triflorum (L.) DC.
[From the Greek *desmos* =chain and Latin *triflorum* = 3-flowered]

Local names: Tick clover; kudaliya (India), hinundupiyali (Sri Lanka), kaliskis dalag (Philippines), topis bubut (Thailand)

Basionym: *Hedysarum triflorum* L. Species Plantarum 2: 749-750. 1753.

Synonyms: *Aeschynomene triflora* Poir., *Desmodium bullamense* G.Don, *Desmodium caespitosum* Bojer, *Desmodium granulatum* Walp., *Desmodium stipulaceum* Hassk., *Hedysarum biflorum* Willd. ex Wall., *Hedysarum granulatum* Schum. & Thonn., *Hedysarum stipulaceum* Burm.f., *Hedysarum triflorum* L., *Hippocrepis humilis* Blco., *Meibomia triflora* (L.) Kuntze, *Nicolsonia reptans* Meisn., *Nicolsonia triflora* (L.) Griseb, *Pleurolobus triflora* (L.) Duchass. & Walp.

Description: It is a perennial herb common in the tropics. The stem is terete, dull light green to dull light violet, and hairy by the apex. The leaves are trifoliolate, spiral and stipulate. The stipule is membranaceous, translucent, 0.5 x 0.2 cm with longitudinal nerves. The rachis is 0.5 cm long and channeled above. The petiolule is 0.1 cm long and hairy. A 0.3 cm long bract is present at the base of the petiolule. The foliole is membranaceous, dull dark green above, recurved at margin, broadly spatulate, acute round at the base, the apex cordate to round, with 3 - 4 pairs of secondary nerves and a polyhedral net of tertiary nerves underneath. The inflorescence is an axillary fascicle. The calyx is 0.3 - 0.4 cm long, pale light green, hairy, with lanceolate lobes. The corolla is 0.5 cm long and whitish-violet. The anthers are pale yellow. The filaments, stigma, style and immature pods green. The fruit is a pod recurved upward, membranaceous, sub-glabrous, with 5 septae, 1.1 x 0.2 cm, each septum 0.25 cm long with a net of nerves forming polyhedral pattern and with an the apex with a 0.2 cm long tip. The calyx is persistent, membranaceous, hairy, the lobes 0.3 x 0.8 cm (Figure 58).

Medicinal Uses: In the Philippines the plant is used as a mouth wash and to treat dysentery, colic and coughs and to heal wounds and sores. In Indonesia, the plant is used to treat diarrhoea and dysentery as in

China. In Taiwan, the plant is used for jaundice, rheumatisms, fever and vaginal infection. In Malaysia, the plant is used to assuage stomach-ache and to treat skin diseases.

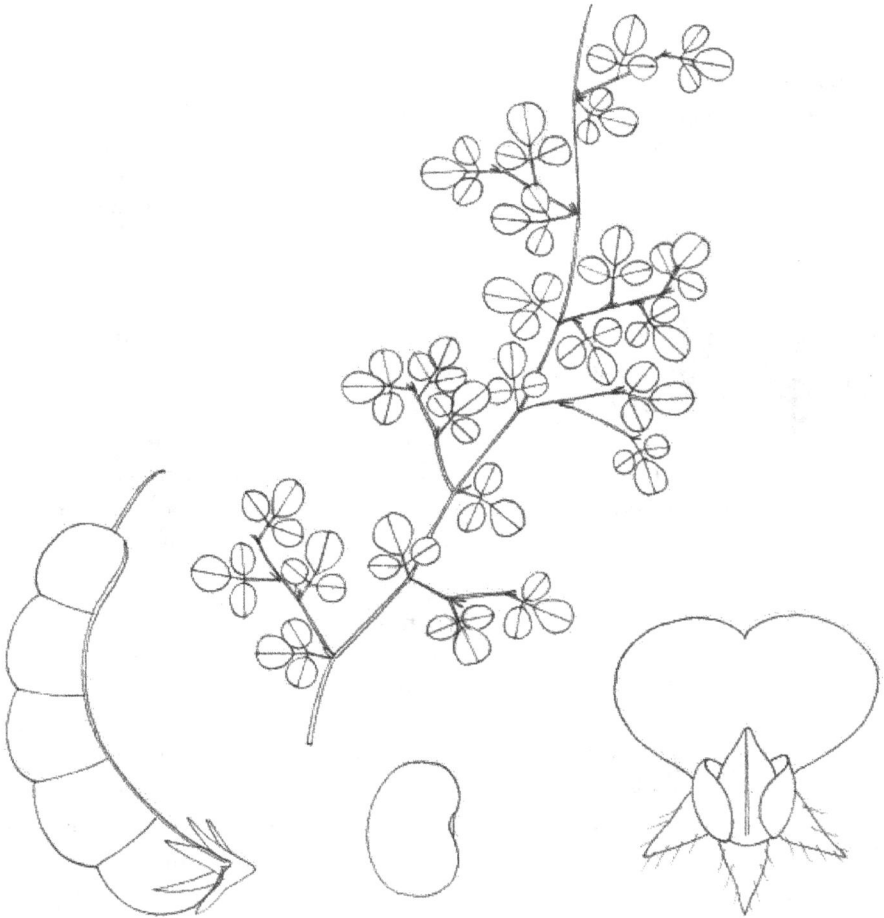

Figure 58: *Desmodium triflorum* (L.) DC.
From: Flora of Thailand, Chiang Mai University Herbarium.
Thailand, Chiang Mai province, Sahngahmpang district, Doi Lohn, West side, Mae Gahm Bawng village, along Mae Gahm Bawng stream. By 18° 5' North - 99° East. Elevation: 1000 m. Date of collection: 23 October 1996. I open disturbed, tea plantation area, disturbed, seasonal; primary evergreen hardwood forest on granite bedrock. Collection and identification: JF Maxwell N° 96-1388.

Pharmacology: An extract of the plant exhibited anthelminthic activity against human *Ascaris lumbricoides* cultured *in vitro* (Raj *et al.*, 1975). The plant contains some alkaloids including beta-phenethylamine, trigonelline, hypaphorine (Ghosal *et al.*, 1971). Analgesic and anti-inflammatory properties of the plant have been confirmed: an extract of the plant elicited inhibition of the writing reflex, increased tail flick time and inhibited carrageenan-induced rat paw oedema (Chowdhury *et al.*, 2005). An extract of the plant protected human skin basal cell carcinoma cell line against adenoviruses (Chiang *et al*, 2003).

References:

Chiang LC, Cheng HY, Liu MC, Chiang W, Lin CC, 2003, Antiviral activity of eight commonly used medicinal plants in Taiwan. Am J Chin Med; 31: 897-905.

Chowdhury KK, Achinto S, Bachar SC, Kundu JK, 2005, Analgesic and anti-inflammatory activities of *Desmodium triflorum* DC. J Biol Sc; 5 581-83.

Ghosal S, Srivastava RS, Banerjee PK, Dutta SK, 1971, Alkaloids of *Desmodium triflorum* Phytochemistry;10:3312-13.

Raj RK, 1975, Screening of indigenous plants for anthelminthic action against human *Ascaris lumbricoides*: Part--II. Indian J Physiol Pharmacol;19:

Desmodium triquetrum (L.) DC.
[From the Greek *desmos* =chain and Latin *triquetrum* = having three corners]

Local names:
Daun duduk (Indonesia), yeyjur (India), lauk thay ywet (Burma)

Basionym:
Hedysarum triquetrum L. Species Plantarum 2: 746. 1753

Synonyms:
Hedysarum triquetrum L., *Pteroloma triquetrum* (L.) DC., *Tadehagi triquetrum* (L.) H. Ohashi

Description:
It is a prostrate herb which grows in a geographical area including India, Nepal, Sri Lanka, Southeast Asia, Papua New Guinea, and the Pacific Islands. The plant grows on sandy and exposed soil. The stem is shaply triangular, reddish at first, with few hairs, 0.3 m in diameter and looks somewhat articulated. The leaves are simple, spiral and stipulated. The stipule is light-green, 0.8 x 0.25 cm, lanceolate, glabrous, and presents longitudinal nervations. The petiole is 1 - 2 x 0.2 - 0.4 cm with a pair of wings the apex of which clasps the base of the leaf-blade. The leaf-blade is 8.8 - 5.5 x 1.1 - 2.1 cm, reddish when young turning dark green, glossy, lanceolate, round at the base, acute at the apex, and presents a conspicuous midrib and 13 -14 pairs of secondary nerves. The inflorescence is a terminal raceme which is 12.5 cm long, with a winged axis which is glabrous. The flower pedicel is 0.4 - 0.5 cm long and hairy. The calyx is reddish green. The corolla is whitish purple and about

1 cm long. The fruit is a green flattish pod recurved upward, pilose, with 4 - 6 septae with are 0.4 cm long and a terminal tail which is 0.6 cm long. The calyx is persistent, minutely hairy, with 5 triangular lobes which are 0.2 x 0.1 cm (Figure 59).

Medicinal Uses: In Burma and China, the plant is used to expel worms from the intestines. In China, it is also used to heal boils and piles. In Indonesia, the plant is used to promote urination.

Pharmacology: The febrifuge and healing uses of the plant have been validated experimentally. The anthelminthic property of the plant could be due to prenylated isoflavones, triquetrumones A, B, and C which exhibited mild anthelminthic property *in vitro* (Xiang *et al*, 2005). An extract of the plant promoted healing in animal model (Shirwaiker *et al.*, 2003).

References: Shirwaiker A, Jahagirdar S, Udupa AL, 2003, Wound healing activity of *desmodium triquetrum* leaves. Indian J Pharm Sc; 65:461-64.

Xiang W, Li RT, Mao YL, Zhang HJ, Li SH, Song QS, Sun HD., 2005, Four new prenylated isoflavonoids in *Tadehagi triquetrum*. J Agric Food Chem.;53:267-71.

Dunbaria scortechinii Prain ex King

[After George Dunbar (1774-1851) and after Benedetto Scortechini (1845-1886) Italian cleric and botanist]

Synonym: *Dunbaria nivea* Miq.

Description: It is a climber which grows wild in Thailand, Malaysia and Indonesia. The stem is terete to angled, hairy, 0.12 cm in diameter, woody at the base and with longitudinal striations. The leaves are trifoliolate, spiral and stipulated. The stipules are deciduous. The rachis is about 6 cm long, ribbed, velvety and 0.2 cm in diameter. The petiolule is velvety, channeled and about 0.4 cm long. The folioles are dark green above, grey underneath, 2.8 - 5 x 5 - 7 cm, membranaceous, the terminal one angled, the lateral one asymmetrical, velvety underneath and with 2 - 3 pairs of secondary nerves. The inflorescence axis is dull greenish. The calyx has reddish areas. The standard is maroon-brown outside, cream yellow inside, with light yellow wings and a keel which is curved and yellowish green. The filaments are whitish green. The pod is linear, green and flattish (Figure 60).

Figure 59: *Desmodium triquetrum* (L.) DC.
From: Flora of Thailand, Prince of Songkla University.
Thailand, Songkla province, Nae Mom district, Khlong Rang Hill. Elevation: 50 m. Date of collection: 30 January 1985. In sandy soil at roadside in full sunlight. Collection and identification: Mark Newman N° 29.

Medicinal Uses:	In Malaysia, the plant is used to heal sores and wounds, to assuage itchiness and to break fever.
Pharmacology:	The plant is unexplored yet for pharmacology. It is noteworthy that an extract of *Dunbaria bella* Prain. inhibited the replication of herpes simplex virus (HSV) types 1 and 2 *in vitro* (Akanitapichat *et al.*, 2006).

Reference: Akanitapichat P, Wangmaneerat A, Wilairat P, Bastow KF., 2006, Anti-herpes virus activity of *Dunbaria bella* Prain. J Ethnopharmacol;105:64-8.

Figure 60: *Dunbaria scortechinii* Prain ex King
From: Flora of Thailand, Prince of Songkla University Herbarium.
Thailand, Songkla province, Muang district, by 8° 5' North - 99° East. In open thicket, disturbed place near the stream. Collection and identification: JF Maxwell Nº 86-3

Eriosema chinense Vogel

[From Greek *erio* = woolly and Latin *chinense* = from China]

Local name:	Sand pea, katil (Indonesia, Philippines), tel (Cambodia), man chaang (Thailand).
Synonym:	*Dolichos biflorus* auct. non L.
Description:	It is an erect perennial herb which grows in waste land and at roadsides to 50 cm tall in India, Burma, Nepal, Thailand, Cambodia, Vietnam, Laos, Indonesia, Philippines, Taiwan, China, Papua New Guinea, and Australia. The plant grows from a tuber which is edible, brown outside, and cream inside. The stem is terete, dull violet, 0.25 cm in diameter, angled at the apex, and hairy, the hairs up to 0.2 cm long. The leaves are simple, spiral and stipulated. The stipule is linear, longitudinally nerved, with a few hair and 0.5 x 0.1 cm. The petiole is pilose and 0.1 cm long. The blade is linear, dull dark green above, hairy above, velvety below, 3.5 - 5 x 0.2 - 0.3 cm, acute at the apex and tapering at the base. The inflorescence is an axillary raceme which is green, about 1 cm long and with few flowers. The calyx is campanulate, green, 0.2 cm long, hairy with linear lobes which are 0.3 cm long. The standard is pale light yellowish-green inside, dull yellow with dense dull reddish streaks outside. The wings are yellow and the keel pale light green with a reddish tip. The pod is light green turning blackish, 0.9 x 0.7 cm, 1-2-seeded, with a little tail and pilose. The seeds are reniform, glossy, 0.35 x 0.2 cm, with a line at one side (Figure 61).
Medicinal uses:	In China, the plant is used to treat coughs, diseases of the lungs and kidneys.
Pharmacology:	The pharmacological property of this plant is unexplored. The members of the genus *Eriosema* are known to elaborate a series of flavonoids with erectile (Drewes *et al.*, 2002), hypoglycemic, vasodilator (Ojewole *et al*, 2006) and antimicrobial properties (Ma *et al.*, 1995; .Awouafack *et al.*, 2008).
References:	Awouafack MD, Kouam SF, Hussain H, Ngamga D, Tane P, Schulz B, Green IR, Krohn K, 2008, Antimicrobial prenylated dihydrochalcones from *Eriosema glomerata*. Planta Med; 74:50-4.
	Drewes SE, Horn MM, Munro OQ, Dhlamini JT, Meyer JJ, Rakuambo NC, 2002, Pyrano-isoflavones with erectile-dysfunction activity from *Eriosema kraussianum*. Phytochemistry; 59:739-47.

Ma WG, Fuzzati N, Li QS, Yang CR, Stoeckli-Evans H, Hostettmann K, 1995, Polyphenols from *Eriosema tuberosum*. Phytochemistry; 39:1049-61.

Ojewole JA, Drewes SE, Khan F, 2006, Vasodilatory and hypoglycemic effects of two pyrano-isoflavone extractives from *Eriosema kraussianum* N. E. Br. [Fabaceae] rootstock in experimental rat models. Phytochemistry; 67: 610-7.

Figure 61: *Eriosema chinense* Vogel

From: Flora of Thailand, Chiang Mai University Herbarium
Thailand, Chiang Mai province, Om Koi district, off highway 1099, near Km 24, south of Nawng Gra Ting village. By 17° 05' North - 99° East. Elevation: 1075 m. Date of collection: 10 August 1996. In open, fire damaged, much degraded, seasonal mixed deciduous dipterocarp - oak hardwood and pine forest, on granite bedrock.

Flemingia macrophylla (Willd.) Kuntze ex Merr.

[After English botanist and physician John Fleming (1747-1829) and from Latin *macrophylla* = with large leaves]

Local names:	Flemingia; serengan jatan (Malaysia), apa-apa (Indonesia), mahae-nok, roh kee (Thailand), malabalatong (Philippines), cay dau ma (Vietnam)
Synonyms:	*Flemingia congesta* Roxb., *Flemingia latifolia* Benth., *Flemingia stricta* Roxb., *Moghania macrophylla* (Willd.) Kuntze.
Description:	It is a shrub native of Southeast Asia and has spread in the tropical regions of the globe. The plant can reach 4 m tall. The stem is terete, hairy, lenticelled, angled at the apex with 4.5 - 5.5 cm long internodes. The leaves are trifoliate, spiral and stipulated. The stipule is deciduous, hairy, lanceolate, and 1 - 1.5 cm long. The rachis is angled, flattish, hairy, grooved above with an oil cell and 6 - 10.5 x 0.2 cm. The petiolule is 0.3 - 0.5 cm, velvety and dotted. The folioles are membranaceous, the middle one broadly elliptic and tapering at the base and the lateral ones are asymmetrical. The folioles are 6 -16 x 4 -7 cm with 7 - 9 pairs of secondary nerves and present some tiny dots and some tertiary nerves which are scalariform. The inflorescence is an axillary raceme which is 4 - 10 cm long and velvety and angled at the apex. The flower pedicel is 0.15 cm long. The calyx is pilose with 5 lobes which are triangular and 0.3 x 0.1 cm. the corolla is 0.7 cm long and purplish. The pod is 1.2 - 0.9 x 0.6 cm, smooth, with short hairs and a 0.2 cm long tail at the apex. The calyx is persistent. The seeds are globose, glossy, black, and 0.2 x 0.35 cm (Figure 62).
Medicinal Uses:	In China, the plant is used to treat swellings and sores. In Taiwan it is used for fever, paralysis and arthritis.
Pharmacology:	The plant produces series of flavonoids of which flemingichromone, 5,7,4'-trihydroxy-6,8-diprenylisoflavone, 5,7,4'-trihydroxy-6,3'-diprenylisoflavone which protected neuronal cells from Abeta-induced damage (Shiao *et al.*, 2005). Flemiflavanone-D from the plant is active *in vitro* against *Staphylococcus aureus* and *Mycobacterium smegmatis* (Mitscher *et al.*, 1985).

Figure 62: *Flemingia macrophylla* (Willd.) Kuntze ex Merr.
From: flora of Thailand, Chiang Mai University Herbarium.
Thailand, Kanchanaburi province, Sangklaburi district, Toong Yai Naresan wildlife reserve, Lai Wo subdistrict, Ban Saneh Pawng area (Karen village). Elevation: 375 m., by 14° 05' North - 99° East. In partly open, fire prone, degraded area in mixed deciduous bamboo forest on rugged limestone terrain.

Flemiflavanone-D

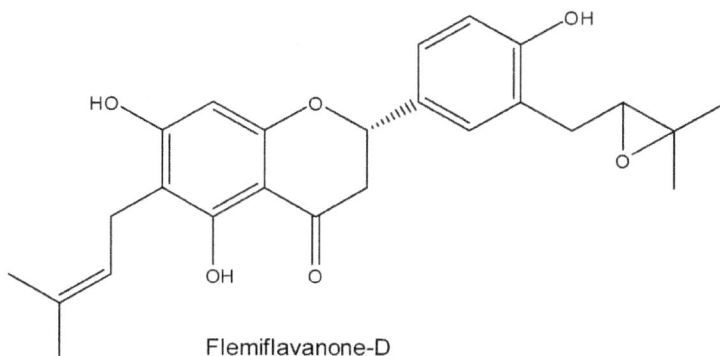

References: Mitscher LA, Gollapudi SR, Khanna IKK, Drake SD, Ramaswamy HT, Rao KVJ, 1985, Antimicrobial agents from higher plants: Activity and structural revision of flemiflavanone-D from *Flemingia stricta*. Phytochemistry; 24: 2885-2887

Shiao YJ, Wang CN, Wang WY, Lin YL.,2005,Neuroprotective flavonoids from *Flemingia macrophylla*. Planta Med; 71(9):835-40.

Indigofera suffruticosa Mill.
[From Latin *Indigofera* = containing indigo and *suffruticosa* = shrubby]

Local names: Anil indigo, nil (Malaysia), khram-thuan (Thailand), tom janti (Indonesia), tina-tinaan (Philippines).

Synonyms: *Indigofera anil* L., *Indigofera comezuelo* Moc. & Sesse ex DC, *Indigofera divaricata* Jacq., *Indigofera drepanocarpa* Bergman, *Indigofera guatimala* Lunan, *Indigofera tinctoria* Mill., *Indigofera truxillensis* Kunth.

Description: It is a shrub which grows up to 2.5 m in open land. The plant is native of tropical America and has spread throughout the tropics. The stem is polyhedral, hairy, flattish and winged at the apex. The leaves are compound, spiral and stipulated. The stipule is linear, 0.3 - 0.5 cm long and hairy. The rachis is angled, hairy, channeled above, 5 -10 cm long and bears 5 - 6 pairs of folioles plus a terminal one. The petiolule is hairy and 0.2 cm long. The folioles are 1 - 4 x 3 -1.5 cm, membranaceous, elliptical, hairy below and without apparent secondary nerves. The inflorescence is an axillary raceme which is angled and hairy and 2 - 6 cm long. The flower pedicel is minute. The calyx is campanulate, 0.7 cm long with triangular lobes. The corolla pinkish-red, the standard is ovate and 0.5 cm long, the wings are 0.4 cm long, and the keel is 0.7 cm long. The pod is hook-shaped, woody, and hairy, about 2 x 0.2 cm and contains 4 - 6 seeds which are angled and about 0.2 cm in diameter (Figure 63).

Figure 63: *Indigofera suffruticosa* **Mill.**
From: Flora of Malaya. Herbarium of University Kebangsaan Malaysia № 08552
Malaysia, Selangor. Collection: Asmah. Determination: Mohd Kassim.

Medicinal Uses: In Malaysia, the plant is used as a remedy for stomachache.

Pharmacology: An extract of the plant inhibited the growth of the Gram-positive *Staphylococcus aureus* (Leite *et al*, 2006). An extract of fruits of

Indigofera suffruticosa Mill. destroys the liver of Balb/c mice and increases the number of cells with aberrant chromosome (Ribeiro *et al.*, 1991). The plant contains a glucoside known as indican which is the precursor of indirubin, dyeing principle of *Indigofera tinctoria* L. Several chemical derivatives of indirubin are being developed in the search for anticancer agents. Some of them abrogated the survival of several human cancers by apoptosis and inhibited the growth of RK3E-ras-induced tumors in Sprague-Dawley rats (KIM *et al*, 2007).

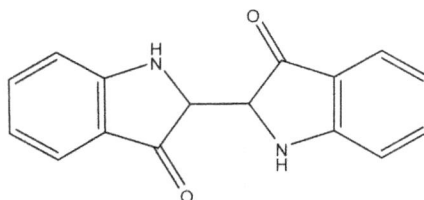

Indirubin

References: Kim SA, Kim YC, Kim SW, Lee SH, Min JJ, Ahn SG, Yoon JH, 2007, Antitumor activity of novel indirubin derivatives in rat tumor model. Clin Cancer Res; 13:253-9.

Leite SP, Vieira JR, de Medeiros PL, Leite RM, de Menezes Lima VL, Xavier HS, de Oliveira Lima E, 2006, Antimicrobial Activity of *Indigofera suffruticosa*. Evidence-based Complement Alternate Med; 3:261-5.

Ribeiro LR, Bautista AR, Silva AR, Sales LA, Salvadori DM, Maia PC, 1991, Toxicological and toxicogenetic effects of plants used in popular medicine and in cattle food. Mem Inst Oswaldo Cruz; 86 Suppl 2:89-91.

Koompassia malaccensis Maing.

[From Malay *kemps* = *Koompassia malaccensis* Maing. And from Latin *malaccensis* = from Malacca]

Local names: Kempas (Malaysia), thang pung (Thailand), impas (Sabah), mengris (Sarawak).

Synonyms: *Koompassia beccariana* Taub., *Koompassia excelsa* Taub.

Description: It is a tree that grows to a height of 60 m in the forest of Malaysia and Indonesia. The bole is straight and buttressed. The bark is dark grey and fissured. The stem is terete, angled, somewhat rough, and hairy at the apex. The internodes are 2.5 - 5 cm long. The leaves are pinnate, spiral and stipulate. The stipule is deciduous. The rachis is about 10 - 20 cm long, not straight, lenticelled, with alternate folioles. The petiolule is about 0.5 cm long, transversally fissured and discretely channeled. The foliole is elliptic, 2 - 3 x 4 - 8 cm, membranaceous, translucent, elliptic, and glaucous below, without visible secondary nerves. The flowers are very small in terminal panicles. The pod is flat, yellowish - green, 9.8 - 12.8 x 3 - 4 cm, with some polyhedral patterns in the middle and winged (Figure 64).

Medicinal Uses: In Malaysia, the plant is used to break fever.

Pharmacology: Kobayashi *et al* (1996) isolated a stilbene from the plant called kompassinol A. Note that kompassinol A from the seeds of *Syagrus romanzoffiana* (Cham.) Glassman (Arecaceae) reduced the glucose levels of Wistar rats in oral glucose challenge (Lam *et al.*, 2008). This result warrants further pharmacological investigation of the plant. Cytotoxic and antimicrobial leads await discovery.

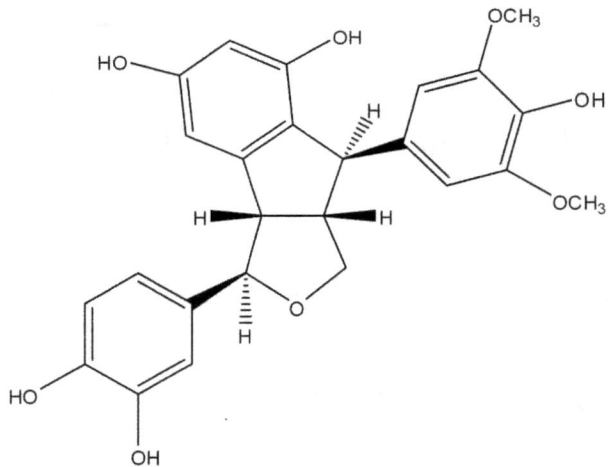

Kompassinol A

References: Kobayashi M, Mahmud T, Yoshioka N, Hori K, Shibuya H, Kitagawa I, 1996. Indonesian medicinal plants. XVIII. Kompasinol A, a new stilbeno-phenylpropanoid from the bark of *Koompassia malaccensis* (Fabaceae). Chem. Pharm. Bull.; 44:2249-2253.

Lam SH, Chen JM, Kang CJ, Chen CH, Lee SS, 2008, Glucosidase inhibitors from the seeds of *Syagrus romanzoffiana*. Phytochemistry; 69:1173-1178

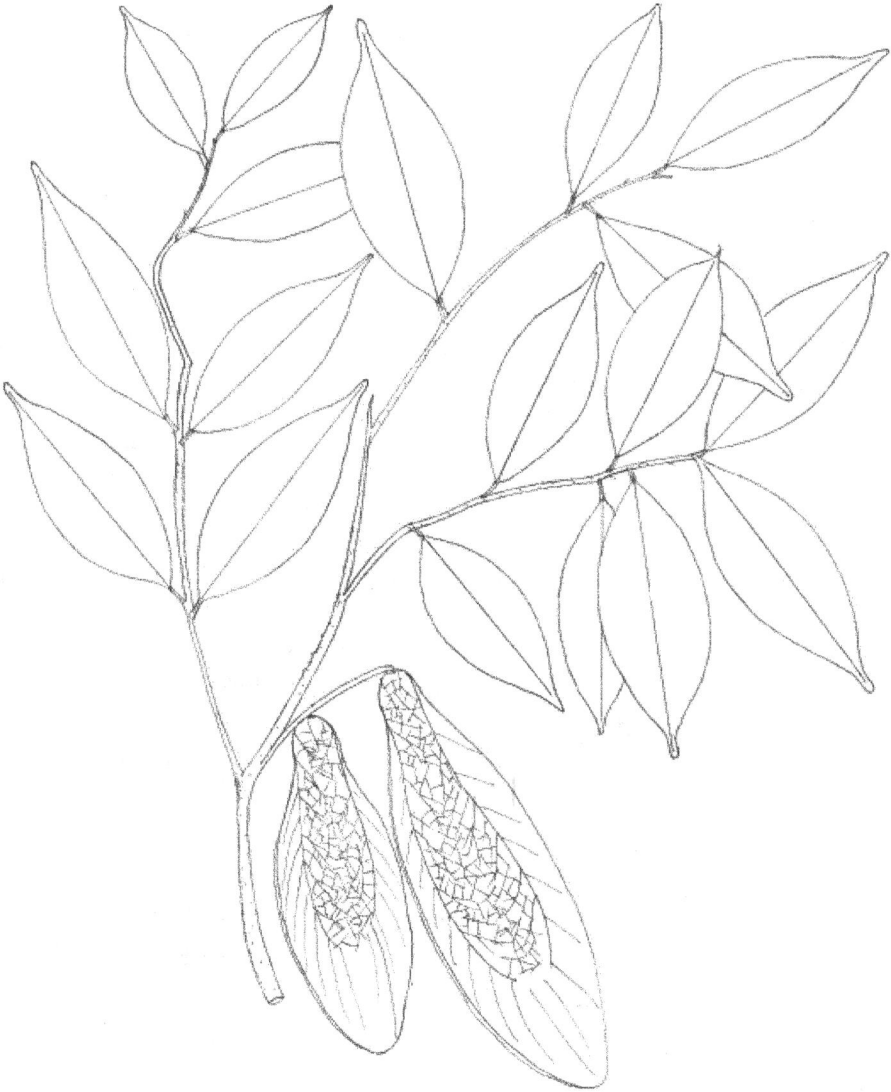

Figure 64: *Koompassia malaccensis* Maing.
From: Herbarium of University Kebangsaan Malaysia Nº 03411
Malaysia, Selangor, in rainforest, Bukit Lajan. Collection and identification: JMM van Balgooy.
Date of collection: 9 February 1975

Millettia sericea (Vent.) Benth.

[After C Millet, 19th century officer of the East India Company and Latin *sericea* = silky]

Local names:	Akar mumbol, akar mambu (Malaysia), cha-nai-kho (Thailand), bori akar (Indonesia)
Synonyms:	*Millettia sericea* Wight & Arn., *Phaseolodes sericeum* (Wight & Arn.) Kuntze
Description:	It is a woody climber which grows to 30 m long in the river bank and sea shore forests of Vietnam, Thailand, Malaysia, and Indonesia. The stem is terete, lenticelled, pitted, 0.1 cm in diameter. The leaves are compound, spiral and stipulate. The young leaves are eaten as salad in Indonesia. The stipule is caducous. The rachis is angled, velvety, 15 x 0.2 cm and bears 4-9 pairs of folioles. The petiolule is velvety, channeled and 0.6 - 0.8 cm long. The foliole is lanceolate, leathery and glossy above, 6 -11 x 2.2 - 4.5 cm, glabrous above, acuminate at the apex, velvety below, round at the base, and with 3 - 5 pairs of secondary nerves. The inflorescence is an axillary raceme which is 14.6 - 29 cm long. The calyx is cup-shaped, 0.4 cm long and truncate. The corolla is violet, with orbicular standard and elliptical wings. The pod is thick, velvety, 8 - 9 x 1.7 - 5 cm with 1-2 seeds which are about 1 cm in diameter (Figure 65).
Medicinal Uses:	In Malaysia, the plant is used to break fever, to promote urination, to assuage toothache, to resolve inflamed eyes and it is given to mothers after childbirth. In Indonesia is used to expel worms from the intestines, to heal infected wounds. It is also used there to stupefy fish.
Pharmacology:	Unknown. One could have some interest in studying the flavonoids of this plant and their activities.

Moghania strobilifera (L.) J. St.-Hil. ex O. Kuntze

[After the Scottish botanist Robert Maughan (1769- 1844) and Latin *strobilifera* = bearing strobils]

Local names:	Gaan (Sabah), pa-apa kebo (Indonesia), khee dang (Thailand) payang-payang (Philippines), duoi chofn. (Vietnam), arana (Papua New Guinea)

Figure 65: *Millettia sericea* (Vent.) Benth.
From: Herbarium of University Kebangsaan Malaysia, Nº 22577
Malaysia. Collection ALM 1310

Basionym: *Hedysarum strobiliferum* L. *Species Plantarum* 2: 746. 1753

Synonyms: *Flemingia bracteata* (Roxb.) Willd., *Flemingia fruticulosa* Wall ex. Benth., *Flemingia fruticulosa* Wall., *Flemingia strobilifera* (L.) Roxb. ex W.T. Aiton, *Hedysarium bracteatum* Roxb., *Hedysarium strobiliferum* L., *Moghania bracteata* (Roxb.) H.L. Li, *Moghania fruticulosa* (Wall.) Mukerjee, *Zornia strobilifera* (L.) Pers.

Description: It is a shrub which grows in a geographical area covering India, Southeast Asia, south China and the Pacific Islands. The plant grows to 3 m, and grows well in savanna and dry waste places. The stem is hairy at the apex 0.2 cm in diameter, and shows internodes 4 – 6 cm long, marked with a minute line. The leaves are simple, spiral and stipulated. The stipule is 0.3 cm long and hairy. The petiole is straight, 1 - 2.5 cm long, hairy, channeled, slightly inflated at both ends. The leaf-blade is 7-13 x 3 -7 cm, membranaceous, subglabrous underneath, broadly lanceolate, minutely cordate at the base, acute at the apex, and shows 7 - 12 pairs of secondary nerves which are straight. The inflorescence is an axillary and terminal raceme which is 9 - 12 cm long and produces series of strobils which are hairy, nerved and numerous. The calyx is subglabrous. The corolla is yellowish-green with an obovate standard. The pod is oblong, 0.7 - 1.5 x 5 - 7 cm, hairy, and contains a pair of orbicular seeds which are oblong, blackish, with an elliptic opening (Figure 66).

Medicinal Uses: In Burma and India, the plant is used to treat epilepsy. In India, plant is used to induce sleep, and to assuage pain. In Malaysia and Papua New Guinea, the plant affords a post-partum remedy and is used for rheumatism. In the Philippines, the plant is also used as a post-partum remedy and provides a treatment for tuberculosis. In Indonesia, the plant is used to expel worms from intestines. In Papua New Guinea, the plant is used to improve walking and talking.

Pharmacology: The plant produces some flavonoids including a flavanone named flemingiaflavanone (8, 3'-diprenyl-5, 7, 4'-trihydroxy flavanone), which inhibited the growth of MRSA *Staphyloccocus aureus*, *Pseudomonas aeruginosa* and *Candida albicans* (Madan *et al.*, 2008). The general medicinal profile of this plant suggests that it warrants further pharmacological studies.

References: Madan S, Singh GN, Kumar Y, Kohli K, Singh RM, Mirc SR, Ahmad S, 2008, A New Flavanone from *Flemingia strobilifera* (Linn) R. Br. and its Antimicrobial Activity. Trop J Pharm Res; 7: 921-27

Figure 66: *Moghania strobilifera* (L.) J. St.-Hil. ex O. Kuntze
From: Flora of Sabah, from Herbarium of University Kebangsaan Malaysia, Nº 26485
Malaysia, Sabah, Papar. Dambahon village, in open area.

Mucuna biplicata Teijsm. & Binnend.
[From Latin *biplicata* = two-folded]

Local names: Lipoi (North Borneo, Dusun name), akar jueh (Malaysia)

Synonym: *Mucuna atropurpurea* Baker

Description: It is a climber which grows in the forests of Vietnam, Malaysia,
                    Indonesia, and Borneo. The stem is terete, glabrous, and pimply
                    at the base, pitted, curved, 0.5 cm in diameter, with lenticels
                    which are 0.05 cm in diameter. The leaves are trifoliolate, spiral
                    and stipulate. The rachis is enlarged at the base, 17 - 20 cm
                    long and 0.3 cm in diameter and sub-glabrous. The petiolule is

swollen, channeled, and 0.2 - 0.9 cm long. The lateral foliole is asymmetrical, round at the base and caudate at the apex. The terminal foliole is elliptic and caudate at the apex. The folioles are 6.3 - 7 x 12 - 14 cm and show 4 - 5 pairs of secondary nerves. Two 0.2 cm long bracts are present at the base of the terminal foliole. One 0.3 cm long bract is present at the base of the lateral folioles. The fruit is a pod which is 6.5 - 7 x 3 - 3.5 cm, covered with 0.3 cm long needle-like hairs which are irritating. The surface of the pod is deeply striated (Figure 67).

Medicinal uses: In Malaysia the plant is used to break fever and stomach-ache. In Indonesia, the seed is used externally as a protective remedy.

Pharmacology: Unknown.

Mucuna gigantea (Willd.) DC.

[From Latin *gigantea* = giant]

Local names: Sea bean, burni bean, krachiap (Thailand), *fue vai (Samoa)*

Basionym: *Dolichos giganteus* Willd. Species Plantarum. Editio quarta 3(2): 1041. 1802

Synonyms: *Carpopogon giganteum* (Willd.) Roxb., *Dolichos giganteus* Willd., *Mucuna grevei* Drake, *Mucuna longipedicellata* Hauman, *Mucuna quadrialata* Baker, *Mucuna tashiroia* Hayata, *Negrieta gigantea* (Willd.) Oker, *Stilzolobium giganteum* (Willd.) Spreng.

Description: It is a large woody climber which grows on the shores and river and lake banks in a geographical area ranging from East Africa to the Pacific Islands. The main stem can reach 15 m long. The stem is terete, with a few hairs. The leaves are trifoliolate, spiral, and stipulate. The stipule is caducous and about 2 cm long. The rachis is 3 - 8 cm long and bears 3 folioles which are dark green above, 4 -12 cm × 2 -8 cm, lanceolate, with 2 - 3 pairs of secondary nerves. The inflorescence is an umbel on a hanging pale greenish axis which is 5 - 20 cm long. The flower pedicel is 1 - 2 cm long. The calyx is greenish, hairy, up to 1 cm long with 5 lobes which are 0.2 - 0.3 cm long. The corolla is pale creamy-green, about 3 cm long with a broadly lanceolate standard and a keel which is constricted at the base. The filament, stigma and style are whitish and the anthers are grey. The pod is oblong, slightly curved, covered with golden hair, to 16 cm long, and containing 4 seeds and present a tail at the apex (Figure 68). The seeds are disseminated by the sea.

Figure 67: *Mucuna biplicata* Teijsm. & Binnend.
From: Flora of Borneo. Herbarium of University Kebangsaan Malaysia
Malaysia, Kimunis - Papar logging road, near river bank. Elevation: 90 m. In lowland
dipterocarp forest on clay soil. Collection and identification: Norhazni Mat Sani № 0069 NMS.
Date of collection: 13 September 1987.

Medicinal Uses: In Guam the seeds are used to increase libido

Pharmacology: The plant probably contains L-dopa (L-3.4-dihydroxyphenylalanine)
                    and indole alkaloids. It could be of interest to study the plant further
                    for its neuropharmacological properties.

Figure 68: *Mucuna gigantea* (Willd.) DC.
From: Flora of Thailand. Prince of Songkla University Herbarium.
Thailand, Songkla province, Chana district. Elevation: sea level. Date of collection: 26 June 1985. In open thicket next to a pond. Collection and identification: JF Maxwell. N° 85-631

Mucuna pruriens (L.) DC.

[From Latin *pruriens* = itching]

Local names: Velvet bean; kekaras gatal (Malaysia), mah moo ee (Thailand), kara benguk (Indonesia), sabawel (Philippines), khnhae (Cambodia), tam nhe (Vietnam),

Basionym:	*Dolichos pruriens* L. *Herbarium Amboinenese* 23. 1754
Synonyms:	*Carpopogon pruriens* (L.) Roxb., *Dolichos pruriens* L., *Mucuna aterrima* (Piper & Tracy) Holland, *Mucuna axillaris* Baker, *Mucuna berneierriana* Baill., *Mucuna deeringia* (Bort) Holland, *Mucuna esquilorii* H. Lev., *Mucuna prurita* Hook, *Mucuna prunita* Wight, *Mucuna utilis* Wall. ex Wight, *Stizolobium aterrimum* Piper & Tracy, *Stizolobium deeringianum* Bort., *Stizolobium pruriens* (L.) Medik., *Stizolobium prurinum* (Wight.)
Description:	It is an elegant climber native to Southeast Asia that has spread in several tropical and subtropical regions of the globe. It is an annual climber, the main stem of which can reach 10 m long. The stem is slender terete with a few hairs. The leaves are trifoliolate, spiral and stipulate. The stipule is caducous, about 0.5 cm long, and hairy. The rachis is about 10 - 20 cm long, pubescent, grooved, and bears 3 folioles. The terminal foliole is broadly lanceolate and the lateral folioles are asymmetrical. The folioles are dark green above, 5 -20 x 3 cm-17 cm, acute at the apex and minutely tipped, with 4 - 7 pairs of secondary nerves and hairy. The inflorescence is an axillary pendulous pale whitish yellow raceme which is about 15 - 30 cm long. The flower pedicel is about 1 cm long. The calyx is light yellowish-green, about 0.5 cm long, hairy with 5 lobes of unequal length. The corolla is about 2 cm long the standard and wings are dark purple, and the keel is white with a yellowish beak. The filaments are whitish with purple anthers The pod is elegantly curved, like a fluffy caterpillar, green with 3 seeds, about 13 cm long. It is densely covered with brownish bristly hairs which are irritating because they contain pruritogenic proteins such as mucunaine. The seed is somewhat polyhedral with an elliptic opening (Figure 69).
Medicinal Uses:	In India, the plant is used for diabetes. The hairs of the pod (Mucuna, British Pharmaceutical Codex, 1934) mixed with honey have been used as an anthelminthic, being given every morning for 2 or 3 days.
Pharmacology:	The plant contain dopamine L-dopa (L-3.4-dihydroxyphenylalanine) (Damodaran *et al.*, 1937) and has some potential for the treatment of Parkinson's disease (Vaidya *et al.*, 1978). A double blind study showed that seed powder possesses advantages over conventional L-dopa preparations. It also synthesises some indole alkaloids including N-dimethyltryptamine which has hallucinogenic properties as

well as tetrahydroisoquinoline alkaloids. The seeds lowered the blood glucose levels in normal and alloxan-diabetic rabbits (Akhtar *et al*, 1990) on account of D-chiro-inositol and galacto-derivatives (Donati *et al.*, 2005). An extract of seeds elicited anti-lipid peroxidation property mediated through the removal of superoxide and hydroxyl radicals (Tripathi *et al.*, 2002). An extract of the plant showed analgesic, anti-inflammatory and antipyretic properties in rats (Iauk *et al.*, 1993).

References:

Akhtar MS, Qureshi AQ, Iqbal J, 1990, Antidiabetic evaluation of *Mucuna pruriens*, Linn seeds. J Pak Med Assoc;40:147-50.

Damodaran M, Ramaswamy R, 1937, Isolation of l-3:4-dihydroxyphenylalanine from the seeds of *Mucuna pruriens*. Biochem J;31:2149-52.

Donati D, Lampariello LR, Pagani R, Guaranty R, Cinci G, Marinello E, 2005, Antidiabetic oligocyclitols in seeds of *Mucuna pruriens*. Phytother Res; 19:1057-60.

Katzenschlager R, Evans A, Manson A, Patsalos PN, Ratnaraj N, Watt H, Timmermann L, Van der Giessen R, Lees AJ, 2004, *Mucuna pruriens* in Parkinson's disease: a double blind clinical and pharmacological study. J Neurol Neurosurg Psychiatry; 75:1672-7

Iauk L, Galati EM, Kirjavainen S, Forestieri AM, Trovato A, 1993, Analgesic and antipyretic effects of *Mucuna Pruriens*. Pharmaceut Biol; 31:213-16.

Misra L, Wagner H, 2004, Alkaloidal constituents of *Mucuna pruriens* seeds. Phytochemistry;65:2565-7.

Tripathi YB, Upadhyay AK, 2002, Effect of the alcohol extract of the seeds of *Mucuna pruriens* on free radicals and oxidative stress in albino rats. Phytother Res;16:534-8.

Vaidya AB, Rajagopalan TG, Mankodi NA, Antarkar DS, Tathed PS, Purohit AV, Wadia NH, 1978, Treatment of Parkinson's disease with the cowhage plant-*Mucuna pruriens* Bak. Neurol India; 26:171-6.

Figure 69: *Mucuna pruriens* (L.) DC.
From: Flora of Thailand, Prince of Songkla University
Thailand, Haadyai, Songkla province Thailand. Elevation: sea level. Date of v\collection: 25
December 1984. In open thick along a river.

Peltophorum pterocarpum (DC.) Backer ex K. Heyne

[from Greek *pelte* = shield, *pherein* = to bear, *pteron* = wing, and *ka.pos* = fruit]

Local name:	Yellow flame, jemerlang laut (Malaysia).
Basionym:	*Inga pterocarpa* DC. *Prodromus Systematis Naturalis Regni Vegetabilis* 2: 441. 1825
Synonyms:	*Brasilettia ferruginea* (Decne) Kuntze, *Caesalpinia ferruginea* Decne., *Caesalpinia inermis* Roxb., *Inga pterocarpa* DC., *Peltophorum inerme* Naves ex Fern.-Vill., *Peltophorum roxburghii* (G.Don) O. Deg., *Poiciana roxburghii* G. Don
Description:	It is a tree which grows to 20 m tall in Southeast Asia and Australia, on sea shores naturally and often grown as a street ornamental. The bark is fissured and cracked. The stem is terete, velvety and lenticelled. The leaves are bipinnate and stipulate. The stipules are linear. The leaves are about 12 - 35 cm long, with 5 - 11 pairs of pinnae. The rachis is inflated at the base, and somewhat winged. The pinnae comprise 9 - 20 pairs of folioles which are asymmetrical, oblong about 1 - 1.5 x 0.6 cm, notched at the apex, hairy below. The inflorescences are terminal racemes, erect, 24 - 40 cm long with red-brown axiss. The peduncles are about 0.2 - 0.8 cm long. The calyx is velvety. The corolla presents 5 petals which are crinkled and yellowish. The pod is 5 - 10 x 2.5 cm, flat, nerved, cupper - brown with 1- 5 seeds (Figure 70).
Medicinal Uses:	In Indonesia, the plant is used as a tonic, an astringent, and to prevent swelling and colic.
Pharmacology:	An extract of the plant showed antibacterial activity against several strains of *Escherichia coli* (Voravuthikunchai *et al.*, 2004).
Reference:	Voravuthikunchai S, Lortheeranuwat A. Jeeju W, Sririrak T, Phongpaichit S, Supawita T, 2004, Effective medicinal plants against enterohaemorrhagic *Escherichia coli* O157:H7. J Ethnopharmacol; 94:49-54.

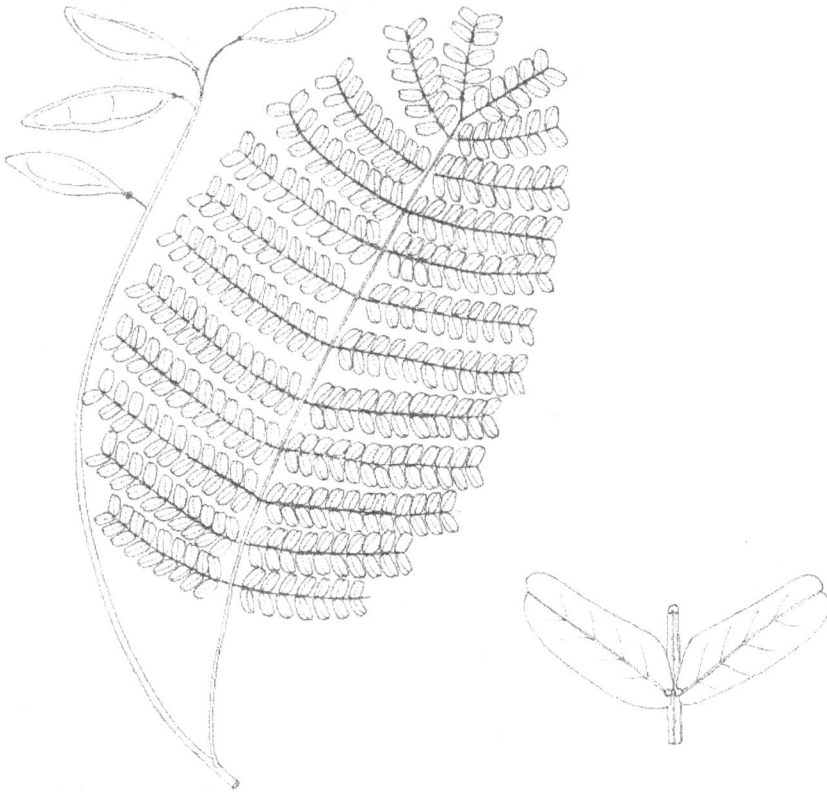

Figure 70: *Peltophorum pterocarpum* **(DC.) Backer ex K. Heyne**
From: Flora of Sabah, Herbarium of the Forest Department, Sandakan No SAN 108503.
Malaysia, Sabah, Bensuluk forest reserve, Beaufort district. Date of collection: 7 March 1985.
On seashore.

Phaseolus lathyroides L.

[From Greek *phaselos* = a little boat and Latin *lathyroides* = like the genus *Lathyrus*]

Local names:	Phasey bean, cow pea, kacang batang (Indonesia), frijolito de los arrozales (Spain)
Synonyms:	*Macroptilium lathyroides* (L.) Urb., Phaseolus psoraleoides Wight & Arnott, Phaseolus semierectus L.
Description:	It is a twining herb which grows to 1.5 m tall in open lands and waste places, often by streams or the sea coast of Malaysia, Thailand, Vietnam, Indonesia, Taiwan, Philippines, Ryukyu Islands, Australia, and Pacific Islands. The plant is native to

tropical America. The stem is terete, 0.4 cm in diameter, pitted, with few hairs, fleshy, pitted and longitudinally striated. The leaves are trifoliolate, spiral and stipulate. The stipules are linear and 0.7 x 0.2 cm. The rachis is hairy and ridged and about 3 cm long. The petiolule is hairy, about 0.6 cm long with 0.2 cm long bracts. The foliole is lanceolate, 3 - 8 x 1 - 3.5 cm membranaceous, with 3 - 8 pairs of secondary nerves, hairy underneath. The inflorescence is an axillary raceme which is fleshy, with few hairs, and that can reach 50 cm long. The calyx is hairy, membranaceous, 0.3 cm long, curved, with triangular lobes, and persistent in fruits. The flower bud is hooked. The corolla is about 1.5 cm long. The standard is purplish - red. The wings and keel are purplish tinged green, red or white. The pod is straight, 5 - 10 cm long and about 0.3 cm wide and contains 18 - 30 seeds which are dark brown, oblong, asymmetrical, about 0.3 cm in diameter and marked by a longitudinal elongated opening (Figure 71).

Medicinal Uses:	In Indonesia, the seeds are known to be poisonous.
Pharmacology:	To date the pharmacological property of the plant remains unexplored.

Phaseolus mungo L.

[From Greek *phaselos* = a little boat and Visayan mungo = *Phaseolus mungo* L.]

Local names:	Mung bean, black gram; pai (Burma), lu tou (China), mu (Nepal), bolaton (Philippines), suphala (Sanskrit), mongo de la India (Spain)
Synonyms:	*Azukia mungo* (L.) Massam., *Phaseolus aureus* Roxb., *Vigna mungo* (L.) Hepper
Description:	It is a climber native to central Asia which is found in most tropical and sub-tropical regions of the globe. The plant is cultivated for its seeds which are edible. The stem is terete, pilose, and about 0.2 cm in diameter. The leaves are compound, spiral and stipulate. The stipules are lanceolate, pilose, longitudinally striated, 0.45 x 0.2 cm, glabrous inside. The rachis is pilose, ribbed to angled, kneeled at the base and about 10 cm long. The petiolule is pilose, short, 0.2 x 0.1 cm, minutely winged. The bracts are 0.2 cm and pilose. The folioles are 2 - 6 x 1 -

Figure 71 : *Phaseolus lathyroides* L.
From: Flora of Singapore. Herbarium of Singapore, Botanical Gardens. National Park Board.
Collection: Joseph Lai, Nº LJ 174. Date of collection: 10 January 1997. In waste ground near construction site in Woodlands.

5 cm, membranaceous, pilose underneath, broadly lanceolate, obovate, and acute at the apex with a tiny tip, round at the base and show about 4 pairs of secondary nerves. The inflorescence is axillary, either sessile or on a 5 - 10 cm long axis which is pilose. The fruit is a pod which is cylindrical to angled, pilose, with 7 - 8 seeds. The pod opens to show angled lodges which are 0.4 x 0.3 cm. The seeds are angled and smooth (Figure 72).

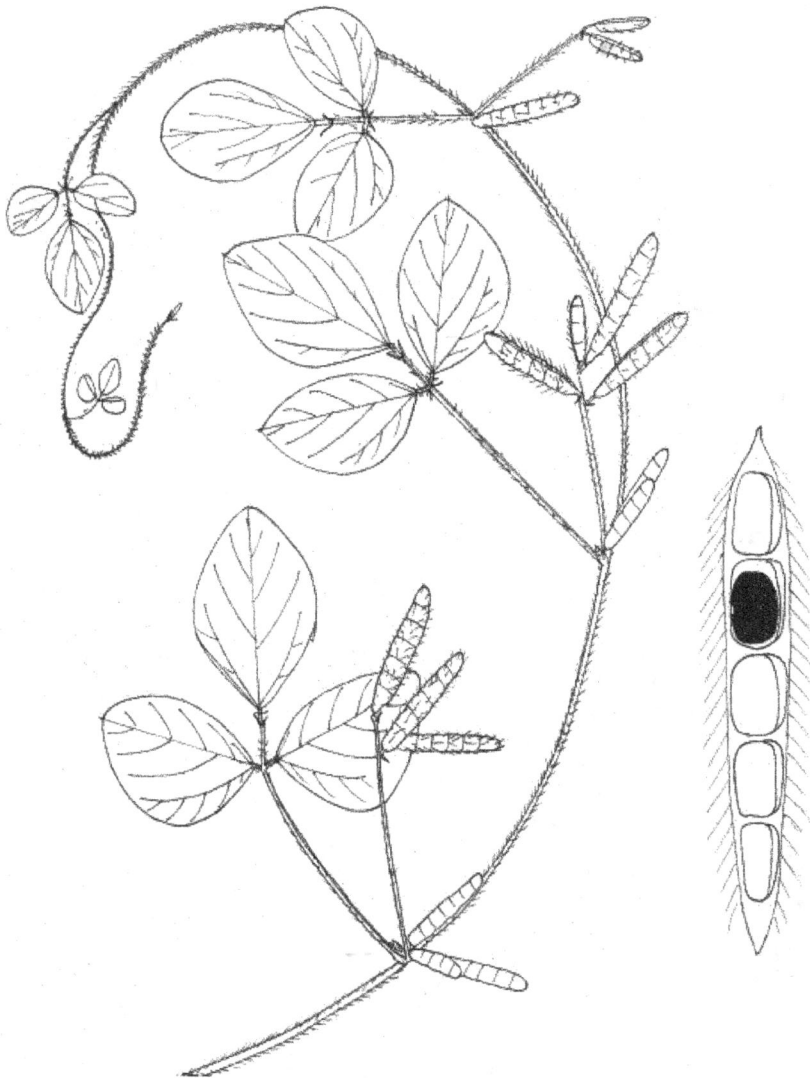

Figure 72: *Phaseolus mungo* L.
From: Herbarium of University Kebangsaan Malaysia № 07310
Malaysia, Tg. Tuan, Port Dickson. Collection and identification: Mohd Kassim. Date of
collection: 28 November 1972.

Medicinal Uses: In China the plant is used to promote digestion, and to control
dysentery as well as smallpox. In Cambodia, Laos and Vietnam, the
plant is used to promote urination. In Malaysia, the plant is used
to treat vertigo. In Indonesia, the plant is used to invigorate.

Pharmacology: Ye *et al* (2000) isolated a protein, mungin, which inhibited the
growth of *Rhizoctonia solani, Coprinus comatus, Mycosphaerella*

arachidicola, Botrytis cinerea, and *Fusarium oxysporum* cultured *in vitro*. The seeds contain a protein, mungoin, with protease inhibitor, antifungal and antibacterial activities (Wang *et al*, 2006). The seeds lowered the blood glucose, serum total lipids, triglycerides and esterified fraction of cholesterol in normal and alloxan-induced diabetic guinea pigs (Srivastava *et al.*, 1999). In addition the seeds contain a polysaccharide which lowers cholesterol-, phospholipid- and triglyceride-levels of rodent rats fed a high fat-high cholesterol diet (Menon *et al.*, 1974).

References:

Menon PVG, P. A. Kurup A, 1974, Hypolipidaemic action of the polysaccharide from *phaseolus mungo* (Blackgram): Effect on glycosaminoglycans, lipids and lipoprotein lipase activity in normal rats. Atherosclerosis; 19: 315-326.

Srivastava A, Joshi LD,1999, Effect of feeding black gram (*Phaseolus mungo*) on serum lipids of normal & diabetic guinea pigs. Indian J Med Res; 92:383-6.

Wang S, Lin J, Ye M, Ng TB, Rao P, Ye X, 2006,Isolation and characterization of a novel mung bean protease inhibitor with antipathogenic and anti-proliferative activities. Peptides; 27: 3129-36.

Ye XY, Ng TB, 2000, Mungin, a novel cyclophilin-like antifungal protein from the mung bean. Biochem Biophys Res Commun; 273:1111-5.

Psophocarpus tetragonolobus (L.) DC.

[From Latin *Psophocarpus* = noisy fruit and *tetragonolobus* = with 4 lobes]

Local names:

Winged bean, kacang botol (Malaysia), tua phot (Thailand), kecipir (Indonesia), sigarillas (Philippines).

Basionym:

Dolichos tetragonolobus L. Systema Naturae, Editio Decima 2: 1162. 1759.

Synonyms:

Botor tetragonoloba (L.) Kuntze, *Dolichos tetragonolobus* L.

Description:

It is a climber which grows to 4 m long. The plant is native to Papua New Guinea and widely cultivated in Burma, India, Sri Lanka, Thailand, Malaysia, Indonesia, Philippines and also found in Africa and America. The stem is slender and glabrous. The leaves are trifoliolate, spiral and stipulate. The stipules are deciduous. The rachis is 15 - 20 cm long and channeled at the apex. The folioles are deltoid, 7 - 15 x 4 - 6 cm, with 4 pairs of secondary nerves. The inflorescence is axillary with 2-10 flowers. The flowers are pale blue, about 2.5 cm long with a broad emarginated standard. The pod is 4-winged, green turning brown and opening noisily, 15 - 25 cm long and containing several elliptic seeds marked with a rind on one side (Figure 73).

Figure 73: *Psophocarpus tetragonolobus* (L.) DC.
From: Flora of Malaya, Herbarium of University Kebangsaan Malaysia
Malaysia, Johor, Pulau Pemagpil, cultivated. Collection and identification: Rahim Hamid

Medicinal Uses: In Malaysia the plant is used to treat smallpox. In Indonesia, the plant is used to heal wounds, and to sooth inflamed eyes. In Papua New Guinea, the plant is used to heal sores, wounds and ulcers.

Pharmacology:	The seeds contain lectins which have been much studied. Note that in rats a lectin caused deleterious effects to the mucosal epithelia of the gastrointestinal tract (Shet *et al.*, 1989). The plant contains a series of pterocarpans (Preston *et al.*, 1977).
References:	Preston NW, 1977,Induced pterocarpans of *Psophocarpus tetragonolobus*.Phytochemistry; 16: 2044-45.
	Shet MS, Madaiah M, Ahamed RN, 1989, Effect of raw winged bean [*Psophocarpus tetragonolobus* (L.) DC] tuber lectin on gastrointestinal tract of growing rats. Indian J Exp Biol; 27:58-61.

Pterocarpus indicus Willd.

[From Greek *pteron* = wing and *karpos* = fruit and Latin *indicus* = from India]

Local names:	Andaman redwood, padauk (Burma), chan kraham (Cambodia), angsana (Malaysia), agana (Philippines), vengai (India)
Synonyms:	*Lingoum indicum* (Willd.) Kuntze, *Lingoum wallichii* (Wight & Arn.) Pierre, *Pterocarpus blancoi* Merr., *Pterocarpus carolinensis* Kaneh, *Pterocarpus pallidus* Blco., *Pterocarpus papuana* F. Muell, *Pterocarpus pubescens* Merr., *Pterocarpus santalinus* Blco., *Pterocarpus wallichii* Wight & Arn.
Description:	It is a tree which grows to 30 m on the sea shores and tidal rivers of India, Burma, Malaysia, Indonesia, the Philippines, South China and Papua new Guinea. The bole is not straight and buttressed. The bark is cream brown and finely fissured. The stem is longitudinally striated, lenticelled, the lenticels being round and 0.1 cm in diameter. The leaves are compound, spiral and stipulate. The rachis is swollen at the base, angled, sub-glabrous, 20 - 25 cm long and bears 5- 9 pairs of folioles. The petiolule is channeled and 0.4 cm long. The foliole is 5 - 10 x 3.8 - 5 cm, glossy, the midrib strongly raised underneath. The inflorescence is an axillary panicle which is 15 cm long. The calyx is 0.6 cm long and hairy. The corolla is golden yellow and 1.5 cm long. The pod is 4.5 - 5 cm in diameter, with papery wings, golden hairy when young and containing several seeds (Figure 74).
Medicinal Uses:	In India, the fruit is used to induce vomiting and is used to heal wounds. In Cambodia, the plant is used against fever, dysentery and as diuretic remedy. The dried sap of the tree makes a resin

Figure 74: *Pterocarpus indicus* Willd.
From: Flora of Malaya. Herbarium of University Kebangsaan Malaysia № 8554
Malaysia, Negeri Sembilan, Gunung Datuk, Rembau. Collection: Asmah

called kino which is used in Southeast Asia to treat diarrhoea, to heal wounds, and as an astringent remedy. In Indonesia, the plant is used for headache.

Pharmacology: An extract from the plant exhibited a broad spectrum of antibacterial activity *in vitro* (Khan *et al.*, 2003) probably due to triterpenes (Rasaga *et al.*, 2005) or phenolic compounds. A polyphenolic substance isolated from the plant showed a carcinostatic effect on mice bearing ascites Ehrlich carcinoma (Takeuchi *et al.*, 1986). An extract of the plant scavenged reactive oxygen species and prevented the alteration of TCA cycle enzymes located in the outer membrane of the mitochondria (Narayan *et al.*, 2007). An extract of the plant showed antibacterial property against *Helicobacter pylori* (Narayan *et al*, 2007a). Kwon *et al* (2006) demonstrated that an extract of the plant abrogated the survival of human cervical adenocarcinoma cell line, HeLa via apoptosis. The wound healing property of the plant is confirmed *in vivo* (Biswas *et al*, 2004). The plant contains series of lignans such as savinin and calocedrin, which significantly inhibited tumour necrosis factor-alpha production in lipopolysaccharide-stimulated RAW264.7 cells, and T cell proliferation elicited by concanavalin (Cho *et al.*, 2001). An extract of the plant lowered the glycemia of diabetic rodents (Kameswara *et al.*, 2001).

References: Biswas TK, Maity LN, Mukherjee B, 2004, The clinical evaluation of *Pterocarpus santalinus* Linn. ointment on lower extremity wounds--a preliminary report. Int J Low Extrem Wounds; 3:227-32.

Cho JY, Park J, Kim PS, Yoo ES, Baik KU, Park MH, 2001, Savinin, a lignan from *Pterocarpus santalinus* inhibits tumor necrosis factor-alpha production and T cell proliferation. Biol Pharm Bull; 24:167-71

Khan MR, Omoloso AD, 2003, Antibacterial activity of *Pterocarpus indicus*. Fitoterapia ;74:603-5.

Kameswara RB, Giri R, Kesavulu MM, Apparao C, 2001,Effect of oral administration of bark extracts of *Pterocarpus santalinus* L. on blood glucose level in experimental animals. J Ethnopharmacol; 74:69-74.

Kwon HJ, Hong YK, Kim KH, Han CH, Cho SH, Choi JS, Kim BW, 2006, Methanolic extract of Pterocarpus santalinus induces apoptosis in HeLa cells. J Ethnopharmacol; 105:229-34.

Narayan S, Devi RS, Devi CS, 2007, Role of *Pterocarpus santalinus* against mitochondrial dysfunction and membrane lipid changes induced by ulcerogens in rat gastric mucosa. Chem Biol Interact;170:67-75

Narayan S, Veeraraghavan M, Devi CS, 2007a, *Pterocarpus santalinus*: an *in vitro* study on its anti-Helicobacter pylori effect. Phytother Res; 21:190-3.

Ragasa CY, De Luna RD, Hofilena JG, 2005,Antimicrobial terpenoids from *Pterocarpus indicus*. Nat Prod Res;19: 305-9.

Takeuchi S, Kono Y, Hadiman, Mizutani T, Maruyama K, Nakayama R, Hiraoka A, Suzuki Y, Watanabe R, Kawarada A, Sasongko S, Adisewojo SS, 1986, A bioactive polyphenolic constituent in the bark of *Pterocarpus indicus*, Willd. I. isolation and characterization; Agric Biol Chem; 50: 569-73

Pueraria mirifica Airy Shaw & Suvat.

[After the Swiss botanist Marc Nicolas Puerari (1766-1845) and Latin *mirificus* = amazing]

Local name: Kwao kreu kao (Thailand).

Description: It is a deciduous woody climber which grows from a massive onion -shaped rhizome in Thailand. The basal stem is about 20 cm in diameter. The bark is thin, vertically cracked. The stem is dull green turning light brown, discretely angled with minute and numerous lenticels and hairy at the apex. The leaves are trifoliolate, spiral and stipulated. The stipule is hairy, somewhat ribbed, irregular at the margin, auricular and 0.9 cm long. The rachis is swollen at the base on 2.5 cm, velvety, about 20 cm long. The folioles are dark green above, about 11.5 - 20 x 10 x 18 cm, wavy at margin, membranaceous with few hairs, dark green above, broadly elliptic, acute at the base, acuminate at the apex and with 4 - 5 pairs of secondary nerves and a few tertiary nerves. The lateral folioles are asymmetrical at the base. The inflorescence is an axillary raceme which is 13 - 17 cm long. The calyx is hairy with 4 lobes of unequal size. The flower is dark purple to pink. The androecium is 0.7 cm long. The pod is about 6 - 8 cm long, pilose, slightly constricted between the seeds and with a tiny tail at the apex (Figure 75).

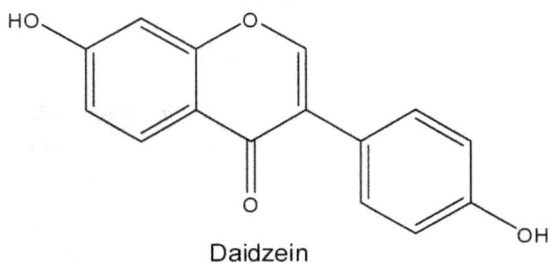

Daidzein

Medicinal Uses: The plant is used to invigorate and it is known to be poisonous. The plant is reputed to enlarge the breast and several products are sold worldwide despite rigorous toxicological study.

Pharmacology: The tuber abounds with isoflavonoids including; puerarin, daidzin, genistin, daidzein, miroestrol and genistein (Chansakaow *et al.*, 2000; Cherdshewasart *et al.*, 2007). Some of these are phytoestrogens and prevented bone loss in orchidectomized rats (Urasopo *et al.*, 2007). The tuber has an oestrogenic effect similar to conjugated equine oestrogen, and can alleviate the climacteric symptoms in perimenopausal women (Chandeying *et al.*, 2007). However, it should be noted that estrogenic substances may induce breast cancer. An interesting topic of research would be to use these phytoestrogens as starting material for the synthesis of anti-oestrogenic molecules which could be used in fighting breast cancer.

Figure 75: *Pueraria mirifica* **Airy Shaw & Suvat.**
From: Flora of Thailand, Chiang Mai University Herbarium.
Thailand, Lampoon province, Mae Tam district, Doi Kuhn Dahn national park, West side, Yaw. Elevation: 900 m. Date of collection: 25 June 1994. In open, fire damaged degraded deciduous forest with numerous bamboos on granite bedrock. Collection and identification: JF Maxwell:

References: Chandeying V, Sangthawan M, 2007, Efficacy comparison of Pueraria mirifica (PM) against conjugated equine estrogen (CEE) with/without medroxyprogesterone acetate (MPA) in the treatment of climacteric symptoms in perimenopausal women: phase III study. J Med Assoc Thai; 90: 1720-6.

Chansakaow S, Ishikawa T, Sekine K, Okada M, Higuchi Y, Kudo M, Chaichantipyuth C, 2000, Isoflavonoids from *Pueraria mirifica* and their estrogenic activity. Planta Med; 66: 572-5.

Cherdshewasart W, Subtang S, Dahlan W, 2007, Major isoflavonoid contents of the phytoestrogen rich-herb *Pueraria mirifica* in comparison with Pueraria lobata. J Pharm Biomed Anal; 43: 428-34.

Urasopon N, Hamada Y, Asaoka K, Cherdshewasart W, Malaivijitnond S, 2007, *Pueraria mirifica*, a phytoestrogen-rich herb, prevents bone loss in orchidectomized rats. Maturitas; 56: 322-31.

Pueraria phaseoloides Benth.

[After the Swiss botanist Marc Nicolas Puerari (1766-1845) and Latin *phaesoloides* = *Phaseolus* - like]

Local names: Tropical kudzu, kudzu tropika (Malaysia), krandang (Malaysia), singkamasaso (Philippines), pied (Laos), thua sian paa (Thailand), dau dai (Vietnam).

Synonyms: *Dolichos phaseoloides* Roxb., *Pueraria javanica* (Benth.) Benth.

Description: It is a perennial herb that originates from Southeast Asia and has spread to the tropics as a crop and vegetable. The roots are edible. The main stem can grow up to 10 m long. The stem is pale light yellowish with blue veins, terete, pilose, and hairy and about 0.15 cm in diameter. The leaves are trifoliolate, spiral and stipulate. The stipule is triangular, linear, pilose and 0.5 cm long. The rachis is pilose, whitish pale light yellowish with blue veins about 10 cm long and bears 3 folioles. The petiolule is pilose and 0.5 cm long. The terminal foliole is deltoid and the lateral folioles are asymmetrical. The folioles are dull dark green above, 2 - 20 x 2 -16 cm, sub-glabrous with 3 - 4 pairs of secondary nerves and with linear bracts at the base. The inflorescence is an axillary raceme which is 10 - 30 cm long, pale light yellowish with blue veins and showing minute globose irregular glands below the pedicels. The flower pedicel is pilose. The calyx is pilose, 0.6 cm long and campanulate. The corolla is violet with an orbicular standard which is whitish and violet inside, 1 - 2 cm in diameter. The keel is whitish. The anther filaments are white. The style is light-green. The pod is linear, terete or compressed cylindrical, about 10 cm long, and containing several angled seeds which are brownish-black, about 0.2 cm in diameter and marked with an elliptic mark the center of which develops a minute conical formation (Figure 76).

Medicinal Uses: In Malaysia, the plant is used to heal boils and infected ulcers.

Pharmacology: The plant has apparently not been studied for pharmacology.

Figure 76: *Pueraria phaseoloides* Benth.
From: Flora of Thailand, Chiang Mai University Herbarium
Thailand, Lampang province, Muang Bahn district, Jar Sawn national park, Mae Bahn. By 18°
North - 98° East. Elevation: 1000 m. Date of collection: 23 October 1995. In open, disturbed
thicket in primary evergreen, seasonal, hardwood forest on granite bedrock. Collection and
identification: JF Maxwell 95-976.

Robinia pseudo-acacia L.

[After French botanist Jean Robin (1550-1629) and Latin *pseudes-acacia* = false, false acacia]

Local name: Black Locust, false acacia; winn (Parish)

Synonym: *Robinia pringlei* Rose

Description: It is a tree native to North America which has been introduced into temperate countries as an ornamental plant, although severely poisonous. The plant can reach a height of about 25 m and yields a wood of good quality. The stem is smooth, longitudinally striated, terete, lenticelled and velvety at the apex . The leaves are spiral, pinnate and stipulated. The stipules are linear, 2 cm long and deciduous. The rachis is flattened, seems to emerge from the stem from a ciliate opening, pilose, terete and up to 30 cm long. The rachis holds 4 to 5 pairs of folioles which are opposite and attached to the velvety, flattish petiolule. The folioles are hairy, elliptic, 2.5 cm- 5 x 1 - 2cm, with a minute tip at the apex. The secondary nerves are inconspicuous. The inflorescences are terminal racemes with numerous flowers which are fragrant. The flower pedicel is hairy. The calyx is 5 - lobed and hairy, fragrant, white, about 2 cm long. The fruit is a pod, which is about 7 x 2.5 cm, thin, marked with transverse lines and pointed at the apex (Figure 77).

Medicinal Uses: In China, the plant is used to make a remedy for the eyes.

Pharmacology: A peptide from the seeds showed antibacterial property against *Corynebacterium michiganense*, *Staphylococcus aureus*, *Bacillus subtilis*, and *Escherichia coli* (Talas-Oğraş *et al.*, 2005). An ethanolic extract of *Robinia pseudoacacia* L. (Fabaceae) contained robinlin, a monoterpene, which abrogated the survival of brine shrimps. The plant contains lectins which might hold some potential in the treatment of cancer (Pusztai *et al.*, 2008).

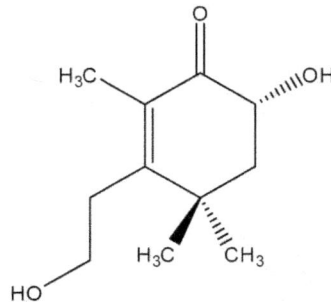

Robinlin

References: Pusztai A, Bardocz S, Ewen SW, 2008,Uses of plant lectins in bioscience and biomedicine.Front Biosci;13: 1130-40.

Talas-Oğraş T, Ipekçi Z, Bajroviç K, Gözükirmizi N, 2005, Antibacterial activity of seed proteins of Robinia pseudoacacia. Fitoterapia; 76:67-72.

Tian F, Chang CJ, Grutzner JB, Nichols DE, McLaughlin JL. Robinlin: a novel bioactive homo-monoterpene from Robinia pseudoacacia L. (Fabaceae). Bioorg Med Chem Lett; 11:2603-6.

Figure 77: *Robinia pseudo-acacia* L.
From: Herbarium of North Louisiana University, Flora of Louisiana.
USA, Louisiana at junction of L.a. 126 and L.a. 505. South Gransville, La., Sec. 15, T13N, R4W. Collector: Keth Kessler Nº 1249. Date of Collection: 16 April 1981.

Sesbania grandiflora (L.) Pers.

[After Persian *sisabaan* = name of a *Sesbania* species and from Latin *grandiflora* = with large flowers]

Local names:	Hummingbird tree, kacang turi (Malaysia), paukpan (Burma), angkea dey (Cambodia), agasti (India, Sanskrit), katurumurunga (Sri Lanka), caturai (Philippines), agatti (India), agati a Grandes Fleurs (France)
Basionym:	*Aeschynomene coccinea* L. f. *Supplementum Plantarum* 330. 1781
Synonyms:	*Agati coccinea* (L.f.) Desv., *Agati grandiflora* (L.) Desv.
Description:	It is a tree which grows wild or cultivated in a geographical zone including India, Southeast Asia, and Australia. The plant grows to about 6 m and is a common sight in Asian villages. The stem is terete, hairy and angled at the apex, the older parts lenticelled and marked with leaf-scars which are linear and about 0.3 cm long. The leaves are compound, spiral and stipulate. The stipules are velvety, 0.5 - 0.6 x 0.2 cm and deciduous. The rachis is 13 cm to 30 cm long, subglabrous, angled, with a hairy sheath at the base with 16 - 30 pairs of folioles which are thinly coriaceous, linear oblong, about 2 x 0.7 cm and opposite to sub-opposite. The apex of the foliole is minutely notched with a hairy bud, and shows underneath 6 to 7 pairs of secondary nerves which are discrete. The petiolule is angled, and wrinkled when dry. The flower buds are glabrous, lenticelled and hairy at the apex. The inflorescences are racemes 2.5 cm long with 2 - 4 flowers. The corolla is 7.5 - 8.8 cm long. The pods are about 36 x 0.6 cm, linear, angled, and edged inflated (Figure 78).
Medicinal Uses:	In India, the plant has manifold medicinal uses. Among other things, it is used to treat tumours, leprosy, rheumatism, painful swelling, anemia, fever, bronchitis and to invigorate. In Cambodia, the plant is used to treat diarrhoea. In Cambodia, Laos and Vietnam, the plant is a tonic and is used for fever. In Malaysia, the plant is used to treat sprains. In Indonesia, the plant is used to make a gargle and to treat dysentery. In the Philippines the plant is used as a laxative and to remove blood from saliva.
Pharmacology:	An extract of the plant attenuated pentylenetetrazol and strychnine- induced seizures in rodents as well as lithium-pilocarpine-induced status epilepticus and showed anxiolytic activity (Kasture *et al.*, 2002). An extract of the plant showed

protective effect against erythromycin estolate (800 mg/kg/day)-induced hepatotoxicity in rats (Pari. *et al.*, 2003). The leaf juice of *S. grandiflora* showed significant antiurolithiatic activity against calcium oxalate-type stones and also exhibited antioxidant properties (Doddola *et al.*, 2008).

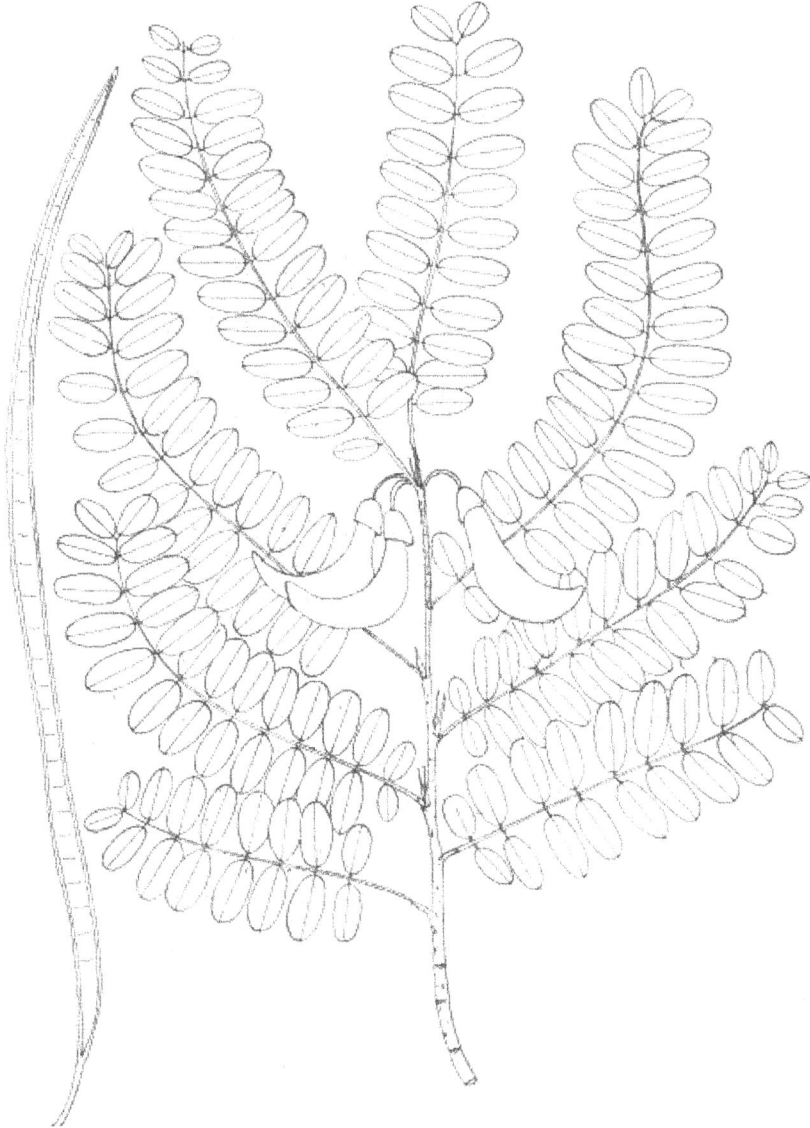

Figure 78: *Sesbania grandiflora* **(L.) Pers.**
From: Flora of Malaya.
Malaysia, Bangi, University Kebangsaan Malaysia Campus. Collection and identification: Habsah Md. Talib. No 16077.

References: Doddola S, Pasupulati H, Koganti B, Prasad KV, 2008, Evaluation of *Sesbania grandiflora* for antiurolithiatic and antioxidant properties. Nat Med (Tokyo), 62:300-7.

Kasture VS, Deshmukh VK, Chopde CT, 2002, Anxiolytic and anticonvulsive activity of *Sesbania grandiflora* leaves in experimental animals. Phytother Res;16:455-60.

Pari L, Uma A, 2003, Protective effect of *Sesbania grandiflora* against erythromycin estolate-induced hepatotoxicity. Therapie; 58:439-43.

Sophora tomentosa L.

[From Arabic *sofera* = name of leguminous plant and from Latin *tomentosa* = tomentose]

Local name: Necklace pod

Synonyms: *Sophora arenicola* Nees, *Sophora havanensis* Jacq., *Sophora littoralis* Schr., *Sophora occidentalis* L., *Sorindeia goudotii* Briq., *Zanthyrsis paniculata* Raf.

Description: It is a shrub or small tree which grows in open areas, often along sea shores, in most tropical countries. The wood is yellow. The stem is terete, hairy, velvety, the oldest parts lenticelled, pitted, stout and about 0.7 cm in diameter. The leaves are compound, spiral and stipulate. The rachis is velvety, forming a sheath at the base, 10.5 - 15 cm long, channeled above and somewhat angled with 6 - 7 pairs of folioles plus a terminal one. The petiolule is 0.2 cm long, wrinkled, hairy and channeled. The folioles are opposite or sub-opposite and about 1.8 x 3 cm, elliptic, coriaceous, glossy, velvety underneath with 3 - 4 pairs of secondary nerves, the margin recurved and the apex minutely pointed. The flower pedicel is densely sericeous. The calyx is 0.7 - 0.9 cm long, tomentose, truncate. The corolla is 1.6 cm long. The pods are 7 - 15 cm long, tomentose, with 6 - 8 seeds separated by narrow joints, and dispersed by sea (Figure 79)

Medicinal Uses: In Malaysia, the plant is used to treat diarrhoea. In Indonesia the plant is used for intestinal upsets and cholera. In the Philippines, the plant is used for stomach-aches.

Pharmacology: The plant contains matrine, cytosine, N-methylcytisine and N-acetylcytisine which are poisonous (Ohmiya *et al.*, 1974) as well as cohorts of flavonoids (Tanaka *et al.*, 1997). The pharmacological property of this plant seems still unexplored.

Figure 79: *Sophora tomentosa* L.
From: Botanical Inventory of Taiwan. Herbarium, Institute of Botany, Academia Sinica, Taipei (HAST)
Taiwan, Taitung Hsien: Lanyu (orchid Island) along coastal highway, 22° 01' North - 121° 35' East. Elevation: 0 m - 50 m. On very exposed coastal rock. Collection and identification: Chi Cheng Liao 1144. Date of collection: 24 February 1993.

References: Ohmiya S, Otomasu H, Murakoshi I, Haginiwa J, 1974, N-acetylcytisine from *Sophora tomentosa*. Phytochemistry; 13: 1016

Tanaka T, Iinuma M, Asai F, Ohyama M,. Burandt CL, 1997, Flavonoids from the root and stem of *Sophora tomentosa*. Phytochemistry; 46:1431-1437

Spatholobus ferrugineus Benth.

[From Greek *spatho* = short sword and *lobos* = lobe and Latin *ferrugineus* = rusty red]

Local names: Akar kelesei (Malaysia), akar kemedu balok, akar jagat (North Borneo)

Description: It is a climber which grows in the forest of Malaysia, Borneo and Indonesia. The stem is terete, velvety and rusty and about 0.4 cm in diameter. The leaves are compound and stipulated. The stipule is 1.3 x 0.7 cm, hairy and broadly lanceolate. The rachis is about 9 cm long. The petiolule is 0.5 x 0.2 cm with a pair of 0.5 cm linear bracts. The foliole is thinly coriaceous, hairy, and shows 8 - 11 pairs of secondary nerves arching at the margin, raised underneath with tertiary nerves. The foliole is 11.2 - 18.2 x 6 - 10.2 cm. The inflorescence is an axillary panicle. The calyx is hairy and presents a 3 dentate lobe. The flowers are brownish yellow. The pods are flat, nerved and about 6 cm long (Figure 80).

Medicinal Uses: In Indonesia, the plant is used to treat colic, irregular menses, coughs and fever.

Pharmacology: To date the pharmacological property of this plant seems to be unknown. Han *et al.*, (2007) isolated (+)-catechin-(4-->8)-(-)-epicatechin and (+)-catechin-(4-->8)-(+)-catechin-(4-->8)-(-)-epicatechin from *Spatholobus suberectus* Dunn which potently inhibited the DNA-topoisomerase-II. These catechins could account for the antiviral activity of an extract of the plant against Coxsackie virus B5, Polio virus I, Echo virus 9 and Echo virus 29 (Guo *et al.*, 2006). The plant elaborates a series of flavonoids, including butin, which inhibited cellular tyrosinase activity and melanin activity in human epidermal melanocytes (Lee *et al.*, 2006).

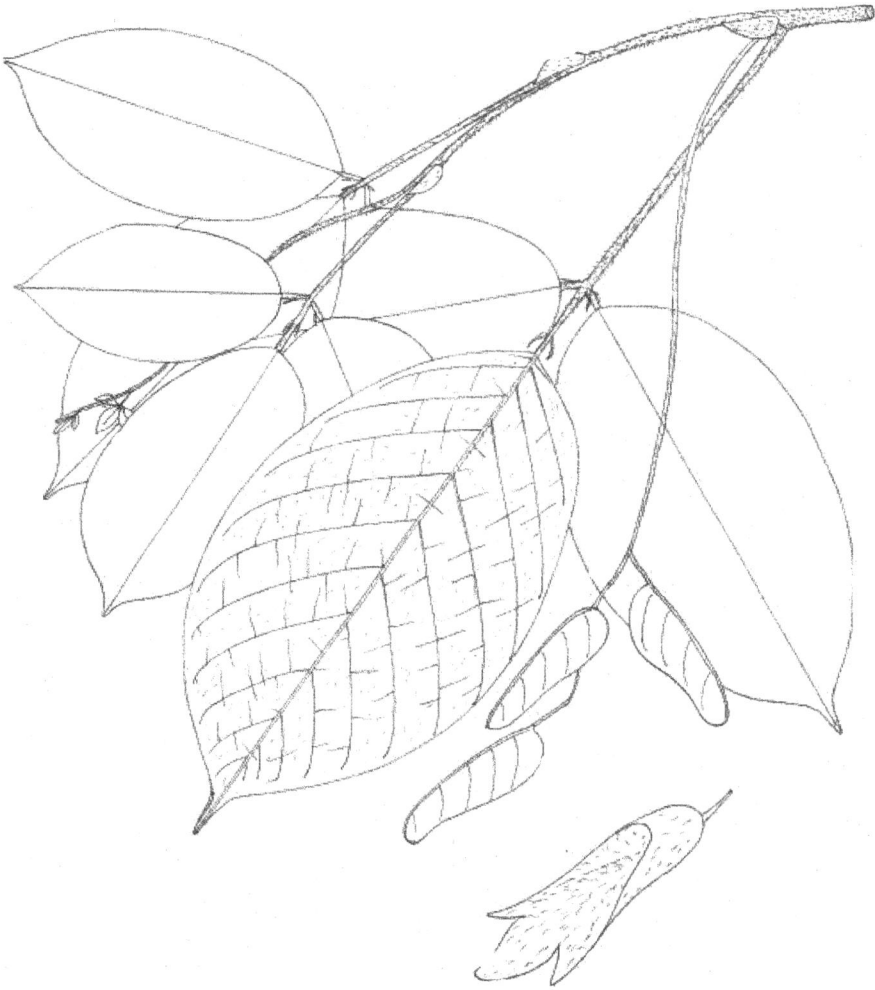

Figure 80: *Spatholobus ferrugineus* Benth.
From: Flora of Sabah, Herbarium of the Forestry Department Sandakan No SAN 110468.
Malaysia, Sabah, Ranau district, Southwest of Mount Kinabalu, below Kota Belud, East of
Ranau. Collection: Amin & Maidil. Date of collection: 20 July 1985. In logging area, on slope.

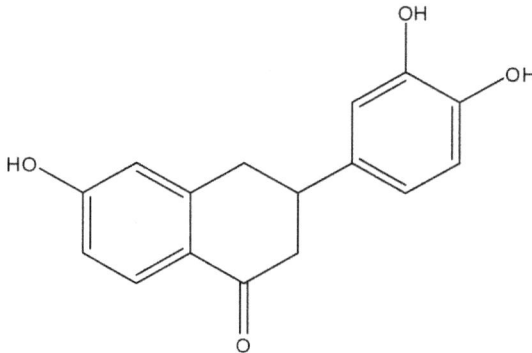

Butin

References: Guo JP, Pang J, Wang XW, Shen ZQ, Jin M, Li JW, 2006, *In vitro* screening of traditionally used medicinal plants in China against enteroviruses. World J Gastroenterol; 12:4078-81.

Han AR, Park HJ, Chen D, Jang DS, Kim HJ, Lee SK, Seo EK. Topoisomerase-II-inhibitory principles from the stems of *Spatholobus suberectus*. Chem Biodivers 2007 4:1487-91

Lee MH, Lin YP, Hsu FL, Zhan GR, Yen KY., 2006, Bioactive constituents of *Spatholobus suberectus* in regulating tyrosinase-related proteins and mRNA in HEMn cells. Phytochemistry; 67:1262-70.

Tephrosia purpurea (L.) Pers.

[From the Greek *tephros* = ash-colored and Latin *purpurea* = purple]

Local names: Purple tephrosia; sarphoka (India), nha troi (Cambodia, Laos, Vietnam), indigo batard (France), sharapunkha (Sanskrit), balatong-pula (Philippines), sila (Sri Lanka), hola (Hawaii)

Basionym: *Cracca purpurea* L. *Species Plantarum* 2: 752. 1753

Synonyms: *Cracca purpurea* L., *Cracca wallichii* (Graham ex Fawcwt & Rendle) Rydb., *Galega diffusa* Roxb., *Galega purpurea* (L.) L., *Glycyrrhiza marei* H-Lev., *Hedysarum lineare* Lour., *Tephrosia crassa* Bojer ex Baker, *Tephrosia diffusa* Wight & Arn, *Tephrosia indigofera* Bertol., *Tephrosia lanceolata* Link., *Tephrosia leptostachya* DC, *Tephrosia pumila* (Lam) Pers., *Tephrosia wallichii* Graham ex Fawcet & Rendle

Description: It is a perennial branched herb which occurs from India to southern China through Southeast Asia to tropical Australia in exposed areas, often in waste places, grassy fields, seashores and rocks. The plant can reach up to 60 cm tall. The stem is pilose, terete, about 0.2 cm in diameter, somewhat slightly zigzag-shaped at the base. The leaves are compound, spiral and stipulate. The stipules are linear, velvety and 0.2 cm long, persistent and triangular. The rachis is about 1.5 - 2 cm long with 7 - 12 pairs of folioles. The petiolule is hairy and minute. The foliole-blade is spathulate, about 0.7 x 0.45, hairy underneath and with 4 pairs of secondary nerves looping at margin. The inflorescences are terminal racemes which are about 8 cm long with 0.6 cm long pedicels which are hairy. The calyx is hairy, about 0.5 x 0.3 cm with 4 lobes which are triangular linear and about 0.2

cm long. The corolla is about 1 cm long, purplish red, with a standard pubescent at the back. The pods are hairy, 2.4 - 4.5 cm, containing 5 - 6 seeds and showing a vestigial style at the apex (Figure 81).

Figure 81: *Tephrosia purpurea* (L.) Pers.
From: Botanical Inventory of Taiwan, Herbarium, Institute of Botany, Academia Sinica, Taipei (HAST)
Taiwan, Pingtung Hsien: Kenting national park: Fench-Chui-Sha, sandy beach. Elevation: 30 m. Clumped on exposed coastal coral rock face. Collector: Chi - Cheng Liao *et al.*, N° 1585. 29 July 1983.

Medicinal Uses: In India, the plant has various uses in Ayurvedic medicine where it is prescribed for numerous ailments including wounds, fever, tumours, leprosy, liver diseases and asthma. The Yunnani medicine used it also for asthma, liver diseases, boils, syphilis and diseases of the lungs. In Sri Lanka, the plant is used to expel worms from intestines. In Burma, the plant is used to promote digestion. In Cambodia, Laos and Vietnam, the plant is used to induce menses.

Pharmacology: The antitumour property of the plant has been validated: Chang
                     et al (1997) isolated from the plant a series of flavonoids including
                     7,4'-dihydroxy-3',5'-dimethoxyisoflavone, (+)-tephropurpurin,
                     (+)-purpurin, pongamol, lanceolatin B, (-)-maackiain,
                     (-)-3-hydroxy-4-methoxy-8,9-methylene-dioxypterocarpan,
                     and (-)-medicarpin which induced quinone reductase
                     activity with cultured Hepa 1c1c7 mouse hepatoma cells. In
                     addition, an extract of the plant inhibited benzoyl peroxide-
                     mediated cutaneous oxidative stress and toxicity and abrogated
                     7,12-dimethyl benz(a)anthracene - 12-O-tetradecanoyl
                     phorbal-13-acetate skin tumour formation in murine skin
                     (Saleem *et al.*, 2001). The wound healing property of the plant
                     has been confirmed: an extract of the plant promoted healing
                     in rats subjected to incision wound, excision wound and dead
                     space wound with resulted comparable to the standard drug
                     fluticasone propionate ointment (Lodhi *et al.*, 2006). Pavana *et
                     al* (2007) demonstrated the an extract from the plant reduced
                     the level of blood glucose and increased the level of plasma
                     insulin as well as normalized the lipids and lipoproteins profile
                     in streptozotocin-induced diabetic rats. Note that flavonoids
                     have been shown to possess anti-asthmatic properties (Liu *et al.*,
                     2007).

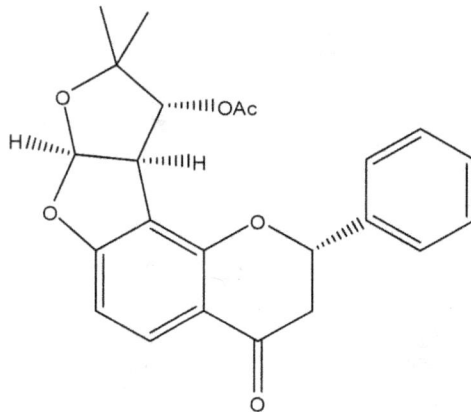

(+)-purpurin

References: Chang LC, Gerhäuser C, Song L, Farnsworth NR, Pezzuto JM,
                     Kinghorn AD, 1997, Activity-guided isolation of constituents
                     of *Tephrosia purpurea* with the potential to induce the phase II
                     enzyme, quinone reductase. J Nat Prod.; 60:869-73.

                     Liu B, Yang J, Wen Q, Li Y, 2008, Isoliquiritigenin, a flavonoid
                     from licorice, relaxiss guinea-pig tracheal smooth muscle *in vitro*

and *in vivo*: Role of cGMP/PKG pathway. Eur J Pharmacol; 587:257.

Lodhi S, Pawar RS, Jain AP, Singhai AK, 2006, Wound healing potential of *Tephrosia purpurea* (Linn.) Pers. in rats. J Ethnopharmacol; 108:204-10.

Pavana P, Manoharan S, Renju GL, Sethupathy S, 2007, Antihyperglycemic and antihyperlipidemic effects of *Tephrosia purpurea* leaf extract in streptozotocin induced diabetic rats. J Environ Biol; 28:833-7.

Saleem M, Ahmed Su, Alam A, Sultana S, 2001, *Tephrosia purpurea* alleviates phorbol ester-induced tumor promotion response in murine skin. Pharmacol Res; 43:135-44.

Uraria crinita (L.) Desv.

[From Greek *ura* = tail - loke and Latin *crinita* = long-haired]

Local name:	Mao wei cao (China)
Basionym:	*Hedysarum crinitum* L. *Mantissa Plantarum* 1: 102. 1767.
Synonyms:	*Doodia crinita* (L.) Roxb., *Hedysarum crinitum* L., *Uraria macrostachya* (Wall.) Schindl.
Description:	It is a shrub which grows up to 2 m tall in dry exposed areas in a geographical region covering India, Bangladesh, Burma, Thailand, Vietnam, Cambodia, Laos, Malaysia, Indonesia and Australia. The stem is striated, hairy and terete. The leaves are compound, spiral and stipulate. The stipules are broadly lanceolate and hairy. The rachis is angular, about 25 cm long and holds 3 pairs of folioles plus a terminal one. The petiolule is 0.3 cm and minutely winged. The folioles are oblong, 8 - 9 x 2.5 - 4 cm, the midrib raised on both surface, minutely cordate at the base, the apex marked with a tiny tip, and with 5 - 6 pairs of secondary nerves plus some tertiary reticulations visible underneath. The inflorescences are about 22 x 3 cm, stout, and pilose. The calyx is shallowly cup-shaped and about 0.3 cm long. The corolla is purple and about 0.6 cm long. The fruits are elliptical pods (Figure 82).
Medicinal uses:	In China, the plant is to check bleeding, break fever, and to treat coughs. In Malaysia, the plant is used to treat diarrhoea, fever, to expel worms from intestines and makes a remedy given

after childbirth. In Taiwan the plant is eaten as a vegetable and used to treat inflammation, cold and stomach-ache.

Figure 82: *Uraria crinita* **(L.) Desv.**
From: University Kebangsaan Malaysia Herbarium Sabah, № 1119
Malaysia, Tampuli, Daerah Tuaran, Sabah. Collection: Takashi Sato, Andau Sanan, Sintiong Gelat

Pharmacology: An extract of the plant inhibited experimentally-induced stress ulcers (Hsu *et al.*, 1983). An ethyl acetate fraction from the plant showed nitric oxide-scavenging and antioxidant activity possibly due to flavonoids such as genistein (Yen *et al.*, 2001). Note that acaricidal and antibacterial activities have been reported from *Uraria picta* (Igboechi *et al*, 1989; Rahman *et al.*, 2007).

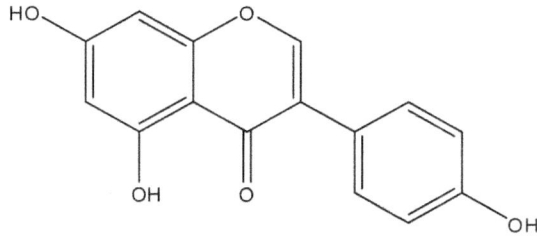

Genistein

References:	Hsu S.Y, Liu KC, 1983, Studies on the anti-ulcer actions of Chinese herbs and folk medicines (III). The annual reports of the national research institutes of Chinese medicine. 31-41.
	Igboechi AC, Osazuwa EO, Igwe UE, 1989, Laboratory evaluation of the acaricidal properties of extracts from *Uraria picta* (Leguminosae). J Ethnopharmacol; 26:293-8.
	Rahman MM, Gibbons S, Gray AI, 2007, Isoflavanones from *Uraria picta* and their antimicrobial activity. Phytochemistry; 68:1692-7.
	Yen GC, Lai HH, Chou HY, 2001, Nitric oxide-scavenging and antioxidant effects of *Uraria crinita* root. Food Chem; 74: 471-478.

Uraria lagopodioides (L.) Desv. ex DC.

[From Greek *ura* = tail - like and *lagos* = a hare and *podioides* = diminutive of feet]

Local names:	Tick trefoil, atiguha (India, Sanskrit), pokok korat tanah (Malaysia), ya hangon (Thailand), kantuy kamprok (Cambodia), duoi chon (Vietnam), ekor tupai (Indonesia), basing karan (Philippines)
Basionym:	*Hedysarum lagopodioides* L. *Species Plantarum* 2: 1198. 1753
Synonyms:	*Doodia lagopoides* (L.) Roxb., *Hedysarum lagopoides* L., *Lespedeza lagopodioides* (L.) Pers., *Uraria equilobata* Hosok
Description:	It is a creeping herb which grows up to 1 m long in a geographical area including India, Nepal, Thailand, Malaysia, Indonesia, China, Australia and Pacific Islands. The plant is common in dry grassland, open forest, waste places, and roadsides. The stem is terete, dull green, subglabrous, lenticelled and angled at the apex. The leaves are trifoliolate, spiral and stipulated. The stipule is linear, pilose and 0.7 cm long. The rachis is hairy

and 2.2 - 3.5 cm long. The petiolule is 1.2 - 2 cm, with linear bracts. The foliole is broadly lanceolate, 2.5 - 10 x 1.5 - 3.2 cm, dull light green above, round at the apex with a minute tip, acute at the base, with about 8 pairs of secondary nerves. The inflorescence is a terminal raceme, which is 2.5 - 7 cm long, with numerous light green ciliate bracts, about 0.4 x 1.8 cm, velvety above, glabrous inside, and marked with longitudinal striations. The calyx is light green turning brown, campanulate and hairy. The petals are whitish-pale light bluish. The standard is broadly obovate, and 0.5 - 0.7 x 0.45 - 0.65 cm. The wings are 0.2 cm long. The pods are blackish, about 0.6 cm long and grayish black (Figure 83).

Medicinal Uses: In India, this plant is used to empty the bowels, to treat asthma, dysentery, delirium, ulcers, tumours, malarial fever, inflammation of the chest, and broken bones. It is also used to induce abortion. In China, the plant is used to heal piles. In Malaysia and Bangladesh, the plant is used to treat dysentery.

Pharmacology: An extract of the plant showed a depressant effect stronger than diazepam in mice (Chakma *et al.*, 2006). This result confirms the psychiatric use of the plant and warrants further study of the principles involved.

Reference: Chakma TK, Khan MTH, Rahman T, Choudri MSK, Rajia S, Alamgir M, 2006, Screening of Bangladeshi medicinal plants for their effects on pentobarbital-induced sleeping time in mice. Ars Pharm; 47: 211-217.

Zornia diphylla (L.) Pers.
[After Johannes Zorn (1739-1799), German apothecary and Latin *diphylla* = with 2 leaves]]

Local name: Melem-mari (India)

Basionym: *Hedysarum diphyllum* L. *Species Plantarum* 2: 747. 1753.

Synonyms: *Hedyserum conjugatum* Willd., *Hedyserum diphyllum* L., *Zoria conjugata* (Willd.) Sm., *Zoria surinamensis* Miq., *Zoria zeylonensis* R.H.

Description: It is an annual herb which grows in the tropics. It is much branched with few leaves, and grows up to 40 cm tall. The stem is terete, glabrous, longitudinally striated and pilose. The leaves are 2-foliolate, spiral and stipulate. The stipule is lanceolate,

Figure 83: *Uraria lagopodioides* **(L.) Desv. ex DC.**
From: Flora of Thailand, Chiang Mai University Herbarium
Thailand, Lampang province, Hahng Chat district, by 18° North - 98° East. North Thailand. Poi
Kuhn Dahn national park, Southeast side Mao Pry station, Waw Giayo subdistrict. Elevation:
350 m. Date of collection: 24 June 1994. In open disturbed, weedy, degraded area in fire
prone deciduous dipterocarp-oak forest, granite bedrock.

acute, nerved, and 0.3 - 1 cm long. The rachis is 1 - 2 cm long,
pilose and channeled. The petiolule is minute, flattish, pilose
and 0.1 cm long. The folioles are lanceolate, round at the base,
pointed at the apex, 1 - 3 x 0.5 - 0.7 cm, subglabrous underneath
with black dots, coriaceous and with discrete secondary nerves
and a prominently raised midrib underneath. The inflorescence

is a spicate pilose raceme which is 2.5 - 10 cm long. The bracts are lanceolate, pilose, nerved, inserted every 0.5 cm, and 0.6 x 0.2 cm long. The calyx is membranaceous with 5 lobes, pilose and about 0.3 cm long. The corolla is glabrous, yellow, with purple lines in the throat, 0.6 - 0.8 cm long with an orbicular standard. The pods are articulated, somewhat pilose thorns, about 0.7 cm long, with conspicuous reticulation (Figure 84).

Figure 84: *Zornia diphylla* (L.) Pers.
From: Flora of Malaya.
Malaysia. Collection: Abdul Latiff ALM 254, A Zainuddin, and Hamid. Determination: A. Zainuddin.

Medicinal Uses: In India, the plant is used to induce sleep and to heal stomach ulcers. In China, the plant is used to heal boils.

Pharmacology: To date, no pharmacological study has evaluated the plant for neuropharmacology. An extract of the plant inhibited spontaneous ileum contractions of rat (Rojas *et al.*, 1999). This would be worth further study.

References: Rojas A, Bah M, Rojas JI, Serrano V, Pacheco S, 1999, Spasmolytic activity of some plants used by the Otomi Indians of Quéretaro (México) for the treatment of gastrointestinal disorders. Phytomed; 6:367-71.

C.Order MYRTALES Lindley 1833

The order Myrtales consists of 12 families and more than 9,000 species of tanniferous herbs, climbers, and tropical trees, the ancestor of which was probably in or near the Rosales. Myrtales are tanniferous, produce some triterpenes, flavonoids and valuable essential oils. This vast group of plants represents quite an untapped reservoir of natural products of pharmaceutical value. In this chapter, medicinal plants from the Sonneriatacea, the Lythraceae, the Myrtaceae, the Onagraceae and the Combretaceae families are presented and pharmaceutical potentials discussed.

1.Family SONNERIATACEAE Engler & Gilg 1924 nom. conserv., the Sonneriata Family

The family Sonneriataceae consists of the genus Sonneratia, with 8 species and *Duabanga* with 2 species. These are tanniferous trees, accumulating ellagic acid, with simple opposite and exstipulate leaves which are often leathery. The flowers are often showy and grouped in cymes. The calyx comprises 4 - 8 sepals, the corolla is made of 4 - 8 petals. The androecium comprises numerous stamens with tetrasporangiate and dithecal anthers. The gynaecium comprises 4 - 20 carpels fused into a plurilocular ovary containing numerous ovules on axile placenta. The fruits are capsules or berries. *Sonneratia* species are common tropical mangrove trees.

The Family is small and has no apparent horticultural or pharmaceutical value. Many mangrove creatures, including bats and fishes and plants depend on *Sonneratia*. A very few pharmacological studies have been undertaken on it. Sharma *et al.* (1974), reported activity against Walker's carcinosarcoma from *Duabanga sonnetarioides*. This little family awaits pharmacological investigation and there may well be the possibility of discovering original phenolic substances of chemotherapeutic and antimicrobial value. *Sonneratia griffithii* Kurtz. is medicinal in the East and is described in this chapter.

References: Sharma SC, Shukla YN, Tandon JS, Dhar MM, 1974, Genkwanin 4'-galactoside and other constituents from *Duabanga sonneratioides* Phytochemistry; 13: 527-528.

Sonneratia griffithii Kurtz.

[After Pierre Sonnerat (1748-1814), French colonial officer and after Dr William Griffith (1810 - 1845) a medical doctor with the British East India Company]

Local name:	Perepat (Malaysia)
Synonym:	*Sonneratia alba* J. Smith
Description:	It is a common mangrove tree of Southeast Asia. The bole is surrounded by pneumatophores arising from roots. The plant is a halophyte. The stem is glabrous, terete, minutely fissured, peeling , 0.4 cm in diameter and somewhat articulated. The nodes are swollen and marked with rings and ovoid leaf-scars. The internodes are irregular, and 1 - 4 cm long. The leaves are simple, opposite, and without stipules. The petiole is stout, glabrous, 0.3 - 0.4 cm x 0.2 cm, and non-channelled. The leaf-blade is roundish, broadly spathulate, 8.5 - 5 cm x 8 - 3 cm, glabrous, woody to somewhat spongy, with 8 - 12 pairs of discrete secondary nerves. The midrib is flattish above and below. The flower is axillary or terminal. The calyx is leathery, conical and produces 6 lobes which are triangular. The corolla consists of 6 petals which are linear - lanceolate and reddish. The fruit is a terminal green nut, about 4 cm long, solitary, glossy, woody, globose and flattish, depressed at the apex and exhibiting a persistent style of about 2 cm, and persistent sepals which are 1.5 x 1.4 cm. The fruit peduncle is about 4 cm long (Figure 85).
Medicinal uses:	In Malaysia the plant is used to treat skin infection.
Pharmacology:	Unknown. The medicinal uses suggest some antibacterial and/or antifungal properties which need to be validated experimentally. The plant's use in combating skin infection is probably on account of tannins such as ellagic acid. This plant would be worth investigating.

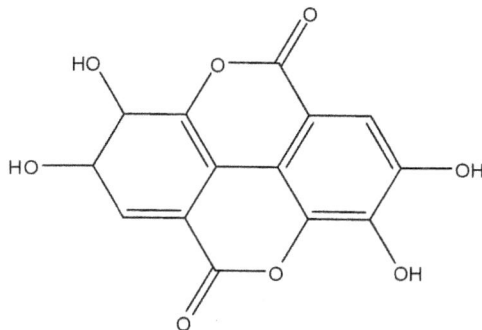

Ellagic acid

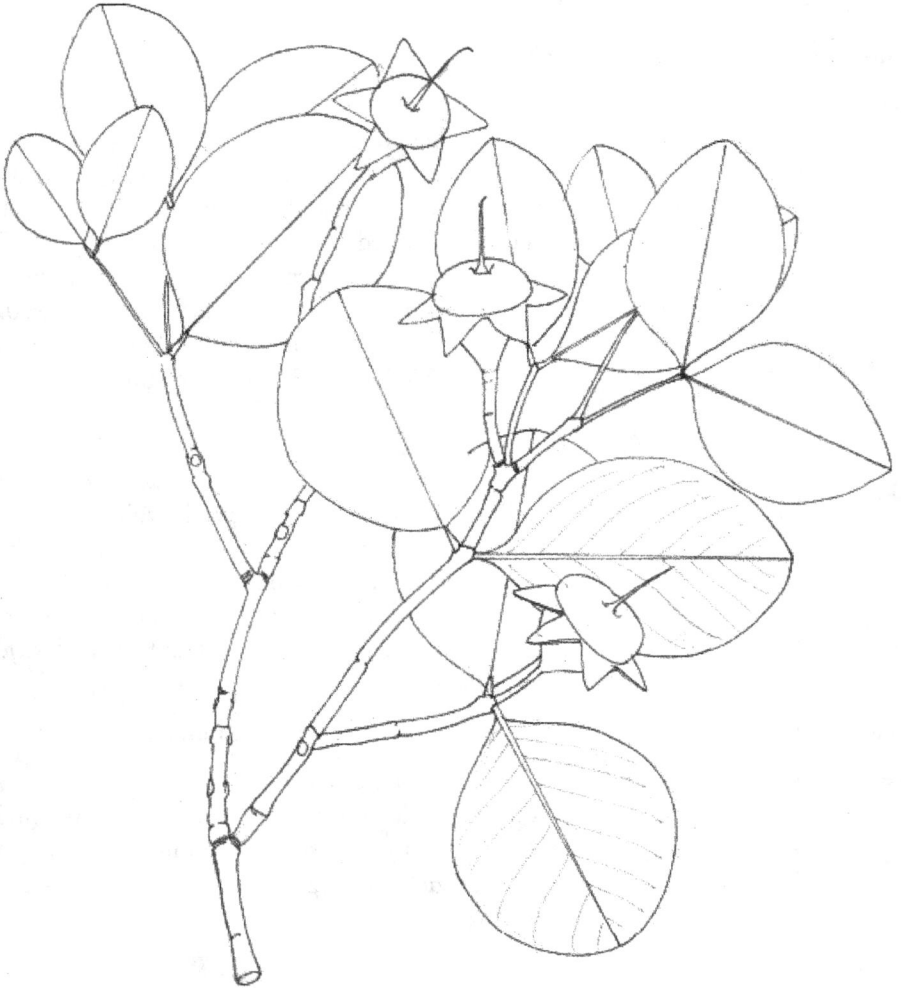

Figure 85: *Sonneratia griffithii* **Kurtz.**
From: Herbarium of University Kebangsaan Malaysia
Malaysia, Negeri Sembilan State, Tanjung Tuan, Port Dickson

2.Family LYTHRACEAE Jaume St. - Hilaire 1805 nom. conserv., the Loosestrife Family

The family Lythraceae consists of about 24 genera and 500 species of herbs, shrubs and trees. The main groups of natural products found in this family are tannins, triterpenes, piperidine and quinazoline alkaloids and a series of naphthoquinones. In terms of botanical features, Lythraceae develop simple, opposite leaves without stipules. The flowers are often 4, 6 or 8 in number, the calyx is tubular, the petals are free and characteristically constricted at the base. The stamens are twice as numerous as the petals and organized into 2 whorls. The gynaecium consists of 2 - 6 carpels fused to form a compound, superior and plurilocular ovary. The ovules are attached to axillary placentas. A nectary disc is present. The fruits are capsules which are dehiscent, and contain several little seeds.

Lythraceae of horticultural value are *Lagerstroemia indica* L. (crape - myrtle) and *Lythrum salicaria* L. (purple loosestrife). The dried leaves of *Lawsonia inermis* L. (Henna, *British Pharmaceutical Codex* 1934) have a long history of use to counteract putrefaction and to dye the skin and the hair due to a naphthoquinone: lawsone. Of recent pharmacological interest in this family is woodfordin C; a dimeric hydrolysable tannin. This is a potent inhibitor of topoisomerase II and has been patented in Japan (Das *et al.*, 2007). The presence of topoisomerase inhibitors in this family suggest that much more is awaiting discovery. *Lagerstroemia indica* L., *Lagerstroemia speciosa* (L.) Pers. are used for medicinal purposes in the East.

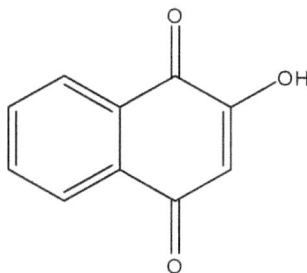

Lawsone

Reference: Das PK, Goswami S, Chinniah A, Panda N, Banerjee S, Sahu NP, Achari B, 2007, *Woodfordia fruticosa*: Traditional uses and recent findings. J Ethnopharmacol; 110: 189-199.

Lagerstroemia indica L.

[After Magnus von Lagerstroem, 18th century Swedish naturalist and Latin *indica* = from India]

Local names:
China privet, crape myrtle, tuong vi bang lang (Vietnam), melindres (Philippines), pavalak (India), zi wei (China)

Synonyms:
Lagerstroemia chinensis Lam; *Murtughas indica* (Linn.) Kuntze.

Description:
It is a small tree which grows in a geographical area covering India, Sri Lanka, Bangladesh, Nepal, Pakistan, Bhutan, Burma, Cambodia , Laos, Thailand, Vietnam, Malaysia, Indonesia, Philippines, China, Taiwan and Japan. It is often cultivated as an ornamental plant. The stem is terete, glabrous, fibrous, fissured longitudinally, peeling, straight, and angled - winged at the apex. The leaves are simple, spiral, exstipulate, sessile. The leaf blade is elliptic, glabrous above except on the midrib, with 2 - 7 pairs of secondary nerves conspicuous underneath plus a few tertiary nerves. The leaf-blade margin is recurved and somewhat minutely ciliate. The inflorescence is a many flowered terminal panicle with angled peduncles. The calyx is about 0.5 cm long, and presents 6 lobes which are lanceolate. The corolla comprises 6 petals which are pink, broad, crumpled and curled on long claws and about 1 cm long. The stamens are numerous. The fruit is a globose hexagonal capsule which is about 0.7 cm in diameter, valved, and containing several seeds which are 0.8 x 0.1 cm and curved (Figure 86).

Medicinal uses:
In India, the plant is used to invigorate and to break fever. In Cambodia, Laos and Vietnam, the plant is used to treat constipation. In China, the plant is used to check bleeding, to treat rheumatism, and colds.

Pharmacology:
The plant is known to produce anthocyanins; delphinidin 3-arabinoside, petunidin 3-arabinoside, and malvidin 3-arabinoside, gallic acid, methyl gallate, ellagic acid, saponins, terpenoids, steroids, and tannins (Saleh, 1973; Castillo *et al.*, 1980). The plant has not yet been tested for antioxidant, cytotoxic or antimicrobial activity. The medicinal uses suggest some anti-inflammatory potential which needs to be validated. Note that an extract of the plant showed high antithrombin activity *in vitro* (Chistokhodova *et al.*, 2002).

References:
Castillo AV, Topacio MR, Balasbas MM, 1980, Physicochemical investigation of *Lagerstroemia indica* Linne. NRCP Research Bulletin; **35**: 201-207.

Chistokhodova N, Chi Nguyen C, Calvino T, Kachirskaia I,Cunningham G, Miles H, 2002, Antithrombin activity of medicinal plants from central Florida. J Ethnopharmacol; 81: 277-280.

Saleh NA, 1973, Anthocyanins of *Lagerstroemia indica* flowers. Phytochemistry; 12: 2304.

Figure 86: *Lagerstroemia indica* **L.**
From: Herbarium of University Kebangsaan Malaysia, No 15825.
Malaysia, Bangi. Collection and identification: Rohana Omar

Lagerstroemia speciosa (L.) Pers.

[After Magnus von Lagerstroem, 18th century Swedish naturalist and Latin *speciosa* = showy]

Local names:	Queens crape-myrtle, bungor (Malaysia), eikmwe (Burma), jarul (India), murutagass (Sri Lanka)
Synonyms:	*Lagerstroemia flos-reginae* Retz., *Lagerstroemia regina* Roxb., *Munchausia speciosa* L.
Description:	It is a tree which grows wild in India, Burma, Thailand, Malaysia, Sri Lanka, Indonesia and Australia. It is a common tropical ornamental roadside tree. The plant can reach up to 18 m tall. The stem is smooth, glabrous, angled, peeling, about 0.5 cm in diameter, with internodes which are about 5 cm long. The leaves are simple, spiral and without stipules. The petiole is woody, stout, clasping the stem, glabrous channelled and about 1.5 cm long. The leaf-blade is thinly coriaceous, elliptic to oblong, minutely acuminate at the apex, 11 - 16 cm x 8.5 - 6 cm, and shows 10 - 12 pairs of secondary nerves prominently raised underneath and united by an intramarginal nerve. The inflorescence is a terminal panicle which is about 30 cm long and much flowered. The calyx is 1.6 cm long, hairy, and produces 6 lobes which are about 0.6 cm long and triangular. The petals are about 3 x 2 cm, purple, membranaceous, clawed, and much undulate. The fruit is capsular, rugose, dehiscent, angled, and minutely apiculate, about 2.2 x 2 cm on a persistent calyx. The seeds are about 0.6 cm long (Figure 87).
Medicinal uses:	In India, the plant is used as an astringent and febrifuge. In the Andamans the plant is used to heal mouth ulcers. In Burma, Cambodia, Laos and Vietnam, the plant is used as an astringent. In Malaysia and Indonesia the plant is used to treat diarrhoea. In the Philippines, the plant is used for headaches and diabetes.
Pharmacology:	The hypoglycemic property has been validated and is due to corosolic acid which was shown to be a glucose transport activator in Ehrlich ascites tumor cells (Murakami *et al.*, 1993). This triterpene stimulates glucose uptake via enhancing insulin receptor phosphorylation (Shi *et al.*, 2008). In a clinical trial, 1% corosolic acid (Glucosol) showed a significant reduction in blood glucose levels (Judy *et al.*, 2003). In addition, an extract from the plant extract showed marked nephroprotective activity (Priya *et al.*, 2007). The astringent property is probably due to tannins which are common in the Myrtales.

Figure 87: *Lagerstroemia speciosa* **(L.) Pers.**
From: Flora of Malaya
Malaysia, Kuala Lumpur, in University of Malaya campus, near Physics department.
Collection and identification: Mohd Kassim

Corosolic acid

References

Judy WV, Hari SP, Stogsdill WW, Judy JS, Naguib YM, Passwater R, 2003, Antidiabetic activity of a standardized extract (Glucosol) from Lagerstroemia speciosa leaves in Type II diabetics. A dose-dependence study. J Ethnopharmacol; 87: 115-7.

Murakami C, Myoga K, Kasai R, Ohtani K, Kurokawa T, Ishibashi S, Dayrit F, Padolina WG, Yamasaki K, 1993, Screening of plant constituents for effect on glucose transport activity in Ehrlich ascites tumor cells. Chem Pharm Bull (Tokyo), 41: 2129-31.

Priya TT, Sabu MC, Jolly CI, 2007, Amelioration of cisplatin induced nephrotoxicity in mice by an ethyl acetate extract of *Lagerstroemia speciosa* (L). J Basic Clin Physiol Pharmacol; 18:289-98.

Shi L, Zhang W, Zhou YY, Zhang YN, Li JY, Hu LH, Li J, 2008, Corosolic acid stimulates glucose uptake via enhancing insulin receptor phosphorylation. Eur J Pharm; 584: 21-29.

3.Family MYRTACEAE A.L. de Jussieu 1789 nom. conserv., the Myrtle Family

The family Myrtaceae is a large group of flowering plants which comprises about 140 genera and 3000 species of shrubs and trees which are found principally in the subtropical and tropical regions of the globe. The most common types of secondary metabolites in this family are fragrant volatile monoterpenes and phenylpropanoids (essential oils), sesquiterpenes, triterpenes, and other phenolic substances. The bark of Myrtaceae is often reddish. The leaves are simple, opposite and without stipules. The leaf-blade presents some oil cells and the secondary nerves are united into a distinct intramarginal nerve. The inflorescences are cymes or racemes. The flowers present a conspicuous nectary disk around which are inserted 4- 5 imbricate sepals, 4-5 imbricate petals, and numerous stamens which are often showy. The anthers are tetrasporangiate and dithecal. The gynaecium consists of 2-5 carpels which are fused to form a compound ovary with 2-5 locules, each locule containing 2-many ovules attached to axil placentas. The fruits are berries, capsules, drupes or nuts.

An example of Myrtaceae is *Myrtus communis* L. (myrtle) which is cultivated for ornament. A number of tropical fruit trees such as *Psidium guavaja* L. belong to this family. Several species are of pharmaceutical value on account of the essential oils they produce. Eucalyptus Oil (*British Pharmacopoeia*, 1963) from fresh leaves of *Eucalyptus globulus* Labill., is used as an antiseptic and deodorant, it contains cineole. Melaleuca Oil (*British Pharmaceutical Codex*, 1949) from the fresh leaves of *Melaleuca leucadendron* L. has been used as antiseptic. Niaouli Oil (*French Pharmacopoeia*, 1965) obtained from the fresh leaves of *Melaleuca viridiflora* Gaertn. has been used as an antiseptic. The flower buds of *Syzygium aromaticum* (L.) Merr. & Perry are cloves from which is obtained an oil (Clove Oil, *French Pharmacopoeia*, 1965) which is used as analgesic and antiseptic in dentistry, the oil contains eugenol.

The taxonomic position and chemical profile of this family indicate it to be a source of natural products with potentials for the treatment of cancer, microbial infection and other life-threatening illnesses. One such compound is pedunculagin, a tannin from *Pimenta dioica* (L.) Merr. which exhibited cytotoxic activity against solid tumor cancer cells. It also had antioxidant activity. It strongly inhibited nitric oxide generation and induced the proliferation of T-lymphocytes and macrophages (Marzouk *et al.,* 2007). Ye *et al.* (2004) isolated 2',4'-Dihydroxy-6'-methoxy-3',5'-dimethylchalcone from *Cleistocalyx operculatus* (Roxb.) Merr. & L.M. Perry. This exhibited a cytotoxic activity against SMMC-7721, 8898, HeLa, SPC-A-1, 95-D and GBC-SD cell lines via apoptosis, and potentiated the cytotoxicity of the chemotherapeutic agent doxorubicin to drug-resistant KB-A1 cells (Qian *et al.*, 2005). *Baeckea frutescens* L., *Decaspermum fruticosum* Forst., *Eugenia aquea* Burm.f., *Eugenia aromatica* O. Ktze, *Eugenia chlorantha* Duthie, *Eugenia jambos* L., *Eugenia longiflorum* (Presl.) F. Vill., *Eugenia oleina* Wight, *Eugenia operculata* Roxb., *Eugenia polyantha* Wight, *Leptospermum flavescens* Smith, *Melaleuca cajuputi* Powell, *Psidium guajava* L., *Rhodamnia cinerea* Jack., and *Rhodomyrtus tomentosa* (Ait.) Hassk. all have medicinal properties in the East.

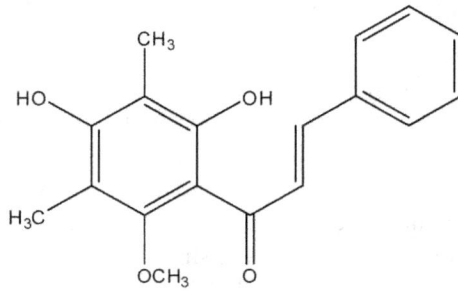

2',4'-Dihydroxy-6'-methoxy-3',5'-dimethylchalcone

References:	Marzouk MS, Moharram FA, Mohamed MA, Gamal-Eldeen AM, Aboutabl EA, 2007, Anticancer and antioxidant tannins from *Pimenta dioica* leaves. Z Naturforsch [C]; 62: 526-36.
	Qian F, Ye CL, Wei DZ, Lu YH, Yang SL, 2005, *In vitro* and *in vivo* reversal of cancer cell multidrug resistance by 2',4'-dihydroxy-6'-methoxy-3',5'-dimethylchalcone. J Chemother; 17: 309-14.
	Ye CL, Liu JW, Wei DZ, Lu YH, Qian F, 2004, *In vitro* anti-tumor activity of 2',4'-dihydroxy-6'-methoxy-3',5'-dimethylchalcone against six established human cancer cell lines. Pharmacol Res; 50: 505-10.

Baeckea frutescens L.

[After Abraham Baeck (1713-95), Swedish naturalist and Latin *frutescens* = shrubby]

Local names:	Baeckea, gang song *(China)*, hujong atap (Malaysia), junjung atap (Indonesia), moreck ansai (Cambodia), son naa, son saai (Thailand)
Synonyms:	*Baeckea chinensis* Gaertn., *Baeckia cochinchinensis* Bl., *Baeckea cumingiana* Schauer, *Baeckea sumatrana* Bl., *Cedrela rosmarinus* Lour.
Description:	It is a shrub which grows up to 2.5 m tall on savannah in a geographical area covering India, Burma, Thailand, Cambodia, Laos, Vietnam, Indonesia, the Philippines, Papua New Guinea and Australia. The stem is cracked, peeling, angled and smooth at the apex. The internodes are 0.2 cm long. The leaves are simple, decussate and exstipulate. The petiole is about 0.2 cm long. The leaf blade is needle-shaped, channelled, grooved, woody, covered with oil cells and about 0.1 x 0.7 cm long. The flower is axillary and solitary on a 0.1 cm long pedicel. The calyx is cup-shaped with 5

little roundish lobes. The corolla comprises 5 white petals which are orbicular and 0.1 cm in diameter. The androecium consists of 10 stamens. The fruit is a conical capsule which is 0.2 cm long with 5 vestigial calyx lobes and contains a few angular seeds (Figure 88).

Medicinal Uses: The plant is used to treat fever in Southeast Asia and China. In Cambodia, Laos and Vietnam, the plant is used for rheumatism and headache. In Malaysia the plant is used as a post-partum remedy. The plant yields an essential oil which has a fragrance of lavender.

Pharmacology: The plant owes its medicinal value to its essential oil which is a counter-irritant and antiseptic and contains several monoterpenes such as fenchol and linalool (Liu *et al*, 2004). An extract of the plant showed antibacterial activity against the cariogenic bacterium *Streptococcus mutans* (Hwang *et al.*, 2004). Fujimoto *et al* (1996), isolated phloroglucinol BF-2 which exhibited strong cytotoxic activity against leukemia cells (L 1210). The compound, 5-Hydroxy-2-isopropyl-7-methoxychromone, exhibited toxicity to the brine shrimp, *Artemia salina*, (Gray *et al.*, 2003). These results suggest further investigation on the anticancer potentials of Baeckea species would be worth while.

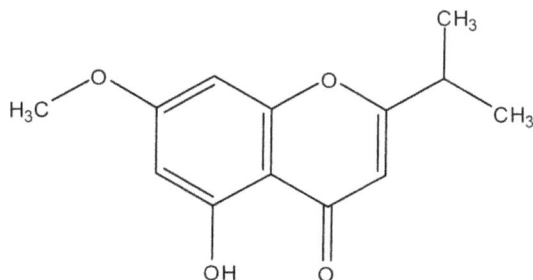

5-Hydroxy-2-isopropyl-7-methoxychromone

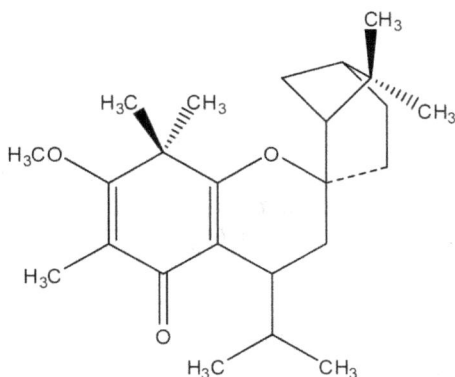

Phloroglucinol BF-2

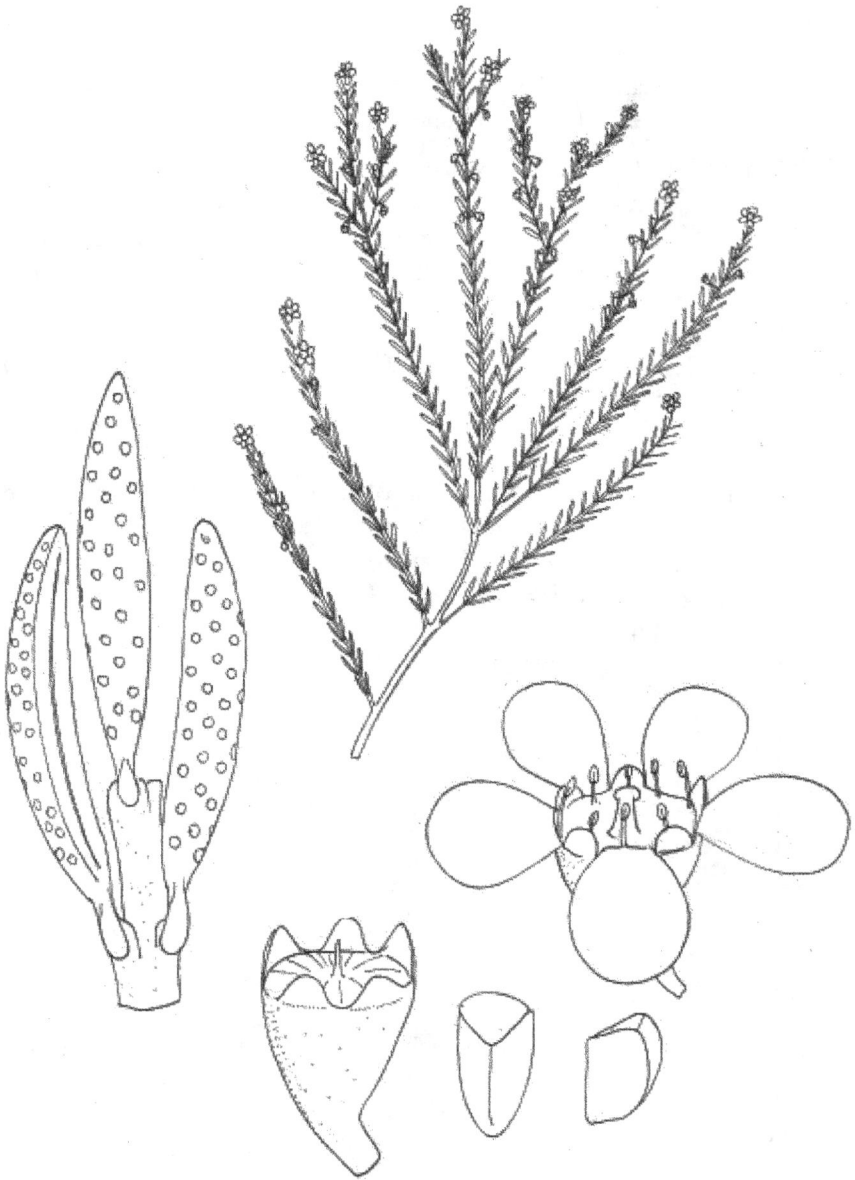

Figure 88: *Baeckea frutescens* **L.**
From: Flora of Thailand, Prince of Songkla University Herbarium
Thailand, Songkla province, Haad Yai district, Klonh Hoy Kong, West of Toong Loong.
Elevation sea level. Date of collection: August 6 1985.

References: Fujimoto Y, Usui S, Makino M, Sumatra M, 1996, Phloroglucinols from *Baeckea frutescens*. Phytochemistry; 41: 923-5.

Gray CA, Kaye PT, Nchinda AT, 2003, Chromone studies, Part 13. Synthesis and electron-impact mass spectrometric studies of 5-hydroxy-2-isopropyl-7-methoxychromone, a constituent of the medicinal plant *Baeckea frutescens*, and side-chain analogues. J Nat Prod; 66: 1144-6.

Hwang JK, Shim JS, Chung JY, 2004, Anticariogenic activity of some tropical medicinal plants against *Streptococcus mutans*. Fitoterapia; 75: 596-8.

Liu BM, Lai MX, Liang KN, Chen Y, Yan KJ, Cai QL, Li YH, 2004, Zhongguo Zhong Yao Za Zhi; 29: 539-42.

Decaspermum fruticosum Forst.
[From Latin *decaspermum* = with 10 seeds and *fruticosum* = bushy]

Local name: Silky myrtle, badaduk (North Borneo), tukang benang (Malaysia), *malagitinggiting (Philippines)*

Synonym: *Decaspermum paniculatum* Kurz., *Legnotis lanceolata* Blco., *Metrosideros pictipetala* Blco., *Nelitris fruticosa* A. Gray, *Nelitris paniculata* Lindl., *Psidium decaspermum* L.f.

Description: It is a shrub or a small tree which grows to a height of 10 m in the forests of India, Burma, Thailand, Malaysia, Indonesia, Philippines, Australia and Pacific Islands. The bark is reddish brown, smooth, velvety with 2 cm long internodes. The stem is reddish and velvety, pitted and about 0.2 cm in diameter. The leaves are simple, opposite and without stipules. Some hairy buds are present at leaf axis. The petiole is about 0.7 cm long, flattish, and channelled. The leaf-blade is oblong, 3 - 9 cm x 0.5 - 4 cm, with about 12 - 13 pairs of secondary nerves plus an intramarginal nerve. The leaf-blade is thinly coriaceous, with a midrib hairy above, and acuminate at the apex, with numerous tiny oil cells. The inflorescence is an axillary and terminal panicle. The calyx is campanulate, about 0.2 cm long, hairy with 4 lobes which are lanceolate. The corolla comprises 5 petals which are white and about 0.3 cm long. The anthers are about 0.15 cm long. The style is about 0.2 cm long The fruit is globose, 0.6 - 1 cm in diameter, ripening purple, and crowned by 5 persistent sepals (Figure 89).

Medicinal uses: In Malaysia, the plant is used to treat dysentery. In Indonesia, the plant is used to deflate swollen gums and to make the teeth firm and the fruits and young leaves are eaten for food. In the Philippines the plant is used to assuage stomach ache.

Pharmacology: Unknown. The plant awaits pharmacological investigation.

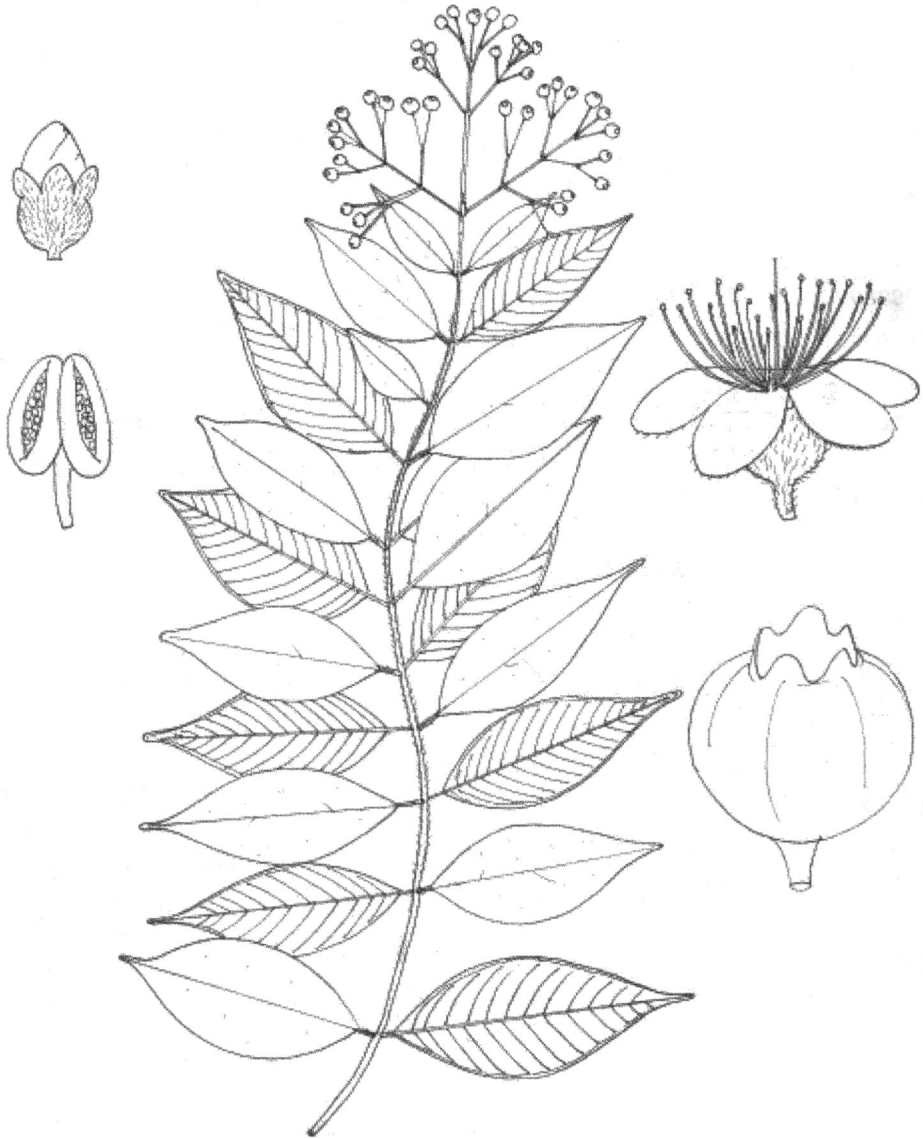

Figure 89: *Decaspermum fruticosum* Forst.
From Flora of Sabah. Herbarium of the Forest Department Sandakan, No SAN 86456.
Malaysia, Sabah, Sipitang district, Merinetaman SFI forest area, on sandy rocky soil.
Collection: Ag. Amin & Haya. Date of collection: 10 February 1985.

Eugenia aquea Burm.f.

[After Francois Eugene de Savoie-Carignan (1663-1736) patron of science and from Latin *aquea* = watery]

Local names:	Water apple; jambu chili, jambu ayer (Malaysia), djamboo aer, djamboo wer (Indonesia), tambis (Philippines), chom phu pa (Thailand)
Synonym:	*Syzygium aqueum* (Burm.) f. Alston
Description:	It is a small tree native to South India which is cultivated throughout tropical Asia to Hawaii as an ornamental and fruit tree. The stem is smooth, glabrous, with internodes which are 4 - 5 cm long. The leaves are simple, decussate and without stipules The petiole is minute, channelled, glabrous, and 0.15 - 0.3 cm long. The leaf blade is papery, 10.5 - 13 cm x 3.8 - 5 cm, glabrous, broadly elliptic, round at the apex, cordate at the base, amplexicaul-like, with minute dots at the apex. The leaf-blade shows a midrib sunken above and prominently raised below, with 8 - 9 pairs of secondary nerves merged with an intramarginal nerve which is 0.7 - 0.8 cm away from the margin. The inflorescence is a terminal cyme, with glabrous pedicels which are flattish, conical and about 0.7 cm long. The flower is white. The calyx is urn-shaped, 0.4 cm in diameter, with 4 lobes which are 0.3 x 0.3 cm. The androecium is conspicuous and about 4 cm in diameter. The fruit is about 2 - 4 cm long, pale pink, glossy, pear-shaped with apical depression (Figure 90).
Medicinal Uses:	The plant is used to make an astringent gargle in Indonesia. In Papua New Guinea the plant is used as a treatment for stomach ache or acute dysentery.
Pharmacology:	The astringent property mentioned above is due to proanthocyanidin samarangenins A and B as well as (-)-epigallocatechin (-)-epigallocatechin 3-O-gallate tannin flavan-3-ols, and complex tannins (Nonaka *et al.*, 1992). The plant is of interest for pharmacology. Note that (-)-epigallocatechin 3-O-gallate from the closely related *Syzygium samarangense* inhibited both the proliferation of human peripheral blood mononuclear cells activated by phytohemagglutinin and IL-2 and IFN-γ production from these cells (Kuo *et al.*, 2004).
References:	Kuo YC, Yang LM, Lin LC, 2004, Isolation and Immunomodulatory Effect of Flavonoids from *Syzygium samarangense*. Planta Med; 70: 1237-1239.
	Nonaka G, Aiko Y, Aritake K, Itsuo N, 1992, Tannins and Related Compounds. CXIX. Samarangenins A and B, Novel Proanthocyanidins with doubly bonded structures, from *Syzygium samarangens* and *S. aqueum*. Chem Pharm Bull; 40: 2671-267.

Figure 90: *Eugenia aquea* **Burm.f.**
From: Flora of Malaya, № 00658.
Malaysia, Campus University Malaya, Collection and determination: Mohd Kassim №236: 19 September 1972

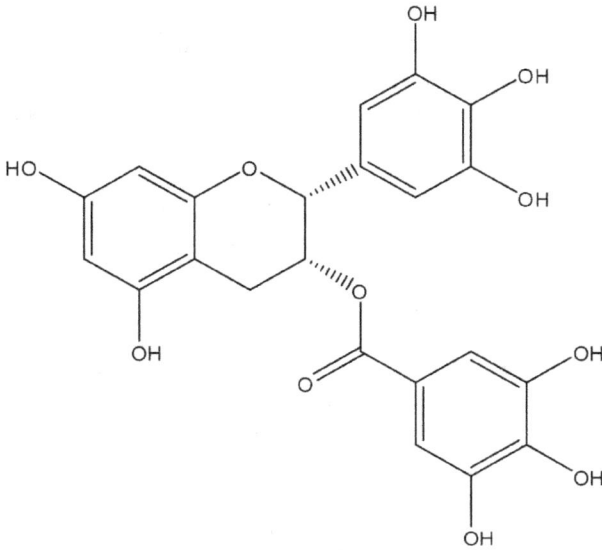

(-)-epigallocatechin 3-O-gallate

Eugenia aromatica O. Ktze

[After Francois Eugene de Savoie-Carignan (1663-1736) patron of science and from Latin *aromatica* = fragrant]

Local names:	Clove; cengkeh (Malaysia and Indonesia), lay hnyin (Burma), kanphlu (Thailand), giroflier (France), kanz ph'u (Laos), khan phluu (Cambodia), clavo de comer (Philippines)
Synonyms:	*Eugenia caryophyllata* Thunb., *Caryophyllus aromaticus* L., *Jambosa caryophyllus* Niedz, *Syzygium aromaticum* (L.) Merr. & Perry
Description:	The clove tree native to the Moluccas was later cultivated and spread to Indonesia and Malaysia by Dutch and British planters. It is a tree which grows up to 20 m. The stem is smooth, glabrous, dotted, glossy, 0.4 cm in diameter and longitudinally fissured. The internodes are about 2 cm long. The stem shows some leaf scars which are 0.1 cm in diameter and heart shaped. The leaves are simple, decussate, crowded near the apex of stem and without stipules. The petiole is slender, reddish, channelled, with oil cells and up to 2.5 cm long. The leaf-blade is leathery, lanceolate, thinly coriaceous, 7 -12 cm x 2.5 - 4.5 cm, pointed at the apex with 20 - 30 pairs of secondary nerves merged to an intramarginal nerve. The flowers are arranged in candelabra-like terminal panicles. The calyx tube is 1 - 1.5 cm x 0.3 cm with 4 lobes. The corolla shows 4 petals. The fruit is oblong 2.5 - 3 cm x 1.3 - 1.5 cm, crowned by 4 vestigial calyx lobes and contains a seed (Figure 91).

Medicinal Uses: Clove, the sun-dried unopened flower buds is a common spice and food flavour. Since ancient times, clove has been highly valued as a spice by the Chinese. During the Middle Ages the spice became increasingly important in Europe. The oil distilled from the flower buds (Clove Oil, *French Pharmacopoeia*, 1965) is used as analgesic and antiseptic in dentistry. Traditionally, cloves are used as carminative, invigorating, to give good breath and to promote menses. In Malaysia, the plant is used for headache and at confinement and to assuage toothache. In Chinese medicine, it is used against cholera and diarrhoea.

Pharmacology: Clove oil has two major components, eugenol and beta-caryophyllene. Eugenol constitutes about 80% of the oil. Numerous pharmacological studies have been reported, sometimes with contradictory results. Of particular interest is the fact that clove oil has trypanocidal (Santoro *et al.*, 2007), chemopreventive (Banerjee *et al.*, 2006), and antifungal (Park *et al.*, 2007) activities, as well as cytotoxic effects (Prashar *et al.*, 2006) against human fibroblasts and endothelial cells. Beta-caryophyllene has anaesthetic properties (Ghelardini *et al.*, 2001).

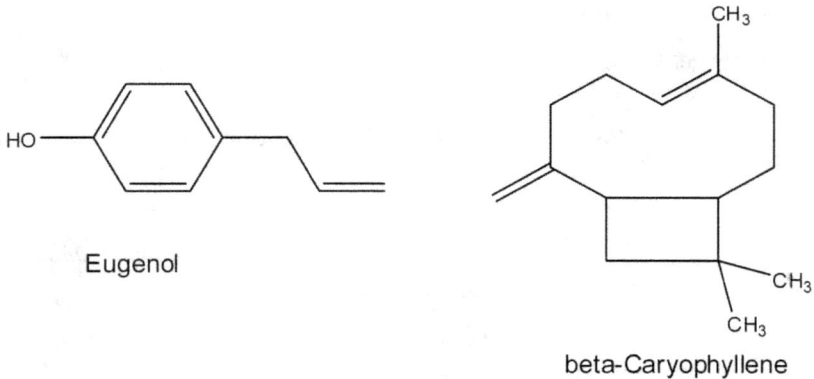

Eugenol

beta-Caryophyllene

References: Banerjee S, Panda CK, Das S, 2006, Clove (*Syzygium aromaticum* L.), a potential chemopreventive agent for lung cancer. Carcinogenesis; 27: 1645-54.

Ghelardini N, Di Cesare G, Mannelli L, Mazzanti G, Bartolini A, 2001, Local anaesthetic activity of beta-caryophyllene. Farmaco; 56: 387-389.

Park MJ, Gwak KS, Yang I, Choi WS, Jo HJ, Chang JW, Jeung EB, Choi IG, 2007, Antifungal activities of the essential oils in *Syzygium aromaticum* (L.) Merr. Et Perry and *Leptospermum petersonii* Bailey and their constituents against various dermatophytes. J Microbiol; 45: 460-5.

Prashar A, Locke IC, Evans CS, 2006, Cytotoxicity of clove (*Syzygium aromaticum*) oil and its major components to human skin cells. Cell Prolif; 39: 241-8.

Santoro GF, Cardoso MG, Guimarães LG, Mendonça LZ, Soares MJ, 2007, *Trypanosoma cruzi*: activity of essential oils from *Achillea millefolium* L., *Syzygium aromaticum* L. and *Ocimum basilicum* L. on epimastigotes and trypomastigotes. Exp Parasitol; 116: 283-90.

Figure 91: *Eugenia aromatica* O. Ktze
From: Herbarium of University Kebangsaan Malaysia
Malaysia, Johor state, Mersing, Pulau Tinggi track from Tg keramat to Kampung Pinang.
Planted tree.

Eugenia chlorantha Duthie

[After Francois Eugene de Savoie-Carignan (1663-1736) patron of science and from Latin *chlorantha* = green-flowered]

Local names:	Kelat merah, kelat gelam (Malaysia), ubah puteh (Borneo)
Synonym:	*Eugenia hullettiana* King, *Syzygium chloranthum* (Duthie) Merr. & Perry, *Syzygium griseum* Airy Shaw
Description:	It is a tree which grows to about 20 m tall in the forest of Cambodia, Laos, Vietnam, Thailand, Malaysia, and Indonesia. The bark is smooth, dark red and finely fissured. The stem is smooth, terete, glabrous with some sorts of lenticels and fissured. The internodes are 3.5 - 6.3 cm. The leaves are simple, decussate and without stipules. The petiole is 1 cm long, glabrous and channelled. The leaf-blade is thinly coriaceous, elliptic, 6 - 20 cm x 2 - 9 cm, pointed at the apex, cuneate at the base, and with about 15-18 pairs of faint secondary nerves merged with an intramarginal nerve about 0.15 cm apart from the margin. The inflorescence is a terminal and axillary panicle with angled peduncles. The flower is greenish white. The stamens are rose-red. The fruit is globose, 1 - 2 cm in diameter, green turning pink-red with vestigial calyx lobes at the apex around an excavation (Figure 92).
Medicinal Uses:	The plant is used to treat skin diseases.
Pharmacology:	Unknown. The antimicrobial and anti-inflammatory properties of this plant need to be investigated. Phenolic principles most probably account for the medicinal uses.

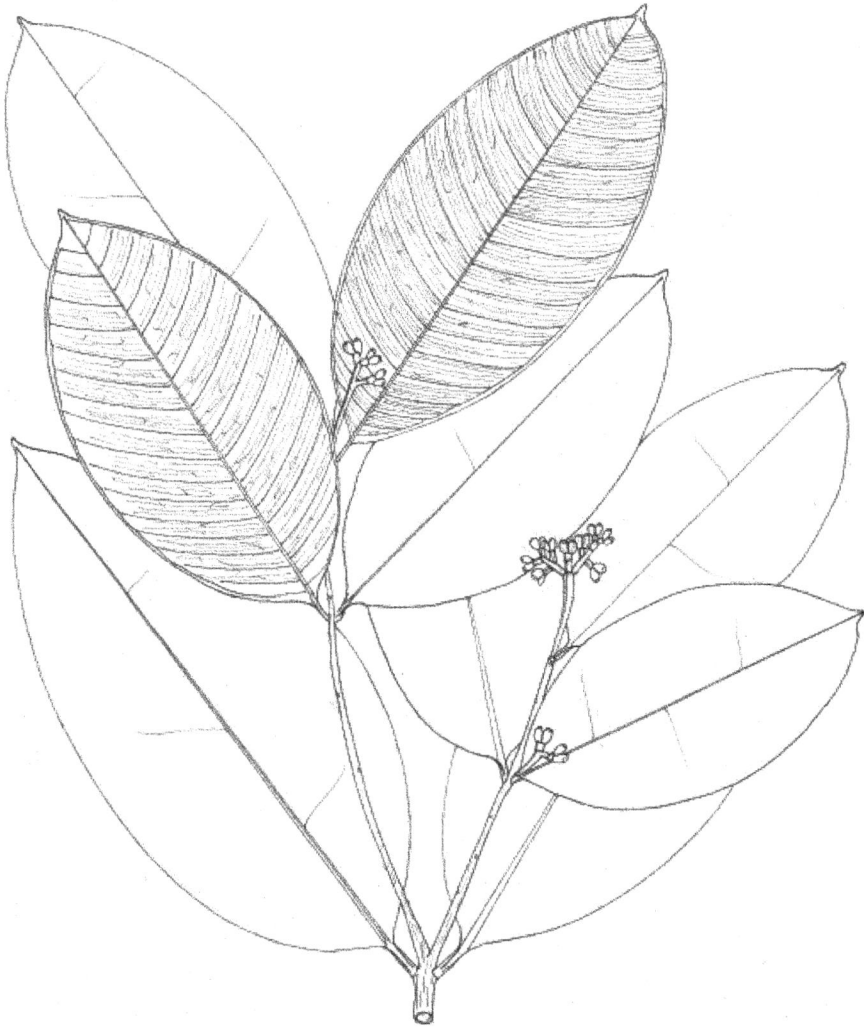

Figure 92: *Eugenia chlorantha* Duthie
From: Flora of Malaya
Malaysia, Kuala Lumpur, Sugai Netas, 76 miles from Kuala Lumpur.
Collection: Zai R. Identification: Katijah.

Eugenia jambos L.

[After Francois Eugene de Savoie-Carignan (1663-1736) patron of science and from Malay jambos = *Eugenia jambos*]

Local names:
: Malay apple, jambu mawar, jambu ayer mawar (Malaysia), thabye (Burma), chompuh sa (Cambodia), jambu (Sri Lanka), jambose (France), mamana rosa (Philippines), jambu (Sanskrit), perunaval (India).

Synonyms:
: *Jambos vulgaris* DC., *Jambosa jambos* (L.) Millsp., *Jambosa vulgaris* DC., *Syzygium jambos* (L.) Millsp., *Myrtus jambos* (L.) Kunth.

Description:
: It is a shrub or tree which is found in India, Southeast Asia, to Australia. The plant is cultivated for its fruits which are edible. The bark is grayish white and scaly. The stem is angled, fissured, peeling with longitudinal flakes. The internodes are 4 - 5 cm long. The leaves are simple, decussate and without stipules. The petiole is 0.6 - 0.7 cm x 0.2 cm, channelled, glabrous, and granular. The leaf-blade is 9 - 21 cm x 2 - 4.8 cm, lanceolate, acute at the base, acuminate at the apex, thinly coriaceous and with about 12 - 18 pairs of secondary nerves merged to an intramarginal nerve which is 0.3 cm away from the margin. The flowers are fragrant, in groups of 2-8 at the end of stems. The flower is 7.5 - 10 cm in diameter with a very conspicuous androecium. The sepals are rounded. The fruit is globose, white to dull yellow pink and about 5 cm wide with 4 vestigial sepals and style at the apex on an angled disk (Figure 93).

Medicinal Uses:
: In India the plant is used for asthma, dysentery, to invigorate and to treat syphilis. In Cambodia, Laos and Vietnam, the plant is used to assuage toothache and to break fever. In Burma, the plant is used to heal inflamed eyes.

Pharmacology:
: The plant abounds with hydrolysable tannins such as 1-O-galloyl castalagin and casuarinin which exhibited cytotoxic property against human promyelocytic leukemia cell line HL-60 via apoptosis (Yang *et al.*, 2000). The anti-inflammatory and analgesic properties of the plant have been validated using inflammatory models in rats with potencies comparable to phenylbutazone (Slowing *et al.*, 1994) and hot plate and formalin tests (Avila-Peña *et al.*, 2007). The plant contains a series of dihydrochalcones with antioxidant properties (Jayasinghe *et al.*, 2007). An extract of bark displayed an antibacterial property (Djipa *et al.*, 2000).

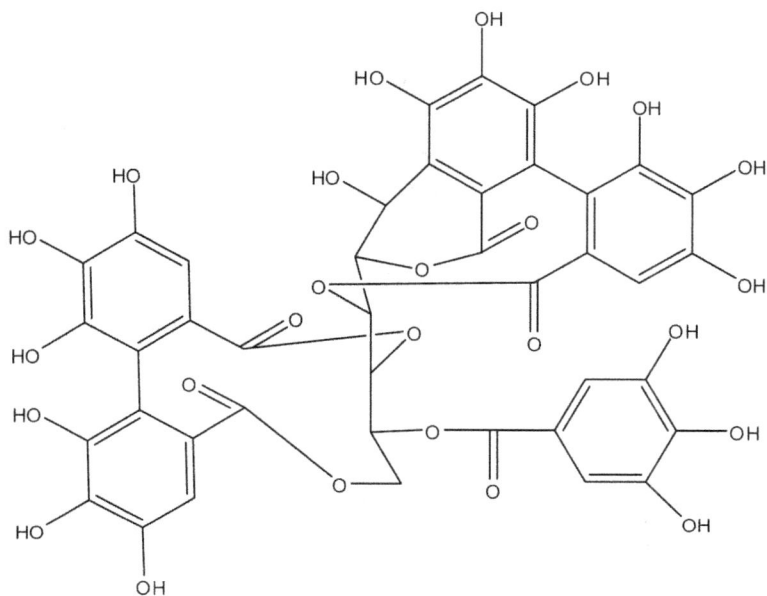

Casuarinin

References: Avila-Peña D, Peña N, Quintero L, Suárez-Roca H, 2007, Antinociceptive activity of *Syzygium jambos* leaves extract on rats. J Ethnopharmacol; 112: 380-5.

Djipa CD, Delmée M, Quetin-Leclercq J, 2000, Antimicrobial activity of bark extracts of *Syzygium jambos* (L.) Alston (Myrtaceae). J Ethnopharmacol; 71: 307-13.

Jayasinghe UL, Ratnayake RM, Medawala MM, Fujimoto Y, 2007, Dihydrochalcones with radical scavenging properties from the leaves of *Syzygium jambos*. Nat Prod Res; 21: 551-4.

Slowing K, Carretero E, Villar A, 1994, Anti-inflammatory activity of leaf extracts of *Eugenia jambos* in rats. J Ethnopharmacol; 43: 9-11.

Yang LL, Lee CY, Yen KY, 2000,Induction of apoptosis by hydrolyzable tannins from *Eugenia jambos* L. on human leukemia cells. Cancer Lett; 157: 65-75.

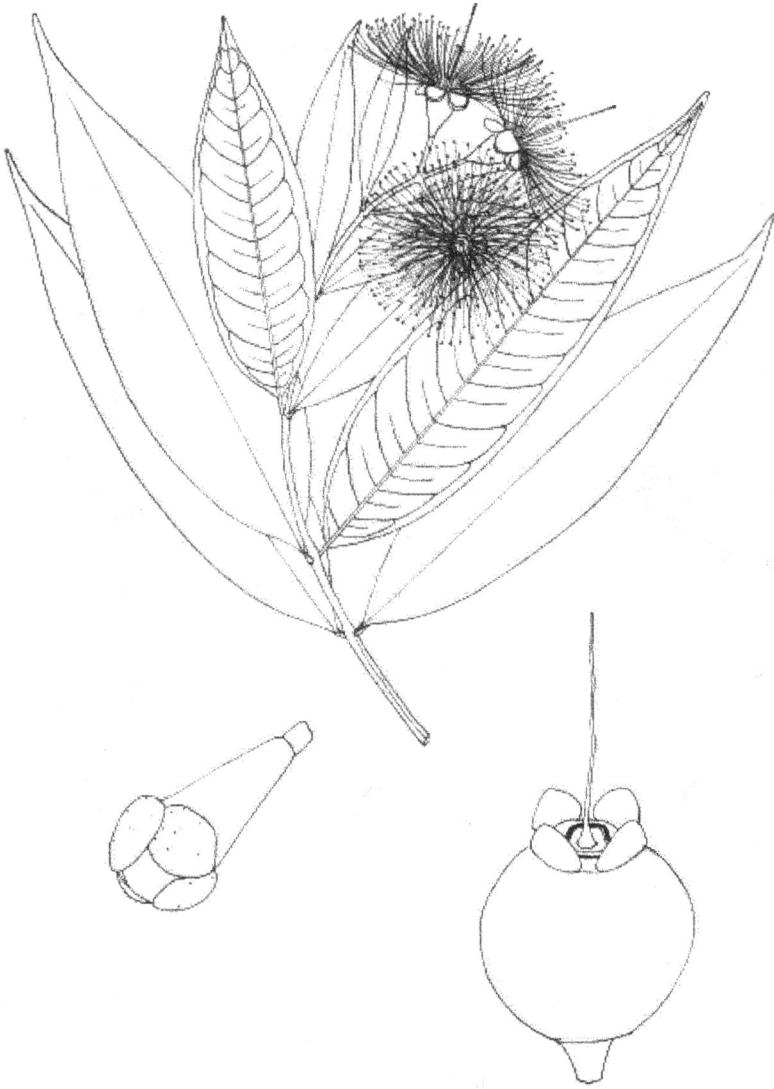

Figure 93: *Eugenia jambos* L.
From: Herbarium of University Kebangsaan Malaysia
Malaysia, Pulau Pinang state, Balek Pulau on the roadside near Hevea plantation.
Determination: Khatyah Hj Hussein. Collection: Za Zah.

Eugenia longiflorum (Presl.) F. Vill.

[After Francois Eugene de Savoie-Carignan (1663-1736) patron of science and from Latin *longiflorum* = with long flowers]

Local name:	Kelat merah (Malaysia)
Synonyms:	*Eugenia lineata* Duthie, *Jambosa lineata* DC., *Syzygium lineatum* (DC.) Merr. & Perr., *Syzygium longiflorum* Presl.
Description:	It is a timber tree which grows up to 20 m tall in the forests of Burma, Cambodia, Laos, Vietnam, Malaysia, and Indonesia. The bark is reddish. The stem is terete, smooth and finely cracked when young, and the older parts show roundish flakes. The leaves are simple, opposite and without stipules. The petiole is channelled, glabrous and about 0.5 cm long. The leaf-blade is coriaceous, 6 - 8 cm x 2 - 3 cm, tapering at the base, pointed at the apex, with 20 - 30 pairs of secondary nerves which are discrete and merged with an intramarginal nerve 0.1 cm away from the margin. The leaf-blade shows some oil cells visible above, and a midrib sunken above. The inflorescence is a light green terminal cyme. The flower pedicels are minute. The calyx is conical, about 0.8 cm long and develops 4 sepals which are translucent at the margin. The corolla consists of 4 petals which are light green turning whitish, membranaceous, dotted, deciduous, round, and 0.6 x 0.2 cm. The stamens are white with light yellow anthers, numerous, showy, and about 0.8 cm long. The style is 1 cm long and white. The fruit is globose, smooth, 0.6 cm in diameter, whitish, with 4 calyx lobes at the apex and containing a single seed (Figure 94).
Medicinal Uses:	In Malaysia, the plant is used at confinement.
Pharmacology:	Unknown. The plant awaits pharmacological investigation.

Figure 94: *Eugenia longiflorum* (Presl.) F. Vill.
From: Flora of Thailand, Prince of Songkla University.
Thailand, Haad Ya district, by 8° 3' North - 99° East. Elevation: 200 m. Date of collection: 25 May 1985. Collection and identification: JF Maxwell № 85-405

Eugenia oleina Wight

[After Francois Eugene de Savoie-Carignan (1663-1736) patron of science and from Latin *oleina* = related to olive, oil?]

Synonym:	*Eugenia myrtifolia* Roxb., *Syzygium myrtifolium* (Roxb.) DC, *Syzygium oleinum* Wall.
Description:	It is a tree that grows on the shores of Burma, Thailand, Malaysia, Borneo and the Philippines. The bark is grey to orange, and flaky. The stem is terete, fissured longitudinally, and peeling. The youngest parts are smooth and minutely winged with oil cells. The leaves are opposite or sub-opposite, simple and without stipules. The petiole is glabrous, channelled and 0.5 - 0.7 cm long. The leaf-blade is 5.7 - 8 cm x 1.7 - 4.7 cm, thinly coriaceous, spathulate, round, recurved at margin, and with about 30 pairs of secondary nerves merged to an intramarginal nerve 0.1 cm away from the margin. The leaf blade is dark green above, glossy and shows a midrib sunken above. The leaf-blade is acute at the apex, and cuneate at the base. The inflorescence is an axillary and terminal green cyme which is about 4 cm long with angled, winged, articulated peduncle covered with oil cells. The flower pedicel is minute. The calyx is conical, yellowish-green, covered with oil cells, 0.7 x 0.4 cm and develops 4 lobes. The corolla comprises 4 petals which are white, broadly lanceolate and almost 1 cm long. The androecium is showy, white and about 0.8 cm long. The style is white, and 1 cm long. The fruit is 0.5 x 0.6 - 0.7 cm, obovoid, red turning black crowned with vestigial calyx lobes and containing a single seed (Figure 95).
Medicinal Uses:	The plant is known as being poisonous in Malaysia.
Pharmacology:	Unknown. Some anthocyanins have been isolated from *Eugenia myrtifolia* Sims (Longo et al., 2007). This tree is worthy of further study.

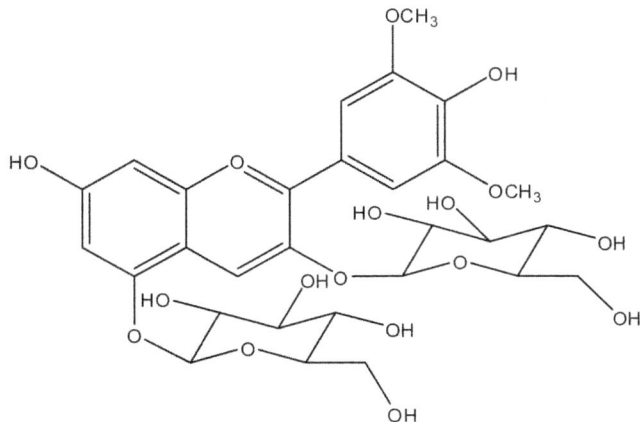

Malvidin 3,5 -O-diglucoside

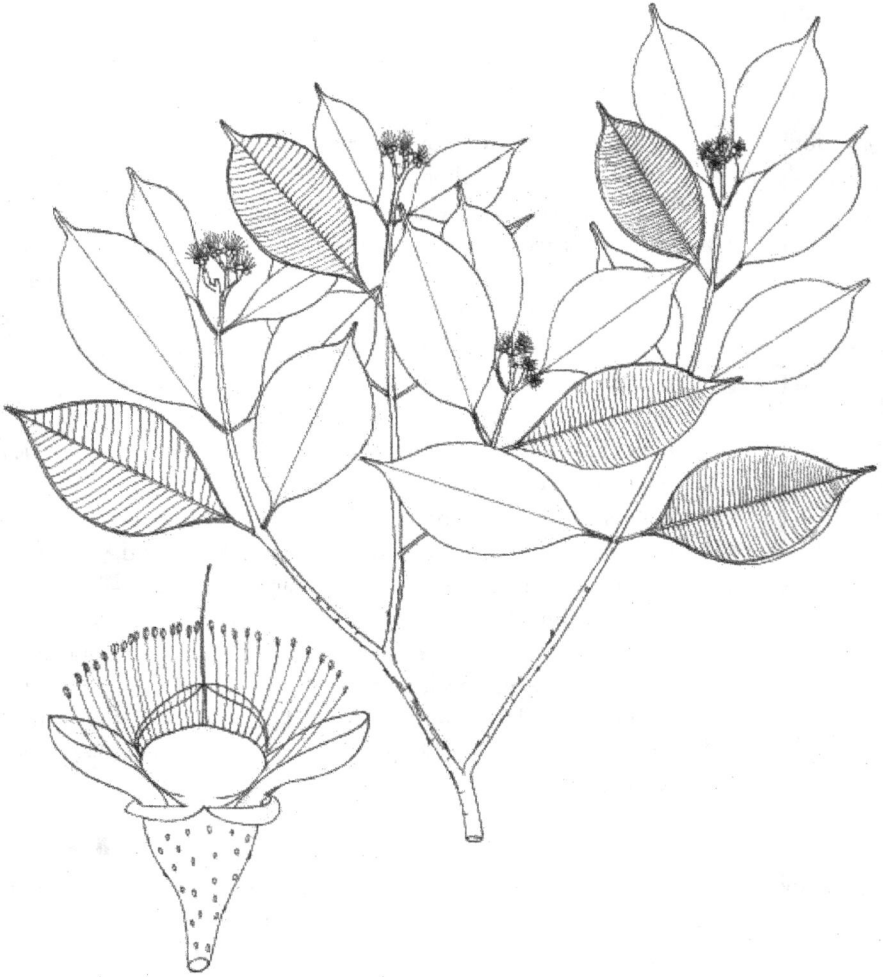

Figure 95: *Eugenia oleina* Wight
From: Flora of Thailand, Prince of Songkla University Herbarium.
Thailand, Trang province, Muang district, Khao Chong national park, by 8° 7'
North - 98° 2' East. Elevation: 325 m. Date of collection: 12 October 1985. In partly
open margins of the primary evergreen forest near the waterfalls. Collection and
identification: JF Maxwell, N° 85-960

References: Longo L, Scardino A, Vasapollo G, Blando F, 2007,
                   Anthocyanins from *Eugenia myrtifolia* Sims. Innov Food Sci
                   Emerging Technol; 8: 329-332.

Eugenia operculata Roxb.

[After Francois Eugene de Savoie-Carignan (1663-1736) patron of science and from Latin *operculata* = with a little cover]

Local names:	Jaman (Sikkim), kyamunaa (Nepal), konthabye (Burma), jamawa (India), voi (Cambodia, Laos, Vietnam), bhumi jambu (Sanskrit), malaruhak (Philippines).
Synonyms:	*Cleistocalyx operculatus* (Roxb.) Merr. & L.M. Perry, *Eugenia cerasoides* Roxb. *Syzygium operculatum* (Roxb.) Nied., Syzygium nervosum DC.
Description:	It is a timber tree that can reach up to 40 m tall with a girth of 2.4 m. It is found in the forest of India, Burma, Cambodia, Laos, Vietnam, Thailand, Malaysia, Indonesia, Philippines and Australia. The bark is pale brown and exfoliating. The stem is smooth, pimply, glabrous, somewhat flattish, articulated, and angular at the apex and with longitudinal leaf-scars. The nodes are a little enlarged and 0.3 cm in diameter. The older stems are fissured and peeling. The leaves are simple, opposite or sub-opposite and without stipules. The petiole is glabrous, channelled, and up to 1.5 cm long. The leaf-blade is somewhat spathulate, 15 - 19 cm x 4 - 6 cm, dark-green above, coriaceous, cuneate at the base, glabrous. The leaf-blade shows a midrib and about 10 pairs of secondary nerves sunken above, and some oil cells are visible underneath. The intramarginal nerve is 0.3 - 0.5 cm away from the margin. The inflorescence is a green, articulated, glabrous, angled panicle on a 3 cm long axe. The flower pedicel is 0.5 cm long. The calyx buds open by dropping a lid. The flower is about 0.8 cm in diameter, white, the petals united to form a calyptra. The fruit is 0.4 - 1 cm in diameter, whitish with pinkish hue, with a disk at the apex the diameter of which is 0.25 - 0.3 cm (Figure 96).
Medicinal Uses:	In India, the plant is used an Ayurvedic remedy for weakness, dysentery, bronchitis and ulcers. The fruits are eaten to assuage rheumatism. In Burma, the plant is used to treat rheumatism. In China, it is carminative and tonic and used to treat leprosy, cholera, jaundice and to expel worms from the intestines. In Cambodia, Laos and Vietnam, the leaves are used to make a tea which is carminative and the plant is used as an antiseptic for wounds.
Pharmacology:	*Eugenia operculata* Roxb. displays a broad range of interesting pharmacological properties. The plant elaborates a series of

flavonoids which are cytotoxic, apoptotic, and antioxidant. Ye *et al.* (2004, 2007) isolated a series of flavonoids including 2',4'-dihydroxy-6'-methoxy-3',5'-dimethylchalcone, 3'-formyl-4',6'-dihydroxy-2'methoxy-5'-methylchalcone, and 8-formyl-5-hydroxy-7-methoxy-6 methylflavanone. These abrogated the survival of SMMC-7721 (liver cancer), 8898 (pancreatic cancer), and 95-D (high metastatic lung carcinoma), cell lines and displayed antioxidant properties. Such antioxidant flavonoids may account for the protection of PC12 cells against the oxidative damage induced by hydrogen peroxide reported by Lu *et al.* (2003). Extracts of the plant increased the force of contraction and lowered the frequency of contraction in an isolated rat heart perfusion system (Woo *et al.*, 2002) and lowered the glucose level of streptozocin-induced diabetic rodents in relation to inhibition of alpha - glucosidase (Mai *et al.*,2007).

References: Lu YH, Du CB, Wu ZB, Ye CL, Liu JW, Wei DZ, 2003, Protective effects of *Cleistocalyx operculatus* on lipid peroxidation and trauma of neuronal cells. Zhongguo Zhong Yao Za Zhi; 28: 964-6.

Mai TT, Chuyen NV, 2007, Anti-hyperglycemic activity of an aqueous extract from flower buds of *Cleistocalyx operculatus* (Roxb.) Merr and Perry. Biosci Biotechnol Biochem; 71: 69-76.

Woo AY, Waye MM, Kwan HS, Chan MC, Chau CF, Cheng CH, 2002,Inhibition of ATPases by *Cleistocalyx operculatus*. A possible mechanism for the cardiotonic actions of the herb. Vascul Pharmacol; 38: 163-8.

Ye CL, Liu JW, Wei DZ, Lu YH, Qian F, 2004, *In vitro* anti-tumor activity of 2',4'-dihydroxy-6'-methoxy-3',5'-dimethylchalcone against six established human cancer cell lines. Pharmacol Res; 50: 505-10.

Ye CL, Liu Y, Wei DZ, 2007, Antioxidant and anticancer activity of 3'-formyl-4', 6'-dihydroxy-2'-methoxy-5'-methylchalcone and (2S)-8-formyl-5-hydroxy-7-methoxy-6-methylflavanone. J Pharm Pharmacol ; 59: 553-9.

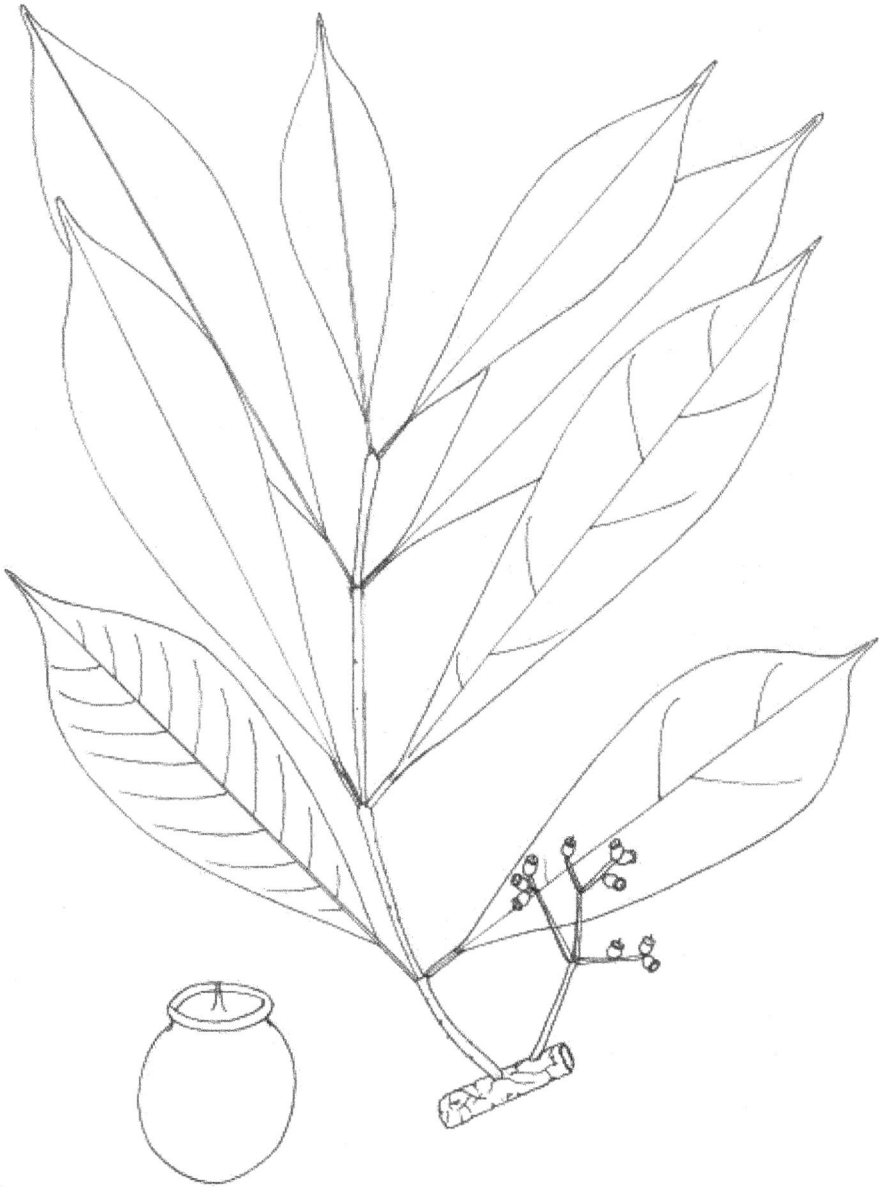

Figure 96: *Eugenia operculata* **Roxb.**
From: Flora of Thailand, Prince of Songkla University
Thailand, Songkla province, Haad Yai district, Dton Nga Chang reserve, by 8° 5' N - 98° 5'
East. Elevation: 50 m. Date of collection: 2 August 1985. In partly open area, rocky place
along river, primary evergreen forest. Collection and identification: JF Maxwell.

Eugenia polyantha Wight

[After Francois Eugene de Savoie-Carignan (1663-1736) patron of science and from Latin *polyantha* = having many flowers]

Local name:	Indonesian bay leaf; salam manting (Indonesia)
Synonyms:	*Aulomyrcia inaequalis* (DC) Amshoff, *Eugenia balsamea* Ridl., *Myrcia inaequiloba* (DC) D Legrand, *Myrciaria polyantha* (Miq.) O. Berg., *Syzygium polyanthum* (Wight) Walp.
Description:	It is a tree that can reach up to 30 m, found Burma, Thailand, Cambodia, Laos, Vietnam, Malaysia and Indonesia. The bark is grey. The stem is terete and glabrous. The leaves are simple, opposite and without stipules. The petiole is 0.5 - 1 cm long. The leaf-blade is thinly leathery, elliptic, 7 - 16 cm x 2.5 - 7 cm, with 7 - 9 pairs of secondary nerves with an intramarginal nerve 0.2 - 0.4 cm away from the margin. The dried leaves are aromatic and used as a spice. The inflorescence is a sessile, articulated panicle which is about 2 cm long with angular pedicels. The calyx is cup-shaped with 5 round lobes. The corolla comprises 5 petals. The androecium is showy with many stamens. The fruit is globose, deep pink, varicose, 0.7 x 0.5 cm with apical persistent calyx lobes around a disk in the middle of which stands a vestigial style and few stamens (Figure 97).
Medicinal uses:	In Malaysia the plant is used to treat itches. In Indonesia, the plant is used to treat diarrhoea.
Pharmacology:	The use of the plant to treat itchiness might account for some antifungal property reported by Mohamed *et al.* (1999). The plant showed very strong activity against *Bursaphelenchus xylophilus* (Mackeen *et al.*, 1999) and strong *in vitro* anti-tumour promoting activity when assayed using Raji cells (Ali *et al.*, 2000).
References:	Ali AM, Lajis NH, Mooi LY, Yih K, Norhanom AW, Saleh K, Yazid AM, 2000, Anti - tumor promoting activity of some Malaysian traditional vegetable (Ulam) extracts by immunoblotting analysis of raji cells. Nat Prod ScI; 6: 147 -150.
	Mohamed S, Saka S, El-Sharkawy SH, Ali AM, Muid S, 1999, Antimycotic screening of 58 Malaysian plants against plant pathogens. Pestic Sci; 47: 259 -264.
	Mackeen MM, Ali AM, Abdullah MA,Nasir RM, Nashriyah B, Mat NB, Abdul R, Razak AR, Kawazu K, 1999, Antinematodal activity of some Malaysian plant extracts against the pine wood nematode, *Bursaphelenchus xylophilus*. Pestic Sci; 51: 165-170.

Figure 97: *Eugenia polyantha* Wight
From: University Kebangsaan Malaysia Herbarium No 01639
Malaysia, Campus of UKM, Bangi, Selangor. Collection and identification: MK and Zai. Date of
collection: 24 September 1973.

Leptospermum flavescens Smith

[From Greek *lepto* = thin and *sperma* = seed and Latin *flavescens* = pale yellow]

Local names:	Tantoon tea tree, yellow tea tree, cina maki, gelam bukit, gelam gunung (Malaysia)
Synonym:	*Leptospermum amboinense* Bl.
Description:	It is a tree with twisted branches which grows in a geographical area covering Burma, Thailand, Malaysia, Indonesia, the Philippines and Australia. The plant varies in size and shape and could be a bush or almost a timber tree. It has ornamental value. The bark is fissured, flaky and grayish-brown. The stem is fissured, cracked, angled to winged and pilose. The internodes are about 0.5 cm long. The leaves are sessile, spiral, and without stipules. The leaf-blade is about 1.3 -2 cm x 0.2 - 0.5 cm, spathulate to linear elliptic, hairy when young, with oil cells underneath, and fragrant with one pair of secondary nerves. The flower is axillary and solitary. The calyx is cup-shaped, green, with 5 white lobes which are 0.25 x 0.3 cm, minutely ciliate, shorter that the petals and dotted with oil cells. The corolla presents 5 petals which are whitish, orbicular and 0.5 cm in diameter. The androecium consists of several, 0.4 cm long stamens, with flattish filaments. The fruit is a small woody conical capsule, 0.4 - 0.6 cm in diameter opening at the apex with 5 slits. The seeds are numerous, thin and linear (Figure 98).
Medicinal uses:	In Malaysia, the plant is used to invigorate, to treat constipation and stomach-ache. In Indonesia, the oil distilled from the leaves is used to treat infection of the lungs and painful joints.
Pharmacology:	The plant owes its tonic and analgesic properties to an essential oil which is counter irritant, antiseptic and carminative. The essential oil of this plant comprises cohorts of terpenes including alpha-pinene and cineole (Perry *et al.*, 1997).
References:	Perry NB, Brennan NJ, Van Klink JW, Harris W, Douglas MH, McGimpsey JA, Smallfield BM, Anderson RE, 1997, Essential oils from New Zealand manuka and kanuka: Chemotaxonomy of *Leptospermum*. Phytochemistry; 44: 1485-94.

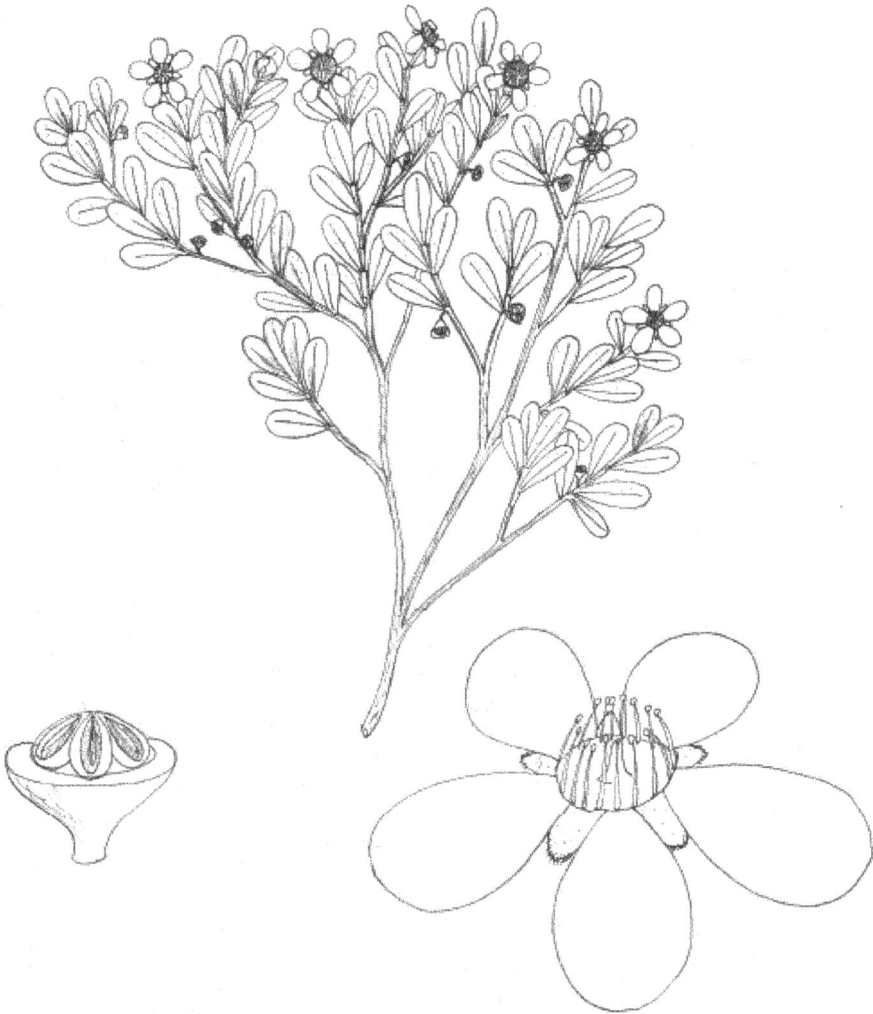

Figure 98: *Leptospermum flavescens* Smith
From: Herbarium of University Kebangsaan Malaysia Herbarium № 04474
Malaysia, Pahang state, Gunung Ulu Kali, near Telecom station.

Melaleuca cajuputi Powell

[from Greek *melas* = black and *leukos* = white, and from Malay-Indonesian *kayu puteh* = white wood]

Local names: Botttle brush, gelam (Malaysia), minyak kayu puteh (Indonesia), bois blanc (France), cham, da ra bo dich (Cambodia, Laos, Vietnam), lothsumbul (Sri Lanka), kaiyappudai (India).

Synonyms:	*Melaleuca cajuputi* Roxb., *Melaleuca minor* Sm. *Myrtus saligna* Burm.f., *Melaleuca leucadendron* (L.) L. var. *minor* (Smith) Duthie.
Description:	It is a large shrub that grows in swampy ground near coasts in India, Malaysia, Cambodia, Laos, Vietnam, and Indonesia. It is a native of the Moluccas and has been cultivated in Asia for several centuries for its essential oil: the cajuput oil. The plant can reach a height of 24 m, and the bole is twisted. The bark is whitish, soft, fissured and with papery flakes which are coarse elongate and shaggy. The stem is smooth, 0.2 cm in diameter, glabrous, terete, with 0.2 x 0.1 cm crescent-shaped leaf-scars, it is hairy and angled at the apex. The internodes are about 1 cm long. The leaves are simple, sessile, spiral and without stipules. The leaf-blade is lanceolate, thick, woody, velvety at first, grayish, 6 - 16.5 cm x 1.7 - 2.6 cm with 5-7 longitudinal nerves and acute at the apex. The flower is sessile on a spike which is velvety at first, 7.5 - 15 cm long, overall and which looks-like a bottle-brush. The calyx is velvety with 5 membranaceous lobes ciliate at the margin. The corolla presents 5 petals which are deciduous, membranaceous and globose. The stamens are numerous and conspicuous and about 0.7 cm long. The style is 1 cm long. The fruit is a 0.2 x 0.4 cm, woody, rough capsule with 3 radial lodges at the apex. The seeds are minute, chip-like and 0.1 cm long (Figure 99).
Medicinal uses:	The leaves yield cajuput oil. In India, the oil is used for rheumatism, eczema and boils. In Sri Lanka, the plant is used to invigorate. In Malaysia, the oil is used to treat diarrhea and cholera. In Burma, the oil is applied as a gout and heart tonic. In China, it is used to clean infected wounds and to assuage joint pain. In Cambodia, Laos and Vietnam, the oil is used to treat influenza, and dropsy. It has several uses in Indonesia where it is held in great esteem. It is used there as analgesic and antiseptic, and is especially used for vertigo, convulsion, and toothache. In the Philippines, the plant is used against asthma. In Papua New Guinea, the oil is used in case of malaria. The oil has been included as Melaleuca Oil (British Pharmaceutical Codex, 1949) employed internally as a carminative and externally as a stimulant and mild counter-irritant in rheumatism.
Pharmacology:	The major constituents of the oil are cineole and terpinen-4-ol which account for the medicinal properties mentioned above. Cineole is a well known antiseptic agent that inhibits the growth of a broad spectrum of bacteria and fungi (Dubey *et al.*, 1983). Other compounds might account for the traditional

anti-inflammatory use of the plant such as triterpenes (Lee *et al.*, 1999). Tsugura *et al.*, (1991), isolated the triterpene ursolic acid, from the fruits and a series of stilbenes including piceatannol and oxyresveratrol which inhibited histamine release from rat mast cells induced by compound 48/80 or concanavalin A. There is mounting evidence indicating that piceatannol, which is closely related to resveratrol, offers serious potential as an anticancer agent. For instance it reduced proliferation rate of human colon carcinoma cell line Caco-2 (Wolter *et al.*, 2002). An extract of fruit displayed *in vitro* and *in vivo* anti-HSV1 activity (Nawawi *et al.*, 1999). An extract of the plant inhibited the enzymatic activity of CYP2D6 (Subehan *et al.*, 2006).

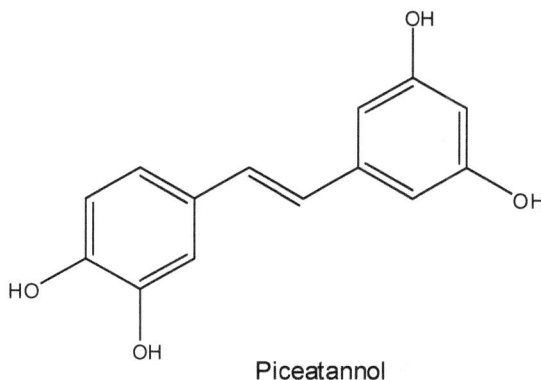

Piceatannol

References:

Dubey NK, Kishore N, Singh SK, Dikshit A, 1983, Antifungal properties of the volatile fraction of *Melaleuca leucadendron*. Trop Agr; 60: 227-28.

Lee CK, Chang MH, 1999, Four new triterpenes from the heartwood of *Melaleuca leucadendron*. J Nat Prod; 62: 1003 -5.

Nawawi A, Nakamura N, Hattori M, Kurokawa M, Shiraki K, 1999, Inhibitory effects of Indonesian medicinal plants on the infection of herpes simplex virus type 1. Phytother Res; 13: 37-41.

Tsuruga T, Chun YT, Ebizuka Y, Sankawa U, 1991, Biologically active constituents of *Melaleuca leucadendron*: inhibitors of induced histamine release from rat mast cells. Chem Pharm Bull (Tokyo); 39: 3276-8.

Subehan TS, Iwata H, Kadota S, Tezuka Y, 2006, Mechanism-the based inhibition of CYP3A4 and CYP2D6 by Indonesian medicinal plants. J Ethnopharmacol; 105: 449-55.

Wolter F, Clausnitzer A, Akoglu B, Stein J, 2002, Piceatannol, a natural analog of resveratrol, inhibits progression through the S phase of the cell cycle in colorectal cancer cell lines. J Nutr; 132: 298-302.

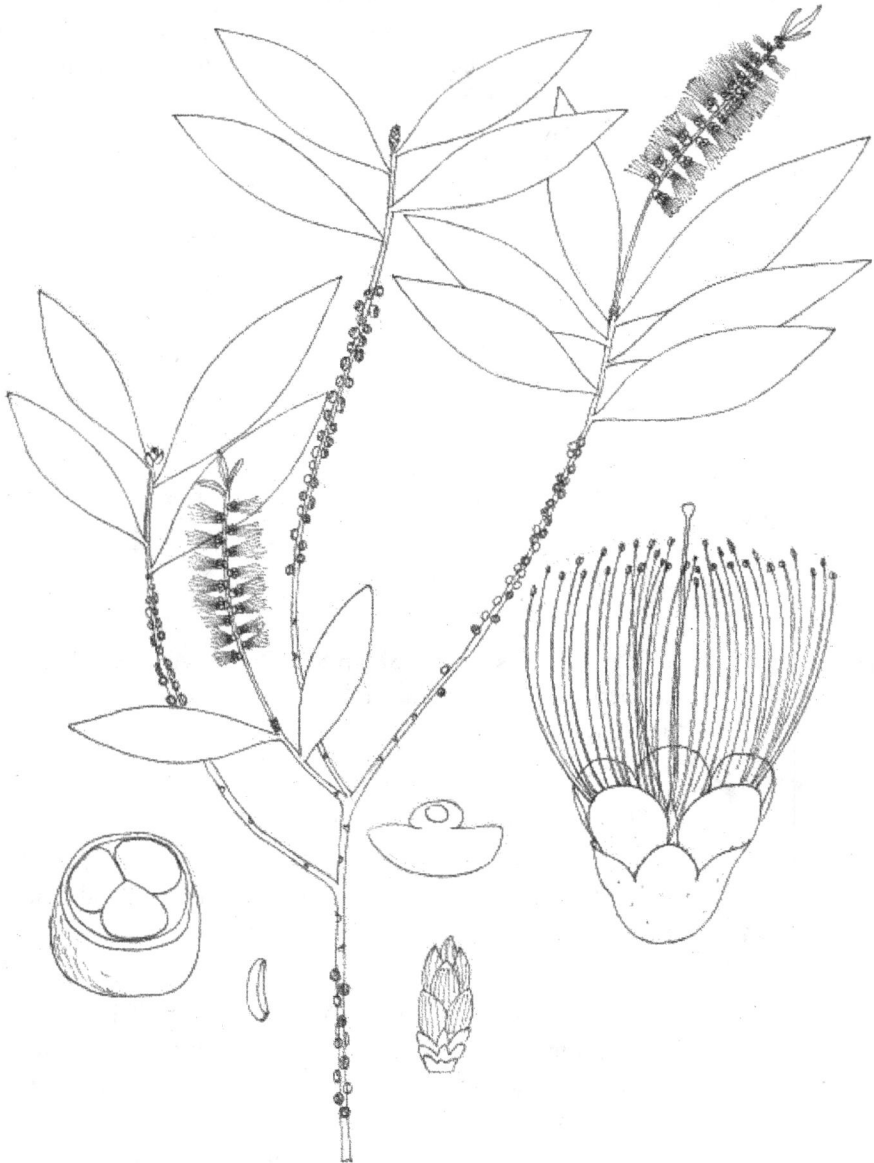

Figure 99: *Melaleuca cajuputi* Powell
From: Flora of Malaya No 0531
Malaysia, Port Dickson, Tanjung Tuan. Collection: Mohd. Kassim, 28 November 1972.
Determination: A Zainuddin, 14 April 1986.

Psidium guajava L.

[From Greek *psidion* = pomegranate and from Spain *guyaba* = *Psidium guajava* L.]

Local names:	Guava tree, amrud (Arabic), malaka (Burma), dfamboe bidji (Indonesia), trabek srok (Cambodia), gay oi (Vietnam), goyavier (France), guyaba (Spain), pera (Sri Lanka), koyya (India)
Synonyms:	*Guajava pyrifera* (L.) Kuntze, *Myrtus guajava* (L.) Kuntze, *Psidium guava* Griseb., *Psidium guayava* Raddi, *Psidium igatemyensis* Barb. Rodr., *Psidium pomiferum* L., *Psidium pumilum* Vahl, *Psidium pyriferum* L.
Description:	It is a large shrub, native to tropical America, which is cultivated as a fruit tree in most tropical countries. The bark is smooth. The stem is quadrangular, winged, 0.5 cm in diameter, smooth, dotted with oil cells and with some hairs at the apex. The internodes are 3 - 3.5 cm long. The leaves are simple, opposite and without stipules. The petiole is channelled, velvety and 0.5 - 0.8 cm x 0.2 cm. The leaf-blade is elliptic, 6 - 13 cm x 4.2 - 6.3 cm, coriaceous, hairy at first, with 16 - 23 pairs of secondary nerves and oil cells visible underneath. The flower is solitary, axillary and terminal. The flower pedicel is hairy, 1.2 - 3 cm long. The flower bud is hairy, 1.5 x 0.4 cm. The calyx is 0.8 x 0.4 cm with 5 sepals which are triangular, velvety, and 0.5 x 0.7 cm. The corolla comprises 5 petals which are pilose with oil cells. The androecium comprises numerous stamens. The style is 1 cm long with a globose stigma. The fruit is a pyriform or globose berry which is edible, about 5 cm in diameter crowned at the apex by vestigial calyx lobes (Figure 100).
Medicinal Uses:	In India the plant is an astringent remedy used to heal wounds, ulcers, to treat diarrhoea and to check bleeding. In most Southeast Asian countries, the plant is used to treat diarrhoea. In Malaysia, it is used to heal wounds. In the Philippines, the plant is used for diabetes, and as an astringent for ulcers, wounds, and diarrhoea. In China the leaves are used to treat diarrhoea, infection of the skin and diabetes mellitus.
Pharmacology:	The plant has been the subject of numerous chemical and pharmacological studies. It demonstrates antioxidant, hepatoprotection, anti-allergy, antimicrobial, antigenotoxic, antiplasmodial, cytotoxic, antispasmodic, cardioactive, anticough, antidiabetic, anti-inflammatory and antinociceptive activities, supporting its traditional uses (Gutiérrez *et al.*, 2008). The antidiarrhoeal property of the plant has been confirmed experimentally. A dose of 0.2 ml fresh leaf extract/kg produced 65% inhibition of propulsion comparable to 0.2 mg/kg of morphine

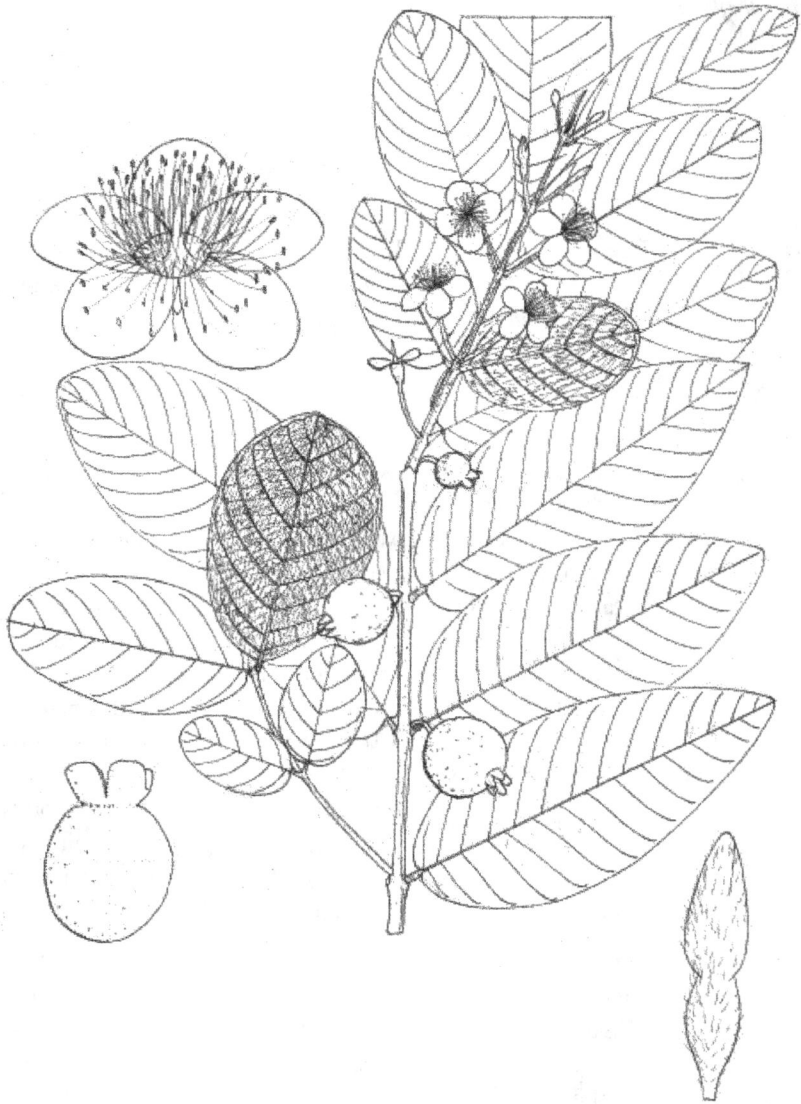

Figure 100: *Psidium guajava* **L.**
From: Flora of Malaya.
Malaysia, Jalan Rawang, Kuang. Date of collection: 20 July 1972. Collection and
identification: Mohd. Kassim

Pharmacology: (contd)	sulphate in rodents (Lutterodt, 1992) probably due to quercetin, and other tannins (Zhang *et al.*, 2003). The plant contains a galactose-specific lectin which binds to *Escherichia coli* preventing its adhesion to the intestinal wall and thus preventing diarrhoea (Coutino *et al.*, 2001). The wound healing and antibacterial activity from the plant

has been validated experimentally (Chah *et al.*, 2006; Qadan *et al.*, 2005). Extracts of the plant showed antigiardiasic activity (Ponce *et al.*, 1994) and hepatoprotective (Roy *et al.*, 2006) activity. Salib *et al.* (2004) isolated phenylethanol glycosides of which mecocyanin which showed cytotoxic activities *in vitro* against Ehrlich ascites carcinoma cells and leukemia P388 cells.

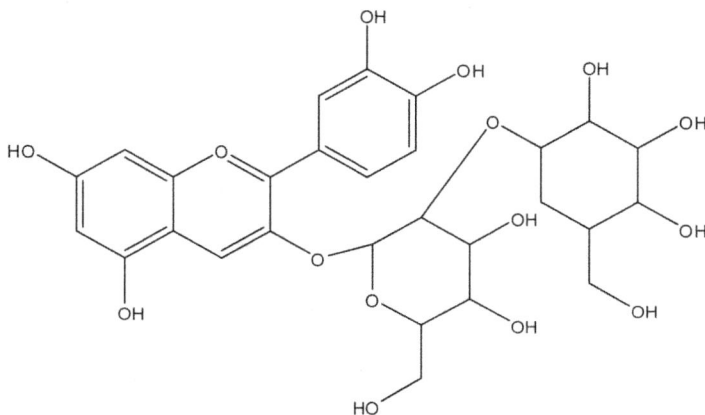

Mecocyanin

References:

Chah KF, Eze CA, Emuelosi CE, Esimone CO, 2006, Antibacterial and wound healing properties of methanolic extracts of some Nigerian medicinal plants. J Ethnopharmacol; 104: 164-167.

Coutino RR, Hernandez, CP, Giles RH, 2001, Lectins in fruits having gastrointestinal activity: their participation in the hemagglutinating property of *Escherichia coli* O157:H7. Arch Med Res; 32: 251-257.

Gutiérrez RMP, Mitchell S, Solis RV, 2008, *Psidium guajava*: A review of its traditional uses, phytochemistry and pharmacology. J Ethnopharmacol; 117: 1-27.

Lutterodt, G.D., 1992. Inhibition of Microlax-induced experimental diarrhoea with narcotic-like extracts of *Psidium guajava* leaf in rats. J Ethnopharmacol; 37: 51-157.

Ponce MM, Navarro AI, Martinez GMN, Alvarez CR, 1994, *In vitro* effect against *Giardia* of 14 plant extracts. Rev Investig Clin; 46: 343-347.

Qadan F,Thewaini AJ, Ali DA, Afifi R, Elkhawad A, Matalka KZ, 2005, The antimicrobial activities of *Psidium guajava* and *Juglans regia* leaf extracts to acne-developing organisms. Am Chin Med; 33: 197-204.

Roy CK, Kamath JV, Asad M, 2006, Hepatoprotective activity of *Psidium guajava* Linn. Ind J of Exp Biol; 44: 305-11.

Salib JY, Michael HN, 2004, Cytotoxic phenylethanol glycosides from *Psidium guaijava* seeds. Phytochemistry; 65: 2091-93.

Zhang WJ, Chen BT, Wang CY, Zhu QH, Mo Z, 2003, Mechanism of quercetin as an antidiarroeal agent. Di Yi Jun Yi Xue Xue Bao; 23: 1029-31.

Rhodamnia cinerea Jack.
[From Greek *rhodo* = rose and *amnion* = bowl and Latin *cinerea* = ash grey]

Local name: Mempoyan (Malaysia)

Synonym: *Rhodamnia trinervia* Bl.

Description: It is a tree which grows up to 10 m tall in forests from Southeast Asia to Australia. The bark is grayish brown. The wood is hard and makes a valuable timber. The stem is glabrous, terete, cracked, peeling, and velvety at the apex. The internodes are 2-4 cm long. The nodes are swollen, giving the stem a bony style. The leaves are simple, opposite and without stipules. The petiole is 0.5 - 0.75 cm, velvety and channelled. The leaf-blade is coriaceous, oblong, elliptic, acuminate at the apex, 6 - 7.2 cm x 2.4 - 2.8 cm, hairy underneath, with about 6 pairs of secondary nerves and intramarginal nerves which are prominent underneath. The flowers are in axillary clusters. The calyx is hairy with 4 sepals. The corolla comprises 4 petals. The stamens are numerous. The fruit is a globose berry which is 0.75 cm in diameter, hairy, with dots, a pair of linear bracts at the base, turning red to black, crowned at the apex with vestigial calyx and contain 3-8 seeds. The fruit pedicel is slender and hairy (Figure 101).

Medicinal Uses: The plant is used after childbirth as a protective remedy. It is also used for scalds and stomach-ache.

Pharmacology: Unknown. The plant probably owes its medicinal properties to tannins and other phenolic compounds. This plant is well worth further study.

Figure 101: *Rhodamnia cinerea* **Jack.**
From: Flora of Thailand, Prince of Songkla University Herbarium.
Thailand, Nakornsitammarat province, Lansagah district, Gabrame falls, Kao Luang national park. Elevation: 200 m. Date of collection: 19 May 1985. In open sandy places, near rivers in primary evergreen forest. Collection and identification: W. Ramsi N° 67.

Rhodomyrtus tomentosa (Ait.) Hassk.

[From Latin *rhodomyrtus* = rose-myrtle and *tomentosa* = tomentose]

Local names:	Downy myrtle, rose myrtle; tao jin niang (China), kemunting (Malaysia, Indonesia), tho (Thailand), karamunting Borneo), sragan (Cambodia), sim (Vietnam)

Basionym: *Myrtus tomentosa* Aiton *Hortus Kewensis*; 2: 159. 1789.

Synonyms: *Myrtus canescens* Lour., *Myrtus tomentosa* Aiton

Description: It is a shrub which grows in open, sandy places, along the shores and on river banks, of India, Burma, Malaysia, Laos, Cambodia, Vietnam, Indonesia, China, Japan, the Philippines and Sri Lanka. It is ornamental, invasive and has spread to Hawaii and the US. The plant can reach up to 3 m tall. The stem is glabrous, fissured longitudinally, and peeling, hairy at the apex, about 0.4 cm in diameter, and with 1.5 - 2 cm long internodes. The leaves are simple, opposite and without stipules. The petiole is 0.25 - 0.5 cm long, velvety, channelled and somewhat angular underneath. The leaf-blade is 2 - 3 cm x 1 - 2 cm, oblong, coriaceous, woody, woolly underneath, dotted with oil cells, and shows 3 longitudinal nerves visible underneath. The flower is axillary and solitary on a peduncle which is about 2 cm long and velvety. The calyx is 5 lobed, velvety and urceolate, the lobes 0.4 cm x 0.4 cm and dotted with oil cells. The corolla comprises 5 petals which are pink and about 1 - 1.3 cm long. The androecium is conspicuous, with pink filaments and yellow anthers. The style is filiform. The fruit is a berry which is oblong, about 0.7 cm in diameter, velvety, purplish and edible (Figure 102).

Medicinal uses: In China, the plant is used to break fever, to check bleeding, to assuage pain in the heart, and to promote digestion. In Malaysia, the plant is used to stop diarrhoea, and as a protective remedy given after childbirth. In Indonesia, the plant is used to heal wounds.

Pharmacology: This common medicinal plant has not been the subject of many pharmacological studies. Most of the medicinal uses mentioned above are probably due to tannins and other phenolics such as rhodomyrtone. Salni *et al*, (2002) isolated rhodomyrtone or 6,8-dihydroxy-2,2,4,4-tetramethyl-7-(3-methyl-1-oxobutyl)-9-(2-methylpropyl)-4,9-dihydro-1*H*-xanthene-1,3(2*H*)-di-one which inhibits the growth of *Escherichia coli* and *Staphylococcus aureus*. The plant contains triterpenes (Hui WH *et al.*, 1975, 1976), the pharmacological potential of which remains unexplored.

Figure 102: *Rhodomyrtus tomentosa* (Ait.) Hassk.
From: Herbaria of Michigan State University, Plants of Borneo.
Malaysia, Sabah state, Kota Kinabalu, bukit Padang district, hills by UKMS campus 5° 58'
North - 116° 06' East. Collection and identification: John H Beaman 6830. Date of collection:
24 August 1984. Elevation: 30 m. Scattered shrubby vegetation. Crocker formation.

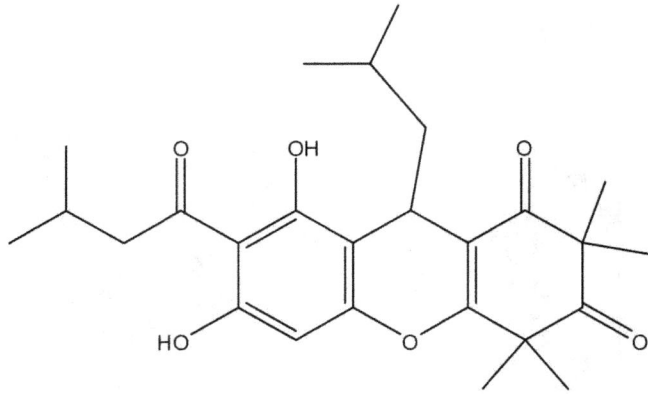

Rhodomyrtone

References:

Hui WH, Li MM, 1976, Two new triterpenoids from *Rhodomyrtus tomentosa* Phytochemistry; 15: 1741-43.

Hui WH, Li MM, Luk K, 1975, Triterpenoids and steroids from *Rhodomyrtus tomentosa*. Phytochemistry; 14: 833-34.

Salni D, Sargent MV, Skelton BW, Soediro I, Sutisna M, White AH, Yulinah E, 2002, Rhodomyrtone, an antibiotic from *Rhodomyrtus tomentosa. Austral J Chem;* 55: 229 - 32.

4.Family ONAGRACEAE A.L. de Jussieu 1798 nom conserv., the Evening Primrose Family

The family Onagraceae consists of 17 genera and 675 species of tanniferous water-loving herbs known to accumulate ellagic and gallic acids. The leaves are simple, opposite or alternate and without stipules. The flowers are often solitary and yellow. The calyx is 4 lobed, the lobes valvate. The corolla is very characteristic and consists of 4 petals which are contorted or imbricate and often clawed and form a yellow cross. The androecium comprises 4 - 8 stamens. The anthers are 2 locular, and open lengthwise. The gynaecium is inferior, comprise 4 carpels fused into a 4 locular ovary, each locule containing several ovules attached to the axil or parietal placenta. The fruits are capsules, berries or nuts containing numerous seeds.

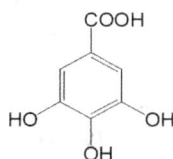

Gallic acid

Onagraceae of the genera *Fuchsia* and *Clarkia* are ornamental. The oil expressed from the seeds of *Oenothera biennis* (evening primrose oil), is sold as a dietary supplement, for premenstrual syndrome. A few pharmacological studies have focused on Onagraceae and the discovery of drugs from this family would not be surprising. Piperine from *Ludwigia hyssopifolia* L. exhibited antitumour and antibacterial activity (DasB *et al.*, 2007). Extracts of several *Epilobium* species showed antiproliferative effect in PZ-HPV-7 human prostatic epithelial cells *in vitro* (Vitalone *et al.*, 2003). Members of the genus *Oenaothera* elaborate interesting series of oligomeric ellagitannins known as oenotheins which showed potent anti-tumour activity and an inhibitory effect on infection by the herpes simplex virus (Taniguchi *et al.*, 2002). *Jussiaea repens* L. and *Ludwigia octovalvis* (Jacq.) Raven are medicinal in the East.

References: Das B, Kundu J, Bachar SC, Uddin MA, Kundu JK, 2007, Antitumor and antibacterial activity of ethylacetate extract of *Ludwigia hyssopifolia* Linn and its active principle piperine. Pak J Pharm Sci; 20: 128-31.

Taniguchi S, Y, Yabu-uchi R, Ito H, Hatano T, Yoshida T, 2002, A macrocyclic ellagitannin trimmer, oenotherin T1, from Oenothera species. Phytochemistry; 59: 191-195.

Vitalone A, Guizzetti M, Costa LG, Tita B, 2003, Extracts of various species of *Epilobium* inhibit proliferation of human prostate cells. J Pharm Pharmacol; 55: 683-90.

Jussiaea repens L.

[After Antoine Laurent de Jussieu, French botanist (1748-1836) and Latin *repens* = having creeping and rooting stems]

Local names:	Water primrose; shui long (China), buang buang (Indonesia), phak pot nam (Thailand), inai pasir (Malaysia), sakot sumbu (North Borneo), agidahano (Papua New Guinea), sigang-dagat (Philippines)
Synonyms:	*Jussiaea adscendens* L., *Jussiaea patibilcensis* Kunth., *Ludwigia adscendens* (L.) Hara, *Ludwigia clavellina* M. Gomez
Description:	It is a perennial herb floating on water found in a geographical area covering India, Nepal, Pakistan, Sri Lanka, Thailand, Malaysia, Indonesia, the Philippines, Papua New Guinea, and Australia. The stem is glabrous, dark red purplish, fleshy, with 1 cm long internodes, and rooting at nodes. The roots are long and fibrous. The leaves are simple, spiral, sessile-like and without stipules. The leaf blade is obovate, spathulate, tapering at the base, round at the apex, 1.5 - 1.7 cm x 0.5 - 0.7 cm, with 6-12 pairs of secondary nerves. The midrib is sunken above and prominent underneath. The flower is axillary. The hypanthium is dark red purplish, long , slender and quadrangular. The calyx comprises 5 green sepals which are lanceolate and about 0.8 cm long. The corolla comprises 5 petals which are cream, yellow at the base, obovate, nerved, emarginated and about 1 cm x 0.8 cm. The androecium consists of 10 stamens which are short. The fruit is an elongated capsule which is about 2 cm long, with dark brown ribs, and containing several tiny seeds (Figure 103).
Medicinal uses:	In China, the plant is used to treat syphilis, rheumatism, pimples, ringworm, and to promote urination. In Taiwan, the plant is used to sooth inflammation. In Cambodia, Laos and Vietnam, it is used to remove ringworm. In Malaysia, the plant is used to treat diseases of the skin. In North Borneo the plant is used as a salad.
Pharmacology:	The plant abounds with phenolic substances, including 2"-4'"-O-n-pentanoyl)-gallate, trifolin 2"-O-gallate, and other flavonoids, some of which have cytotoxic activity against Ehrlich ascites carcinoma cells (Markous *et al.*, 2007) which probably accounts for the antibacterial property measured by Ahmed *et al.* (2005) and the medicinal uses mentioned above. The antiviral and antioxidant properties of this herb are worth further study.

Figure 103: *Jussaeia repens* L.
From: Flora of Malaya. University Kebangsaan Herbarium
Malaysia, Malacca state, Telkom Mass, in rice field, floating on water. Collection: A. Zainuddin
and Hamid Salleh, 4109. Determination: A Zainuddin. Date of collection: 23 January 1992

References: Ahmed F, Selim MS, Shilpi JA, 2005, Antibacterial activity of *Ludwigia adscendens.* Fitoterapia; 76: 473-5.

Marzouk MS, Soliman FM, Shehata IA, Rabee M, Fawzy GA, 2007, Flavonoids and biological activities of *Jussiaea repens.* Nat Prod Res; 21: 436-43.

Ludwigia octovalvis (Jacq.) Raven

[After German botanist Christian Gottlieb Ludwig (1709-1773) and Latin *octovalvis* = with 8 valves]

Local names: Primrose willow; lakom air (Malaysia), cacabean (Indonesia), tayilakton (Philippines), thian nam (Thailand).

Basionym: *Oenothera octovalvis* Jacq. *Enumeratio Systematica Plantarum* 19. 1760

Synonyms: *Jussiaea angustifolia* Lam., *Jussiaea didymosperma* H. Pierrer, *Jussiaea ligustrifolia* Kunth., *Jussiaea linearis* Hochst, *Jussiaea macropoda* C. Presl., *Jussiaea octovalvis* (Jacq.) Sw., *Jussiaea pubescens* L., *Jussiaea suffruticosa* L., *Jussiaea villosa* Lam., *Ludwigia pubescens* L. Hara, *Ludwigia suffruticosa* (L.) M. Gomez, *Oenothera octovalvis* Jacq.

Description: It is a perennial herb found in marshes throughout the tropics of the world. The plant is robust and much branched. The stem is woody, angled, glabrous, longitudinally striated with few lenticels and somewhat minutely winged. The internodes are 3 - 5 cm long. The leaves are simple, alternate, and without stipules. The leaf-blade is 0·6 -14 cm × 0·1 - 4 cm, linear lanceolate with a prominent midrib underneath and about 6 - 8 pairs of secondary nerves. The flower is axillary on a 1.5 cm long pedicel. The hypanthium is 2.2 cm and hirsute. The calyx comprises 4 sepals which are lanceolate, glabrous and about 0.7 x 0.2 cm long. The corolla shows 4 petals which are 3-17 x 2-17 mm, yellow, obovate, nerved and emarginated. The androecium comprises 8 stamens which are short. The fruit is a capsule which is about 2.5 cm long with 8 ribs and contains several tiny globose seeds which are muricate and 0.1 cm in diameter (Figure 104).

Medicinal Uses: In Cambodia, Laos and Vietnam the plant is used to treat dysentery. In Malaysia, the plant is used to treat syphilis. In Indonesia, the plant is used to heal pimples and boils.

Figure 104: *Ludwigia octovalvis* **(Jacq.) Raven**
From: Herbarium of University Kebangsaan. Flora of Borneo
Malaysia, Sabah, Penampang, Kampung Kodunungan in paddy field. Date of collection: 25
December 1989. Collection and identification: Z.H. Harith

Pharmacology:

The general medicinal profile of the plant indicates that it contains antibacterial compounds. The antibacterial property has been validated as an extract inhibited the growth of cariogenic *Streptococcus mutans* (Chen *et al.*, 1989). Chang *et al.*, (2004) isolated oleanane-type triterpenes from the plant, which displayed cytotoxic activity against oral epidermoid carcinoma KB and colorectal carcinoma HT29 cell-lines. Murugesan *et al.* (2000), measured, antidiarrhoeal and antitussive properties. Kuo *et al*, (1999), reported that the plant inhibited human mesangial cell proliferation activated by interleukin-1beta (IL-1beta) and IL-6 and decreased IL-1beta and tumour necrosis factor (TNF-alpha) production. An extract of the plant showed hepatoprotective activity (Yang *et al.*, 1987).

References:

Chang CI, Kuo CC, Chang JY, Kuo YH, 2004, Three new oleanane-type triterpenes from *Ludwigia octovalvis* with cytotoxic activity against two human cancer cell lines. J Nat Prod; 67: 91-3.

Chen CP, Lin CC, Namba T, 1989, Screening of Taiwanese crude drugs for antibacterial activity against *Streptococcus mutans*. J Ethnopharmacol; 27: 285-95.

Kuo YC, Sun CM, Tsai WJ, Ou JC, Chen WP, Lin, CY, 1999, Blocking of cell proliferation, cytokine production and gene expression following administration of Chinese herbs in the human mesangial cells. Life Sc; 64: 2089-99.

Murugesan T, Ghosh L, Mukherjee K, Das J, Pal M, Saha BP, 2000, Evaluation of antidiarrhoeal profile of *Jussiaea suffruticosa* linn. extract in rats. Phytother Res; 14: 381-3.

Yang LL, Yen KY, Kiso Y, Hikino H, 1987, Antihepatotoxic actions of Formosan plant drugs. J Ethnopharmacol; 19: 103-10.

5.Family COMBRETACEAE R. Brown 1810 nom. conserv., the Indian Almond Family

The family Combretaceae consists of 20 genera and about 400 species of tanniferous trees, shrubs or woody climbers which grow in the tropical regions of the world. The leaves are simple, without stipules, opposite, alternate or verticillate. The inflorescences are terminal and axillary racemes, spikes or heads. The flowers are often difficult to see because they are very small, unisexual or bisexual, and epigynous. The calyx consists of 4-8 sepals, on the hypanthium. The corolla consists of 5 small, imbricate or valvate petals. The androecium consists of 4-18 stamens with tetrasporangiate and dithecal anthers opening by long longitudinal slits. The flower is a disk. The gynaecium consists of 2-5 carpels merged in a 1 - locular and inferior ovary containing 2-6 pendulous ovules. The fruits are often winged and indehiscent or almond shaped.

Examples of ornamental Combretaceae are *Quisqualis indica* L. (Rangoon creeper) and *Terminalia cattapa* L. (Indian almond). Note that *Quisqualis indica* L. is a poison. The dried immature fruits of *Terminalia chebula* Retz. (Myrobalan, *British Pharmaceutical Codex*, 1934) are used as a an equivalent of gall as a commercial source of tannins in India. The dried leaves of *Combretum micranthum* (Kinkeliba, *French Pharmacopoeia* 1965), was reputed to be of value in fevers. Other examples of Combretaceae with pharmaceutical usefulness are *Anogeissus latifolia* Wall. (gum *ghatti*), *Combretum butyrosum*, *Terminalia bellirica* Roxb. (*bahera* tree), *Terminalia tomentosa* W. & A. (*asan* wood), and *Terminalia angustifolia* Jacq. (*bois* benzoin). In regards to the pharmacological potential of this family, several phenolic substances with cytotoxic activity have been isolated, and the isolation of a chemotherapeutic and antiviral agent from this family could become soon a reality. De Leo *et al.* (2006) isolated a series of flavonoid glycosides: myricetin 3-O-alpha- L-rhamnopyranoside, myricetin 3-O-beta-D-galactopyranoside, myricetin 3-O-(6"-galloyl)-beta-D-galactopyranoside, myricetin 3-O-beta-D-xylopyranoside, myricetin 3-O-alpha-L-arabinofuranoside; and gallocatechin which exhibited cytotoxic effects against DU-145 human prostate cancer cells. Casuarinin from the bark of *Terminalia arjuna* induces apoptosis and cell cycle arrest in human breast adenocarcinoma MCF-7 cells (Kuo *et al.*, 2005). Arjunic acid from *Terminalia arjuna* abrogated the survival of human oral (KB), ovarian (PA 1) and liver (HepG-2 & WRL-68) cancer cell lines (Saxena *et al.*, 2007). Combretastatin-A4 is a phenolic compound isolated from *Combretum caffrum* (Pettit *et al.*, 1987) which disrupts tubulin polymerization, alters the morphology of endothelial cells and causes vascular shutdown and regression of tumour vasculature (Srivastava *et al.*, 2005). Punicalagin, from *Combretum molle* (R. Br. ex. G. Don.) Engl & Diels and inhibited the replication of HIV-1 (Asres *et al.*, 2005). *Combretum extensum* Roxb. ex G. Don, *Combretum sundaicum* Miq., *Combretum trifoliatum* Vent., *Terminalia bellirica* (Gaertn.) Roxb., *Terminalia calamansanai* (Blco.) Rolfe, and *Terminalia citrina* (Gaertn.) Roxb. are medicinal Combretaceae in the East.

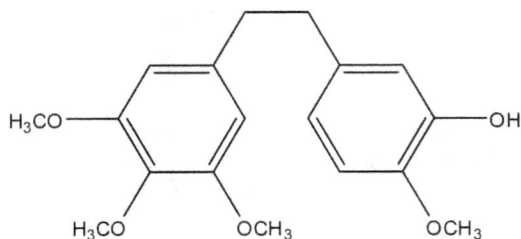

Combretastatin-A4

References:

Asres K, Bucar F, 2005, Anti-HIV activity against immunodeficiency virus type 1 (HIV-I) and type II (HIV-II) of compounds isolated from the stem bark of *Combretum molle*. Ethiop Med J; 43: 15-20.

De Leo M, Braca A, Sanogo R, Cardile V, DeTommasi N, Russo A, 2006, Antiproliferative activity of *Pteleopsis suberosa* leaf extract and its flavonoid components in human prostate carcinoma cells. Planta Med; 72: 604-10.

Kuo PL, Hsu YL, Lin TC, Lin LT, Chang JK, Lin CC, 2005, Casuarinin from the bark of *Terminalia arjuna* induces apoptosis and cell cycle arrest in human breast adenocarcinoma MCF-7 cells. Planta Med; 71: 237-43.

Pettit GR, Cragg GM, Singh SB, 1987, Antineoplastic Agents, 122. Constituents of *Combretum caffrum*. J Nat Prod; 50: 386 - 391.

Saxena M, Faridi U, Mishra R, Gupta MM, Darokar MP, Srivastava SK, Singh D, Luqman S, Khanuja SP, 2007, Cytotoxic agents from *Terminalia arjuna*. Planta Med; 73: 1486-90.

Srivastava V, Negi AS, Kumar JK, Gupta MM, Suman PS, Khanuja SPS, 2005, Plant-the based anticancer molecules: A chemical and biological profile of some important leads. Bioorg Med Chem; 13: 5892-5908.

Combretum extensum Roxb. ex G. Don

[From Latin word *combretum* used by Pliny = climbing plant and *extensum* = stretched out]

Local name:	Kuo ye feng che zi (China)
Synonyms:	*Combretum cyclophyllum* Steud., *Combretum. formosum* Griff., *Combretum. horsfieldii* Miq., *Combretum latifolium* Bl., *Combretum. leucanthum* Van Heurck & Müller Arg., *Combretum macrophyllum* Roxb., *Combretum micropetalum* Llan., *Combretum platyphyllum* Van Heurck & Müller Arg., *Combretum rotundifolium* Roxb., *Combretum wightianum* Wall. ex Wight & Arn. *Embryogonia latifolia* (Bl.) Bl.
Description:	It is a stout woody climber which grows in the forests of India, Sri Lanka, Bangladesh, Burma, Laos, Thailand, Vietnam, China, Malaysia, Indonesia, the Philippines, and New Guinea. The stem is terete, glabrous with a few lenticels. The leaves are simple, opposite and without stipules. The petiole is about 1.5 cm long, stout and flattish above. The leaf-blade is broadly lanceolate, 6 -20 cm × 4 -12 cm, glabrous, acuminate at the apex, and with 4- 8 pairs of secondary nerves. The inflorescence is an axillary, many - flowered, fragrant, comb-like spike which is about 7 cm long. The calyx tube is conical, about 1 cm long, adaxially with a few hairs, and 4 lobes which are triangular. The corolla consists of 4 petals which are about 0.1 cm long, clawed and white. The stamens are exerted. The fruit is glossy, ovoid, 4-winged, about 3 cm long cm, and with a few hairs (Figure 105).
Pharmacology:	Unknown. The plant probably contains combretastatin-like substances or other phenolic substances of chemotherapeutic value.
Medicinal Uses:	The plant is used to invigorate in Cambodia, Laos and Vietnam. In India, it used for the treatment of cancer.

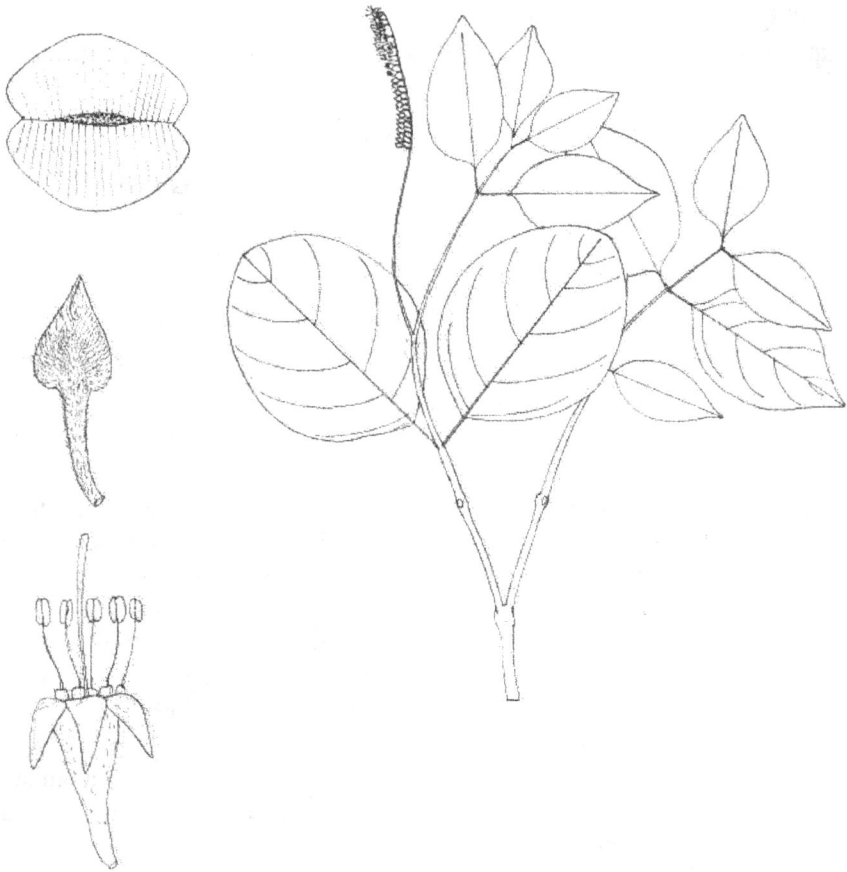

Figure 105: *Combretum extensum* Roxb. ex G. Don

Combretum sundaicum Miq.

[From Latin word *combretum* used by Pliny = climbing plant and *sundaicus* = from Sunda, Indonesia]

Local names:	Lan xing feng che zi *(*China*)*, akar gambir-gambir (Malaysia), sungsung ayer (Indonesia)
Synonym:	*Combretum oliviforme* A.C. Chao
Description:	It is a woody climber which grows in dry sandy open places of Malaysia, Thailand, Vietnam, Malaysia and Indonesia . The plant can be 30 m long with a basal stem of 10 cm in diameter. The bark is thin, smooth, and brown. The stem is terete, about 0.8 cm in diameter, striated longitudinally, peeling in linear flakes, and slightly angled at the apex with tiny circular lenticels. The leaves are simple, opposite and without stipules. The petiole is about 1 cm long. The leaf-blade is broadly elliptic, 5.5 - 11

cm x 2.5 - 5 cm, caudate at the apex, glabrous, with 6-8 pairs of secondary nerves which are sunken above. The inflorescence is terminal and axillary and about 10 cm long. The calyx is hairy and presents 4 lobes which are about 0.2 cm long. The corolla comprises 4 petals which are white, oblong-elliptic and about 0.1 cm long. The androecium includes 8 stamens. The fruit is somewhat heart-shaped, 4-winged, pale light green, developing reddish areas, and about 3 cm long (Figure 106).

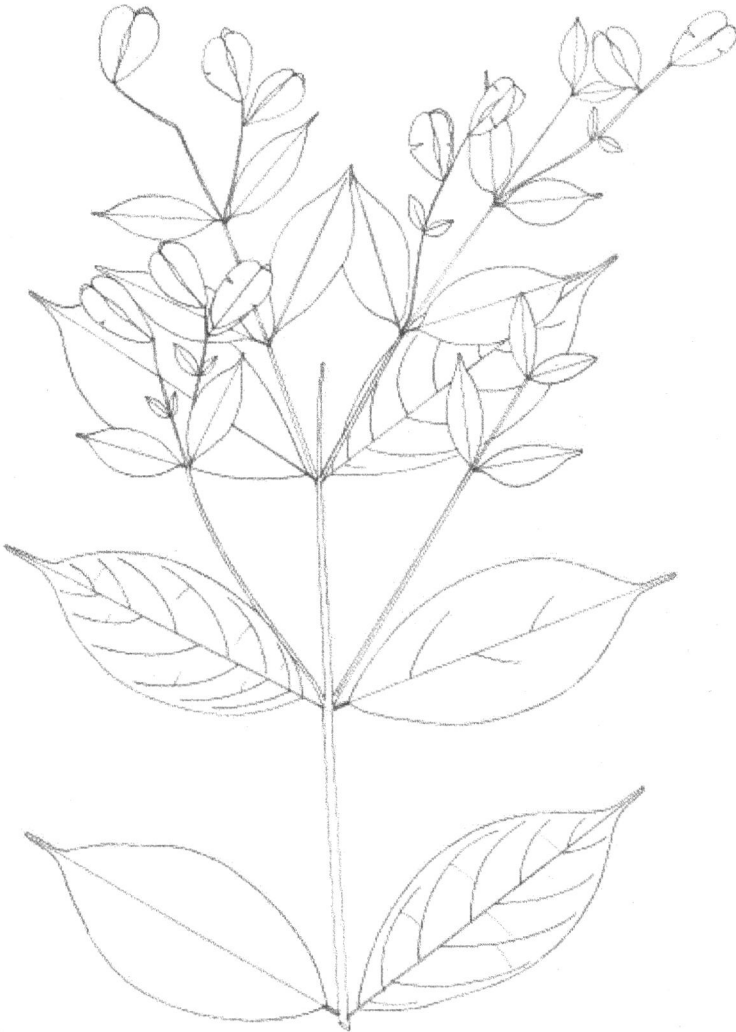

Figure 106: *Combretum sundaicum* **Miq.**
From: Flora of Thailand, Chiang Mai University Herbarium
Thailand, Lampang province, Muang Ban district, Jae Sawn national park, along the dirt road to Bahmiang village. Elevation: 650 m. Date of collection: 28 March 1991. In open rocky alluvial area along the stream in mixed evergreen deciduous forest on shale bedrock. Collection and identification: JF Maxwell N° 96-432

Medicinal uses: In Malaysia the plant is used to treat boils, opium addiction and headaches.

Pharmacology: Unknown. A neuropharmacological study would be worth being performed since the plant may contain opioid derivatives.

Combretum trifoliatum Vent.
[From Latin word *combretum* used by Pliny = climbing plant and *trifoliatum* = with 3 leaves]

Local names: Sonsong harus (Malaysia), tro (Cambodia), ben nam (Laos), .chut (Thailand)

Synonym: *Combretum lucidum* Bl.

Description: It is a scandent shrub which grows in the forests of a geographical area covering Burma, Cambodia, Laos, Vietnam, Thailand, Malaysia, Indonesia, Papua New Guinea and Australia. The stem is terete, longitudinally fissured, peeling, glabrous with internodes which are 5-6 cm long. The leaves are simple, opposite or in whorls of 3, and without stipules. The petiole is short, stout, glabrous, curved and about 0.4 cm long. Some axillary fluffy buds of 0.1 cm in diameter are present. The leaf-blade is coriaceous, glabrous, elliptic, about 3.5 - 5 cm x 12.5 - 15 cm, with a midrib sunken above, and 11-12 pairs of secondary nerves prominent on both surface. The inflorescence is a green axillary and terminal spike which is about 9 cm long. The flower pedicel is hairy and 0.15 cm long. The calyx is light green, cup - shaped, 0.2 cm in diameter, hairy, 5 lobed, the lobes triangular. The androecium comprises 10 stamens which are filamentous. The style is straight and about 0.3 cm long. The fruits are woody, green, 5-winged, like little carambola and about 2.6 x 1 cm (Figure 107).

Medicinal Uses: The plant is used to treat inflammation of the mouth, dysentery, and to check bleeding in Cambodia, Laos and Vietnam. In Malaysia, the fruits are sold to expel worms from the intestines.

Pharmacology: Unknown. The astringency of tannins or other phenolic substances could account for the anti-inflammatory, anti-dysenteric and styptic property of the plant.

Figure 107: *Combretum trifoliatum* Vent.
From: Flora of Thailand, Prince of Songkla University.
Thailand, Pattalung province, Khuan Kanoon district, Ban Talay Noi, near the lake. Elevation: sea level. Date of collection: 16 October 1985. In partly open to mostly shaded thickets near rice field. Collection and identification: JF Maxwell, N° 85-986.

Terminalia bellirica (Gaertn.) Roxb.

[From Latin *terminus* = at the end and from *bellirica* latinization of an Indian or Arabic word]

Local names:	Bastard myrobalan, bedda nuts, beleric myrobalan; balilaj (Arabic), pangan (Burma), bulu (Sri Lanka), behara (India), bamg nut (Vietnam), jelawai (Malaysia), aksha (Sanskrit), akkam (India)
Basionym:	*Myrobalanus bellirica* Gaertn. De Fructibus et Seminibus Plantarum.2: 90. 1791.
Synonyms:	*Myrobalanus bellerica* Gaertn., *Myrobalanus laurinoides* (Teijsm. & Binn.) Kuntze, *Terminalia attenuata* Edgew., *Terminalia belerica* Roxb., *Terminalia eglandulosa* Roxb. ex C.B. Clarke, *Terminalia gella* Dalzell., *Terminalia laurinoides* Teijsm. & Binn., *Terminalia punctata* Roth.
Description:	It is a deciduous tree which grows to a height of 21 m and a diameter of 40 cm at the base. It is common in a geographical area covering India, Burma, Sri Lanka, Cambodia, Laos, Vietnam, Thailand, Malaysia, and Indonesia. The bark is thin, roughly cracked, flaking and brown. The stem is stout, 1 cm in diameter, rough, corky with heart-shaped leaf scars, fissured, cracked, velvety by the apex and slightly angled. The leaves are simple, spiral, at the apex of stems and without stipules. The petiole is slender 4 - 7 x 0.15 cm. The leaf-blade is obovate to spathulate, thinly coriaceous, waxy above, tapering at the base, slightly asymmetrical, 14 - 15 cm x 9 - 10 cm, with 6 - 9 pairs of secondary nerves and tertiary nerves raised underneath. The mature leaf-blades are glabrous and punctuated above. The inflorescence is a dull light green axillary spike which is about 15 cm long. The flower pedicel is ovoid, 0.4 cm and velvety. The calyx is cup - shaped, yellowish, hairy outside, woolly inside, 0.4 cm long, and with 5 triangular lobes. The corolla is absent. The androecium shows 10 conspicuous stamens which are about 0.4 cm long. The fruit is a woody, obscurely 5 - lobed drupe, velvety, with a tiny disc at the apex. The seed is narcotic (Figure 108).
Medicinal uses:	In India, the plant is used to treat inflammation and asthma, eye diseases, fever, piles, hair loss, and to invigorate. It used for tanning. In Burma, the plant is used to treat eye disease. In Cambodia, Laos and Vietnam, the plant is used to invigorate. In Indonesia, the plant is used at childbirth.

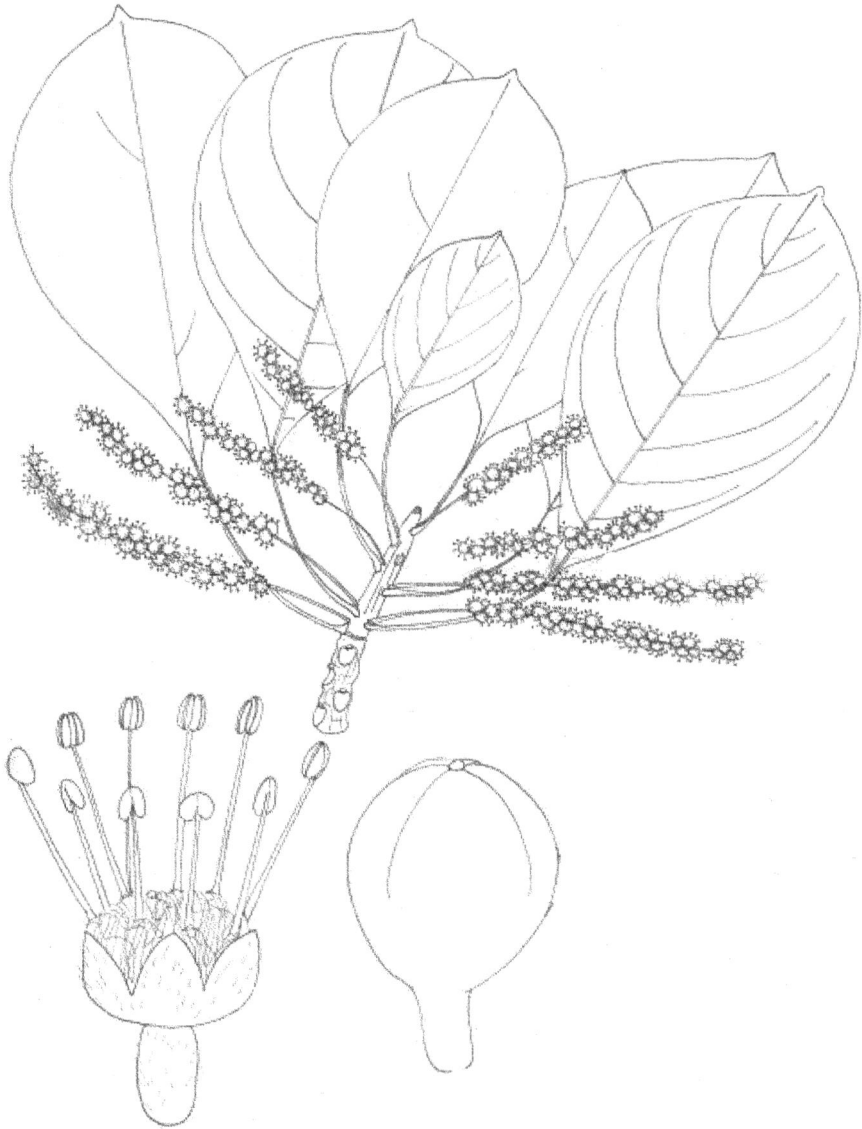

Figure 108: *Terminalia bellirica* **(Gaertn.) Roxb.**
From: Flora of Thailand, Chiang Mai University Herbarium
Thailand, Lampang province, Muang Bahn district, Jae Sawn national park, off the main dirt
road to Bah Miang village. Elevation: 1150 m. Date of collection: 29 March 1996. Collection
and identification: JF Maxwell No 96-451

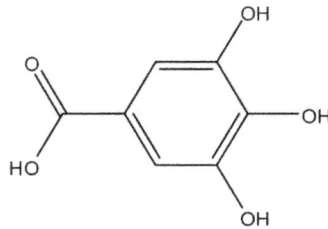

3,4,5-trihydroxy benzoic acid

Pharmacology:	The narcotic property mentioned above has not been validated yet. However, an extract of the plant elicited a significant antidepressant effect in mice using the forced swim test and tail suspension test (Dhingra *et al.*, 2007), suggesting the presence of a neuroactive principle, which is yet to ne isolated. The fruit is an antioxidant (Soubir, 2007) probably due to tannins or other phenolic substances such as gallic acid (3,4,5-trihydroxy benzoic acid) which also exhibited hepatoprotective activity against carbon tetrachloride liver poisoning (Anand *et al.*, 1997). An extract of the plant lowered cholesterol levels in hypercholesterolemic - induced rabbits (Shaila *et al.*, 2007). The anti-asthmatic property is yet to be confirmed.

References:

Anand KK, Singh B, Saxena AK, Chandan BK, Gupta VN, Bhardwaj V, 1997, 3,4,5-Trihydroxy benzoic acid (gallic acid), the hepatoprotective principle in the fruits of *Terminalia belerica*-bioassay guided activity. Pharmacol Res; 36: 315-21.

Dhingra D, Valecha R, 2007, Evaluation of antidepressant-like activity of aqueous and ethanolic extracts of *Terminalia bellirica* Roxb. fruits in mice. Ind J Exp Biol; 45: 610-6.

Shaila HP, Udupa AL, Udupa SL, 1995, Preventive actions of *Terminalia belerica* in experimentally induced atherosclerosis. Int J Cardiol; 49: 101-6.

Soubir T, 2007, Antioxidant activities of some local Bangladeshi fruits (*Artocarpus heterophyllus, Annona squamosa, Terminalia bellirica, Syzygium samarangense, Averrhoa carambola* and *Olea europa*.Sheng Wu Gong Cheng Xue Bao; 23: 257-61.

Terminalia calamansanai (Blco.) Rolfe

[From Latin *terminus* = at the end and from *kalamansanai* = Philippine name of the plant]

Local names: Philippine almond; jelawai mentalun (Malaysia), kalamansanai (Philippines). chugalam (Andamans), leinben (Burma)

Synonyms: *Gimbernatia calamansanai* Blco., *Terminalia bialata* F.-Vill., *Terminalia pyrifolia* (Presl.) Ktze

Description: It is a tree which grows in the Andamans, Burma, Cambodia, Laos, Vietnam, Thailand, Indonesia and the Philippines. The bole is fluted and buttressed. The bark is grey to pale yellow-brown, cracked and flaking. The stem is longitudinally striated, peeling, glabrous, and with conspicuous elliptical leaf-scars. The leaves are simple, alternate and crowded at the ends of stems. The petiole is 1.5 - 2.5 cm long, slender, lenticelled and velvety. The leaf-blade is 7.5 - 10 cm x 2.5 - 3.5 cm, somewhat spathulate, coriaceous, and shows a midrib raised above and 4 - 7 pairs of secondary nerves recurved at margin and raised underneath. The inflorescence is an axillary spike which is velvety and about 12 cm long. The flower is tiny, cream and sessile. The calyx lobes are hairy within. The ovary and calyx are densely pubescent. The fruit is 2 - winged, broad, striate, 5.5 - 10.2 cm x 1.7 - 3.3 cm and pubescent (Figure 109).

Medicinal uses: In the Andamans the bark is used to invigorate the heart. In the Philippines the plant is used as an astringent and lithotritic remedy.

Pharmacology: The plant contains a series of ellagitannins including ellagitannin dimmers calamanin B and C (Tanaka *et al.*, 1991), which account for the astringent property and which might hold cytotoxic and antiviral properties. This plant merits further assessment for cardiotonic and urolithiasic potentials.

Reference: Tanaka T, Morita A, Nonaka GI, Lin TC, Nishioka I, Ho FC, 1991, Tannins and related compounds. CIII isolation and characterization of new monomeric, dimeric, and trimeric ellagitannins, calamansin and calamanins A, B and C from *Terminalia calamasaninai* (Blco.) Rolfe. Chem Pharm Bull; 39: 60-6.

Figure 109: *Terminalia calamansanai* **(Blco.) Rolfe**
From: Flora of Malaya
Malaysia, Perlis state, Kangar, Jalan Batu Pahat. Collection and identification: A Zainuddin *et al*. Date of collection: 24 January 1994

Terminalia citrina (Gaertn.) Roxb.

[From Latin *terminus* = at the end and from *citrina* = lemon-like]

Local names:	Citrine myrobalan; jelawai belang rimau (Malaysia), kyu (Burma), smo (Vietnam)
Synonyms:	*Terminalia arborea* Koord. & Val., *Terminalia comintana* Merr.
Description:	It is a tree which grows throughout a geographical area covering India, Burma, Cambodia, Laos, Vietnam, Malaysia, Indonesia and the Philippines. Tannins can be extracted from the fruits and bark and both yield a blue dye. The tree grows to about 20 m tall and 60 cm in diameter. The bark is smooth and grayish. The stem is terete, about 0.4 cm in diameter, glabrous, fissured, lenticelled, and slightly angled at the apex. The leaves are simple, sub-opposite and without stipules. The petiole is glabrous, 1.2 -1.5 cm long, channelled, and presents a sort of gland near the leaf blade. The leaf-blade is dark green above, 5 - 11 cm x 2 cm, elliptic, coriaceous, glabrous, punctuated above, and with 9 - 11 pairs of secondary nerves. The infructescence axis is brownish. The calyx is 5 lobed, and hairy inside. The fruit is yellowish green almond-shaped, smooth, obscurely 5 -angled and about 4 cm x 1.7 cm (Figure 110).
Medicinal Uses:	In Indonesia and the Philippines, the plant is used for digestive ailments. In India, the plant is used for diarrhoea, inflamed throat, asthma, and sores.
Pharmacology:	The plant produces tannins which probably account for the antidiarrhoeal, anti-inflammatory and healing property mentioned above. The fruit abound with tannins such as corilagin, 1,3,6-tri-O-galloyl-beta-D-glucopyranose, chebulagic acid, and 1,2,3,4,6-penta-O-galloyl-beta-D-glucopyranose and punicalagin, the latter being antibacterial (Burapadaja *et al.*, 1995). Tannins and other phenolics could account for inhibition of Heinz body induction and antioxidant activity reported by Palasuwan *et al*, (2005) and the anti HSV-1 activity reported by Akanitapichat *et al.* (2002).
References:	Akanitapichat P, Kurokawa M, Tewtrakul S, Pramyothin P, Sripandidkulchai B, Shiraki K, Hattori M, 2002, Inhibitory activities of Thai medicinal plants against herpes simplex type 1, poliovirus type 1, and measles virus. J Trad Med; 19: 174-80. Burapadaja S, Bunchoo A, 1995, Antimicrobial activity of tannins from *Terminalia citrina*. Planta Med; 61: 365-6.

Palasuwan A, Soogarun S, Lertlum T, Pradniwat P, Wiwanitkit V, 2005, Inhibition of Heinz body induction in an *in vitro* model and total antioxidant activity of medicinal Thai plants. Asian Pac J Cancer Prev; 6: 458-63.

Figure 110: *Terminalia citrina* **(Gaertn.) Roxb.**
From: Flora of Thailand, prince of Songkla University Herbarium
Thailand, Songkla province, Haad Yai district, Ko Hong Hill, southeast side, at the reservoir.
Elevation: 25 m. Date of collection: 27 December 1985. In shaded place, secondary forest.
Collection and identification: JF Maxwell N° 85-1174

D. Order RHIZOPHORALES Van Tieghem & Constantin 1918

The Order consists only of the family Rhizophoraceae.

1.Family RHIZOPHORACEAE R. Brown in Flindlers 1814 nom. Conserv., the Red Mangrove Family

The Family Rhizophoraceae consists of 14 genera and about 100 species of heavily tanniferous trees widely distributed in tropical regions either growing in mangroves or inland. Most species belong to the genus *Cassipourea*. Common secondary metabolites found in this family are ellagic acid, proanthocyanidins, pyrrolidine, pyrrolizidine, and tropane alkaloids. Kaurane and pimmarane, beyerane diterpenes and triterpenes are also present. The leaves are simple, entire, opposite and stipulate. The flowers are solitary or in cymes, and actinomorphic. The perianth comprises 4 - 5 or more sepals and petals, valvate and fleshy. The stamens are 2, 3 or 5 times as numerous as the petals. A nectary disk is present. The anthers are tetrasporangiate, bilocular and dithecal. The gynoecium comprises 2 - 6 carpels united to form a compound ovary with as many locules as carpels. Each locule contains 2 ovules attached to apical-axillary placentas. The fruits are capsular, baccate, with 1 or few seeds.

To date the Rhizophoraceae represents an interesting field of pharmacological research since antiradical, cytotoxic and even anti-HIV activities have been observed in members of this family. Phuwapraisirisan *et al* (2006), fractionated the bark of *Carallia brachiata* using an antioxidant-based assay. They isolated the trimeric proanthocyanidin, carallidin, along with mahuannin A, both of which exhibited xanthine oxidase *in vitro* and strong antiradical activity. Antiradical properties were also observed with 3,7-O-diacetyl (-)-epicatechin, 3-O-acetyl (-)-epicatechin, 3,3',4',5,7-O-pentaacetyl (-)-epicatechin , (+)-afzelechin, (+)-catechin, cinchonain Ib, and proanthocyanidin B2 isolated from *Rhizophora stylosa* (Li *et al*, 2007).

Diterpenes cassipourol and cassipouryl acetate from *Cassipourea madagascariensis* inhibited the growth of A2780 human ovarian cancer cells cultured *in vitro* (Chaturvedula *et al.*, 2006). Premanathan *et al* (1996, 1999), showed that extracts of mangrove Rhizophoraceae protected MT-4 cells against HIV virus adsorption. Further investigation resulted in the isolation and characterization of a polysaccharide from the leaf of *Rhizophora apiculata*. This polysaccharide inhibited HIV-1 or HIV-2 strains in different cell cultures and completely blocked the binding of HIV-1 virions to MT-4 cells.

Southeast Asian traditional medicine uses *Rhizophora mucronata* Lamk., *Rhizophora apiculata* Bl. (*Rhizophora candelaria* DC.), *Anisophyllea disticha* (Jack) Baill., *Carallia brachiata* (Lour.) Merr. (*Carallia integerrima* DC, *Carallia lucida* Roxb.) *Carallia suffruticosa* Ridl., *Ceriops tagal* (Perr.) C. B. Rob., *Bruguiera gymnorrhiza* (L.) Lamk.

(*Bruguiera conjugata* Merr.), *Bruguiera sexangula* (Lour.) Poir. (*Bruguiera eriopetata* W. & A. Arn.) and *Gynotroches axillaris* Bl. These are often used as astringent remedies. Bboth *Ceriops decandra (Griffith) Ding Hou* and *Ceriops tagal* (Perr.) C. B. Rob are also used as a source of black dye for the making of batik.

References: Chaturvedula VS, Norris A, Miller JS, Ratovoson F, Andriantsiferana R, Rasamison VE, Kingston DG, 2006, Cytotoxic diterpenes from *Cassipourea madagascariensis* from the Madagascar rainforest. J Nat Prod; 69: 287-9.

Li DL, Li XM, Peng ZY, Wang BG, 2007, Flavanol derivatives from *Rhizophora stylosa* and their DPPH radical scavenging activity. Molecules; 12: 1163-9.

Premanathan M, Nakashima H, Kathiresan K, Rajendran N, Yamamoto N, 1996, *In vitro* anti human immunodeficiency virus activity of mangrove plants. Indian J Med Res; 103: 278-81.

Mariappan Premanathan M, Arakaki R, Izumi H, Kathiresan K, Nakano M, Yamamoto N, Nakashima H, 1999, Antiviral properties of a mangrove plant, *Rhizophora apiculata* Bl., against human immunodeficiency virus. Antiviral Research; 44: 113-122

Phuwapraisirisan P, Sowanthip P, Miles DH, Tip-pyang S, 2006, Reactive radical scavenging and xanthine oxidase inhibition of proanthocyanidins from *Carallia brachiata*. Phytotherapy Research; 20: 458 – 461.

Bruguiera gymnorhiza (L.) Lamk.

[After Jean Guillaume Bruguière (1750-1798), botanical artist and plant collector, and from Greek *gymnos* =naked and Latin *rhiza* = root]

Local name: Black mangrove, mu lan (China), prasak tooch (Cambodia), bakauan (Philippines), putut (Indonesia), bakau besar (Malaysia), mangoro (Papua New Guinea), pang ka h¹a sum (Thailand), vet den (Vietnam)

Basionym: *Rhizophora gymnorhiza* L. Species *Plantarum* 1: 443. 1753.

Synonym: *Bruguiera capensis* Bl., *Bruguiera conjugata* (L.) Merrill; *Bruguieria eriopetala* Wight & Arn., *Bruguiera gymnorhiza* (L.) Savigny , *Bruguieria rhedii* Tul, *Bruguieria rhedii* Bl., *Bruguieria rumphii* Bl., *Bruguieria wightii* Bl., *Bruguieria zippelii* Bl., *Rhizophora conjugata* L., *Rhizophora gymnorhiza* L. *Rhizophora palun* DC., *Rhizophora tinctoria* Blco.

Description: It is a tree of the coastal sea mangrove ranging from East Africa to North Australia including Taiwan, Cambodia, India, Indonesia, Japan, Malaysia, Burma, the Philippines, Sri Lanka, Thailand, Vietnam; and India. The tree grows up to 20 m tall with a girth of 60 cm. The bark is gray, deeply fissured. The stem is glabrous, smooth, articulate, somewhatw angled and 0.5 cm in diameter. The internodes are about 3.5 cm long. The leaves are simple, opposite and stipulate. The stipules are often reddish, 4 cm, interpetiolar, and caducous. The petiole is channelled, 3 - 5 cm long, about 0.2 cm in diameter and longitudinally striated. The leaf blade is 20 - 16 cm x 4.5 - 5.6 cm, leathery, elliptic - lanceolate, acute at the base and the apex, with 11-12 pairs of inconspicuous secondary nerves looping at the margin which is discretely wavy. The margin of the leaf blade is recurved. The inflorescences are axillary, terminal and solitary on a 1.5 cm long pedicel. The flowers are reddish and about 3 cm long. The calyx is reddish, about 4 cm long, with 10-14 linear, 1.5-2 cm lobes which are glabrous. The corolla comprises 12 -14 petals of about 1.5 cm long, fringed with white silky hairs at the margin. The stamens are twice as many as petals, with linear anthers. The disk is cup-shaped. The stigma presents 3-4 lobes. The fruits are ribbed, cigar-shaped, and 15 cm x 1.4 cm. the calyx in fruit is about 4.5 cm long, the lobes being 2 cm x 0.2 cm (Figure 111).

Medicinal Uses: In Cambodia, Laos and Vietnam the bark is boiled to make a drink taken to treat diarrhoea and fever. A dark brown dye is obtained from the bark.

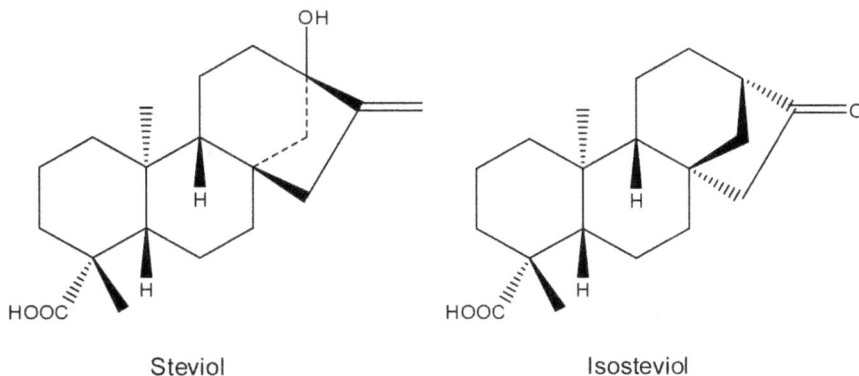

Steviol   Isosteviol

Pharmacology: *Bruguiera gymnorrhiza* is known to elaborate a series of ent-kaurane, ent-beyerane and pimarene diterpenes (Subrahmanyam *et al*, 1999; Han *et al.*, 2004), that are worth exhaustive investigation for pharmacology. Pimmarene diterpene (5R, 9S, 10R, 13S, 15S)-ent-8(14)-pimarene-1-oxo-15R,16-diol showed some levels of cytotoxicity against L-929 cell lines (Han *et al.*, 2005). One such diterpene is steviol, the aglycone of stevioside which tastes about 300 times sweeter than sucrose and is used as sweetener in several countries. Isosteviol (*ent*-16-ketobeyeran-19-oic acid) inhibited DNA replication and prevented the growth of human cancer cells, and caused a marked reduction in TPA (12-*O*-tetradecanoylphorbol-13-acetate)-induced inflammation in rodents.

Figure 111: *Bruguiera gymnorhiza* (L.) Lamk.
From: Flora of Malaya.
Malaysia, Johor State, Mersing, Pulau Tinggi, Kampung Pinang. 18° North, 104 °7· East. Sea level on volcanic mangrove. Determination: A. Zainuddin, December 1995. Date of collection: 7 November 1995.

References: Han L, Huang X, Sattler I, Dahse HM, Fu H, Lin W, Grabley S, 2004, New diterpenoids from the marine mangrove Bruguiera gymnorrhiza. J Nat Prod; 67: 1620-3.

Han L, Huang X, Sattler I, Dahse HM, Fu H, Grabley S, Lin W, 2005, Three new pimarene diterpenoids from marine mangrove plant, *Bruguiera gymnorrhiza*. Pharmazie; 60: 705-7.

Mizushina Y, Akihisa T, Ukiya M, Hamasaki Y, Murakami-Naka Ci, Kuriyama I, Takeuchi T, Sugawara F, Yoshida H, 2005, Structural analysis of isosteviol and related compounds as DNA polymerase and DNA topoisomerase inhibitors. Life Sc; 77: 2127-2140.

Subrahmanyam C, Venkateswara BV, Ward RS, Hursthouse MB, Hibbs DE, 1999, Diterpenes from the marine mangrove *Bruguiera gymnorhiza* Phytochemistry; 51: 83-90.

E. Order EUPHORBIALES Lindley 1833

The order Euphorbiales consists of 4 families and about 8,000 species of trees, shrubs, herbs and climbers, most of which belong to the family Euphorbiaceae.

1. Family EUPHORBIACEAE A.L. de Jussieu 1789, the Spurge Family

The family Euphorbiaceae consists of 300 genera and about 7,500 species of plants of diverse vegetative and chemical features. These are trees, shrubs, herbs, climbers or even cactus - shaped plants, often exuding a milky poisonous latex, and known to produce hydrolysable tannins, ellagitannins, proanthocyanins, various sorts of phenolic compounds and terpenes, cyanogen glycosides, as well as aporphine, pyridine, indole, and tropane type alkaloids. The leaves are simple or compound, alternate and may or may not be stipulate. The inflorecences are diverse. The flowers are small and male or female. The perianth comprises 5 tepals which are distinct or connate and often much reduced. The androecium consists of 5 or more stamens which are tetrasporangiate, dithecal, and open by longitudinal slits. A disc is present. The gynaecium consists of 3 carpels merged into a compound and 3 - locular ovary with 3 distinct styles, each lodge containing 1- 2 ovules. The fruits are characteristic dehiscent trilobed capsules.

Examples of Euphorbiaceae are *Hevea brasiliensis* Muell. Arg. (Hevea rubber). tapioca (*Manihot esculenta* Crantz), and *Ricinus communis* L. which provide castor oil, which has been used since a remote period of time to relieve constipation and is used in industry. Several members in this family, like *Excoecaria oppositifolia*, are toxic on account of complex diterpenoid esters of the tigliane, ingenane or daphnane-type which cause anaphylactic reactions and promote skin tumours. One such compound is 12 - *O* - tetradecanoylphorbol - 13 - acetate. Other toxic principles are proteins (phytoxins), such as curcin from *Jatropha curcas*, and ricin from *Ricinus communis* L. The oil expressed from the seeds of *Croton tiglium* (Croton Oil, *British Pharmaceutical Codex*, 1949) has been used as a purgative and externally as a counter-irritant. Of recent pharmaceutical interest in this family is the isolation of cytotoxic principles including jatrophane polyesters (Duarte *et al*, 2008), abietane diterpenes (Lee *et al*, 2008), triterpenes (Tanaka *et al.*, 2006), and stilbene flavonoids (Yoder, *et al.*, 2007). Hippomanin A from *Phyllanthus urinaria* inhibited HSV-2 infection *in vitro* (Yang *et al.*, 2007).

References: Duarte N, Lage H, Ferreira MJ, 2008, Three new jatrophane polyesters and antiproliferative constituents from *Euphorbia tuckeyana*. Planta Med; 74: 61-8.

Lee CL, Chang FR, Hsieh PW, Chiang MY, Wu CC, Huang ZY, Lan YH, Chen M, Lee KH, Yen HF, Hung WC, Wu YC, 2008, Cytotoxic ent-abietane diterpenes from *Gelonium aequoreum*. Phytochemistry; 69: 276-87.

Tanaka R, Wada S, Yamada T, Yamori T, 2006, Potent antitumor activity of 3,4-seco-8betaH-Ferna-4(23),9(11)-dien-3-oic acid (EC-2) and 3,4-seco-Oleana-4(23),18-dien-3-oic acid (EC-4), evaluated by an *in vitro* human cancer cell line panel. Planta Med; 72: 1347-9.

Yang CM, Cheng HY, Lin TC, Chiang LC, Lin CC, 2007, Hippomanin A from acetone extract of Phyllanthus urinaria inhibited HSV-2 but not HSV-1 infection *in vitro*. Phytother Res; 21: 1182-6.

Yoder BJ, Cao S, Norris A, Miller JS, Ratovoson F, Razafitsalama J, Andriantsiferana R, Rasamison VE, Kingston DG, 2007, Antiproliferative prenylated stilbenes and flavonoids from *Macaranga alnifolia* from the Madagascar rainforest. J Nat Prod; 70: 342-6.

Elateriospermum tapos Bl.

[From Greek *elaterios* = driving and *sperma* = seed and *tapos*, a Sundanese plant name]

Local names:	Perah (Malaysia), pra (Thailand)
Synonym:	*Elateriospermum rhizophorum* Boerl. & Koord.
Description:	It is a timber tree which grows in the forests of Thailand, Malaysia and Indonesia. The plant can reach up to 30 m tall, with a grey bark which is scaly. A copious white latex is present. The stem is terete, with showy circular leaf-scar, glabrous, and fissured longitudinally. The leaves are simple and spiral. The petiole is 3 - 5 cm long, kneeled near the base, slender, glabrous, channelled and with a pair of 0.8 cm circular gland by the apex. The leaf-blade is oblong, bright red at first, 8.8 - 19 cm x 2.3 - 5.5 cm, glabrous, glossy above, with 10 - 18 pairs of secondary nerves looping at margin. The inflorescence is axillary cyme which is 8 - 10 cm long and cream. The male flower is 0.2 cm across with 4- 6 sepals and 10 -20 stamens. The female flower is 0.5 cm across with 6 sepals, with a 2-4 lobed ovary and 3 broad stigmas. The fruit is oblong, 3-lobed, bony-woody capsule, 5 - 6.3 cm long, brownish-pink with 4 cm long oily seeds which are poisonous fresh but are edible after roasting or boiling (Figure 112).
Medicinal Uses:	In Indonesia the sap is used is used to heal putrefied wounds.

Figure 112: *Elateriospermum tapos* Bl.

From: Flora of Malaya
Malaysia, Terengganu state, Dungun, Kg Jerangau village area. Collection and determination:
A Zainuddin. Date of collection: 18 May 1992.

Pharmacology: The plant contains a series of taraxerane triterpenes, including 2,3-seco-taraxer-14-ene-2,3,28-trioic acid 2,3-dimethyl ester which was cytotoxic against NCI-H187 and BC cell lines and also showed *in vitro* antimycobacterial activity against *Mycobacterium tuberculosis.*(Pattamadilok *et al.*, 2008).

Reference: Pattamadilok D, Suttisri R, 2008, Seco-terpenoids and other constituents from *Elateriospermum tapos*. J Nat Prod; 71: 292-4.

Excoecaria cochinchinensis Lour.

[From Latin *excoecare* = to deprive of sight and *cochinchinensis* = from Cochinchina]

Local names:	Chinese croton, buta (Malaysia), ka buea (Thailand), don mat troi (Vietnam), daun sambang darah (Indonesia).
Synonym:	*Excoecaria bicolor* (Hassk.) Zoll. ex Hassk., *Excoecaria orientalis* Pax & Hoffm., *Sapium cochinchinense* (Lour.) Kuntze
Description:	It is a shrub that grows along streams and disturbed places in Burma, Thailand, Malaysia, Cambodia, Laos, Vietnam, and China. The plant is native to Indochina and has spread out to Southeast Asia as an ornament for gardens. The bark is grey and fissured. The sap is highly irritating. The stem is terete, fissured, warty and angled at the base. The leaves are simple, opposite or sub-opposite. The stipule is ovate and 0.1 cm long. The petiole is 0.3 - 0.8 cm long and glabrous. The leaf-blade is asymmetrical, elliptic, 5.2 - 12.5 cm x 2 - 3.4 cm, with 6-10 pairs of secondary nerves, a midrib sunken above, serrate, attenuate at the base, acuminate at the apex, and purplish-red underneath. The inflorescence is an axillary spike which is about 3 cm long. The calyx comprises 3 sepals which are light greenish. The 3 anthers are cream colored and tiny and the filaments are white. The ovary comprises 3 minute styles fused at the base. The fruit is a 3-lobed capsule which is 1 cm in diameter with brownish seeds (Figure 113).
Medicinal Uses:	In Indonesia, the plant is used to check gynecological bleeding. In Thailand, the plant is used to stimulate the uterus. In Cambodia, Laos and Vietnam, the plant is used to treat skin diseases.
Pharmacology:	The irritating property of the plant is due to a series of diterpenes of tigliane, ingenane or daphnane type. Other constituents are megastigmane glucosides: excoecariosides A and B (Giang *et al.*, 2005). An aqueous extract of the plant exhibited a strong antibacterial activity against clindamycin resistant *Staphylococcus aureus* (P31 and Fl14) isolated from patients (Leelapornpisid *et al.*, 2005). An extract of the plant also displayed potent cytotoxic effects *in vitro* (Park *et al.*, 2005).
References:	Giang PM, Son PT, Matsunami K, Otsuka H, 2005, New megastigmane glucosides from *Excoecaria cochinchinensis* LOUR. var. *cochinchinensis*. Chem Pharm Bull; 53: 1600-3.
	Leelapornpisid P, Chansakao S, Ittiwittayawat T, Pruksakorn S, 2005, Antimicrobial activity of herba; extracts on *Staphylococcus aureus* and *Propionibacterum acnes*. In III WOCMAP Congress on Medicinal and Aromatic Plants - Volume 5: Quality, Efficacy, Safety, Processing and Trade in Medicinal and Aromatic Plants.

Park Glee EJ ,Min HY, Choi HY, Han AR, Lee SK, Seo EK, 2002, Evaluation of Cytotoxic Potential of Indonesian Medicinal Plants in Cultured Human Cancer Cells. Nat Produ Sci; 8: 165-69.

Figure 113: *Excoecaria cochinchinensis* **Lour.**
From: Flora of Thailand, prince of Songkla University.
Thailand, Pattani province, Koke Po district. Elevation: 50 m. Date of collection: 3 June 1985. In shaded, disturbed place along a stream, primary evergreen forest. Collection and identification: JF Maxwell No 85-561

Glochidion eriocarpum Champ. ex Benth.

[From Greek *glochin* = a point and *erio* = woolly and *carpum* = fruit]

Local names:	Ubah (Malaysia), khrai mot (Thailand), mao guo suan pan zi (China)
Synonyms:	*Diasperus anamiticus* Kuntze, *Diasperus eriocarpus* (Champ. ex Benth.) Kuntze, *Diasperus villicaulis* (Hook.f.) Kuntze, *Glochidion anamiticum* Kuntze, *Glochidion annamense* Beille, *Glochidion esquirolii* Lévl, *Glochidion vilicaule* Hook.f., *Phyllanthus eriocarpus* (Champ.) Müll.Arg.
Description:	It is a small tree which grows up to 5 m tall in the open lands and waste areas of Thailand, Cambodia, Laos, Vietnam, Taiwan, Indonesia and the Philippines. The bark is thickened, roughly vertically ridged, and brown. The stem is terete, longitudinally striated, and angled and velvety at the apex. The leaves are simple, alternate and stipulate. The stipule is triangular, up to 0.4 cm long, and caducous. The petiole is 0.3 cm long and hairy. The leaf-blade is dark green above, 7.2 - 10.8 cm x 4.7 - 5.2 cm, coriaceous, asymmetrical, broadly elliptic, acuminate at the apex. It is hairy underneath, glabrous above except for the midrib, with 5 - 7 pairs of secondary nerves. The inflorescence is an axillary pedicel which is 2 - 5 cm long. The flower is minute, greenish-yellow fragrant with 6 light yellow oblong sepals which are 0.2 - 0.3 cm long. The male flower shows 3 stamens with grayish anthers. The female flower exhibits a 4 - 5 lobed ovary which is hairy, and about 0.2 cm long. The fruit is a 3 lobed capsule which is pilose, and contains 6 seeds which are triangular and orange - red (Figure 114).
Medicinal Uses:	In China, the plant is used for urticaria, eczema, toothache, dysentery, excessive bleeding of the uterus and colic.
Pharmacology:	The plant contains lupane triterpenes, of which glochidonol, glochidiol exhibited a strong inhibitory effect against MCF-7, NCI-H-460 cancer cell lines via apoptosis (Puapairoj *et al.*, 2005). The medicinal uses is probably due to tannins such as gallic acid
References:	Hui WH, Li MM, 1976, Lupene triterpenoids from *Glochidion eriocarpum*. Phytochemistry; 15: 561-562.
	Puapairoj P, Naengchomnong W, Kijjoa A, Pinto MM, Pedro M, Nascimento MS, Silva AM, Herz W, 2005, Cytotoxic activity of lupane-type triterpenes from *Glochidion sphaerogynum* and

Glochidion eriocarpum two of which induce apoptosis. Planta Med; 71: 208-13.

Figure 114: *Glochidion eriocarpum* **Champ. ex Benth.**
From: Flora of Thailand, Chiang Mai University Herbarium
Thailand, Chiang Mai, Chiang Dao district, Doi Chiang Dao animal sanctuary, Southwest side between Bah Chia and Huay Mae Gawk stations. Elevation: 1325 m. Date of collection: 9 September 1995. In open disturbed, fire damaged area in mixed, seasonal evergreen hardwood and pine forest on granite bedrock. Collection and identification: JF Maxwell N° 95612

Glochidion obscurum (Roxb. ex Willd.) Bl.

[From Greek *glochin* = a point and Latin *obscurum* = indistinct]

Local name: Khram (Thailand), dempoel lelet (Indonesia)

Basionym: *Phyllanthus obscurus* Roxb. ex Willd. Species *Plantarum. Editio quarta* 4: 581. 1805

Synonyms: *Glochidion roxburghianum* Müll.Arg, *Phyllanthus obscurus* Roxb. ex Willd

Description: It is a small tree which grows up to 5 m tall in open forests of Cambodia, Laos, Vietnam, Thailand, Malaysia, and Indonesia. The bark is cracked, flaking and grey brown. The stem is terete, hairy with few lenticels. The leaves are simple, alternate, and stipulate. The stipule is triangular and up to 0.15 cm long. The petiole is 0.3 cm long and hairy. The leaf-blade is thinly coriaceous, lanceolate, asymmetrical, glabrous above except for the midrib. It is subglabrous underneath, 5 - 2.5 cm x 2.2 - 0.7 cm, with 5 - 8 pairs of secondary nerves recurved at the margin. The flower is axillary, minute on a 0.3 cm pedicel. The corolla comprises 6 yellow sepals which are elliptic, hairy and about 0.1 - 0.2 cm long. The male flower shows 4-5 stamens with light green anthers. The female flower presents a 6 angled ovary which is about 0.6 cm long. The fruit pedicel is 1.2 - 1.3 cm long. The fruit is globose, yellowish-green, 0.8 - 1 cm across with a 0.2 cm long tube at the apex, with tiny sharp-lobes and contains 5 seeds which are about 0.4 cm long and red (Figure 115).

Medicinal Uses: In Indonesia, the plant is used to treat dysentery. In Malaysia, it is used to treat diarrhoea, and stomachache

Pharmacology: The plant has not been explored yet for pharmacology.

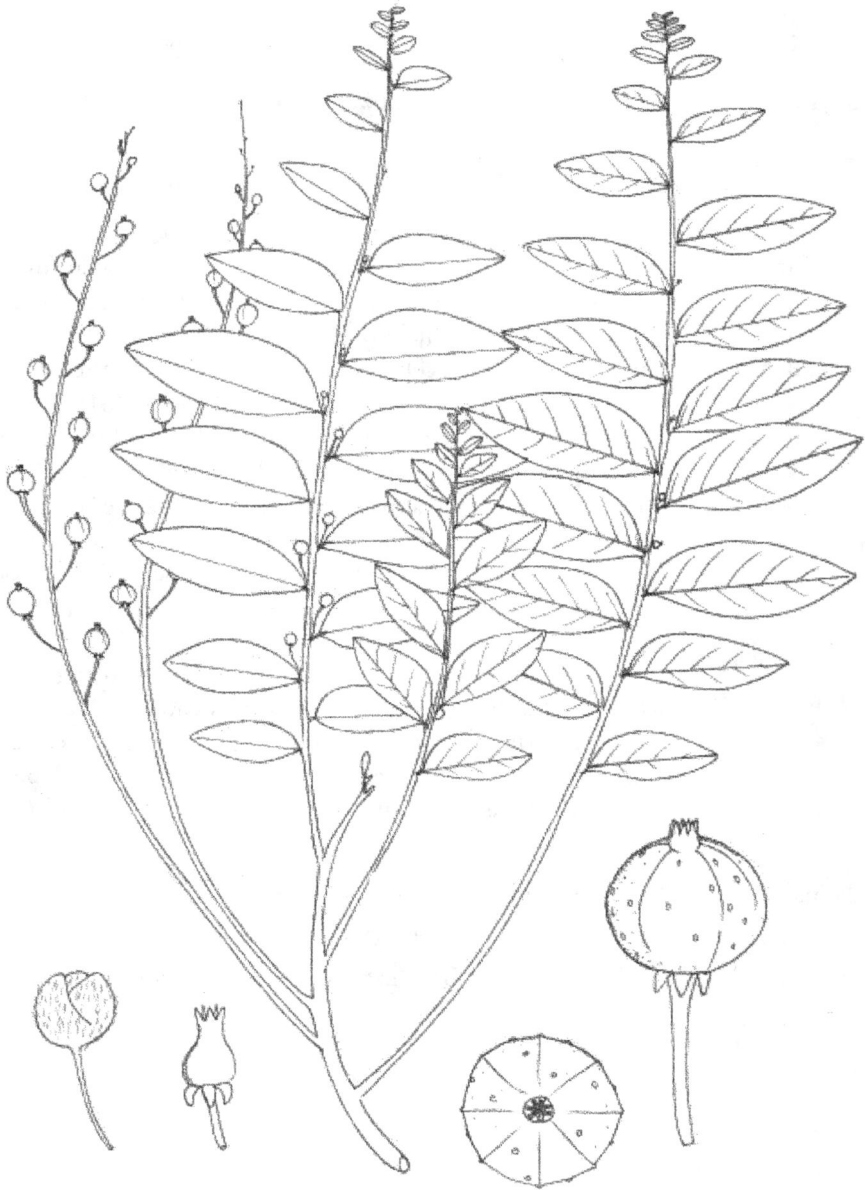

Figure 115: *Glochidion obscurum* **(Roxb. ex Willd.) Bl.**
From: Flora of Malaya № 00146
Malaysia, Jalan Rawang, Kluang. Elevation: 60 m. Collection and identification: Mohd Kassim

Glochidion sericeum (Bl.) Zoll. & Moritzi
[From Greek *glochin* = a point and Latin *sericeum* = silky]

Local names: Khrai tai (Thailand), nyam (Indonesia)

Basionym: *Glochidionopsis sericea* Bl. *Bijdragen tot de flora van Nederlandsch Indië* 588. 1826.

Synonym: *Glochidionopsis sericea* Bl.

Description: This is a shrub or small tree up to 5 m tall found in Thailand, Malaysia, Indonesia and the Philippines. The plant grows in disturbed areas, open forest and waste lands. The stem is velvety, slightly angled, zigzag shaped, with 1 cm long internodes. The leaves are simple, alternate and stipulate. The stipule is broadly triangular, to 0.2 cm long and silky. The petiole is hairy and 0.2 cm long. The leaf-blade is lanceolate, membranaceous, 3.5 - 6 cm x 1.3 - 2.2 cm with 5 - 8 pairs of secondary nerves, acute at the apex and hairy below. The inflorescence is an axillary fascicule. The male flower shows 6 sepals which are about 0.2 cm long and 3 stamens. The female flower has a pair of sepals which are about 0.2 cm long, and a 3 - locular ovary which is about 0.3 cm long. The fruit is a red, silky, 5-lobed capsule, containing 10 seeds which are glossy, red, triangular, leathery and microscopically muricate (Figure 116).

Medicinal Uses: In Malaysia, the plant is used to expel worms.

Pharmacology: Unknown

Glochidion wallichianum Müll. Arg.
[From Greek *glochin* = a point and after botanist Nathaniel Wallich (1786-1854)]

Local name: Man pu (Thailand)

Synonyms: *Glochidion curtisii* Hook.f., *Glochidion desmocarpum* Hook.f., *Phyllanthus wallichianus* (Müll.Arg.) Müll.Arg.,

Description: It is a tree which grows up to 15 m tall in Thailand, the Malay Peninsula and Indonesia. The stem is terete, fissured, lenticelled, zigzag-shaped, and velvety at the apex. The stipule is triangular, and 0.1 cm long. The petiole is hairy and 0.2 cm long. The blade is dark green above, lanceolate, papery, 9.5 - 4.9 cm x 4.5 - 2.5 cm, velvety below, and with 5 -6 pairs of secondary nerves

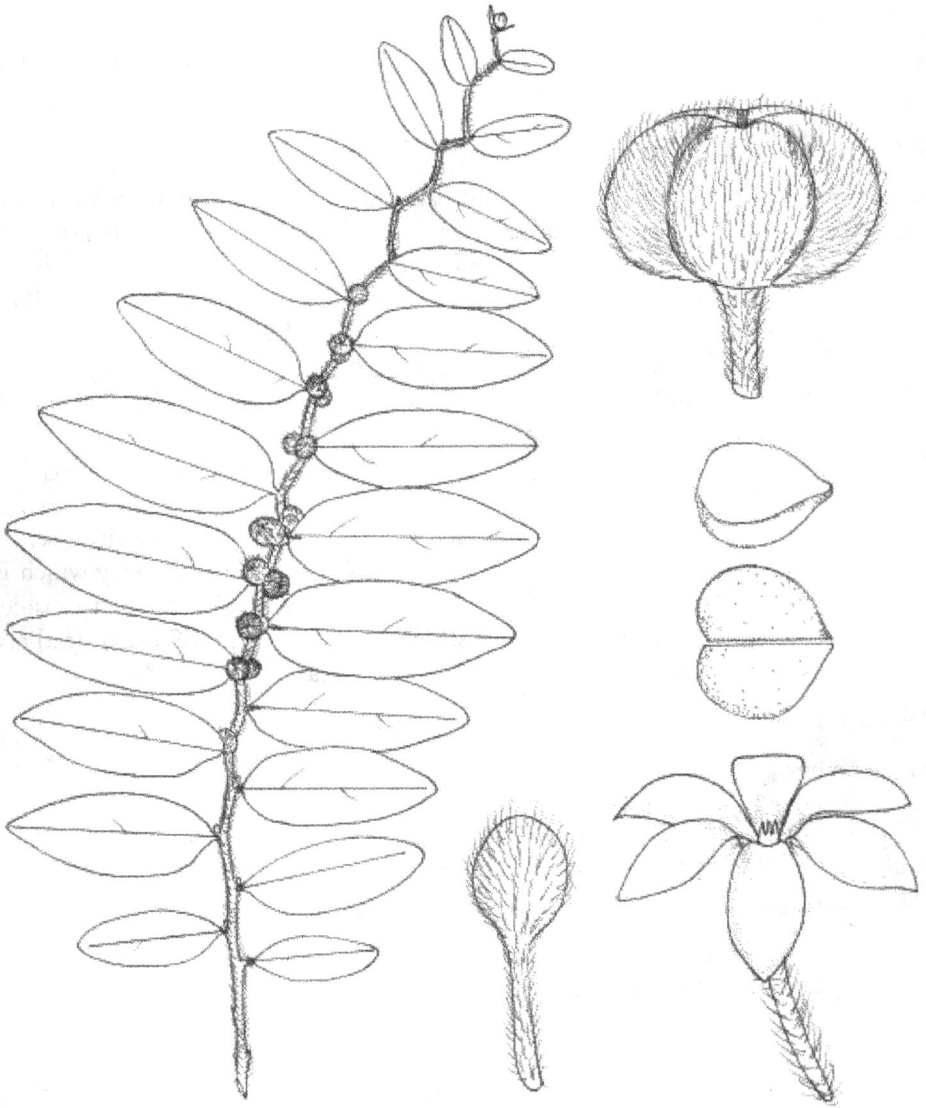

Figure 116: *Glochidion sericeum* **(Bl.) Zoll. & Moritzi**
From: Herbarium of University Kebangsaan Malaysia
Malaysia, Kelantan, Jeli, Upper Sungai, Peangau, on weathered granite. Collection: Abdul Latiff
et al., ALM 1808. Date of collection: 25 September 1986. Determination: A. Zainuddin

looping at the margin. The inflorescence is an axillary fascicule of tiny whitish - green flowers. The flower presents 6 elliptic sepals which are about 0.8 cm long. The male flowers include 3 stamens. The female flower presents a 3 locular ovary which is about 0.9 cm long. The fruit pedicel is 0.5 cm long. The fruit is white with pinkish hue, 0.8 cm in diameter, hairy, 6 - lobed, and contains 6 seeds which are triangular, 0.2 cm long, glossy and woody (Figure 117).

Medicinal Uses: In Malaysia, the plant is medicinal.

Pharmacology: Unknown

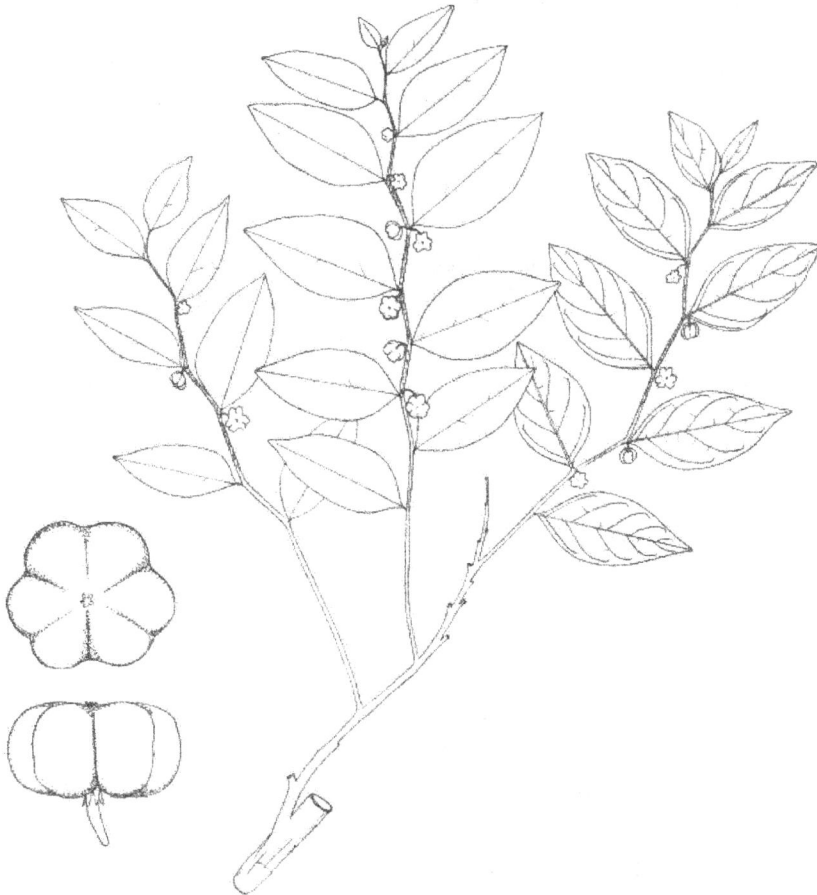

Figure 117: *Glochidion wallichianum* Müll. Arg.
From: Flora of Thailand, prince of Songkla University
Thailand, Songkla province, Rattapoon district, Dton Nga Chang reserve. Elevation: 200 m.
Date of collection: 2 October 1984. In partly open rocky area in the evergreen forest near a river

Jatropha gossypiifolia L.

[From Greek *iatros* = doctor and *trophe* = food and Latin *gossypiifolia* = cottoned leaves]

Local names:	Cotton-leaved physic nut, bellyache bush, adalai (India), sabuu daeng (Thailand), nhao luat (Laos), jarak hitam (Malaysia), jarak kosta merah (Indonesia), lansi-lansinaan (Philippines).
Synonym:	*Jatropha elegans* (Pohl) Klotzsch
Description:	The plant is native to tropical America and has been introduced as an ornamental into tropical Africa and Asia. It grows wild along roads and waste places. It is a shrub which grows up to 2 m tall and is covered with yellowish - red glands. The stem is angled and covered with glands. The leaves are simple, spiral and stipulate. The petiole is slender 12 -15 cm long, channelled and covered with glands. The leaf blade is palmately 3 - 5 lobed, covered with glands at the margin, membranaceous, 9 - 10 cm x 10 - 13 cm, each lobe with 9 - 12 pairs of secondary nerves. The inflorescence is a corymbose cyme which is opposite the leaves. The male flower has 5 elliptical lobes which are about 0.25 cm long, 5 petals which are 0.35 cm long and red and 8 - 12 stamens. The fruit is a 3 - lobed capsule which is about 1 cm in diameter containing 0.7 cm long seeds (Figure 118).
Medicinal Uses:	In India, the plant is used to induce menses, to heal boils, itches, and to induce vomiting. It is also used to treat headache, and as a laxative. In Indonesia, the plant is used as a purgative.
Pharmacology:	Extracts of the plant abrogated the survival of *Plasmodium falciparum in vitro* (Gbeassor *et al.*, 1989), showed a hypotensive effect in rodents (Abreu *et al.*, 2003) and wound healing properties (Santos *et al.*, 2006). The plant contains a macrocyclic diterpene, jatrophenone which is antibacterial (Ravindranath *et al.*, 2003).
References:	Abreu IC, Marinho AS, Paes AM, Freire SM, Olea RS, Borges MO, Borges AC, 2003, Hypotensive and vasorelaxant effects of ethanolic extract from *Jatropha gossypiifolia* L. in rats. Fitoterapia; 74: 650-7.
	Gbeassor M, Kossou Y, Amegbo K, de Souza C, Koumaglo K, Denke A, 1989, Antimalarial effects of eight African medicinal plants. J Ethnopharmacol; 25: 115-8.
	Ravindranath N, Venkataiah B, Ramesh C, Jayaprakash P, Das B, 2003, Jatrophenone, a novel macrocyclic bioactive diterpene from *Jatropha gossypifolia*. Chem Pharm Bull (Tokyo); 51: 870-1.

Santos MF, Czeczko NG, Nassif PA, Ribas-Filho JM, Alencar BL, Malafaia O, Ribas CA, Trautwein VM, Henriques GS, Maia JM, Bittencourt RC, 2006, Evaluation of the use of raw extract of *Jatropha gossypiifolia* L. in the healing process of skin wounds in rats. Acta Cir Bras; 21 Suppl 3: 2-7.

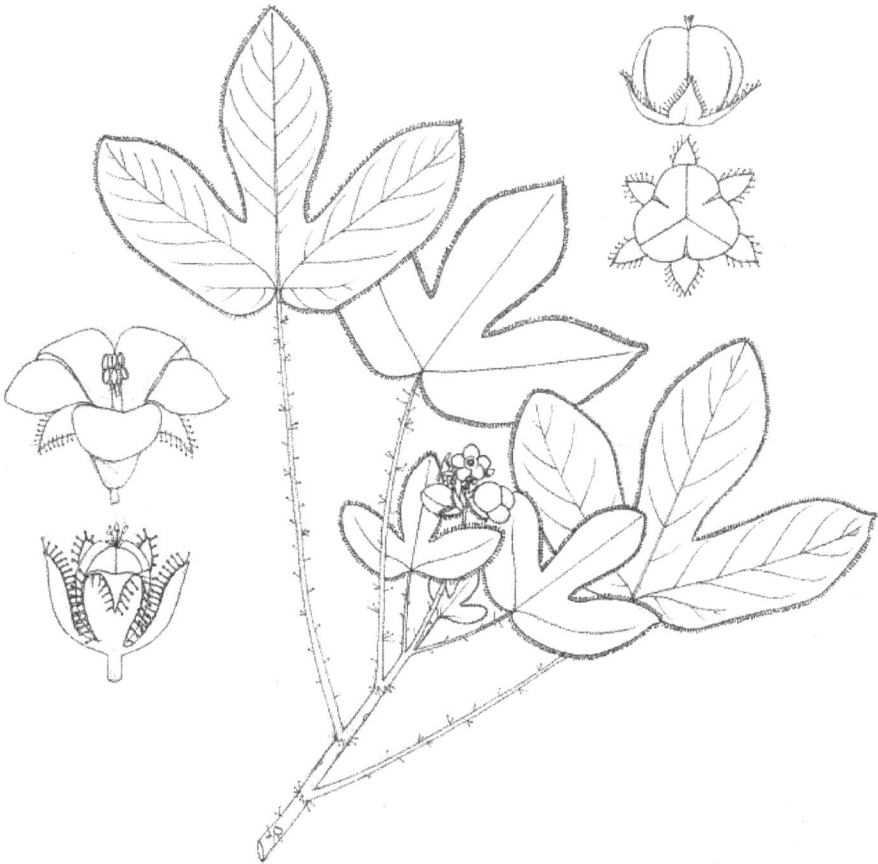

Figure 118: *Jatropha gossypiifolia* L.
From: Herbarium of University Kebangsaan Malaysia No 00830
Malaysia, Selayang, Kuala Lumpur. Collection: MK Zai. Determination: Mohd Kassim. Date of collection: 6 July 1973.

Macaranga hullettii King ex Hook. f.

[From *macaranga* a native name from Madagascar and from after William Hullett (1843-1914) member of Singapore gardens committee]

Local name:	Mahang (Malaysia)
Synonym:	*Macaranga bartlettii* Merr
Description:	It is a tree which grows up to 20 m tall in the secondary forests of Thailand, Malaysia, and Indonesia. The stem is terete, 0.5 cm in diameter, glabrous or hairy, articulate, flattish near the apex, with conspicuous leaf scars, hollowed and ant-inhabited. The leaves are simple, spiral and stipulate. The stipule is conspicuous, up to 1 cm long, and persistent. The petiole is constricted at the base, straight, with 11 - 13 pairs of secondary nerves, and 12.5 - 15 cm long. The leaf-blade is triangular, 17 - 20 cm x 10.5 cm, papery, peltate, rounded at the base, laxly serrate, acute at the apex. The inflorescence is 10 - 30 cm long, axillary, paniculate for male flowers, or in clusters of female flowers. The male flower is minute, sessile; with 3 hairy sepals, and a single anther. The female flower is about 0.5 cm long, with a hairy calyx, and a 4-5 lobed ovary. The fruit is subglobose, about 1 cm in diameter, sessile, with 5 - 6 horn-like appendages by the apex and 5-6 lobed vestigial stigma. The seeds are about 0.5 cm, ovoid, black with a red aril (Figure 119).
Medicinal Uses:	In Malaysia, the plant is used to treat stomachache.
Pharmacology:	Unknown.

Macaranga hypoleuca (Rchb. f. & Zoll.) Müll. Arg.

[From *macaranga* a native name from Madagascar and from Latin *hypoleuca* = whitish or pale beneath]

Local names:	Mahang puteh (Malaysia), lo (Thailand)
Synonyms:	*Mappa hypoleuca* Rchb.f. & Zoll., *Tanarius hypoleucus* (Rchb.f. & Zoll.) Kuntze
Description:	It is a tree which grows up to 30 m tall in Thailand, Malaysia and Indonesia. The bark is greenish white. The stem is stout, hollowed, angular, glaucous, with conspicuous leaf scars, articulated and ant-inhabited. The leaves are simple, spiral and stipulate. The stipule is triangular, glaucous and up to 1 cm long. The petiole is straight, constricted at the base, 4.5 - 20 cm and

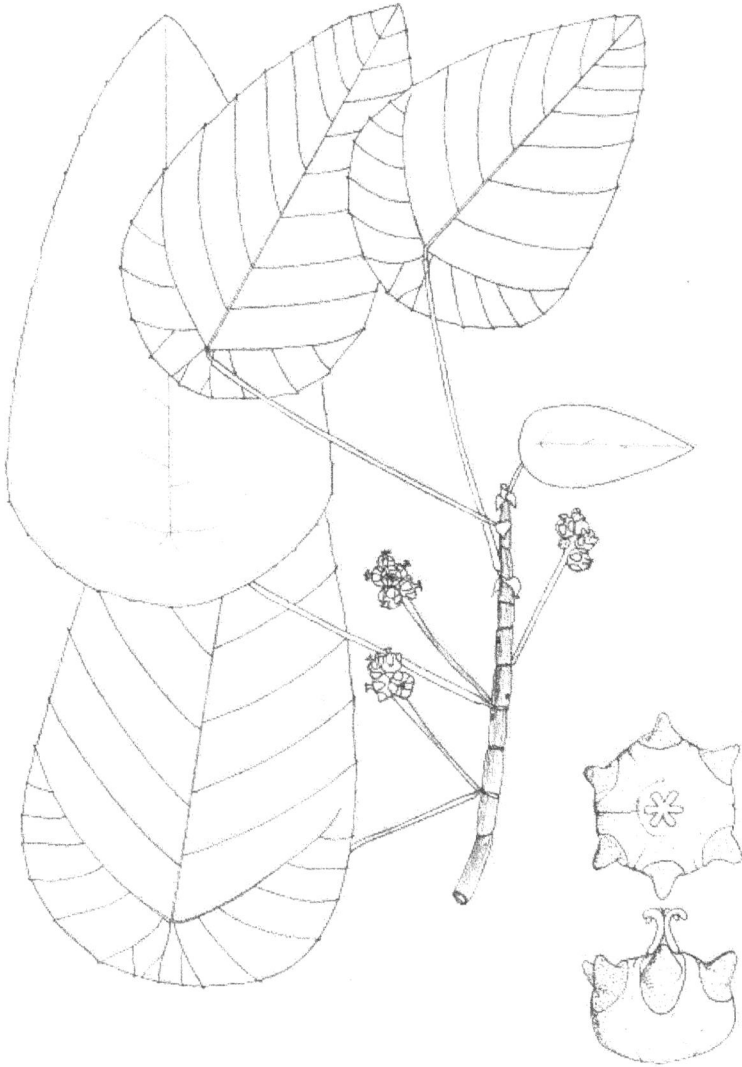

Figure 119: *Macaranga hullettii* **King ex Hook. f.**
From: Herbarium of University Kebangsaan Malaysia № 02911
Malaysia, Bukit Koman, Raub Pahang. Collection and identification: Mohd Kassim, MK 999.
Date of collection: 27 December 1973

glaucous. The leaf blade is intensely white glaucous underneath, 10 - 22 cm x 12 - 30 cm. It is peltate, thinly coriaceous, deeply 3 -lobed, rounded at the base, with 9 - 10 pairs of secondary nerves per lobes, the margin slightly and laxly toothed. Male inflorescence glabrous or scurfy. The male inflorescence is an axillary panicle to 35 cm long, glaucous, hairy at the apex. The flowers are minute with 3 hairy sepals and one stamen. The female inflorescence is an axillary panicle up to 15 cm long with angled pedicels. The female flower is 0.2 - 0.3 cm long, glaucous, hairy, with a 3-lobed ovary. The fruit is a 3-shouldered capsule with 6 dull yellow sticky bosses, 0.5 - 0.6 cm x 0.6 - 0.8 cm, glaucous, hairy and open to release black ovoid seeds with a red aril (Figure 120).

Medicinal Uses: In Indonesia, the plant is used as an insecticide and piscicide.

Pharmacology: Unknown.

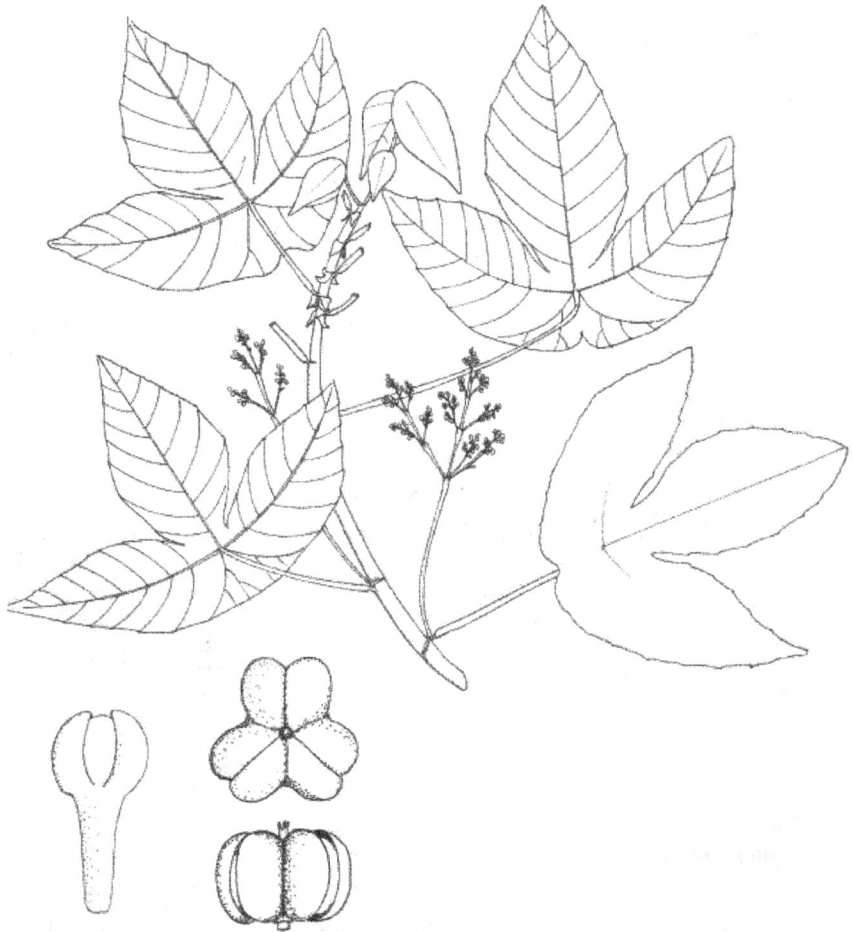

Figure 120: *Macaranga hypoleuca* **(Rchb. f. & Zoll.) Müll. Arg.**
From: Herbarium of University Kebangsaan Malaysia, No 00543
Malaysia, Genting Sampah, Selangor. Elevation 400 m. Collection and identification: Mohd Kassim. Date of collection: 14 May 1972.

Mallotus barbatus (Wall.) Müll. Arg.

[From Latin *mallotus* = woolly and from Latin *barbatus* = bearded]

Local names:	Balek angin (Malaysia), salapang bai yai (Thailand)
Basionym:	*Rottlera barbata* Wall. A Numerical List of Dried Specimens 7822. 1828.
Synonym:	*Mallotus conspurcatus* Croizat, *Mallotus croizatianus* F.P.Metcalf, *Mallotus esquirolii* H.Lév, *Mallotus leveillei* Fedde ex H.Lév., *Mallotus lotingensis* F.P.Metcalf, *Mallotus luchenensis* F.P.Metcalf *Rottlera barbata* Wall.
Description:	It is a shrub or tree which grows up to 9 m tall in a geographical area covering India, Burma, Thailand, Cambodia, Laos, Vietnam, Malaysia and China. The bark is thin, smooth, and grayish The stem is terete and hairy at the apex. The leaves are simple, alternate and stipulate. The stipule is linear triangular and 0.6 -1 cm long. The petiole is hairy and 3 -20 cm long. The leaf blade is dull dark green above, ovate, or 3 dentate 10 - 35 cm x 8 - 25 cm, peltate at the base, denticulate at margin, hairy underneath with 3 - 8 pairs of secondary nerves and scalariform tertiary nerves. The inflorescence is cream light yellowish pendulous, terminal, and 30 - 40 cm long. The male flowers are about 0.8 cm in diameter with 4-5 sepals and more than 50. The female flower is about 0.5 cm in diameter yellowish red with 4-5 sepals The fruit is a globose capsule which is about 2 cm in diameter, dull light yellowish, and covered with long hairs. The seeds are about 0.5 cm in diameter (Figure 121).
Medicinal Uses:	In Malaysia, the plant is used externally to treat intestinal ailments.
Pharmacology:	The plant seems not to have been explored for pharmacology.

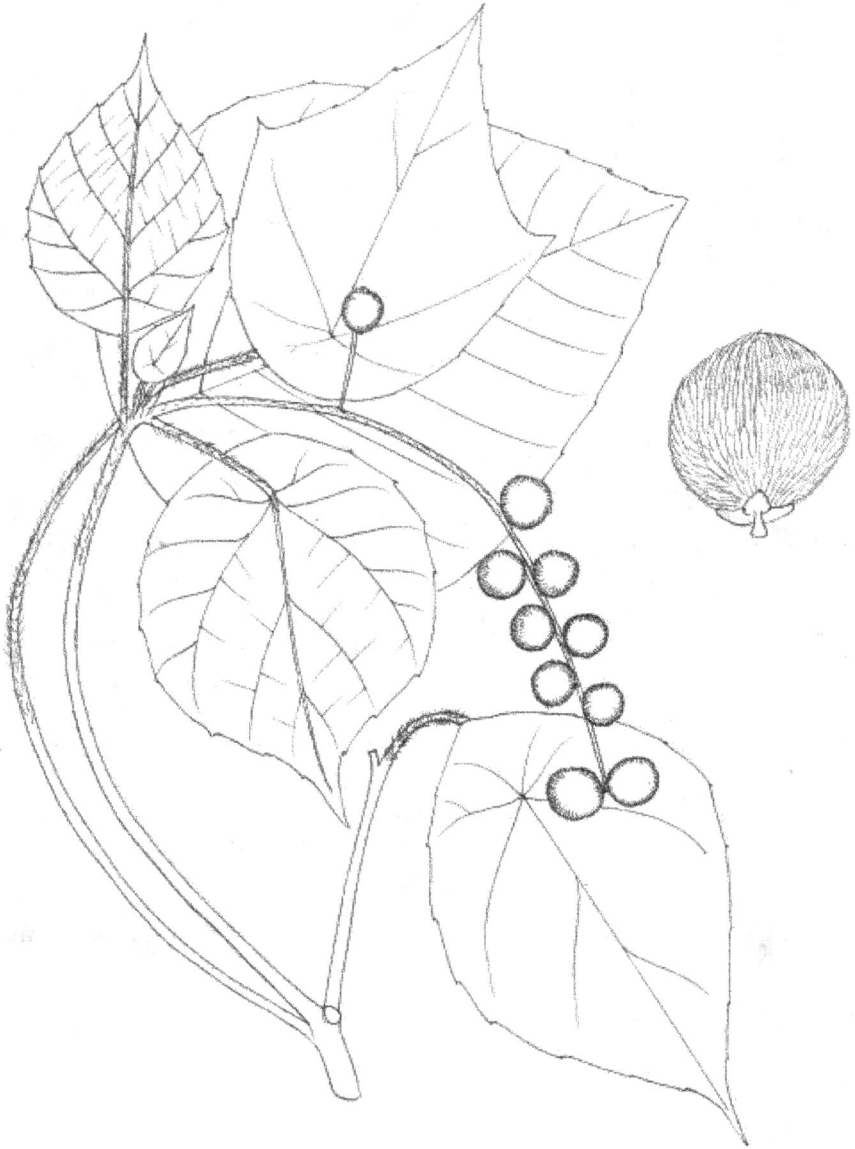

Figure 121: *Mallotus barbatus* **(Wall.) Müll. Arg.**
From: Flora of Thailand, Chiang Mai University Herbarium
Thailand, Lampang province, Muang Bahn district, Jae Sawn national park, East of park
headquarters near Jae Sawn village. Elevation: 450 m. Date of collection: 31 May 1996. In
open, disturbed, mixed evergreen and deciduous hardwood thicket near a small stream. Shale
bedrock. Collection and identification: JF Maxwell, Nº 96-764.

Mallotus japonicus (L. f.) Müll. Arg.

[From Latin *mallotus* = woolly and from Latin *japonicus* = from Japan]

Local name:	Ye wu tong (China), akame-gashiwa (Japan)
Synonyms:	*Croton japonicus* L., *Croton japonicum* Thunb.
Description:	It is a tree which grows in thickets and secondary forests in China, Japan and Taiwan. The stem, petiole and spike are covered with hairs, The leaves are simple, alternate and stipulates. The petiole is as long as the blade. The leaf blade is 7 - 14 cm x 5 - 10 cm, ovate, broad, acute at the apex and with 3 - 6 pairs of secondary nerves. The inflorescence is a spike which is 5 - 18 cm long. The female flower comprises 4-5 sepals which are triangular, 0.25 cm and hairy. The style is hairy and about 0.4 cm long. The fruit is a 3 locular capsule which is granular, echinate, and 0.8 x 0.5 cm. The seeds are black, globose and compressed (Figure 122).
Medicinal Uses:	In Japan, the plant is used for back-ache, stomachache, inflammation, and to remove tumours and to expel worms from the intestines. In Taiwan, the plant is used as an anti-inflammatory.
Pharmacology:	The plant contains bergerin which showed hepatoprotective effects against D-galactosamine in rodents (Lim *et al.*, 2001). The fruit contains mallotojaponin, which suppressed the tumour promoting effect of 12-O-tetradecanoylphorbol-13-acetate on skin tumour formation in mice initiated with 7,12-dimethylbenz-[a]anthracene (Satomi *et al.*, 1994). An extract of the plant inhibited the reverse-transcriptase activity of HIV virus (Min *et al.*, 2001). The plant contains phloroglucinol isomallotochromanol and isomallotochromene inhibit pro-inflammatory cytokine production and mRNA expression via suppression of NF-kappaB activation in activated macrophages(Ishii *et al.*, 2003). Mallotinic acid, mallotusinic acid, corilagin and geraniin, exhibited strong antioxidant activity in the DPPH radical-scavenging, superoxide radical-scavenging, and hydroxyl radical-scavenging assays (Tabata *et al.*, 2008).
References:	Ishii R, Horie M, Saito K, Arisawa M, Kitanaka S, 2003, Inhibition of lipopolysaccharide-induced pro-inflammatory cytokine expression via suppression of nuclear factor-kappaB activation by *Mallotus japonicus* phloroglucinol derivatives. Biochim Biophys Acta; 1620: 108-18.
	Lim HK, Kim HS, Choi HS, Choi J, Kim SH, Chang MJ, 2001, Effects of bergenin, the major constituent of *Mallotus*

japonicus against D-galactosamine-induced hepatotoxicity in rats. Pharmacology; 63: 71-5.

Min BS, Kim YH, Tomiyama M, Nakamura N, Miyashiro H, Otake T, Hattori M, 2001, Inhibitory effects of Korean plants on HIV-1 activities. Phytother Res; 15: 481-6.

Satomi Y, Arisawa M, Nishino H, Iwashima A, 1994, Antitumor-promoting activity of mallotojaponin, a major constituent of pericarps of *Mallotus japonicus*. Oncology; 51: 215-9.

Tabata H, Katsube T, Tsuma T, Ohta Y, Imawaka N, Utsumi T, 2008, Isolation and evaluation of the radical-scavenging activity of the antioxidants in the leaves of an edible plant, *Mallotus japonicus*. Food Chemistry; 109: 64-71.

Figure 122: *Mallotus japonicus* (L. f.) Müll. Arg.
From: Flora of Taiwan, National Ping Tung Herbarium.
Taiwan. Collection and identification: Ching-en Chang 16859. Date of collection: 6 April 1985

Mallotus macrostachyus (Miq.) Müll. Arg.

[From Latin *mallotus* = woolly and from Greek *macro* = large and *stachus* = spike]

Local names:	Common pom-pom tree, balik angin (Malaysia), lo khon (Thailand)
Basionym:	*Rottlera macrostachya* Miq. *Flora van Nederlandsch Indie, Eerste Bijvoegsel* 454. 1816.
Synonyms:	*Mallotus albus* auct. non Müll.Arg, *Mallotus insignis* Müll.Arg, *Rottlera macrostachya* Miq.
Description:	It is a tree which grows up to 15 m tall in secondary forests in Thailand, Malaysia, and Indonesia. The stem is terete and covered with hairs. The leaves are simple, opposite or alternate and stipulate. The stipule is triangular and about 0.2 cm long. The petiole is slender, 4 - 16 cm long constricted and angled at the base, and produces a pair of glands which are 0.1 cm in diameter at the apex. The leaf blade is ovate triangular, 19 - 6 cm x 17 - 6 cm, with 7 - 10 pairs of secondary and scalariform tertiary nerves, denticulate at the margin, caudate at the apex, and hairy underneath. The inflorescence is a spike opposite the leaf which can reach 1 m long. The male flowers are about 0.4 cm in diameter, yellowish and fragrant and present 4 sepals and 50-70 stamens. The female flower is about 0.2 cm in diameter, light greenish with 3 - 6 lobes. The fruit is a capsule which is globose, hairy, about 1.5 cm in diameter, seated on a cupular vestigial calyx, light yellowish with vestigial stigma at the apex. The seeds are ovoid, black and about 0.5 cm in diameter (Figure 123).
Medicinal Uses:	In Malaysia, the plant is used to heal boils, wounds, and to break fever.
Pharmacology:	Unknown.

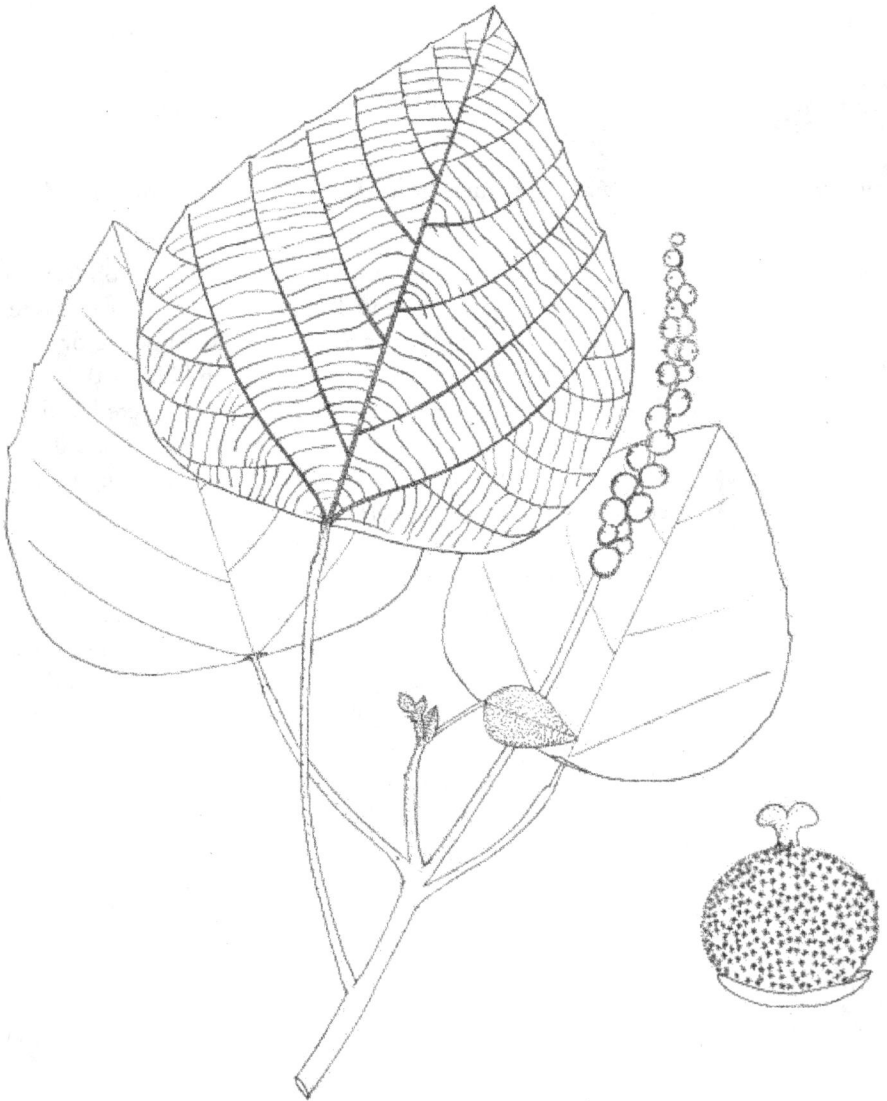

Figure 123: *Mallotus macrostachyus* (Miq.) Müll. Arg.
From: Flora of Malaya, Herbarium of University Kebangsaan Malaysia Nº 08813
Malaysia, Genting Highland, Miles 2, by the roadside. Collection: Mohd Kassim. Date of
collection: 19 December 1973.

Mallotus philippensis (Lam.) Müll. Arg.

[From Latin *mallotus* = woolly and from *Latin philippensis* = from the Philippines]

Local names:	Kamala tree, monkey face tree; tanthieden (Burma), *balek* (Malaysia), kamala (India), sala (Philippines).
Basionym:	*Croton philippensis* Lam. *Encyclopédie Méthodique, Botanique* 2: 206. 1786
Synonym:	*Croton philippensis* Lam.
Description:	It is a tree which grows to a height of 9 m in open lands in a geographical zone including West Himalayas, Sri Lanka, Formosa, South China to New Guinea, Solomon Islands and Australia. The stems, young leaves and inflorescences are covered with red glands. The stem is terete and lenticelled. The leaves are simple, alternate, and stipulate. The petiole is 2.5 - 5 cm long, terete, and slender and with a pair of glands at the apex. The leaf blade is ovate, trinerved, and 5 - 20 cm x 1 - 5 cm. The margin is entire or sinuate - lobed. The leaf-blade is covered on the lower surface with red glands. The apex is acuminate and the base acute. Tertiary nerves are scalariform. The inflorescence is an axillary raceme of spikes. The calyx is 4 - lobed. The stigma is characteristically fluffy. The androecium comprises several stamens. The fruits are depressed, globose, trilobed, 0.6 - 0.7 cm diameter capsules covered with scarlet glands (Figure 124).
Medicinal Uses:	Kamala powder is a dull reddish - brown tasteless and odourless powder which has been used to expel intestinal worms since historical times. The Arab physicians became acquainted with it at an early date, and through them it appears to have reached Europe, and to have been known to the Greek physicians in about the 7th century. This powder consists of red radiating groups of unicellular curved trichomes which cover the capsules (kamala, *Glandulae Rottlerae, British Pharmaceutical Codex*, 1934). Ibn Sina writes "it is a grain like sand, red,…,hot and dry in the third degree". In India, kamala powder is used to expel worms, and to treat ringworm, scabies and other skin diseases. It is also used to heal ulcer, wounds and to remove tumours, to abort and provide a dye. In Burma, kamala powder is used as a laxative and to heal wounds. In China, the plant is used to treat colds and kamala powder is used to expel intestinal worms. In Indonesia, kamala powder is used to expel intestinal worms. In Malaysia, the plant is used to prevent bed - wetting in children.

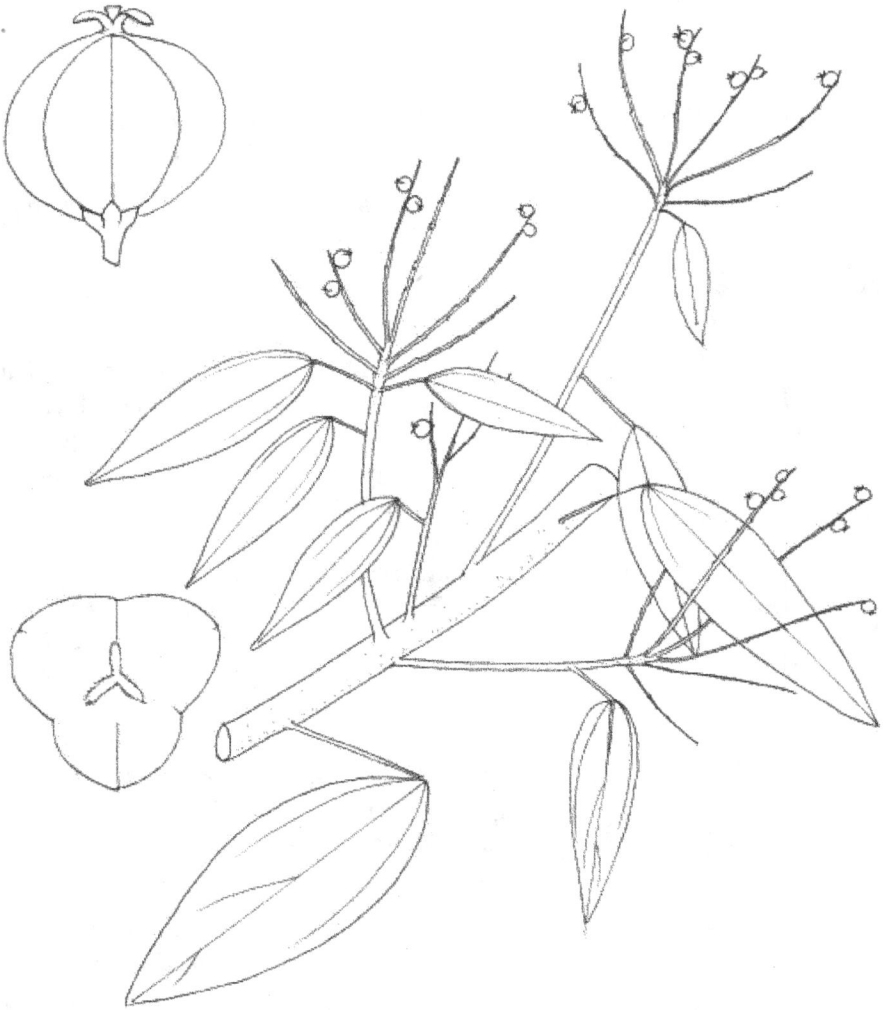

Figure 124: *Mallotus philippensis* **(Lam.) Müll. Arg.**
From: Botanical Inventory of Taiwan. Herbarium, Institute of Botany, Academia Sinica, Taipei (HAST).
Taiwan, Kaoshsiung Hsien, Taoyuan Hsiang, Southern Cross, Island Hwy, between Meishan and Likuan. Broad leaf forest. 23° 15' 46" North - 120° 50' 58" East. Elevation 1120 m. On slope below the road. Collection and identification: Tsui-Ya Liu. Date of collection: 12 May 1994

Pharmacology: The plant produces a series of friedelanes-type triterpenes including 3alpha-hydroxy-D:A-friedooleanan-2-one which inhibited Epstein-Barr virus early antigen activation induced by 12- O-tetradecanoylphorbol 13-acetate (Tanaka *et al.*, 2008). An extract of seeds reduced serum FSH and LH and oestradiol levels via hypothalamic/pituitary axis in rats which adversely affected fertility (Thakur *et al.*, 2005). The dyeing principles of *kamala* powder are phloroglucinol derivatives such as rottlerin (mallotoxin) and isorottlerin. Aqueous and ethanolic extracts of leaves of *Mallotus philippensis* (Lamk.) Muell. Arg. inhibit the spontaneous mobility of *Setaria cervie* microfilariae (Singh *et al.*, 1997). This property is most probably due to rottlerin. This is known to destroy efficiently intestinal worms possibly through inhibition of calmodulin - dependent protein kinase III (Parmer *et al.*, 1997) which phosphorylates a number of substrates which regulate the proliferation of cells upon mitogen stimulation. Rottlerin is a specific PKCdelta inhibitor, which potentiates death receptor- mediated apoptosis and protected murine fibrosarcoma L929 cells, against TNF-induced necrosis (Byun *et al.*, 2008).

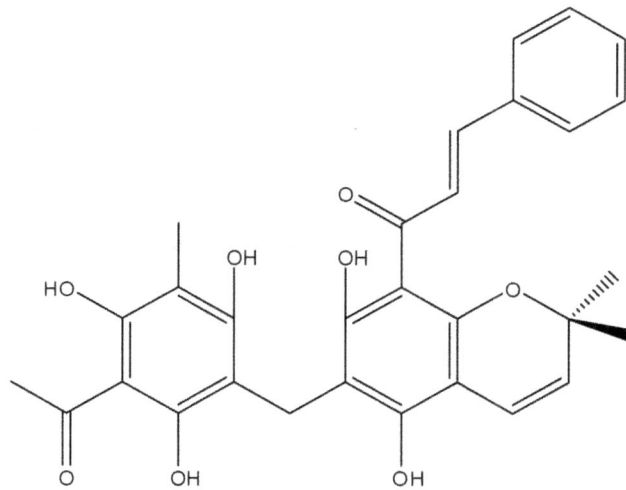

Rottlerin

References:

Byun HS, Won M, Park KA, Kim YR, Choi BL, Lee H, Hong JH, Piao L, Park J, Kim JM, Kweon GR, Kang SH, Han J, Hur GM, 2008, Prevention of TNF-induced necrotic cell death by rottlerin through a Nox1 NADPH oxidase. Exp Mol Med; 40: 186-95.

Parmer TG, Ward MD, Hait WN, 1997, Effects of rottlerin, an inhibitor of calmodulin-dependent protein kinase III, on cellular proliferation, viability, and cell cycle distribution in malignant glioma cells. Cell Growth Differ; 8: 327-34.

Singh R, Singhal KC, Khan NU, 1997, Antifilarial activity of *Mallotus philippensis* Lam. on Setaria cervie (Nematoda: Filarioidea) in vitro. Indian J Physiol Pharmacol; 41: 397-403.

Tanaka R, Nakata T, Yamaguchi C, Wada S, Yamada T, Tokuda H, 2008, Potential anti-tumor-promoting activity of 3alpha-hydroxy-D:A-friedooleanan-2-one from the stem bark of *Mallotus philippensis*. Planta Med; 74: 413-6.

Thakur SC, Thakur SS, Chaube SK, Singh SP, 2005, An etheral extract of Kamala (*Mallotus philippinensis* (Moll.Arg) Lam.) seed induces adverse effects on reproductive parameters of female rats. Reprod Toxicol; 20: 149-56.

Mercurialis leiocarpa Sieb. & Zucc.

[After Mercury, the Roman messenger god and from Greek *leios* = smooth and *spermus* = seed]

Local name:	Mercury, t'ou ku taso (Japan), shan dian (China)
Synonym:	*Mercurialis transmorrisonensis* Hayat.
Description:	It is a herb which grows in the forests of India, Nepal, Thailand, China, Taiwan, and Japan. The plant can grow up to 1 m tall. The stem is terete, glabrous, striated, swollen at nodes, somewhat articulated, and with 4.5 - 7 cm long internodes. The leaves are opposite, simple, and stipulate. The stipules are about 0.2 cm long. The petiole is 1.3 - 5.5 cm long, slender, glabrous with conical minute glands near the blade. The leaf blade is broadly lanceolate, hairy at first then subglabrous, 3 -13 cm x 1.5 - 5.5 cm, asymmetrical, wedge-shaped at the base, membranaceous, acuminate at the apex and with 5 - 10 pairs of secondary nerves. A blue dye is obtained from the leaves. The inflorescence is an axillary spike up to 12 cm long. The male flower presents 3 sepals which are valvate and ovate, up to 0.2 cm long, and 10 - 20 showy stamens which are 0.2 cm long. The female flower comprises 3 sepals, 0.18 cm, 2 glandular cisks and a subglobose ovary. The fruit is a capsule which is about 0.3 cm long on a vestigial calyx and containing a few globose seeds which are 0.25 cm in diameter (Figure 125).
Medicinal uses:	In Japan, the plant is used to treat fever and to counteract poisoning.
Pharmacology:	Masui *et al.* (1985) isolated 3,3'-bis-(1,1'-dimethyl-2,2'-dioxo-4,4'-dimethoxy-5,5'-dihydroxy-5,5'-dimethoxycarbonyl-3-pyrroline from the plant.

Reference: Masui Y, Kawabe C, Mastumoto K, Abe K, Miwa T, 1986,
               A 2-oxo-3-pyrroline dimer from *Mercurialis leiocarpa*.
               Phytochemistry; 25: 1470-71.

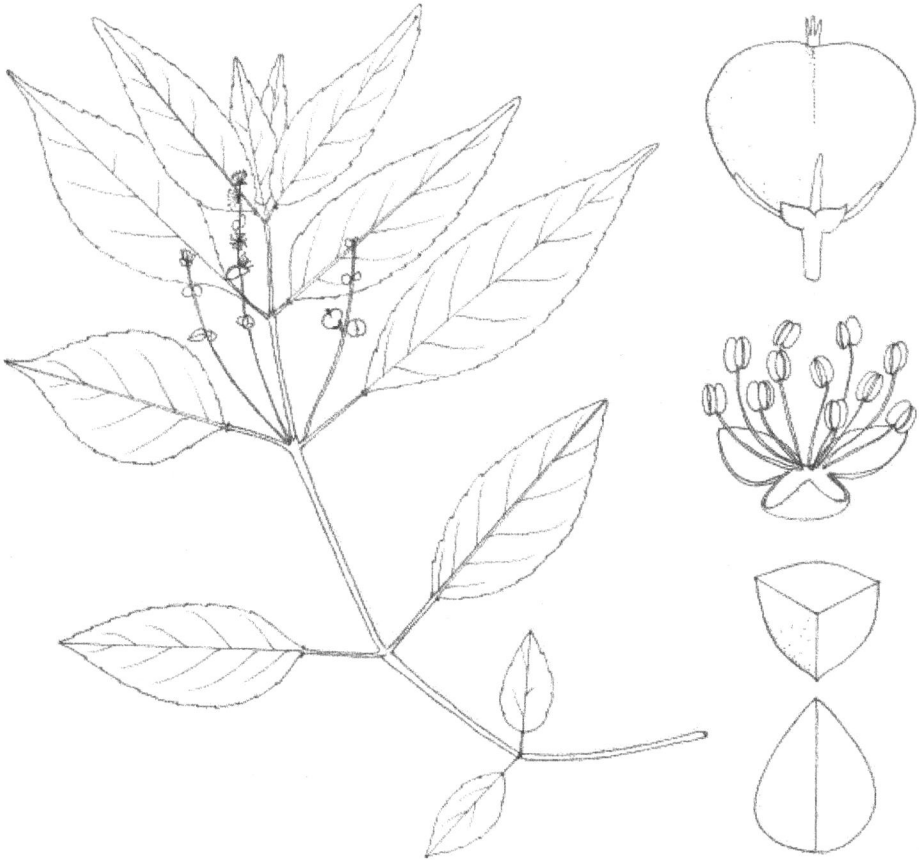

Figure 125: *Mercurialis leiocarpa* **Sieb. & Zucc.**
From: Botanical Inventory of Taiwan, Herbarium, Institute of Botany, Academia Sinica, Taipei
(HAST)
Taiwan, Pingtung Hsien: Wutai Hsiang, hiking entrance of Wu tou mountain to mount summit
broadleaf forest. 120° 48' 23" East - 22° 41' 53" North. Elevation: 1560 m. By small forest
trail. Collection and identification: Yih Ren Lin 187. Date of collection: 14 October 1993.

Phyllanthus elegans Juss.

[From Greek *phullon* = leaf and *anthos* = flower and Latin *elegans* = elegant]

Local name:	Ton tai bai (Thailand)
Synonyms:	*Phyllanthus elegans* Juss., *Phyllanthus glaucifolius* Ridl., *Phyllanthus gomphocarpus* Ridl.
Description:	It is a shrub which grows up to 3 m tall in Burma, Cambodia, Laos, Vietnam and Malaysia. The bark is thin, finely cracked, and light brown. The stem is terete and glabrous. The leaves are simple, alternate and stipulate. The stipule is about 0.3 cm long. The petiole is about 0.3 cm long. The blade is falcate, dark green above, membranaceous, 6 -15 cm x 2.5 -5 cm, coriaceous, acuminate at the apex, glabrous below, with 8 -12 pairs of secondary nerves. The inflorescence is an axillary fascicle. The flower pedicel is whitish-pale light pinkish and 0.2 - 0.25 cm long. The male flower has 4 pale light green disc glands, 4 pale light maroon sepals with fimbriate margin to 0.25 cm long and 4 stamens with cream colored anthers. The female flower has 6 pale light maroon sepals, fimbriate at the margin, up to 0.35 cm long, with a glabrous ovary and a 0.5 cm long stigma. The fruit is an inflated capsule on a 3 cm long pedicel. The capsule is bright light green, 1 - 2 cm in diameter and contains trigonous seeds which are about 0.5 cm long (Figure 126).
Medicinal Uses:	In Cambodia, Laos and Vietnam, the plant is used to invigorate, and to break fever.
Pharmacology:	Unknown.

Phyllanthus frondosus Wall. ex Müll. Arg.

[From Greek *phullon* = leaf and *anthos* = flower and Latin *frondosus* = leafy]

Local name:	Ya xian ye xia zhu (China)
Synonyms:	*Phyllanthus annamensis* Beille; *Phyllanthus campanulatus* Ridl. *Phyllanthus coriaceus* Wall. ex J. D. Hook; *Phyllanthus klossii* Ridl., *Phyllanthus oxyphyllus* Müll. Arg., *Phyllanthus pachyphyllus* Mull-Arg.
Description:	It is a shrub which grows up to 4 m in Malaysia, Thailand, Vietnam and China. The stem is grey-brown and angled.

Figure 126: *Phyllanthus elegans* **Juss.**
From: Flora of Thailand, Chiang Mai University Herbarium
Thailand, Ranong province, Kaper district, Iahm Sohn national park headquarters, Bahn Bain village area, below the summit of Bahn Bain Hill, Muang Gluang district. Elevation: 125 m. Date of collection: 29 November 1996. In partly open, disturbed area, in degraded seasonal primary evergreen forest on granite bedrock. Collection & identification: JF Maxwell N° 96-1560

The leaves are simple, alternate, and stipulate. The stipule is triangular and 0.1 cm long. The petiole is 0.2 - 0.3 cm long. The leaf blade is ovate-lanceolate, purplish violet when young, 3 - 15 cm × 1.5 cm- 3.5 cm, thinly leathery, acuminate at the apex, with 4 -5 pairs of secondary nerves. The inflorescence is axillary and solitary. The male flower is about 0.4 cm in diameter with 6 light greenish sepals and 3 stamens. The female flower is 0.4 cm in diameter with 6 obovate sepals which are 0.15 cm long with an ovoid yellow ovary which is about 0.15 cm across. The fruit is a 3-5-lobed capsule which is 0.4 cm and contains red seeds (Figure 127).

Medicinal Uses: In Malaysia, the plant is used for fever, as a protective remedy after childbirth, and to treat gonorrhea.

Pharmacology: Unknown.

Phyllanthus pulcher Wall. ex Müll. Arg.

[From Greek *phullon* = leaf and *anthos* = flower and Latin *pulcher* = beautiful]

Local name: Kra thuep yop (Thailand), kelurut tanjong (Malaysia), yun gui ye xia zhu (China)

Synonyms: *Diasperus pulcher* (wall. ex Mull-Arg) Kuntze, *Epistylum pulchrum* Baill., *Phyllanthus asteranthos* Croizat

Description: It is a shrub which grows to 1.5 m in open forests of Burma, Cambodia, Laos, Vietnam, Malaysia and Indonesia. The stem is terete and hairy by the apex. The leaves are simple, alternate and stipulate. The stipule is triangular and to 0.4 cm long. The petiole is about 0.1 cm long. The leaf-blade is dark green above, asymmetrical, oblong, 1.8 - 3 cm × 0.8 - 1.3 cm, membranaceous, with 4-6 pairs of secondary nerves which are inconspicuous. The Inflorescence is an axillary fascicle. The flower pedicels, calyx and disk are maroon. The male flower has 4 sepals which are lanceolate, ciliate at margin and up to 0.3 cm long, 2 pinkish stamens; and 4 disk glands. The female flower has 6 sepals which are triangular, up to 0.4 cm long, ciliate at the margin and a globose ovary. The fruit is a 3-lobed brownish capsule on a 2.5 cm long pedicel (Figure 128).

Medicinal Uses: In Cambodia, Laos and Vietnam, the plant is used as a disinfectant. In Malaysia, the plant is used for stomach-ache and tooth-ache, and it is applied to boils, swellings and ulcers.

Pharmacology: The plant has not been studied for pharmacology. Tannins are probably responsible for the medicinal uses of the plant.

Figure 127: *Phyllanthus frondosus* Wall. ex Müll. Arg.
From: Flora of Malaya. Herbarium of University Kebangsaan Malaysia
Malaysia, Selangor, Genting Simpah. Collection and identification: Abdul Latiff. Date of
collection: 17 September 1973.

Figure 128: *Phyllanthus pulcher* Wall. ex Müll. Arg.
From: Flora of Thailand, prince of Songkla University
Thailand, Songkla province, Nah Mawn district, Klong Rang hill. Elevation: 25 m. Date of collection: 10 December 1985. In shaded, wet area, along the stream with secondary growth in sand. Collection and identification: JF Maxwell N⁰ 85-1097.

Sapium sebiferum (L.) Roxb.

[From Latin *sapium* = a plant name, *sebum* = fat and *fer* = producing]

Local name:	Chinese tallow tree, gerah (Malaysia), wu chi (China), agaru (Sanskrit, India)
Basionym:	*Croton sebifer* L. *Species Plantarum* 2: 1004. 1753
Synonyms:	*Croton sebifer* L., *Croton sebiferus* L., *Excoecaria sebifera* (L.) Mull-Arg, *Triadica sebifera* (L.), *Stillingia sebifera* Michx.
Description:	It is an invasive small tree of Southern China and Taiwan. The latex is abundant and vesicant. The stem is glabrous, slender and terete. The leaves are simple, and spiral. The petiole is 2 - 5 cm long. The blade is thin, rhomboid - ovate, with numerous secondary nerves, and 5 - 9 cm, shortly acuminate at the the apex. The the base is acute and shows a pair of glands. The margin is serrate. The inflorescence is a terminal, 7 - 12 cm long yellowish spikes, the male flowers at the base and the female flower at the apex. The fruits are nearly globose, 1.5 cm x 7 mm, glaucous, fleshy capsules turning black and mucronate at the apex. The seeds are 6.5 mm; white and waxy (Figure 129).
Medicinal Uses:	The plant is used in China to relieve constipation and to promote urination. In Vietnam, the seeds are used to treat hair and skin diseases.
Pharmacology:	*Sapium sebiferum* (L.) Roxb. contains geraniin and 6 - O - galloyl - D - glucose which are hypotensive in spontaneously hypertensive rats (Chen *et al.*, 1994; Hsu *et al.*, 1994). The vesicant property of the plant is owed to phorbol esters which stimulate protein kinase C and are tumourigenic (Brooks *et al.*, 1987).
References:	Brooks G, Morrice NA, Ellis C, Aitken A, Evans AT, Evans FJ Toxic phorbol esters from Chinese tallow stimulate protein kinase C. Toxicon; 25: 1229-33. Cheng JT, Chang SS, Hsu FL, 1994,Antihypertensive action of geraniin in rats. J Pharm Pharmacol. 1994 Jan;46:46-9. Hsu FL, Lee YY, Cheng JT, 1994,Antihypertensive activity of 6-O-galloyl-D-glucose, a phenolic glycoside from Sapium sebiferum. J Nat Prod; 57:308-12.

Figure 129: *Sapium sebiferum* **(L.) Roxb.**
From: Flora of Malaya, Herbarium of University Kebangsaan Malaysia
Malaysia, Kedah state, Alor Setar, Kg Gunung Kerian, in sawa padi area. Collection: Mohd.
Noor. Identification: Razali Jaman. Date of collection: 7 September 1984.

Securinega virosa (Roxb. ex Willd.) Baill.

[From Latin *secur* = axe and *negare* = to deny, and *virosa* = poisonous]

Local name:	Membeti (Malaysia)
Synonyms:	*Fluegga virosa* (Roxb. ex Willd) Baill., *Flueggia microcarpa* (Bl.) M.A.
Description:	It is a small tree which grows on open places, especially along rivers. The plant originated from the old world tropics and is found in the tropical and sub-tropical belt. The bark is thin, finely cracked and light brown. The main stem is spiny from old stem the base. The stem is zigzag shaped. The leaves are simple, alternate, in two ranks. The petiolule is 0.2 cm long. The blade is dark green above, small, obovate, 1.7 cm x 0.7 cm, papery, glabrous with 2-3 pairs of secondary nerves. The inflorescence is a small axillary cluster. There are 5 sepals. The male flower has 5 disk glands and 3-5 stamens. Female flowers have a toothed disk ring. The fruit is 0.5 cm across, white, 3-lobed and pulpy (Figure 130).
Medicinal Uses:	The plant is used for boils and wounds in China and the Philippines
Pharmacology:	The plant contain virosecurinine which is a strychnine-like poison in rodents (Hill *et al.*, 1976). Virosecurinine and viroallosecurinine are cytotoxic (Tatematsu, *et al*, 1991). An extract of the plant showed antitrypanosomal activity (Freiburghaus *et al.*, 1996) and antiplasmodial activity, probably on account of bergerin (Nyasse *et al*, 2004). The plant contains bergerin which is anti-arrhythmic (Pu *et al*, 2002). An extract of the plant showed potent antimicrobial activity (Dickson *et al*, 2006).
References:	Dickson RA, Houghton PJ, Hylands PJ, Gibbons S, 2006, Antimicrobial, resistance-modifying effects, antioxidant and free radical scavenging activities of *Mezoneuron benthamianum* Baill., *Securinega virosa* Roxb. & Willd. and *Microglossa pyrifolia* Lam. Phytother Res; 20:41-5.

Freiburghaus F, Goal EN, Nkunya MH, Kaminsky R, Brun R, 1996,*In vitro* antitrypanosomal activity of African plants used in traditional medicine in Uganda to treat sleeping sickness. Trop Med Int Health;1:765-71.

Hill L, Holdsworth D, Small R, 1976, Pharmacological investigations of virosecurinine. P N G Med J; 18:157-61.

Kaou AM, Mahiou-Leddet V, Hutter S, Aïnouddine S, Hassani S, Yahaya I, Azas N, Ollivier E, 2008, Antimalarial activity of crude extracts from nine African medicinal plants. J Ethnopharmacol; 116:74-83.

Nyasse B, Nono J, Sonke B, Denier C, Fontaine C, 2004,Trypanocidal activity of bergenin, the major constituent of *Flueggea virosa*, on *Trypanosoma brucei*. Pharmazie; 59:492-4.

Pu HL, Huang X, Zhao JH, Hong A, 2002, Bergenin is the antiarrhythmic principle of *Fluggea virosa*.Planta Med; 68:372-4.

Tatematsu H, Mori M, Yang TH, Chang JJ, Lee TT, Lee KH, 1991,Cytotoxic principles of *Securinega virosa*: virosecurinine and viroallosecurinine and related derivatives. J Pharm Sci; 80:325-7.

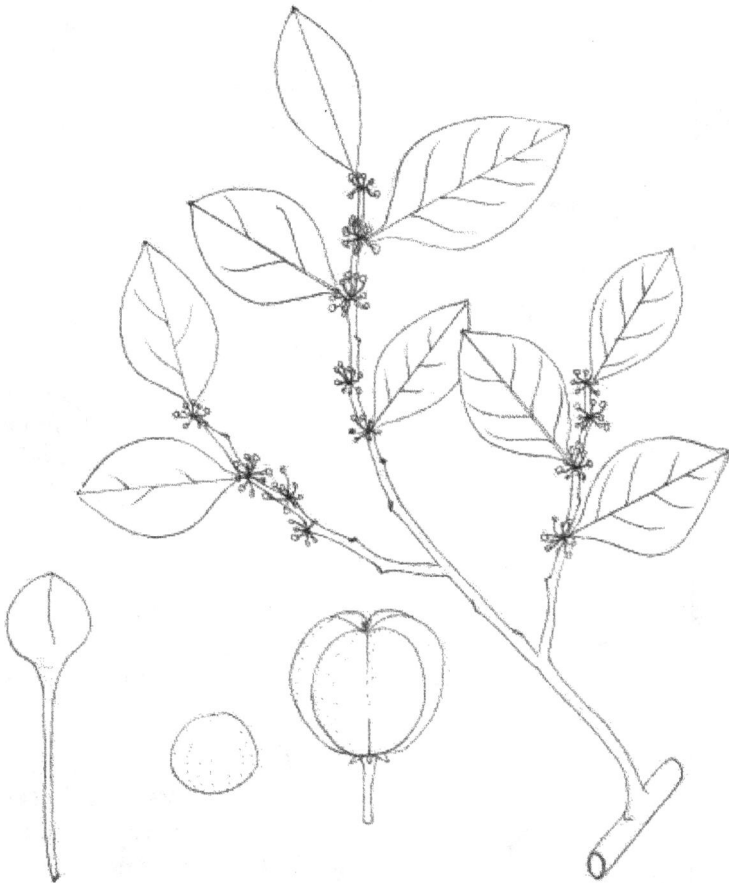

Figure 130: *Securinega virosa* **(Roxb. ex Willd.) Baill.**
From: Flora of Thailand, Chiang Mai University Herbarium
Thailand, Lampoon province, Mae Tah district, Doi Kuhn Dahn national park, pah Dtoop falls area. Elevation: 1050 m. Date of collection: 30 April 1994. In partly shaded, fire damaged area in primary evergreen hardwood forest on granite bedrock.

Trigonostemon longifolius Baill.

[From Greek *trigonostemon* = 3 angled stamen and Latin *longifolius* = with long leaves]

Local name:	Thao yaai mom paa (Thailand)
Description:	It is a small tree which grows up to 5 m in the open forest of Burma, Malaysia and Indonesia. The stem is ribbed and hairy. The leaves are simple, spiral and stipulate. The stipule is up to 0.3 cm long, The petiole is 1 - 2 cm long. The leaf-blade is spathulate, 22 - 50 cm x 3 - 15 cm, glabrous, hairy underneath; attenuate at the base, serrate at margin, caudate at the apex with 16-25 pairs of secondary nerves. The inflorescence is an axillary spike up to 25 cm long and a red axis. The male flower shows 5 oblong sepals, up to 0.25 cm long, hairy, a corolla of 5 petals which are ovate, up to 0.2 cm long, and dark purple; 5 disc glands and 3 stamens with large appendages, cream colored anthers and dark purple connective. The female flower has 5 sepals which are elliptic, up to 0.25 cm long, hairy; 5 petals up to 0.3 cm long; an annular disk and an hirsute ovary. The fruit is a capsule which is 1 cm in diameter with trigonous seeds (Figure 131).
Medicinal Uses:	In Malaysia, the juice of the plant is applied to stings.
Pharmacology:	The plant has not been much studied for pharmacology.

Medicinal Plants from the East

Figure 131: *Trigonostemon longifolius* **Baill.**
From: Flora of Thailand, prince of Songkla University
Thailand, Songkla province, Raad Yai district, Ko Hong Hill, West slope. Elevation: 100 m.
Date of collection: 27 April 1986. In shaded rocky area in the secondary forest along a
stream. Collection and identification: JF Maxwell N° 86-265

F. Order SAPINDALES Bentham and Hooker 1852

The order Sapindales consists of 15 families and about 5,400 species of trees, shrubs, climbers or herbs known to contain a series of bitter oxygenated triterpenes (limonoids, quassinoids), essential oils, saponins, phenolic compounds including biflavonoids, coumarins, tannins and cohorts of alkaloids. The Sapindaceae and the Rutaceae are the largest families in this order.

1.Family SAPINDACEAE A. L. de Jussieu 1789, nom conserv. The Soapberry family

The Family Sapindaceae consists of 140 genera and 1500 species of climbers, shrubs and trees which are known to abound with saponins. The leaves are pinnate, alternate and without stipules. The inflorescence is axillary or terminal and cymose. The flowers are very small with 4- 5 sepals and petals, a disk, 8 stamens, and 3 carpels united into a compound plurilocular ovary with 1-2 axil pendulous ovules per locules. The fruit is fleshy or dry, dehiscent or indehiscent.

Examples of Sapindaceae are the ornamental golden rain tree *Koelreutia paniculata* Laxm., *Sapindus saponaria* L. the berries of which can be used as soap and *Paullinia cupuna* HBK, or guarana, the roasted seeds of which are used for making a caffeine drink and as an ingredient of Guarana (*British Pharmaceutical Codex*, 1934) which has been used for headache, and as an astringent in diarrhoea. Of recent pharmacological interest is the isolation of 1-O-[2",3",4"-tri-O-acetyl-alpha-L-rhamnopyranosyl-(1-->2)-beta- D-glucopyranosyl]-hexadecanol (cupanioside) from *Cupania glabra* which exhibited cytotoxic activity against Hep G2, MDA-MB-231, Hs 578T, MCF-7, and PC-3 cells, and antibacterial activity against *Bacillus cereus, Staphylococcus aureus*, and *Escherichia coli* (Setzer *et al.*, 2005). Other principles of interest are cytotoxic polyisoprenes and glycosides of long-chain fatty alcohols from *Dimocarpus fumatus* (Voutquenne *et al.*, 1999). An extract of *Dodonaea angustifolia* L.f., afforded cell protection from HIV induced cytopathic effect *in vitro* (Asres *et al.*, 2001). This large family holds some significant potential as a source of molecules of therapeutic value.

References:

Asres K, Bucar F, Kartnig T, Witvrouw M, Pannecouque C, De Clercq E, 2001, Antiviral activity against human immunodeficiency virus type 1 (HIV-1) and type 2 (HIV-2) of ethnobotanically selected Ethiopian medicinal plants. Phytother Res; 15: 62 -69

Setzer WN, Vogler B, Schmidt JM, Petty JL, Haber WA, 2005, Isolation of cupanioside, a novel cytotoxic and antibacterial long-chain fatty alcohol glycoside from the bark of Cupania glabra. Planta Med; 71:686-8.

Voutquenne L, Catherine Laved C, Georges Massiot G, Sevenet T, Hadi AD, 1999, Cytotoxic polyisoprenes and glycosides of long-chain fatty alcohols from *Dimocarpus fumatus*. Phytochemistry; 50: 63-69

Allophylus cobbe (L.) Raeusch.

[From Latin *Allophylus* = of another tribe and from the Sri Lankan name of the plant *kobbae*]

Local names:	Allophylus, tippan (India), kobbae (Sri Lanka), kulimpapa burung (Malaysia)
Basionym:	*Rhus cobbe* L.
Description:	It is a small tree that grows in coastal and inland forest of India, Sri Lanka, to Southeast Asia and South China. The stem is terete, glabrous and lenticelled. The leaves are trifoliolate, spiral and without stipules. The rachis is 2 - 11 cm and subglabrous. The foliole is lanceolate to ovate and serrate and shows about 8 pairs of secondary nerves. The inflorescence are axillary spikes of tiny flowers. The flower is 0.2 cm long. The calyx includes 4 sepals. The corolla presents 4 petals grouped one side. The fruit is round and fleshy (Figure 132).
Medicinal Uses:	The plant is astringent and is used in India to treat diarrhoea. In Malaysia, the plant is used to treat stomach ailments. In Vietnam, the plant is used after childbirth and provides a medicine to stimulate the appetite.
Pharmacology:	Extracts of the plant exhibited antifeedant (Jayasinghe *et al*, 2003a) and nematocidal activity (Jayasinghe *et al*, 2003b).
References:	Jayasinghe UL, Kumarihamy BM, Bandara AG, Waiblinger J, Kraus W, 2003a, Antifeedant activity of some Sri Lankan plants. 2003 Jan; 17:5-8.
	Jayasinghe UL; Kumarihamy BM; Bandara AG; Vasquez EA; Kraus W, 2003b, Nematocidal Activity of some Sri Lankan Plants. Nat Prod Res.; 17:259 - 262.

Cardiospermum halicacabum L.

[From Latin *cardiospermum* = heart-shaped seed and *halicacabus* = a plant known of Plinius]

Local names:	Balloon vine, heart pea; malalai (Burma), peri belun (Malaysia), barcolon (Philippines), ketipes (Indonesia), karavi (Sanskrit, India), pois de coeur (France), phong thuyen kat (Cambodia, Laos, Vietnam), penelvel (Sri-Lanka).
Synonyms:	*Cardiospermum corindum* L., *Cardiospermum microcarpum* Kunth, *Cardiospermum molle* Kunth.

Figure 132: *Allophylus cobbe* (L.) Raeusch.
From: Herbarium of University Kebangsaan Malaysia
Malaysia, Johor state, Mersing, Pulau Tinggi, Kampung Pinang, 2° 18' North – 104° 7'
East. Collection: Zulkifli Mohamad & Azani. Identification: A Zainuddin. Date of collection: 7
November 1995.

Description: It is a slender climber native to tropical America which has
spread throughout the world by roadside, open lands. The stem
is slender, and produces long tendrils which are 7-10 cm long.
The leaves are alternate, alternate, and compound. The petiole
is 1.5-3 cm long. The petiolule is 0.5 - 1 cm long. The folioles
are 3-partite and pinnately lobed, lobes and the apex acuminate.
The inflorescence is an axillary, on a 7-10 cm long axe which
is hairy, with a pair of tendrils. The flower is zygomorphic. The
calyx comprises 4 sepals which are broadly ovate, about 0.2 cm
long, with red patches. The corolla comprises 4 petals which
are orbicular, the 2 upper emarginate at the apex, about 0.2

cm x 0.15 cm and whitish - yellow. The androecium comprises 8 stamens, which are about 0.5 cm long. The ovary is angled with a 3-lobed stigma, The fruit is a pyriform, trigonous and papery capsule, which includes 3 locules. The seeds are globose, arillate, 0.4 cm in diameter, dull-black, smooth, glabrous, with a white cordate pattern on one side (Figure 133).

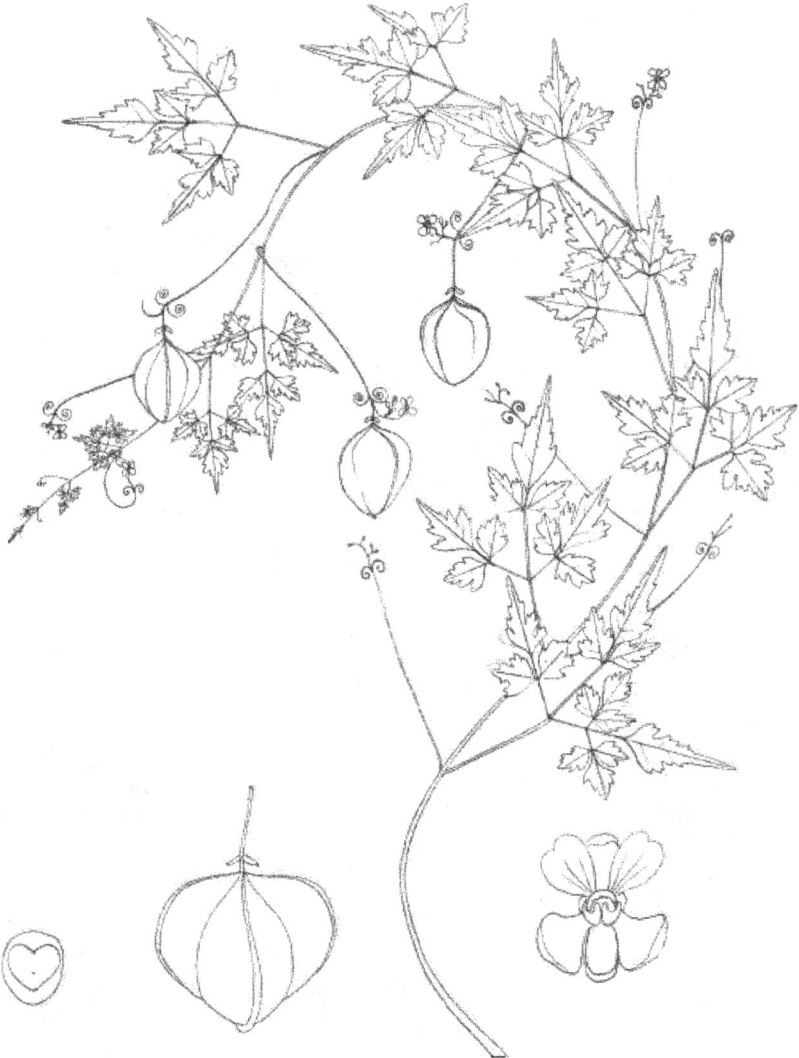

Figure 133: *Cardiospermum halicacabum* L.
From: Herbarium of University Kebangsaan Malaysia N° 04228
Malaysia, Batu 8, Jalan Klang. Collection: Sulong. Date of collection: 18
November 1972

Medicinal Uses: In India, the plant is used to break fever, to promote urination, to treat lung diseases, rheumatisms, irregular menses, tumours, and as an antidote for snake bite. In Cambodia, Laos and Vietnam, the plant is used to promote urination, vomiting and as a laxative and to sooth sore eyes. In the Philippines, the plant is used to treat rheumatism. In China, the plant is used as an antiseptic and a remedy for itchiness. In Malaysia, the plant is used for inflamed eyes and to heal boils. In Indonesia, the plant is used for headaches.

Pharmacology: The plant accumulates series of triterpenoids (Ferrara *et al*, 1996). The antipyretic property of the plant has been confirmed: extracts of the plant lowered yeast-induced fever in rodents (Asha *et al.*, 1999). The anti-inflammatory property has also been confirmed: an extract showed an anti-inflammatory effect in male albino rats using carrageenan-induced rat paw edema. The anti-inflammatory effect is probably due to inhibition of phospholipase (Sadique *et al*, 1987). An extract of the plant inhibited gastric ulcer induced by ethanol in rats and exhibited potent *in vitro* hydroxyl radical scavenging and inhibition of lipid peroxidation activities (Sheeba *et al.*, 2006). Extracts of the plant exhibited a broad spectrum of parasiticidal activity against microfilariae of *Brugia pahangi in vitro* (Khunkitti *et al.*, 2000), *Plasmodium falciparum* (Waako *et al.*, 2005), and larvae of *Strongyloides stercoralis* (Boonmars *et al.*, 2005). Extracts of the plant displayed antidiarrhoeal effects in castor oil-induced diarrhoea, and cessation of intestinal secretions in PGE2-induced peristaltic movement in the charcoal meal test (Rao *et al*, 2006).

References: Asha VV, Pushpangadan P, 1999, Antipyretic activity of *Cardiospermum halicacabum*. Indian J Exp Biol;37:411-4.

Boonmars T, Khunkitti W, Sithithaworn P, Fujimaki Y, 2005, *In vitro* antiparasitic activity of extracts of *Cardiospermum halicacabum* against third-stage larvae of *Strongyloides stercoralis*. Parasitol Res; 97:417-9.

Ferrara L; Schettino O, Montesano D, 1996, Triterpenoids from *Cardiospermum halicacabum* L. Phytother Res; 10(supplement): S192-S194

Khunkitti W, Fujimaki Y, Aoki Y, 2000, *In vitro* antifilarial activity of extracts of the medicinal plant *Cardiospermum halicacabum* against *Brugia pahangi*. J Helminthol; 74:241-6.

Rao NV, Prakash KC, Kumar SM, 2006, Pharmacological investigation of *Cardiospermum halicacabum* (Linn) in different animal models of diarrhoea. Indian J Pharmacol; 38:346-349

Sadique J, Chandra T, Thenmozhi V, Elango V, 1987, Biochemical modes of action of *Cassia occidentalis* and *Cardiospermum halicacabum* in inflammation. J Ethnopharmacol. 1987; 19:201-12.

Sheeba MS, Asha VV, 2006, Effect of *Cardiospermum halicacabum* on ethanol-induced gastric ulcers in rats J Ethnopharmacol; 106:105-10.

Waako PJ, Gumede B, Smith P, Folb PI, 2005, The *in vitro* and *in vivo* antimalarial activity of *Cardiospermum halicacabum* L. and *Momordica foetida* Schumch. Et Thonn. J Ethnopharmacol; 99:137-43.

Dimocarpus longan Lour.

[From Latin *dimocarpus* = two-lobed fruit and the Chinese name of the fruit *longan*]

Local name:	Longan, kyet mouk (Burma), mata kucing (Malaysia), medaru (Indonesia), lamyai pa (Thailand), lengkeng (Malaysia), mien (Cambodia), nam nhai (Laos), nhan (Vietnam) mato dot tungau (North Borneo), oeil de dragon (France)
Synonyms:	*Euphoria cinerea* Radlk. *Euphoria longan* (Lour.) Steud., *Euphoria longana* Lam., *Euphoria nephelioides* Radlk., *Euphoria scandens* Winit & Kerr., *Nephelium longana* Camb., *Nephelium echinulatum* Ridl., *Nephelium longan* (Lour.) Hook, *Nephelium malaiense* Griff.
Description:	It is a tree native to South China which is found in Southeast Asia. The plant grows up to 40 m. The stem is terete, lenticelled, grooved, and hairy by the apex. The leaf is compound, spiral and without stipule. The rachis grows up to 20 cm long and bears 2 - 6 pairs of folioles which are alternate. The petiolule is 0.5 - 3 cm. The foliole is elliptical, 10 - 20 cm x 3.5 - 5 cm, glossy, leathery, ovate oblong, with 9 - 15 pairs of secondary nerves, and hairy underneath, and blunt at the apex. The inflorescence is a terminal panicle. The flower pedicel is about 0.2 cm long. The calyx comprises 5 lobes which are about 0.3 cm long. The corolla consists of 5 petals which are 0.15 - 0.5 cm x 0.05 - 0.2 cm and hairy. The androecium comprises 8 stamens inserted on a disk. The fruit is a drupe which is warty. 1 - 3 cm in diameter and contains a globose, dark brown glossy seed embedded in a translucent aril (Figure 134).

Figure 134: *Dimocarpus longan* Lour.
From: Plants of Borneo, Herbarium of University Kebangsaan Malaysia
Malaysia, Sabah, Kampung Melangkap Tomis, Mandahatan Ridge on hill. Collection: Laurence
Lugas 2604.

Medicinal Uses:	In China, the plant is used to invigorate various organs and to expel worms from the intestines. It is also used for nervous and kidney problems as well as gonorrhea.
Pharmacology:	The fruit contains gallic acid, corilagin and ellagic acid (Rangkadilok *et al*, 2005). These tannins probably account for

the *in vitro* antioxidant effect of a peel extract reported by Pan *et al.*, 2008. Corilagin lowered blood pressure in rodents through the reduction of noradrenaline release and vasorelaxation (Cheng *et al.*, 1995). An extract of flowers suppressed nitric oxide and prostaglandin E2 production in a lipopolysaccharide-stimulated RAW 264.7 cell model (Ho *et al*, 2007). The plant contains adenosine which elicited an anxiolytic-like effect in Vogel-type anti-conflict method in mice (Okuyama *et al*, 1999).

References:

Cheng JT, Lin TC, Hsu FL, 1995,Antihypertensive effect of corilagin in the rat. Can J Physiol Pharmacol; 73:1425-9.

Ho SC, Hwang LS, Shen YJ, Lin CC, 2007, Suppressive effect of a proanthocyanidin-rich extract from longan (*Dimocarpus longan* Lour.) flowers on nitric oxide production in LPS-stimulated macrophage cells. J Agric Food Chem. 2007; 55:10664-70.

Pan Y, Wang K, Huang S, Wang H, Mu X, He C, Ji X, Zhang J, Huang F, 2008, Antioxidant activity of microwave-assisted extract of longan (*Dimocarpus Longan* Lour.) peel. Food Chem; 106:1264-70.

Okuyama E, Ebihara H, Takeuchi H, Yamazaki M., 1999,Adenosine, the anxiolytic-like principle of the arillus of *Euphoria longana*. Planta Med; 65:115-9.

Rangkadilok N, Worasuttayangkurn L, Bennett RN, Satayavivad J.,2005, Identification and quantification of polyphenolic compounds in Longan (*Euphoria longana* Lam.) fruit. J Agric Food Chem; 53:1387-92.

Erioglossum rubiginosum (Roxb.) Bl.

[From Latin *erioglossum* = woolly tongue and *rubiginosum* = rust-colored]

Local names: Mertajam (Malaysia), kilalayu (Indonesia), kalayo (Philippines)

Basionym: *Sapindus rubiginosus* Roxb. *Plants of the Coast of Coromandel* 1: 44, pl. 62. 1795

Synonyms: *Erioglossum edule* Bl., *Lepisanthes hirta* Ridl., *Lepisanthes rubiginosa* (Roxb.) Leenh.

Description: It is a tree which grows up to 10 m tall in the forests of a geographical area ranging from India to Australia, including Southeast Asia, South China and Papua New Guinea. The plant is often cultivated as a fruit tree, the young shoots of which are edible. The stem is hairy, terete, pitted and lenticelled. The leaves are alternate, compound and without stipule. The rachis is woolly and bears 4-6 pairs of folioles. The folioles are 10 - 12.5 cm x 3.5 - 4.5 cm, lanceolate, asymmetrical blunt or acute at the apex, with 4 - 10 pairs of secondary nerves which are woolly. The inflorescence is a terminal raceme of spikes of minute flowers which are 0.7 cm in diameter. The calyx comprises 5 sepals hairy outside, and the corolla 4 petals. The androecium includes 8 stamens. The fruit is a 1.5 cm long red drupe.

Medicinal Uses:	In Malaysia, the plant is used to treat fever, coughs and skin diseases. In Indonesia, the plant is used to treat insomnia and as post-partum remedy.
Pharmacology:	The plant contains a tetrasaccharide derivative of farnesol named rubiginoside and a series of triterpenoid saponins (Adesanya *et al.*, 1999). Sattar *et al* (1989) studied the effect of an extract of the plant on the central nervous system. The plant needs to be studied further, especially in regards to its hypnotic property.
References:	Adesanya SA, Martin MT, Hill B, Dumontet V, Van Tri M, Sévenet T, Païs M, 1999, Rubiginoside, a farnesyl glycoside from *Lepisanthes rubiginosa*. Phytochemistry; 51:1039-41.
	Sattar MA, Gan EK, Loke SE, Mah KF, Wong WH, 1989, Effect of an extract of *Erioglossum edule* on the central nervous system. J Ethnopharmacol.; 25:217-20.

Guioa pleuropteris (Bl.) Radlk.
[After J. Guio a 18th century Spain botanist and Greek *pleuron* = a rib and *pteron* = a wing]

Local name:	Tanggianuk (Malaysia)
Synonyms:	*Cupania griffithiana* Kurz., *Cupania pleuropteris* Bl., *Guioa aptera* Radlk., *Guioa forbesii* Baker f., *Guioa lasiothyrsa* Radlk., *Guioa subapiculata* Radlk.
Description:	It is a tree which grows up to 10 m tall in the coastal and swampy forests of Burma, Cambodia, Laos. Vietnam, Thailand, Malaysia, Indonesia and the Philippines. The stem is terete and glabrous. The leaves are pinnate, alternate and without stipules. The rachis is ribbed to winged and bears 2 - 3 pairs of folioles,

which are sessile, 6 - 14 cm x 3 - 5.5 cm, asymmetrical, with 4 - 6 pairs of secondary nerves and hairy underneath. The inflorescence is axillary. The flower is 0.3 cm in diameter. The calyx and corolla include 5 sepals and 5 petals respectively. The petals are whitish and hairy. A notched disk is present. The fruit is 2-3-lobed, up to 2 cm in diameter, red, and splits to release 2 -3 seeds which are smooth, blackish and embedded in a fleshy yellow-orange aril. The calyx is persistent (Figure 135).

Figure 135: *Guioa pleuropteris* (Bl.) Radlk.
From: Herbarium of University Kebangsaan Malaysia
Malaysia, Sabah, Moyog. Elevation: 200 m. Collection: Takashi Sato. Date of collection: 8 February 1981. Determination: PC Welsen, 14 October 1986.

Medicinal Uses: In Malaysia, the plant is used to treat fever and stomach-ache.

Pharmacology: Unknown.

Harpullia arborea (Blco.) Radlk

[From Bengal name *harpulli* and Latin *arborea* = tree - like]

Local names:	Tulip-wood tree, pus tree, pacat (Malaysia, Indonesia), uas (Philippines), neikottei (India)
Synonyms:	*Blancoa arborea* Bl., *Harpullia imbricata* Thwaites, *Harpullia cupanioides* F.-Vill., *Harpullia Blancoi* F.-Vill., *Harpullia tomentosa* Ridl., *Ptelea arborea* Blco., *Seringia lancolata* Blco
Description:	It is a tree which grows up to 20 m in Sri Lanka, Malaysia, Thailand, Vietnam, Indonesia, Philippines, Australia, and the Pacific Islands. The bark is smooth and brownish. The stem is hairy when young. The leaves are paripinnate, alternate and without stipule. The rachis bears 2 - 4 pairs of folioles which are sessile, alternate, 12 - 20 cm x 4.5 - 6 cm, elliptic, acute both at the apex and the base, hairy underneath and with 6 - 8 pairs of secondary nerves. The inflorescence is axillary. The calyx comprises 5 sepals which are broadly lanceolate. The corolla consists of 5 petals bending downward and pointed at the apex. The androecium consists of 5 stamens which are showy. The fruit is a bilobed glossy green turning reddish capsule which is 2 - 4 cm in diameter, splitting into 2 halves to show a pair of globose seeds with an aril covering the basal region (Figure 136).
Medicinal Uses:	In the Philippines, the plant is used to wash the hair, as a leech repellent, to stupefy fish and to treat rheumatism .
Pharmacology:	The pharmacological property of this plant is yet unknown. The plant is known to produce a new norhopane triterpenoid, 3beta-eicosanoyl-6beta-hydroxy-21alpha *H*-24-norhopan-4(23),22(29)-diene (Thanakijcharoenpath *et al.*, 2008).
Reference:	Thanakijcharoenpath W, Ratchanee Poovapatthanachart R, 2008. A new norhopane from *Harpullia arborea* Fitoterapia; in press.

Litchi chinensis Sonner

[From the Chinese name of the fruit *li chih* and from Latin *chinensis* = from China]

Local names:	Lytchee, litchi, kyetmauk (Burma), laici (Malaysia), see raaman (Thailand), vai (Thailand), kulen (Cambodia), litsi (Indonesia), letsias (Philippines), litchi (France).
Synonyms:	*Dimocarpus litchi* Lour., *Litchi sinense* J. Gmelin, *Nephelium litchi* Cambess. *Euphoria didyma* Blco, *Litchi philippinensis* Radlk.

Figure 136: *Harpullia arborea* (Blco.) Radlk
From: Flora of Sabah, Herbarium of the Forest Department Sandakan, SAN № 100238. Malaysia, Sabah, Nabutan, Ranau district. Collection: Amin G. & Amat. Date of collection: 25 August 1983.

Description:　　　　It is a tree that grows up to 30m tall, native of South China and is grown in Southeast Asia and Pacific Islands for its fruits which are edible and of economic importance. The bole is short and the bark is thin, finely roughened and grey. The stem is terete, and glabrous and 0.3 cm in diameter. The leaves are pinnate, alternate and without stipules. The rachis is glabrous, elliptic, acuminate at the apex, and bears 2-4 pairs of folioles. The petiolule is 0.3 - 0.8 cm long and dark brown. The foliole is dark green above, glaucous below, 6 - 13 - 2 - 3 cm, the midrib sunken above, and without apparent secondary nerves. The inflorescence is a terminal and axillary pendulous panicle which is many flowered and up to 30 cm long. The flower is tiny and yellowish white, and either male or female. The calyx comprises 4 lobes. The corolla is absent. A disk in present and supports 6 - 7 stamens The fruit is a drupe which is 3.5 cm x 3 cm, green turning red, with a muricate pericarp and containing 1 seed which is brown, glossy and enclosed in a white sweet aril (Figure 137).

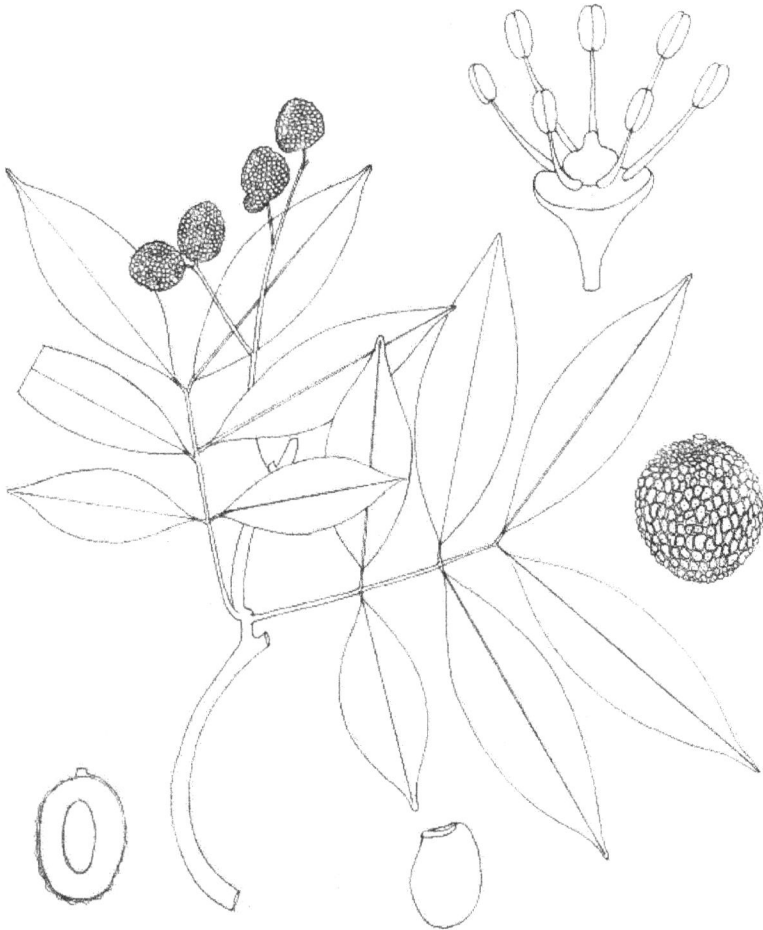

Figure 137: *Litchi chinensis* Sonner
From: Flora of Thailand, Chiang Mai University Herbarium
Thailand, Chiang Mai province, Sahn Gahn Pang district, Doi Lohn, West side , Mae Galm Bawng village, Huay Gaye subdistrict. Elevation: 1000 m. Date of collection: 22 May 1996. In open fruit orchard, disturbed, seasonal, primary evergreen hardwood forest cultivated in the village for edible aril on granite bedrock. Collection and identification: JF Maxwell N° 96-708.

Medicinal Uses:	In India, the plant is used to invigorate. In Cambodia, Laos and Vietnam, the plant is used as a carminative, and provides a remedy for smallpox and sore throat. In Malaysia, the plant is used to treat nervous disorders and infection of the testes. In China, the plant is used against tumours, and is used as a gargle. In the Pacific Islands the plant is used for coughs.
Pharmacology:	The pericarp contains a series of flavonoids such as epicatechin, procyanidin (or proanthocyanidin) B2, and B4 which displayed significant antioxidant activities and cytotoxic properties (Li *et al*, 2007) and induced mouse splenocyte stimulatory effects (Zhao *et al.*, 2007). A petroleum ether extract of leaves displayed anti-inflammatory, analgesic and antipyretic activity in rodents (Besra *et al.*, 1996).

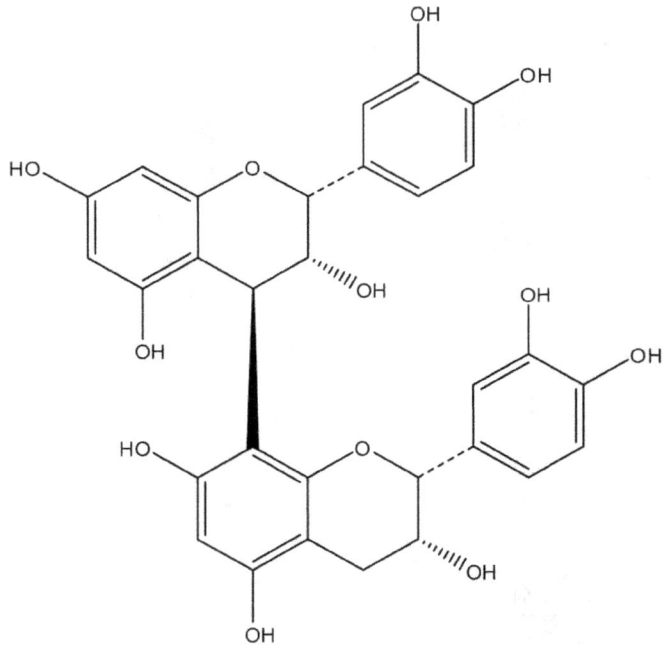

Proanthocyanidin B2

References:	Besra SE, Sharma RM, Gomes A, 1996, Antiinflammatory effect of petroleum ether extract of leaves of *Litchi chinensis* Gaertn. (Sapindaceae).J Ethnopharmacol; 54:1-6.
Li J, Jiang Y, 2007, Litchi flavonoids: isolation, identification and biological activity. Molecules; 12:745-58.
Zhao M, Yang B, Wang J, Liu Y, Yu L, Jiang Y, 2007, Immunomodulatory and anticancer activities of flavonoids extracted from litchi (*Litchi chinensis* Sonn) pericarp. Int Immunopharmacol; 7:162-6.

Mischocarpus sundaicus Bl.

[From Greek *mischos* = a stalk and *karpos* = a fruit and from Latin *sundaicus* = from the Sunda islands]

Local names:	Red pear-fruit, sugi, medang serai (Malaysia), khaokwang (Thailand), sandek prei (Cambodia), ki howe (Indonesia), bing guo mu (China), malasalab (Philippines)
Synonyms:	*Cupania erythrorhachis* Miq., *Mischocarpus lessertianus* Ridl., *Schleichera revoluta* Turcz.
Description:	It is a tree which grows 3 - 6 m tall often on sandy coasts, islands and estuaries and swamps and also inland, in a region covering India, Southeast Asia and Australia. The stem is terete, darkish red, glabrous and, according to locals, can be eaten when young. The leaves are paripinnate, alternate and exstipulate. The rachis is 10 - 20 cm long and bears 1-3 pairs of folioles. The petiolule is about 1 cm long. The foliole is 6.5 - 15 cm x 2.5 - 7 cm, elliptic lanceolate, glossy above, marked with a prominent midrib, with 4-6 pairs of secondary nerves plus some internerves, and some hairs are present at axils of secondary nerves with the midrib underneath. The inflorescence is an axillary or terminal panicle up to 12 cm long and hairy. The flower pedicel is 0.1 - 0.3 cm long. The flower is minute, 0.15 cm in diameter. The calyx comprises 5 triangular lobes around a disk on which is inserted 8 stamens with glabrous filaments. The ovary is hairy. The fruit is a pear-shaped capsule green at first, which is1.5 - 0.7 cm with a distinct stipe which is 0.6 cm long, slightly sticky, and contains one seed which is globose and embedded in a thin waxy-pulp layer (Figure 138).
Medicinal Uses:	The plant is used to treat headache in Cambodia, Laos and Vietnam. In Malaysia, the plant is used to treat coughs.
Pharmacology:	The pharmacological property of *Mischocarpus sundaicus* Bl. Is to date unexplored. Note that Mizushina *et al* (2005) isolated a unusual triterpene dicarboxylic acid: mispyric acid, which inhibits the enzymatic activity of DNA polymerase.

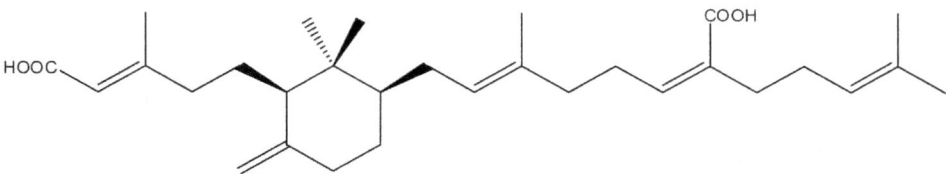

Mispyric acid

Reference: Mizushina Y, Takikawa H, Imamura Y, Sasaki M, Mori K, Yoshida H, 2005 , Inhibitory effect of mispyric acid on mammalian DNA polymerases. Biosci Biotechnol Biochem.; 69:1534-8.

Figure 138: *Mischocarpus sundaicus* Bl.

From: Flora of Thailand, Prince of Songkla University.
Thailand, Songkla province, Muang district, Keo Moi, Songkla. Elevation 50 m. Date of collection: 16 November 1984. In secondary forest, scrub, partly shaded area. Collection: JF Maxwell N° 84-426

Nephelium mutabile Bl.

[From Greek *nephelion* = like a cloud and from Latin *mutabile* = varied]

Local name:	Rambutan king, pulasan (Malaysia), kapoelasan (Indonesia), bulala (Philippines)
Synonyms:	*Nephelium chryseum* auct. non Bl., *Nephelium ramboutan-ake* (Labill.) Leenh
Description:	It is a tree which is native to Malaysia and cultivated in Southeast Asia for its fruits which are edible. The tree can reach 15 m. The stem is hairy at the apex and 0.3 - 0.7 cm in diameter. The petiolule is 0.3 - 1.1 cm long and channeled. The leaves are compound, spiral and without stipule. The rachis is 15 - 30 cm and bears 2 - 5 pairs of sub-opposite folioles. The folioles are dark green above, lanceolate, 6 - 15 cm x 2 - 5 cm long, hairy underneath and with 6 - 8 pairs of secondary nerves. The inflorescence is a terminal or axillary panicle of tiny yellowish flowers. The calyx comprises 5 lobes which are hairy. The androecium comprises 5-8 stamens. The fruit is ovoid, dark purplish, 4 - 6 cm x 3 - 5 cm, covered with oblong tubercles. The seed is ovoid, oblong about 2.5 cm long and embedded in a translucent aril (Figure 139).
Medicinal Uses:	In Malaysia, the plant is used to treat fever and to expel worms from the intestines.
Pharmacology:	Unknown

Sapindus rarak DC.

[From Latin *Sapindus* = for soap and *rarak* an Indonesian name for the plant]

Local names:	Mao ban wu huan zi (China), mah sahk (Thailand), lerak, rarak (Indonesia)
Synonyms:	*Dittelasma rarak* Hook. f. ex Hiern, *Dittelasma rarak* (DC) Hiern.
Description:	It is a timber tree which grows up to 20 m in Bhutan, Burma, Thailand, Malaysia, Cambodia, Laos, Vietnam, Indonesia, China and Taiwan. The bark is slightly thickened, roughened and grey. The stem is stout, terete and hairy at the apex. The leaves are spiral, dropping, compound and without stipule. The rachis is 20 - 35 cm long, terete, reddish and bears 7 - 12 pairs

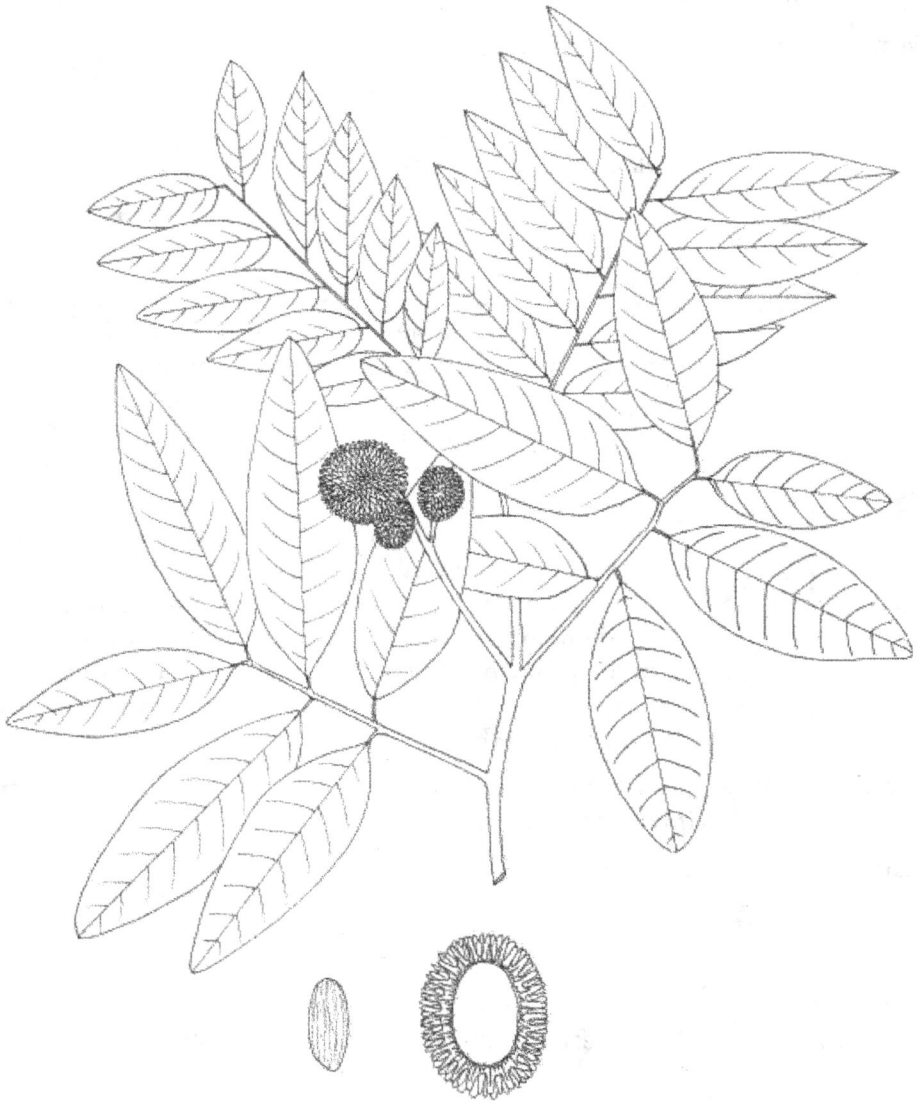

Figure 139: *Nephelium mutabile* **Bl.**
From: Herbarium of University Kebangsaan Malaysia № 42455
Malaysia, Sabah, Pulau Tiga, . Elevation: 250 m. Collection: Fatimah. Determination: E Rahim.
Date of collection: 7 June1982.
& From: Flora of Malaya, Pahang state, Jerantut, Jalan Maran. Collection: Mohd Kassim.
Determination: Abdul Latiff

Description (contd.)   of folioles which are subopposite. The petiolule is 0.5 - 0.8 cm long.
The foliole is 7 - 15 cm x 1.5 - 5 cm, dull dark green above, dull
pale light green underneath, obtuse at the base, acute at the apex,
with about 12 pairs of secondary nerves slightly prominent on both
surfaces. The inflorescence is dull dark brown-grey, and hairy. The

flower pedicel is 0.15 cm. The calyx comprises 5 sepals which are oblong, about 0.3 cm long and with few hairs. The corolla consists of 4 petals which are hairy, lanceolate and about 0.4 cm long. The fruit is a brown-red schizocarp which is 2.5 cm in diameter, each locule containing a dull black seed (Figure 140).

Figure 140: *Sapindus rarak* DC.
From: Flora of Thailand, Chiang Mai University Herbarium
Thailand, Lampang province, Muang Bahn province, Jae Sawn national park, Langgah village-Bahn Dohn Noon village road. Elevation: 1025 m. In open, fire damaged, mostly secondary growth bordering agricultural fields in seasonal evergreen hardwood forest on granite bedrock. Collection and identification: JF Maxwell, No 96-54.

Medicinal Uses:

In Indonesia, the plant is used to treat itchiness caused by scabies and to stupefy fish.

Pharmacology:

The medicinal property is probably due to the saponins which abound in the plant. Extracts of the plant showed some levels of fibroblast protection against *Heterometrus laoticus scorpion* venom treatment (Uawonggul *et al.*, 2006), affected rumen fermentation (Wina *et al.*, 2005) and displayed antifungal activity (Phongpaichit *et al.*, 1992). The pericarp contains a sweet tasting sesquiterpene glycoside: mukurozioside IIb (Chung *et al*, 1998). The plant contain cytotoxic and molluscicidal saponins (Hamburger *et al.*, 1992).

References:

Chung MS, Kim NC, Long L, Shamon L, Ahmad WY, Sagrero-Nieves L, Kardono LBS, Kennelly EJ, Pezzuto JM, Soejarto DD, A. Kinghorn D, 1998, Dereplication of saccharide and polyol constituents of candidate sweet-tasting plants: isolation of the sesquiterpene glycoside mukurozioside IIb as a sweet principle of *Sapindus rarak*. Phytochem Anal; 8:49 -54.

Hamburger M, Slacanin I, Hostettmann K, Dyatmiko W, Sutarjadi, 1992, Acetylated saponins with molluscicidal activity from *Sapindus rarak*: Unambiguous structure determination by proton nuclear magnetic resonance and quantitative analysis. Phytochem Anal; 3: 231 – 237

Phongpaichit S; Suvannarat N; Petcharat V; Ongsakul M, Nilrat L; Wiriyachitra P, 1992, Antifungal activities of extracts from *Maesa ramentacea*, *Sapindus rarak* and *Sapindus emarginatus*; Rit tan ra khong san sakat chak bai kraduk kai (*Maesa ramentacea*) lae phon makham-di-khwai (*Sapindus rarak* lae S. *emarginatus*). Sonklanakarin J Sci Technol; 14:361-66.

Uawonggul N, Chaveerach A, Thammasirirak S, Arkaravichien T, Chuachan C, Daduang S, 2006, Screening of plants acting against *Heterometrus laoticus* scorpion venom activity on fibroblast cell lysis. J Ethnopharmacol; 103:201-7.

Wina E, Muetzel S, Hoffmann E, Makkar HPS, Becker K, 2005, Saponins containing methanol extract of *Sapindus rarak* affect microbial fermentation, microbial activity and microbial community structure *in vitro*. Anim Feed Sci Technol; 121, 159-174.

Schleichera trijuga Willd.

[After J. C. Schleicher, a Swiss botanist and Latin *trijuga* = three jugate]

Local names: Sri Lanka oak, kobin (Burma), vanamra (Sanskrit, India), kon (Sri Lanka).

Synonyms: *Pistacia oleosa* Lour., *Schleichera oleosa* (Lour.) Oken

Description: It is a deciduous tree which grows up to 20 m tall in India, Sri Lanka, Nepal, Burma, Cambodia, Vietnam, Laos, Thailand, Malaysia, Indonesia and Australia. The bark is pale brown, scaly and thin. The stem is terete, lenticelled and glabrous. The leaves are pinnate, alternate and exstipulate. The leaves can reach 40 cm long. The rachis bears 2 - 4 pairs of folioles which are 4 - 20 cm x 1 - 4 cm, elliptic with 10 - 12 pairs of conspicuous secondary nerves. The inflorescence is a raceme which is 7.5 - 12.5 cm long and opposite the leaves. The calyx presents 5 sepals which are triangular. Five stamens are inserted on a disk around a bottle -shaped ovary. The fruits are ovoid, beaked, 2.5 - 3.8 cm long and contain 1-2 seeds which are 1.5 cm long, smooth and brown (Figure 141).

Medicinal Uses: In India, the plant is used to treat skin diseases including leprosy, ulcers, itch, boils. It also used there for cholera, headache, worms, and as a tonic. In Cambodia, the plant is used to heal boils and to promote the growth of hair. In Cambodia, Laos and Vietnam, the plant is used against malaria and boils. In Indonesia, the plant is used to heal wounds and to promote the growth of hair. The oil expressed from the seed, kusum oil, has been used for making laundry soaps in Europe.

Pharmacology: The plant produces a series of sterols of which schleicherastatins 1-7 inhibited the growth of P-388 lymphocytic leukemia cell line (Pettit *et al*, 2000).

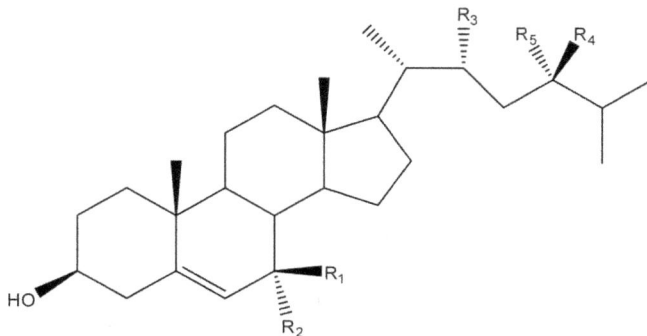

Schleicherastatins

Reference: Pettit GR, Numata A, Cragg GM, Herald DL, Takada T, Iwamoto C, Riesen R, Schmidt JM, Doubek DL, Goswami A, 2000, Isolation and structures of schleicherastatins 1-7 and schleicheols 1 and 2 from the teak forest medicinal tree Schleichera oleosa. J Nat Prod.; 63:72-8.

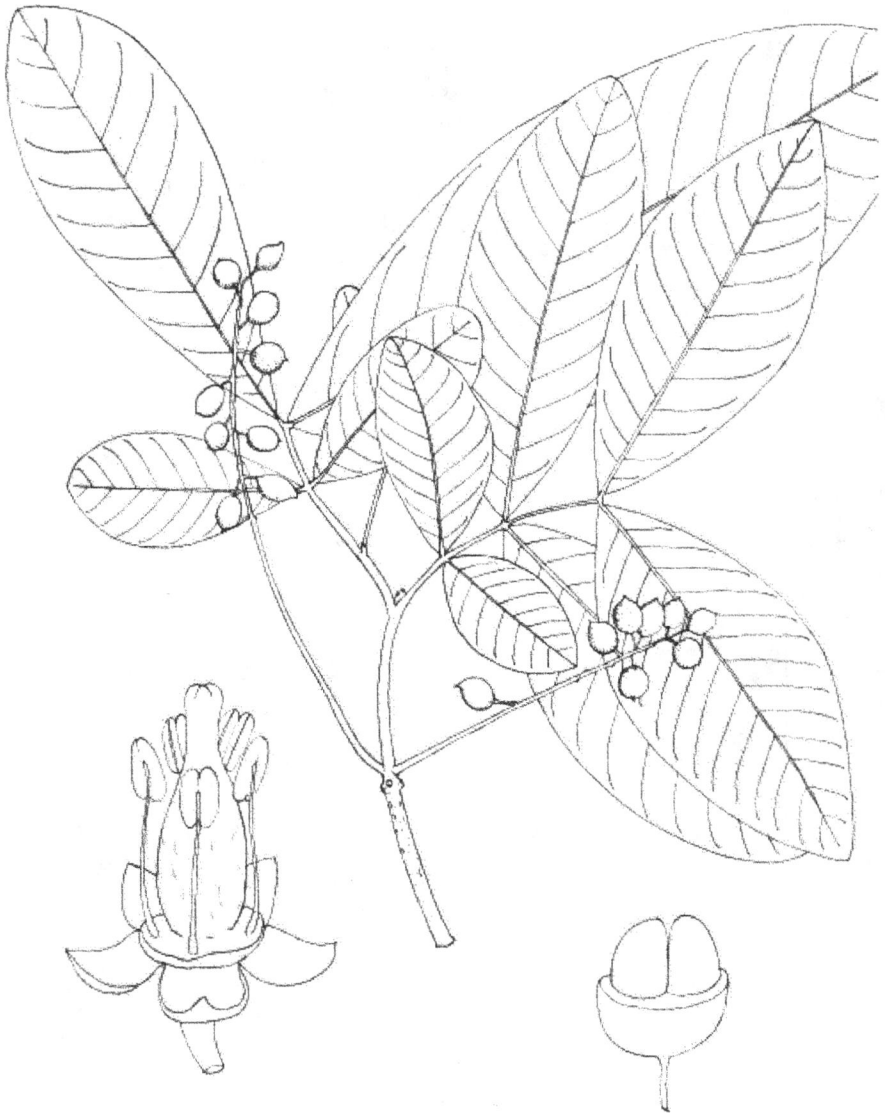

Figure 141: *Schleichera trijuga* Willd.

From: Flora of Thailand

Thailand, Kanchanaburi province, Songklaburi district, Toon Yai wildlife reserve, Ban Saneh Pang area (Karen village). Elevation: 250 m. Date of collection: 10 April 1974. Collection and identification: JF Maxwell No 94-474. In partly open, degraded, fire prone area in deciduous forest with much bamboo on rugged limestone terrain.

2.Family ANACARDIACEAE Lindley 1830 nom conserv., the Sumac Family

The family Anacardiaceae consists of about 60 genera and 600 species of tropical trees, climbers or shrubs, the resinous exudatation of which is often extremely vesicant. Phenolic compounds such as tannins, biflavonoids, and alkylphenols abound in this group. The leaves are mostly alternate, simple or compound, coriaceous, with straight secondary nerves. Stipules are absent. The inflorescences are panicles. The flowers minute, whitish to green, with 5 sepals, 5 petals and 10 stamens and present a well - developed 5 - lobed nectary disc. The anthers are tetrasporangiate and dithecal, and open by longitudinal slits. The gynaecium comprises 1 - 5 carpels fused into a 1 - 3 locular ovary, each locules containing a single ovule. The fruits are drupes.

In this family are several fruit trees such as *Mangifera indica* L. (mango), *Anacardium occidentale* L (cashew - nut), and *Pistacia vera* (pistachio nut). Other species of economic value are *Pistacia lentiscus* var. chia that produces mastic, *Rhus coriaria* (dyeing and tanning Sumac), and *Rhus succedanea* (Japan wax tree). The dried berries of *Rhus glabra* (Pennsylvanian sumac) have been used as mouthwash (Rhus, *British Pharmaceutical Codex*, 1934). The sap of several members of this family contain alkylated phenolic compounds or urushiols which produce anaphylactic shock. Such poisonous members include *Anacardium melanorrhoea* (rengas tree), *Toxicodendron vernis* (poison sumac), *Toxicodendron radicans* (poison ivy), and *Gluta* species. Of particular pharmacological interest in this family are the anticancer and antiviral properties of phenolic compounds. The compound 1,3-Dihydroxy-5-(tridec-4',7'-dienyl) benzene from *Lithraea molleoides* abrogated the survival of hepatocellular carcinoma cell line-Hep G2, mucoepidermoid pulmonary carcinoma cell line-H292 and mammary gland adenocarcinoma cell line -MCF7 (Lopez *et al,* 2005). Lanneanol: a dihydroalkylcyclohexenol and from *Lannea nigritana* (Sc. Ell.) Keay exhibited cytotoxic effects (Kapche et al., 2007). Chlorogenic acid butyl ester and 2-O-Caffeoyl-(+)-allohydroxycitric acid from *Spondias mombin* showed antiviral activities against *Coxsackie* and *Herpes simplex* viruses, respectively (Corhourt *et al,* 1992).

References   Corthout J, Pieters L, Claeys M, Berghe DV, Vlietinck A,1992, Antiviral caffeoyl esters from *Spondias mombin* Phytochemistry; 31: 1979-1981

Kapche GDWK , Laatsch H, Fotso S, Kouam SF, Wafo P, Ngadjui BT, Abegaz BM, 2007, Lanneanol: A new cytotoxic dihydroalkylcyclohexenol and phenolic compounds from *Lannea nigritana* (Sc. Ell.) Keay. Biochem System Ecol; 35: 539-43.

López P, Ruffa MJ, Cavallaro L, Campos R, Martino V, Ferrar G, 2005, 1,3-dihydroxy-5-(tridec-4',7'-dienyl)benzene: a new cytotoxic compound from *Lithraea molleoides*. Phytomedicine; 12:108-11

Bouea macrophylla Griff.

[After German botanist A. Boue (1794 - 1881) and Latin *macrophylla* = large - leaved]

Local names:	Kundang daun besar (Malaysia), ma praang (Thailand), gandaria (Indonesia)
Description:	It is a tree which grows up to 35 m in Thailand, Malaysia, and Indonesia. The bark is dark grey to brownish-red. The tree is resinous. The stem is angled, and fissured. The leaves are simple, opposite and without stipules. The petiole is 1 - 2.5 cm long and stout. The leaf-blade is oblong, 10 - 30 cm x 2.5 - 11 cm, acuminate at the apex, cuneate at the base, with 15 - 25 pairs of secondary nerves. The inflorescence is an axillary panicle of tiny flowers. The flowers are light yellowish-green. The corolla comprises 4 minute petals which are oblong spathulate. The fruit is a drupe which is globose, 3.5 - 5cm and green turning yellow. The fruit is edible (Figure 142).
Medicinal Uses:	In Malaysia, the plant is used for headaches and as a mouthwash.
Pharmacology:	Unknown, likewise for the genus *Bouea*

Buchanania lucida Bl.

[After Scottish botanist Buchanan-Hamilton (1762-1829) and Latin *lucida* = glossy]

Local name:	Little gooseberry tree, sparrows' mango otak udang tumpul, rengas (Malaysia)
Synonym:	*Buchanania arborescens* (Bl.) Bl.
Description:	It is a tree which grows up to 30 m on the sea shores and tidal river of a geographical area covering Tenasserim, Andaman Islands, Thailand, Cambodia, Laos, Vietnam, Malaysia, Indonesia, Australia and the Pacific Islands. The bark is grayish-brown. A resin exudes when the bark is incised. The stem is darkish grey. The leaves are simple, spiral and exstipulate and crowded at the apex of the stems. The petiole is 1.25 - 2.5 cm long with discrete wings. The blade is coriaceous, pink when young, spathulate, 5 - 25 cm x 2 - 7 cm, cuneate at the base, acuminate at the apex, with 7 - 20 pairs of secondary nerves which are conspicuous on both surfaces. The inflorescence is an axillary panicle of tiny flowers. The calyx is 5 lobed and persistent in fruit. The corolla comprises 5 petals. The fruit is a greenish-purple drupe which is elliptic (Figure 143).

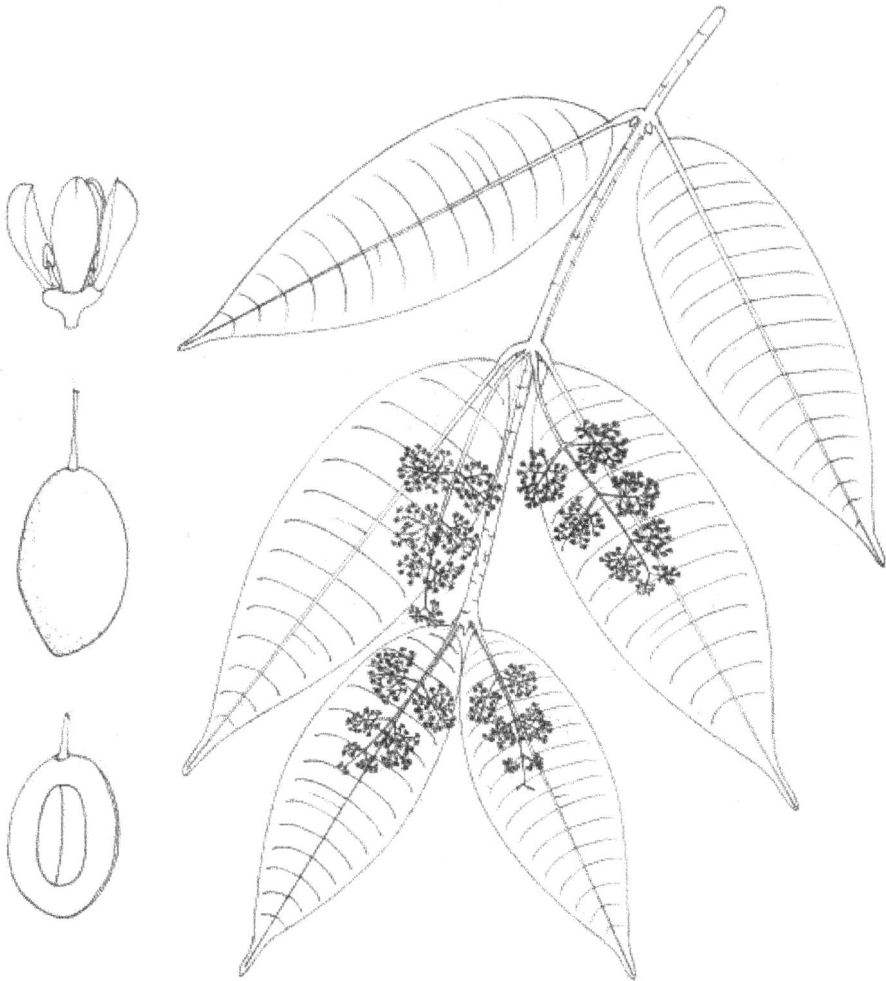

Figure 142: *Bouea macrophylla* **Griff.**
From: Flora of Malaya, from University Kebangsaan Herbarium
Malaysia, Kedah, Pulau Langkawi. Collection: Rasman Alif. Identification: Mohd Kassim. Date
of collection: 11 November 1980

Figure 143: *Buchanania lucida* Bl.
From: Herbarium of University Kebangsaan Malaysia
Malaysia, Bangi. Date of collection: 24 January 1980.

Medicinal Uses: In Malaysia, the plant is used to assuage headache.

Pharmacology: The pharmacological property of *Buchanania lucida* Bl. and of
the genus *Buchanania* remains unexplored.

Rhus succedanea L.

[From a Greek name *rhus* and Latin *succedanea* = substituted]

Local names: Crab's claw, Japan wax tree, ranivalai (Nepal), arkhar (India).

Synonym: *Toxicodendron succedanueum* (L.) Kuntze.

Description: It is a tree which grows up to 40 m tall in India, Burma, Thailand, Cambodia, Vietnam, Laos, Malaysia, China and Taiwan. The bark is grey brown. The stem is glaucous and terete. The leaves are spiral, compound and without stipule. The rachis is reddish, bears 4 - 8 pairs of folioles and a terminal one. The leaf can reach 60 cm long. The foliole is elliptic, lanceolate, asymmetrical, 4 - 8 cm x 1 - 2.5 cm with 10-15 pairs of secondary nerves marked by a reddish gland at axil with the midrib underneath. The inflorescence is a lax axillary panicle. The flower pedicel is 0.25 - 0.5 cm long and hairy. The calyx shows 5 ovate lobes. The corolla comprise 5 petals which are oblong. The disk is 5 lobed. The flower is cream-colored, 0.38 cm in diameter. The fruit is ovate, flattened and 0.5 - 0.75 cm in diameter, light brown and waxy (Figure 144).

Medicinal Uses: In India, the plant is used to treat diarrhoea. In China, the wax expressed from the drupe, or Japan wax, is used for the making of an external remedy.

Pharmacology: The plant produces a series of biflavonoids of which Hinokiflavone is cytotoxic (Lin *et al*, 1989) and inhibits HIV-1 reverse transcriptase (Lin *et al*, 1997). Another biflavonoid of interest is robustaflavone, which is a potent inhibitor of hepatitis B virus (Zembower *et al*, 1998). The compounds 10'(Z),13'(E),15'(E)-heptadecatrienylhydroquinone, 10'(Z),13'(E)-heptadecadienylhydroquinone, and 10'(Z)-heptadecenylhydroquinone isolated from the plant showed antioxidant and cytotoxic properties (Wu PL *et al.*, 2002).

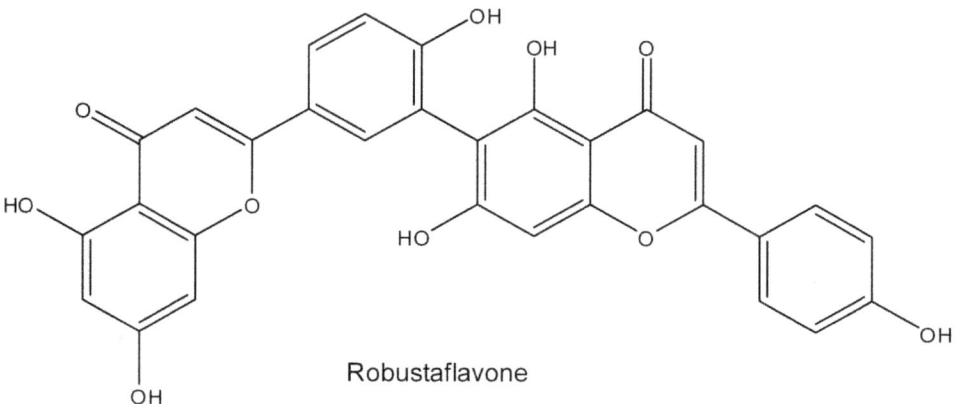

Robustaflavone

References: Lin YM, Chen FC, Lee KH, 1989, Hinokiflavone, a cytotoxic principle from Rhus succedanea and the cytotoxicity of the related biflavonoids. Planta Med; 55:166-8.

Lin YM, Anderson H, Flavin MT, Pai YH, Mata-Greenwood E, Pengsuparp T, Pezzuto JM, Schinazi RF, Hughes SH, Chen FC, 1997, In vitro anti-HIV activity of biflavonoids isolated from *Rhus succedanea* and *Garcinia multiflora*. J Nat Prod; 60:884-8.

Wu PL, Lin SB, Huang CP, Chiou RY, 2002, Antioxidative and cytotoxic compounds extracted from the sap of Rhus succedanea. J Nat Prod; 65:1719-21.

Zembower DE, Lin YM, Flavin MT, Chen FC, Korba BE, 1998, Robustaflavone, a potential non-nucleoside anti-hepatitis B agent. Antiviral Res; 39:81-8

Figure 144: *Rhus succedanea* L.
From: Botanical Inventory of Taiwan. Herbarium Institute of Botany, Academia Sinica, Taipei Taiwan, Taipei City, neihu, on the mountain road from Chinlungshih (a temple) to Vaishuanghsi, 121° 34' 53" East - 25° 06' 47"North. Elevation 250 m. On semi-shaded site beside road. Collection and identification: Yi Chung Chen.

Spondias pinnata (L. f.) Kurz

[From a Greek plant name *spondias* and Latin *pinnata* = pinnate]

Local names:	Hog plum, kywae (Burma), amara (Nepal), umrah (Malaysia), amrata (Sanskrit, India), emberella (Sri Lanka), libas (Philippines)
Basionym:	*Mangifera pinnata* L. f. *Supplementum Plantarum* 156. 1781 [1782].
Synonyms:	*Mangifera pinnata* L.f., *Poupartia pinnata* (L.f.) Blco., *Spondias acuminata* Roxb., *Spondias bivenomarginalis* K.M. Feng & Mao, *Spondias mangifera* Willd., *Tetrastigma megalocarpum* W.T. Wang
Description:	It is a tree which grows up to 10 m in India, Burma, Indonesia, China, Thailand, Malaysia, Cambodia, Laos, Vietnam, Indonesia, the Philippines and the Pacific Islands. The plant is cultivated for its fruits. The bark is light grey with some vertical cracks. The leaves are compound, spiral and exstipulate. The rachis is 10 - 20 cm long and smooth and bears 3-5 pairs of folioles plus a terminal one. The petiolule is 0.5 - 0.6 cm long. The foliole is dull dark greenish above, 7.5 - 15 cm x 3 - 5 cm, oblong, acuminate at the apex with 14 - 25 pairs of secondary nerves which merge into an intramarginal nerve. The inflorescence is a terminal tan panicle up to 35 cm long. The flowers are cream-white on a 0.1 - 0.4 cm long stalk. The calyx shows minute triangular lobes. The corolla comprise 5 petals which are 0.25 - 0.3 cm long, and oblong. The disk is 10 crenate. The androecium shows 10 stamens smaller than the petals. The fruit is an ovoid pale yellowish sour fruit which is about 3.8 cm long (Figure 145).
Medicinal Uses:	In India, the plant is used as an aphrodisiac, and provides a remedy for rheumatism, ulcers, blood diseases, dysentery and dyspepsia. In Burma, the plant is used for dyspepsia. In Cambodia, Laos and Vietnam, the plant is used to treat malaria. In Malaysia, the plant is used as an astringent. In Indonesia, the plant is used for dysentery, dysmenorrhoea, constipation, infected wounds and coughs.
Pharmacology:	The plant seems unexplored in terms of its pharmacology.

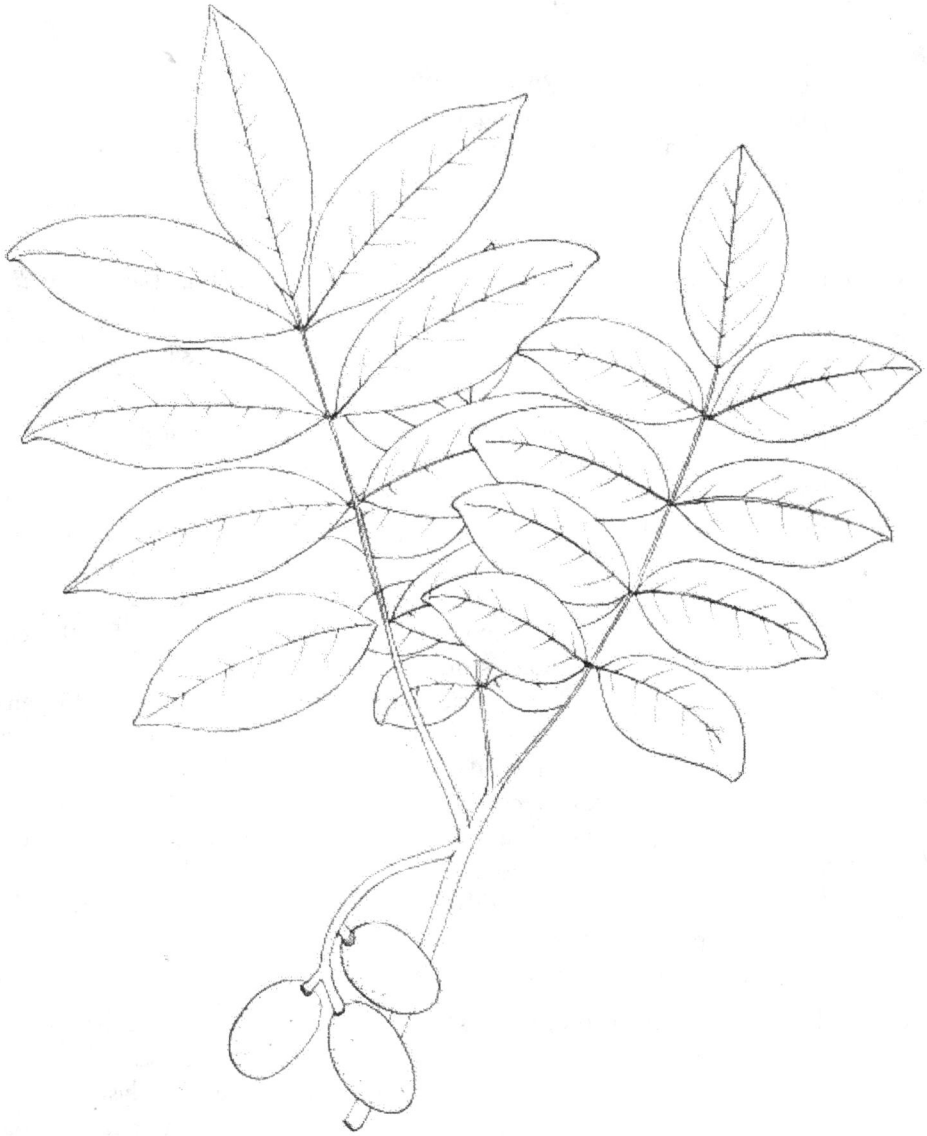

Figure 145: *Spondias pinnata* **(L. f.) Kurz**
From: Flora of Thailand, Prince of Songkla University
Thailand, Nakornsitammarat province, Lansagah district,, Gahrome falls, Khao Luang national park. Elevation 150 m. Date of collection: 16 December 1985. In open thicket, margins of primary evergreen forest on granite bedrock along a river. Collection and identification: JF Maxwell N° 85-1144

3.Family MELIACEAE A.L. de Jussieu nom. conserv., the Mahogany family

The family Meliaceae consists of 51 genera and 550 species of tropical trees known to produce bitter oxygenated triterpenoids including limonoids and furanocoumarins. The leaves are pinnate, alternate or spiral and without stipule. The inflorescence are axillary racemes of numerous tiny flowers. The calyx includes 3 - 5 valvate sepals. The corolla comprises 3 - 5 petals which are alternate with the sepals. The androecium is tubular with 6 - 10 stamens. The anthers are tetrasporangiate and dithecal. The gynaecium consists of 2 - 5 carpels fused into a compound, plurilocular ovary, and each locule containing 2 ovules attached to an axil placenta. The fruits are scepticidal or loculicidal capsules or berries or drupes containing several seeds which are occasionally winged.

The family Meliaceae contains a number of trees the wood of which is of economic value: *Swietenia mahogani* (L.) Jacq. (mahogany) and *Cedrela odorata* L. *Azadirachta indica* A. Juss. (Azadirachta, India*n Pharmaceutical Codex*) or margosa, neem, the dried stem bark, root bark and leaves of which were used in India as a bitter flavor and against fever as well as for cosmetic purpose. The limonoids of Meliaceae have attracted a great deal of interest on account of their cytotoxic properties. Limonoids from the seeds of *Chisocheton siamensis* exhibited antiplasmodial, antimycobacterial and cytotoxic activity against NCI-H187 (human small cell lung cancer), KB (oral human epidermal carcinoma) and MCF-7 (breast cancer) cancer cell lines (Maneerat *et al.*, 2008).

Reference: Maneerat W, Laphookhieo S, Koysomboon S, Chantrapromma K, 2008, Antimalarial, antimycobacterial and cytotoxic limonoids from *Chisocheton siamensis*. Phytomedicine; (In Press)

Dysoxylum acutangulum Miq.

[From Greek *dyes* = unpleasant and *xylon* = wood and Latin *acutangulum* = sharply angular]

Local name: Langkang (Indonesia)

Synonyms: *Alliaria acutangula* (Miq.) Kuntze, *Alliaria schultzii* (C.DC.) Kuntze, *Dysoxylum foveolatum* Radlk., *Dysoxylum schultzii* C.DC.

Description: It is a tall tree which grows up to 40 m in the forest of Thailand, Malaysia, Indonesia, Philippines, Papua New Guinea, Australia and the Pacific Islands. The bark is smooth and yellowish. The stem is terete, smooth, with minute hairs and angled at the apex. The leaves are opposite, paripinnate and without stipules, The rachis is 9.8 - 23 cm, sharply quadrangular, with minute hairs, and bears 4 - 7 pairs of folioles without domatia. The petiolule is flat above, and 0.6 - 0.8 cm long. The foliole is elliptic, 7.4 - 11 cm x 4 - 4.5 cm, thick, granules, with about 14 pairs of secondary nerves which are discrete and a midrib prominent underneath. The inflorescence is a panicle up to 8 cm long. The corolla comprises 4 petals which are yellowish. The androecium includes 8 stamens. The fruit pedicel is 2 - 3 cm long. The fruit is a pyriform smooth, 3 - lobed capsule which is 4.5 - 6 cm x 3.7 - 5 cm, yellow-orange with 3 black seeds (Figure 146).

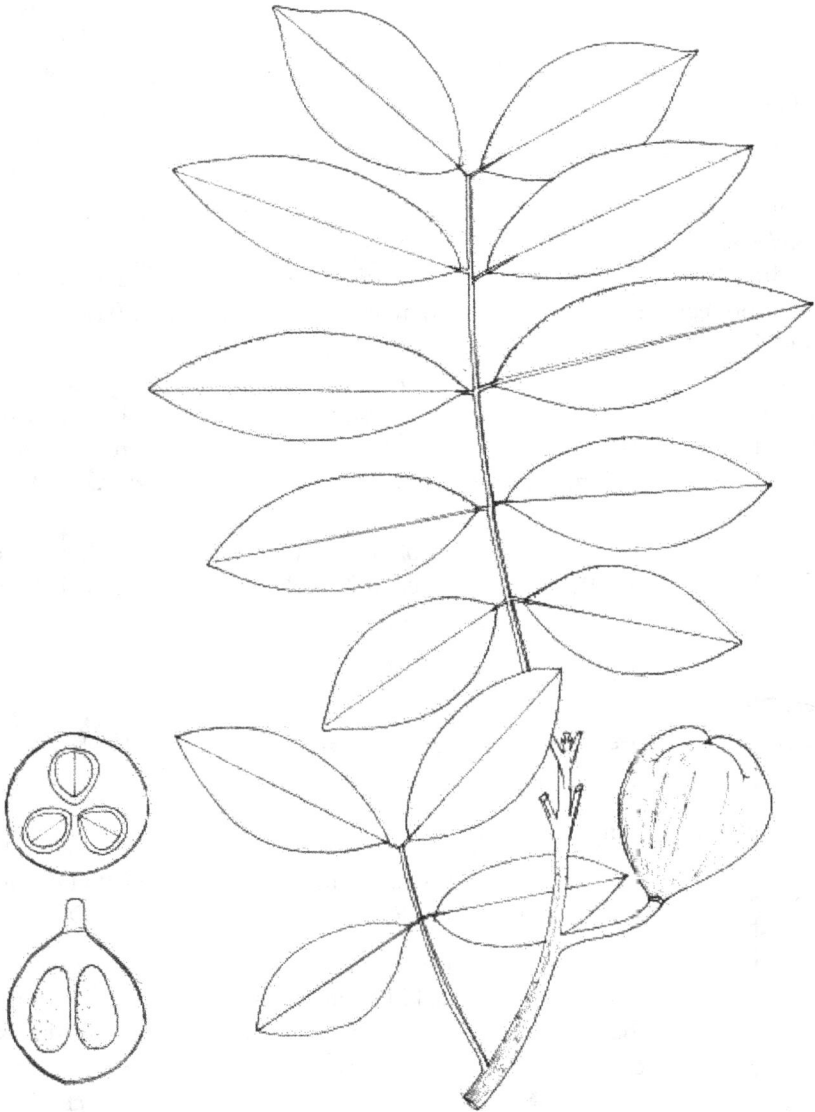

Figure 146:*Dysoxylum acutangulum* Mic.
From: Herbarium of University Kebangsaan Malaysia
Malaysia. Elevation: 60 m. Collection and identification: A. Zainuddin AZ 4349.
Date of collection: 17 November 1992.

Medicinal Uses:	The seeds are used as a poison in Indonesia.
Pharmacology:	The plant contains (+)-8-hydroxycalamenene, a sesquiterpene phenol which is toxic to fish (Nishizawa *et al.*, 1983).
Reference:	Nishizawa M, Inoue A, Sastrapradja S, Hayashi Y, 1983, (+)-8-Hydroxycalamenene: A fish-poison principle of *Dysoxylum acutangulum* and *D. Alliaceum*. Phytochemistry; 22: 2083-85.

Lansium domesticum Corrêa

[From Malay *langsat* = lansium and Latin *domesticum* = cultivated]

Local names:	Duku langsak (Burma), langsat (Malaysia), kokosan (Indonesia), lansones (Philippines), longkong (Thailand), bon-bon (Vietnam)
Synonyms:	*Aglaia domestica* (Correa) Pell., *Aglaia dookoo* Griff.
Description:	It is a tree up to 15 m tall, probably originating from Malaysia, which is cultivated or found wild throughout Southeast Asia to Papua New Guinea. The plant presents small buttresses. The bark is light reddish with tubercles of old inflorescence. The stem is smooth. The leaves are pinnate, spiral and without stipule. The rachis bears 5 - 7 alternate folioles. The folioles are leathery, 7-20 cm long, dark green above. The inflorescence is a panicle originating from stem and up to 20 cm long. The calyx is 5 - lobed. The corolla comprises 5 yellowish petals. The anthers are grouped in a staminal tube, 10 in a single whorl. The fruit is a brown 5 - seeded berry with a soft pericarp which is about 3 cm in diameter. The seeds are embedded in a thick whitish edible aril (Figure 147)
Medicinal Uses:	In Malaysia, the plant is used to treat dysentery, fever and to expel worms. In Indonesia, the plant is used to promote urination. In the Philippines, the plant is used to treat diarrhoea and tuberculosis.
Pharmacology:	The plant contains series of triterpenes, some of which are active against *Plasmodium falciparum* (Saewan *et al.*, 2006). The compound 3-oxo-24-cycloarten-21-oic acid, inhibited the activity of skin-tumor promotion on the basis of Epstein Barr virus activation (Nishizawa *et al*, 1989).

Figure 147: *Lansium domesticum* Corrêa
From: Herbarium University Kebangsaan Malaysia
Malaysia, Terengganu, Kuala Berang, Kampung Sekayu. Collection and identification: A
Zainuddin. Date of collection: 31 January 1991.

References: Nishizawa M, Emura M, Yamada H, Shiro M, Chairul, Hayashi Y,
Harukuni TV, 1989, inhibitors. Tetrahedron Lett, 30:5615-18.

Saewan N, Sutherland JD, Chantrapromma K, 2006,
Antimalarial tetranortriterpenoids from the seeds of *Lansium
domesticum* Corr. Phytochemistry; 67:2288-93.

Melia dubia Cav.

[From Latin *melia* = flowering ash and *dubia* = doubtful]

Local names:	Giant neem tree, arangaka (India), lapshi (Nepal), gango (Philippines)
Synonyms:	*Melia candollei* Juss., *Melia azedarach* Blco., *Melia composita* Willd.
Description:	It is a tall tree which grows in thickets and secondary forests, in tropical Africa, India, Cambodia, Laos, Vietnam, China and tropical Australia. The stem is hairy. The leaves are bi- or tri- pinnate, spiral and without stipules. The leaf can reach 75 cm long, each pinna with 2 - 5 pairs of folioles and a terminal one. The petiolule is 0.3 - 0.6 cm long. The foliole is ovate lanceolate, 2 - 7.5 cm x 0.5 - 3.5 cm with 7 - 8 pairs of secondary nerves. The inflorescence is axillary or terminal panicle which is many flowered. The calyx is tomentose, 5 - lobed, and minute. The corolla comprises 5 petals which are white to purplish, 0.5 cm long, linear, and subglabrous. The staminal tube is 0.6 cm long, subglabrous, and 10 toothed. The stigma is 5 toothed. The fruit is an ovoid drupe which is about 3 cm in diameter, smooth and yellowish and contains 5 seeds which are smooth and brown (Figure 148).
Medicinal Uses:	In India, the plant is used to treat colic and infected wounds
Pharmacology:	Pettit *et al*, (2002) isolated from the plant a series of euphane-type triterpenes including meliastatins 1-5 and methyl kulonate, kulinone, 16-hydroxybutyrospermol, and kulactone which inhibited the growth of the P388 lymphocytic leukemia cell line. The antiseptic property of the plant has been confirmed, as an essential oil from the plant inhibited the growth of *Pseudomonas aeruginosa*, *Escherichia coli*, *Klebsiella pneumoniae* and *Fusarium oxysporum* and *Candida albicans* cultured *in vitro* (Nagalakshmi *et al.*, 2003). An extract of the plant showed mild anti-Herpes activity *in vitro* (Vijayan *et al.*, 2004).
References:	Nagalakshmi MA, Thangadurai D, Pullaiah T, 2003, *In vitro* antimicrobial efficacy of leaf essential oils of *Chukrasia tabularis* Adr Juss and *Melia dubia* Cav (Meliaceae).Phytother Res; 17:414-6.
	Pettit GR, Numata A, Iwamoto C, Morito H, Yamada T, Goswami A, Clew low PJ, Cragg GM, Schmidt JM, 2002, Antineoplastic agents. 489. Isolation and structures of meliastatins 1-5 and related euphane triterpenes from the tree *Melia dubia*. J Nat Prod; 65:1886-91

Vijayan P, Raghu C, Ashok G, Dhanaraj SA, Suresh B, 2004, Antiviral activity of medicinal plants of Nilgiris. Indian J Med Res; 120:24-9.

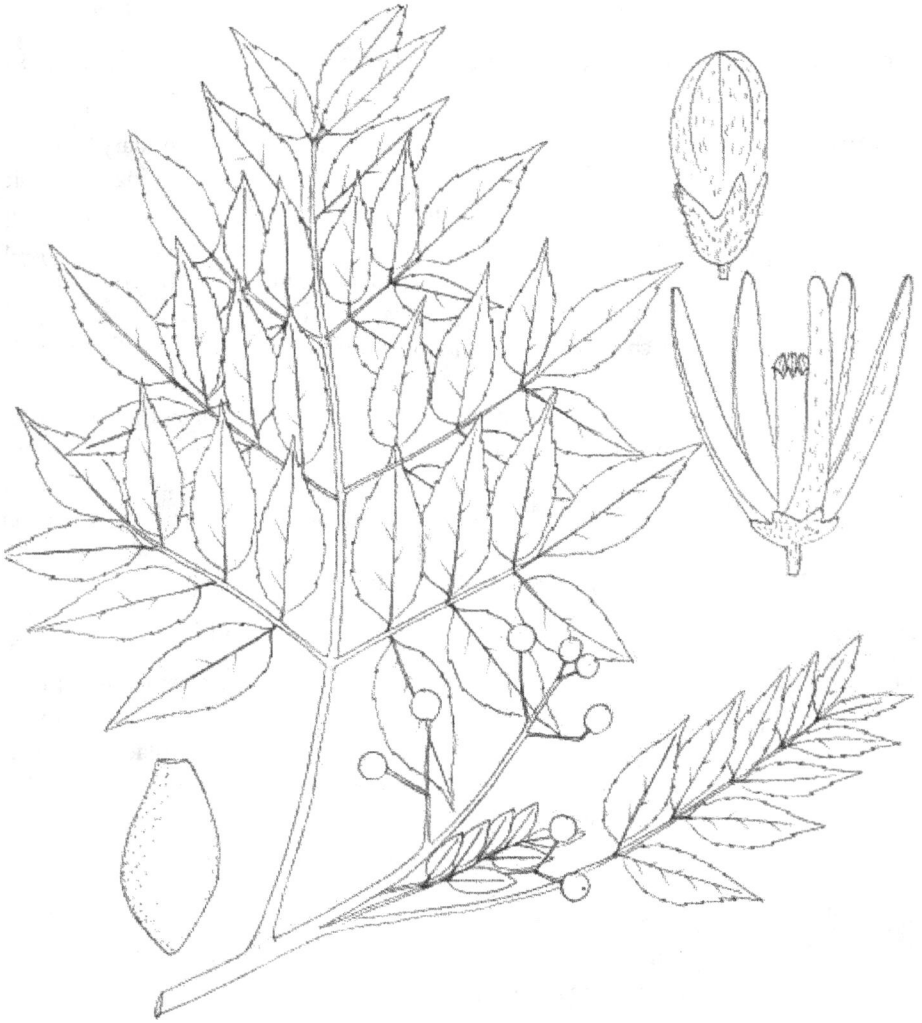

Figure 148: *Melia dubia* **Cav.**
From: Flora of Malaya. Herbarium of University Kebangsaan Malaysia, № 10996
Indonesia, Kalimantan, Collection and identification: T. Khuzzan

Xylocarpus granatum J. König

[From Greek *xylon* = wood and *karpon* = fruit and Latin *granatum* = pomegranate]

Local name:	Cannonball mangrove, nyireh bunga (Malaysia), dhundul (Bengladesh), tabigi (Philippines), mu guo lian (China)
Synonym:	*Carapa moluccensis* sensu Ridl. non Lam, *Carapa obovata* Bl., *Carapa granatum* (Koenig) Alston, *Xylocarpus minor* Ridl., *Xylocarpus obovatus* Juss.
Description:	Small tree up to 15 m tall in mangroves from East Africa to the Pacific Islands. Buttresses snake-like, bark smooth, and scaling. The stem is terete, zigzag shaped, longitudinally striated, 0.4 cm in diameter, with 1.5 cm internodes. The leaf scars are conspicuous. The leaves are paripinnate, spiral, and without stipule. The rachis is 2 - 7 cm long and striated. The petiolule is 0.4 cm long. The folioles is obovate, thick, glossy, recurved at margin, 5.5 - 9 cm x 3.7 - 4.3 cm, withering orange red, and with 8 pairs of secondary nerves. The inflorescence is an axillary raceme. The flower pedicel is angular. The calyx is 4 - lobed, the sepals 0.15 cm x 0.1 cm. The corolla shows 4 petals which are obovate, and 0.3 cm x 0.15 cm. The fruit is an obovoid, pear-shaped dehiscent woody capsule which is about 5 cm long and contain several polyhedral seeds (Figure 149).
Medicinal Uses:	The plant is used to treat cholera, swelling and itches in Indonesia. The plant is used against dysentery in Southeast Asia. In the Philippines, the plant is used against diarrhoea.
Pharmacology:	The plant contains a series of limonoids (Cui *et al*, 2007; Li *et al.*, 2007, Yin *et al*, 2007, Wu *et al*, 2006) such as gedunin, which inhibits the growth of CaCo-2 colon cancer cell, cultured *in vitro* (Uddin *et al.*, 2007).
References:	Cui J, Wu J, Deng Z, Proksch P, Lin W, 2007, Xylocarpins A-I, limonoids from the Chinese mangrove plant *Xylocarpus granatum*. J Nat Prod; 70:772-8.
	Li M, Wu J, Zhang S, Xiao Q, Li Q, 2007, Xylocarpins A and B, two new mexicanolides from the seeds of a Chinese mangrove *Xylocarpus granatum*: NMR investigation in mixture. Magn Reson Chem;45:705-9.
	Uddin SJ, Nahar L, Shilpi JA, Shoeb M, Borkowski T, Gibbons S, Middleton M, Byres M, Sarker SD, 2007, Gedunin, a limonoid from *Xylocarpus granatum*, inhibits the growth of CaCo-2 colon cancer cell line *in vitro*. Phytother Res; 21:757-61

Yin S, Wang XN, Fan CQ, Lin LP, Ding J, Yue JM, 2007, Limonoids from the seeds of the marine mangrove *Xylocarpus granatum*. J Nat Prod; 70:682-5.

Wu J, Zhang S, Li M, Zhou Y, Xiao Q, 2006, Xylogranatins A-D, new mexicanolides from the fruit of a Chinese mangrove *Xylocarpus granatum*. Chem Pharm Bull Tokyo; 54:1582-5.

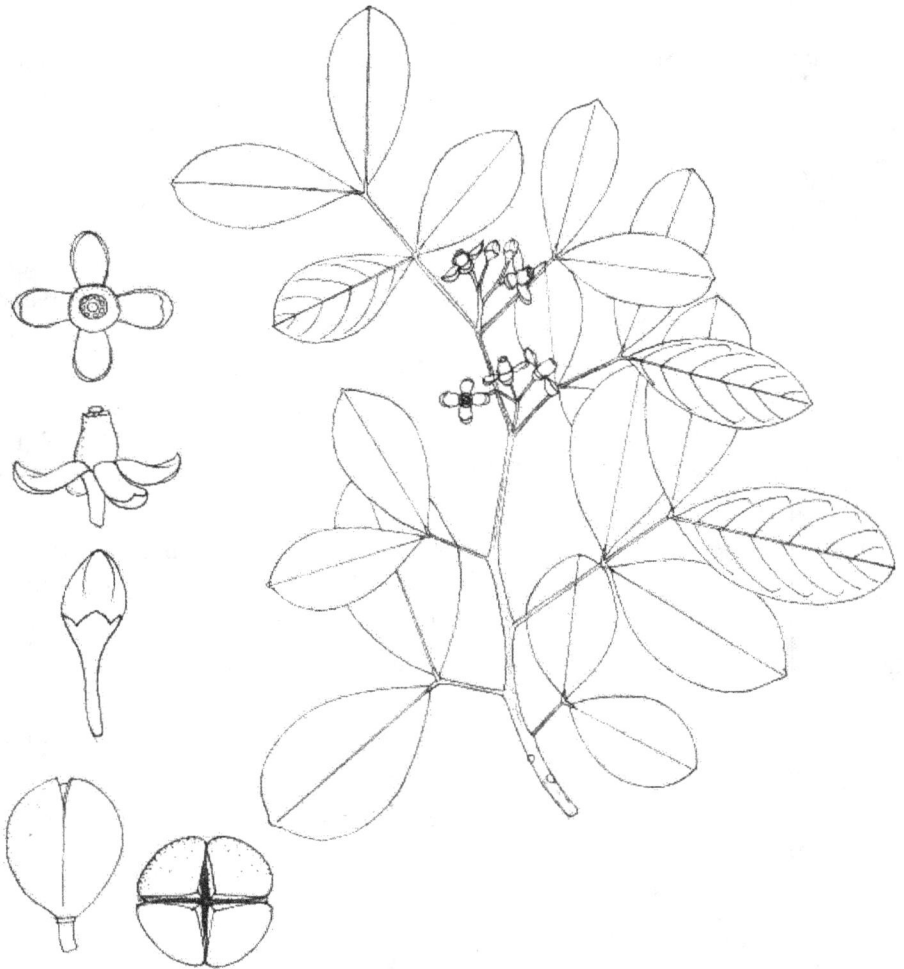

Figure 149: *Xylocarpus granatum* **J. König**
Malaysia, Sabah, Likas, along Iraman river near Sungai Puai. Elevation: 0 m. Collection and identification: Sukup Akin, SA 3067. Date of collection: 16 October 1994.

Xylocarpus moluccensis (Lamk.) Roem.

[From Greek *xylon* = wood and *karpon* = fruit and Latin *moluccensis* = from the Moluccas]

Local name:	Cedar mangrove, nyireh batu (Malaysia)
Synonyms:	*Carapa moluccensis* Lam. *Xylocarpus australasicus* Ridl., *Xylocarpus gangeticus* (Prain.) C.E. Parkinson, *Xylocarpus mekongensis* Pierre
Description:	It is a tree which grows up to 18 m in the mangroves ranging from East Africa, India to Australia and the Pacific Islands. The plant presents some pneumatophores. The bark is strongly fissured, and brownish-yellow. The leaves are paripinnate, spiral and without stipule. The rachis is up to 10 cm long and bears 3 - 4 pairs of folioles. The petiolule is 0.2 - 0.5 cm long. The foliole is elliptic - ovate, up to 12 cm x 5 cm, wedge-shaped at the base, acuminate at the apex with 3- 5 pairs of secondary nerves. The inflorescence is a lax raceme of cymes by the apex of the stems. The calyx is about 0.3 cm long with 4 sepals which are rounded. The corolla comprises 4 petals which are about 0.5 cm long and elliptical. The staminal tube is about 0.5 cm long. The fruit is 8 - 20 cm in diameter with several angled seeds which are 4 - 8 cm long (Figure 150).
Medicinal Uses:	The plant is used to treat cholera, swelling and itches in Indonesia. The plant is used against dysentery in Southeast Asia. In the Philippines, the plant is used against diarrhoea.
Pharmacology:	An extract of the plant displayed moderate inhibitory activity against *Escherichia coli*, *Vibrio cholerae*, *Staphylococcus aureus*, *Staphylococcus epidermis*, *Shigella dysenteriae*, *Staphylococcus pyogenes*, *Salmonella typhi*, *Pseudomonas aeruginosa* and *Enterobacter aerogenes* and showed antidiarrhoeal activity in both castor oil- and magnesium sulphate-induced diarrhoea models in mice (Uddin *et al*, 2005). In addition, an extract showed CNS depressant activity in pentobarbitone-induced hypnosis, reduction of locomotor and exploratory activities in the open field, hole cross, head-dip and evasion tests (Sarker *et al*, 2007).
References:	Sarker SD, Uddin SJ, Shilpi JA, Rouf R, Ferdous ME, Nahar L, 2007, Neuropharmacological properties of *Xylocarpus moluccensis*. Fitoterapia; 78:107-11.
	Uddin SJ, Shilpi JA, Alam SM, Alamgir M, Rahman MT, Sarker SD, 2005, Antidiarrhoeal activity of the methanol extract of the barks of *Xylocarpus moluccensis* in castor oil- and magnesium sulphate-induced diarrhoea models in mice. J Ethnopharmacol; 101:139-43.

Figure 150: *Xylocarpus moluccensis* **(Lamk.) Roem.**
From: Herbarium of University Kebangsaan Malaysia
Malaysia. Collection and identification: A Zainuddin. Date of collection: 19 December 1988

Walsura pinnata Hassk.

[From the India name *walsura* and from Latin *pinnata* = pinnate]

Local name:	Yue nan ge she shu (China)
Synonyms:	*Heynea cochinchinensis* Baill., *Napeodendron altissimum* Ridl., *Walsura cochinchinensis* (Bail..) Harms, *Walsura neurodes* Hiern, *Walsura yunnanensis* C.Y. Wu
Description:	It is a tree which grows in the forests of Burma, Thailand, Cambodia, Laos, Thailand, Malaysia, Indonesia, China, and the Philippines. The bark is dark brown. The stem is longitudinally fissured, with conspicuous leaf-scar, angled with rufous indumentums at the apex. The leaves are imparipinnate, and spiral. The the base of the rachis is spoon-shaped, articulated and swollen at nodes. The leaf is about 30 cm long with 3 pairs of folioles plus a terminal one. The petiolule is 1 - 1.2 cm long. The foliole is coriaceous, glaucous, asymmetrical, with 8 - 10 pairs of secondary nerves, 10 - 18 cm x 3 - 5 cm, lanceolate, acuminate at the apex, and with 14 pairs of secondary nerves. The inflorescence is an axillary panicle which is 15 - 30 cm long. The flower includes 5 sepals which are hairy, 5 petals and 10 stamens united at the base. The fruit is dull green grey oblong, 1.8 - 3 - 1 - 2 cm with a pair of poisonous seeds in a sweet aril (Figure 151).
Medicinal Uses:	The seeds are used as a poison in Malaysia.
Pharmacology:	The plant contains walsucochins A and B which exhibited significant cell protecting activities against H2O2-induced PC12 cell damage (Zhou *et al.*, 2008). The compounds, 9-O-alpha-L-arabinopyranosides (-)-isolariciresinol and 3,5-dihydroxyphenyl 6-O-(4-hydroxy-3,5-dimethoxybenzoyl)-beta-D-glucopyranoside, displayed significant antioxidant activities (Luo *et al.*, 2006). The plant synthesises series of tetranortriterpenoids (Luo *et al.*, 2000).
References:	Luo XD, Wu SH, Ma YB, Wu DG, 2000, Tetranortriterpenoids from *Walsura yunnanensis*. J Nat Prod; 63:947-51.
	Luo XD, Wu DG, Cai XH, Kennelly EJ, 2006, New antioxidant phenolic glycosides from *Walsura yunnanensis*. Chem Biodivers; 3:224-30
	Zhou ZW, Yin S, Zhang HY, Fu Y, Yang SP, Wang XN, Wu Y, Tang XC, Yue JM, 2008, Walsucochins A and B with an unprecedented skeleton isolated from *Walsura cochinchinensis*. Org Lett; 10:465-8.

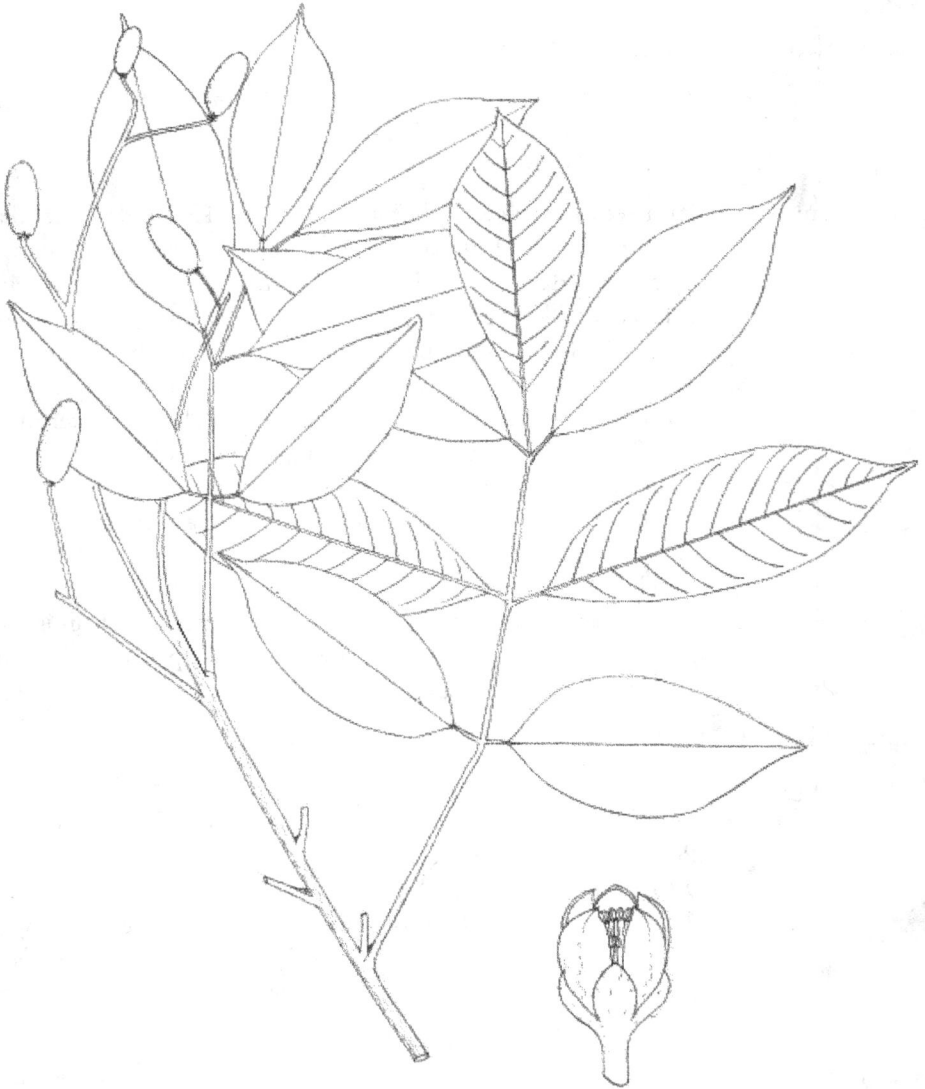

Figure 151: *Walsura pinnata* **Hassk.**
From: Herbarium of University Kebangsaan Malaysia № 24336
Malaysia, Kelantan state, Jeli, Sungai Long intake via dam site. Elevation: 770 m. In over logged lowland dipterocarp forest on granite.

4.Family RUTACEAE A. L. de Jussieu 1789 nom. conserv., the Rue Family

The family Rutaceae consists of 150 genera and 1,500 species of small aromatic trees or shrubs producing essential oils (limonene), bitter oxygenated triterpenes (limonoids), flavonoids (hesperidin), furanocoumarins, and several kinds of alkaloids including notably carbazole and acridone alkaloids. The leaves are simple compound, spiral, alternate or opposite, without stipules with a petiole often winged or knee - shaped. Leaves of Rutaceae are dotted with translucent essential oil cells.. The flowers are white and fall off quickly. The calyx consists of 4 - 5 sepals which are imbricate, free or connate. The corolla is made of 4 - 5 petals which bend downward and are slightly fleshy. The androecium is more or less partially tubular and consists of 4 - 10 stamens which originate from a conspicuous nectary disc dotted with oil cells. The gynaecium consists of 4 - 5 carpels merged into a compound, plurilocular and superior ovary. Each locules containing 1 - 2 ovules attached to axil placentas. The styles are free or connate. The stigma is protruding, globose and glossy. The fruits are baccate or succulent (hesperidia) or capsular. The peel of hesperidia is rich in essential oils.

The oil distilled from the peel of *Citrus limon* (L.) Burm. f. (lemon), *Citrus aurantium* L. (sour orange), *Citrus sinensis* (L.) Osbeck (sweet orange), *Citrus aurantifolia* (Chaistm.) Swingle (lime) is aromatic and of commercial and pharmaceutical value as a flavoring agent. Bergamot oil (*Oleum Bergamottae, British Pharmaceutical Codex,* 1949) obtained by expression from the fresh peel of the fruit of *Citrus bergamia* has been used in perfumery in preparations for the hair (Cologne Spirit or *Spiritus Coloniensis*) and to flavor tea. Other Rutaceae are used medicinally but are of lesser importance. These include *Pilocarpus jaborandi* Holmes, *Ruta graveolens* L., *Agathosma betulina, Peganum harmala, Zanthoxylum americanum* and *Zanthoxylum clavaherculis. Pilocarpus jaborandi* Holmes produces an imidazole alkaloid, pilocarpine, which is used to treat glaucoma. The dried leaves of *Agathosma betulina* (*Barosma betulina* or *buchu*) are diuretic. The leaves of *Murraya koenigii* (curry leaves) are used to flavor Asian food. Of particular pharmacological interest in this family are a series of quinoleic alkaloids which displayed a broad spectrum of activities such as acronycine and rutaeocarpine. Bergamot oil expressed from *Citrus aurantium* L. *ssp. bergamia* (Wight. and Arnott) Engler contains furanocoumarins which induce severe phototoxic reactions. Of recent interest is the isolation of anti-HIV decarine, γ-fagarine, and (+)-tembamide *Zanthoxylum ailanthoides*

Reference: Cheng MJ, Lee KH, Tsai IL, Chen IS, 2005, Two new sesquiterpenoids and anti-HIV principles from the root bark of *Zanthoxylum ailanthoides*. Bioorg Med Chem; 13:5915-20.

Boenninghausenia albiflora (Hook.) Rchb. ex Meisn.

[After German homeopathic practitioner Clemens Maria Franz Von *Boenninghausen* (1785-1864) and Latin *albiflora* = with white flower]

Local name:	Chou jie cao (China)
Basionym:	*Ruta albiflora* Hook. *Exotic flora* 1: , pl. 79. 1823
Synonyms:	*Boenninghausenia brevipes* (Franch.) H. Lév., *Boenninghausenia japonica* Siebold. ex Miq., *Boenninghausenia schizocarpa* S.Y, Hu, *Boenninghausenia sessilicarpa* H. Lév., *Bodinieria thalictrifolia* H. Lév., *Bodinieria japonica* Sib. ex Miq; *Bodinieria. schizocarpa* S. Y. Hu; *Bodinieria. sessilicarpa* H. Lév; *Podostaurus thalictroides* Jungh., *Ruta albiflora* Hook.
Description:	It is a fragrant shrub which grows 1.5 m tall in India, Bhutan, Kashmir, Nepal, Pakistan, Burma, Laos, Vietnam, Cambodia, Malaysia, Indonesia, Japan and China. The stem is slender and light brown by the apex. The leaves are cordate to spatulate, dull dark green above, marked with oil cells, about 0.3 x 0.8 cm and with 3 pairs of secondary nerves. The inflorescence is dull dark violet and few flowered. The flower is ovoid in bud. The calyx is green with sepals which are about 0.1 cm long. The corolla has 4 petals which are elliptic, white, dotted with oil cells, and up to 0.6 cm long. A disk is present. The stamens are longer than the corolla, the anthers are grayish and the filaments white. A 0.15 cm long pale light greenish gynophore is present. The style and stigma are light green. The fruit is a group of follicles which is about 0.5 cm in diameter, each follicle containing a kidney - shaped muricate seed (Figure 152).
Medicinal Uses:	The plant is used against malaria. In Taiwan, the plant is used to check bleeding.
Pharmacology:	The plant contains series of acridone alkaloids (Rózsa *et al.* 1975) including 1,3-dihydroxy-4-(2'-hydroxy-3'-hydroxymethyl-3',4'-epoxy-butyl)-N-methylacridone, 1,3-dihydroxy-4-[(Z)-3'-hydroxy-3'-methyl-buten-1'-yl]-N-methylacridone, and cohorts of coumarins with levels of cytotoxicity against cancer cells (Chaya *et al.*, 2004).
References:	Chaya N, Terauchi K, Yamagata Y, Kinjo J, Okabe H, 2004, Antiproliferative constituents in plants 14. Coumarins and acridone alkaloids from *Boenninghausenia japonica* NAKAI. Biol Pharm Bull; 27:1312-6
	Rózsa Z, Szendrei K, Novák I, Reisch J, Minker E, 1975, Acridone alkaloids as constituents in the roots of *Boenninghausenia albiflora* Reichb. Pharmazie; 30:753-4.

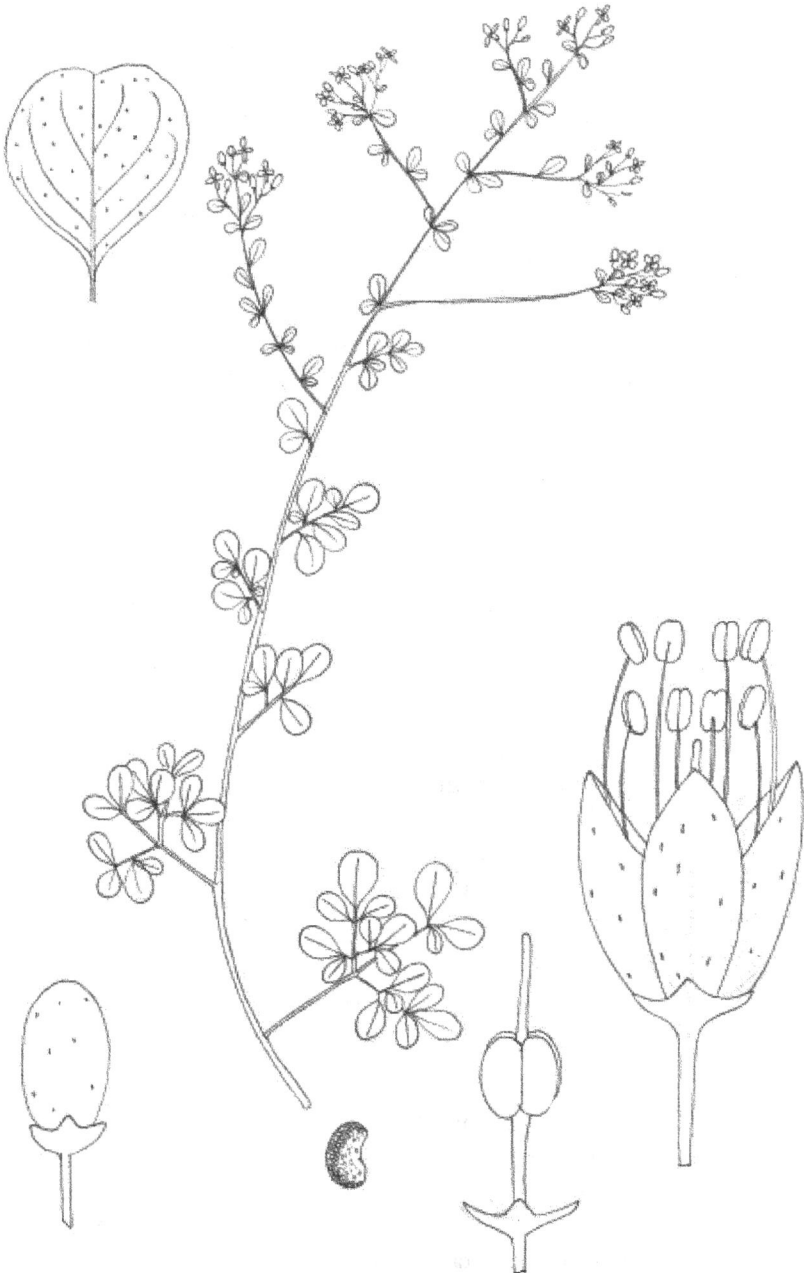

Figure 152: *Boenninghausenia albiflora* (Hook.) Rchb. ex Meisn.
From: Flora of Thailand. Chiang Mai University Herbarium
Thailand, Chiang Mai province, Jawn Tong district, Doi Intanon national park, Giew Mae Bahn meadow, grassland, West of the Royal stupas. Elevation: 2250 m. Date of collection: 10 September 1994. in open fire prone area next to primary evergreen hardwood grassland meadow area on granite bedrock.

Citrus limon (L.) Burm. f.

[From Greek *kedromelon* =apple of cedar and Arabic *al-limun* = lemon]

Local names:	Lemon, ning meng (China), citron (France), limau mata kerbau (Malaysia)
Basionym:	*Citrus medica* var. *limon* L. *Species Plantarum* 2: 782. 1753
Synonyms:	*Citrus medica* var. *limon* L., *Citrus limonum* Riso., *Citrus limonelloides* Hayata, *Citrus limonia* (L.) Osbeck
Description:	It is a small tree cultivated throughout the sub-tropical and tropical belt for its fruit. The stem is smooth with oil cells, thorns, zigzag shaped with about 2.5 cm long internodes and angled at the apex. The thorn is straight, at axil of leaf and stem, and 0.15 - 0.3 cm long. The leaves are simple, alternate, and without stipule. The petiole is 0.5 - 0.7 cm long and flat above. The leaf blade is broadly elliptic, 2.2 - 5 cm x 4.4 - 10.5 cm, dark green above, coriaceous, with oil cells, serrate at the margin and with 6 - 8 pairs of secondary nerves. The flower is fragrant, solitary or part of a fascicle. The calyx is cup-shaped, 0.4 x 0.9 cm with 5 lobes. The corolla comprises 5 petals which are 1.5 x 0.5 cm, somewhat fleshy, recurved, with oil cells, and pure white. The androecium includes several yellow stamens distributed in groups. The stigma is protruding, light green and glossy. The fruit is yellow, ovoid, fragrant, and rough to the touch, dotted with oil cells, and includes 8 - 11 fleshy segments, a thick pericarp, and several seeds (Figure 153).
Medicinal Uses:	The plant is used as antidotal, to invigorate and to promote digestion. Lemon oil (*Oleum Limonis, British Pharmaceutical Codex*, 1963) from the fresh lemon peel (*Citrus limon, Citrus limonia, Citrus medica*) is carminative and used as a flavoring agent.
Pharmacology:	*Citrus* limonoids are known to have cytotoxic effects (Tian *et al*, 2001). Limonoid glucosides; limoin 17beta D-glucopyranoside, obacunone 17beta D-glucopyranoside; nomilinic acid, 17beta D-glucopyranoside, and deacetylnomilinic acid 17beta D-glucopyranoside scavenged superoxide radical. Limoin, 17beta D-glucopyranoside; and obacunone, 17beta D-glucopyranoside were cytotoxic against undifferentiated human SH-SY5Y neuroblastoma cells *in vitro* via apoptosis (Poulose *et al.*, 2005).
References:	Poulose SM, Harris ED, Patil BS, 2005, *Citrus* limonoids induce apoptosis in human neuroblastoma cells and have radical scavenging activity. J Nutr; 135:870-7.

Tian Q, Miller EG, Ahmad H, Tang L, Patil BS, 2001, Differential inhibition of human cancer cell proliferation by *citrus* limonoids. Nutr Cancer; 40:180-4.

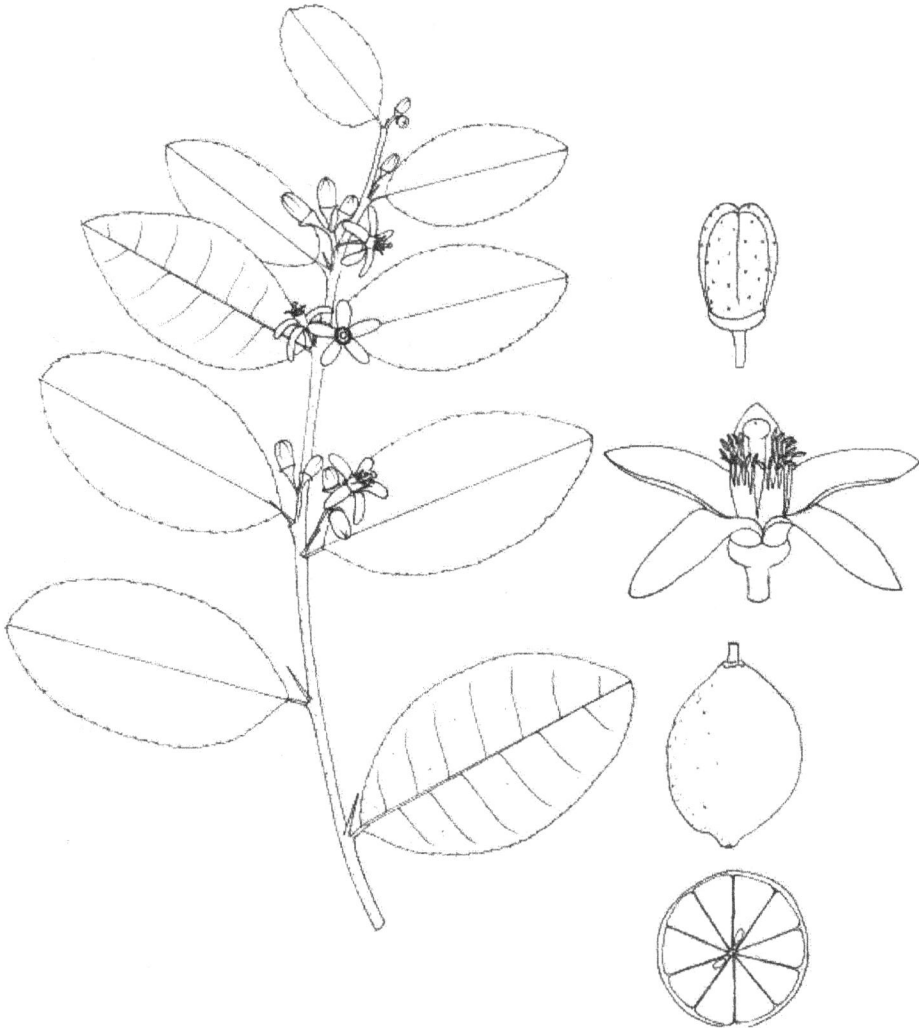

Figure 153: *Citrus limon* **(L.) Burm. f.**
From: Herbarium of University Kebangsaan Malaysia
Malaysia, UPM farm, Serdang Malaysia

Citrus sinensis (L.) Osbeck

[From Greek *kedromelon* =apple of cedar and Latin *sinensis* = from China]

Local names:	Valencia orange, sweet orange, navel orange, thung chin thi (Burma), pandil (India), kroch posat (Cambodia), somtra (Thailand), cam (Vietnam), kiengz (Laos), limau cula (Malaysia), suan cheng (China), jeruk manis (Indonesia), kahel (Philippines)
Basionym:	*Citrus aurantium* var. *sinensis* L. *Species Plantarum* 2: 783. 1753
Synonym:	*Citrus aurantium* var. *sinensis* L.
Description:	It is a tree which grows up to 15m tall in several tropical and subtropical countries where it is cultivated for its fruits. The stem is smooth and angular at the apex. The leaves are simple, alternate, and without stipule. The petiole is about 1 - 3 cm long and discretely winged. The leaf-blade is elliptic, 5 - 15 cm x 2 - 8 cm wide, dotted with oil cells, crenate with 5 pairs of secondary nerves. The flower is fragrant solitary or in an axillary fascicle. The calyx is cup shaped. The corolla comprises 5 lobes which are linear, dotted with oil cells, white and about 1 cm long. The fruit is globose, orange, rough to the touch, dotted with oil cells up to 12 cm in diameter with about 10 partitions inside and several seeds (Figure 154).
Medicinal Uses:	In India the plant is used as a tonic, diuretic and an aphrodisiac. In Cambodia, the plant is used for bronchitis. The peel is used to check bleeding and to prevent intestinal worms. The oil obtained by mechanical means from the fresh peel of the fresh orange *Citrus sinensis* (Orange oil, *Oleum Aurantii, British Pharmaceutical Codex*, 1963) has been used as a flavoring agent and in perfumery.
Pharmacology:	An extract of orange juice inhibited the proliferation of fibroblast and epithelial prostate cells (Vitali *et al.*, 2006). The peel contains polymethoxyflavones which exert proapoptotic activity in human breast cancer cells (Sergeev *et al.*, 2007).
References:	Sergeev IN, Ho CT, Li S, Colby J, Dushenkov S., 2007, Apoptosis-inducing activity of hydroxylated polymethoxyflavones and polymethoxyflavones from orange peel in human breast cancer cells. Mol Nutr Food Res; 51:1478-84.

Vitali F, Pennisi C, Tomaino A,Bonina F, De Pasquale A, Saija A, Tita B, 2006, Effect of a standardized extract of red orange juice on proliferation of human prostate cells *in vitro*. Fitoterapia; 77:151-55.

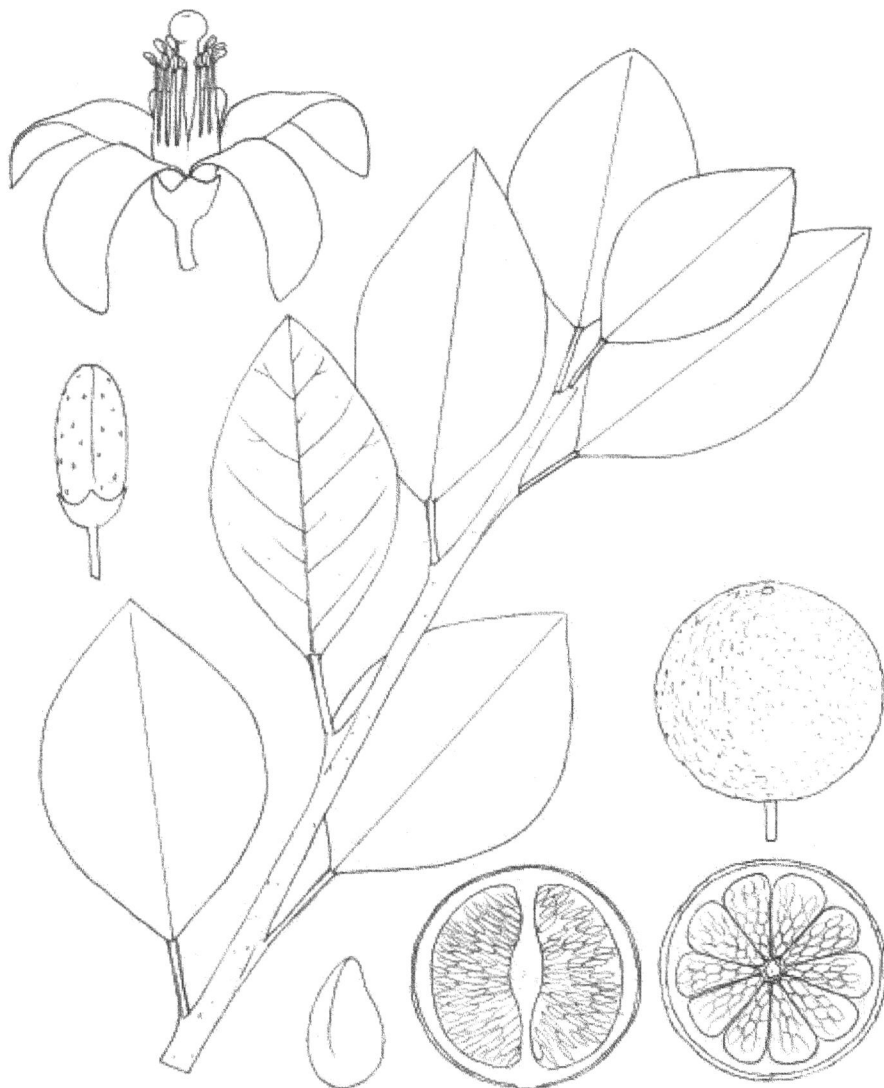

Figure 154: *Citrus sinensis* **(L.) Osbeck**

From: Flora of Malaya
Malaysia, UPM farm, Serdang, Selangor. Collection: D. Jones & Zai.

Clausena lansium (Lour.) Skeels

[After Clausen, a botanist known to Burman and Malay *langsat* = lansium]

Local name:	Wampee, wampi (Malaysia), huang p'i (China), uampit (Philippines)
Basionym:	*Quinaria lansium* Lour. *Flora Cochinchinensis* 1: 272. 1790
Synonyms:	*Quinaria lansium* Lour; *Clausena wampi* (Blco.) Oliver; *Cookia wampi* Blco..
Description:	It is a fragrant tree which grows up to 10 m tall in China and Vietnam and is cultivated in Asia for its resinous fruits. The stem is pustular. The rachis is about 10 - 15 cm, and bears 5 - 11 folioles which are sub-opposite. The petiolule is about 0.5 cm long. The folioles are asymmetrical elliptic, glossy above, acuminate at the apex, 5 - 10 cm x 3 - 7 cm and with 2 to 5 pairs of discrete secondary nerves. The inflorescence is terminal and paniculate. The flower is 0.8 cm in diameter. The calyx comprises 5 sepals which are ovate, and 0.1 cm long. The corolla comprises 5 petals which are white, elliptic, pointed at the apex, and 0.5 cm long. The androecium includes 10 showy stamens. A disk is present. The ovary is hirsute. The fruit is dull yellowish-green, globose, 1 - 2 cm long, covered with glands of fragrant oil, and containing a single seed. The fruits are copious in pendant inflorescence (Figure 155).
Medicinal Uses:	In Vietnam, the plant is used for bronchitis and hair care. In China, the plant is used as a carminative, an anti-inflammatory, and as a diuretic. In Taiwan, the plant is used to treat bronchitis.
Pharmacology:	The plant contains a series of coumarins of which clausenacoumarine lowers blood glucose levels both in normal mice and alloxan diabetic mice (Shen *et al.*, 1989). Other main secondary metabolites are alkaloids (Li S *et al.*, 1991). Clausenamide inhibited liver lipid peroxidation caused by alcohol (Liu *et al.*, 1991) and exhibited nootropic effects in rodents (Tang *et al.*, 2004)
References:	Li WS, Chesney JD, El-Feraly FS, 1991, Carbazole alkaloids from *Clausena lansium*. Phytochemistry, 30:343-346.
	Liu Y, Shi CZ, Zhang JT, 1991, Anti-lipid peroxidation and cerebral protective effects of clausenamide, Yao Xue Xue Bao; 26:166-70.
	Shen ZF, Chen QM, Liu HF, Xie MZ, 1989, The hypoglycemic effect of clausenacoumarine, Yao Xue Xue Bao; 24:391-2.

Tang K, Zhang JT, 2004, Mechanism of (-)clausenamide induced calcium transient in primary culture of rat cortical neurons. Life Sci; 74:1427-34

Figure 155: *Clausena lansium* (Lour.) Skeels
From: Flora of Malaya
Malaysia, yard of Heng Hup shop, Jalan F.R.I. 7¹/² miles, Kepong, Selangor.
Collection and identification: D. Jones & Zai № 2212

Euodia meliaefolia Bth.

[From Greek *eu* = good and *odion* = smell and Latin *meliaefolia* = with leaves like a Melia]

Local name:	Pepauh (Malaysia)
Synonyms:	*Boymia glabrifolia* Champ. ex Benth., *Euodia glauca* Miq., *Megabotrya meliifolia* Hance ex Walp., *Phellodendron burkillii* Steen., *Tetradium glabrifolium* (Champ. ex Benth.) T. Hartley
Description:	It is a tree which grows up to 20 m tall in the forests of Himalaya, Malaysia, Cambodia, Laos, Vietnam, Indonesia, Philippines, Taiwan, Japan and China. The stem is terete and smooth. The leaves are opposite, compound and without stipules. The rachis bears 9 - 13 pairs of folioles. The petiolule is about 0.2 cm long. The foliole is asymmetrical, lanceolate, 6 - 2 cm x 12 - 3 cm, with 6 - 8 pair of secondary nerves which are discrete. The inflorescence is a terminal cyme which is 9 - 19 cm long, with numerous tiny white flowers. The calyx is 5 lobed and minute. The corolla comprises 5 petals which are oblong, 0.3 cm long with a few hairs and green-white. The androecium includes 5 stamens longer than the petals. The fruit is a 0.3 - 0.35 cm long trigonous capsule with appressed pubescent follicles containing one black and glossy seed per follicle. The seed is 0.25 - 0.4 cm long (Figure 156).
Medicinal Uses:	In China, the plant is used to heal sores. In Taiwan, the plant is used to heal ulcers and to assuage stomachache.
Pharmacology:	The plant contains megastigmane glucosides, called euodionosides A-G (Yamamoto *et al.*, 2008) as well as series of benzo[*c*]phenanthridine alkaloids (Wu *et al*, 1995) including rutaecarpine which is a vaso- and utero-relaxant (Ko *et al.*, 2006).
References:	Ko HC, Chen KT, Chen CF, Su JP, Chen CM, Wang GJ, 2006, Chemical and biological comparisons on Euodia with two related species of different locations and conditions. J Ethnopharmacol. 2006 24; 108:257-63.
	Wu TS, Yeh JH, Wu PL, 1995, The heartwood constituents of *Tetradium glabrifolium*. Phytochemistry, 40: 121-124.
	Yamamoto M, Akita T, Koyama Y, Sueyoshi E, Matsunami K, Otsuka H, Shinzato T, Takashima A, Aramoto M, Takeda Y, 2008, Euodionosides A-G: megastigmane glucosides from leaves of *Euodia meliaefolia*.Phytochemistry; 69:1586-96.

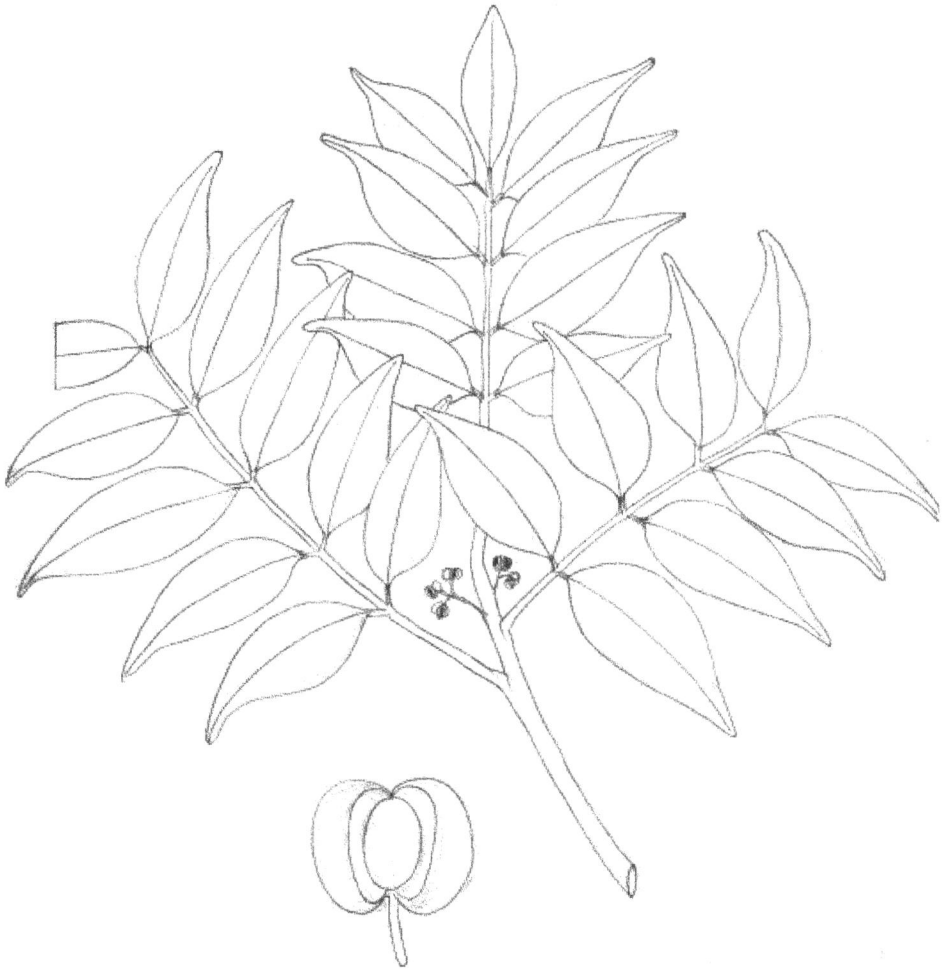

Figure 156: *Euodia meliaefolia* **Bth.**
From: Botanical Inventory of Taiwan. Herbarium Institute of Botany, Academia Sinica, Taipei Taiwan, Kaohsiung Hsien: Taoyuan Hsiang: Chuyunshan forest. Road at mileage 26 Km. In broadleaf forest. Elevation: 1600 m. Beside sunny road slope. Collection: Tsui-Ya Lui. Date of collection: 19 July 1993. Determination: Jenn-Che Wang.

Glycosmis ovoidea Pierre

[From Greek *glucus* = sweet and *osme* = smell and Latin *ovoidea* = ovoid]

Local name:	Guang ye shan xiao ju (China)
Synonyms:	*Glycosmis craibii* var. *glabra* (Craib) Tanaka, *Glycosmis singuliflora* Craib var. *glabra* Craib
Description:	It is a tree which grows up to 10 m tall with a girth of 9 cm in Thailand, Vietnam and China. The bark is thin, smooth, and dark grey. The stem is terete and zigzag shaped. The leaves are imparipinnate, alternate and without stipules. The petiolule is 0.2 - 0.6 cm long. The folioles are elliptic lanceolate, blades oblong, 5 - 10 cm × 2 - 3.5 cm, slightly coriaceous, and with about 10 pairs of secondary nerves underneath. The inflorescence is an axillary or terminal cyme. The calyx is slightly 5 - lobed. The corolla comprises 5 petals which are pale light green to white, about 0.5 cm long and somewhat spatulate. The androecium comprises 10 stamens with white filaments and cream colored anthers. The stigma is much exerted and cream colored. The fruit is orange, 1.5 cm in diameter, with 1-2 seeds (Figure 157).
Medicinal Uses:	In Vietnam, the plant is used to heal wounds.
Pharmacology:	Unknown

Luvunga scandens (Roxb.) Buch.-Ham. ex Wight & Arn.

[From Latin *scandens* = climbing]

Local name:	San ye teng (China), akar keeping (Malaysia), dhira (India)
Basionym:	*Limonia scandens* Roxb. *Flora indica*; or, *descriptions of Indian Plants* 2: 380. 1832.
Synonyms:	*Limonia scandens* Roxb., *Luvunga nitida* Pierre.
Description:	It is a woody climber which grows on the forest riverbanks of China, Cambodia, India, Laos, Malaysia, Burma, Thailand, and Vietnam. The main stems are spiny. The stem is terete and smooth. The leaves are trifoliate, alternate and without stipules. The petiole is 2 - 9 cm long. The petiolule is 0.3 - 1 cm long. The foliole is spatulate, 6 - 20 cm × 3 - 9 cm and shows about 5 pairs of secondary nerves. The inflorescence is axillary and short.

Figure 157: *Glycosmis ovoidea* Pierre
From: Flora of Thailand, Chiang Mai University Herbarium
Thailand, Kanchanapuri province, Songklaburi district, Toong Yai wildlife reserve, Iai Ko sub-district, Ban Saneh Paung area (Karen village), along Ro Kee stream. Elevation: 225 m. Date of collection: 15 April 1995. In shaded, seasonally flooded deciduous hardwood forest on rugged limestone terrain,

Description (contd.) The calyx is 4 - lobed and to 0.4 cm long. The corolla includes 4 petals which can reach 1 cm in length. The androecium comprises 8 stamens. A disk is present. The fruit is a yellow, elliptic berry up to 5 cm in diameter which contains up to 4 seeds which are ovoid and 2 - 3 cm long (Figure 158).

Medicinal Uses: In India, the plant is used as an aphrodisiac and a treatment for fever and yields a fragrant oil named kakala. In Malaysia, the plant is used as a protective remedy given after childbirth.

Pharmacology: The essential oil from the fruits displayed some levels of antifungal activity against *Arthroderma benhamiae*, *Microsporum gypseum*, *Trichophyton mentagrophytes* and *Ctenomyces serratus* (Garg *et al.*, 1999).

Reference: Garg SC, Jain R, 1999, Antifungal activity of Luvunga scandens against some keratinophilic fungi. India J Pharm Sc; 61: 248-9

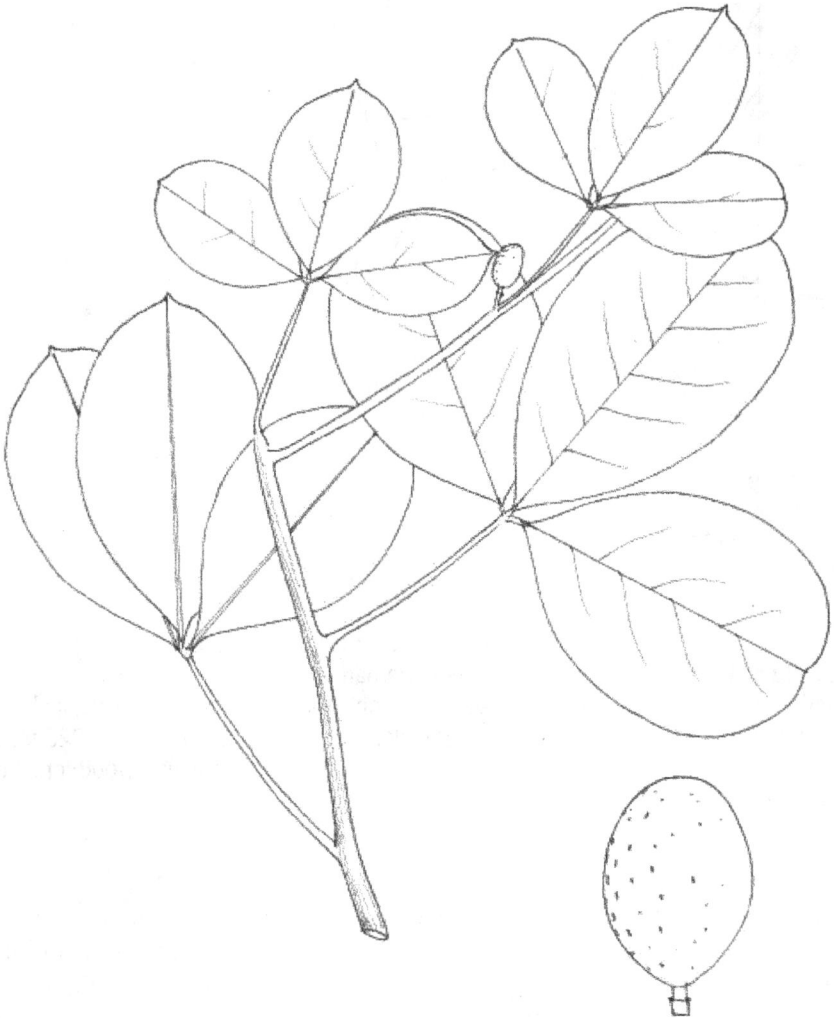

Figure 158: *Luvunga scandens* **(Roxb.) Buch.-Ham. ex Wight & Arn.**
From: Herbarium of University Kebangsaan Malaysia, No 02834
Malaysia, Pulau Bumbun, Kedah state. Collection: A Rahim Hj Othman. Date of collection: 19 February 1975. Determination: Benjamin C. Stone.

Ruta angustifolia (L.) Pers.

[From Latin *ruta* =herb of grace and *angustifolia* = having narrow foliage

Local names:	Garuda (Malaysia), godong minggu (Indonesia)
Description:	It is a fragrant herb native to Southern Europe which has been introduced into India, Southeast Asia and China as an ornamental and/or medicinal plant. The plant grows up to 1 m tall. The stem is terete and glabrous. The leaves are sessile, minute, oblong, dotted with oil cells and about 1 x 0.5 cm. The inflorescence is a cyme which is axillary. The flowers are minute, with 4 triangular sepals which are about 0.2 cm long, 4 oblong ciliate yellow petals to 1 cm long, 8 stamens as long as the petals and a 4 lobed ovary dotted with oil cells. The fruit is 4 lobed capsule dotted with oil cells (Figure 159).
Medicinal Uses:	In China, the plant is used as a salad. In Cambodia, Laos and Vietnam, it is used as an emmenaguoge, antispasmodic, anthelminthic and as a counter-irritant remedy in rheumatism, neuralgia, pains and is used to awake fainting people. In Malaysia, the plant is used to calm itchiness. In Indonesia, the plant is used externally to quiet convulsions and to treat jaundice. Note that an infusion of *Ruta graveolens* L. (common rue, herb of grace) has been used in Europe to promote menses. The oil of rue has also been used to stop spasms, and to produce skin irritation (Rue, *British Pharmaceutical Codex*, 1934).
Pharmacology:	The plant abounds in phototoxic furanocoumarins such as psoralen, xanthotoxin, bergapten, and isopimpinellin (Milesi *et al.*, 2001) as well as quinoline alkaloids (Vasudevan *et al.*, 1968).
References:	Milesi S, Massot B, Gontier E, Bourgaud F, Guckert A, 2001, *Ruta graveolens* L.: a promising species for the production of furanocoumarins. Plant Sci.; 161:189-199.
	Vasudevan TN, Luckner M, 1968, Alkaloids from Ruta angustifolia Pers., *Ruta chalepensis* L., *Ruta graveolens* L. and *Ruta montana* Mill, Pharmazie. 23:520-1.

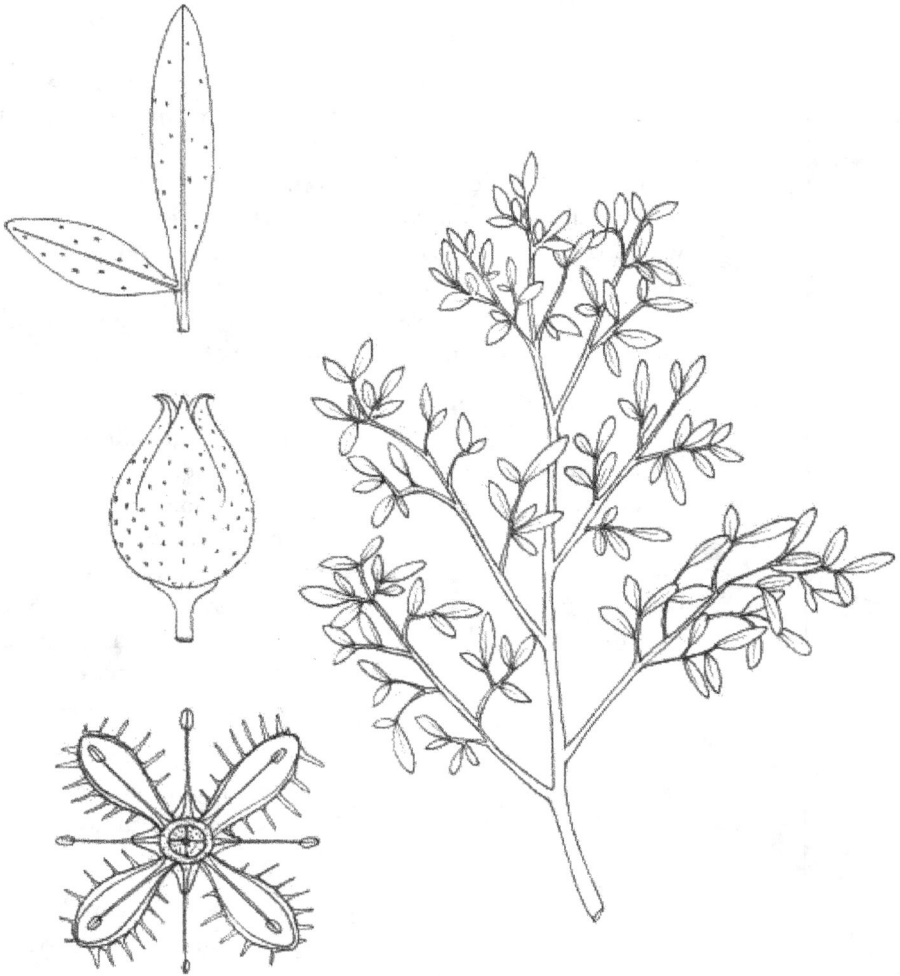

Figure 159: *Ruta angustifolia* (L.) Pers.
From: Flora of Malaya. Herbarium of University Kebangsaan Malaysia
Malaysia, Pahang state, Genting Highland, near Masjid Yayasan Mohd. Noah, planted near the resident house

Zanthoxylum acanthopodium DC.

[From Greek *zanthos* = yellow, *xylon* = wood and Latin *acanthopodium* = spiny foot]

Local name:	Sichuan peppercorn, ci hua jiao (China)
Description:	It is a shrubby climber which grows up to 6 m tall in the forests of India, Bhutan, Bangladesh. Burma, Bhutan, Nepal, Laos, Vietnam, Thailand Malaysia, Indonesia and China. The bark is grayish black. The stem is pubescent, rusty or with prickles which are straight. The leaves are spiral, compound and without stipules. The rachis is winged, about 10 cm long with 2 - 3 pairs of folioles and a terminal one. The folioles are sessile, 6 - 10 cm x 2 - 4 cm, lanceolate, papery, serrate at the margin, rusty pubescent and with 10 - 30 pairs of secondary nerves. The inflorescence is axillary with few flowers on hairy pedicels. The flower presents a series of 6 petals which are linear, yellowish green, and to 1.5 cm long. The male flowers include 5 or 6 anthers reddish at first, and twice as long as the petals. The gynaecium presents 2- 5 carpels. The fruit is a follicle with few oil cells, dull reddish, about 0.5 cm in diameter, glabrous and opens to release a black seed (Figure 160).
Medicinal Uses:	In Cambodia, Laos and Vietnam, the plant is used to treat fever and to promote sweating. Note that *Zanthoxylum americanum* (northern prickly ash) and *Zanthoxylum clavaherculis* (southern prickly ash) have been used to treat flatulence (Zanthoxylum, toothache bark, Xanthoxylum, *British Pharmaceutical Codex*, 1934).
Pharmacology:	The plant is known to contain a lignan that inhibits germination (Roy *et al.*, 1977). Sukari *et al*, (1996) reported some preliminary pharmacological properties of the plant.
References:	Roy S, Guha R, Chakraborty DP, 1977, Acanthotoxin: a germination inhibiting lignan from *Zanthoxylum acanthopodium* D.C. Chemistry and Industry; 6: 231-32.
	Sukari A, Rahmani M, Haron MNB, Ali J, Ahmad JH, 1996, Chemical constituents of the Leaves of *Zanthoxylum Acanthopodium* and its biological activity. Oriental J Chem; 12: 135-36

Figure 160: *Zanthoxylum acanthopodium* DC.
From: Flora of Thailand, Chiang Mai University Herbarium
Thailand, Chiang Mai province, Kuang district, Doi-Sutep-Pui National Park, summit area of Doi Pui. Date of collection: 17 July 1994.

G. Order APIALES Nakai 1930

The order Apiales consists of 2 families: the Araliaceae and Apiaceae, and about 3,700 species of saponiferous plants, mostly herbs, climbers and shrubs, the common ancestry of which stands near or in the Sapindales. The key botanical feature in this order are inflorescences which are umbels and palmatilobed or deeply dissected leaf blades. Some Apiaceae abound with piperidine alkaloids derived from lysine such as the deadly poisonous coniine alkaloids (*Conium maculatum* L., hemlock) which took Socrates' life. Others are used as spice *Pimpinella anisum*. The Araliaceae came first in the Apiales.

1. Family ARALIACEAE A. L. de Jussieu 1789 nom. conserv., the Ginseng Family

The family Araliaceae consists of about 70 genera and 700 species of tropical trees, shrubs, woody climbers or herbs containing a series of pentacyclic triterpenoid saponins of the ursane, oleananes, and dammarane types, tetracyclic triterpenoid saponins of the protostane type, and acetylenic fatty acids.

The leaves of Araliaceae are large, alternate, and very characteristically palmatilobed or pinnately compound, and with or without stipules The petiole is slender and clasping the stem. The flowers are small, regular, and arranged in umbels. The corolla comprises 5 petals and the androecium 5 stamens. A nectary disc is present. The gynaecium consists of 2- 5 or more carpels fused into a compound and inferior ovary containing 2- 5 locules, each locule containing a single, apical, axillary, pendulous and epitropous ovule. The fruits are drupaceous or dry. The seeds are oily.

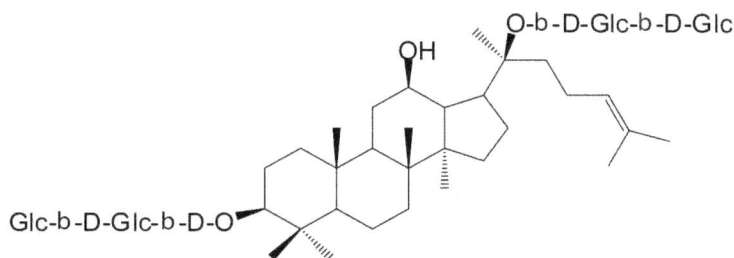

Ginsenoside Rb - (1)

Several plant species in this family are ornamental such as *Hedera helix* L. (English ivy), *Schefflera actinophylla* (umbrella tree), *Schefflera elegantissima* (false aralia) and *Fatsia japonica* (Japan Aralia). Members of this family have strong neuropharmacological, immunological and oncological potentials. The Araliaceae family includes *Panax ginseng* C. A. Meyer (Ginseng or schinseng, Japan Pharmacopoeia, 1961-1962) ginseng), *Panax quinquefolium* L. (American ginseng), *Panax notoginseng* Burk. (*san*

- *chi* ginseng), *Panax pseudoginseng* Wall. species *Japonicus* Hara: *Panax japonicus* C. A. Meyer (Japan or *chikusetsu* ginseng, Japan Pharmacopoeia 1961-1962), *Panax pseudoginseng* Wall. species *himalaicus* (Himalayan ginseng) and *Eleutherococcus senticosus* Maxim: *Acanthopanax senticosus* (Siberian ginseng). These are all commercially available as OTC for their stimulating properties against aging-related disorders mainly due to the ginsenosides such as ginsenosides Rg 1 and Rb1 which modulate neurotransmission. Xue *et al.* (2006), demonstrated that Rb1 promotes neurotransmitter release by increasing the phosphorylation of synapsins through the Protein Kinase A (PKA) pathway, whereas the similar effects observed with Rg1 are independent of the phosphorylation of synapsins which are abundant phosphoproteins essential for regulating neurotransmitter release (Xue *et al.*, 2006). Ginsenoside Rb₁ showed some level of protection of dopaminergic neurons against glutamate (Radad *et al.*, 2004). In Asia - Pacific, about 50 species of plants species classified within the family Araliaceae are medicinal. Most of these plants are used to counteract putrefaction, to allay fever, to promote expectoration and to invigorate.

References: Radad K, Gille G, Moldzio R, Saito H Wolf-Dieter Rausch WD, 2004, Ginsenosides Rb1 and Rg1 effects on mesencephalic dopaminergic cells stressed with glutamate. Brain Res; 1021: 41-53.

Xue JF, Liu ZJ, Hu JF, Chen H, Zhang JT, Nai-Hong Chen NC, 2006, Ginsenoside Rb1 promotes neurotransmitter release by modulating phosphorylation of synapsins through a cAMP-dependent protein kinase pathway. Brain Res;1106: 91-98

Hedera himalaica Tob.

[From Latin *hederacea* = of or pertaining to ivy and *himalaica* = from Himalaya]

Local name: Nepal ivy; chang chun teng (China)

Synonym: *Hedera nepalensis* K. Koch, *Hedera. potaninii* Pojarkova; *Hedera. robusta* Pojarkova; *Hedera. shensiensis* Pojarkova; Hedera. sinensis (Tobler) Handel-Mazzetti.

Description: It is a small epilithic or epiphytic tree which grows in forests, roadsides and on rocky slopes of Himalaya, Nepal, China, Cambodia, Laos, and Vietnam. It grows to a height of 1.5 m with a basal diameter of 5 cm. The plant has ornamental value. The bark is thin, grey, with scattered pustular lenticels. The leaves are simple, alternate and without stipules. The petiole is slender, channeled, and 1 - 2 cm long. The leaf blade is dull dark green above, light green underneath, triangular, glabrous, with about 3 to 5 pairs of secondary nerves conspicuous on both surfaces, recurved at the margin, the margin entire and wavy, and 2 - 4.3 cm x 3.9 - 7.2 cm. The inflorescences are terminal umbels on 2 cm peduncles. The umbels are about 2 cm in diameter. The flower pedicel is about 1 cm long. The fruit is about 0.3 cm long, dull green, covered with starry hairs and green and conical at the apex (Figure 161).

Medicinal Uses: In China, the plant is used to treat inflamed skin. In Cambodia, Laos and Vietnam, the plant is used to heal abscesses and resolve insect bites.

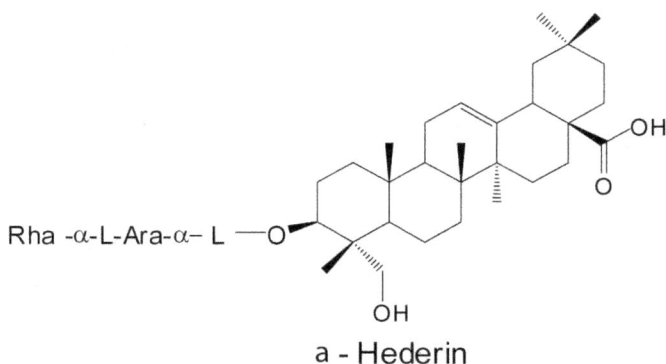

Rha -α-L-Ara-α- L

a - Hederin

Pharmacology: The plant abounds with hederagenin saponins (Kizu *et al,* 1985) which are probably responsible for the anti-inflammatory properties mentioned above. Some of these saponins have spermicidal properties (Panwar *et al.*, 1988). Tang *et al.*, (2007) isolated antimicrobial principles from the plant. An extract of *Hedera himalaica* Tob. was active against the agricultural pest *Aphis craccivora* Koch (Tewary *et al.*, 2005). Note that alpha - hederin which is widespread in the genus *Hedera* protected lymphocytes cultured *in vitro* against mutation caused by doxorubicin and inhibits the growth of mouse B16 melanoma cells and non - cancer mouse 3T3 fibroblasts cultured *in vitro* (Amara - Mokabe *et al.*, 1996; Danloy. *et al.*, 1994) and modified the cellular contents and cell membrane of *Candida albicans* after 24 hours exposure (Moulin - Traffort *et al.*, 1998). It is also hepatoprotective (Liu *et al.* 1997) and antiviral (Calabrese *et al.*, 1975).

References: Amara-Mokrane YA, Lehucher-Michel MP, Balansard G, Duménil G, Botta A, 1996, Protective effects of alpha-hederin, chlorophyllin and ascorbic acid towards the induction of micronuclei by doxorubicin in cultured human lymphocytes. Mutagenesis; 11:161-7.

Calabrese AI, 1975, Letter: Antiviral activity of hederin. J Pharm Sci; 64:VIII.

Danloy S, Quetin-Leclercq J, Coucke P, De Pauw-Gillet MC, Elias R, Balansard G, Angenot L, Bassleer R, 1994, Effects of alpha-hederin, a saponin extracted from *Hedera helix*, on cells cultured in vitro. Planta Med ; 60:45-9.

Kizu H., Kitayama S, Nakatani F, Tominori T, Namba T, 1985, Studies on Nepalese crude drugs. III. On the Saponins of *Hedera nepalensis* K. KOCH. Chem Pharm Bull (Tokyo); 33: 3324-3329.

Liu YP, Liu J, 1997, Effect of alpha-hederin on hepatic detoxifying systems in mice. Zhongguo Yao Li Xue Bao; 18:33-6.

Moulin-Traffort J, Favel A, Elias R, Regli P, 1998, Study of the action of alpha-hederin on the ultrastructure of *Candida albicans*. Mycoses. 41: 411-6.

Pant G, Panwar MS, Rawat MS, Negi DS, 1988, Spermicidal glycosides from *Hedera nepalensis* K. Koch (inflorescence). Pharmazie; 43:294.

Tang Yl, Liu X, Tang X, 2007, An analysis of effective component and antimicrobial effect of *Hedera nepalensis*. Chin J Vet Med, 43: 51-73.

Tewary DK, Bhardwaj A, Shanker A, 2005, Pesticidal activities in five medicinal plants collected from mid hills of Western Himalayas. Ind Crops Prod; 22: 241-247.

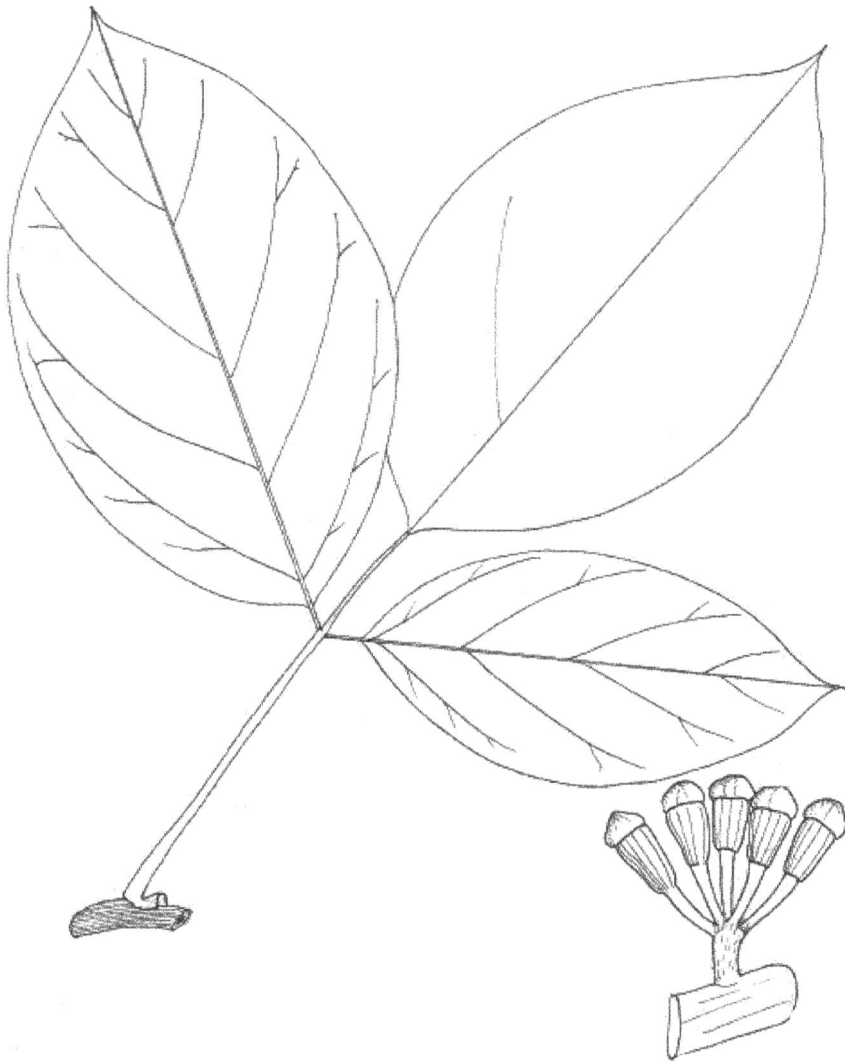

Figure 161: *Hedera himalaica* Tob.
From: Flora of Thailand, Chiang Mai University Herbarium.
Thailand, Chiang Mai Province, Chiang Dao district, Doi Chiang Dao Animal Sanctuary, upper valley below summit of Doi Luang. North of Thailand by 18° North 98° East . Altitude 1950 m.
Date of collection: 10 November 1995. Collection and Identification: JF Maxwell.

Schefflera subulata (Miq.) Vig.

[After J.C. Scheffler, 19th century botanist and from Latin *subulata* = awl-shaped]

Local name:	Jolok hantu (Malaysia)
Basionym:	*Paratropia subulata* Miq. Annales Museum Botanicum Lugduno-Batavi 1: 22.1863.
Synonyms:	*Heptapleurum subulatum* (Miq.) Seem., *Heptapleurum subracemosum* King, *Heptapleurum subulatum* (Miq.) Seem., *Schefflera klossii* Ridl. *Schefflera subulata* (Seem) Ridl., *Schefflera oxyphylla* var. *oxyphylla*, *Schefflera subracemosa* (King) R.Vig.
Description:	It is a slender to moderately stout climber which grows in the rainforest of Malaysia. Stems are terete, longitudinally striated and pitted. The leaves are 3 - 5 foliolate, mostly 3, spiral and without stipules. The folioles are broadly elliptic, acuminate at the apex and the base, 6.5 - 11 cm x 14 - 19 cm. The petiolule is 1.2 cm long. The rachis is 10 - 14 cm long swollen and clasping the stem. The folioles are glabrous, coriaceous, and present 5 pairs of secondary nerves raised on both surface, the first basal pair well marked. The inflorescences are stout, spreading, over 10 cm long, few branched with a spike like appearance, tiny umbels. Fruits are 5 – locular, 0.2 x 0.1 cm on 0.2 cm long hairy pedicels. The body of the fruit is striated and the upper part is vaguely conical (Figure 162).
Medicinal uses:	The plant is used as a sedative and to break fever.

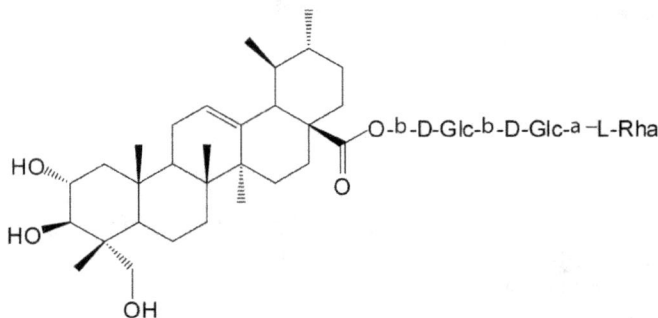

O-b-D-Glc-b-D-Glc-a –L-Rha

Asiaticoside

Pharmacology:	To date the plant has not been subject to any pharmacological testing. The sedative property mentioned above may be due to polyacetylene derivates and/or saponins which abound in *Schefflera* species. Baur *et al.* (2005) demonstrated that polyacetylene derivatives isolated from an African Araliaceae, *Cussonia zimmermannii* Harms, elicited positive allosteric modulation of $GABA_A$ receptors. Majonoside-R2 a saponin from Vietnamese ginseng exhibited anxiolytic activity in the laboratory involving $GABA_A$ receptor (Huong NT *et al.*, 1998).

It is noteworthy that the asiaticoside characterized from *Schefflera octophylla* (Lour.) Harms bark (Sung *et al.*, 1992) is responsible for the anti - inflammatory property of *Centella asiatica* L.

References:

Baur R, Simmen U, Senn M, Séquin U, Sigel E, 2005, Novel plant substances acting as beta subunit isoform-selective positive allosteric modulators of GABAA receptors. Mol Pharmacol; 68:787-92.

Huong NT, Matsumoto K, Watanabe H, 1998,The antistress effect of majonoside-R2, a major saponin component of Vietnamese ginseng: neuronal mechanisms of action. Methods Find Exp Clin Pharmacol; 20:65-76.

Figure 162: *Schefflera subulata* **(Miq.) Vig.**
From: Herbarium University Malaya
Malaysia, Ulu Gombak forest reserve, Batu 22, Selangor. Altitude 300 m. Collection: Mohd. Kassim. Date of collection: 5 October 1974.
Determination: Benjamin C. Stone, December 1979.

III. Subclass ASTERIDAE Takhtajan 1966

The subclass Asteridae consists of 11 orders, 49 families, and nearly 60,000 species of plants which are thought to have originated by development from or near to the order Rosales during the Tertiary period. The Asteridae is the most evolved subclass of Dicotyledons. About a third of the species in this group belong to the family Asteraceae. The general morphological tendency observed in Asteridae is fusion of sepals, petals and carpels into a tubular perianth and single ovaries. The chemical weapons used in this Subclass are alkaloids; monoterpenoid indole alkaloids and pyrrolizidine alkaloids, terpenes; iridoid glycosides, monoterpenes (volatile oils) diterpenes, sesquiterpenes, triterpenoid and steroid saponins, and phenolic compounds; phenylethanoid glycosides, naphthoquinones, and cohorts of flavonoids. The order Gentianales is primitive in the Asteridae and a common ancestor for the Rubiales, Dipsacales and Asterales (Appendix I).

A.Order GENTIANALES Lindley 1833

The order Gentianales consists of 6 families and about 5,500 species of plants thought to have originated from the order Rosales

1.Family GENTIANACEAE A. L. de Jussieu 1789 nom. conserv., the Gentian Family

The family Gentianaceae consists of about 75 genera and about 1,000 species of annual or perennial herbs, known to produce xanthones and secoiridoid glycosides. Most Gentianaceae belong to the genus *Gentiana* with about 400 species. The leaves of Gentianaceae are simple, opposite, without stipules, often connate at the the base or connected by a transverse line. The flowers are actinomorphic, often blue, and tubular. The calyx is tubular or made of free imbricate sepals. The corolla is 4 - 12 - lobed, the lobes mostly contorted. The androecium comprises as many stamens as the corolla lobes and is inserted on the corolla between the lobes. There are 2 locular anthers opening lengthwise. The gynaecium consists of a pair of carpels fused into a superior, and single - locular ovary containing numerous ovules attached to a pair of parietal placentas. The style is simple. The fruits are capsular and contain numerous tiny seeds.

Several plant species in the Gentianaceae are ornamental, such as *Exacum affine*, the handling of which may induce eczema in sensitive individuals. Secoiridoid glycosides such as gentiopicroside are intensely bitter and numerous plant species in the Gentianaceae have been used in Western medicine to promote appetite on account of their bitterness: *Sabatia angularis* (American centaury), *Centaurium erythraea* Rafn. (European centaury), the dried fermented rhizome and root of *Gentiana lutea* L. (yellow gentian) (Gentian, *British Pharmacopoeia*, 1963), *Gentiana catesbaei*,

Gentiana macrophylla, Gentiana punctata, and *Gentiana purpurea,* the dried flowering tops of the common centaury *Centaurium minus (Centaurium umbellatum, Erythraea centaurium)* and other species of *Centaurium* (Petite Centaurée, *French Pharmacopoeia,* 1965). *Centaurium beyrichii* (rock centaury) and *Centaurium calycosum* (Buckley centaury) are poisonous to cattle. An interesting chemical feature of Gentianaceae is the production of xanthones, namely aglycones and *O* - glycosides, the distribution of which is quite restricted to a few families in the Magnoliopsida. Xanthones have attracted a great deal of interest on account of their ability to inhibit the enzymatic activity of monoamine oxidase, microbial infection, and inflammation and platelet aggregation.

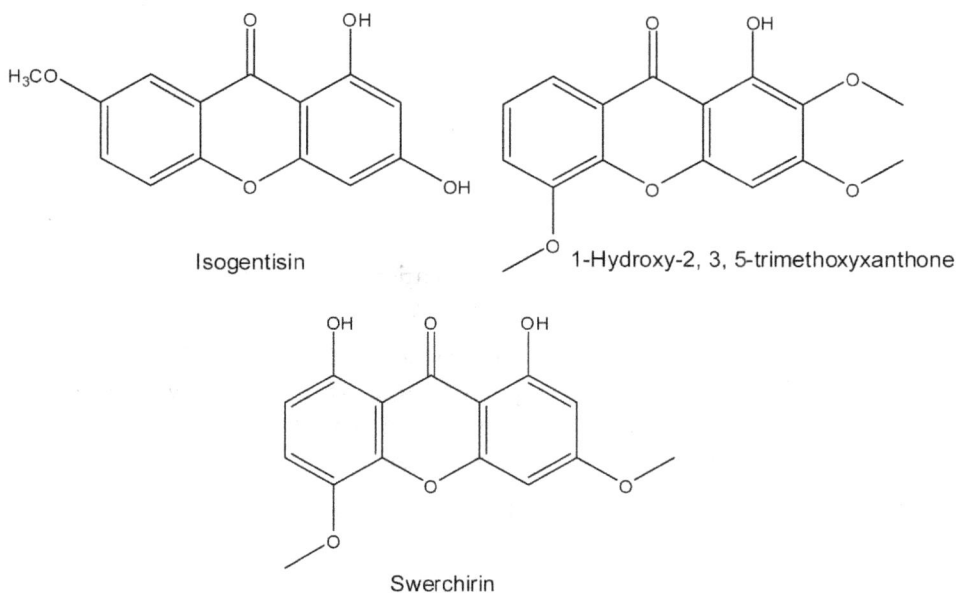

Isogentisin

1-Hydroxy-2, 3, 5-trimethoxyxanthone

Swerchirin

One such xanthone is isogentisin (1,3-dihydroxy-7-methoxyxanthone) from *Gentiana lutea* (Yellow Gentian) which protects human vascular endothelial cells against lethal effects of cigarette smoke chemicals by activating cellular repair functions (Schmieder *et al,* 2006). Another xanthone, 1-Hydroxy-2, 3, 5-trimethoxyxanthone from *Halenia elliptica,* relaxes rat coronary artery via both an endothelium-dependent mechanism involving nitric oxide and an endothelium-independent mechanism by inhibiting Ca (2+) influx through L-type voltage-operated Ca(2+) channels. Iridoids of Gentianaceae, such as swerchirin, are also of pharmacological interest. Swerchirin from *Swertia longifolia* reduced the elevation of aspartate aminotransferase, alanine aminotransferase and alkaline phosphatase of paracetamol-induced hepatotoxicity in rodents (Hajimehdipoor *et al.,* 2006) and exhibited hypoglycemic properties (Asthana *et al.,* 1991). Flavonoids from *Gentiana lutea* inhibited the enzymatic activity of monoamine oxidase (Haraguchi *et al.,* 2004). Another flavonoid isoorientin, showed hypoglemic activity in hyperglycemic and streptozotocin-induced diabetic rats (Sezik *et al.,* 2005). About 20 plant species classified within the family Gentianaceae are medicinal in Asia - Pacific. These are often used to invigorate, to allay fever, to stimulate appetite and urination, to relieve constipation and to counteract putrefaction of the skin. *Exacum tetragonium* Roxb. is a good example.

References: Asthana RK, Sharma NK, Kulshreshtha DK, Chatterjee SK, 1991, A xanthone from *Swertia chirayita*. Phytochem; 30: 1037-39.

Hajimehdipoor H, Sadeghi Z, Elmi S, Elmi A, Ghazi-Khansari M, Amanzadeh Y, Sadat-Ebrahimi SE, 2006, Protective effects of *Swertia longifolia* Boiss. and its active compound, swerchirin, on paracetamol-induced hepatotoxicity in mice. J Pharm Pharmacol; 58:277-80.

Haraguchi H, Tanaka Y, Kabbash A, Fujioka T, Ishizu T, Yagi A, 2004, Monoamine oxidase inhibitors from *Gentiana lutea*. Phytochemistry; 65: 2255-60.

Schmieder A, Schwaiger S, Csordas A, Backovic A, Messner B, Wick G, Stuppner H, Bernhard D, 2007, Isogentisin – a novel compound for the prevention of smoking-caused endothelial injury. Atherosclerosis; 194: 317-25.

Ekrem Sezik E, Mustafa Aslan M, Erdem Yesilada E, Shigeru Ito S, 2005, Hypoglycemic activity of *Gentiana olivieri* and isolation of the active constituent through bioassay- directed fractionation techniques. Life Sci; 76: 1223-38.

Wang Y, Shi JG, Wang MZ, Che CT, Yeung JH, 2007,Mechanisms of the vasorelaxant effect of 1-hydroxy-2, 3, 5-trimethoxy-xanthone, isolated from a Tibetan herb, *Halenia elliptica*, on rat coronary artery. Life Sci; 81:1016-23.

Exacum tetragonum Roxb.

[From Greek *tetragonia* = four angled]

Local name:	*Zao bai nian* (China)
Description:	It is a herb which grows to a height of 1 m. It is found by roadsides and in meadows from an altitude of 200 m to 1500 m in China, Cambodia, India, Laos, Malaysia, Burma, Nepal, New Guinea, Philippines, Vietnam; Australia. The stem is erect, light green, quadrangular, glabrous, smooth, and somewhat swollen. Internodes 6.3 - 9.3 cm long. Leaves simple, sessile, opposite and without stipules. The leaf blade is membranaceous, dark green above, 1.7 - 2.6 cm x 3.8 - 6 cm, ovate-lanceolate to ovate, and shows a pair of secondary nerves. The flowers are arranged in terminal cymes on 0.3 - 1 cm long pedicels. The calyx is 5 - 6 mm long with lanceolate calyx lobes with spiny the apex. The corolla 1.5-2.5 cm long; tubular , the tube yellowish green, with 4 lilac blue lobes which are elliptic and 1.1-1.7 cm long. Filaments linear, pale light green and 0.15 - 2 cm long. The anthers are orange, lanceolate and 0.7 - 0.8 cm long. Style linear, pale light greenish, and 1 - 1.2 cm long. The stigma lobes are orbicular. The fruits are subglobose capsules which are 0.4 - 0.5 cm in diameter. The seeds are ellipsoid, and tiny (Figure 163).
Medicinal Uses:	In Burma the plant is used to break fever.
Pharmacology:	The pharmacological properties of this plant are still unexplored. An extract of *Exacum affine*, showed anti-influenza virus type A activity *in vitro* (Mothana *et al*, 2006). Das *et al* (1984) isolated secoiridoids gentiopicroside and methylgrandifloroside from *Exacum tetragonum* Roxb.

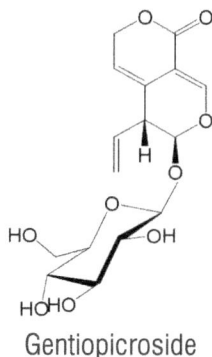

Gentiopicroside

References:	Das S, Barua RN, Sharma RP, Baruah JN, Kulanthaivel P, Herz W, 1984, Secoiridoids from *Exacum tetragonum*. Phytochem; 23:908-09.

Mothana RA, Mentel R, Reiss C, Lindequist U, 2006, Phytochemical screening and antiviral activity of some medicinal plants from the island Soqotra. Phytother Res; 20:298-302.

Figure 163: *Exacum tetragonum* **Roxb.**

From: Flora of Thailand.
Thailand, Chiang Mai province, Chiang Dao district, Doi Chiang Dao animal sanctuary, above Sop Huay Pah Dahng, Huay Nah Lao station, along the road to Muang Kawng. Altitude 800 m. Date of collection: 11 October 1995. Collection and botanical identification: JF Maxwell No 95-891.

2.Family APOCYNACEAE A. L. de Jussieu 1789 nom. conserv., the Dogbane Family

The family Apocynaceae consists of about 250 genera and 2,000 species of soft wooded tropical trees, shrubs, woody climbers or herbs which are easily detectable in the field by 3 botanical features: leaves simple, opposite and exstipulate, presence of abundant white latex, and tubular flowers with 5 contorted lobes. Apocynaceae are well known and valued for the vast array of indole alkaloids of enormous pharmaceutical value, some of which of which used in hospitals to treat leukemia.

Other types of secondary metabolites found in Apocynaceae are poisonous cardiotonic glycosides, steroidal alkaloids and iridoid glycosides. The inflorescences are cymes or cymose panicles. The stamens are inserted on the corolla, as many as the lobes and alternate with them and comprise 2 - locular anthers opening lengthwise. The gynaecium consists of two carpels more or less united to form a superior, and 2 - locular or unilocular or 2 - carpellate ovary containing 2 to many ovules. The fruits are pairs of berries, drupes or follicles containing several winged or tufted seeds in splitting fruit.

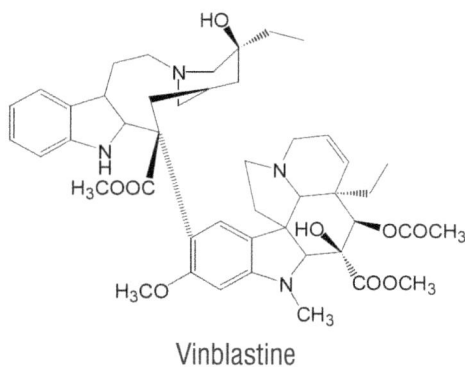

Vinblastine

Several Apocynaceae are ornamental: *Plumieria* species (frangipani), *Thevetia peruviana* (Pers.) K. Schum. (yellow oleander) and *Nerium oleander* L. (oleander) which are commonly used to decorate gardens. In regards to the pharmaceutical interest of this family, binary complex monoterpenoid indole alkaloids are of therapeutic value. Both vinblastine and vincristine, from *Catharanthus roseus* G. Don (periwinkle) interfere with the assembly of the mitotic spindle and are included in combination chemotherapy protocols for the treatment of acute leukemia, lymphoma, and a number of solid tumors such as breast and lung cancers. Vinblastine (Velbe®) is particularly useful to treat Hodgkin's disease whereas vincristine sulphate (Oncovin®) is used to treat acute leukemia in children.

Echitamine and villastonine are cytotoxic. A methanol extract of roots of *Alstonia macrophylla* inhibits the proliferation of human lung cancer cell - lines MOR - P (adenocarcinoma) and COR L - (23) (large cell carcinoma) using the SRB assay. This effect is probably due to villastonine which destroys both cell - lines with IC_{50} value inferior to 5 μM (Keawpradub *et al.*, 1997).

Corymine extracted from the leaves of *Hunteria zeylanica* (Retz.) Gardn. & Thw. is interesting because it potentiates the convulsions induced by either strychnine or picrotoxin, at doses of 2, 8 and 15 mg/Kg in mice (Leewanich *et al.*, 1996) and inhibits glycine - gated chlorine - channels by interacting with a site different from that of 4,4' - diisothiocyanostilbene - 2,2' - disulfonic acid (Leewanich *et al.*, 1998, 2005).

An interesting feature of *Ochrosia* species is that they elaborate indole alkaloids such as ellipticine and 9 - methoxyellipticine (Peube - Locou et al., 1972) which are of chemotherapeutic value. These alkaloids are planar and inhibit topoisomerase II activity by DNA intercalation. The 9 - Hydroxy - 2 - *N* - *ellipticinium* obtained by quaternarization of 9 - hydroxyellipticine is a semisynthetic anticancer agent of clinical value in a number of forms of breast cancer. A methanol extract of stem bark *Ochrosia glomerata* inhibits *Plasmodium falciparum in vitro* with an IC50 value inferior to10 µg/mL (Horgen *et al.*, 2001).

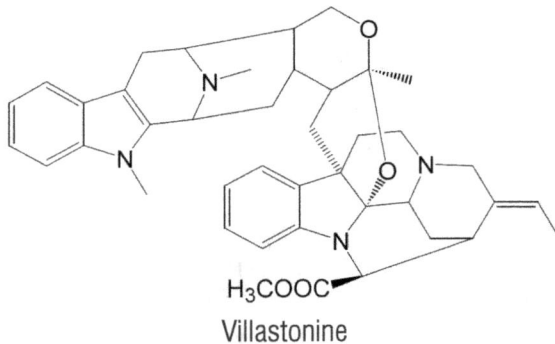

Villastonine

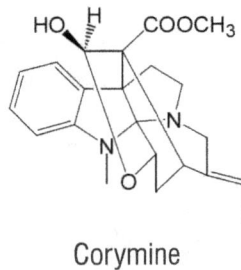

Corymine

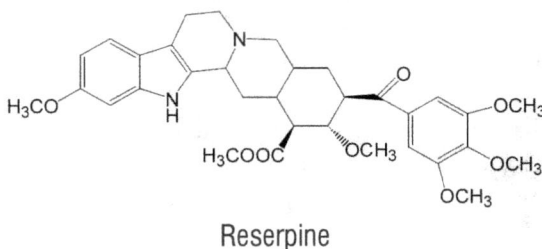

Reserpine

The dried roots of *Rauvolfia serpentina* (L.) Benth. ex Kurz (Rauwolfia, *British Pharmaceutical* Codex, 1963) contains reserpine, an indole alkaloid which has been used in the past as a neuroleptic and hypotensive drug which blocks the adrenergic transmission by depleting noradrenaline from sympathetic neurons. Ibogaine from *Tabernanthe iboga*, is another example of a neuroactive alkaloid which protects the *N* - methyl - aspartate (NMDA) neuron receptors against excessive release of excitatory amino acids and represents therefore a potential therapeutic agent for the treatment of Alzheimer's disease, Huntington chorea and other brain degenerative syndromes.

Ouabain   Conessine

Thevetiosigenin

Ouabain (Ouabain, *British Pharmacopoeia*, 1958) from the seeds of *Strophanthus gratus*, or from the wood of *Acokanthera schimperi* or *Acokanthera ouabaio*, has been used to treat acute congestive heart failures. The dried bark from the stem and roots containing not less than 2% of total alkaloids (Holarrhena, *British Pharmaceutical Codex*, 1949), has been used in the form of a liquid extract to treat amoebic dysentery. Conessine hydrobromide (*French Pharmacopoeia*, 1965) has been used to treat amoebic dysentery but it has been dropped on account of severe neuropsychiatric effects. The seeds of *Thevetia peruviana* (Pers.) K. Schum. are known to abound with cardiac glycosides of the cardenolide type: thevetosides and gentiobiosyl - thevetosides of digitoxigenin (thevetin B). Thevetin is digitalis - like in action and is effective 4 to 6 hours after being taken *per os*. It has been used in continental Europe and is considered particularly useful to treat mild myocardial insufficiency and to treat digitalis - intolerance.

About 80 species of Apocynaceae are medicinal in Asia - Pacific. Note that the latex of many of these plant species is used to treat gastrointestinal ailments, to allay fever and pains, and to treat diabetes and infectious diseases.

References:

Horgen FD, Edrada A, de los Reyes, Agcaoili F, DA Madulid DA, V Wongpanich V, Angerhofer, CK, Pezzuto JM, Soejarto DD, Farnsworth, NR, 2001, Phytomedicine; 8: 71 - 81.

Keawpradub, N, Houghton, PJ, Eno-Amooquaye, E, Burke, PJ, 1997, Activity of extracts and alkaloids of Thai Alstonia species against human lung cancer cell lines. Planta Med; 63: 97 - 101.

Leewanich P, Tohda M, Matsumoto K, Subhadhirasakul S, Takayama H, Aimi N, Watanabe H, 1996, Behavioral studies on alkaloids extracted from the leaves of *Hunteria zeylanica*. Biol Pharm Bull; 19:394-9.

Leewanich P, Tohda M, Matsumoto K, Subhadhirasakul S, Takayama H, Aimi N, Watanabe H, 1998, A possible mechanism underlying corymine inhibition of glycine-induced Cl- current in *Xenopus* oocytes. Eur J Pharmacol; 348:271-7.

Leewanich P, Tohda M, Takayama H, Sophasan S, Watanabe H, Matsumoto K, 2005, Corymine potentiates NMDA-induced currents in *Xenopus* oocytes expressing NR1a/NR2B glutamate receptors. J Pharmacol Sci; 98:58-65.

Amalocalyx microlobus Pierre ex Spire

[From Latin *microlobus* = with tiny lobes]

Local name:	Mao che teng (China), jim kah (Thailand), mak sim (Laos)
Synonym:	*Amalocalyx burmanicus* Chatt., *Amalocalyx yunnanensis* Tsiang
Description:	It is a climber which grows in the forests of China, Laos, Burma, Thailand and Vietnam. The stem is terete, dull light green, hairy, 0.4 cm in diameter, and velvety at the apex. The internodes are about 20 cm long and the nodes present a ring of minute hairs. The plant is laticiferous and produces a copious white latex upon excision. The leaves are simple, opposite and without stipules. The petiole is slender, channeled, hairy, enlarged and clasping at the base and about 1 - 4.5 cm long. The blade is obovate, hairy, cordate at the base, apiculate at the apex, wavy at the margin, 13 - 16 cm x 8 - 10 cm, with a midrib sunken at the apex, and 7 to 8 pairs of secondary nerves. The inflorescences are axillary the light green cymes which are about 6 - 14 cm long. The pedicels, calyx and corolla are white. The calyx and corolla lobes have both faint pinkish hue. The calyx is about 0.7 cm long with 5 linear lobes which are linear and about 0.4 x 0.2 cm. The corolla is about 2.2 - 2.8 cm long. The fruits are pairs of elongated follicles which are 8 -12 cm x 1 -1.5 cm which contain several seeds which are ovate, about 1 cm long and bearing a tuft of hairs which is about 4 cm long (Figure 164).
Medicinal uses:	The plant has medicinal uses in Vietnam and is known to be toxic.
Pharmacology:	Unknown

Figure 164: *Amalocalyx microlobus* **Pierre ex Spire**
From: Flora of Thailand, Chiang Mai University Herbarium
Thailand, Han province, Tah Wahng Pah district, Doi Pu Kah national park, the base of the
West side of Doi Yao, at Ban Nam, Yam subdistrict. Elevation 400 m. Date of collection: 23
July 1994. In open disturbed, fire prone thickets bordering agricultural field on shale bedrock.
Collection and identification: JF Maxwell Nº 94-796.

Melodinus orientalis Bl.

[From Latin *orientalis* = from the East]

Synonym:	*Melodinus citriformis* King & Gamble, *Melodinus laxiflorus* Bl.
Description:	It is a climber which grows in the forest of Malaysia and Indonesia. The stem is terete, slender at the apex, 0.2 cm in diameter, longitudinally striated and glabrous. The internodes are 2 - 3 cm long. The plant is laticiferous and exudes an abundant latex upon incision. The leaves are simple, opposite and without stipules. The petiole is cracked transversally, about 0.5 cm long, and channeled. The leaf blade is lanceolate, acute at the base, 6 - 10 cm x 1.5 - 3 cm, acuminate at the apex, recurved and wavy at margin, with a midrib sunken above and about 10 pairs of secondary nerves visible underneath with a discrete intramarginal nerve. The inflorescences are small axillary cymes on about 0.5 cm long peduncles. The calyx is 0.1 cm long and sepals are ciliate and round. The corolla is 0.1 cm long. The mature fruits are pairs of orange follicles which are 5 cm long and containing several 3 cm long seeds (Figure 165).
Medicinal Uses:	In Indonesia the sap is used as an external remedy.
Pharmacology:	Unknown. Members of the genus are known to produce a series of alkaloids, some of them called melodinus alkaloids, such as meloscine (Schultz *et al.*, 1999). The plant might contain rhazinilam isolated in *Melodinus australia*, which induces a non-reversible assembly of tubulin by inhibiting the cold-induced disassembly of microtubules. This plant could be of interest in studying for its alkaloidal contents and cytotoxic activity (Banwell *et al.*, 2000).

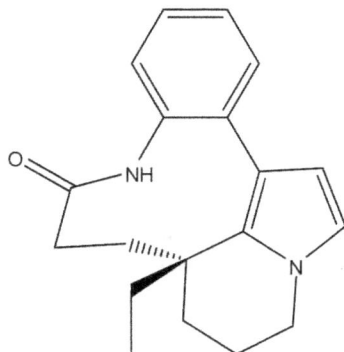

Rhazinilam

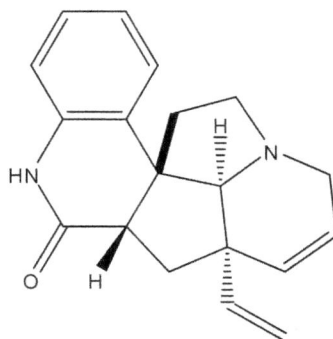

Meloscine

References: Banwell M, Edwards A, Smith J,Hamel E, Verdier-Pinard P, 2000, Convergent synthesis and preliminary biological evaluation of (±)-B-norrhazinal. J. Chem. Soc., Perkin Trans. 1, 2000, 1497-1499.

Schultz AG, Dai M, 1999, Asymmetric synthesis of the core structure of the Melodinus alkaloids. Tetrahedron Lett; 40: 645-648.

Figure 165: *Melodinus orientalis* Bl.

From: Plants of Borneo, Michigan State University
Malaysia, Sabah, Penampang district: crocker Range, Km 40 on Kota Kinabalu-Tabunan road, 5° 51' North - 116° 16' East. Elevation 1000 m. In hilly dipterocarp forest on ridge top. Crocker formation. Collection: John H. Beaman *et al* 8314. Date of Collection: 20 January 1984. Determination: JC Regalado, 1986.

Paravallaris macrophylla Pierre ex Hua

[From Greek para = beside and Latin *vallaris* = a wall and Latin *macrophylla* = large-leaved]

Local names:	Dao ying mu (China), khua Khau khuai (Vietnam)
Synonyms:	*Kibatalia anceps* (Dunn & R. Williams) Woodson, *Paravallaris yunnanensis* Tsiang & P. T. Li; *Trachelospermum anceps* Dunn & R. Williams; *Vallaris anceps* (Dunn & R. Williams) C. E. C. Fischer; *Vallaris. arborea* C. E. C. Fischer.
Description:	It is a tree which grows to about 10 m tall withd a bole of 14 cm in diameter, near streams and alluvial areas, in the forests of China, Cambodia, Laos, Burma, Thailand, and Vietnam. The bark is thin, smooth and gray. The stem is smooth, flattish, almost glossy, with a few lenticels, winged, 0.8 cm in diameter and with internodes which are about 6 cm long. The plant is laticiferous and exudes an abundant pure white latex upon incision. The leaves are simple, opposite and exstipulate. The petiole is stout, channeled, and about 1 - 1.5 cm x 0.3 cm. The leaf blade is dark green above, leathery, oblong or elliptic, 11-38 × 4-13 cm, thinly coriaceous, recurved and wavy at the margin, the midrib and about 15 pairs of secondary nerves sunken above, and raised underneath with a few tertiary nerves. The inflorescence is an axillary cyme which is about 2.5 - 5 cm long. The calyx is 0.3 cm long. The corolla is about 2.5 cm long, white, with 5 lobes which are 1.1 -1.4 cm, and puberulent on both surfaces. The fruits are pairs of bright green follicles which are narrowly ellipsoid, 8 -24 cm × 0.7 - 0.9 cm containing several seeds which are equipped with an umbrella like formation (Figure 166.
Medicinal Uses:	In Cambodia, Laos and Vietnam, the latex is used to check bleeding.
Pharmacology:	The plant contains a paravallarine-type steroidal alkaloid called 20-epi-kibataline (Ngoc *et al.*, 1984). The pharmacological property of this tree is unknown.
References:	Ngoc PH, Kutschabsky L, Phuong NM, Adam G, 1984, IX, Natural Products from Vietnamese Plants. 20-Epi-kibataline, a New Steroidal Alkaloid from Paravallaris macrophylla. Planta Med; 50:269-70.

Figure 166: *Paravallaris macrophylla* Pierre ex Hua
From: Flora of Thailand
Thailand, Lampang province, Muang Bahn (pan) district, Jae Sawn national Park, east side .
Park headquarters area, along Mae Sawn stream, just below Jae Sawn Falls. Elevation: 535
m. Date of collection: 23 August 1995. In open alluvial area along the stream in fire damaged,
much degraded deciduous forest (teakless) with much bamboo, on granite bedrock.

Parsonsia laevigata (Moon) Alston

[After James Parsons (1705-1770), a London doctor, and Latin laevigata = smooth or slippery, lustrous or shining

Local name:	akar labu dendang (Malaysia), hai nan tong xin jie (China), houraikagami (Japan)
Basionym:	*Echites laevigatus* Moon *A Catalogue of the Indigenous and Exotic Plants Growing in Sri Lanka* 20. 1924.
Synonym:	*Echites laevigata* Moon; *Heligme spiralis* (Wall. ex G. Don) Thwait; *Parsonsia helicandra* Hook. & Harn., *Parsonsia helicandra* Hooker & Arnott; *Parsonsia howii* Tsiang; *Parsonsia spiralis* Wallich ex G. Don. *Periploca alboflavescens* Dennst;
Description:	It is a woody climber which grows up to 10 m long in the forests of India, China, Solomon Islands, Taiwan, Cambodia, India, Indonesia, Malaysia, Japan, Laos, Burma, Philippines, Sri Lanka, Thailand, and Vietnam. The stem is terete, about 0.3 cm, glabrous, with a few conspicuous lenticels, longitudinally striated, angled at the apex, with very few tiny hairs, and 2 to 3.5 cm internodes. The nodes show some sort of microscopical membranes, which look like stipules. The plant is laticiferous and exudes an abundant latex upon excision. The leaves are simple, opposite and without stipules. The petioles are channeled, flattish at the base, with few minute hairs, and about 1 - 2 cm long. The leaf blade is ovate or elliptic, thinly coriaceous, wavy and recurved at the margin, 5.5 - 8 cm x 2.2 - 4.2 cm, the base cuneate, with 5-7 secondary nerves which are discrete, looping at some distance from the margin, and visible underneath. The the apex of the leaf blade presents a tiny gland-like formation. The inflorescence is an axillary cyme on a 3 - 9 cm long peduncle. The calyx is cup-shaped, 0.2 cm long, 5 lobed, the lobes, 0.1 cm long, broadly lanceolate and minutely ciliate. The corolla is white with a short tube producing 5 oblong lobes which are contorted, and about 0.5 x 0.1 cm. The anthers are merged into a fusiform structure which is about 0.3 cm long. The stigma is mitreform. The fruits are pairs of follicles which are about 15 x 1 cm long, elongated with a terminal and containing several seeds which are about 1.3 cm long with a tuft of hairs which is about 4 cm long (Figure 167). *Parsonsia laevigata* (Moon) Alston is a food plant for larvae of *Idea leuconoe* Erichson, the largest butterfly in Japan.

Medicinal Use: In India the plant is given for insanity. In the Solomon Islands the plant is used to treat swellings.

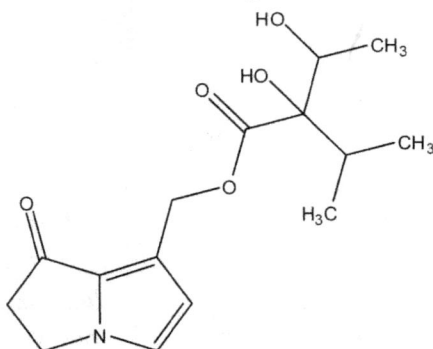

Parsonine

Pharmacology: The plant is known to contain a series of pentacyclic taraxerane and lupane type triterpenes (Ogihara *et al.*, 1987) as well as pyrrolizidine alkaloids such as parsonine and macrocyclic pyrrolizidine alkaloids such as parsonsianine, parsonsianidine and methylparsonsianidine (Abe *et al.*, 1991). Note that butterflies sequester these alkaloids and concentrate them in their exocrine defensive secretions. The plant produces some lignan glycosides (Abe *et al.*, 1989). The pharmacological property of this common climber is still unexplored. There is the possible role of parsonine still in the anti-inflammatory properties of the plant (Gosh *et al.*, 1974).

References: Abe F, Yamauchi T, 1989, Lignan glycosides from *Parsonsia laevigata*. Phytochemistry; 28: 1737-1741.

Abe F, Nagao T, Okabe H, Yamauchi T, 1991,Macrocyclic pyrrolizidine alkaloids from *Parsonsia laevigata*. Phytochemistry; 30: 737-1739.

Ghosh MN, Singh H, 1974, Inhibitory effect of a pyrrolizidine alkaloid, crotalaburnine, on rat paw oedema and cotton pellet granuloma. Br J Pharmacol; 51: 503-508.

Ogihara K, Higa M, Hokama K, Suga T, 1987,Triterpenes from the leaves of *parsonsia laevigata*.Phytochemistry; 26: 783-785.

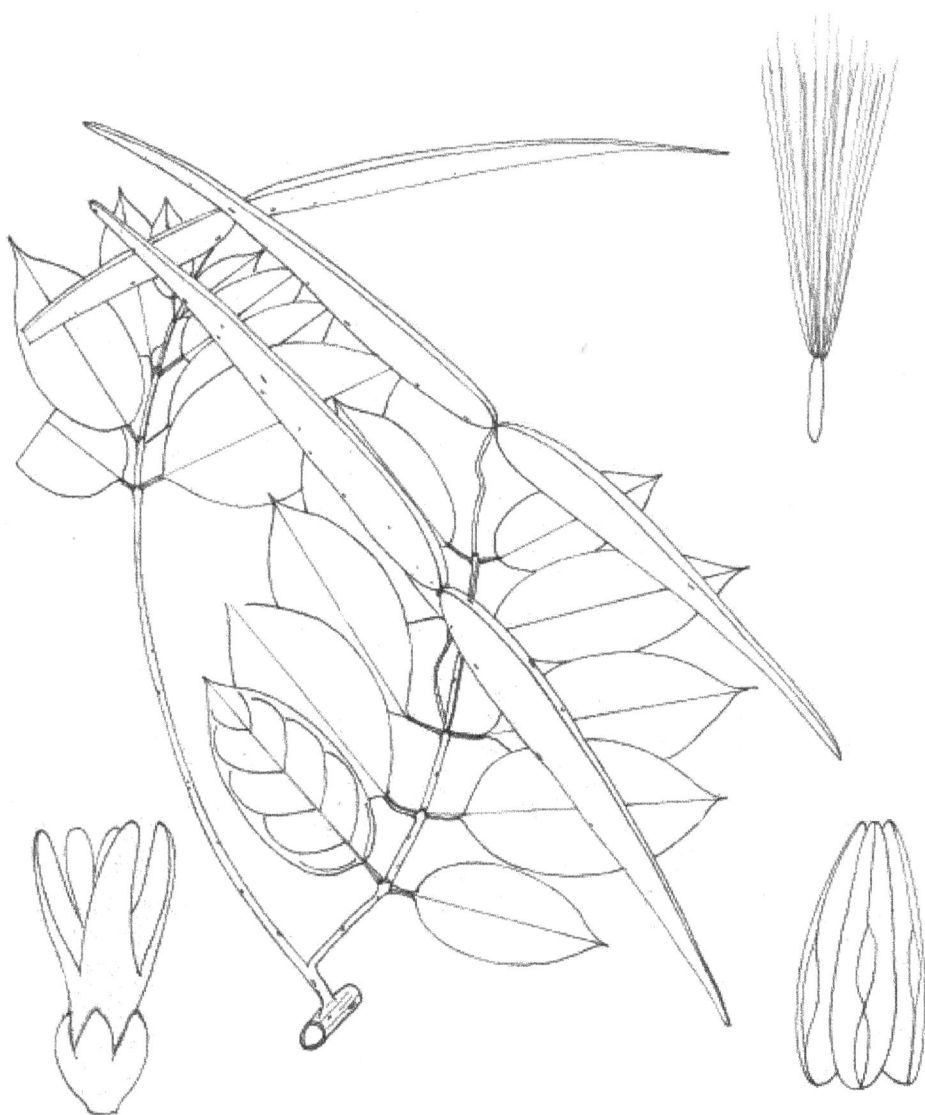

Figure 167: *Parsonsia laevigata* (Moon) Alston
From: Herbarium of University of the Ryukyus
Japan, Ryukyu, seashore of Pinishi-Juna, Komi, Iriomotejima, Yaeyama Island. Climber on limestone area. Date of Collection: 29 July 1984. Collection: Shimabuku K & Y. Miyasi N° 5659

Tabernaemontana cylindrocarpa (King & Gamble) Merr.

[After J. T. Mueller or Tabernaemontanus, a German botanist of the 16th century and Latin *cylindrocarpa* = with cylinder - shaped fruits]

Synonym: *Ervatamia cylindrocarpa* King & Gamble

Description: It is a common shrub which grows to a height of 3 m in the rainforest of Malaysia. The stem is terete, about 0.3 cm in diameter, with few lenticels and exudes an abundant latex upon incision. The internode forms a sort of little tube. The leaves are simple, decussate, sessile, and without stipules. The leaf blade is membranaceous, broadly elliptic, tapering at the base, apiculate at the apex with a little tail that can reach 2 cm long. The leaf blade is 3 - 5 cm x 7 - 12.5 cm and presents underneath about 5 pairs of secondary nerves which are arching at a distance from the margin. The secondary nerves are sunken above. The leaf blade shows under microscopic examination some sort of digitations. The flowers are grouped in terminal cymes. The flowers are white, with 5 contorted lobes. The fruits are a pair of elliptic carpels beaked at the apex and about 7 x 1.5 cm (Figure 168).

Medicinal uses: The plant is used by Malays as an external remedy for itchiness, eczema and beriberi. It is also applied to the skin of syphilitics.

Pharmacology: The medicinal use of the plant is probably due to some counterirritant effects of the latex. It would be of interest to study the property of the plant against *Treponema pallidum*, the agent of Syphilis. Note that several species in the genus *Tabernaemontana* are used to treat syphilis throughout Southeast Asia (Van Beek *et al.*, 1984).

References: Van Beek TA, Verpoorte R, Svendsen AB, Leeuwenberg AJ, Bisset NG, 1984, *Tabernaemontana* L. (Apocynaceae): a review of its taxonomy, phytochemistry, ethnobotany and pharmacology. J Ethnopharmacol; 10:1-156. Review.

Figure 168: *Tabernaemontana cylindrocarpa* **(King & Gamble) Merr.**
From: Herbarium of University Kebangsaan Malaysia N0 00791
Malaysia, Bangi. Collection and Identification: Mohd. Kassim. Date of Collection: 11May 1973.

Tabernaemontana malaccensis Hook f.

[After J. T. Mueller or Tabernaemontanus, a German botanist of the 16th century and Latin *malaccensis* = from Malacca]

Local name:	Lada-lada (Malaysia), prachek. (Sri Lanka)
Synonym:	*Ervatamia malaccensis* (Hook f.) king & Gamble
Description:	It is a common large shrub which grows to about 2.5 m in the rainforest of Malaysia. The stem is terete, glabrous, with few lenticels, about 0.25 cm in diameter and with 2 - 6.5 cm long internodes. The internodes show some sort of triangular membranes above the petiole. The plant is laticiferous, the latex is pure white and abundant. The leaves are simple, opposite and without stipules. The petiole is about 0.5 - 0.7 cm long, slender and channeled. The leaf blade is elliptic, cuneate at the base, acuminate at the apex, 2.2 – 5 cm to 6 - 13 cm with 5 to 6 pairs of secondary nerves which are conspicuous and straight underneath. The flowers are white, tubular and with 5 contorted lobes. The fruits are pairs of follicles which are orange-red, somewhat fleshy, about 3.8 x 1.2 cm on a 2.5 cm long pedicel (Figure 169).
Medicinal uses:	The plant is used to heal syphilitic ulceration of the nose and to heal boils and pimples. A root paste of the whole plant is applied on aching and painful parts. The latex is used for the making of arrow-poison in Malaysia.
Pharmacology:	The plant produces a series of indole alkaloids including N (1)-methoxy-19,20-dehydroervatamine, 19,20-dehydroervatamine, N(l)-methoxymethuenine, methuenine, dregamine, 6-oxomethuenine, 16-epimethuenine, 20- epiervatamine (Clivio *et al.*, 1990). Cumulative dose-response experiments and coaxial stimulation of the guinea pig ileum in an organ bath showed that methuenine is a non-competitive antagonist against acetylcholine and histamine (Bakana *et al.*, 1985), hence the curare activity of latex.

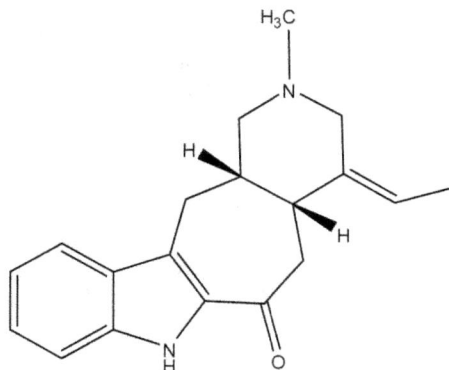

Methuenine

References:

Bakana P, Laekeman GM, Totte J, Herman AG, Vlietinck AJ, 1985, Stereochemical considerations in relation to the pharmacological activity of *Pterotaberna* alkaloids. J Nat Prod; 48:766-71.

Clivio P, Richard B, Zeches M, Le Men-Olivier L, Goh SH, David B, Sevenet T, 1990, Alkaloids from the leaves and stem bark of *Ervatamia malaccensis*. Phytochemistry; 29:2693-2696.

Figure 169: *Tabernaemontana malaccensis* **Hook.f.**
From: Flora of Malaya, Herbarium of University Kebangsaan Malaysia, Nº 12913
Malaysia, Gunung Brinchang, Cameron Highland, Pahang state. Collection: Willis K Little.
Determination: Mohd Kassim. Date of collection: July 1976.

Tabernaemontana peduncularis Wall

[After J. T. Mueller or Tabernaemontanus, a German botanist of the 16th century and Latin *peduncularis* = with a distinct stalk]

Local name:	Dejarang (Malaysia), phut dong (Thailand)
Synonym:	*Tabernaemontana graciliflora* Wall., *Ervatamia graciliflora*, (Wall.) Lace, *Ervatamia repeuensis* Pierre, *Ervatamia peduncularis* (Wall.) King & Gamble.
Description:	It is a common small tree which grows to a height of 3 m in the forest of Burma, Thailand, Cambodia, Vietnam, and Malaysia. The stem is rough at the base, 0.3 to 0.4 cm in diameter, glabrous, with 1 - 3.5 cm long internodes. The plant is laticiferous and exudes an abundant latex upon incision. The leaves are simple, opposite and without stipules. The petioles are channeled, clasping the stem, and about 1 cm long. The leaf blade is elliptic lanceolate, 2.3 - 4 cm x 8 - 15 cm, thinly coriaceous, caudate at the apex, recurved and wavy at the margin and shows a midrib and 9 to 11 pairs of secondary nerves sunken above and prominent underneath. The inflorescences are axillary cymes on a 5 - 8 cm long peduncle. The flowers are white, tubular and 5 lobed, the lobes contorted. The fruit consist of a pair of obliquely ellipsoid orange, red, yellow or green, 1-2-seeded, follicles (Figure 170.
Medicinal uses:	In Malaysia the plant is used to heal syphilitic ulceration of the nose. The plant is well known in Malaysia to be poisonous. In Thailand, the plant is used for inflammation and fever.

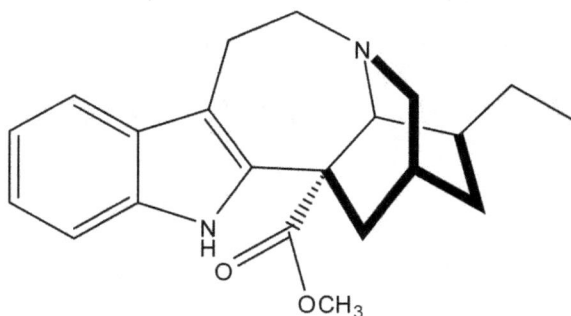

Coronaridine

Pharmacology:	The plant elaborates a series of indole alkaloids such as pedunculine, peduncularidine, coronaridine, coronaridine hydroxyindolenine, eglandine, heyneanine, eglandulosine,

heyneanine hydroxyindolenine and N(1)-methyl-aspidospermidine (Zèches-Hanrot *et al.*, 1995). Coronaridine is common in the genus *Tabernaemontana* has been the subject of several pharmacological studies which have unambiguously demonstrated cytotoxic (Kupchan *et al.*, 1963), antifertility (Meyer *et al.*, 1973), muscle relaxant (Perera *et al.*, 1985), analgesic and hypothermic (Okuyama *et al.*, 1992), and anticholinesterase activities (Andrade *et al.*,2005). Heyneanine is cytotoxic against A2780 ovarian cancer cell line.(Prakash Chaturvedula *et al.*, 2003),

References:

Andrade MT, Lima JA, Pinto AC, Rezende CM, Carvalho MP, Epifanio RA, 2005,Indole alkaloids from *Tabernaemontana australis* (Muell. Arg) Miers that inhibit acetylcholinesterase enzyme. Bioorg Med Chem;13:4092-5.

Kupchan SM, Bright A, Macko E, 1963, Tumor inhibitors. II. Alkaloids of Ervatamia dichotoma. Isolation, crystallization, and pharmacological properties of coronaridine. J Pharm Sci; 52:598-9

Meyer WE, Coppola JA, Goldman L, 1973, Alkaloid studies. 8. Isolation and characterization of alkaloids of *Tabernaemontana heyneana* Wall and antifertility properties of coronaridine. J Pharm Sci; 62:1199-201.

Okuyama E, Gao LH, Yamazaki M, 1992,Analgesic components from bornean medicinal plants, *Tabernaemontana pauciflora* Bl. and *Tabernaemontana pandacaqui* Poir. Chem Pharm Bull (Tokyo); 40:2075-9.

Perera P, Kanjanapothy D, Sandberg F, Verpoorte R, 1985, Muscle relaxant activity and hypotensive activity of some *Tabernaemontana* alkaloids. J Ethnopharmacol; 13:165-73.

Prakash Chaturvedula VS, Sprague S, Schilling JK, Kingston DG, 2003, New cytotoxic indole alkaloids from *Tabernaemontana calcarea* from the Madagascar rainforest. J Nat Prod.; 66:528-31

Zèches-Hanrot M, Nuzillard JM, Richard B, Schaller H, Hadi HA, Sévenet T, Le Men-Olivier L, 1995, Alkaloids from leaves and stem bark of *Ervatamia peduncularis*. Phytochemistry; 40: 587-591

Figure 170: *Tabernaemontana peduncularis* Wall
From: Flora of Malaya, Herbarium of University Kebangsaan Malaysia, No 26665
Malaysia, Negeri Sembilan state, Gemencheh, dam site. Collection A. Zainuddin. Dare of
collection: 8 September 1992 Determination: MMJ van Balgooy. Date of identification: 17
February 1997.

Strophanthus wallichii A. DC

[From Greek *strophos* = twisted cord and *anthos* = flower and after Nathaniel Wallich (1786 - 1854) East India Company's botanist in Calcutta].

Local name:	Yun nan yang jiao miu (China)
Description:	It is scandent shrub which grows in Malaysia, Bangladesh, India, Laos, Thailand, and Vietnam The stem is terete, stout, lenticelled, about 0.5 cm in diameter, with about 4.5 - 5.5 cm long internodes marked with a tiny line. The plant is laticiferous, the latex being pure white. The leaves are simple, decussate and without stipules. The petiole is about 0.5 cm long, and channeled. The leaf blade is broadly lanceolate, 6.5 - 7 cm x 3 - 5 cm, with 5 to 6 pairs of secondary nerves, round at the base, and acuminate at the apex. The inflorescences are cymose on a 5 - 7 cm long peduncle. The calyx is tubular with 5 linear lobes which are about 1 cm long. The corolla is about 3.2 cm long, purplish, with 5 linear lobes around a patched throat. The stigma is mitreform. The fruits are pairs of massive oblong, about 12 x 4.5 cm, follicles which are lenticelled (Figure 171)
Medicinal Uses:	The plant is used in India for medicinal purposes.
Pharmacology:	Unknown. The plant probably contains abundant cardiotonic glycosides.

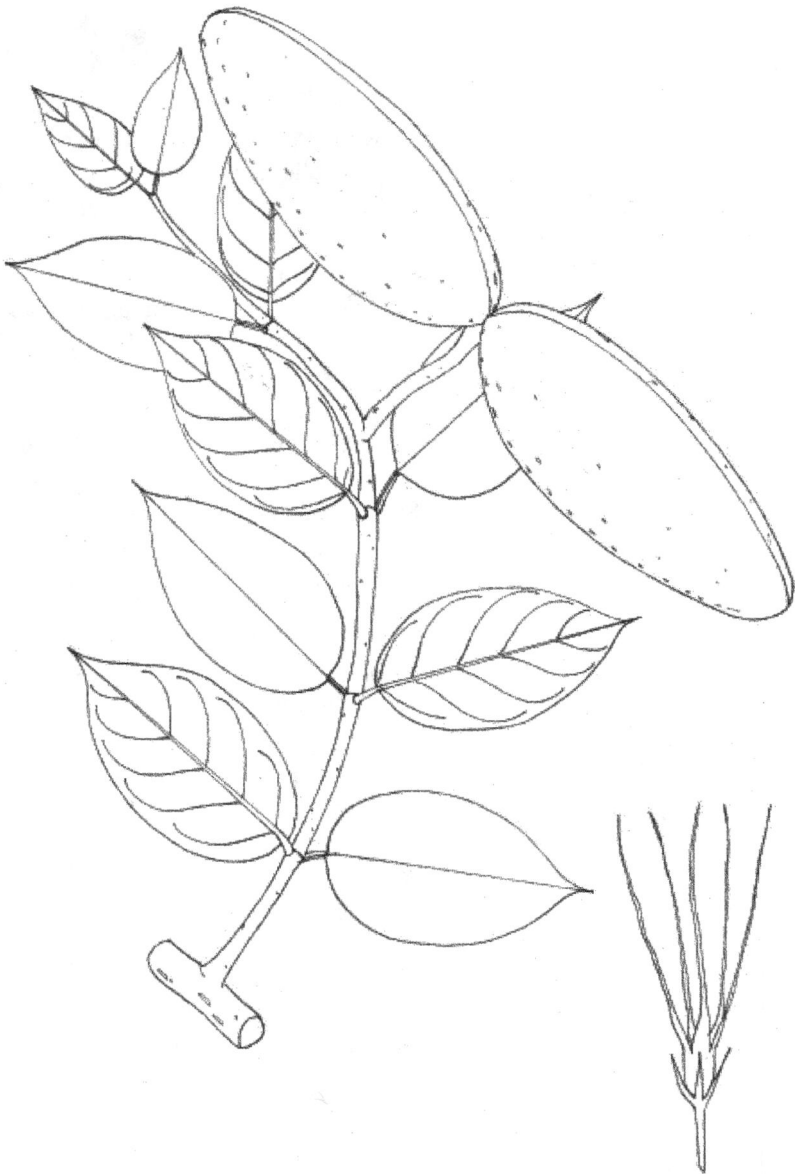

Figure 171: *Strophanthus wallichii* **A. DC**
From: Herbarium of University Kebangsaan Malaysia
Malaysia, Pulau Langkawi, Tg Rhu, Grand Pool Hotel site, sandy soil. Collection: Abdul Latiff
et al. date of Collection: 14 February 1986. Identification: A Zainuddin.

3.Family ASCLEPIADACEAE R. Brown 1810 nom. conserv., the Milkweed Family

The family Asclepiadaceae consists of about 250 genera and 2,000 species of laticiferous, poisonous, tropical shrubs, herb and climbers which at first glance look very much like members of the Apocynaceae family; with which it shares the opposite simple leaves without stipules, the production of a white latex, and a 5 lobed corolla. The fruits are a pair of follicles, filled with comose seeds. The main difference is at the flower level. Flowers of Asclepiadaceae are very characteristic as they comprise a unique type of organs known as pollinia. The calyx shows tiny glands at the base of the lobes inside. The androecium consists of 5 stamens, the filaments of which usually connate into a staminal tube. In regards to the phytochemical pattern of Asclepiadaceae, oxypregnane cardiotonic glycosides , indole, piperidine and phenanthroindolizidine alkaloids are predominant.

Asclepias curassavica L. (blood-flower), *Calotropis procera* (Ait.) Ait. f. (giant milkweed), *Hoya carnosa* R. Br (Wax Plant,), *Hoya pubicalyx* Merr. and *Hoya kerrii* Craib. (sweetheart Hoya) are grown as tropical garden ornamental plants.

The dried stem bark of *Marsdenia cundurango* Rchb. f. (Condurango, *British pharmaceutical Codex*, 1934) has been used as an aromatic bitter and gastric sedative in the form of a tincture. The dried roots of *Hemidesmus indicus* (Hemidesmus, *British Pharmaceutical Codex*, 1934) were used to treat syphilis, rheumatism, psoriasis and eczema in Western medicine.

Members of the family Asclepiadaceae, and particularly *Asclepias, Calotropis, Carissa, Cryptostegia, Gomphocarpus, Menabea, Periploca* and *Xysmalobium* species accumulate a series of cardiotoxic glycosides of the pregnane type. One such glycoside is periplocin (*British Pharmaceutical Codex*, 1967), characterized from the bark of *Periploca graeca*. Periplocin which has been used in Russia instead of digitalin (1 mL ampoule of 0.25 mg). Pregnanes and pregnane glycosides have drawn much attention in recent years because of their antitumor and anticancer activities (De Leo *et al.*, 2005; Hamed, *et al*, 2006;). A cytotoxic activity was exhibited by 3-O-(beta-glucopyranosyl) acovenosigenin A isolated from *Streptocaulon griffithii* against human gastrointestinal cancer cell lines HGC-27, A549, MCF-7, and Hela cells (Zhang *et al*, 2007).

Asclepiadaceae have attracted a great deal of interest on account of their phenanthroindolizidine alkaloids which might hold some potential for the treatment of cancer. Tylocrebine, from *Tylophora crebiflora* displayed promising signs of anti - tumor property but heavy side effects precluded the continuation of further clinical studies. However, there may be other phenanthroindolizidine alkaloids of clinical value as the family offers a vast array of structures such as tylophoridicines C-F, R-(+)-deoxytylophorinidine, tylophorinine and tylophorinidine, from *Tylophora atrofolliculata*. The structures exhibited cytotoxic activity *in vitro* on HCT-8 cell (Huang *et al.*, 2004). Antofine, a phenanthroindolizidine alkaloid isolated from *Cynanchum paniculatum* is cytotoxic with G2/M cell cycle arrest (Lee *et al.*, 2003). Members of this family could be of interest in looking for neuroprotective agents since a biacetophenone cynandione A from *Cynanchum wilfordii* protects cultured cortical neurons from toxicity induced by H_2O_2, L-glutamate, and kainite (Lee *et al.*, 2000). Note that the latex and the leaves of Asclepiadaceae are often used to make arrow - poison, to counteract putrefaction, to assuage pain, to allay fever, to induce vomiting and to relieve constipation. In Asia - Pacific about 50 Asclepiadaceae plant species are used for medicinal purpose.

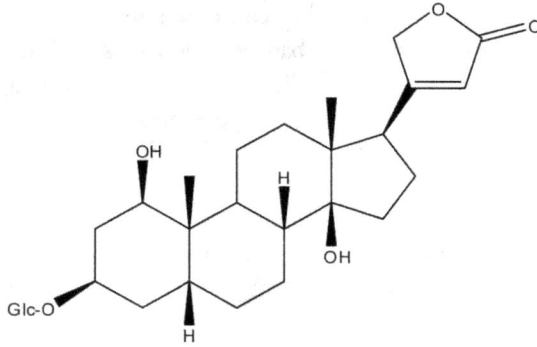

3-O-(b-glucopyranosyl)acovenosigenin A

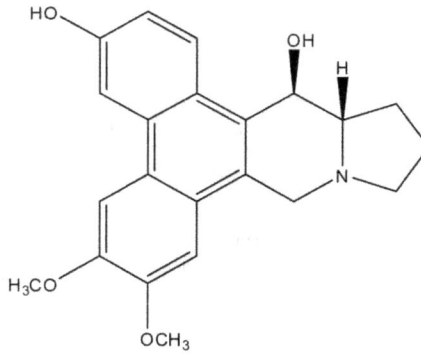

Tylophoridicine E

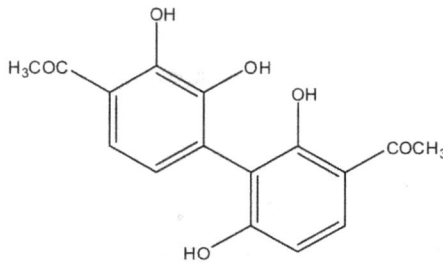

Cynandione A

References: De Leo M, De Tommasi N, Sanogo R, Autore G, Marzocco S, Pizza C, Morelli I, Braca A, 2005, New pregnane glycosides from *Caralluma dalzielii*. Steroids; 70:573-585.

Hamed AI, Plaza A, Balestrieri ML, Mahalel UA, Springuel IV, Oleszek W, Pizza C, Piacente S, 2006, Cardenolide glycosides from *Pergularia tomentosa* and their proapoptotic activity in Kaposi's sarcoma cells. J Nat Prod; 69:1319-22.

Huang X, Gao S, Fan L, Yu S, Liang X, 2004, Cytotoxic alkaloids from the roots of *Tylophora atrofolliculata*. Planta Med; 70:441-5.

Lee MK, Yeo H, Kim J, Markelonis GJ, Oh TH, Kim YC, 2000, Cynandione A from *Cynanchum wilfordii* protects cultured cortical neurons from toxicity induced by H2O2, L-glutamate, and kainate. J Neurosci Res; 59:259-64.

Lee SK, Nam KA, Heo YH, 2003, Cytotoxic activity and G2/M cell cycle arrest mediated by antofine, a phenanthroindolizidine alkaloid isolated from *Cynanchum paniculatum*. Planta Med; 69:21-5.

Zhang XH, Zhu HL, Yu Q, Xuan LJ, 2007, Cytotoxic cardenolides from *Streptocaulon griffithii*. Chem Biodivers; 4:998-1002

Cryptolepis buchananii Roem. & Schult.

[From Greek *kryptos* = hidden and Latin *lepis* = a scale and after Francis Buchanan, (1762-1829) British scientific explorer]

Local name: Karanta (India)

Synonym: *Trachelospermum cavaleriei* H. Lév,

Description: It is a woody climber which grows to a length of 5 m with a basal diameter of 8 cm in the forests of China, India, Kashmir, Laos, Burma, Nepal, Pakistan, Sri Lanka, Thailand, and Vietnam. The bark is smooth, peeling-flaking, and blackish. The stem is flaking, peeling, terete, 0.4 cm in diameter, and produce abundant white latex upon incision. The leaves are simple, opposite and exstipulate. The petiole is slender and 0.6 - 1.3 cm long. The leaf-blade is oblong or elliptic, membranaceous, 10-19 cm × 4.5 - 7.5 cm, rounded at the base, acuminate at the apex, with about 25 - 30 pairs of secondary nerves visible underneath.

The inflorescences are paniculate cymes. The flower pedicels are glabrous and about 0.4 cm long. The calyx is glabrous, with 5 lobes which are 0.15 cm long, ovate and subacute. The corolla is greenish yellow with a 0.2 cm long tube and 5 lobes which are 0.6 cm long and linear-lanceolate. The corona lobes are club-shaped. The fruits are pairs of follicles which are 5 - 10 cm x 1.3 - 2 cm, straight, cylindrical and pointed at the apex. The seeds are brownish, ovate-oblong, 0.6 - 0.8 cm long, with a tuft of white hairs which is 2.5 - 3.5 cm long (Figure 172).

Medicinal Uses: In India, the plant is used to treat rickets, paralysis, and to promote the production of milk in young mothers. In China, the plant is used to treat chills and oedema . In Thailand, the plant is used for the treatment of inflammation, including arthritis, and muscle and joint pain.

Pharmacology: The plant elaborates a series of cardenolides including cryptosin which is a potent positive inotropic agent (Yeau *et al.*, 1963; Rao *et al.*, 1990). The plant is immunostimulating: an extract of the plant given orally produced a significant stimulation of the delayed type hypersensitivity reaction and humoral antibody production in rodents (Kaul *et al.*, 2003). The anti-inflammatory property of the plant has been validated: an extract reduced carrageenan-induced rat paw oedema and eicosanoid production from calcium ionophore A23187-stimulated rat peritoneal leukocytes (Laupattarakasem *et al.*, 2006). The plant contains nicotinoyl glucosides (Sunil *et al*, 1978, 1980). Note that cryptolepine, an indoloquinoline alkaloid isolated in members of the genus *Cryptolepis* : *Cryptolepis sanguinolenta* is cytotoxic due to its ability to intercalate into DNA, and has exhibited potent antiplasmodial activities *in vitro* (Seville *et al.*, 2007).

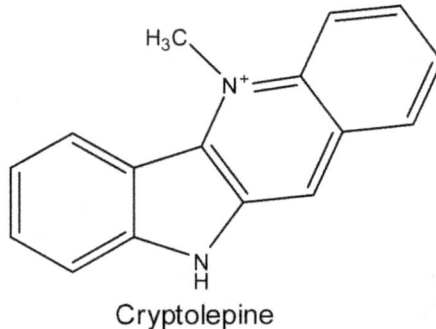

Cryptolepine

Figure 172: *Cryptolepis buchananii* **Roem. & Schult.**
From: Flora of Thailand, Chiang Mai University Herbarium
Thailand, Lampang province, Nao Ta district, by 17o North, Mae Moh Basin at Fah Mayo
reservoir, Koa Setah subdistrict. Elevation: 325 m. Date of Collection: 17 december 1994.
In open disturbed, degraded, deciduous dipterocarp-oak scrub forest margin bordering the
reservoir on sand bedrock.

References: Dutta SK, Sharma BN, Sharma PV, 1978, Buchananine, a novel
               pyridine alkaloid from *Cryptolepis buchanani*. Phytochemistry;
               17:2047-2048.

               Dutta SK, Sharma BN, Sharrial PV, 1980, A new nicotinoyl
               glucoside from *Cryptolepis buchanani*. Phytochemistry; 19:
               1278.

               Kaul A, Bani S, Zutshi U, Suri KA, Satti NK, Suri OP, 2003,
               Immunopotentiating properties of *Cryptolepis buchanani* root

extract. Phytother Res; 17:1140-4.

Laupattarakasem P, Wangsrimongkol T, Surarit R, Hahnvajanawong C, 2006, *In vitro* and *in vivo* anti-inflammatory potential of *Cryptolepis buchanani*. J Ethnopharmacol; 108:349-54.

Rao VR, Banning JW, 1990, Interactions of cryptosin with mammalian cardiac beta-adrenoceptors. Drug Chem Toxicol; 13:173-94.

Seville S, Phillips RM, Shnyder SD, Wright CW, 2007, Synthesis of cryptolepine analogues as potential bioreducible anticancer agents. Bioorg Med Chem; 15: 6353-6360.

Yeau KL, Chou YS, Young DS, 1963, The cardiotonic effect of a glycoside from *Cryptolepis buchanani*. Yao Xue Xue Bao; 10:561-5.

Dischidia nummularia R. Br.

[From Latin *numularia* = resembling a coin]

Local name:	Button orchid, yuan ye yan shu lian (China), jeh po prih (Thailand)
Synonyms:	*Collyris minor* Vahl., *Dischidia gaudichaudii* Decne, *Dischidia minor* (Vahl.) Merr., *Dischidia orbicularis* Decne.
Description:	It is a succulent epiphyte which grows in the forests of India, Indonesia, Laos, Malaysia, Sri Lanka, Thailand, Vietnam, Australia, and the Pacific Islands. The plant has ornamental value. The stem is slender, 0.2 cm in diameter, laticiferous, creeping, rooting at nodes, and clustered, light yellowish and up to 1.5 m long. The internodes are about 1.5 - 2.5 cm long. The leaves are simple, opposite and without stipules. The petiole is minute and about 0.15 cm long. The leaf blade is orbicular, thick, dull yellowish above, pale light greenish underneath and about 1 x 0.4 cm. The inflorescences are minute axillary heads about 0.5 cm long. The calyx is urceolate with 5 lobes. The corolla is white, minute and develops 5 lobes which are ovate-triangular. The fruits are pairs of follicles which are lanceolate and about 3 - 4 cm × 0.5 cm (Figure 173).
Medicinal Uses:	In Malaysia and Indonesia, the plant is used to assuage the pain caused by spiny fish.

Pharmacology: The plant probably contains series of pentacyclic triterpenes (Chen *et al.*, 1993; Ma *et al.*, 2008). The pharmacological properties of this plant are still unexplored.

References: Chen ZS, Lee GH, Kuo YH, 1993, Disformone and dischidiol from *Dischidia formosana.* Phytochemistry; 34: 783-786.

Ma X, Yang C, Zhang Y, 2008, Complete assignments of (1) H and (13)C NMR spectral data for three polyhydroxylated 12-ursen-type triterpenoids from *Dischidia esquirolii*; Magn Reson Chem; 46:571-575.

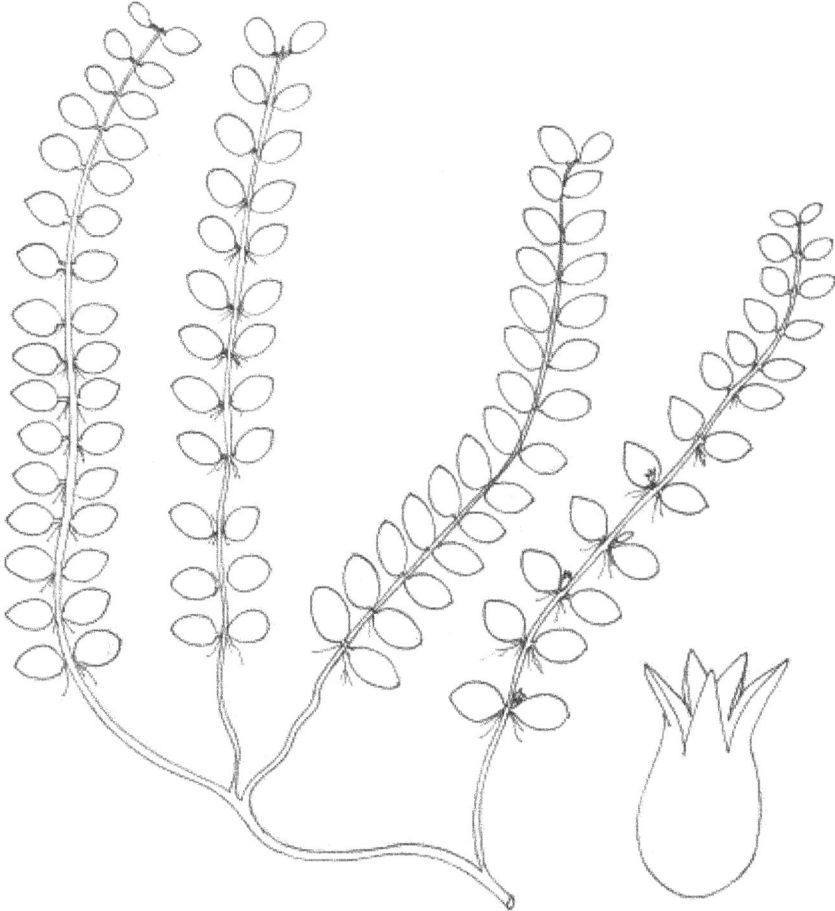

Figure 173: *Dischidia nummularia* R. Br.
From: Flora of Thailand, Chiang Mai University Herbarium
Thailand, Chiang Mai province, Wieng Hang district, Doi Neum, East side, near Mae Haht falls in the vicinity of Wieng nang town. Elevation 850 m. Date of collection: 21 April 1995. In open forest.
& from: Plants of Borneo, Michigan University Herbarium,
Borneo, 5° 02' North - 115° 31 East. Collection: John Beaman.

Gymnema alterniflorum (Lour.) Merr.

[From Greek *gymnos* = naked and Latin *alterniflorum* = with alternate flowers]

Local name:	Periploca of the woods, small Indian ipecacuanha; barkista (Arabic), gurmar, adigam (India), ajaballi (Sanskrit), chi geng teng (China).
Basionym:	*Apocynum alterniflorum* Lour. *Flora Cochinchinensis* 168. 1790
Synonyms:	*Asclepias curassavica* Lour., *Gymnema affine* Decne., *Gymnema parviflorum* Wall.
Description:	It is a large woody climber which grows in Taiwan, China, India, Indonesia, Japan, Malaysia, Sri Lanka, Vietnam, Africa and Australia. The stem at the top is slender, terete, 0.3 cm in diameter, lenticelled, glabrous, hairy at the apex with 1 - 3 cm long internodes. The plant is laticiferous and exudes white latex upon excision. The leaves are simple, opposite and without stipules. The petiole is 0.6 - 1.3 cm long with a few hairs and channeled. The leaf blade is obovate to oblong, 3.2 - 5 cm x 1.3 - 3.2 cm, acute to acuminate at the apex, recurved at the margin with 4 to 5 pairs of secondary nerves. The inflorescences are small axillary cymes on a 0.5 - 0.7 cm long peduncle. The calyx is cup-shaped, with 5 triangular lobes, with few hairs and about 0.3 cm long. The corolla is yellow, campanulate, with 5 lobes and 0.5 cm across. The fruits are single or paired follicles, which are woody, 4 - 7 cm long, containing several flat winged, 0.7 - 0.9 cm x 0.4 - 0.5 cm comose seeds (Figure 174).
Medicinal Uses:	In Taiwan the plant is an antidote for snake bite. In India the plant is used to expel worms from intestines, to clear opaque cornea, to sooth inflamed parts and for asthma and bronchitis. The plant is used to treat diabetes, abscesses and snake bite. In China, the plant is used for the treatment of rheumatism, blood-vessel inflammation, haemorrhoids, and snake bites.
Pharmacology:	The plant contains a series of pentacyclic triterpenoid saponins which account for its medicinal uses. The antidiabetic property of the plant has been validated by several pharmacological studies and the plant is used in preparations for the treatment of diabetes (Porchezhian *et al.*, 2003; Leach *et al.*, 2007). Gymnemic acid IV from the plant showed a hypoglycemic effect comparable to that of glibenclamide, and increased plasma insulin levels in streptozotocin-diabetic mice (Sugihara *et al.*, 2000). The antiseptic effect of the plant has been validated: an extract abrogated the survival of *Bacillus pumilis*, *Bacillus subtilis*,

Pseudomonas aeruginosa and *Staphylococcus aureus* cultured *in vitro* (Satdive *et al*, 2003).

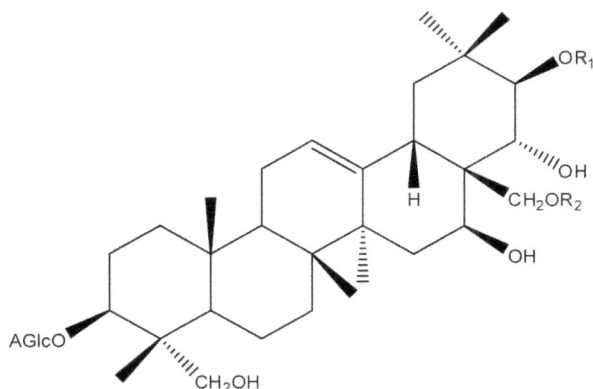

Gymnemic acids

References: Leach MJ, 2007, *Gymnema sylvestre* for diabetes mellitus: a systematic review. J Altern Complement Med; 13:977-83.

Porchezhian E, Dobriyal RM, 2003, An overview on the advances of *Gymnema sylvestre*: chemistry, pharmacology and patents. Pharmazie; 58:5-12.

Satdive RK, Abhilash P, Fulzele DP, 2003, Antimicrobial activity of *Gymnema sylvestre* leaf extract. Fitoterapia; 74:699-701.

Sugihara Y, Nojima H, Matsuda H, Murakami T, Yoshikawa M, Kimura I, 2000, Antihyperglycemic effects of gymnemic acid IV, a compound derived from *Gymnema sylvestre* leaves in streptozotocin-diabetic mice. J Asian Nat Prod Res; 2:321-7.

Figure 174: *Gymnema alterniflorum* **(Lour.) Merr.**
From Flora of Taiwan, Herbarium National Pingtung Institute of Agriculture.
Taiwan, Hengchim, Kenting. Collection: C.L. Yeh. Date of Collection: 24 July 1984.

B. Order SOLANALES Lindley 1833

The order Solanales consists of 8 families and about 5,000 species of herbs, shrubs and climbers often producing tropane alkaloids derived from ornithine, steroidal alkaloids, indole alkaloids and lignans. Most plant species in the Solanales belong to the family Solanaceae and the family Convolvulaceae.

1. Family CONVOLVULACEAE A. L. de Jussieu 1789 nom. conserv., the Morning - glory Family

The family Convolvulaceae consists of 50 genera and 1,500 species of tuberous climbers known to produce glucoresins, lignans, indole, pyrrolizidine and tropane alkaloids and polyhydroxytropanes derived from ornithine. Flavonoids such as kaempferol and quercetin and their glycosides are common in this family which also produces some flavonoid sulfates. Note also the presence of phenylpropanoid glycosides. The leaves are simple, often cordate at the base, without stipules, entire and lobed. The flowers are infundibuliform and colorful. The calyx consists of 5 sepals which are free, imbricate and persistent in fruits. The corolla is membranaceous and more or less 5-lobed. The androecium consists of 5 stamens attached to the base of the corolla tube and alternate with the lobes. The anthers are 2 - celled and open lengthwise. The gynaecium consists of 2 - 5 carpels which merge into a superior and 1 - 4 - locular ovary each locules containing 1 or 2 ovules attached to basal or axile placentas. A nectary disc is present. The fruits are indehiscent, succulent or capsular. The seeds are occasionally hairy and curved.

Several species in this family are ornamental, such as *Ipomoea tricolor* Cav. (heavenly-blue morning-glory), *Ipomoea alba* L. (moon flower), *Ipomoea quamoclit* L. (cypress vine), and *Ipomoea sloteri* (House) Ooststr. (cardinal climber). Several members of this family have been included in European pharmacopoeias as drastic laxatives on account of their glucoresin: *Ipomoea orizabensis* (Ipomoea, British Pharmaceutical Codex, 1963), *Ipomoea purga* (Wender.) Hayne (Jalap, British Pharmaceutical Codex, 1963), *Convolvulus scammonia* L. (scammony), *Operculina turpethum* (L.) Silva Manso, *Operculina macrocarpa* (Ipomoea tuberosa; Brazilian Jalap, Portuguese Pharmacopoeia, 1936) and *Ipomoea hederacea* (British Pharmaceutical Codex, 1949). An interesting feature of Convolvulaceae is their tendency to elaborate serotoninergic lysergic acid diethylamide - like indole alkaloids which impart hallucinogenic properties to the plant. Such psychoactive principles are found in the seeds of *Rivea corymbosa* (L.) Hall (ololiuqui) and *Ipomoea violacea* L. (tlitlitzin) which have both been used by South American shaman to induce narcosis. In regards to the recent pharmacological findings in this family, a series of macrocyclic glucoresins named ipomoeassin A-F isolated from *Ipomoea squamosa* inhibited the growth of A2780 human ovarian cancer cultured *in vitro* (Cao *et al* 2007). An extract of *Erycibe elliptilimba* Merr. & Chun abrogated the survival of MDA-MB435 human breast cancer cells with arrest at G2/M phase (Kummalue *et al.*, 2007). Bonabiline A, a monoterpenoid 3alpha-acyloxytropane from the roots of *Bonamia spectabilis* showing M3 receptor antagonist activity (Ott *et al.*, 2006). Clycosin, erythrinin B, deguelin and rotenone isolated from *Erycibe expansa* inhibited lipopolysaccharide-activated nitric oxide production in mouse peritoneal macrophages.(Morikawa *et al.*, 2006). An extract of *Convolvulus pluricaulis* elicited antidepressant-like effect in mice by a mechanism involving the adrenergic, dopaminergic, and serotoninergic systems and with potencies comparable to that of imipramine and fluoxetine. (Dhingra *et al*, 2007). An ethyl acetate extract of roots of *Ipomoea stans* Cav. given to mice, reduced spontaneous motor activity, antagonized pentylenetetrazole-induced convulsion, and increased the hypnotic effect induced by pentobarbital via increase of release of GABA in brain cortex of mice suggesting some potentials for the development of anxiolytic drugs (Herrera-Ruiz *et al.*, 2007). About fifty plant species from this family are used for medicinal purpose in Asia - Pacific. Note that many of these plants are used to purge the bowels, to invigorate, to treat dropsy, to heal sores and broken bones, to counteract gynecologic putrefaction, to expel intestinal worms, to heal haemorrhoids and to assuage headache.

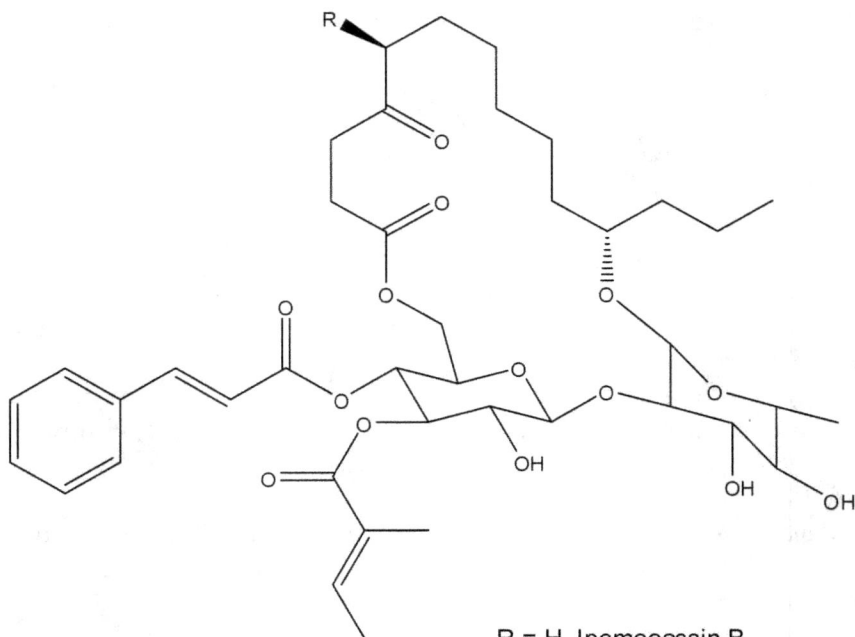

R = H, Ipomoeassin B
R= OAc, Ipomoeassin E

References: Cao S, Norris A, Wisse JH, Miller JS, Evans R, Kingston DG, 2007, Ipomoeassin F, a new cytotoxic macrocyclic glycoresin from the leaves of *Ipomoea squamosa* from the Suriname rainforest. Nat Prod; 21:872-6.

Dhingra D, Valecha R, 2007, Evaluation of the antidepressant-like activity of *Convolvulus pluricaulis* choisy in the mouse forced swim and tail suspension tests. Med Sci Monit; 13:155-61

Herrera-Ruiz M, Gutiérrez C, J. Jiménez-Ferrer JE, Tortoriello J, Mirón G, León I, 2007, Central nervous system depressant activity of an ethyl acetate extract from *Ipomoea stans* roots J Ethnopharmacol; 112: 243-247.

Kummalue T, O-charoenrat P, Jiratchariyakul W, Chanchai M, Pattanapanyasat K, Sukapirom K, Iemsri S, 2007, Antiproliferative effect of *Erycibe elliptilimba* on human breast cancer cell lines. J Ethnopharmacol; 110:439-43.

Morikawa T, Xu F, Matsuda H, Yoshikawa M, 2006, Structures of new flavonoids, erycibenins D, E, and F, and NO production inhibitors from *Erycibe expansa* originating in Thailand. Chem Pharm Bull (Tokyo); 54:1530-4.

Ott SC, Jenett-Siems K, Pertz HH, Siems K, Witte L, Eich E, 2006, Bonabiline A, a monoterpenoid 3alpha-acyloxytropane from the roots of *Bonamia spectabilis* showing M3 receptor antagonist activity. Planta Med; 72:1403-6.

Argyreia maingayi (C.B. Clarke) Hoogl.

[From Greek *argyro* = silvery and after Alexander Carroll Maingay, (1836-1869) Physician Botanist]

Description: It is a climber which grows in the rainforest of Malaysia. The stem is terete, pilose, and woody with longitudinal striations and about 3 mm in diameter. The leaves are simple, spiral and without stipules. The petiole is slender, 0.2 cm in diameter, channeled and about 2 cm long. The leaf blade is elliptic lanceolate, acute at the base, acuminate at the apex, subglabrous, 8.5 - 10 cm x 2.6 - 3.6 cm and shows about 6 pairs of secondary nerves which are conspicuous underneath. The apex of the blade is minutely tufted. A few scalariform tertiary nerves are visible underneath the leaf blade. The inflorescences are axillary cymes on about 1 cm hairy peduncles, with conspicuous bracts. The bracts are hairy and about 0.7 x 0.2 cm. The calyx consists of 5 sepals which are hairy at the apex and persistent in fruits and about 1 x 0.3 cm. Fruits purplish with persistent green calyx (Figure 175).

Medicinal Uses: In Malaysia, the roots are boiled in water and the decoction obtained is smeared on painful bones.

Pharmacology: The pharmacological property of *Argyreia maingayi* (C.B. Clarke) Hoogl. is unexplored. Antioxidant properties have been reported from extracts of bark of *Argyreia cymosa* (Badami *et al.*, 2008). Oral administration of the ethanolic extract of *Argyreia speciosa* root significantly enhanced the production of circulating antibody in mice in response to sheep red blood cells and ameliorated the total white blood cell count (Gokhale *et al*, 2003). Phenylpropanoid derivatives *p*-hydroxycinnamate and scopoletin isolated from *Argyreia speciosa* showed some antifungal properties against *Alternaria alternate* (Shukla *et al.*, 1999).

References: Badami S, Vaijanathappa V, Bhojraj S, 2008, *In vitro* antioxidant activity of *Argyreia cymosa* bark extracts. Fitoterapia; (in press).

Gokhale AB, Damre AS, Saraf MN, 2003, Investigations into the immunomodulatory activity of *Argyreia speciosa*. J Ethnopharmacol; 84: 109-114.

Shukla YN, Srivastava A, Kumar S, Kumar S, 1999, Phototoxic and antimicrobial constituents of *Argyreia speciosa*. J Ethnopharmacol; 67: 241-245.

Figure 175: *Argyreia maingayi* **(C.B.Clarke) Hoogl.**
From: Flora of Malaya.
Malaysia, Pahang State, Kuala Nipis, Merapoh district, Taman Negara, Sungai Relau.
Upstream. Altitude 200 m. In Lowland dipterocarp forest. Collector: A Zainuddin. Date of
collection: 13th December 1994.

Ipomoea batatas (L.) Lamk.

[From the Greek *ips* = a worm, and *homoios* = like and from Spain word *batata* = sweet potato]

Local names:	Sweet potato, *keledek* (Malaysia), *kaswan* (Burma), *dam long* (Cambodia), fan chu (China), patate douce (France), camote (Philippines), batata doce (Portuguese), kandagranthi (Sanskrit).
Basionym:	*Convolvulus batatas* L. Species Plantarum 1: 154. 1753
Synonyms:	*Anisea martinicensis* var. *nitens* (Choisy) O' Donnell, *Batatas edulis* var *porphyrorhiza* (Grisb.) Ram. Goyena, *Convolvulus apiculata* M. Martens & Galeotti, *Convolvulus attenuatus* M. Martens & Galeotti, *Convolvulus batatas* L., *Convolvulus candidans* Sol. Ex Sims, *Convolvulus denticulatus* Desr., *Convolvulus edulis* Thunb., *Convolvulus esculentus* Salisb., *Convolvulus hederaceus* Sesse & Moc., *Convolvulus tuberosus* Vell., *Convolvulus varius* Vell., *Ipomoea angustisecta* Engl., *Ipomoea batatas* var. *edulis* (Thunb.) Makino, *Ipomoea batatas* var *lobata* Gagnep. & Courchet, *Ipomoea bolusiana* Schinz, *Ipomoea bolusiana* var *pinnatipartita* Verdc., *Ipomoea confertifolia* Standl., *Ipomoea davidsoniae* Standl., *Ipomoea denticulata* (Desr.) Choisy, *Ipomoea edulis* (Thunb.) Makino, *Ipomoea fastigiata* (Roxb.) Sweet, *Ipomoea mesenteroides* Hallier f., *Ipomoea praetermissa* Rendl., *Ipomoea purpusii* House, *Ipomoea setifera* Poir., *Ipomoea simplex* Hook, *Ipomoea vulsa* House.
Description:	It is an annual herb native of tropical America which is cultivated worldwide in tropical and sub-tropical regions. The tubers are red, white or yellow, and elongated. The stem is green or purplish, slightly angled and rooting at nodes. The leaves are simple, alternate and without stipules. The petiole is slender, channeled, slightly enlarged at the base and 5.5 - 10.5 cm long. The leaf is ovate-cordate, acute angular or more or less lobed, yellowish light green, 4 -13 cm x 3 -13 cm and presents 5 to 10 pairs of secondary nerves. The inflorescences are axillary, 1-7-flowered; 2 -10.5 cm long, and angular. The flower pedicel is 0.2 -1 cm long. The sepals are elliptic, shortly acuminate, sparingly hairy, discretely nerved, glabrous, and 0.7 - 1.3 cm long. The corolla is pink, white, and pale purple to purple, with a darker center, infundibuliform, membranaceous, and 3 cm-4 cm, glabrous. Stamens are included. The ovary is subglabrous and 4 - celled. The fruits are capsules which are globose (Figure 176).

Medicinal Uses:

Ipomoea batatas (L.) Lamk. (sweet potato), the tubers of which are edible and it is a productive and adaptable crop. In China the plant is used to invigorate digestion and urination. In Malaysia, the roots are given to allay thirst in fever. In Cambodia, Laos and Vietnam, it is used in case of fever. In Indonesia, the plant is used to treat inflammation, dysentery, burns and diabetes. In Papua New Guinea, the plant the plant is used for stomachache and asthma. In India, the tuber is used as aphrodisiac, laxative, and to abrogate thirst.

Pharmacology:

The tubers of *Ipomoea batatas* (L.) Lamk. (sweet potato) have been used as a source of pharmaceutical starch in Japan. Its tubers are an important source of food and raw material for producing alcohol (Bovell-Benjamin 2007). Recent pharmacological studies on this plant have revealed antidiabetic, immunostimulating, cytotoxic, antioxidant, antifungal and vasorelaxant properties. The antidiabetic property of the plant has been confirmed: it contains a glycoprotein which showed antidiabetic activity in streptozotocin-induced diabetic rats, yellow KK, db/db mice and Zucker fatty rats (Kusano *et al.*, 2000; 2001). Chang *et al* (2007) observed that consumption of leaves of this plant increased the proliferation responsiveness of peripheral blood mononuclear cells, the cytotoxic activity of nature killer (NK) cells, and the secretion of interferon (IFN)-gamma. The tuber contains a (1-->6)-alpha-D-glucan which stimulates the immune system of mice via proliferation of lymphocytes and serum IgG concentration (Zhao *et al.*, 2005). The plant contains a trypsin inhibitor which inhibited cellular growth of NB4 promyelocytic leukemia cells with cell cycle arrest at the G1 phase by apoptosis through a mitochondria-dependent pathway involving the activation of the pathway of caspase-3 and -8 cascades (Huang *et al*, 2007). An extract of the plant induced G1 cell cycle arrest in human colon carcinoma cell lines HCT116 cell line after 48 h of treatment (Kaneshiro *et al.*, 2005). The tuber contains a number of phenolic substances including 4,5-di-O-caffeoyldaucic acid which is a strong antioxidant *in vitro* (Dini *et al.*, 2006) as well as 3,5-dicaffeoylquinic acid which is antifungal against *Rhizopus stolonifer* cultured *in vitro* (Stange *et al.*, 2001). The presence of these phenolic substances might account for the anti-inflammatory use of the plant. The antiasthma property of the plant has not been studied. There could be some myorelaxing activity as an extract of the plant exhibited a relaxing effect on aortic ring preparations (Runnie I *et al.*, 2004). The leaves contain tiliroside, astragalin, rhamnocitrin, rhamnetin and kaempferol (Luo *et al.*, 2005).

Figure 176: *Ipomoea batatas* (L.) Lamk.
From: Harvard University Herbarium.
Malaysia, Johor state, Pemanggil Island
Collection: Shafee Daud. Identification: G. Staples, February 1985.

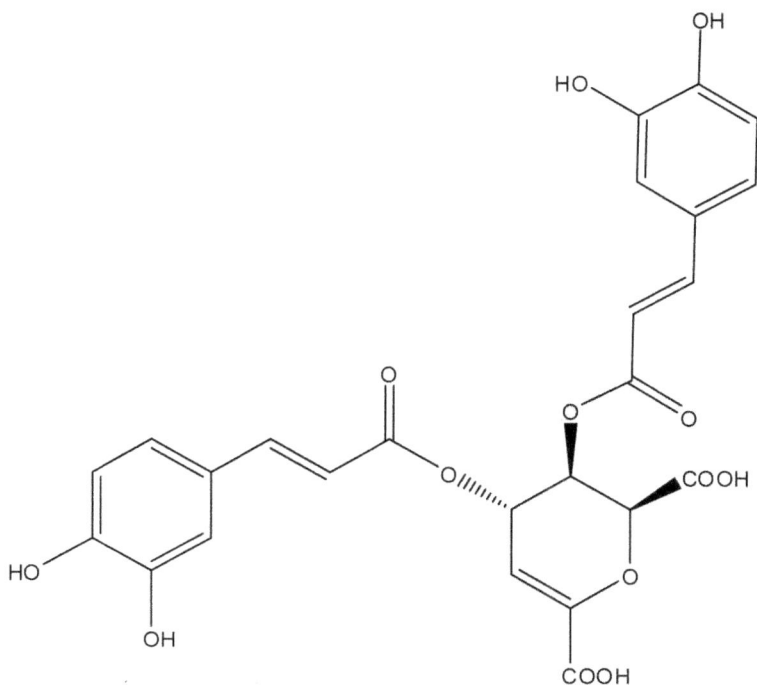

4,5-di-O-caffeoyldaucic acid

References:

Bovell-Benjamin AC, 2007, Sweet potato: a review of its past, present, and future role in human nutrition. Adv Food Nutr Res; 52:1-59.

Chang WH, Chen CM, Hu SP, Kan NW, Chiu CC, Liu JF, 2007, Effect of purple sweet potato leaves consumption on the modulation of the immune response in basketball players during the training period. Asia Pac J Clint Nutr; 16:609-15.

Huang GJ, Shea MJ, Chen HJ, Chang YS, Lin YH, 2007, Growth inhibition and induction of apoptosis in NB4 promyelocytic leukemia cells by trypsin inhibitor from sweet potato storage roots. J Agric Food Chem; 55:2548-53.

Kaneshiro T, Suzuki M, Takamatsu R, Murakami A, Hibachi H, Fuji no T, Yoshimi N, 2005, Growth inhibitory activities of crude extracts obtained from herbal plants in the Ryukyu Islands on several human colon carcinoma cell lines. Asian Pac J Cancer Prev; 6:353-8.

Kusano S, Abe H, 2000, Antidiabetic activity of white skinned sweet potato (*Ipomoea batatas* L.) in obese Zucker fatty rats. Biol Pharm Bull; 23:23-6.

Kusano S, Abe H, Tamura H, 2001,Isolation of antidiabetic components from white-skinned sweet potato (*Ipomoea batatas* L.). Basic Biotechnol Biochem; 65:109-14.

Luo JG, Kong LY, 2005, Study on flavonoids from leaf of Ipomoea batatas. Zhongguo Zhong Yao Za Zhi; 30:516-8.

Runnie I, Salleh MN, Mohamed S, Head RJ, Abeywardena MY, 2004, Vasorelaxation induced by common edible tropical plant extracts in isolated rat aorta and mesenteric vascular bed. J Ethnopharmacol; 92:311-6.

Strange RT, Midland SL, Holmes GJ, Sims JJ and Mayer T, 2001, Constituents from the periderm and outer cortex of *Ipomoea batatas* with antifungal activity against *Rhizopus stolonifer*, Postharvest Biol Technol; 23: 85-92.

Zhao G, Kan J, Li Z, Chen Z, 2005, Characterization and immunostimulatory activity of an (1-->6)-a-D-glucan from the root of *Ipomoea batatas*. Int Immunopharmacol; 5:1436-45.

Ipomoea digitata L.

[From the Greek ips = a worm, and homoios = like and from Latin digitata = lobed like fingers]

Local names:	Giant potato, *pakong kertas, kang kong laut, keledek hutan* (Malaysia), *kazun* (Burma), *vidari* (Sanskrit), *nilappuchani* (India)
Synonyms:	*Convolvulus paniculatus* (Burm.f.) Kuntze, *Convolvulus paniculatus* L., *Ipomoea paniculata* (L.) R. Br., *Quamoclit digitata* (L.) G. Don
Description:	It is a perennial herb which grows in several tropical countries, including tropical Asia. The roots are large and tuberous. The stem is angled, woody, stout, and glabrous. The internodes are 1 to 2 cm long. The flowers are simple, alternate and without stipules. The petiole is slender , channeled, glabrous, enlarged at the base and 2.4 to 6 cm long and 1 mm in diameter. The blade is deeply palmately divided, 4 - 8 cm x 6 - 4 cm, recurved and wavy at the margin, sub-glabrous, dark green above, with 5 to 7 lobes, each lobe lanceolate, asymmetrical except the middle one. The inflorescences are axillary, in many-flowered corymbosely paniculate cymes, the axes up to 15 cm long. The flower pedicels are 0.6 - 2 cm long. The sepals are 0.6 mm - 0.8 mm long,

orbicular and glabrous. The corolla is infundibuliform, light pink and dark pink at throat, 3.8 - 6.3 cm long, and discretely 5 lobed. The fruits are ovoid capsules which are 0.8 - 1.3 cm long, 4 valved, and surrounded by the sepals. The seeds are hairy and about 0.6 cm long (Figure 177).

Medicinal Uses: In Cambodia, Laos and Vietnam, the tubers are used as an aphrodisiac, to invigorate, to prevent obesity and to treat hypermenorrhoea. In India, the plant is used to promote the secretion of milk, to stimulate urination and venereal appetite, to invigorate, and to empty the bowels.

Pharmacology: An extract of the plant exhibited scavenging activity *in vitro* against nitric oxide generated *in vitro* by sodium nitroprusside (Jagetia *et al*, 2004). The seed gum has been found to have a structure and properties similar to guar gum and locust bean gum which are gums of pharmaceutical importance (Singh *et al.*, 2004). Some have been pharmacological studies (Matin *et al*, 1962, 1969).

References: Jagetia GC, Baliga MS, 2004,The evaluation of nitric oxide scavenging activity of certain Indian medicinal plants *in vitro*: a preliminary study. J Med Food; 7:343-8.

Matin MA, Tewari JP, Kalani DK, 1969,Pharmacological investigations of *Ipomoea digitata* Linn. Indian J Med Sci; 23:479-82.

Matin MA, Tewari JP, Kalani DK, 1969, Pharmacological effects of paniculatin--a glycoside isolated from *Ipomoea digitata* Linn. J Pharm Sci; 58:757-9.

Mishra SS, Datta KC, 1962, A preliminary pharmacological study of *Ipomoea digitata* Linn. Indian J Med Res; 50:43-5.

Singh V, Srivastava V, Sethi R, 2004, *Ipomoea digitata* Seed Gum and the Gum-g-polyacrylamide: Potential Pharmaceutical Gums. Pharmaceut Biol; 42: 230-233.

Figure 177: *Ipomoea digitata* L.
From: Flora of Malaya, *University* Kebangsaan Malaysia Herbarium.
Malaysia, Terengganu state, Dungun, Kuala Abang, Batu Jara sea coast. Collection and
identification: A. Zainuddin. AZ 2978. Date of collection: 4th of August 1989.

Ipomoea nil (L.) Roth

[From the Greek *ips* = a worm, and homoios = like and from Arabic *habunnil* = *Ipomoea nil*]

Local name:	Indian Jalap, white edge morning-glory, early call morning glory, imperial Japan morning-glory, qian niu (China), napalkot (Korea), habunnil (Arabic), kakkattan (India)
Basionym:	*Convolvulus nil* L. *Species Plantarum, Editio Secunda* 1: 219. 1762.
Synonyms:	*Convolvulus hederaceus* L., *Convolvulus nil* L., *Convolvulus tomentosus* Vell., *Ipomoea cuspidata* Ruiz & Pav., *Ipomoea hederacea* Baker & Rendle, *Ipomoea hederacea* Jacq., *Ipomoea hederacea* var. *integriuscula* A. Gray, *Ipomoea longicuspis* Meisn., *Ipomoea nil* var *setosa* (Bl.) Boerl., *Ipomoea scabra* Forsk., *Ipomoea setosa* Bl., *Ipomoea trichocalyx* Steud., *Ipomoea vaniotiana* H. Lev., *Ipomoea villosa* Ruiz & Pav., *Pharbitis cuspidata* (Ruiz & Pav.) G. Don. *Pharbitis nil* (L.) Choisy
Description:	It is an annual creeping herb of tropical American origin which grows in most tropical and subtropical regions of the world. It has ornamental value and several varieties with diverse flower colours are available. The stem is hairy, terete, light green with dark violet areas, longitudinally striated and twining and can be 2.5 m long. The internodes are about 10 to 12 cm long. The leaves are simple, alternate and without stipules. The petiole is flattish, finely channeled, and hairy at the base and 2 -15 cm long. The leaf blade is dull dark green above, dull light green underneath, subglabrous, shows 5 pairs of secondary nerves raised on both surfaces, and tertiary nerves which are scalariform and visible underneath only. The leaf blade is broadly ovate or nearly circular, 4 -15 cm x 4.5 -14 cm, cordate at the base, 3-lobed, and acuminate at the apex. The inflorescence is an erect axis, which is light green, axillary, 4 - 5 cm long and 1 or few flowered. The flower pedicel is 0.2 -1 cm long. The sepals are light green, hairy at the base, linear, 1 - 2.5 cm long. The corolla is infundibuliform, membranaceous, the midpetaline area whitish, the other parts and all of inside blue, 3.8 - 5 cm long and glabrous. The stamens are white included, unequal and the filaments are white. The pistil is included; and the ovary is glabrous, 3-loculed and white. The stigma is 3-lobed. The fruits are capsular, straw colored, globose, 0.8 -1 cm in diameter and glabrous. The seeds are black, ovoid-trigonous, 0.5 - 0.6 cm, and gray (Figure 178)

Medicinal Uses: The plant is listed under the name of *Ipomoea hederacea* in the 1949 edition of the *British Pharmaceutical Codex* as purgative. Kaladana, or the dried seeds, is a purgative with an action similar to jalap. The seeds have been included on the *Chinese Pharmacopoeia*, Indian *Pharmacopoeia* (1955), and *Japanese Pharmacopoeia* (1961). The seeds are used in India as a laxative, anthelminthic, an antipyretic and an anti-inflammatory. In China, Cambodia and Laos the seeds are used to abort, to empty the bowels and to promote urination. In the Bismarck Archipelago the leaves are used to heal sores and smoothes skin rashes.

Pharmacology: The plant elaborates a series of dicarboxylic acids: butanedioic acid, pentanedioic acid, hexanedioic acid, heptanedioic acid, octanedioic acid, nonanedioic acid, decanedioic acid, undecanedioic acid, dodecanedioic acid, tridecanedioic acid, tetradecanedioic acid, pentadecanedioic acid, hexadecanedioic acid, which abrogated the mutagenicity of 2-(2-furyl)-3-(5-nitro-2-furyl)acrylami(dAeF -2) in the *Salmonella typhimurium* TA1535/pSK1002 *umu* test.

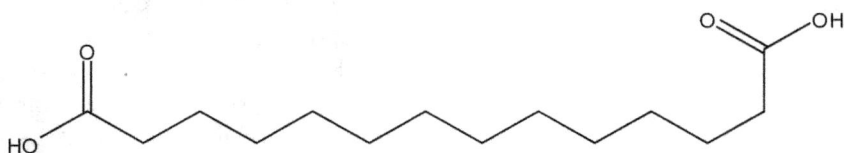

Tetradecanedioic acid

Tetradecanedioic acid suppressed the effects of other mutagenic agents (Miyazawa *et al.*, 1995). Ko *et al* (2004) studied the antitumor effects of *Ipomoea nil* (L.) Roth on AGS gastric cancer cell line and showed that an extract of this plant abrogated the survival of these cells dose dependently via apoptosis. The natural product involved here is still unknown.

References: Ko SG, Koh SH, Jun CY, Nam CG, Bae HS, Shin MK, 2004, Induction of apoptosis by *Saussurea lappa* and *Pharbitis nil* on AGS gastric cancer cells. Biol Pharm Bull; 27:1604-10.

Miyazawa M, Shimamura S, Nakamura S, and Kameoka H, 1995, Partial suppression of SOS-inducing activity of furylfuramide by dibasic acids from *Ipomoea nil* in the *Salmonella typhimurium* TA1535/pSK1002 umu test. J Agric Food Chem; 43: 284-287.

Figure 178: *Ipomoea nil* (L.) Roth
From: Flora of Thailand, Chiang Mai University Herbarium
Thailand, Sahngahmpang district, Doi Lohn, West side, at the Mae Gahm Bawng Village,
along Mae Gahm Bawng stream. Elevation: 1000 m,. Date of collection: 23 October 1996.
Collection and identification: JF Maxwell, N° 96-1383

Ipomoea quamoclit L.

[From the Greek *ips* = a worm, and homoios = like and from Mexican *qnamo chitl*]

Local name:	Red Jasmine, cardinal creeper, hummingbird vine or star glory, *myatlaeni* (Burma), *agao* (Philippines), *kamalata* (Sanskrit), *mayirmanikkam* (India)
Synonyms:	*Convolvulus quamoclit* (L.) Spreng., *Quamoclit quamoclit* (L.) Britton, *Quamoclit pinnata* L., *Quamoclit pennata* Voigt.
Description:	It is a slender twinning annual herb that originates from tropical America which grows wild or as an ornamental in several tropical countries. The stem is terete, light green if not translucent, glabrous, about 1.5 mm in diameter, and up to 60 cm long The leaves are deeply pinnate, giving a fragile feathery appearance, alternate and without stipules. The leaf blade is 7.5 - 12.5 cm x 5 x 7.5 cm, curling at the apex. The inflorescences are axillary 1-3 flowered on 2 - 4.5 cm long conical and somewhat fleshy and glossy axes. The sepals are unequal, elliptic, 0.4 - 0.8 cm x 0.15 -0.2 cm with few nervations and a minute thorn at the apex. The corolla is membranaceous, intensely crimson, about 1 cm long, with a slender conical tube which develops 5 triangular lobes forming a star. The stamens are slightly protruding from the throat of the corolla. The fruit is a papery capsule which is globose, 0.6 cm in diameter, and 4-celled. The sepals are persistent in fruit. The seeds are glabrous, tiny, and grey or black (Figure 179).

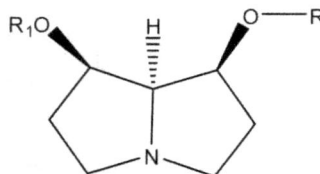

Ipanguline-type alkaloid

Medicinal Uses:	In India the plant is used to heal bleeding piles and carbuncles. It is also considered there as cooling. In Cambodia, Laos and Vietnam, the seeds are eaten to empty the bowels and to assuage stomachaches. In Indonesia a paste of leaves is used externally to treat piles, ulcers, inflamed skin and sores.
Pharmacology:	The roots contain small amounts of pyrrolizidine alkaloid namely anhydroplatynecine, ipanguline D10 and ipanguline X2

(Jenett-Siems *et al.*, 2005). It may be of some interest to study the plant for pharmacology. Wagner *et al* (1983) studied the chemical constituents of the resin plant and found jalapinolic acid glycosides.

Figure 179: *Ipomoea quamoclit* L.
From: Harvard University Herbarium. Flora of Malaya No 06265.
Malaysia, Negeri Sembilan state, Jelebu, Kampung Kuala Pah. Collector: Noraini Mansor (032). Identification: G. Staples, February 1985.

H₂N... rendered structure:

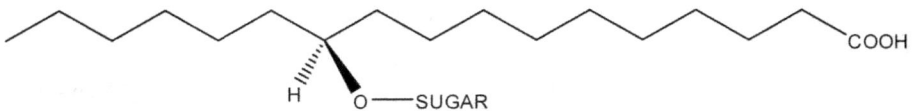

Jalapinolic acid glycoside

References: Jenett-Siems K, Ott SC, Schimming T, Siems K, Müller F, Hilker M, Witte L, Hartmann T, Austin DF, Eich E, 2005, Ipangulines and minalobines, chemotaxonomic markers of the infrageneric *Ipomoea* taxon subgenus Quamoclit, section Mina. Phytochemistry; 66: 223-231

Wagner H, Schwarting G, Varljen J, Bauer R, Hamdard ME, El-Faer MZ, Beal J, 1983, Chemical Constituents of the Convolvulaceae-Resins IV1. Planta Med; 49: 154-7

Merremia hederacea (Burm. f.) Hallier f.
[After German naturalist and botanist Basius Merrem (1761-1824), and Latin *hederacea* = of or pertaining to ivy]

Local name: Ivy wood rose, li lan wang (China)

Basionym: *Evolvulus hederaceus* Burm. f. *Flora Indica . . . nec non Prodromus Florae Capensis* 77, pl. 30, f. 2. 1768.

Synonym: *Convolvulus acetosellifolius* Desr., *Convolvulus chryseides* (Ker Gawl.) Spreng., *Convolvulus dentatus* Vahl, *Convolvulus flavus* Willd., *Convolvulus lapathifolius* Spreng., *Evolvulus hederaceus* Burm.f., *Ipomoea acetosellifolia* (Desr.) Choisy, *Ipomoea dentata* (Vahl.) Roem & Moritzi, *Lepistemon glaber* Hand.-Muzz, *Lepistemon muricatum* Spar., *Merremia chryseides* (Ker Gawl.) Hallier f., *Merremia convolvulacea* Dennst. ex Hallier f.

Description: It is a vine which grows by grassy roadsides in a geographical area ranging from East Africa to the Pacific Islands including China, Taiwan, Bangladesh, Cambodia, India, Indonesia, Japan, Laos, Malaysia, Burma, Nepal, New Guinea, Pakistan, Philippines, Sri Lanka, Thailand, Vietnam and North Australia. The stem is glabrous, slender and terete and about 0.15 cm in diameter. The internodes are about 9 cm long. The leaves are simple, alternate and without stipules. The petiole is about 2 - 3 cm long, subglabrous and slender. The leaf blade is cordate-ovate,

1.5 -7.5 cm x 1 - 5 cm, cordate at the base, irregularly crenate and wavy at the margin, with about 4 pairs of secondary nerves and minutely spiny at the apex. The inflorescences are cymose on a peduncle about 3 cm long. The flower pedicel is about 0.2 - 0.5 cm long. The calyx consists of 5 sepals which are hairy, lanceolate to elliptic and marked at the apex with a small dorsal growth. The corolla is yellow, infundibuliform, about 4 cm long, membranaceous and obscurely 5 lobed, the lobes dentate and slightly nerved. The androecium presents 5 stamens which are white and bend inward. The stigma globose and as white as the androecium. The fruit is a capsule which globose, about 0.5 cm in diameter, and subglabrous. The seeds are trigonous-globose, and minute (Figure 180).

Medicinal Uses: In China it is used to treat tonsillitis. In Malaysia, a paste of leaves is applied to cracks in hands and feet.

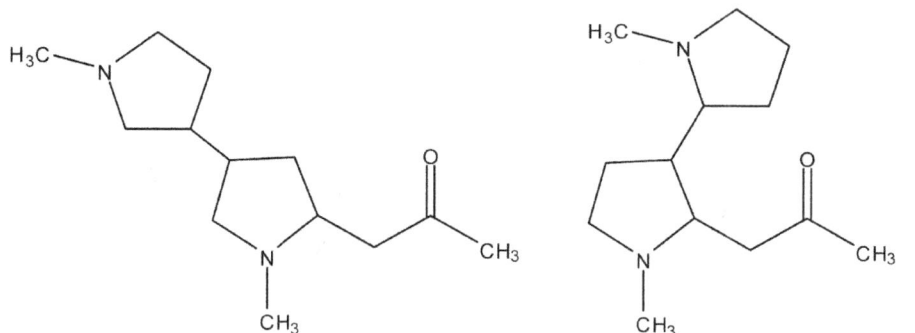

2',4-N-Methylpyrrolidinylhygrine   2',3-N-Methylpyrrolidinylhygrine

Pharmacology: The plant has not yet been studied for pharmacology. It is known to contain some pyrrolidine alkaloids derived from ornithine such as : phygrine, nicotine, hygrine, cuscohygrine, 2', 3 -N-methyl pyrrolidinyllhygrine and 2', 4 -N-methyl pyrrolidinyllhygrine (Jennett-Siems et al., 2005).

References: Jenett-Siems K, Weigl R, Böhm A, Mann P, Tofern-Reblin B,. Otta SC, Ghomian A, Kaloga M, Siems K, Witte L, Hilker M, Müller F, Eicha E, 2005, Chemotaxonomy of the pantropical genus Merremia (Convolvulaceae) the based on the distribution of tropane alkaloids. Phytochemistry; 66: 1448-64.

Figure 180: *Merremia hederacea* **(Burm. f.) Hallier f.**
From: Flora of Malaya
State of Selangor, Simpang Cheras, Ulu Langat, Jajang. Collection and identification: Zainuddin (AZ 1832).

Merremia peltata (L.) Merr.

[After German naturalist and botanist Basius Merrem (1761-1824), and Latin *peltata* = shield-shaped]

Local name:	Big leaf rope, akar balaan (Malaysia), bulakan (Philippines), fue lautetele (Samoa), en luen (Thailand), kebeas (Palau), veliyana (Fiji).
Basionym:	*Convolvulus peltatus* L. *Species Plantarum* 2: 1194. 1753
Synonym:	*Convolvulus bufalinus* Lour., *Convolvulus peltatus* L., *Convolvulus crispatulus* Wall,. *Ipomoea bufalina* Choisy, *Ipomoea nymphaeifolia* Bl., *Ipomoea peltata* (L.) Choisy, *Ipomoea petaloidea* Choisy, *Merremia borneensis* Merr., *Merremia bufalina* Merr. & Rendle, *Merremia distillatoria* (Blco.) Merr., *Merremia elmeri* Merr., *Merremia nymphaeifolia* (Dietr.) Hall., *Operculina bufalina* Hall. f. *Operculina peltata* (L.) Hall. f., *Operculina petaloidea* Ooststr., *Spiranthera peltata* (L.) Bojer.
Description:	It is an invasive vine that strangles vegetation in logged or burned forests up to an altitude of 300 m. It ranges from East Africa to Madagascar, Mauritius, Reunion and Pemba Island, Bangladesh, Indonesia, Malaysia, the Philippines and northern Queensland, to the Pacific Islands. The stem is woody, up to 30 m long with white sap, glabrous, and lenticelled. In the Philippines the stem is sometimes used for tying purposes. The internodes are of variable length but around 5 cm long. The leaves are simple, alternate, and without stipules. The petiole is about 8 cm long. The leaf blade is dull light green, peltate cordate; wavy at the margin, 13 - 19 cm x 10 cm x 15 cm, acuminate at the apex, and shows 7-10 pairs of secondary nerves and tertiary nerves which are conspicuous on both surface. The secondary nerves are reddish underneath The inflorescences are large, fleshy, axillary, corymbs on 5 - 8 cm long conical peduncles with many flowers. The calyx comprises 5 fleshy, lanceolate subequal, sepals which are 1.8 -2.5 cm long. The corolla is infundibuliform, membranaceous, pure white 4 - 6 cm long, and discretely 5 - lobed. The androecium consists of 5 stamens with elongated anthers. The stigma presents 2 broad lobes. The fruits are ovoid capsules which are 2.5 - 3 cm long and containing 4 trigonous seeds (Figure 181).
Medicinal uses;	In Indonesia, the sap of the plant is used for washing the hair, it is taken orally to relieve constipation, to treat coughs and to expel worms and is used for sore eyes. The leaves are used to assuage inflamed skin. In Malaysia the tubers are reputed to cause purging and the juice of plant given to treat internal injury. In the Philippines the sap is used as purgative and is applied to sore breasts, ulcers, and wounds.

Pharmacology: The pharmacological potential of this common medicinal plant is yet unknown and it could be worth studying. Traces of alkaloids derived from ornithine hygrine, nicotine, cuscohygrine, cyclotropine, and tropan 3-ol have been detected in the plant (Jenett-Siems *et al.*, 2005). Resin from the sap could account for the purgative property mentioned above as well as counter-irritant effects in inflamed skin.

References: Jenett-Siems K, Weigl R, Böhm A, Mann P, Tofern-Reblin B, Otta SC, Ghomian A, Kaloga M, Siems K, Witte L, Hilker M, Müller F, Eicha E, 2005, Chemotaxonomy of the pantropical genus *Merremia* (Convolvulaceae) the based on the distribution of tropane alkaloids. Phytochemistry; 66: 1448-64.

Figure 181: *Merremia peltata* (L.) Merr.

From: Plants of Borneo
Malaysia, Sabah, Beaufort district, Beaufort Hill, 5° 22' North - 115° 45' West. Altitude 250 m.
Collector: John H. Beaman 9641, 6 May 1984.
Identification: J.C. Regalado, 1987.

Merremia tridentata (L.) Hallier f.

[After German naturalist and botanist Basius Merrem (1761-1824), and Latin *tridentata* = three-toothed]

Local name:	*Kong kang pasir* (Malaysia), *prasarini* (Sanskrit), *savolikkoti* (India)
Basionym:	*Convolvulus tridentatus* L. *Species Plantarum* 1: 157. 1753
Synonym:	*Convolvulus arvensis* sensu Lour., *Convolvulus oligodontus* Baker, *Convolvulus tridentatus* L., *Ipomoea angustifolia* Jacq., *Ipomoea tridentata* (L.) Roth., *Merremia alapites* Dammer, *Merremia hastata* Hallier f., *Xenostegia tridentata* (L.) D.F. Austin & Staples
Description:	It is a perennial herb which grows in East Africa, India, Cambodia, Laos, Vietnam, Taiwan, and Malaysia. The stem is prostate, slender, angular, glabrous, and about 1.5 mm in diameter. The internodes are about 2 to 6 cm long. The leaves are simple, alternate, amplexicaul and without stipules. The leaf blade is linear, 2 - 3 cm x 0.5 - 0.3 cm, and develops two lobes at the base which are dentate. The inflorescences are axillary, on 2.5 - 3.3 cm peduncles. The sepals are lanceolate, 0.4 x 0.08 cm and show some innervations. The corolla is infundibuliform, 5 lobed, pale yellow and about 2 cm long. The fruits are capsular, globose, about 0.4 cm in diameter and opens to release blackish seeds (Figure 182).
Medicinal Uses:	In India, the plant is used to treat rheumatism, piles, constipation, and dysuria. In Cambodia, Laos and Vietnam, the seeds are ingested to expel worms from the intestines, and to promote urination. In Malaysia, a paste of the plant is used externally to break fever. In the Philippines the plant is used for toothaches. In East Africa, the plant is used against snake bites.

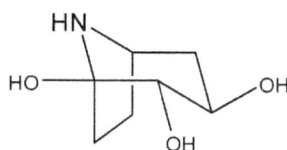

Calystegine A3   Calystegine B1   Calystegine B2

Pharmacology:	To date the pharmacological properties of this plant are not quite fully unexplored. Hatapakki *et al* (2004) showed that the plant has healing properties. Note that *Merremia* species are known to contain the polyhydroxytropanes calystegines A3, B1

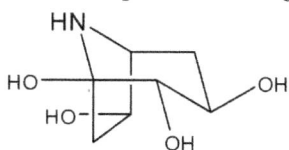

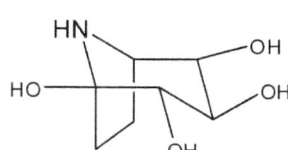

and B2 (Schimming *et al.*, 1998). Calystegines possess potent glycosidase inhibitory properties (Molyneux *et al.*, 1993). The plant contains traces of alkaloids derived from ornithine: hygrine and nicotine (Jenett-Siems *et al.*, 2005).

References:

Hatapakki BC, Hukkeri V, Patil DN, Chavan MJ, 2004, Wound healing activity of aerial parts of *Merremia tridentata*. Indian Drugs; 41: 532.

Jenett-Siems K, Weigl R, Böhm A, Mann P, Tofern-Reblin B, Otta SC, Ghomian A, Kaloga M, Siems K, Witte L, Hilker M, Müller F, Eicha E, 2005, Chemotaxonomy of the pantropical genus *Merremia* (Convolvulaceae) the based on the distribution of tropane alkaloids. Phytochemistry; 66: 1448-64.

Molyneux RJ, Pan YT, Goldmann A, Tepfer A, Elbein AD, 1993, Calystegins, a novel class of alkaloid glycosidase inhibitors. Arch Biochem Biophys; 304: 81-88.

Schimming T, Tofern B, Mann P, Richter A, Jenett-Siems K, Dräger B, Asano N, Gupta MP, Correa MD, Eich E, 1998, Distribution and taxonomic significance of calystegines in the Convolvulaceae. Phytochemistry: 49: 1989-1995

Figure 182: *Merremia tridentata* (L.) Hallier f.
From: Herbarium, Institute of Botany, Academia Sinica, Taipei. Botanical Inventory of Taiwan.
Taitung Hsien: Chihpen forest path. Altitude 50 m.

Merremia umbellata (L.) Hall. f.

[After German naturalist and botanist Basius Merrem (1761-1824), and from Latin *umbellata* = bearing an umbel]

Local names:	Yellow merremia, yellow wood rose; shan zhu cai (China), sovivi (Fijian)
Basionym:	*Convolvulus umbellatus* L. *Species Plantarum* 1: 155. 1753
Synonyms:	*Convolvulus aristolochiifolius* Mill., *Convolvulus caracassanus* Willd. ex Roem. & Schuldt., *Convolvulus cymosus* Desr., *Convolvulus luteus* M.Martens & Galeotti, *Convolvulus multiflorus* Mill., *Convolvulus sagittifer* Kunth., *Convolvulus umbellatus* L., *Ipomoea cymosa* (Desr.) Roem. & Schult., *Ipomoea mollicoma* Miq., *Ipomoea polyanthes* Willd. Ex Roem. & Schult., *Ipomoea portobellensis* Beurl., *Ipomoea sagitiffer* (Kunth.) G.Don, *Ipomoea umbellata* (L.) G. Mey
Description:	It is a perennial, twining vine which grows in thickets and on edges of forest from near sea level to about 400 m by roadsides, forested valleys, thickets; in China, Taiwan, Bangladesh, Cambodia, Indonesia, Laos, Malaysia, Burma, Nepal, New Guinea, Philippines, Sri Lanka, Thailand, Vietnam; East Africa, South India, North Australia, Pacific Islands, and tropical America. The stem is slender, angled, hairy, laticiferous, and woody at the base. The internodes are 2 to 5.5 cm long. The leaves are simple, spirally arranged and without stipules. The petioles are slender, hairy, and 1.5 - 3 cm long. The leaf blades are entire, broadly ovate, 1.5 - 3.7 cm x 3 - 6.5 cm, cordate at the base, usually long-acuminate at the apex, hairy underneath and show 6 to 7 pairs of secondary nerves. The flowers are arranged in axillary umbels on 1 cm long axes which are hairy. The flower peduncles are about 1 cm long. The calyx comprises 5 sepals which are broadly elliptic, and 0.5 -1cm long. The corolla is infundibuliform, to 3.5 cm long, yellow, and with 5 lobes which are emarginated. The fruits are ovoid to conical, about 0.7 x 0.3 cm, containing 4 dark brown seeds which are 0.5 - 0.65 cm long, and densely pubescent (Figure 183).
Medicinal Uses:	In China, the plant is used to treat infections. The latex is eaten as a purgative in Cambodia, Laos and Vietnam. The Malays make a paste of leaves which is applied to burns. The same paste is used in Indonesia to treat cracks of the feet. In the Philippines the plant is used to remove blood from urine.
Pharmacology:	Grosvenor *et al*, (1995) reported a modest antibacterial activity from this plant against *Staphylococcus aureus*. The plant contains alkaloids derived from ornithine: hygrine, 5-(2-hydroxypropyl) hygrine, 5-(2-hydroxypropyl) hygroline, cuscohygrine and tropane 3 beta ol (Jenett-Siems *et al.*, 2005).

References: Grosvenor PW, Supriono A, Gray D, 1995, Medicinal plants from Riau Province, Sumatra, Indonesia. Part 2: antibacterial and antifungal activity. J Ethnopharmacol: 45: 97-111

Jenett-Siems K, Weigl R, Böhm A, Mann P, Tofern-Reblin B, Otta SC, Ghomian A, Kaloga M, Siems K, Witte L, Hilker M, Müller F, Eicha E, 2005, Chemotaxonomy of the pantropical genus *Merremia* (Convolvulaceae) the based on the distribution of tropane alkaloids. Phytochemistry; 66: 1448-64.

Figure 183: *Merremia umbellata* **(L.) Hall. f.**

From: Harvard University Herbarium.
Malaysia, Bukit Takun, Taman Templer. Collector: Arishah. Date of collection: 2 January 1980.
Identification: G.W. Staples. February 1985.

C.Order LAMIALES Bromhead 1838

The order Lamiales consists of 4 families and about 7,800 species of herbaceous plants which are thought to have originated along with Solanales during the Post Eocene period from an ancestry near to or in the Gentianales. The chemical weapons used here are numerous but there is a tendency towards terpenes, iridoid glycosides, and lignans with a normal lot of flavonoids inherited from the Gentianales. Note that Lamiales differ from Solanales by producing iridoids, by seldom using alkaloid weapons, and by the zygomorphic specialization for pollination by specific insects or birds (hummingbirds). Boraginaceae have appeared during the Oligocene and is the oldest family in Lamiales, although it stands somewhat apart both chemically and physically from the Verbenaceae and Lamiaceae.

1.Family BORAGINACEAE A. L. de Jussieu 1789 nom. conserv., the Borage Family

The family Boraginaceae consists of about 100 genera and 2,000 species of herbs, shrubs and occasionally trees which are cosmopolitan in distribution. The secondary metabolites often found in this family are principally ornithine derived pyrrolizidine alkaloids, naphthoquinones, and rosmarinic acid. Pyrrolizidine alkaloids are strongly hepatotoxic.

The leaves are simple, covered with bristly calcified or silified hairs, alternate, and without stipules. The inflorescences are scorpioid cymes. The flowers, often blue, star - shaped, actinomorphic and are principally hermaphrodite. The calyx, corolla and androecium comprise 4 - 6 sepals, petals and stamens respectively. The anthers are 2 - celled, open lengthwise and are attached to the corolla tube. The anthers alternate with the corolla lobes. The gynaecium consist of a pair of carpels more or less fused in a superior, 4 - locular ovary, each locule containing a single ovule attached to axile placenta. The fruits are nutlets, berries or drupes.

Several species of Boraginaceae are ornamental, *Myosotis arvensis* (forget-me-not) which been grown as a garden ornamental plant since the middle ages in England. The Boraginaceae contain a number of medicinal plants: *Pulmonaria officinale* (Jerusalem Cowslip) has been used in Europe for the treatment of lung diseases, The seeds of *Borago officinalis* L. (borage) (*Borago officinalis oleum raffinatum*, European Pharmacopoeia) can be used to nourish and moisturize dry and problem skin. The dried roots of *Cynoglossum officinale* L. (Cynoglossum Root, *Spanish Pharmacopoeia*, 1954) have been used in Western medicine to soothe inflammation, to alleviate coughs and to stop diarrhoea. The dried roots and rhizomes of *Symphytum officinale* L.) (Comfrey, *British Pharmaceutical Codex*, 1934), which contain allantoin, have been used to heal wounds and ulcer. Allantoin promotes the proliferation of cells and is used to make cosmetics. It is also found in *Plantago* species in the Lamiales. The dried roots of *Alkanna tinctoria* Tausch. (Alkanna, British Pharmaceutical Codex, 1949) contains a red dye, alkannin which is used for coloring toilet preparation of an oily nature. Alkannin is a naphthoquinone.

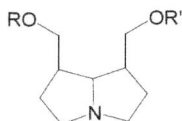

Pyrrolizidine alkaloid

The family Boraginaceae has been the subject of several interesting pharmacological studies and one might foresee the discovery of drugs from this taxon in the coming decades. Bioassay guided studies on Boraginaceae often result in the isolation of prenylated naphthoquinones which are cytotoxic and antimicrobial. Shikonin from *Lithospermum erythrorhizon* Sieb. & Zucc. inhibits proliferation, promotes apoptosis and blocks cell cycle progression of rat vascular smooth muscle cell (Zhang *et al.*, 2005). Beta-dimethylacrylshikonin isolated from *Onosma leptantha*, abrogated the survival of L1210 murine lymphoblastic leukemia cell line and elicited some levels of anti-inflammatory properties in rodents (Kundakovic *et al*, 2006). Leyva *et al.* (2000) studied the efficacy of oncocalyxones A and C isolated from *Auxemma oncocalyx* (Boraginaceae) and reported that oncocalyxones were cytotoxic to leukemia cells and multidrug-resistant cells *in vitro* and may be a promising novel class of chemotherapeutic agents effective against multidrug resistant tumours. Shikonin and alkannin derivatives from *Lithospermum erythrorhizon* Sieb. et Zucc. and *Macrotomia euchroma* (Royle) Pauls. exhibited extremely potent growth inhibitory activities against both types of cancer cells HCT 116 cells and Hep G2 cells (Cui *et al.*, 2007).

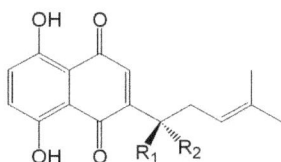

(R-) Shikonin (R$_1$= OH, R$_2$= H)
(S-) Alkannin (R$_1$= H, R$_2$=OH)

Rajbhandari M *et al* (2007) isolated a series of antimicrobial naphthoquinones from *Maharanga bicolor*. Alkannin and alkannin beta-acetoxyisovalerate inhibited the growth of multi resistant human pathogenic *Staphylococcus* and *Enterococcus* species and deoxyalkannin, alkannin beta-hydroxyisovalerate and alkannin beta-acetoxyisovalerate showed antiviral activity against herpes simplex virus type-1. *Cordia spinescens* L. exhibited some anti-HIV potentials *in vitro* (Matsuse *et al.*, 1998). Other pharmacological properties reported from this family are antidiabetic (Ortiz-Andrade *et al.*, 2007), anti-inflammatory (Perianayagam *et al.*, 2006) and anti-oxidative (Cadirci *et al.*, 2007).

In Asia - Pacific, about 30 species of Boraginaceae used for medicinal purposes await further pharmacological investigations. These plants are often used to allay fever, to stop diarrhoea, to heal wounds and boils, to assuage pains, to resolve swellings and to treat several sorts of viral infections.

References: Cadirci E, Suleyman H, Kasey H, Halici Z, Ozgen U, Koc A, Ozturk N, 2007, Effects of *Onosma armeniacum* root extract on ethanol-induced oxidative stress in stomach tissue of rats. Chem-Biol Interact; 170: 40-48.

Cui XR, Tsukada M, Suzuki N, Takeshi Shimamura T, Gao L, Koyanagi J, Komada F and Saito S, 2007, Comparison of the cytotoxic activities of naturally occurring hydroxyanthraquinones and hydroxynaphthoquinones. Euro J Medicinal Chem; (In Press).

Kundakovic T, Fokialakis N, Dobric S, Pratsinis H, Kletsas D, Kovacevic N, Chinou I, 2006, Evaluation of the anti-inflammatory and cytotoxic activities of naphthazarine derivatives from *Onosma leptantha*. Phytomedicine; 13: 290-4.

Leyva A, Pessoa C, Boogaerdt F, Sokaroski R, Lemos TL, Wetmore LA, Huruta RR, Moraes MO, 2000, Oncocalyxones A and C, 1,4-anthracenediones from *Auxemma oncocalyx*: comparison with anticancer 1,9-anthracenediones. Anticancer Res; 20: 1029-31.

Matsuse IT, Lim YA, Hattori M, Correa M, Gupta MP, 1998, A search for anti-viral properties in Panamanian medicinal plants: The effects on HIV and its essential enzymes. J Ethnopharmacol; 64: 15-22.

Ortiz-Andrade RR, Rodríguez-López V, Garduño-Ramírez ML, Castillo-España P, Estrada-Soto S, 2005, Anti-diabetic effect on alloxanized and normoglycemic rats and some pharmacological evaluations of *Tournefortia hartwegiana*. J Ethnopharmacol; 101: 37-42

Perianayagam JB, Sharma SK, Pillai KK, 2006, Anti-inflammatory activity of *Trichodesma indicum* root extract in experimental animals. J Ethnopharmacol; 104: 410-414.

Rajbhandari M, Schoepke TH, Mentel R, Lindequist U, 2007, Antibacterial and antiviral naphthazarins from *Maharanga bicolor*. Pharmazie; 62:633-5

Zhang ZQ, Cao XC, Zhang L, Zhu WL, 2005, Effect of shikonin, a phytocompound from *Lithospermum erythrorhizon*, on rat vascular smooth muscle cells proliferation and apoptosis in vitro. Zhonghua Yi Xue Za Zhi; 85: 1484-8.

Cordia subcordata Lamk.

[After Valerius Cordus, a German botanist of the 16th Century, and Latin *subcordata* = rather heart-shaped]

Local names:	Sea trumpet, beach cordial; kerosene wood (Papua New Guinea), kou (Hawaii), ironwood (Australia), koa (Guam), cheng hua po bu mu (China)
Description:	It is a handsome, tree which grows to a height of 3 m in sandy, open woodland of India, Indonesia, Thailand, Malaysia, Vietnam; East Africa, and the Pacific Islands. The plant is apparently native to Malaysia but has been spread by the sea. The wood is used to make crafts and ornaments in the Pacific Islands and is very resistant to termites. The bark is yellow-brown. The stem is brown, cracked horizontally, 0.4 cm in diameter, and lenticelled. The petiole is slender, yellowish-orange, channeled, 3 - 6 cm long and glabrous. The leaf blade is irregularly shaped, dark green above with whitish sunken nerves, whitish light green below, thinly coriaceous, somehow translucent, glossy, ovate to sub-cordate, 8 - 18 cm × 4 - 13 cm, obtuse and slightly asymmetrical at the base, the margin entire to sub undulate, and acuminate to acute at the apex. The leaf blade shows about 4 to 5 pairs of secondary nerves and tertiary nerves which are prominent underneath. The inflorescences are axillary cymes on a 3 to 4 cm axis. The flower pedicels are about 1 cm long. The calyx is tubular 1. 3 × 0.8 cm, with little lobes. The corolla is orange, infundibuliform, to 4.5 cm long tube; a 4 cm wide throat and presents 5 lobes which are triangular-orbicular. The fruit is drupaceous, almost round, green when young, and brown and hard at maturity, about 2.5 cm long, and contains up to 4 white seeds, each about 1 to 1.3 cm long (Figure 184).
Medicinal Uses:	Indonesians use the leaves of the plant to assuage the pain caused by poisonous fish stings. In Papua New Guinea, the plant is used to treat rheumatism.
Pharmacology:	An ethanol extract of the plant exhibited some antiplasmodial effects *in vitro* (Rasoanaivo *et al.*, 2004). The active principle involved is yet unknown but could be due to naphthoquinones derivatives such as a meroterpenes which abound in the genus. On such compound is (1aS*,1bS*,7aS*,8aS*)-4,5-dimethoxy-1a,7a-dimethyl-1,1a,1b,2,7,7a,8,8aoctahydrocyclopropa[3,4]cyclopenta[1,2b]naphthalene-3,6-dione isolated from *Cordia globosa* which displayed a strong trypanocidal (*Trypanosoma cruse*) and cytotoxic activity against five cancer cell lines activity *in vitro* (Vieira *et al.*, 2008).

Figure 184: *Cordia subcordata* L.
From: Flora of Malaya, University of Malaya Herbarium
Malaysia, Pulau Langkawi, Tg Rhu. Collector: Rita Manurung N°50. Date of Collection: 20 August 1972.

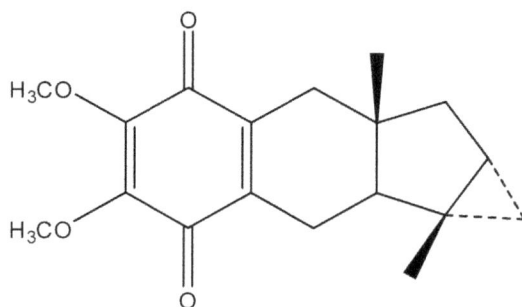

(1aS*,1bS*,7aS*,8aS*)-4,5-dimethoxy-1a,7a-dimethyl-1,1a,1b,2,7,7a,8,8a-octahydrocyclopropa[3,4]cyclopenta[1,2b]naphthalene-3,6-dione

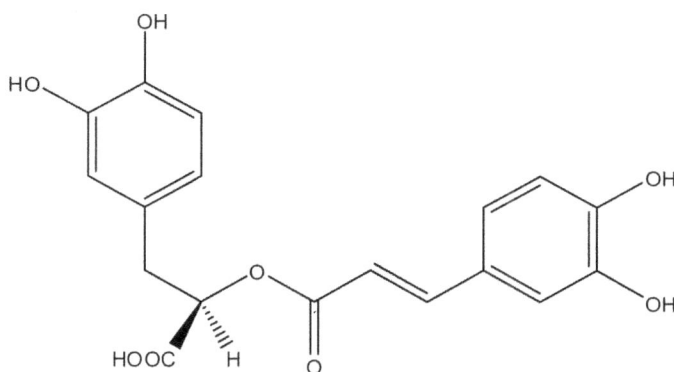

Rosmarinic acid

Note that meroterpenes from *Cordia linnael* are antifungal (Ioset *et al.*, 1998). Significant *in vitro* toxicity against Yoshida ascite sarcoma have been found in other *Cordia* species: *Cordia martinicensis*, *Cordia myxa* and *Cordia ulmiflora* (Gabbrielli *et al.*, 1993).

The anti-inflammatory property of the plant has not been yet substantiated but it is very likely since an extract of *Cordia verbenacea* exhibited potent anti-inflammatory effects *in vivo* (Sertié *et al.*, 1991) possibly on account of rosmarinic acid. The antidotal activity of *Cordia subcordata* Lam. against fish sting has not been confirmed experimentally but the role of rosmarinic acid might be important here since it has been identified as a snake antidote from *Cordia verbenacea* by inhibition of phospholipase A2 which is a key enzyme of inflammation (Ticli *et al.*, 2003; 2005).

References: Gabbrielli G, Trovato A, Rapisarda A, Ragusa S, 1993, In vitro cytotoxic effect of the leaves of some species of *Cordia*. Pharmacol Res; 27, Suppl. 1:115-16.

Ioset JR, Marston A, Mahabir P. Gupta MP, Hostettmann K, 1998, Antifungal and larvicidal meroterpenoid naphthoquinones and a naphthoxirene from the roots of *Cordia linnael*. Phytochemistry; 47:729-734.

Rasoanaivo P, Ramanitrahasimbola D, Rafatro H, Rakotondramanana D, Robijaona B, Rakotozafy A, Ratsimamanga-Urverg S, Labaïed M, Grellier P, Allorge L, Mambu L, Frappier F, 2004, Screening extracts of Madagascan plants in search of antiplasmodial compounds. Phytother Res; 18: 742 - 47.

Sertié JAA, Basile AC, Panizza S, Oshiro TT, Azzolini CP, Penna SC, 1991, Pharmacological assay of *Cordia verbenacea* III: Oral and topical anti-inflammatory activity and gastrotoxicity of a crude leaf extract. J Ethnopharmacol; 31: 239-247.

Ticli FK, Soares M, Pereira PS, Sampaio SV, 2003, Inhibition of the myotoxic and edematogenic activity of crude *Bothrops jararacussu* venom and of the BthTX-I and II toxins by rosmarinic acid isolated from the plant *Cordia verbenacea* (Boraginaceae) Toxicol Letts; 144 Suppl. 1:69.

Ticli FK, Lorane, Hage IS, Cambraia RS, Pereira PS, Magro AJ, Fontes MRM, Stábeli RG, Giglio JR, França SC, Soares AM, Sampaio SV, 2005, Rosmarinic acid, a new snake venom phospholipase A_2 inhibitor from *Cordia verbenacea* (Boraginaceae): antiserum action potentiation and molecular interaction. Toxicon; 46: 318-27

Vieira NC, Espíndola LS, Santana JM, Veras ML, Pessoa ODL, Pinheiro SM, de Araújo RM, Lima MAS, Silveira ER, 2008, Trypanocidal activity of a new pterocarpan and other secondary metabolites of plants from Northeastern Brazil flora. Bioorg Med Chem; 16: 1676-82.

Cynoglossum zeylanicum (Vahl) Thunb. Ex Lehman

[From Greek *kynos* = dog and *glossa* = tongue and from Latin *zeylanicum* = from Sri Lanka]

Local names:	Sri Lanka hound's tongue, liu li cao, t'ieh ku san (China), kanike kuro, thina (Nepal)
Basionym:	*Anchusa zeylanica* Vahl ex Hornem.Hortus Regius Botanicus Hafniensis1: 176.1813.
Synonyms:	*Cynoglossum coeruleum* Buch.-Ham. ex D. Don, *Cynoglossum furcatum* Wall., *Echinospermum zeylanicum* (Vahl) Lehm., *Rochelia zeylanica* Roem. & Schult.
Description:	It is a herb which grows to a height of 60 cm on forest meadows and sunny slopes in from Eat Africa, Sri Lanka, India, Afghanistan, Himalaya, China, Taiwan, Pakistan, Malaysia, Philippines, Thailand, Vietnam, Hawaii, and Japan. The plant has ornamental value. The stem is terete, hairy, about 0.3 cm in diameter. The leaves are simple, hairy, spiral, and without stipules. The basal and lower stem leaves are petiolate. The upper stem leaves are sessile. The basal and lower leaf blades are oblong-lanceolate, 15 -20 cm × 3-5 cm. The upper stem leaves are sessile, oblong lanceolate, without visible nervations and about 1.5 x 0.2 cm. The inflorescences are terminal and axillary, dichotomously branching; and slender cymes which are about 15 cm long with a fruit or flower every 0.5 cm. The flower pedicles are minute. The calyx is 0.15 -0.2 cm with 5 lobes which are ovate and hairy. The corolla is blue, infundibuliform, and 0.35 - 0.45 cm wide at the base; 5 lobed. The fruits are 4 -lobed capsules which are ovoid-globose, about 0.3 cm in diameter, and covered with digitate trichomes. The calyx lobes are persistent (Figure 185)
Medicinal Uses:	In Nepal, the flowers are used to heal boils and the leaf juice is used as eye drops to treat conjunctivitis. In China and Taiwan, the plant is reputed to be poisonous. In Ethiopia, the plant is used to treat fever, headache and sweating.
Pharmacology:	The plant abounds with a series of pyrrolizidine alkaloids including isoechinatine, echinatine, neocoramandaline, lactodine and viridinatine (Ravi *et al.*, 2000, 2008; Ravikumar *et al.*, 2004). These alkaloids probably account for the poisonous property and the medicinal uses mentioned above (Ghosh *et al.*, 1974). It is interested to note that pyrrolizidine alkaloids are tumorigenic and hepatotoxic.

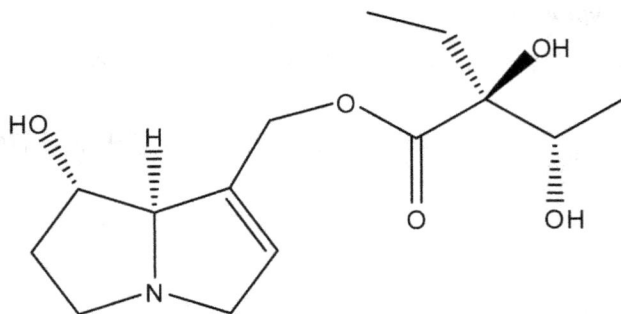

echinatine

References: Ghosh MN, Singh H, 1974, Inhibitory effect of a pyrrolizidine alkaloid, crotalaburnine, on rat paw oedema and cotton pellet granuloma. Br J Pharmacol; 51: 503-8.

Ravi S, Lakshmanan AJ, 2000, Neo coramandaline, a pyrrolizidine alkaloid from *Cynoglossum furcatum*. Ind J Chem Section B; 39: 80-82.

Ravikumar R, Lakshmanan AJ, 2004, Isoechinatine, a pyrrolizidine alkaloid from *Cynoglossum furcatum*. Indian J Chemi, Sect. B: 43: 406-409.

Ravi S, Ravikumar R, Lakshmanan AJ, 2008,Pyrrolizidine alkaloids from *Cynoglossum furcatum*. J Asian Nat Prod Res

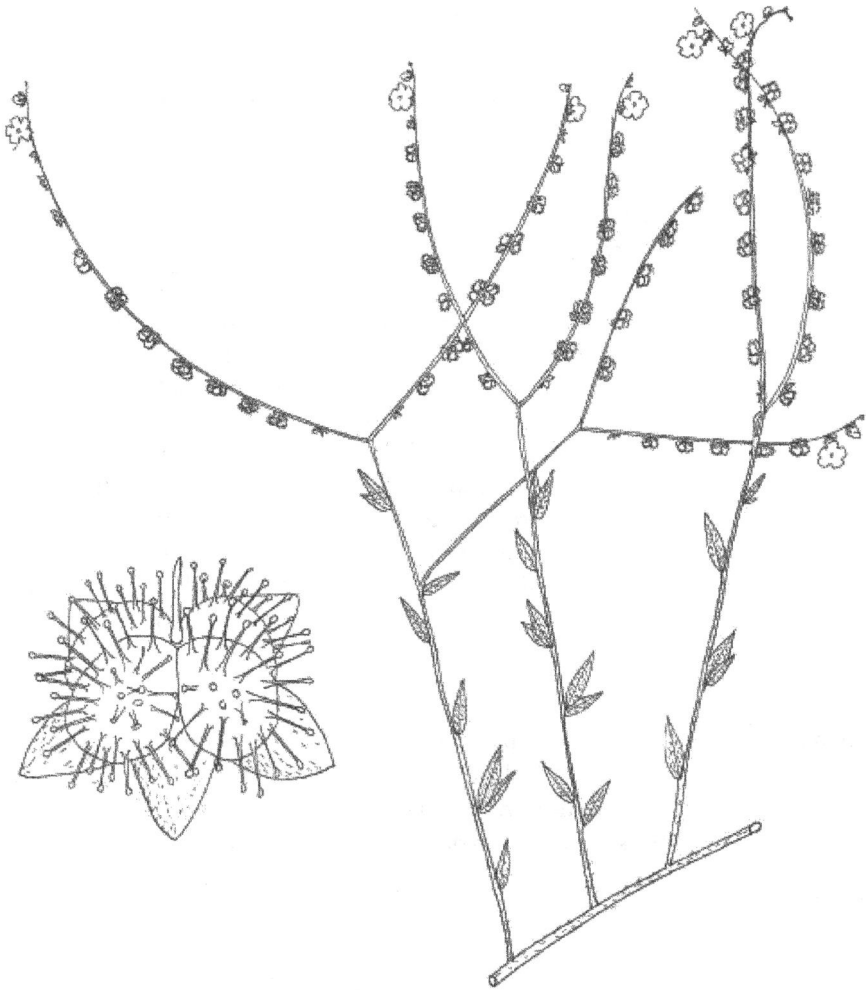

Figure 185: *Cynoglossum zeylanicum* (Vahl) Thunb. Ex Lehman
From: Herbarium, Institute of Botany, Academia Sinica, Taipei (HAST),Botanical
Inventory of Taiwan. Taiwan, Miali Hsien Taiwan Hsiang from Hushan, mineral
spring to taian mineral spring. Elevation: 500 m - 600 m. Date of collection: 29
September 1990. Collector and Identification: Chi-Hsien Lin N°551
          ; 10:307-10.

Rotula aquatica Lour.

[from Latin *rotula* = small wheel and *aquatica* = aquatic]

Local name: Lun guan mu (China), gada peh, ker dap eh (Thailand), buntut-buaya (Philippines), pashanabhed (India)

Synonym: *Carmona viminea* (Wall.) G. Don, *Ehretia viminea* Wall., *Rhabdia lyciodes* Mart., *Rhabdia viminea* (Wall.) Dalziel ex Hook., *Rhabdia viminea* (Wall.) Dalziel & Gibs.

Description: It is a shrubby bush that grows over gravel bars in stream beds, alluvial areas, and rock crevices in China, India, Indonesia, Malaysia, Burma, Philippines, Thailand, and Vietnam. The plant grows to a height of 3 m. The stem is glabrous, terete, 0.2 - 0.4 cm in diameter, with a few lenticels, light green turning violet, the oldest stem light brown. The leaves are simple, without stipules, subsessile and packed in small groups along the stem. The petiole is about 0.2 cm long. The leaf blade is spathulate, 0.5-2.5 cm × 0.2 -1 cm, and somewhat coriaceous. The inflorescences are terminal cymes. The calyx comprises 5 linear sepals which are hairy and 0.4 to 0.5cm long. The corolla is purple or pink, tubular with 5 lobes, and 0.6 - 0.7 cm ×0.6 - 0.7 cm. The fruit is ovoid, glossy, about 0.4 cm in diameter, with a vestigial style ate the apex and persistent calyx. The fruit are yellow- to brownish red, about 4 mm in diameter and contain 4 seeds (Figure 186).

Medicinal Uses: In India, the plant is used by vaidyas to treat cancer. The Karen people of Thailand boil the stem in water until the water becomes red and the drink obtained is taken as a purgative. In the Philippines the stem is used in decoction as a sudorific and diuretic.

Pharmacology: An extract of the plant exhibited a strong cytotoxic effect against HPAF-II, BxPC-3, and CAPAN-2 pancreatic cancer cell lines, confirming the anticancer property of the plant (Patil *et al.*, 2004). This effect could be mediated by polyphenols which have marked antioxidant activity (Patil *et al.*, 2003). These polyphenols might account for the protective effect of a decoction of the plant on male Westar rats against experimentally induced urolithiasis (Christina *et al.*, 2002; Prashad *et al.*, 1993).

References: Christina AJ, Priya Mole M, Moorthy P, 2002, Studies on the antilithic effect of *Rotula aquatica* lour in male Wistar rats. Methods Find Exp Clin Pharmacol; 24: 357-9.

                   Patil S, Jolly C, Narayanan S, 2003, Free Radical Scavenging Activity of *Acacia catechu* and *Rotula aquatica*: Implications in Cancer Therapy. Indian Drugs-Bombay; 40: 328.

Narayanan S, Eibl G, Jolly CI, 2004, Evaluation of antimitotic activity of *Rotula aquatica* (Lour): A traditional herb used in treatment of cancer. Indian J Exp Biol; 42: 893-899.

Prasad KVSRG, Bharathi K, and Srinivasan KK, 1993, An experimental evaluation of *Rotula aquatica* Lour for antilithiatic activity in albino rats. Indian Drugs; 30: 398-404.

Figure 186: *Rotula aquatica* **Lour.**
From: Flora of Thailand, Chiang Mai University Herbarium.
Thailand, Kanchanaburi province, Sangklaburi district, Toon Yai Naresuan wildlife reserve, Lei Wo subdistrict, Ban Senoh Pawng village, by 15° North and 98° East. Altitude 200 m. Date of collection: 12 January 1994. Collection and identification: JF Maxwell, N° 94-18.

Trichodesma zeylanicum (Burm. f.) R. Br.

[From Greek *tricho-* = hairy and *desmos* = a band or bundle and from Latin *zeylanicum* = from Sri Lanka]

Local names:	Sri Lanka borage , Camel bush, cattle bush, late weed , dilang-usa (Philippines), andhahuli (India)
Basionym:	*Borago zeylanica* Burm. f. Flora Indica . . . nec non Prodromus Florae Capensis 41.1768.
Synonyms:	*Borago zeylanica* Burm. f., Borago africana Blco., Borago indica Blco.
Description:	It is a densely bristly-hairy annual shrubby herb which grows to 1.8 m by roadsides and on abandoned lands in a geographical area ranging from East and South Africa to the Pacific Islands including Madagascar, the Comoros, Mauritius, India, Sri Lanka, Thailand, Malaysia, Indonesia, the Philippines, Papua New Guinea, and Australia. The basal stem is woody at the base and 3.5 cm in diameter. The bark is thin, smooth, lenticelled, grey and covered with irritating hairs. Younger stems are 0.4 cm in diameter, articulated, somewhat articulated, hairy at the apex. The internodes are 1.2 to 2 cm, with swollen nodes presenting discrete longitudinal lines curving downward. The leaves are simple, decussate and without stipules. The petiole is 0.4 - 0.7 cm long, hairy and deeply channeled. The leaf blade is oblong to lanceolate , 4.4 - 12cm x 1.2 - 4.1 cm, lanceolate, thinly coriaceous, tapering at the base, recurved and wavy at the margin, densely covered with bristly hairs which are rugose to touch. The leaf-blade is dull dark green above, dull light green underneath, shows 5- 9 pairs of secondary nerves and a few tertiary nerves visible underneath. The inflorescences are axillary and terminal cymes which are about 11 cm long and 12 cm in diameter. The calyx presents 4 lanceolate sepals which are bristly hairy, enlarging in fruit, about 0.7 x 1.2 - 1.8 cm and bending inward. The corolla is membranaceous, blue, hairy inside, glabrous outside, and about 0.7 - 0.9 x1.3 cm. The anthers are protruding and united into a cone which is about 0.8 cm long. Internal corolla gland brown. Stigma and style cream. The fruits are 0.4 cm in diameter, comprise 4 nutlets in persistent calyx, which are smooth and shiny (Figure 187).
Medicinal Uses:	In the Philippines the flowers are used to induce sweating in fever and to treat diseases of the lungs. In India, a paste of leaves is used as an emollient. In Africa, the young leaves are edible, and the plant is used to treat lung diseases, and to heal boils, wounds and snake bites.

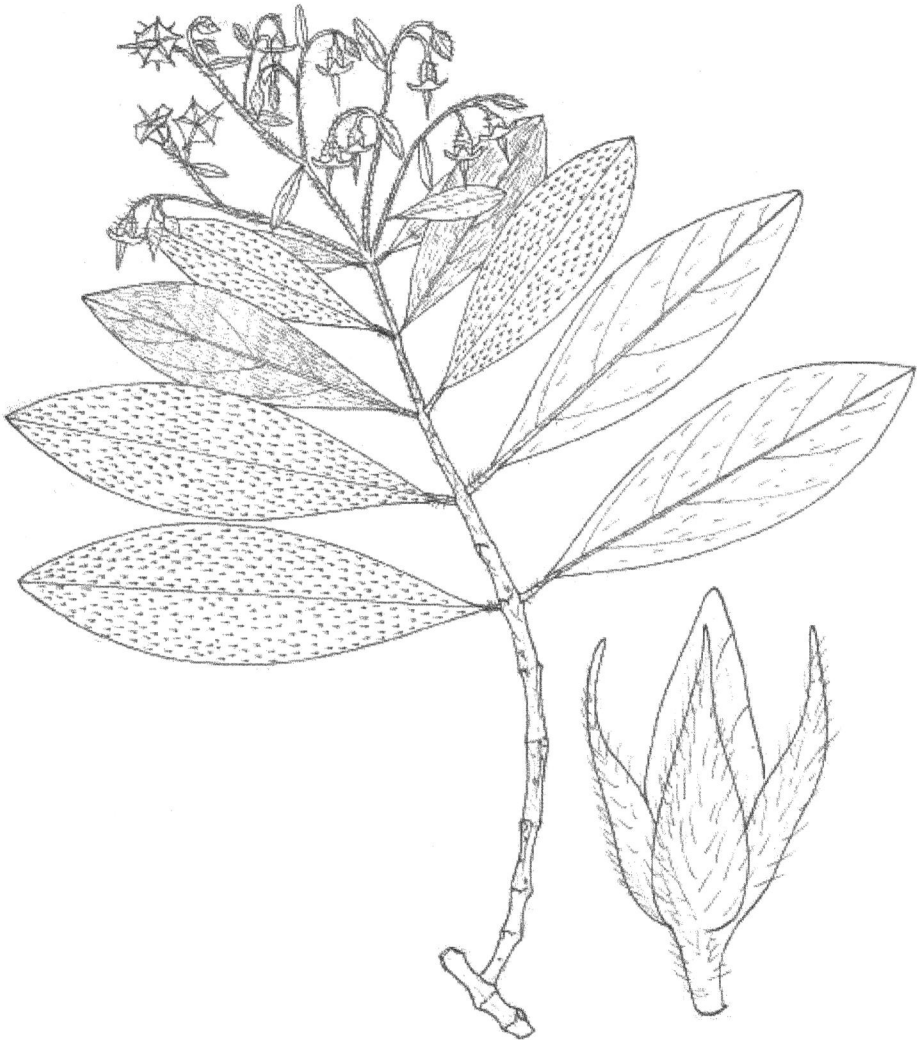

Figure 187: *Trichodesma zeylanicum* **(Burm. f.) R. Br.**
From: Flora of Thailand, Chiang Mai University.
Thailand, Chiang Mai province, Chiang Dao district, Doi Chiang Dao wildlife sanctuary, eastern part of Doi Luang Valley, West of the summit of Doi Chiang Dao. Altitude 1850 m. Date of collection: 1st February 1996. Collection and identification: JF Maxwell N° 96-170.

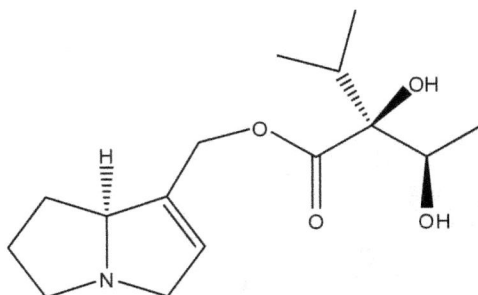

Supinine

Pharmacology: The pharmacological property of this plant is still unexplored. However, anti-inflammatory properties have been reported from other Trichodesma species. A chloroform extract of *Trichodesma indicum* exhibited pronounced anti-inflammatory activity in the carrageenan-induced rat paw oedema (Perianayagam *et al.*, 2006), probably on due to alkanoic acid (Singh *et al.*, 2006). The seeds contain ricinoleic acid, malvalic acid, and sterculic acid. The plant also contains poisonous pyrrolizidine alkaloids such as trichodesmine and supinine (O' Kelly *et al.*, 1961).

References: Hosamani KM, 1994, Ricinoleic and cyclopropene acids in *Trichodesma zeylanicum* seed oil. Phytochemistry; 37: 1621-1624.

O' Kelly J, Sargeant K, 1961, Supinine from the seeds of *Trichodesma zeylanicum* R. Br. J. Chem Soc; 484.

Perianayagam JB ,Sharma SK, Pillai KK, 2006, Anti-inflammatory activity of *Trichodesma indicum* root extract in experimental animals. J Ethnopharmacol; 104: 410-414.

Singh B, Sahu PM, Lohiya RK, Sharma MK, Singh HL, Singh S, 2006,   Anti-inflammatory activity of alkanoids and triterpenoids from *Trichodesma amplexicaule* Roth. Phytomedicine; 13:152-156

2.Family LAMIACEAE Lindley 1836 nom. conserv., the Mint Family

The family Lamiaceae (or Labiatea or Labiae) consists of about 200 genera and 3,200 species of hairy and aromatic herbs or shrubs which are cosmopolitan in distribution. Common secondary metabolites encountered in this family are monoterpene (volatile oils), diterpenes (abietane), triterpenes and flavonoids. The stem is quadrangular and the leaves are simple, mostly decussate and without stipules and variously crenate or toothed at the margin. The inflorescences are racemes or cymes which are terminal or axillary. The flowers are perfect and zygomorphic and beautiful. The calyx consists of 5 variously united sepals which persist in fruits. The corolla is tubular, blue or white, bilabiate with 5 imbricate lobes. The androecium consists of 2 - 4 stamens which originate from the corolla. The gynaecium consists of a pair of carpels fused into a 4 - locular and superior ovary, each locule containing a single ovule attached to a basal axile placenta. The style originates from the inner the base of the carpels (gynobasic) and the stigma is bifid. The fruits consist of 4 achene - like nutlets which are packed in the calyx.

This family is of economic value as a source of ornamental plants and of a volatile oil for perfumery and medicine. The family Lamiaceae contains cohorts of ornamental plants such as *Caryopteris incana* (California lilac), *Ajuga pyramidalis* (pyramidal bugleweed), *Lavandula angustifolia* (English Lavender) and *Physostegia virginiana* (obedient plant). Several plant species in the Lamiaceae are of pharmaceutical value because of their volatile oils which have carminative and flavouring properties: *Mentha piperita*, (Peppermint, British Pharmaceutical Codex, 1954), *Mentha viridis* L., *Mentha spicata* (Spearmint Oil, British Pharmaceutical Codex, 1963). *Lavendula intermedia, Lavendula officinalis* (Lavender Oil, British Pharmaceutical Codex, 1963), *Rosmarinus officinalis* L. (Rosemary Oil, British Pharmaceutical Codex, 1963), *Salvia officinalis* (Sage, British Pharmaceutical Codex, 1934). The volatile oil of *Hyssopus officinalis* L. (Hyssop, Portuguese Pharmacopoeia, 1936) has been used in conjunction with other herbs as a carminative and cough remedy. It is also used in perfumery. The volatile oil of *Thymus vulgaris* L. (Thyme Oil, British Pharmaceutical Codex, 1949) is antiseptic, antispasmodic and carminative and has been used as an ingredient for cough mixtures. The volatile oil of *Origanum vulgare* or marjoram (Origanum, Polish Pharmacopoeia, 1954) as been used as an aromatic, a carminative for coughs and externally to heal wounds. *Scutellariae Radix* is ancient drug in traditional Chinese medicine, prepared from the roots of *Scutellaria baicalensis* (Japan Pharmacopeia JPXIII and Chinese Pharmacopeia) which has been prescribed for bronchitis, hepatitis, diarrhoea, and tumours. The volatile oil of *Mentha pulegium* (Pulegium oil, British Pharmaceutical Codex, 1934) as been used as an mmenagogue. The volatile oil of *Melissa officinalis* is carminative and diaphoretic (French Pharmacopoeia, 1965). Examples of oils used in perfumery are patchouli oil (*Pogostemon heyneanus* Bth.), lavender oil, hyssop oil, marjoram oil, rosemary oil, melisa oil, sage oil, and thyme oil.

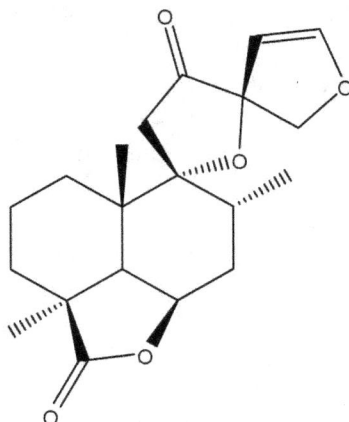

Cytotoxic diterpene of *Marrubium* sp.

Of recent interest is the isolation of several series of cytotoxic diterpenes. Cytotoxic labdane diterpenes were isolated from *Marrubium* species active against MOLT-4 (T cell leukemia), DAUDI (B cell leukemia), RAJI (B cell leukemia), K562 (granulocytic leukemia), MCF-7 (breast cancer), HeLa (cervix cancer) and FM3 (melanoma) (Karioti et al., 2007). Dai et al. (2008) isolated the neo-clerodane diterpenoid scutebarbatines I-L from *Scutellaria barbata* which showed significant cytotoxic activities against HONE-1 nasopharyngeal, KB oral epidermoid carcinoma, and HT29 colorectal carcinoma cells. Ent-16-Kauren-19-ol and ent-16-kauren-19-oic acid isolated from *Plectranthus strigosus* Benth displayed ant-herpetic property (Gaspar-Marques et al., 2008).

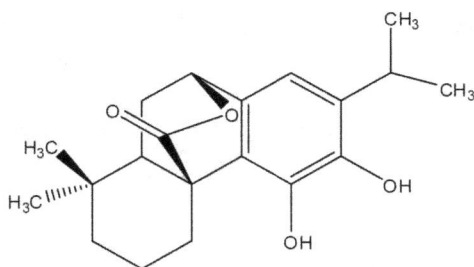

Carnosol

Carnosol, a phenolic diterpene from *Rosmarinus officinalis*, protected cultured dopaminergic cells against rotenone through down regulation of caspase-3 increase of tyrosine hydroxylase, Nurr1, an extracellular signal-regulated kinase suggesting that carnosol may have potential as a possible compound for the development of new agents to treat Parkinson's disease (Kim et al., .2006; Izumi et al., 2007)

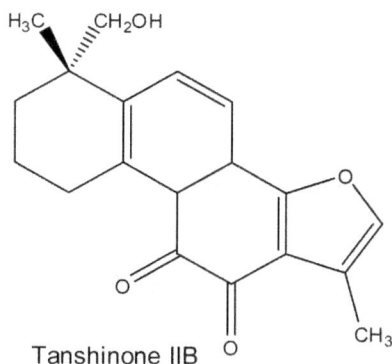

Tanshinone IIB

Another neuroprotective agent is tanshinone IIB from *Salvia miltiorrhiza,* which significantly reduced the focal infarct volume, cerebral histological damage and apoptosis in rats subjected in experimentally induced stroke (Yu *et al.*, 2007). About 60 species of plants classified within the family Lamiaceae are used for medicinal purposes in Asia - Pacific. These plants are often used to facilitate digestion, to assuage spasms, to counteract putrefaction, to promote urination and to regulate menses.

References:

Dai SJ, Liang DD, Ren Y, Liu K, Shen L, 2008, New neo-clerodane diterpenoid alkaloids from *Scutellaria barbata* with cytotoxic activities. Chem Pharm Bull (Tokyo); 56: 207-9.

Gaspar-Marques C, Simões MF, Valdeira ML, Rodríguez B, 2008, Terpenoids and phenolics from *Plectranthus strigosus*, bioactivity screening. Nat Prod Res; 22: 167-77.

Izumi M, Satoh T, Inukai Y, Tutumi Y, Nakayama N, Kosaka K. Itoh K, 2007, Carnosic acid and carnosol as neuroprotective electrophilic compounds. Neurosci Res; 58, Supplement 1: S208.

Karioti A, Skopeliti M, Tsitsilonis O, Heilmann J and Skaltsa H, 2007, Cytotoxicity and immunomodulating characteristics of labdane diterpenes from *Marrubium cylleneum* and *Marrubium velutinum* Phytochemistry; 68: 1587-1594.

Kim SJ, Kim JS, Cho HS, Lee HJ, Kim SY, Kim S, Lee SY, Chun HS, 2006, Carnosol, a component of rosemary (Rosmarinus officinalis L.) protects nigral dopaminergic neuronal cells. Neuroreport; 17: 1729-33.

Yu XY, Lin SG, Zhou ZW, Chen X, Liang J, Duan W, Yu XQ, Wen JY, Chowbay B, Li CG, Sheu FS, Chan E, Zhou SF, 2007, Tanshinone IIB, a primary active constituent from *Salvia miltiorrhza*, exhibits neuro-protective activity in experimentally stroked rats. Neurosci Lett; 417: 261-5.

Anisomeles indica (L.) O.K

[From Greek *aniso* = unequal and *melo* = limb and Latin *indica* = from India]

Local name: Gopali (India), chine ts'ao (China), talingharap, kabling-parang
                      (Philippines)

Basionym: *Nepeta indica* L. *Species Plantarum* 2: 571-572. 1753

Synonyms: *Anisomeles ovata* R. Br., *Epimeredi indica* (L.) Roth; *Marrubium
                      indicum* (L.) Burm.f., *Nepeta indica* L., *Phlomis indica* Blco.

Description: It is an erect herb which grows to a height of 1.5 m in open
                      disturbed thicket, in alluva waste areas of tropical Africa,
                      India, China, Cambodia, India, Laos, Malaysia, Burma,
                      Philippines, Thailand, and Vietnam. The stem is hairy, sharply
                      quadrangular, branched, 0.2 cm at the apex and with 9.3 - 14
                      cm long internodes. The stem is slightly swollen right above
                      the internodes. The leaves are simple. decussate, and without
                      stipule. The petiole is 1.3 - 2.2 cm. The leaf blade is triangular,
                      membranaceous, crenate at the margin, with 3 to 4 pairs of
                      secondary nerves and some tertiary nerves visible underneath,
                      and 1.2 - 3.8 cm x 4.5 - 6.8 cm, acute at the apex and acuminate
                      at the base. The inflorescences are axillary and terminal spikes
                      which are 3.5 - 5.5 cm in diameter. The calyx is membranaceous,
                      hairy, conspicuously nerved, about 0.6 cm long, with 5 purple-
                      red, triangular-lanceolate teeth. The corolla is 1.6 cm long,
                      tubular, bilabiate, the upper lip short, both side of the upper
                      lip and filaments pale light greenish, lower lip whitish tinted
                      violet. The stamens and style protrude out of the corolla. The
                      anthers are dark maroon, style and stigma light maroon. The
                      fruits are 0.15 - 0.25 cm nutlets packed in a persistent calyx
                      (Figure 188).

Medicinal Uses: In India the plant is used to promote digestion, to invigorate and
                      to treat uterine affections. In the Philippines, the plant is used to
                      treat abdominal pains, to break fever, to assuage rheumatic pain
                      and to promote digestion. In China, it is used for rheumatism,
                      influenza, abdominal pain, skin sores, and as an antidote for
                      snake bite. In Taiwan, the plant is used to break fever and to
                      promote urination. In Cambodia, Laos and Vietnam, the plant
                      is used to treat abdominal complaints and to dress the hair.
                      Indonesians use the plant to treat urine stones.

Pharmacology: The   plant   contains   a   diterpene,   ovatodiolide,
                      3,7,11,15_17.-cembratetraene-16,2:19,6-diolide,   which
                      exhibited anti-HIV activity *in vitro* (Shahidul *et al.*, 2000). An

extract of the plant demonstrated strong anti-*Helicobacter pylori* activities *in vitro* (Wang *et al.*, 2005). The anti-inflammatory, analgesic and diuretic properties of the plant have been validated experimentally. Extracts of the plant significantly inhibited the production of NO radicals, and pro-inflammatory cytokines (TNF-alpha, and IL-12) induced by LPS/IFN-γ in a dose dependent manner and elicited cytotoxic effects against colon, prostate, hepatoma and breast cancer cell lines (Hsieh *et al.*, 2008). Aqueous extracts of the plant showed analgesic and diuretic activity in rats (Dharmasiri *et al.*, 2003; 2003a).

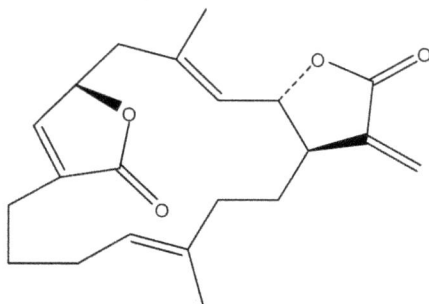

Ovatodiolide

References:

Dharmasiri MG, Ratnasooriya WD, Thabrew MI, 2003, Water extract of leaves and stems of preflowering but not flowering plants of *Anisomeles indica* possesses analgesic and antihyperalgesic activities in rats. Pharmaceut Biol; 41: 37- 44.

Dharmasiri MG, Ratnasooriya WD, Thabrew MI, 2003a, Diuretic activity of leaf and stem decoction of *Anisomeles indica*. J Trop Medicinal Plants; 4: 43-45.

Hsieh SC, Fang SH, Rao YK, Tzeng YM, 2008, Inhibition of pro-inflammatory mediators and tumor cell proliferation by *Anisomeles indica* extracts. J Ethnopharmacol. (In press).

Shahidul Alam M, Quader MA, Rashid MA, 2000, HIV-inhibitory diterpenoid from *Anisomeles indica*. Fitoterapia; 71: 574-6.

Wang YC, Huang TL., 2005, Screening of anti-Helicobacter pylori herbs deriving from Taiwanese folk medicinal plants. FEMS Immunol Med Microbiol; 43: 295-300.

Figure 188: *Anisomeles indica* **(L.) O.K**
From: Flora of Thailand, Chiang Mai University Herbarium
Thailand, Kanchanaburi province, Sangklaburi district, Toong Yai Neresuan wildlife reserve,
Lai Mo subdistrict, Ban Saneh Pawng, Karen village. Altitude 200 m. Date of collection: 12
January 1994.

Hyptis brevipes Poit.

[From the Greek *huptios* = turned back and Latin *brevipes* = with a short stalk]

Synonym:	*Mesosphaerum brevipes* (Poiteau) Kuntze.
Local names:	Duan bing diao qiu cao (China), pandasan onini (Borneo)
Description:	It is an erect, annual herb that grows to a height of 1 m in open waste areas and roadsides in China, Taiwan, Thailand, Malaysia, Philippines, Pacific Islands, and tropical America, where it is native. The stem is slender, 0.1 - 0.3 mm in diameter, somewhat rigid, quadrangular, with few hairs and 2.2 - 5 cm long internodes.
	The leaves are simple, decussate, subsessile, and without stipule. The leaf blade is linear oblong to linear lanceolate, 1.2 - 3 cm × 1.5-0.5 cm, narrowly cuneate at the base, serrate at the margin, acute to acuminate at the apex, with 3 to 4 pairs of secondary nerves, hairy with oil cells underneath. The inflorescences are globose axillary heads of about 1 cm in diameter. The calyx is tubular, with a few hairs, striated and presents 5 linear lobes, which are about 2.5 mm long. The corolla is white, 0.35 cm long, puberulent, bilabiate, lower lip 3 lobed; middle lobe larger, concave, circular, constricted at the base, and bending inward. The stamens are slightly exerted. The fruits are dark brown nutlets adaxially ribbed, packed in a persistent calyx, with 2 basal white scars (Figure 189).
Medicinal Uses:	Malays use the plant to expel intestinal worms, and as a post partum remedy. In Indonesia, the plant is used to heal wounds. In the Philippines, the plant is used to relieve headache.
Pharmacology:	Goun *et al.* (2003) reported antibacterial activity from the plant, confirming the wound healing use mentioned above. A methylene chloride extract was particularly active against *Staphylococcus aureus* and the agricultural fungus *Phytophthora parasitica*. The plant contains 6-hydroxycaleic acid (Pedersen *et al.*, 2000).
References:	Goun E, Cunningham G, Chu D, Nguyen C, Miles D, 2003, Antibacterial and antifungal activity of Indonesian ethnomedical plants. Fitoterapia; 74: 592-6.
	Pedersen JA, 2000, Distribution and taxonomic implications of some phenolics in the family Lamiaceae determined by ESR spectroscopy. Biochem System Ecol; 28: 229-253

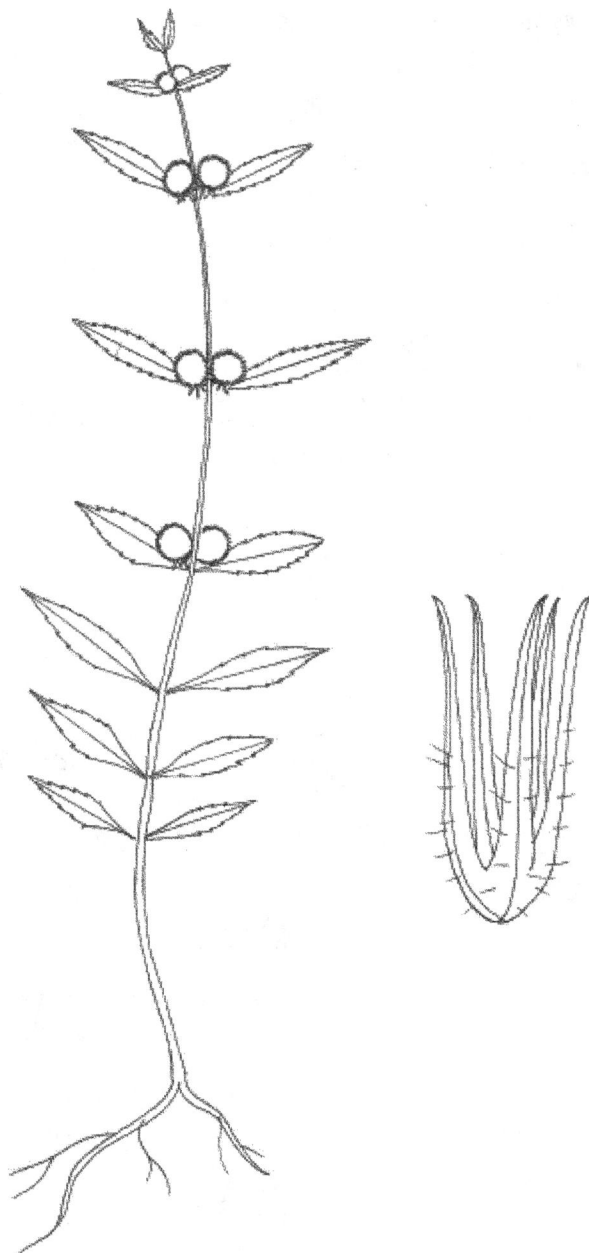

Figure 189: *Hyptis brevipes* **Poit.**
From: Plants of Borneo, Herbarium of Michigan State University
Malaysia, Sabah, Tambunan district, Crocker Range, Km 55 on Kota Kinabalu-Tanbunan
road, 5° 49', North - 116° 20', West. Altitude 1675 m. Collection: John H. Beaman, Reed S
Beaman, Teofila E Beaman, Jody Kennard, and Frederick M Shelton. 6917. Date of Collection:
4 September 1983

Hyptis capitata Jacq.

[from the Greek *huptios* = turned back and Latin *capitata* = capitate]

Local names:	Knobweed, cartagena amarilla (Spain), botonesan (Philippines)
Synonyms:	*Clinopodium capitatum* Sw., *Mesosphaerum capitatum* (Jacq.) Kuntze, *Pycnanthemum decurrens* Blco, *Thymus virginicus* Blco
Description:	It is an erect, somewhat woodish herb native to tropical America which grows by roadsides and on disturbed areas in a geographical area enclosing Thailand, Malaysia, Indonesia, Vietnam, Papua new Guinea, Australia, Pacific Islands, Martinique, Antilles and tropical America. The stem is hollowed, strongly quadrangular, with 7 - 10 cm long internodes, and up to 1 m tall. The leaves are opposite, simple and without stipule. The petiole is about 2 - 3 cm long. The leaf blade is 10.5 - 4 cm x 2.2 - 0.5 cm, broadly lanceolate, irregularly serrate at the margin, acuminate at the base, acute at the apex, and with about 5 pairs of secondary nerves clearly visible underneath. The inflorescences are axillary, globose 1.5-2.5 cm diameter heads on 3 to 3.5 cm pedicels. The calyx is tubular, membranaceous, hairy at the base, with striations, 0.4 x 0.2 mm with 5 linear lobes which are 0.1 cm long. The corolla is white with faint purplish spots on the upper lip, 0.5 to 0.6 cm long, with 5 lobes, the median lower one hairy underneath and turned back. The stamens and stigma protrude out of the corolla tube. The fruits are brownish-black nutlets packed in the persistent calyx (Figure 190).
Medicinal Uses:	In the Philippines the plant is used to heal wounds, to promote menses and to assuage headaches. In Taiwan the plant is used to treat tuberculosis, malaria and influenza.
Pharmacology:	The plant contains series of bioactive triterpenes which might be involved in the wound healing and anti-tuberculosis uses mentioned above. Hyptatic acid-A 2alpha,3beta,24-trihydroxyolean-12-en-28-oic acid showed some levels of antibacterial activity *in vitro* (McRae JM *et al.*, 2008). Hyptatic acid A and 2alpha-hydroxyursolic acid (2alpha,3/I-dihydroxyurs-12-en-28-oic acid) demonstrated significant *in vitro* cytotoxicity in human colon HCT-8 tumour cells (Yamagishi *et al.*, 1991). The plant elaborates some lignans such as 2,3-di(3',4'-methylenedioxybenzyl)-2-buten-4-olide, and large amount of rosmarinic acid (Almtorp *et al.*, 1991). Rosmarinic acid is widely distributed in the Lamiaceae: it has been reported to possess anti-inflammatory activity and used in cosmetics as a skin conditioner (Engleberger *et al.*, 1988).. To date the anti-malarial property of *Hyptis capitata* Jacq. has not been validated but

Chukwujekwu *et al.* (2005), isolated an abietane-type diterpenoid endoperoxide, 13alpha-*epi*-dioxiabiet-8(14)-en-18-ol, with potent antiplasmodial activity.

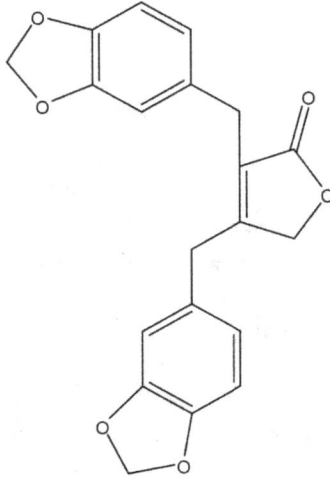

2,3-di(3',4'-methylenedioxybenzyl)-2-buten-4-olide

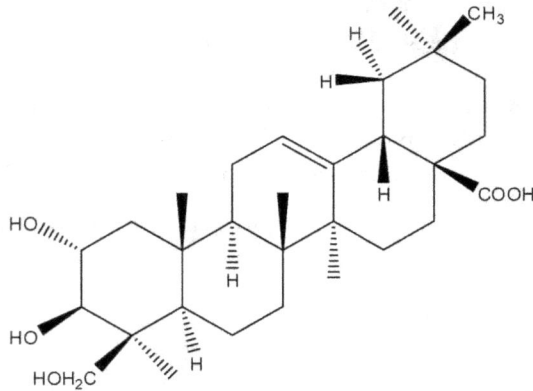

Hyptatic acid A

References:

Almtorp GT, Hazell AC, Kurt BG, Torssell KBG, 1991, A lignan and pyrone and other constituents from *Hyptis capitata*. Phytochemistry; 30: 2753-2756.

Chukwujekwu JC, Smith P, Coombes PH, Mulholland DA, van Staden J, 2005, Antiplasmodial diterpenoid from the leaves of *Hyptis suaveolens*. J Ethnopharmacol; 102: 295-297.

Engleberger W, Hadding U, Etschenberg E, Graf E, Leyck S, Winkelmann J, Parnham MJ, 1988, Rosmarinic acid: a new inhibitor of complement C3-convertase with anti-inflammatory activity. Int. J. Immunopharmacol; 10: 729-737.

McRae JM, Yang Q, Crawford RJ, Palombo EA, 2008, Antibacterial compounds from *Planchonia careya* leaf extracts. J Ethnopharmacol; 116: 554-60.

Yamagishi T, De-Cheng Zhang DC, Jer-Jang Chang JJ, Donald R, McPhail DR, McPhai AT, Kuo-Hsiung Lee KH, 1991, The cytotoxic principles of *Hyptis capitata* and the structures of the new triterpenes hyptatic acid-A and -B Phytochemistry; 27: 3213-3216.

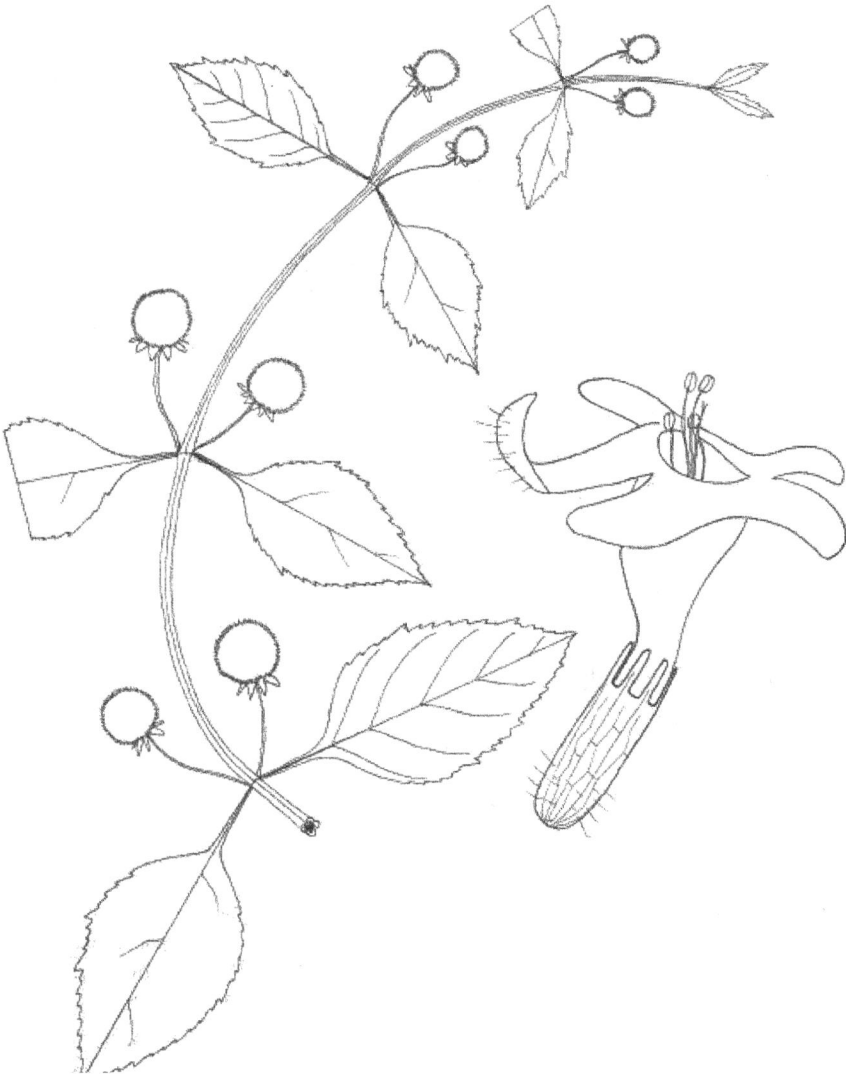

Figure 190: *Hyptis capitata* **Jacq.**
From: University Kebangsaan Malaysia Herbarium. Flora of Borneo.
Malaysia, Sabah, Tambunan, Km 64, Tambunan, Kota Kinabalu road. Altitude 1250 m.
Collection and identification: Char Hor Kuan, № CHK 14. Date of collection: 30 July 1989.

Leonurus sibiricus L.

[From Greek *leon* = lion and *oura* = a tail and from Latin *sibiricus* = from Siberia]

Local name:	Lion's tail, Siberian motherwort , Chinese motherwort; gros tombé (France). Indonesia: gin jean (Javanese), dendereman, si saratan (Indonesia), seranting, tebungaga (Malaysia), kacangma (North Borneo). Philippines: kamariang-sungsong (Philippines), khanchaa thet, saa saa, saa nam (Thailand), yakumosou (Japan)
Synonym:	*Leonurus japonicus* Houtt., *Leonurus heterophyllus* Sweet, *Leonurus artemisia* (Lour.) S.Y. Hu, *Leonurus manshuricus* Yabe; *Leonorus sibiricus* L. *sibiricus* var. *grandiflora* Benth.
Description:	It is an erect branching annual herb, native to temperate Asia, which grows up to 1 m tall on stony or sandy grasslands of a geographical area covering Mongolia, Russia, Siberia, China, Korea, Japan, India, Mascarenes, Malaysia ,Sumatra, Indonesia and the Philippines. The stem is quadrangular, light green, pitted, 0.3 - 0.5 cm in diameter and with a few lenticels. The leaves are simple, decussate and without stipules. The petiole is light green, slender 3 to 4.3 cm and channeled. The leaf blade is deeply incised, with secondary nerves sunken above, 8 - 13 cm x 12 - 9 cm. The inflorescences are globose axillary heads which are many flowered, and 3 -3.5 cm in diameter. The calyx is dark green, sessile, hairy, campanulate 0.5 cm long., with spiny lobes. The corolla is hairy, 0.8 cm long, pink, the lower lip 4 lobed with violet streak and 2 midlobes entirely violet inside, with a few hairs, upper lip oblong, straight, concave. The stamens are visible under the upper lobe, the anthers are tan and the filament pale light pink with light violet streaks. The fruits are brown, oblong, triquetrous tiny nutlets in a persistent calyx (Figure 191).
Medicinal Uses:	In Korea, the plant is used as a tonic remedy and to check intestinal bleeding. In China, the plant is used to promote menses and urination, and to invigorate the uterus. In Vietnam and Japan the plant is used to promote menses. In Cambodia, Laos and Vietnam, the plant s used to invigorate blood circulation. Indonesia, it is used to make a tincture to expel vermin.
Pharmacology:	The plant contains some flavonoids and iridoids (Hayashi *et al.*, 2001; Pan *et al.*, 2006), alkaloids (Luo *et al.*, 1985) and diterpenes known as sibiricinones (Boalino *et al.*, 2004) . The plant exhibited some effects on preneoplastic and neoplastic

mammary gland growth in multiparous GR/A mice (Nagasawa *et al.*, 1990, 1992). An extract of the plant was cytotoxic against several cancer cell lines *in vitro* via apoptosis (Chinwala *et al.*, 2007). Effects are probably mediated by some cytotoxic furanoditerpene-lactones which are known to occur in the plant (Sato *et al.*, 2003; Romero-González *et al.*, 2006). A labdane diterpene known as prehispanolone (Hon *et al.*, 1991) is a platelet activating factor receptor antagonist (Lee *et al.*,1991) and stimulates the proliferation of lymphocytes T and B (Xu *et al.*, 1002).Shi *et al.*, (1995) validated the uterotonic property of the plant. This activity is due to the stimulation of H1-receptor and alpha-adrenergic. Islam *et al.* (2005) reported that intraperitoneal injection of an extract of the plant showed a significant analgesic effect in acetic acid-induced writhing in mice. Extracts of the plant exhibited an antibacterial property against a broad spectrum of bacteria (Ahmed *et al.*, 2006). Note that the seeds contain a heat-stable antibacterial and antifungal protein, designated LJAMP2 (Yang *et al.* 2006). An extract of the plant decreased the time of onset of sleep and potentiated the pentobarbital induced sleeping time in mice (Ahmed *et al.*, 2005). The plant contains a series of cyclopeptides including the dodecapeptide, cycloleonurinin, cyclo (-Gly-Pro-Thr-Gln-Tyr-Pro-Pro-Tyr-Tyr-Thr-Pro-Ala-), which showed potent immunosuppressive effect on human peripheral blood lymphocytes (Morita *et al.*, 1997). An extract of the plant stimulated the scavenging activity of superoxide dismutase in keratinocytes caused by the acceleration of SOD production and it suppressed UVB-induced oxidative damage in keratinocytes (Tanaka *et al.*, 2001).

References:

Ahmed F, Islam MA, Choudhuri MSK, 2005, Nigerian J Nat Prods Med; 9: 35-7.

Ahmed F, Islam MA, Rahman MM, 2006,Antibacterial activity of *Leonurus sibiricus* aerial parts. Fitoterapia; 77: 316-7.

Boalino DM, McLean S, Reynolds WF, Tinto WF, 2006, Labdane diterpenes of *Leonurus sibiricus*. J Nat Prod; 2004 67: 714-7.

Chinwala MG, Gao M, Dai J, Shao J, 2003, In vitro anticancer activities of *Leonurus heterophyllus* sweet (Chinese motherwort herb). J Altern Complement Med; 9: 511-8.

Hayashi K, Ikoma R, Deyama T, 2001, Phenolic Compounds and Iridoids from *Leonurus sibiricus*. Nat Med; 55: 276.

Hon PM, Lee CM, Shang HS, Cui YX, Wong HNC, Chang HM, 1991, Prehispanolone, a labdane diterpene from *Leonurus heterophyllus*. Phytochemistry; 30: 354-356.

Islam MA, Ahmed F, Das AK, Bachar SC, 2005, Analgesic and anti-inflammatory activity of *Leonurus sibiricus*. Fitoterapia; 76: 359-62.

Lee CM, Jiang LM, Shang HS, Hon PM, He Y, Wong HNC, 1991, Prehispanolone, a novel platelet activating factor receptor antagonist from *Leonurus heterophyllus*. Brit Pharmacol; 103: 1719-1724.

Luo SR, 1985, Separation and determination of alkaloids of *Leonurus sibiricus,* Zhong Yao Tong Bao; 10: 32-5.

Morita H, Gonda A, Takeya K, Itokawa H, Hirano T, Oka K, Osamu Shirota O, 1997, Solution state conformation of an immunosuppressive cyclic dodecapeptide, cycloleonurinin. Tetrahedron; 53: 7469-7478.

Nagasawa H, Onoyama T, Suzuki M, Hibino A, Segawa T, Inatomi H, 1990, Effects of motherwort (*Leonurus sibiricus* L) on preneoplastic and neoplastic mammary gland growth in multiparous GR/A mice. Anticancer Res; 10: 1019-23.

Nagasawa H, Inatomi H, Suzuki M, Mori T, 1992, Further study on the effects of motherwort (*Leonurus sibiricus* L) on preneoplastic and neoplastic mammary gland growth in multiparous GR/A mice. Anticancer Res; 12: 141-3.

Pan SM, Ding HY, Chang WL, Lin HC, 2006, Phenols from the aerial parts of *Leonurus sibiricus*. Zhonghuá Yáoxué Zázhì; 58: 35-40.

Romero-González R, Jorge L, Ávila-Núñez JL, Lianne Aubert L, Miguel E, Alonso-Amelot ME, 2006,Labdane diterpenes from *Leonurus japonicus* leaves. Phytochemistry; 67: 965-970.

Satoh M, Satoh Y, Isobe K, Fujimoto Y, 2003, Studies on the constituents of *Leonurus sibiricus* L. Chem Pharm Bull (Tokyo); 51: 341-2.

Shi M, Chang L, He G, 1995, Stimulating action of *Carthamus tinctorius* L., *Angelica sinensis* (Oliv.) Diels and *Leonurus sibiricus* L. on the uterus. Zhongguo Zhong Yao Za Zhi; 20: 173-5, 192.

Tanaka H, Yamaba H, Okada T, Katada T, Nakata S, 2001, Stimulating Effects of Yakumosou (*Leonurus sibiricus* L.) on intracellular SOD Activity in skin. J Japan Cosmetic Sci Soc; 25: 74-80.

Yang X, Li J, Li X, Rong SR, Yan PY, 2006, Isolation and characterization of a novel thermostable non-specific lipid transfer protein-like antimicrobial protein from motherwort (*Leonurus japonicus* Houtt) seeds. Peptides; 27: 3122-3128.

Xu HM, Lee CM, Hon PM, Chang HM, 1992, Proliferation of lymphocytes T and B by prehispanolone LC-5504 of *Leonurus heterophyllus* Sweet. Acta Pharm Sinica; 27: 812-816.

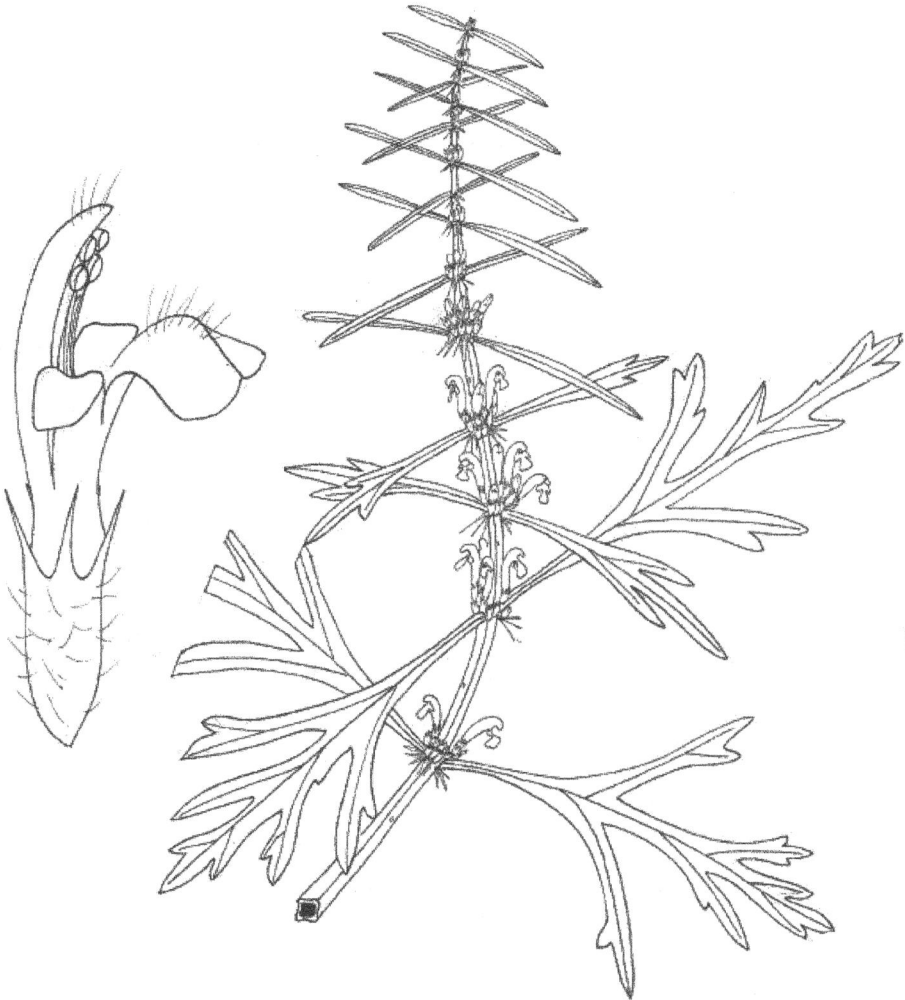

Figure 191: *Leonurus sibiricus* L.

From: Flora of Thailand
Thailand, Lampang province, Jae Sawn national park, Bah Miang village, next to the school.
Elevation: 1025 m. Date of collection: 23 May 1996. Collection and identification; JF Maxwell, No 96-734.

Leucas lavandulifolia Sm.

[From Greek *leukos* = white and *lavendulifolia* = lavender-like leaves

Local names:	Leucas, ketumbak (Malaysia), halkusha, mosappullu, (India), xian ye bai rong cao (China), solasolasihan (Philippines), paci-paci (Indonesia), armoise blanche (France)
Synonyms:	*Leonurus indicus* Burm.f; *Leucas indica* (L.) Vatke, *Leucas lavandulaefolia* , *Leucas linifolia* (Roth) Spreng; *Phlomis linifolia* Roth.
Description:	It is an erect annual herb, which grows to 0.8 m in sunny areas, roadsides and riverbanks, in a geographical area ranging from East Africa to India, Indonesia, Malaysia, Philippines, and Thailand. The stem is pubescent, quadrangular, about 0.2 cm in diameter, and branching. The leaves are sessile, simple, opposite and without stipules. The leaf blade is linear, hairy, 2.5 - 9 cm × 0.3 -1.2 cm, attenuate at the base, serrate at the margin, obtuse at the apex, sunken at midrib, with 2- 3 pairs of secondary nerves which are inconspicuous. The inflorescence is a terminal raceme which is about 1.5 - 2.5 cm in diameter. The bracts are linear, and spiny at the apex. The calyx is obovoid, about 0.5 mm long, hairy and longitudinally striated, the mouth oblique with irregular teeth. The corolla is pure white, about 1.5 cm long hairy outside, the lower lip larger than the upper and 3 lobed. The fruits are brown nutlets packed in the calyx (Figure 192).
Medicinal Uses:	In the Philippines the plant is used to heal inflamed wounds, and to promote digestion. In India, the plant is used for fever; it is a stimulant, diaphoretic, and is used for rheumatism and snakebite. In Malaysia, the plant is used to heal sores and to wash the nostrils, to expel intestinal worms and to treat vertigo. In Indonesia the plant is used to treat nervous disorders, coughs and epileptic seizures.
Pharmacology:	The chloroform extract of *Leucas lavandulaefolia* at oral doses of 200 mg/kg and 400 mg/kg exhibited significant protection against D(+)galactosamine induced liver damage in rats (Chandrashekar *et al.*, 2007). This effect could be mediated by phenylpropanoid glycosides which exhibited potent antioxidant activity *in vitro* (Mostafa *et al.*, 2007). The sedative, antipyretic, wound healing and anti-coughing properties of the plant have been confirmed experimentally. An extract of the plant reduced the spontaneous activity and exploratory behavioral pattern of

rodents and potential pentobarbitone induced sleeping time in mice (Mukherjee *et al.*, 2002). A methanol extract of *Leucas* lowered body temperature in experimentally yeast-infected rodents as effectively as paracetamol (Mukherjee *et al.*, 2002). A methanol extract of the plant elicited wound healing properties comparable to that of nitrofurazone (Saha *et al.*, 1997). A methanol extract of the plant also reduced the cough induced by sulfur dioxide gas in mice with an activity comparable to that of codeine phosphate (Saha *et al.*, 1997).

References:

Chandrashekar KS, Prasanna KS, Joshi AB, 2007, Hepatoprotective activity of the Leucas lavandulaefolia on D(+) galactosamine-induced hepatic injury in rats. Fitoterapia; 78: 440-2.

Mostafa M, Nahar N, Mosihuzzaman M, Makhmoor T, Choudhary MI, Rahman AU, 2007, Free radical scavenging phenylethanoid glycosides from *Leucas indica* Linn. Nat Prod Res; 21: 354-61.

Mukherjee K, Saha BP, Mukherjee PK, 2002, Psychopharmacological profiles of *Leucas Lavandulaefolia* Rees. Phytother Res; 16 696-9.

Mukherjee K, Saha BP, Mukherjee PK, 2002, Evaluation of antipyretic potential of *Leucas lavandulaefolia* (Labiatae) aerial part extract. Phytother Res; 16: 686-8.

Saha K, Mukherjee PK, Das J, Pal M, Saha BP, 1997, Wound healing activity of *Leucas lavandulaefolia* Rees. J Ethnopharmacol; 56: 139-144.

Saha K, Pulok K, Mukherjee PK, Murugesan T, Saha BP, Pal M, 1997, Studies on *in vivo* antitussive activity of *Leucas lavandulaefolia* using a cough model induced by sulfur dioxide gas in mice. J Ethnopharmacol; 57: 89-92.

Figure 192: *Leucas lavandulifolia* Sm.
From Flora of Thailand, Prince Songkla University
Thailand, Songkla province, Muang district, in front of Suan Dtoon falls. Elevation sea level.
Date of collection: 5 October 1984. Collection and identification: JF Maxwell N° 84-301

Mosla dianthera (Buch.-Ham. ex Roxb.) Maxim.

[From Latin *di-* = two and *anthera* = anther]

Local names:	False skullcap, miniature beefsteak plant; xiao yu xian cao (China)
Basionym:	*Lycopus diantherus* Buch.-Ham. ex Roxb. Flora Indica; or descriptions of Indian Plants 1: 144. 1820
Synonyms:	*Cunila nepalensis* D.Don, *Hedeoma nepalensis* (D.Don) Benth., *Lycopus dianthera* Buch.-Ham. ex Roxb., *Melissa nepalensis* (D.Don) Benth., *Mosla ocimoides* Buch.-Ham Benth., *Mosla punctata* Maxim., *Mosla remotiflora* Sun, *Orthodon diantherus* (Buch.-Ham ex Roxb.) Hand.-Mazz, *Orthodon grosseserratum* (Maxim.) Kudo, *Orthodon punctatus* var. *tetrantherus* Hand.-Mazz., *Orthodon punctatum* (Thunb.) Kudo var. *tetrantherus* Hand.-Mazz, *Orthodon punctatum* (Thunb.) Kudo var. *tetrantherus* Hand.-Mazz., *Orthodon punctulatus* (J.F Gmel.) Ohwi,
Description:	It is an annual herb which grows near water up to 1 m tall in a geographical area which covers China, Taiwan, Bhutan, India Japan, Malaysia, Burma Nepal, Pakistan, and Vietnam. The plant is native to Asia and has spread to the eastern USA. The stem is quadrangular, with a few short hairs. It is much branched, slender, 0.2 cm near the apex, and presents 2.3 - 5.7 cm long internodes. The leaves are simple, decussate and without stipule. The petiole is channeled, 0.3 - 0.7 cm, and with a few hairs. The leaf blade is lanceolate linear, thinly coriaceous, with oil cells underneath, 2 - 2.2 cm x 0.7 cm, with 2 - 3 pairs of secondary nerves visible underneath only and serrate at the margin. The inflorescences are terminal spikes which are about 1 to 4 cm long. The calyx is tubular, curved, about 0.4 cm long, with hairy nerves, triangular lobes, and little glossy oil glands. The corolla is purplish, about 0.5 cm long, bilabiate, with 5 discrete lobes. The fruits are gray-brown, subglobose, 0.1 cm in diameter nutlets packed in the persistent calyx (Figure 193).
Medicinal Uses:	In China the plant is used to remove parasites from the skin and to promote digestion. In Cambodia, Laos and Vietnam, the plant is used to assuage headache.
Pharmacology:	An aqueous extract of *Mosla dianthera* (Buch.-Ham. ex Roxb.) Maxim. attenuated phorbol 12-myristate 13-acetate (PMA) and calcium ionophore A23187-stimulated TNF-alpha, IL-8 and IL-6 secretion in human mast cell (Lee

et al., 2006). The plant accumulate some essential oils principally consisting of (±)-carvone and (±)-limonene , (*Z*)-limonene oxide, beta-caryophyllene, and alpha-humulene (Kim *et al.*, 2000), which explain the carminative property mentioned above. These oils are most probably antibacterial (Sandri *et al.*, 2007). The plant contains rosmarinic acid, 4,5-dimethoxy-2,3-methylenedioxy-1-propenylbenzene, 4,5-dimethoxy-2,3-methylenedioxycinnamaldehyde, and 4,5-dimethoxy-2,3-methylenedioxybenzaldehyde together with 2,4,5-trimethoxybenzaldehyde, the triterpenes: beta-sitosterol and stigmasterol, betulinic acid, oleanolic acid, ursolic acid, arjunolic acid, beta-sitosteryl glucopyranoside, and luteolin (Kuo *et al.*, 1999).

References:

Kim SH, Eun JS, Shin TY, 2006, *Mosla dianthera* inhibits mast cell-mediated allergic reactions through the inhibition of histamine release and inflammatory cytokine production. Toxicol Appl Pharmacol; 216: 479-84.

Kim TH, Thuy NT, Shin JH, Baek HH, Lee HJ, 2000, Aroma-Active compounds of miniature beefsteakplant (*Mosla dianthera* Maxim.), J. Agric. Food Chem; 48: 2877 -81.

Kuo YH, Lin SL,1999, Chemical Components of the Whole Herb of *Mosla dianthera*. Chem Pharm Bull (Tokyo); 47: 1152-1153.

Sandri IG, Zacaria J, Fracaro F, Delamarec APL, Echeverrigaray S, 2007, Antimicrobial activity of the essential oils of Brazilian species of the genus *Cunila* against foodborne pathogens and spoiling bacteria. Food Chem; 103: 823-828.

Figure 193: *Mosla dianthera* (Buch.-Ham. ex Roxb.) Maxim.
From: Botanical Inventory of Taiwan. Herbarium, Institute of Botany, Academia Sinica Taipei (HAST)
Taiwan, Hsinchu Hsien, Chienshih Hsiang, Meihua Sheshu, along the river. Altitude 300 m - 400 m. Collector: Chi Hsien Lin 497. Date of Collection: 12 August 1990.

Perrila frutescens (L.) Britt.

[from Latin *frutescens* = shrubby]

Local name:	Beefsteak plant, Chinese basil , Rattlesnake weed, winn (Parish), pérille de Nankin (France), hojiso, shiso (Japanese), tia to (Vietnam),nga (Laos), kemangi (Indonesia), deulkkae (Korea), zi su (China), nga-khimon (Thailand).
Synonyms:	*Melissa rugosa* Lour., *Ocimum frutescens* L., *Perilla nankinensis* Decne., *Perilla ocymoides* L.
Description:	It is a herb which grows to a height of 2 m in open fields and roadsides of China, Taiwan, Bhutan, Cambodia, India, Indonesia, Japan, Korea, Laos, Vietnam and North America. The plant has commercial value as ornamental and as a spice. The stem is erect, quadrangular, subglabrous, green or purple, and with 4 to 6.8 cm long internodes. The leaves are simple, decussate and without stipules. The petiole is slender, hairy, grooved and 1.4 - 5.2 cm long. The leaf blade is broadly ovate to circular, 4.5 -13 cm x 2.8 -10 cm, green above, purplish underneath, hairy, the base wedge-shaped, serrate and recurved at the margin, with 4 - 7 pairs of secondary nerves, with a few oil cells underneath, the midrib filled with hairs above, and acuminate at the apex. The inflorescence is an axillary spike up to 15 cm long with green and hairy bracts. The calyx is green turning dark violet, and about 0.3 cm long with linear lobes and long hairs at the base. The corolla is bilabiate, light violet, about 0.5 cm long with 5 lobes which are hairy at the margin. The fruits are tiny nutlets which are gray-brown or tawny (Figure 194).
Medicinal Uses:	In Korea, the plant is used as a carminative, for colds, and coughs. In China, it is used for morning sickness, to break fever, to treat colds, rheumatism and asthma, to calm, and to promote urination.
Pharmacology:	The essential oil of this plant and the flavonoid luteolin isolated from the plant have antibacterial properties (Zhang *et al.*, 1990; Yamamoto *et al.*, 2002). Note that luteolin is anti-inflammatory and anti-allergic (Ueda *et al.*, 2002). *Perrila frutescens* (L.) Britt. elaborates caffeic esters: (Z,E)-2-(3,4-dihydroxyphenyl) ethenyl ester and (Z,E)-2-(3,5-dihydroxyphenyl)ethenyl ester of 3-(3,4-dihydroxyphenyl)-2-propenoic acid which strongly inhibited xanthine oxidase *in vitro* (Nakanishi *et al.*, 1990). Monoterpene glucosides, perillosides A and C, obtained from the

leaves inhibited the enzymatic activity of aldose reductase which is considered to be a key enzyme in diabetic complications such as cataract (Fujita *et al.*, 1995). Caffeic acid, methyl caffeate, rosmarinic acid, and luteolin 7-O-glucuronide-6"-methyl ester from the plant inhibited platelet derived growth factor-induced mesangial cell proliferation (Makino *et al.*, 1998). An aqueous extract of the plant showed significant inhibitory effects against HIV-1 induced cytopathogenicity in MT-4 cells (Yamasaki *et al.*, 1998) probably due to Pf-gp6, a 6 kDa glycoprotein (Kawahata *et al.*, 2002). Prenyl 3-benzoxepin derivatives, perilloxin and dehydroperilloxin, inhibited the enzymatic activity of cyclo-oxygenase 1 (Liu *et al.*, 2000). The plant inhibited mast cell-mediated degranulation in rats (Shin *et al.*, 2000).

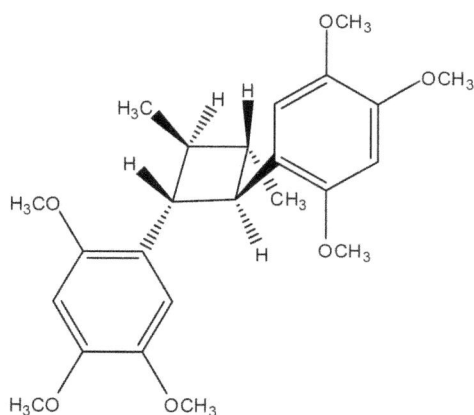

Magnosalin

Two lignans, magnosalin and andamanicin isolated from the plant inhibited inhibition of nitric oxide synthase and tumour necrosis factor-alpha expression in murine macrophage cell line RAW 264.7 (Ryu *et al.*, 2002). Takeda *et al.*, 2002 showed that rosmarinic acid which is present in the plant had antidepressive effects in rodents. Rosmarinic acid reduced lipopolysaccharide (LPS)-induced liver injury in D-galactosamine (D-GalN)-sensitized mice (Osakabe *et al.*, 2002) and inhibited skin tumorigenesis induced by 7,12-dimethylbenz[a]anthracene (DMBA) and promoted by application of 12-tetradecanoylphorbol 13-acetate (TPA) in rodents (Osakabe *et al.*, 2004). An extract of the plant showed an antiproliferative effect in human hepatoma HepG2 cells via apoptosis (Lin *et al.*, 2007)

References: Fujita T, Ohira K, Miyatake K, Nakano Y, Nakayama M, 1995, Inhibitory effects of perillosides A and C, and related monoterpene glucosides on aldose reductase and their structure-activity relationships. Chem Pharm Bull (Tokyo); 43: 920-6.

Honda G, Koezuka Y, Tabata M, 1988, Isolation of dillapiol from a chemotype of *Perilla frutescens* as an active principle for prolonging hexobarbital-induced sleep. Chem Pharm Bull (Tokyo), 36: 3153-5.

Kawahata T, Otake T, Mori H, Kojima Y, Oishi I, Oka S, Fukumori Y, Sano K, 2002, A novel substance purified from *Perilla frutescens* Britton inhibits an early stage of HIV-1 replication without blocking viral adsorption. Antivir Chem Chemother; 13: 283-8.

Lin CS, Kuo CL, Wang JP, Cheng JS, Huang ZW, Chen CF, 2007, Growth inhibitory and apoptosis inducing effect of *Perilla frutescens* extract on human hepatoma HepG2 cells. J Ethnopharmacol; 112: 557-67.

Liu J, Steigel A, Reininger E, Bauer R, 2000, Two new prenylated 3-benzoxepin derivatives as cyclooxygenase inhibitors from *Perilla frutescens* var. acuta. J Nat Prod; 63: 403-5.

Makino T, Ono T, Muso E, Honda G, 1998, Inhibitory effect of *Perilla frutescens* and its phenolic constituents on cultured murine mesangial cell proliferation. Planta Med; 64: 541-5.

Nakanishi T, Nishi M, Inada A, Obata H, Tanabe N, Abe S, Wakashiro M, 1990, Two new potent inhibitors of xanthine oxidase from leaves of *Perilla frutescens* Britton var. acuta Kudo. Chem Pharm Bull (Tokyo); 38: 1772-4.

Osakabe N, Yasuda A, Natsume M, Sanbongi C, Kato Y, Osawa T, Yoshikawa T, 2002, Rosmarinic acid, a major polyphenolic component of *Perilla frutescens*, reduces lipopolysaccharide (LPS)-induced liver injury in D-galactosamine (D-GalN)-sensitized mice. Free Radical Biol Med; 33: 798-806.

Osakabe N, Yasuda A, Natsume M, Yoshikawa T, 2004, Rosmarinic acid inhibits epidermal inflammatory responses: anticarcinogenic effect of *Perilla frutescens* extract in the murine two-stage skin model. Carcinogenesis; 25: 549-57.

Ryu JH, Son HJ, Lee SH, Sohn DH, 2002, Two neolignans from *Perilla frutescens* and their inhibition of nitric oxide synthase and tumor necrosis factor-alpha expression in murine macrophage cell line RAW 264.7. Bioorg Med Chem Lett; 12: 649-51.

Shin TY, Kim SH, Kim SH, Kim YK, Park HJ, Chae BS, Jung HJ, Kim HM, 2000, Inhibitory effect of mast cell-mediated immediate-type allergic reactions in rats by *Perilla frutescens*. Immunopharmacol Immunotoxicol; 22 :489-500.

Takeda H, Tsuji M, Matsumiya T, Kubo M, 2002, Identification of rosmarinic acid as a novel antidepressive substance in the leaves of *Perilla frutescens* Britton var. acuta Kudo (*Perillae Herba*). Nihon Shinkei Seishin Yakurigaku Zasshi; 22: 15-22.

Ueda H, Yamazaki C, Yamazaki M, 2002, Luteolin as an anti-inflammatory and anti-allergic constituent of *Perilla frutescens*. Biol Pharm Bull; 25: 1197-202.

Zhang Z, Su C, Chen D, 1990, Comparison of bacteriostatic ability of oleum of *Perilla frutescens* (L.) Britt., Cinnamomum cassia Presl and nipagin A. Zhongguo Zhong Yao Za Zhi; 15(2): 95-7.

Yamamoto H, Ogawa T, 2002, Antimicrobial activity of perilla seed polyphenols against oral pathogenic bacteria. Biosci Biotechnol Biochem; 66: 921-4.

Yamasaki K, Nakano M, Kawahata T, Mori H, Otake T, Ueba N, Oishi I, Inami R, Yamane M, Nakamura M, Murata H, Nakanishi T, 1998, Anti-HIV-1 activity of herbs in Labiatae. Biol Pharm Bull; 21: 829-33.

Figure 194: *Perrila frutescens* (L.) Britt.
From: Herbarium of Northeast Louisiana University, Monroe. Flora of Louisiana
USA, in woods along USFS 530 at Rattan Creek, Southwest of Pacton Kisatchie National
Forest, Sec. 23. Collection and identification: Keith H Kessler.

Scutellaria discolor Colebr.

[From Latin *scutella* = a small dish and from *discolor* = without color]

Local name:	Yenakhat (India), yi se huang qin (China), nilo butte ghans, daampaate (Nepal), jawer kotok, amperu lemah, daun kukur (Indonesia), nilam bukit, toma (Malaysia).
Synonym:	*Scutellaria discolor* Wallich ex Bentham, *Scutellaria cyrtopoda* Miq., *Scutellaria heteropoda* Miq., *Scutellaria zollingeriana* Briq.
Description:	It is a little delicate erect herb which grows, mostly on shaded grassy slopes, streamsides and roadsides in a geographical area covering North India, China, Cambodia, India, Indonesia, Laos, Malaysia, Burma, Nepal, Thailand, Papua New Guinea, and Vietnam. The herb is perennial, hairy, rhizomatous and grows to about 30 cm tall. The stem is erect, slender, hairy, light green, and few branched. The leaves are simple, opposite and without stipules. The petiole is 2 - 6 cm long and minutely grooved, dull light violet and winged. The leaf blade is elliptic-ovate to broadly elliptic, 3 - 5.2 cm x 1.5 -2 cm, papery, dull green above, light green underneath, acute to round at the base, and the apex, crenate at the margin, with 3 - 4 pairs of secondary nerves. The inflorescences are terminal spikes which are about 10 cm long. The calyx is light green, about 0.2 cm long, bilobed, hairy at the base, curved and with a scale on its back. The corolla is bilabiate, 0.7 - 1 cm long, the upper lip blue, the lower blue with white palate ridges, the base of the tube bent. The lower pair of stamens protrude out of the corolla along the lower lip. The fruits are brown nutlets which are ovoid-ellipsoid, about 1 mm in diameter (Figure 195).
Medicinal uses:	In Nepal the plant is used for colds, cuts, and insect stings. In Indonesia, the plant is used to assuage pains.
Pharmacology:	To date the pharmacological property of *Scutellaria discolor* Colebr. are unexplored. The plant contains a series of flavonoids including chrysin, wogonin, apigenin, luteolin, 5,7-dihydroxy-8,2'-dimethoxyflavone, 5,7,4'-trihydroy-8-methoxyflavone, 5,7-dihydroxy-8,2', 6'-trimethoxyflavone and chrysin 7-O-glucuronide, 5,7,8-trihydroxyflavone 8-O-beta-D-glucuronopyranoside and 5,7,2', 6'-tetrahydroxy-8-methoxyflavone 2'-O-beta-D-(2-O-caffeoyl)glucopyranosidepinocembrin, 7-hydroxy-5,8-dimethoxyflavone, 5,7,4'-trihydroxy-8-methoxyflavone, 5,7,2'-trihydroxy-8,6'-dimethoxyflavone, norwo-

gonin 7-O-beta-D-glucuronopyranoside, 7-hydroxy-5,8,2'-tri-methoxyflavone and 5,7-dihydroxy-8,2', 6'-trimethoxyflavone (Tomimori *et al.*, 1985, 1986, 1988) and neoclerodane diterpenes (Ohmo *et al.*, 1996) . Wogonin is probably involved in the anti-inflammatory use mentioned above.

References: Lin CC, Shieh DE, 1996, The anti-inflammatory activity of *Scutellaria rivularis* extracts and its active components, baicalin, baicalein and wogonin. Am J Chin Med. 1996; 24: 31-6.

Ohno A, Kizu H, Tomimori T, 1996, Studies on Nepalese crude drugs. XXXI. On the diterpenoid constituents of the Aerial Part of *Scutellaria discolor* COLEBR. Chem Pharm Bull; 44: 1540-1545.

Tomimori T, Miyaichi Y, Imoto Y, Kizu H, Namba T, 1985, Studies on Nepalese crude drugs. V. on the flavonoid constituents of the root of *Scutellaria discolor* Colebr. (1). Chem. Pharm. Bul; 33: 4457-4463.

Tomimori T, Miyaichi Y, Imoto Y, Kizu H, Namba T, 1986, Studies on Nepalese crude drugs. VI. On the flavonoid constituents of the root of *Scutellaria discolor* Colebr. (2). Chem. Pharm. Bul. 34: 406-08.

Tomimori T, Miyaichi Y, Imoto Y, Kizu H, Namba T, 1988, Studies on the Nepalese rude Drugs. XI. : On the Flavonoid Constituents of the Aerial Parts of *Scutellaria discolor* COLEBR. Chem Pharm Bull (Tokoy); 36: 3654-58.

Figure 195: *Scutellaria discolor* Colebr.
Thailand, Chiang Mai (Province), Doi Chiang Dao animal sanctuary, East of Huny Hae, Gawk Station. Altitude 1500 m. Date of collection: 10 September 1995. Collector and identification: JF Maxwell N° 93-646.

Scutellaria rivularis Wall. ex Benth.

[From Latin *scutella* = a small dish and from *rivularis* = growing by streams]

Local name: Skullcap, ban zhi lian (China).

Synonyms: *Scutellaria adenophylla* Miq; *Scutellaria cavaleriei* H. Lév. & Vaniot; *Scutellaria komarovii* H. Lév. & Vaniot; *Scutellaria minor* L. var. *indica* Benth;

Description: It is an erect herb which grows in moist mud, rice fields, and open watery areas of the Himalayas, Nepal, India, China, Taiwan, Japan, Korea, Laos, Burma, Thailand, and Vietnam. The stem is erect, green, up to 50 cm tall, and glabrous. The leaves are simple, decussate and without stipules. The petiole is about 0.2 cm long and slender. The leaf blade is dark green above, triangular-ovate to ovate-lanceolate, 0.2 - 0.4 cm x 0.7 - 3.2 cm, broadly cuneate at the base, laxly crenate at the margin, and acute at the apex. The flowers are axillary. The flower pedicel is 0.1 - 0.2 cm long. The calyx is about 0.2 cm long and maroon at the margin. The corolla is bilabiate, lilac, 0.9 -1.3 cm long, and the middle lobe of lower lip is rectangular. The anthers are purple. The fruits are brown nutlets, which are, warty, tiny and packed in a persistent calyx (Figure 196)

Medicinal Uses: In China, the plant is used is used to treat internal injuries and lumbago.

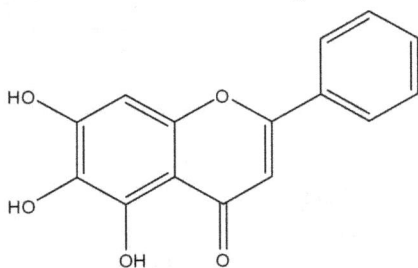

Baicalein

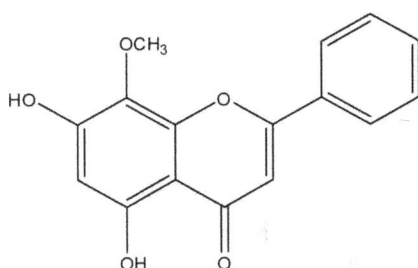

Wogonin

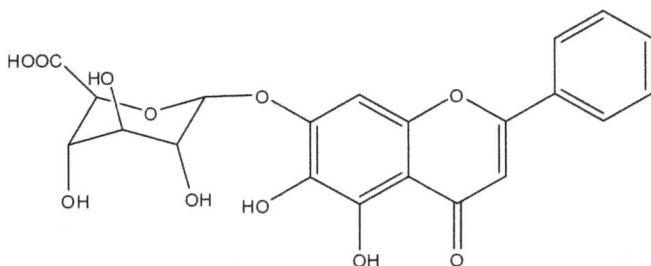

Baicalein

Pharmacology:

An aqueous extract of *Scutellaria rivularis* Wall. ex Benth. protected rats against carbon tetrachloride-induced liver fatty degeneration and cell necrosis (Chiu *et al.*, 1992). This effect is probably mediated by flavonoids which abound in the plant, such as baicalin, baicalein and wogonin. Wogonin inhibited the enzymatic activity of cyclooxygenase-2 both *in vitro* and *in vivo* (Park *et al.*, 2001). Baicalin exhibited anti-inflammatory activity against carrageenan-induced paw oedema in rats (Lin *et al.*, 1996). Baicalein, baicalin and wogonin are antioxidants and inhibit the enzymatic activity of xanthine oxidase. Baicalein and baicalin exhibited scavenging activity for superoxide radicals (Lin *et al.*, 1996). Baicalein, baicalin and wogonin are cytotoxic. Baicalin exhibited a strong antiproliferative activity against human bladder cancer cell lines (KU-1 and EJ-1) and a murine bladder cancer cell line (MBT-2). Wogonin and baicalein inhibited the proliferation of several cancer cell lines and the plant has been described as crude clinical antitumour drug (Sonoda *et al.*, 2004). Baicalin exhibited a remarkable cytotoxic effect against acute lymphoblastic leukemia CCRF-CEM cell line cultured *in vitro* via fragmentation of cellular DNA and arrest of the cell cycle at G(0)/G(1) phase and activation of caspase-3 (Shieh *et al.*, 2006). The flavonoids induced apoptosis in human promyelocytic leukemia HL-60 cells (Lu *et al.*, 2007). Wogonin is antiviral against respiratory syncytial virus (Ma *et al.*, 2002), and exerted anxiolytic effect through positive allosteric modulation of the GABA$_A$ receptor in rodent (Hui *et al.*, 2002). Baicalein prevented neurotoxicity induced by both glutamate and glucose deprivation (Lee *et al.*, 2003) and wogonin inhibited excitotoxic and oxidative neuronal damage in primary cultured rat cortical cells (Cho *et al.*, 2004). Wogonin is antiviral against hepatitis B virus activity *in vitro* and *in vivo* (Guo *et al.*, 2007).

References:

Chiu HF, Lin CC, Yen MH, Wu PS, Yang CY, 1992, Pharmacological and pathological studies on hepatic protective crude drugs from Taiwan (V): The effects of *Bombax malabarica* and *Scutellaria rivularis*. Am J Chin Med. 1992; 20: 257-64.

Cho J, Lee HK, 2004,Wogonin inhibits excitotoxic and oxidative neuronal damage in primary cultured rat cortical cells. Eur J Pharm; 485: 105-110.

Guo Q, Zhao L, You Q, Yang Y, Gu H, Song G, Lu N, Xin J, 2007, Anti-hepatitis B virus activity of wogonin *in vitro* and *in vivo*. Antiviral Res; 74: 16-24.

Hui KM, Huan MSY, Wang HY, Zheng H, Sigel E, Baur R, Ren H, Li ZW, Wong TF, Hong Xue H, 2002, Anxiolytic effect of wogonin, a benzodiazepine receptor ligand isolated from Scutellaria baicalensis Georgi. Biochem Pharmacol; 64: 1415-1424.

Ikemoto S, Sugimura K, Yoshida N, Yasumoto R, Wada S, Yamamoto K, Kishimoto T, 2000, Antitumor effects of Scutellariae radix and its components baicalein, baicalin, and wogonin on bladder cancer cell lines. Urology; 55: 951-955.

Lee HH, Yang LL, Wang CC, Hu SY, Chang SF, LeeYH, 2003, Differential effects of natural polyphenols on neuronal survival in primary cultured central neurons against glutamate- and glucose deprivation-induced neuronal death. Brain Research; 986: 103-113.

Lin CC, Shieh DE, 1996, The anti-inflammatory activity of Scutellaria rivularis extracts and its active components, baicalin, baicalein and wogonin. Am J Chin Med; 24: 31-6.

Lu HF, Hsueh SC, Ho YT, Kao MC, Yang JS, Chiu TH, Huamg SY, Lin CC, Chung JG, 2007, ROS mediates baicalin-induced apoptosis in human promyelocytic leukemia HL-60 cells through the expression of the Gadd153 and mitochondrial-dependent pathway. Anticancer Res; 27: 117-25.

Ma SC, Du J, But PPH, Deng XL, Zhang YW, Ooi VEC, Xu HX, Lee SHS, Lee SF, 2002, Antiviral Chinese medicinal herbs against respiratory syncytial virus. J Ethnopharmacol; 79: 205-211.

Park BK, Heo MY, Park H, Kim HP, 2001, Inhibition of TPA-induced cyclooxygenase-2 expression and skin inflammation in mice by wogonin, a plant flavone from Scutellaria radix. Eur Journal Pharm; 425: 153-157.

Shieh DE, Cheng HY, Yen MH, Chiang LC, Lin CC, 2006, Baicalin-induced apoptosis is mediated by Bcl-2-dependent, but not p53-dependent, pathway in human leukemia cell lines. Am J Chin Med; 34: 245-61.

Son D, Lee P, Lee J, Kim H, Kim SY, 2004, Neuroprotective effect of wogonin in hippocampal slice culture exposed to oxygen and glucose deprivation. Eur J Pharm; 493: 99-102.

Sonoda M, Nishiyama T, Matsukawa Y, Moriyasu M, 2004, Cytotoxic activities of flavonoids from two Scutellaria plants in Chinese medicine. J Ethnopharmacol; 91: 65-8.

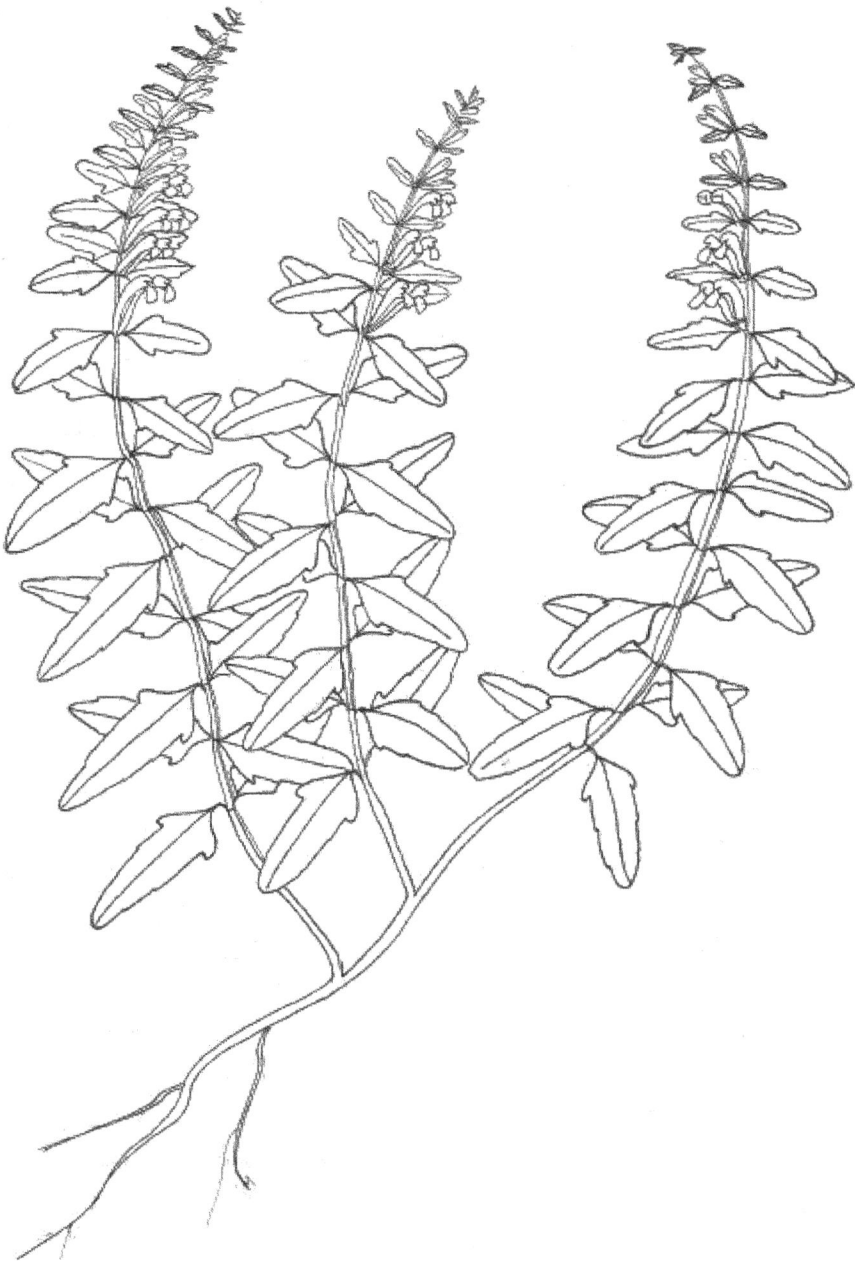

Figure 196: *Scutellaria rivularis* **Wall. ex Benth.**
From: Flora of Thailand, prince of Songkla University
Thailand, Chien Mai province, Mae Jun district, Ban Haipattana, Nongbagaio subdistrict.
Elevation 600 m. Date of collection: 23 August 1985. Collection and identification: JF Maxwell,
N° 85-823.

Teucrium viscidum Bl.

[After Teucer, first king of Troy and Latin *viscidum* = viscid]

Local name:	Sticky germander; xue jian chou (China)
Synonym:	*Teucrium stoloniferum* Roxb.
Description:	It is a deciduous perennial herb which grows in moist forests, ravines and thickets on slopes in a geographical area covering China, Taiwan, India, Indonesia, Japan, Korea, Thailand, Burma and the Philippines. The plant grows to a height of 1.5 m. The stem is dull green, quadrangular, hirsute, velvety. Internodes 6.5 to 8 cm long , the node with a sunken ring. Leaves simple, decussate and without stipules. The petiole is dull green, hairy and 1 - 3 cm long. The leaf blade is dull dark green above, dull light green beneath, oblong lanceolate, rounded at the base, acute at the apex, serrate at the margin with 6 pairs of secondary nerves, 1.6 - 3 cm x 4.2 - 7.5 cm, hairy. The secondary nerves are inconspicuous above. The inflorescence is a terminal and axillary dull dark maroon spike, which is hairy, and 3.5 - 7 cm long. The calyx is dull dark maroon, campanulate tubular, hairy, 5 lobed and 0.4 cm long. The corolla is whitish mixed with bluish and lilac, 0.7 x 0.3 m long with a prominent lower lip, The stamens and style protrude out of the corolla tube. The anthers are orange. The filament, stigmas and style are very pale light greenish. The fruits are tiny yellow-brown nutlets (Figure 197).
Medicinal uses:	In China, the plant is used as an antidote for poison, and to treat boils, ulcers and other skin diseases. In Cambodia, Laos and Vietnam, the plant is used to break fever and to invigorate.

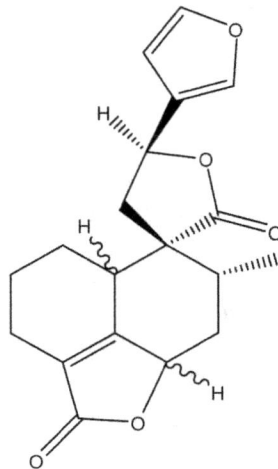

6 b = H, 10 b = H, Teucvin
6 a = H, 10 a = H, Teucvidin

Pharmacology: *Teucrium viscidum* Bl. is known to contain series of diterpenoids including teucvin, teuflin and teucvidin (Node *et al.*, 1981) but it has not been studied for pharmacology. Other members of the genus *Teucrium* have been the subject of several pharmacological and toxicological studies which revealed antipyretic properties in both yeast and carrageenan pyrexia in rats (Autore *et al.*, 1984). Hypoglycemic (Gharaibeh *et al.*, 1988), anti-inflammatory (Tariq *et al.*, 1989), hypolipidemic (Rasekh *et al*, 2001), analgesic (Abdollahi *et al.*, 2003), anti-oxidant (Kadifkova Panovska *et al.*, 2005), and antimicrobial effects have been observed (Ahmad *et al.*, 2008). Note that the plant is most probably hepatotoxic (Dourakis *et al.*, 2002)

References: Abdollahi M, Karimpour H, Monsef-Esfehani HR, 2003, Antinociceptive effects of *Teucrium polium* L total extract and essential oil in mouse writhing test. Pharmacol Res; 48: 31-5.

Ahmad B, Shah SM, Bashir S, Begum H, 2008, Antibacterial and antifungal activities of *teucrium royleanum* (Labiatea). J Enzyme Inhib Med Chem. 23: 136-9.

Autore G, Capasso F, De Fusco R, Fasulo MP, Lembo M, Mascolo N, Menghini A, 1984, Antipyretic and antibacterial actions of *Teucrium polium* (L.). Pharmacol Res Commun; 16: 21-9.

Dourakis SP, Papanikolaou IS, Tzemanakis EN, Hadziyannis SJ, 2002, Acute hepatitis associated with herb (*Teucrium capitatum* L.) administration. Eur J Gastroenterol Hepatol; 14: 693-5.

Gharaibeh MN, Elayan HH, Salhab AS, 1988, Hypoglycemic effects of *Teucrium polium*. J Ethnopharmacol; 24: 93-9.

Kadifkova Panovska T, Kulevanova S, Stefova M, 2005, *In vitro* antioxidant activity of some *Teucrium* species (Lamiaceae); 55: 207-14.

Node N, Sai M, Fujita E, 1981, Isolation of the diterpenoid teuflin (6-epiteucvin) from *Teucrium viscidum* var. *miquelianum*. Phytochemistry; 20: 757-760.

Rasekh HR, Khoshnood-Mansourkhani MJ, Kamalinejad M, 2001,Hypolipidemic effects of *Teucrium polium* in rats. Fitoterapia; 72: 937-9.

Tariq M, Ageel AM, al-Yahya MA, Mossa JS, al-Said MS, 1989, Anti-inflammatory activity of *Teucrium polium*. Int J Tissue React; 11: 185-8.

Figure 197: *Teucrium viscidum* Bl.

From Flora of Thailand
Thailand, Chiang Mai province, Muang district, Doi Sutep-Pui national park. Altitude 1550 m.
Date of collection: 27 december 1995. Collection and identification: JF Maxwell. Nº 95-1305

3.Family VERBENACEAE Jaume St. - Hilaire 1805 nom. conserv., the Verbena Family

The family Verbenaceae regroups about 100 genera and 2,600 species of herbs, climbers, shrubs or trees known to produce iridoids glycosides, phenolic glycosides (orobranchin), flavonoids, oleananes triterpenes, clerodane diterpenes and naphthoquinones. The stem is quadrangular. The leaves are compound, decussate and without stipules. The inflorescences are often terminal and cymose or racemose. The flowers are zygomorphic and colourful. The Perianth comprises a tubular and 5 - lobed calyx and a tubular corolla. The corolla is 5 lobed and often bilabiate. The androecium is made of 4 stamens, the anthers of which are dithecal, tetrasporangiate and open by longitudinal slits. The filaments are attached to the corolla and alternate with the lobes. The gynoecium consists of 2 carpels joined to form a 4 locular ovary, each locule enclosing a single ovule attached to axile placentas. The fruits are berries or capsules.

Several Verbenaceae are ornamental. One of these is *Lantana camara* (yellow sage, common Lantana) the fruits of which have been responsible for poisoning of children on account of pentacyclic triterpene derivative lantadene A and B which provoke cholestasis, hepatic necrosis, gastroenteritis with bloody, watery faeces, weakness, paralysis of the limbs and death in 3-4 days. Trees are not so common in this family but *Tectona grandis* L. s. provides the commercial teak wood. The dried leaves of *Aloysia triphylla* (L'Hérit.) Britt. (*Lippia citriodorata* H.B. and K.) or lemon verbena is used to treat digestive and nervous ailments. *Vitex agnus - castus* L. (chaste tree) has been used medicinally since Ancient Greek times and is still used for the treatment of premenstrual syndrome and menopause. About 50 species of plants classified within the family Verbenaceae are of medicinal value in Asia - Pacific. To date the pharmacological potential of this large family is yet to be fully explored. The oleanane pentacyclic triterpenoid, oleanolic acid, isolated from a hexane fraction of *Lantana hispida* showed promising results against *Mycobacterium tuberculosis* H37Rv strain (Jiménez-Arellanes *et al*, 2007). Other oleananes of interest isolated from this family are maslinic acid and its diacetyl derivative which showed human DNA topoisomerase I inhibitory activity against various human solid tumour cell lines (Pungitore *et al.*, 2007) a series of cytotoxic clerodane diterpenes, including premnone C, have been isolated from this family (Chin *et al.*, 2006; Jones *et al.*, 2007). Adebajo *et al.* (2007), isolated 6beta-hydroxyipolamide, ipolamide and isoverbascoside with exhibited hypoglycemic properties *in vitro*.

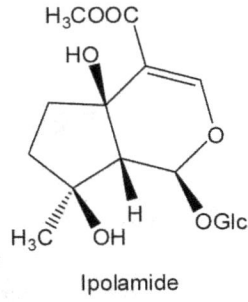

Ipolamide

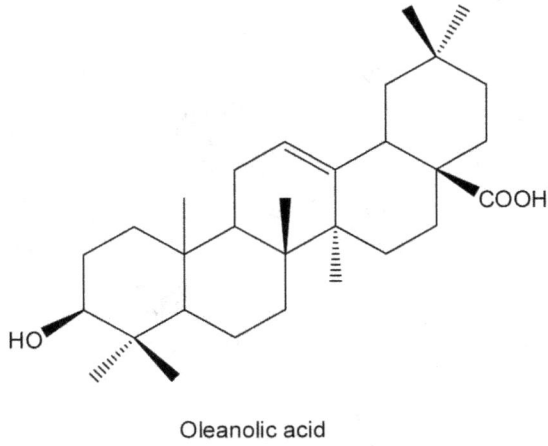

Oleanolic acid

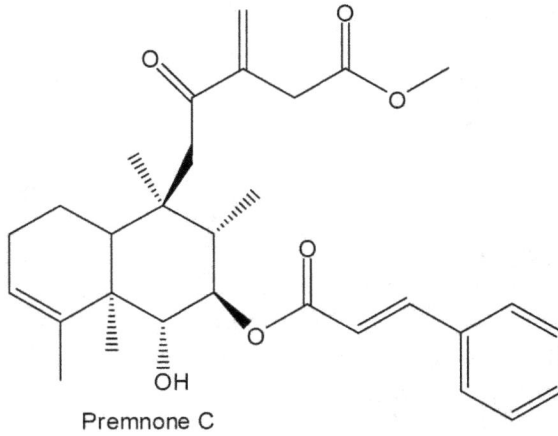

Premnone C

References:

Adebajo AC, Olawode EO, Omobuwajo OR, Adesanya SA, Begrow F, Elkhawad A, Akanmu MA, Edrada R, Proksch P, Schmidt TJ, Klaes M, Verspohl EJ, 2007, Hypoglycemic constituents of *Stachytarpheta cayennensis* leaf. Planta Med; 73: 241-50.

Chin YW, William, Jones WP, Mi Q, Rachman I, Riswan S, Kardono LBS, Chai HB, Farnsworth NR, Cordell GA, Swanson SM, Cassady JM, Kinghorn AD, 2006, Cytotoxic clerodane diterpenoids from the leaves of *Premna tomentosa* Phytochemistry, 67: 1243-48.

Jiménez-Arellanes A, Meckes M, Torres J, Luna-Herrera J, 2007, Antimycobacterial triterpenoids from *Lantana hispida* (Verbenaceae). J Ethnopharmacol; 111: 202-5.

Jones WP, Lobo-Echeverri T, Mi Q, Chai HB, Soejarto DD, Cordell GA, Swanson SM, Kinghorn AD, 2007, Cytotoxic constituents from the fruiting branches of *Callicarpa americana* collected in southern Florida. J Nat Prod; 70: 372-7.

Pungitore CR, Padron JM, Leon LG, Garcia C, Ciuffo GM, Martin VS, Tonn CE, 2007, Inhibition of DNA topoisomerase I and growth inhibition of human cancer cell lines by an oleanane from *Junellia aspera* (Verbenaceae). Cell Mol Biol; 53: 13-7.

Callicarpa candicans (Burm.f.) Hochr

[From the Greek *kallos* = beautiful and *karpos* = fruit and from Latin *candicans* = white]

Local name:	callicarpa; liwu liwu (Dusun), bai mao zi zhu (China)
Basionym:	*Urtica candicans Burm.* f. Flora Indica . . . nec non Prodromus Florae Capensis 197. 1768.
Synonyms:	*Callicarpa cana* L., *Urtica candicans* Burm. f.
Description:	It is a perennial shrub which grows up to 2 m tall in open land in a geographical area including Burma, Cambodia, Laos, Vietnam, Malaysia, India, Indonesia, Philippines, Thailand, Australia and the Pacific Islands. The stem is terete, hairy, and 0.2 to 0.3 cm in diameter The internodes are 4.5 - 6 cm long, and the nodes present a discrete ring. The leaves are simple, decussate and without stipule. The petiole is channeled, hairy, slender, 1 to 3.1 cm, minutely angular, and slightly kneeled near the stem. The leaf blade is papery, elliptic lanceolate, to spathulate, crenate at the margin except at the base, 12 - 18 cm x 2.8 - 5 cm , with about 10 pairs of secondary nerves conspicuous and hairy underneath. The inflorescences are 2 -4 cm across axillary and hairy cymes of tiny flowers. The calyx is cup -shaped, 0.2 cm long and covered with hairs. The corolla is pinkish to pink, tubular and about 2 mm long and 5 lobed. The stamens are about 0.4 cm long and protrude out of the corolla. The fruit is black-purple, glossy, and about 0.2 cm in diameter (Figure 198).
Medicinal Uses:	In Cambodia, Laos and Vietnam, the plant is used to stimulate the appetite of new mothers. Malays use the plant to assuage abdominal discomfort. In Indonesia the plant is used to heal wounds and boils and to promote menses. In the Philippines the leaves are used for asthma and stomachache. In India the plant is used for skin diseases.
Pharmacology:	The plant is known to contain a powerful fish poison: callicarpone, some hemisynthetic derivative of which exhibited antimycobacterial activity (McChesney *et al.*, 1979). Note that *Callicarpa* species including *Callicarpa candicans* (Burm.f.) Hochr merit further study since *Callicarpa* species elaborate phenylethanoid glycosides with neuroprotective properties. Such compounds are forsythoside B, acteoside, 2'-acetylacteoside, poliumoside, brandioside, echinacoside, isoacteoside, cistanoside H and E-tubuloside E and Z-tubuloside E from *Callicarpa dichotoma* which exhibited significant neuroprotective activity

against glutamate-induced neurotoxicity in primary cultured rat cortical cells (Koo *et al.*, 2005). Acteoside inhibited glutamate-induced intracellular Ca^{2+} influx resulting in overproduction of nitric oxide and reduced the formation of reactive oxygen species. It also preserved the mitochondrial membrane potential and the activities of antioxidative enzymes, such as superoxide dismutase, glutathione reductase and glutathione peroxidase which are reduced by glutamate. It was followed by the preservation of the level of glutathione and finally the inhibition of membrane lipid peroxidation (Koo *et al.*, 2006). Other interesting aspect of *Callicarpa* species is their tendency to elaborate a series of diterpenes with cytotoxic properties against several cancer cell - lines (Jones *et al.*, 2007).

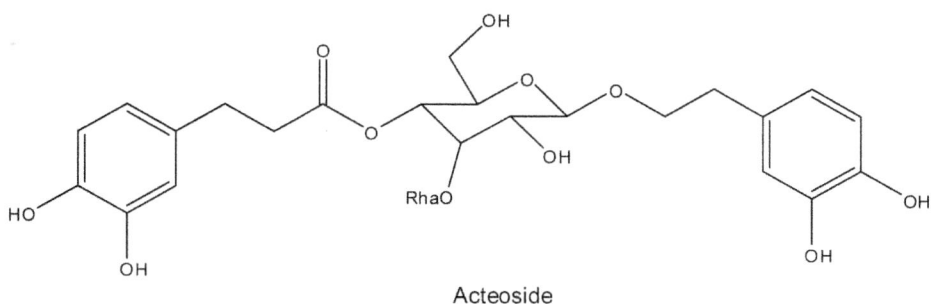

Acteoside

References:

Jones WP, Lobo-Echeverri T, Mi Q, Chai HB, Soejarto DD, Cordell GA, Swanson SM, Kinghorn AD, 2007, Cytotoxic constituents from the fruiting branches of *Callicarpa americana* collected in southern Florida. J Nat Prod. 70: 372-7.

Koo KA, Sung SH, Park JH, Kim SH, Lee KY, Kim YC, 2005, In vitro neuroprotective activities of phenylethanoid glycosides from *Callicarpa dichotoma*. Planta Med; 71: 778-80.

Koo KA, Kim SH, Oh TH, Kim YC, 2006, Acteoside and its aglycones protect primary cultures of rat cortical cells from glutamate-induced excitotoxicity. Life Sci; 79: 709-16.

McChesney JD, Kabra PM, Fraher P, 1979, Simple analogs of the toxin callicarpone. J Pharm Sci.; 68: 1116-20.

Figure198: *Callicarpa candicans* **(Burm.f.) Hochr**
From: Flora of Sabah
Sabah, Poring. Collector Joseph Punis Guntivid N° JPG-05

Callicarpa formosana Rolfe

[From the Greek *kallos* = beautiful and *karpos* = fruit and from Latin *formosana* = from Formosa]

Local names:	Taiwan beauty berry plant, du hong hua (China), balilli (Philippines)
Description.	It is a shrub which grows to a height of 3 m in a geographical area including China, Taiwan, Japan, and the Philippines. The plant has ornamental value. The stem petioles, and cymes are woolly. The stem is terete and about 0.4 cm in diameter. The internodes are 5 to 6 cm long. The leaves are simple, decussate and without stipules. The petiole is channeled, stout, and 1 - 2.5 cm long. The leaf blade is 13 - 19 cm x 4.7 - 12 cm, elliptic ovate, acute at the base and the apex, serrate at the margin. From near the base, shows about 8 pairs of woolly secondary nerves visible underneath. The inflorescences are axillary cymes of tiny flowers, which are about 3 - 8 cm across on a 1.5 -2.5 cm long peduncle. The calyx is cup-shaped, hairy, with 4 triangular lobes. The corolla is purple to purplish, about 0.25 cm long and 4 lobed. The anthers are 0.5 cm long with the style from the corolla protruding. The fruits are 0.2 cm glossy and purplish (Figure 199)
Medicinal uses:	In Taiwan the plant is used to check bleeding wounds, to treat venereal diseases and to promote menses. In the Philippines, the plant is used for asthma and it is considered as an indispensable companion in fishing sorties as it is used as fish poison.
Pharmacology:	Unknown.

Figure 199: *Callicarpa formosana* **Rolfe**
From: Flora of Taiwan, Herbarium, National Pintung Institute of Agriculture.
Philippines, Botel Tobago. Collector: C.E. Chang 16837. Date of collection: 6 April 1965.

Callicarpa longifolia Lamk.

[From the Greek *kallos* = beautiful and *karpos* = fruit and from Latin *longifolia* = with long leaves]

Local name: Long-leaved beauty-berry; chang ye zi zhu (China)

Synonym: *Callicarpa lanceolaria* Roxb., *Callicarpa albida* Bl., *Callicarpa roxburghiana* Roem. & Schult. , *Callicarpa attenuifolia* Elmer

Description: It is a shrub which grows in a geographical area covering Taiwan, China, India, Indonesia, Laos, Malaysia, Burma, Philippines, Thailand, and Vietnam. The plant reaches about 3 m tall. The stem is terete, obscurely angled, lenticelled, striated, the young parts hairy and about 0.4 cm in diameter. The internodes are 4.5 to 5 cm long. The nodes present a transverse scar. The leaves are simple, opposite and without stipules. The petiole is flattish, hairy, channeled, 0.7 to 1.5 cm long. The leaf blade is subglabrous, 6.7 - 14.5 cm x 2 - 4.8 cm, with 7 pairs of secondary nerves, and a few tertiary nerves, membranaceous, spathulate, tapering at the base, acuminate at the apex, serrate at the margin from near the base. The inflorescences are axillary cymes which are 2 - 3 cm across on, 0.5 -1.5 cm long peduncles. The calyx is cup-shaped, about 1 mm long, truncate and hairy. The corolla is pale purple, 0.2 cm long, and 5 lobed, the lobes ovate. The stamens protrude out of the corolla as well as the style. The fruit is globose, white pulpy, 0.15 cm in diameter and stellate pubescent (Figure 200).

Medicinal Uses: In Taiwan, the plant is used to heal wounds. Malays use the plant to treat abdominal complaints, fever, syphilis, sprue, and as a post-partum remedy. In Indonesia, the plant is used to heal wounds and check diarrhoea.

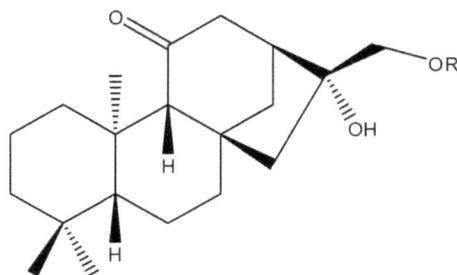

R = H, calliterpenone
R = OAc, calliterpenone monoacetate

Pharmacology: The pharmacological property of this plant is unknown. Subramaniam *et al.* (1974), isolated kaurane diterpenes; calliterpenone and calliterpenone monoacetate or, ent-1 l-oxokaurane-16,17-diol and its 17-acetate and a triterpene ursolic acid and traces of flavonoids. It would be of interest to assess the pharmacological properties of calliterpenone.

Reference: Subramanian SS, Nair AGR, Vedantham TNC, 1974, Terpenoids and flavones of *Callicarpa macrophylla* and *C. longifolia*. Phytochemistry; 13: 306-7.

Figure 200: *Callicarpa longifolia* Lamk.
From: Plants of Borneo, herbaria of Michigan State University.
Malaysia, Sabah, Ladah Datu district, near Segama river at confluence with Danum river. 5° 01' North - 117° 48' East. In logged forest.

Clerodendrum cyrtophyllum Turcz.

[From Greek *klero* = chance and *dendrum* = tree, *kyrtos* = arch and *phullon* = leaf

Local name: Da qing (China)

Description: It is a shrub or small tree that grows up to a height of 10 m in Korea, Malaysia, and Vietnam from an altitude of 500 to1700 m. The stem is terete, glabrous, with a few lenticels, 0.4 cm in diameter, yellow-brown, and with 2 - 2.5 cm internodes. The leaves are simple, opposite, decussate, and without stipules. The petiole is slender, deeply channeled, 2 - 3.3 cm long. The leaf blade is coriaceous, oblong - elliptic, or ovate-elliptic, 3.7 - 5.9 cm x 10 - 16 cm, papery, cuneate at the base, acuminate at the apex and shows 8 to 10 pairs of secondary nerves and a midrib sunken above. The leaf blade presents a few tertiary scalariform nerves underneath. The inflorescences are large, at the apex of stems, and corymbose, The flowers are fragrant. The calyx is yellow-brown, 0.3 - 0.4 cm, with 1 mm long lobes. The corolla is white, about 1 cm long with a slender tube from which originate 5 linear lobes which are 0.5 cm long. The stamens and style protrude from the corolla. The anthers are purple and the filaments green. The fruits are blue-purple, globose, 0.5 -1cm diameter glossy drupes (Figure 201)

Medicinal Uses: In Taiwan the plant is used to break malarial fever.

Pharmacology: *Clerodendrum cyrtophyllum* Turcz contain a pheophorbide derivative which exhibited some levels of cytotoxicity against human lung carcinoma (A549), ileocecal carcinoma (HCT-8), kidney carcinoma (CAKI-1), breast adenocarcinoma (MCF-7), malignant melanoma (SK-MEL-2), ovarian carcinoma (1A9), and epidermoid carcinoma of the nasopharynx (KB) cell lines cultured *in vitro* (Cheng H *et al.*, 2001).

References: Cheng HH, Wang HK, Ito J, Bastow KF, Tachibana Y, Nakanishi Y, Xu Z, Luo TY, Lee KH, 2001, Cytotoxic pheophorbide-related compounds from *Clerodendrum calamitosum* and *C. cyrtophyllum*; J Nat Prod, 64: 915-9.

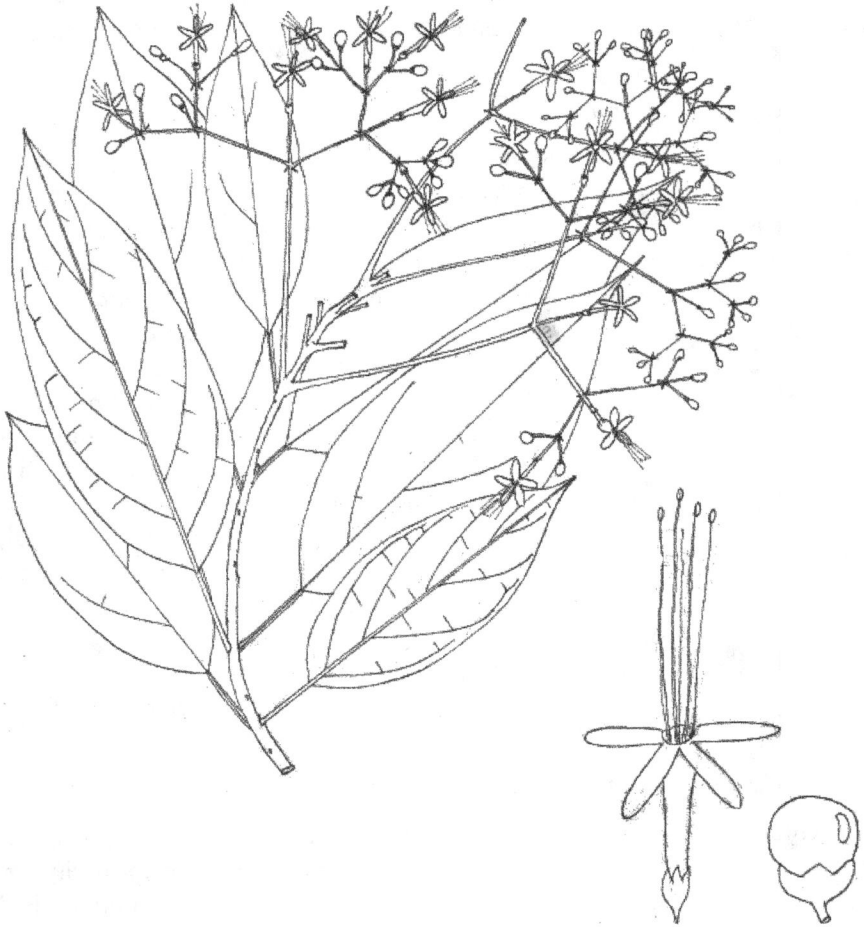

Figure 201: *Clerodedrum cyrtophyllum* Turcz.
From: Botanical Inventory of Taiwan.
Taiwan, Keelung city, Tawulunshan, Chingjenhu. 121° 42' 13" East - 25° 09' 37' North. Altitude 150 m. Collector: Wen-Pen Leu, WH HU and CY Leu. Date of collection: 1986.

Clerodendrum fragrans (Vent.) Willd.

[From Greek klero = chance and *dendrum* = tree and from Latin *fragrans* = fragrant]

Local names:	Glory bower, stick bush, chong ban xiu mo li (China)
Synonyms:	*Ovieda fragrans* (Willd.) Hitchc., *Clerodendrum chinense* (Osb.) Mabberley, *Clerodendrum fragrans* var. multiplex (Sweet) Moldenke, *Clerodendrum philippinum* Schauer
Description:	It is a shrub which grows to a height of 1.5 cm in China and Southeast Asia and is cultivated as a garden ornamental. The stem is discreetly quadrangular, glabrous except at the apex. The internodes are 1 - 6 cm long. The petiole is 5 - 10 cm long, 0.6 cm in diameter, hairy and channeled. The leaf blade is membranaceous, triangular, 6 - 12 cm x 10 - 17 cm, with 4 - 5 pairs of secondary nerves, some scalariform tertiary nerves underneath, the margin wavy and minutely toothed, velvety below. The inflorescences are terminal, dense corymbose cymes on a 3.5 cm long pedicel and look like a bunch of white roses. The bracts are dark pink. The cyme is about 6 cm in diameter. The pedicles and petioles are dark violet. The flower is fragrant. The calyx is maroon about 0.6 cm long cm, deeply 5-lobed. The corolla tube is cream about 2 cm long and produces 5 whitish pink broadly lanceolate lobes. The anthers are maroon. Anthers and style protrude from the corolla tube (Figure 202).
Medicinal Uses:	In China, the plant is used to treat weak legs, and skin diseases. In Cambodia, Laos and Vietnam, the plant is used to remove smallpox. In Malaysia, the plant is used to assuage rheumatism pains, swellings, to treat skin diseases and at childbirth.
Pharmacology:	*Clerodendrum fragrans* (Vent.) Willd., is known to contain caffeic acid, kaempferol, 5,4'-dihydroxy-kaempferol-7-O-beta-rutinoside, acteoside and leucoseceptoside A (Gao *et al.*, 2003) as well as iridoid diglucoside, 5-O-beta-glucopyranosyl-harpagide (Kanchanapoom *et al.*, 2005) and cholestane sterols (Akihisa *et al.*, 1988). The plant may have some value for the treatment of certain acute myelocytic leukemia putatively caused by a block in the myeloid differentiation process since promyelocytic cell line HL-60 exposed to an extract of the plant differentiated into morphologically and functionally mature monocytoid cells (Chen PM *et al.*, 1988).
References:	Akihisa T, Ghosh P, Thakur S, Oshikiri S, Tamura T, Matsumoto T, 1988, 24beta-methylcholesta-5,22E,25-trien-3beta-ol and 24alpha-ethyl-5alpha-cholest-22E-en-3beta-ol from *Clerodendrum fragrans*, Phytochemistry, 27: 241-244.
	Chen PM, Yung LL, Hsiao KI, Chen CM, Yeh HM, Chuang MH, Tzeng CH, 1988, *In vitro* induction of differentiation in HL-60

leukemic cell line by *clerodendron fragrans*. Am J Chin Med. 16: 139-44.

Gao LM, Wei XM, He YQ., 2003,Studies on chemical constituents in leafs of *Clerodendron fragrans,* Zhongguo Zhong Yao Za Zhi; 28: 948-51.

Kanchanapoom T, Chumsri P, Kasai R, Otsuka H, Yamasaki K, 2005, A new iridoid diglycoside from *Clerodendrum chinense.* J Asian Nat Prod Res; 7: 269-72.

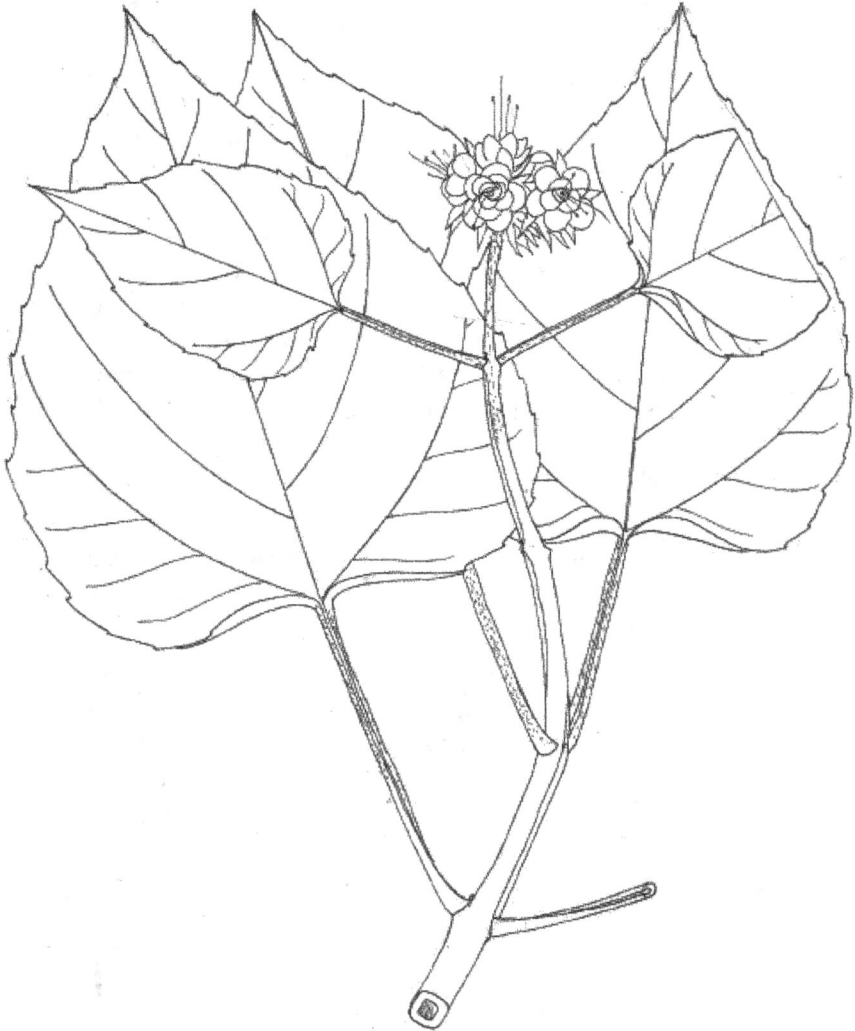

Figure 202:*Clerodendrum fragrans* (Vent.) Willd.,
From: Flora of Thailand, Chiang Mai University Herbarium.
Thailand, Lampang province, Muang Bahn (Pan), Jao Sawn National Park, Dah Niang Village area.
Elevation 1100 m. Date of collection: 28 May 1996. Collection and identification: JF Maxwell.

Clerodendrum infortunatum L.

[From Greek *klero* = chance and dendrum = tree]

Local names:	Ghetu flower, Indian Bhat tree, bhanti (Sanskrit), hka.aung:kri (Burma), perugilai (India), paw kwaw (Thailand).
Description:	It is shrub which grows to a height of 2.5 m in India, Burma, Thailand and Malaysia. The bark is thin. The stem is quadrangular and 0.5 cm diameter, and hairy at the apex. The leaves are simple, decussate and without stipules. The petiole is 0.35 - 0.4 cm x 9.5 cm and with a few hairs at first. The leaf-blade is dull green above, cordate to broadly lanceolate, thinly coriaceous, 5.2 - 11.5 cm x 15 - 20.2 cm, wavy at the margin, pilose on both surface, and presents about 6 - 10 pairs of secondary and tertiary nerves underneath. The inflorescences are about 20 cm long terminal cymes with dull maroon or pinkish axes. Flowers are fragrant. The calyx is red and 1.5 x 1 cm with lanceolate lobes. The corolla tube is dull red with 5 whitish lobes around a pink throat. The anthers are dark brown, with white filaments and protruding, with the style, out of the corolla tube (Figure 203).
Medicinal Uses:	In Burma, the plant is used as a tonic, an anthelminthic, a bitter and a febrifuge. In Cambodia, Laos and Vietnam, the plant is used as a remedy for angina and vaginal infection.
Pharmacology:	The plant contains clerodin, a bitter clerodane diterpene first isolated by Banerjee in 1936 and structurally indentified by Sim *et al.* (1961) and Paul *et al.* (1962). Four new crystalline compounds, clerodolone, clerodone, clerodol and a sterol, previously isolated but not characterized and now designated clerosterol, have been isolated from the root of *Clerodendron Infortunatum* Bhat. The plant contains a bitter diterpene, clerodin, which has insect antifeedant property. The pharmacological properties of clerodin and congeners needs further study.
References:	Banerjee AK, 1936, Clerodin from *Clerodendron infortunatum*. Science and Culture, 2, 163.
	Manzoor-Khuda M, Sarela S, 1965, Constituents of *clerodendron infortunatum* (bhat)-I Isolation of clerodolone, clerodone, clerodol and clerosterol. Tetrahedron, 21: 797-802.
	Paul IC, Sim GA, Hamor TA, Robertson JM, 1962, J. Chem. Soc, 4133 - 4145
	Sim A, Hamor A, Paul IC, Robertson JM, 1961, Proc. Chem. Soc, 75.

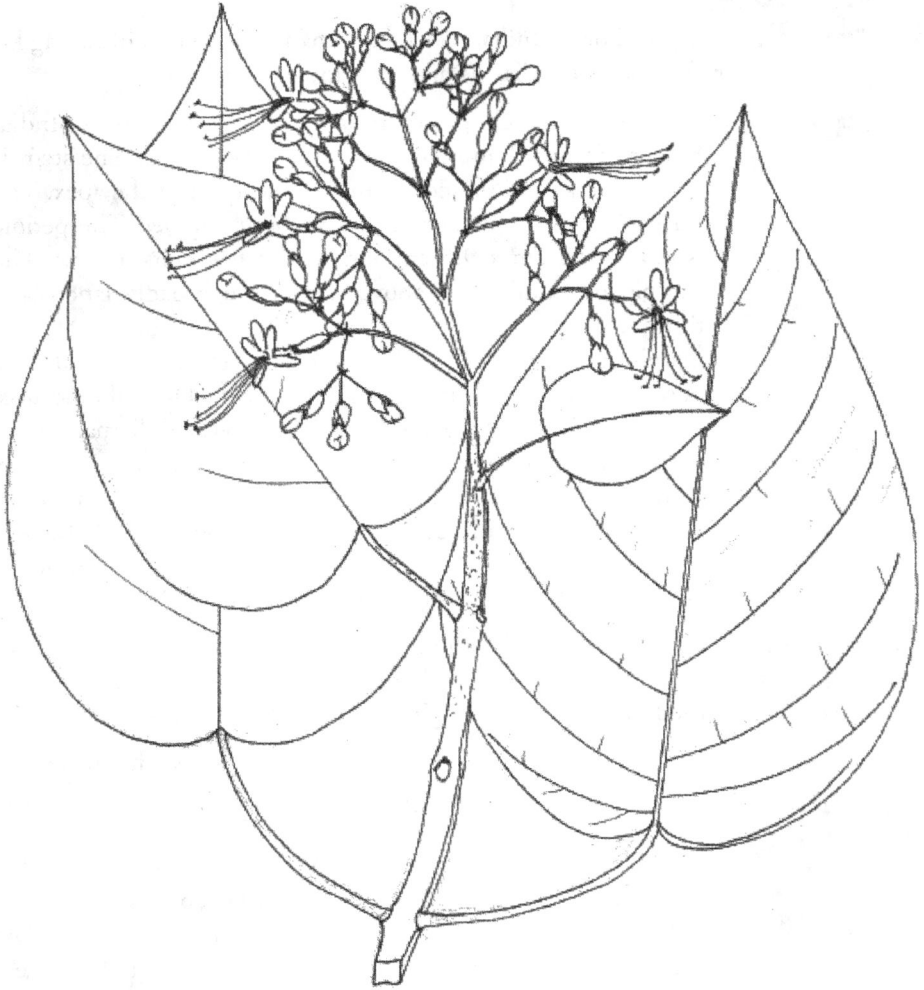

Figure 203:*Clerodendrum infortunatum* L.
From: Flora of Thailand, Chiang Mai University Herbarium
Kanchanaburi province, Sangklaburi district, Toong Yai Nareswan wildlife reserve. Lai Wo
subdistrict, Ban Saneh Pawng (Karen village), near Ro Kee stream. Altitude 200 m. Date of
collection: 15 April 1994.

Clerodendrum serratum (L.) Moon

[From Greek *klero* = chance and *dendrum* = tree, and from Latin serratum = Toothed like a saw]

Local names:	Blue fountain bush, bharngi (Sanskrit), sirutekku (India), lampin Badak (Malaysia), san dui jie (China).
Basionym:	*Volkameria serrata* L., *Mantissa Plantarum* 1: 90. 1767
Description:	It is a shrub which grows to a height of 4 m in China, Southeast Asia, India and East Africa from an altitude of 200 - 1800 m.

The stem is quadrangular, minutely hairy at the apex, lenticelled, fleshy with 4 - 6.5 cm long internodes. The leaves are opposite, simple and without stipules. The petiole is 0.7 cm long and non-channeled. The leaf blade is spathulate, serrate, acuminate at the apex, tapering at the base, 3 - 5.7 cm x 12 - 23.5 cm and presents 10 - 12 pairs of secondary nerves and a few tertiary nerves underneath. The inflorescences are terminal racemes of densely yellow-brown pubescent, cymes. The bracts are sessile, ovate to broadly ovate, and 1.5 - 4.5 cm x 0.5 - 1.8 cm. The calyx is tubular, glabrous, membranaceous, about 0.4 cm long and minutely 5-dentate. The corolla white, bluish, or purplish, 0.9 cm long, with 5 lobes which are oblong to obovate, and about 1 cm long. The stamens are 2 - 4 cm long and exerted. The style is long and exerted. The fruits, which are subglobose, are black and glossy (Figure 204).

Medicinal Uses: In India, the plant is used to treat in asthma, coughs, fever, worms, burning sensation of the body and wounds. In Burma, the plant is used to treat venereal diseases. In Cambodia, Laos and Vietnam, the plant is used for toothache. In Malaysia, the plant is given at childbirth, it also used as remedy for skin diseases, headaches, fever, arthritis, beriberi and leprosy. Indonesians use the plant to promote urination in venereal diseases. The plant is also used to expel worms from intestines, and to treat coughs.

Pharmacology: The anti-inflammatory effect of the plant has been assessed experimentally but the results obtained so far are somewhat contradictory. An ethanol extract of roots produced antinociceptive, anti-inflammatory and antipyretic activities in rodents (Narayanan N *et al.*, 1999) and prolonged administration of a plant saponin induced antihistamine and anti-allergic activities in rodents. (Gupta, 1968). However, an aqueous extract increased acid phosphatase and myeloperoxidase activity as well as a significant increase in the production of nitric oxide, hydrogen peroxide, and O_2 by macrophages cultured *in vitro*. Oral administration of this extract to rodents increased the total leukocyte count, which is a sign of pro-inflammation (Juvekar *et al.*, 2006). The healing properties of the plant have been assessed by Vidya *et al.* (2005). An ethanol extract of *Clerodendrum serratum* inhibited the growth of *Streptococcus pyogenes*-A and *Proteus mirabilis* (Narayanan *et al.*, 2004). An ethanol extract of roots exhibited hepatoprotective activity in male Wistar strain rats exposed to carbon tetrachloride (Vidyam *et al.*, 2007). The plant contains iridoid glycosides (Wei *et al.*, 2000), phenylpropanoid glycoside (serratumoside A) (Yang *et al.*, 2000), oleanolic acid. queretaroic acid, and serratagenic acid, (Rangaswami *et al.*, 1969)

References:

Gupta SS, 1968, Development of antihistamine and anti-allergic activity after prolonged administration of a plant saponin from Clerodendron serratum. J Pharm Pharmacol; 20: 801-2.

Juvekar AR, Nachankar RS, Hole RC, Wakade AS, Kulkarni MP, Ambaye RY, 2006, *In vitro* and *in vivo* immunomodulatory activity of aqueous extract of *Clerodendrum serratum* L. roots. Planta Med; 72.

Narayanan N, Thirugnanasambantham P, Viswanathan S, Vijayasekaran V, Sukumar E, 1999, Antinociceptive, anti-inflammatory and antipyretic effects of ethanol extract of *Clerodendron serratum* roots in experimental animals. J Ethnopharmacol; 65: 237-41.

Narayanan N, Thirugnanasambantham P, Viswanathan S, Rajarajan S, Sukumar E, 2004, Comparative antibacterial activities of *Clerodendrum serratum* and *Premna herbacea*, Indian J Pharm Sci; 66: 453-54.

Rangaswami S, Serengan S, 1969, Sapogenins of *Clerodendron serratum* Constitution of a new pentacyclic triterpene acid, serratagenic acid, Tetrahedron; 25: 3701-05.

Vidya, SM, Krishna V, Manjunatha BK, Singh SDJ, Mankani KL, 2005, Evaluation of wound healing activity of root and leaf extracts of *Clerodendrum serratum* L Indian Drugs-Bombay; 42: 609-13.

Vidya SM, Krishna V, Manjunatha BK, Mankani KL, Ahmed M, Singh SD, 2007, Evaluation of hepatoprotective activity of *Clerodendrum serratum* L. Indian J Exp Biol; 45: 538-42.

Wei, X. M. Zhu, Q. X. Chen, J. C. Cheng, D. L. , 2000, Two new iridoid glucosides from *Clerodendrum serratum*. Chin Chem Lett; 11: 415-16.

Yang H, Hou AJ, Mei SX, Peng LY, Sun HD, 2000, A new phenylpropanoid glycoside: Serratumoside A from *Clerodendrum serratum*, Chin Chem Lett; 11: 323-26.

Figure 204: *Clerodendrum serratum* **(L.) Moon**
From: Flora of Malaya, University Kebangsaan Malaysia Herbarium
Malaysia, Batu 20, Gombak, Selangor. Collection and identification: Hamid S., № 12616

Congea tomentosa Roxb.

[From Latin *tomentosa* = densely covered with matted wool or short hair]

Local names:	Wooly Congea, shower orchid, rong boa teng (China), eluvia de orquídeas (Spain)
Synonym:	*Congea tomentosa* var. *oblongifolia* Schauer.
Description:	It is a woody climber which grows at an altitude of 600 to 1200 m in China, Bangladesh, India, Laos, Burma, Thailand, Vietnam, and Malaysia. The plant is ornamental and several varieties have been produced. The basal stem is about 10 cm in diameter; the bark is thin, finely cracked and light brown. The stem is densely yellowish tomentose when young, becoming grayish, terete, lenticelled and slightly swollen and marked with a thin horizontal line. The internodes are about 7 cm long. The petiole is 0.5 - 1.3 cm, channeled, densely tomentose. The leaf blade is dull dark green, elliptic - lanceolate, with a minutely cordate the base, an acuminate the apex, 3.3 - 5.5 cm x 6.8 x 11.5 cm, thinly coriaceous, tomentose underneath, slightly wavy at the margin, and presents 5 - 6 pairs of secondary nerves, adaxially prominent. The inflorescences are axillary panicles of packed cymes of about 25 cm long, with dull grayish green. The involucral bracts are 3 or 4, white or grayish and turning purplish pink, oblong, obovate-oblong, or broadly elliptic, 2 -3 cm x 0.8 -1.2 cm, nerved, and tomentose. The calyx is light green, urceolate, tomentose, about 0.7 cm with minute triangular sepals. The corolla is white with red lines, bilabiate, about 0.6 cm long. The stamens are didynamous, and exerted with the style. The fruit is a drupe in a persistent calyx (Figure 205).
Medicinal Uses:	In Thailand, the roots of the plant are used to empty the bowels
Pharmacology:	To date not much is known about the pharmacological properties of *Congea tomentosa* Roxb. Leitao *et al.* (1997) found that the plant has some antiviral properties.
Reference:	Leitao, SG, Delle Menache F, Goncalves JLS, Wigg MD, 1997, Antiviral activity of *Congea tomentosa* leaf extracts. Boll. Chim. Farmaceut; 136: 120.

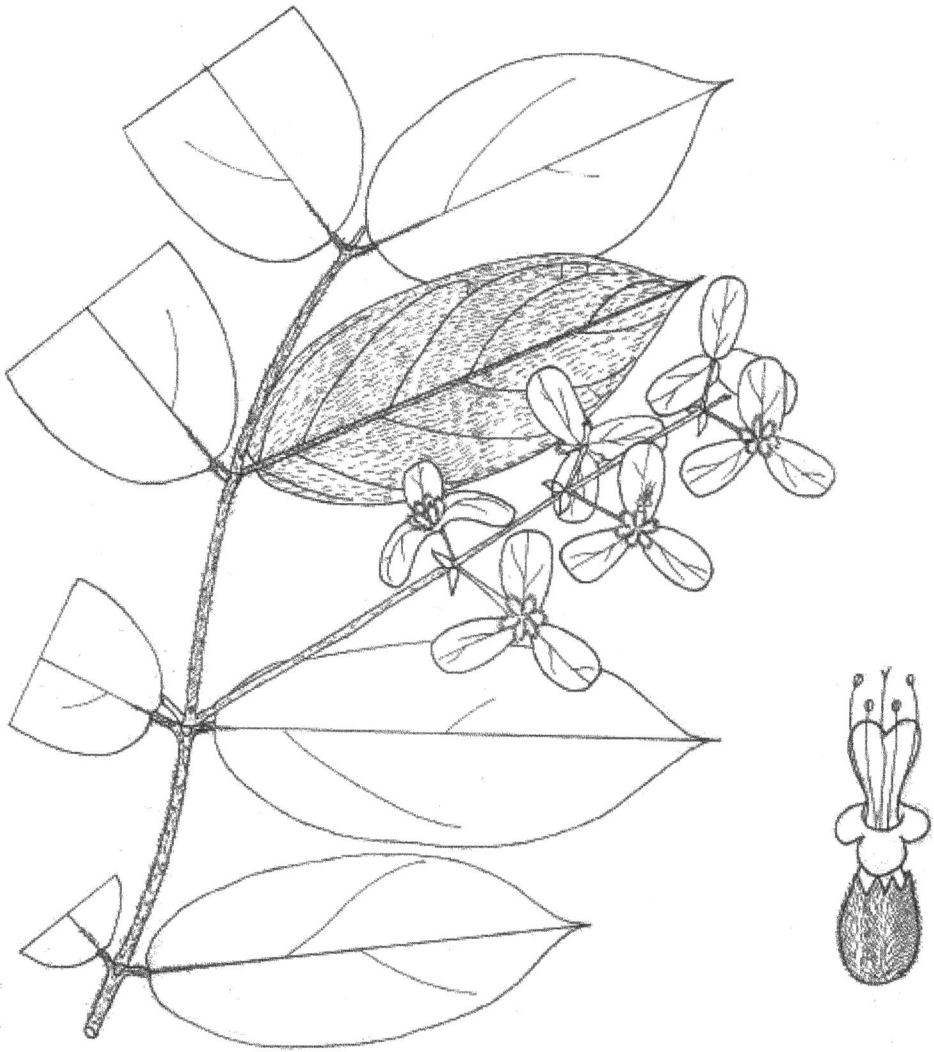

Figure 205: *Congea tomentosa* Roxb.
From: Flora of Thailand, Chiang Mai University Herbarium (HUKM N° 31489)
Thailand, Sukoh province, Kiriat district, Ramkahmbang National Park, the base of the East
side of Kao Lung, near Bin Panhg Falls. Along the main dirt road to park headquarter. Elevation
2225 m. Date of collection 2 February 1995.

Gmelina villosa Roxb.

[From Indian *gumudu* and Latin *villosa* = hairy]

Local names:
Parrot's Beak, bulangan (Malaysia), talungun (Philippines), rais Madre de Dios (Portuguese).

Synonym:
Gmelina elliptica Sm., *Gmelina asiatica* L. var. villosa (Roxb.) Bakh.

Description:
It is a tree of about 6m tall which grows in open thickets, along streams in Southeast Asia. The stem is terete, fissured longitudinally, with few lenticels, hairy to tomentose near the apex. Internodes are 4 - 6 cm long, the nodes being slightly swollen. Leaves are simple, exstipulate, sub-opposite, of different size by pairs, and without stipules. The petioles are slender, grooved above and tomentose at first, 2.5 - 4.5 cm x 1 mm. The leaf blade is broadly lanceolate, tomentose underneath, glossy above, wavy at the margin, 4 - 6 cm x 5.5 - 9 cm, broadly lanceolate with 3 - 4 pairs of secondary nerves sunken above. The tertiary nerves are visible on both surfaces of the leaf-blade. The inflorescence is a terminal tomentose raceme. The flower is small. The calyx is 0.6 x 0.1 cm. The corolla is 0.4 cm long. The fruit is ovoid, 1 - 1.5 cm x 0.3 - 0.1 cm and yellow (Figure 206).

Medicinal Uses:
Malays use the plant externally to treat headaches, heal swelling and to promote the growth of hair. Eating the leaves helps empty the bowels. Indonesians use the juices expressed from the fruits or leaves to assuage earaches.

Pharmacology:
To date knowledge on the pharmacological potential of *Gmelina villosa* Roxb is non-existent. Some studies refer to chemical constituents such as iridoids (Hosny *et al.*, 1998), phenolic glycosides (Satyanarayana *et al.*, 1985), lignans and flavonoids of related species. Lignans are interesting from a pharmaceutical point of view as they are know to be cytotoxic. It may be of interest to assess the cytotoxic properties of the lignans from this plant (Anjaneyulu *et al.*, 1975, 1977). An extract of *Gmelina asiatica* displayed a broad spectrum of antibacterial activities (Sudhakar *et al.*, 2006) and prominent oral antipyretic activity (Ikram *et al.*, 1987).

References:
Anjaneyulu ASR, Madhusudhana Rao A, Kameswara Rao V, Ramachandra Row L, Pelter A, Ward RS, 1977, Novel hydroxy lignans from the heartwood of *gmelina arborea*. Tetrahedron; 33: 133-43.

Anjaneyulu ASR, Rao KJ, Kameswara Rao VL, Ramachandra Row L, Subrahmanyam C, Pelter A, Ward RS, 1975, The structures of lignans from *Gmelina arborea* Linn. Tetrahedron; 31: 1277-85.

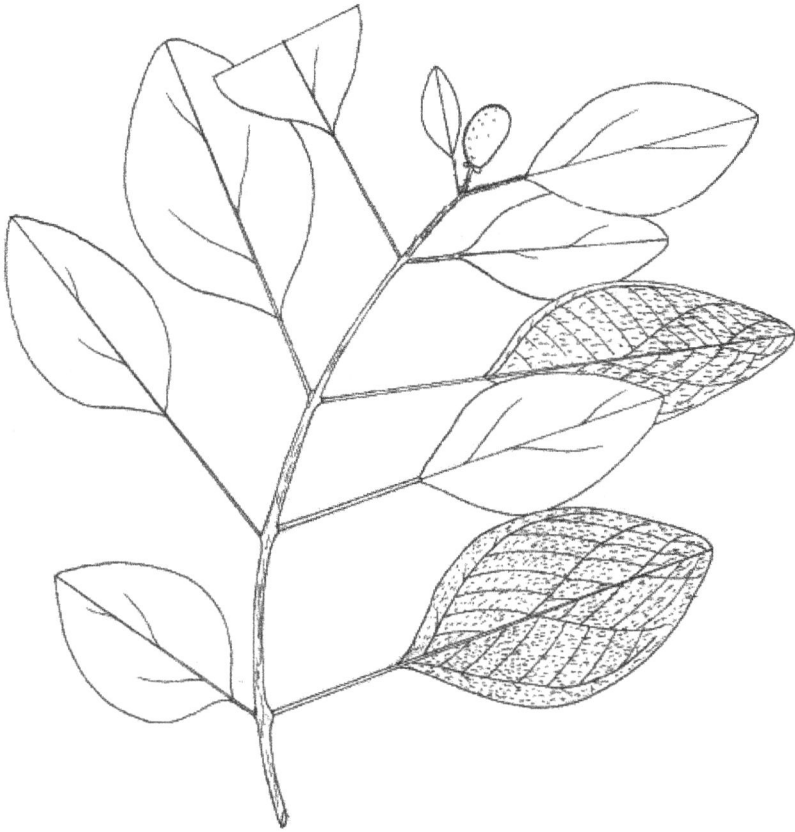

Figure 206: *Gmelina villosa* **Roxb.**
From: Flora of Thailand, Price of Songkla University, Herbarium UKM.
Thailand, Songkla province, Suan Dtoon Falls, Muang district. Elevation 200 m. Date of collection: 12 February 1985. Collection and Identification: JF Maxwell.

Hosny M, Rosazza JP, 1998, Gmelinosides A-L, twelve acylated iridoid glycosides from *Gmelina arborea*. J Nat Prod; 61: 734-42.

Ikram M, Khattak GS, Gilani SN, 1987, Antipyretic studies on some indigenous Pakistani medicinal plants: II. J Ethnopharmacol; 19: 185-92.

Satyanarayana P, Subrahmanyam P, Kasai R and Tanaka O, 1985, An apiose-containing coumarin glycoside from *Gmelina arborea* root Phytochemistry; 24: 1862-63.

Sudhakar M, Rao CV, Rao PM, Raju DB, 2006, Evaluation of antimicrobial activity of *Cleome viscosa* and *Gmelina asiatica*. Fitoterapia; 77: 47-9.

Premna corymbosa (Burm. f.) Rottler & Willd.

[From Greek *premnon* = dwarf stature and from Latin *corymbosa* = provided with corymbs]

Local names:	Muney-kerai (India), kaar (Marshall), serpoli (Bangladesh), taung-tan-kri, taung-taunggi (Burma)
Basionym:	*Cornutia corymbosa* Burm. f. *Flora Indica* . . . nec non Prodromus Florae Capensis 132, pl. 41, f. 1. 1768
Synonyms:	*Citharexylum paniculatum* Poir., *Cornutia corymbosa* Burm.f., *Premna cordifolia* Wight, *Premna integrifolia* L., *Premna scandens* Bojer, *Premna serratifolia* L., *Premna spinosa* Roxb.
Description:	It is a deciduous tree which grows to a height of about 12 m on the sandy beaches of India, Southeast Asia and Pacific Islands. The bole is curved and the bark is lenticelled. The stem is terete, glabrous, about 0.5 cm in diameter, and longitudinally striated. The nodes are minutely marked with a transversal ring. The internodes are 1 to 4 cm long. The leaves are simple, opposite, and without stipules. The petiole is glabrous, channeled above and 1.8 - 2.1 cm long. The leaf blade is 4.5 - 6.8 cm x 11.5 x 14 cm, broadly elliptic, obtuse, glabrous, thinly coriaceous, and wavy at the margin and presents about 4 - 6 pairs of secondary nerves which are slightly raised on both surfaces. Some tertiary nerves, sunken on both surfaces of the blade are visible. The inflorescences are terminal axillary corymbs on about 4 cm long pedicels. The corymbs are about 6 - 10 cm in diameter. The flowers are tiny, 2 mm in diameter. The calyx is cupular, hairy and presents a few teeth at the apex. The corolla is tubular with minute round lobes, greenish-white, and hairy at the throat. The androecium presents 4 stamens which protrude, with the style, discretely from the corolla . The fruit is glossy, globose, 3 mm in diameter, 3-4 seeded on a persistent calyx (Figure 207).
Medicinal Uses:	In Vietnam, the leaves and the roots are used in treating fever, diarrhoea, to promote digestion and urination, to assuage rheumatic pains and also as a galactagogue . It is used as a galactagogue in Cambodia, and Laos. In Burma the plant is used as a laxative, carminative, and stomachic. A decoction of the plant is drunk for fevers, rheumatism and neuralgia. In China, the plant is used for malaria. In Taiwan it is applied to contusions. In Indonesia the plant is used to treat infection of the lungs. In the Philippines, a tea of leaves is drunk to promote digestion and urination. In India, the plant is used for diabetes.

Pharmacology:

The antidiabetic property of the plant has been experimentally confirmed. An ethanol extract of *Premna corymbosa* (Burm. f.) Rottler & Willd brought down close to normal the fasting level of alloxan in diabetic albino rats (Kar A *et al.*, 2001). The extract was found to produce marked reduction in blood glucose concentration at tested dose levels in a dose dependant manner in both normoglycemic and alloxan induced hyperglycemic albino rats (Dash *et al.*, 2005). Note that the plant contains an anti-inflammatory anioxazale alkaloid which occurs also in *Gmelina arborea* L. This alkaloid reduced cotton pellet-induced granuloma formation in rats as efficiently as phenylbutazone (Barik *et al.*, 1992) and might be involved in the anti-inflammatory properties mentioned above. Other alkaloids are premnine, ganiarine, and ganikarine. Ganiarine and premnine have a sympathomimetic action. The plant is known to produce a series of phenylethanoid glycosides including premnafolioside (Yuasa *et al.*, 1993). Kurup *et al.* (1964), report the presence of some antibiotic substances from this plant.

References:

Alamgir M, Rokeya B, Hannan JM, Choudhuri MS, 2001, The effect of *Premna integrifolia* Linn. (Verbenaceae) on blood glucose in streptozotocin induced type 1 and type 2 diabetic rats. Pharmazie; 56: 903-4.

Kar A, Choudhary BK, Bandyopadhyay NG, 2003, Comparative evaluation of hypoglycemic activity of some Indian medicinal plants in alloxan diabetic rats J Ethnopharmacol; 84: 105-108.

Barik BR, Bhowmik T, Dey AK, Patra A, Chatterjee A, Joy S, Susan T, Alam M, Kundu AB, 1992, Premnazole, an isoxazole alkaloid of *Premna integrifolia* and *Gmelina arborea* with anti-inflammatory activity. Fitoterapia 63: 295-299.

Dash GK, Patro CP, Maiti AK, 2005, A study on the anti-hyperglycemic effect of *Premna corymbosa* Rottl. J Natural Remedies; 5: 31-4.

Yuasa K, Ide T, Otsuka H, 1993, Premnafolioside a new phenylethanoid, and other phenolic compounds from stems of *Premna corymbosa* var. obtusifolia. J Natural Prod; 56:1698-99.

Kurup KK, Kurup PA, 1964, Antibiotic substance from the root bark of *Premna Integrifolia;* Naturwissenschaften; 51: 484-484.

Otsuka H, Watanabe E, Yuasa K, Ogimi C, Takushi A, Takeda Y, 1961, A verbascoside iridoid glucoside conjugate from *Premna corymbosa* var. *obtusifolia*. Phytochemistry; 32: 983-86.

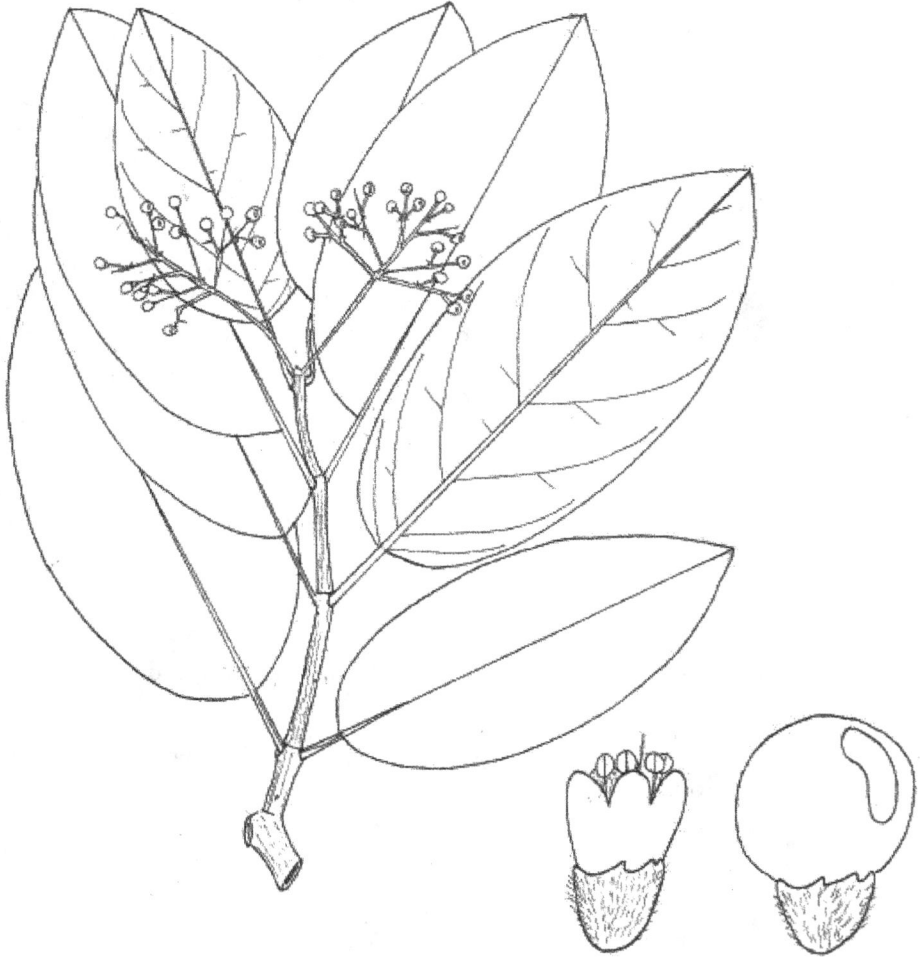

Figure 207: *Premna corymbosa* (Burm. f.) Rottler & Willd
From: Flora of Malaya No 06962
Malaysia, sea level, Pulau Rendang, Terengganu state. Collector KC Liew 173.

Verbena officinalis L.

[From Latin *verbena* = common European vervain and *officinalis* = sold as an herb]

Local names:	Common vervain, verveine (France), verbena (Spain, Italian, Portuguese), ma pien tsao (China), faristarium (India).
Synonym:	*Verbena setosa* M. Martens & Galeotti
Description:	It is a perennial herb which grows in temperate and subtropical regions. The stem is dull green, erect, up to 1 m high, decumbent at the base, quadrangular and subglabrous. The leaves are simple, opposite, and sessile. The leaf blade is deeply incised to tripartite, hairy, recurved at the margin, the nervations deeply sunked above. The inflorescences are dull green, sticky, hairy, with hairy bracts, spikes up to 25 cm long which are much flowered at the apex. The calyx is cupular, 0.1 - 0.4 cm, hairy, with 5 linear lobes. The corolla is dull dark violet-lilac and hairy, 0.4 - 0.8 cm, with 5 subquadrate lobes. The fruit is a dry ribbed pyrene with a vestigial style at the apex (Figure 208).
Medicinal Uses:	The plant was used during the Neolithic period as a medicine. It was known to Pliny who mentioned its use as an antidote for snake poison. *Verbena officinalis* L. (BHMA 1983 *British Herbal Pharmacopoeia*) has been traditionally used as a diuretic, sedative, and skin anti-inflammatory and it was known at the time of the Roman emperor Theodosius (4th century AD) to remove tumours. In India, the plant is used to heal wounds, to break fever, to invigorate, and to promote menses. In Europe the plant was used for treating fever, colds, and nervous disorders. In Cambodia, Laos and Vietnam, the plant is used to treat nervous illnesses. In several parts of Asia, the plant is also used for skin diseases, digestive troubles and genito-urinary disorders.

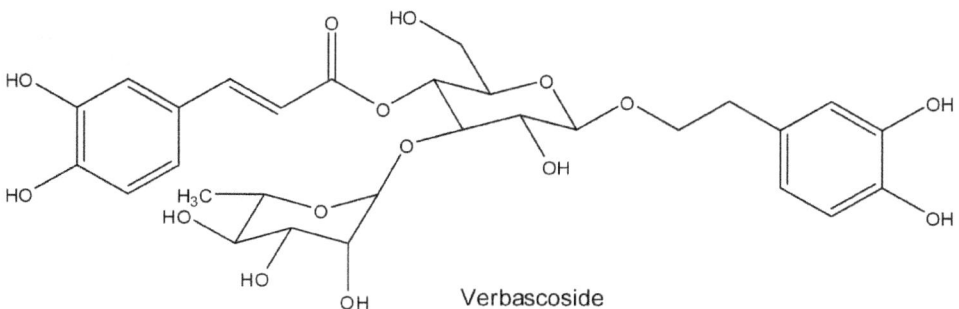

Verbascoside

Pharmacology:	The plant contains the phenyl propanoid glycoside, verbascoside; iridoid glycosides, hastatoside and verbenalin; as well as beta-

sitosterol, ursolic acid, oleanolic acid, 3-epiursolic acid, and 3-epioleanolic acid and a volatile oil. Verbascoside is a powerful antioxidant common in the Lamiales that has been the subject of numerous pharmacological studies. It exhibited cytotoxic effects against human gastric adenocarcinoma MGc80-3 cells, reversed MGc80-3 cells' malignant phenotypic characteristics and induced redifferentiation of MGc80-3 cells (Li *et al.*, 1997). It also elicited neuroprotective effects against 1-methyl-4-phenylpyridinium ion (MPP+) induced apoptosis and oxidative stress in PC12 neuronal cells (Sheng *et al.*, 2002), and cardiotonic properties (Pennacchio M *et al.*, 1996), modulation of telomerase activity (Zhang *et al.*, 2002), immunomodulatory activity (Akbay *et al.*, 2002) and antibacterial property against *Staphylococcus aureus* (Avila *et al.*, 1999) .

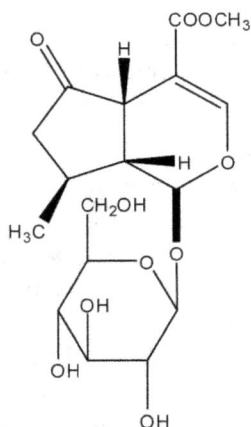

Verbenalin

Verbenaline exhibited hepatoprotective effects in rodents (Singh *et al.*, 1998). Citral, from the volatile oil, induced apoptosis in several hematopoietic cancer cell lines with DNA fragmentation and induction of caspase-3 (Dunai *et al.*, 2005; Calvo, 2006). Extracts of *Verbena officinalis* L. exhibited anti-inflammatory activity in the carrageenan paw oedema test and skin inflammation (Deepak *et al.*, 2000). Lai *et al.* (2006) showed aqueous extracts of *Verbena officinalis* L. exhibited cytoprotective effects against beta-amyloidal (Abita) peptide and dithiothreitol in primary cultures of cortical neurons.

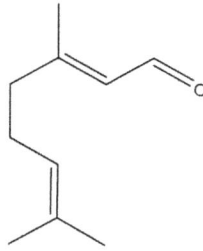

Citral

References: Akbay P, Calis I, Ündeger U, Basaran N, Basaran AA, 2002, *In vitro* Immunomodulatory activity of verbascoside from *Nepeta ucrainica* L. Phytother Res; 16: 593 – 595.

Avila JG, de Liverant JG, Martínez A, Martínez G, Muñoz JL, Arciniegas A, Romo de Vivar A, 1999, Mode of action of *Buddleja cordata* verbascoside against *Staphylococcus aureus.* J Ethnopharmacol.; 66: 75-8.

Calvo MI , 2006, Anti-inflammatory and analgesic activity of the topical preparation of Verbena officinalis L. J Ethnopharmacol; 107: 380-382.

Deepak M, Handa SS, 2000, Antiinflammatory activity and chemical composition of extracts of *Verbena officinalis*. Phytother Res; 14: 463-5.

Dudai N, Weinstein Y, Krup M, Rabinski T, Ofir R, 2005, Citral is a new inducer of caspase-3 in tumor cell lines. Planta Med; 71: 484-8.

Lai SW, Yu MS, Yuen WH, Chang RC, 2006,Novel neuroprotective effects of the aqueous extracts from *Verbena officinalis* Linn. Neuropharmacology; 50: 641-50.

Ji L, Yun Z, Hong Z, Baoning S, Rongliang Z, 1997, Differentiation of Human Gastric Adenocarcinoma Cell Line MGc80-3 Induced by Verbascoside. Planta Med; 63: 499-502.

Sheng GQ, Zhang JR, Pu XP, Ma J, Li CL, 2002, Protective effect of verbascoside on 1-methyl-4-phenylpyridinium ion-induced neurotoxicity in PC12 cells. Eur J Pharm; 451: 119-24.

Pennacchioa M, Alexandera E, Syahb YM, Ghisalbertib EL, 1996,The effect of verbascoside on cyclic 3',5'-adenosine monophosphate levels in isolated rat heart . Eur J Pharmy; 305:169-171.

Singh B ;Saxena A, Chandran BK , Anand KK, SuriI OP, SuriI KA, Satti NK. 1998, Hepatoprotective activity of verbenalin on experimental liver damage in rodents. Fitoterapia; 69: 135-40.

Zhang F, Jia1 Z, Deng Z, Wei Y, Zheng R, Yu L, 2002, *In vitro* Modulation of telomerase activity, telomere length and cell cycle in MKN45 cells by verbascoside. Planta Med; 68: 115-18.

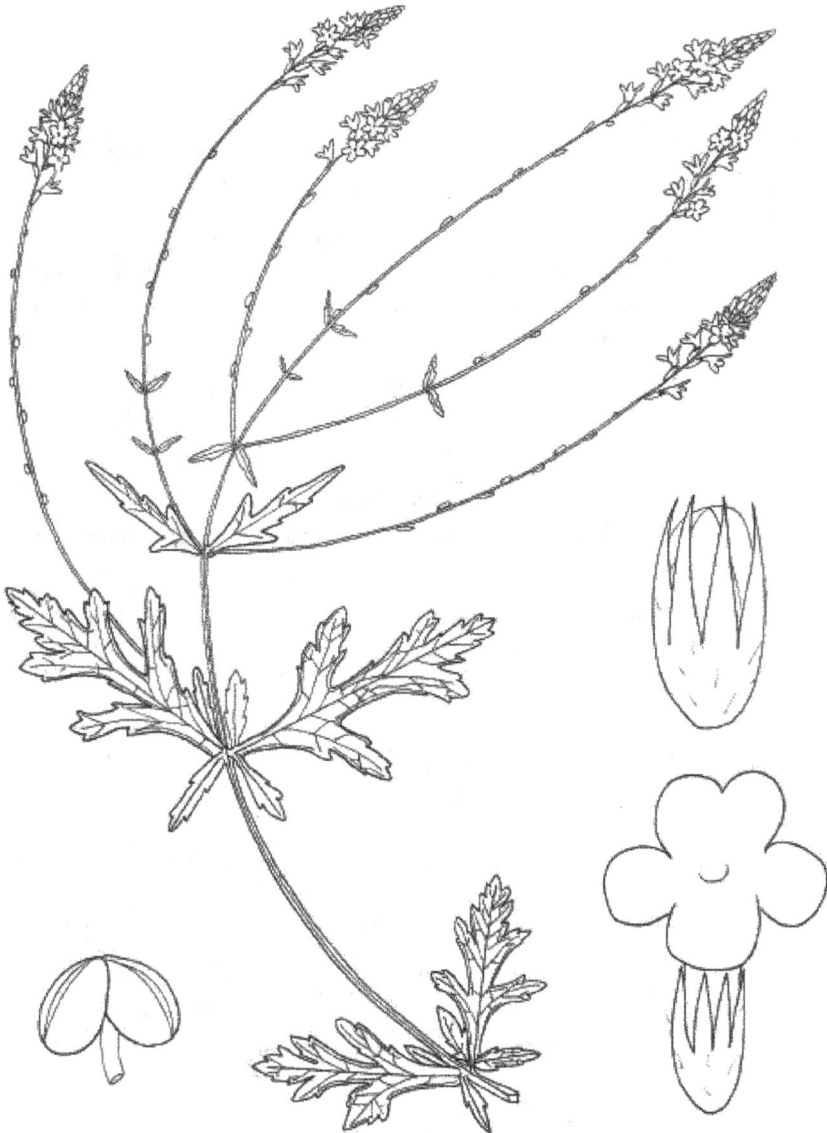

Figure 208: *Verbena officinalis* L.
From: Flora of Thailand, Chiang Mai University Herbarium
Thailand, Chiang Mai province, Chiang Dao, Doi Chiang Dao animal sanctuary, valley West of Doi Luang, east of Huay Mae Gawk station. Altitude 1600 m. Date of collection: 3 March 1995. Collection and identification: JF Maxwell Nº 95-193

D. Order PLANTAGINALES Lindley 1833

The order consists of the single family Plantaginaceae

1.Family PLANTAGINACEAE A L de Jussieu 1789 nom. Conserv., the Plantain Family.

The Family Plantaginaceae consists of 3 genera: *Plantago*, *Littorella*, and *Bougueria*. The genus Plantago is by far the largest genus of this family with 250 species of herbs. The leaves of *Plantaginaceae* are simple, basal and without stipules. The flowers are minute and packed in spikes. The calyx, corolla and androecium are tetramerous. The corolla lobes are imbricate. The stamens alternate with the lobes of the corolla tube, the filament attached to the corolla tube. The anthers are tetrasporangiate and dithecal. The gynoecium consists of 2 carpels fused to form a bilocular superior ovary containing several ovules attached to an axillary placenta. The fruits are capsular often circumscissile and containing numerous tiny mucilaginous seeds.

The genus *Plantago* yields a substantial number of medicinal products. The seeds of *Plantago psyllium* (Sand Plantain) and of *Plantago arenaria* (Branched Plantain) (*Plantago indica*) (Psyllium, *British Pharmaceutical Codex*, 1963).is used as demulcent. It absorbs and retains water and is therefore used as a bulk-providing medium in the treatment of chronic constipation (dose: 4 to 16 g). Another official demulcent is Plantago Seed (United States National Formulary, 1965) which consists of the seed of *Plantago psyllium*, *Plantago arenaria*, or *Plantago ovata* (Blond Psyllium). *Plantago major* var. *asiatica* (*Japanese Pharmacopoeia*,1962) is used in Japan for the same purpose. *Plantago coronopus* (buck's-horn plantain) has been used in Europe to dissolve renal calculi and promote urination (Brit.med.J./1965, 1544). Several slimming and laxative preparations containing *Plantago* seeds are available. Of recent interest is the fact that *Plantago* species have shown promising anticholesterolaemic (Chung *et al.*, 2008), antidiabetic (Galisteo *et al.*, 2005), anti-obesity (Salas-Salvadó *et al.*, 2007), antidiabetic (Hannan *et al.*, 2006), and antitumoral effects (Ozaslan *et al.*, 2007) experimentally. In Southeast Asia, *Plantago major* L., *Plantago asiatica* L., *Plantago depressa* Wiild., and *Plantago lanceolata* L. are medicinal for various ailments.

References: Chung MJ, Park KW, Kim KH, Kim CT, Baek JP, Bang KH, Choi YM, Lee SJ, 2008,Asian plantain (Plantago asiatica) essential oils suppress 3-hydroxy-3-methyl-glutaryl-co-enzyme A reductase expression *in vitro* and *in vivo* and show hypocholesterolaemic properties in mice. Br J Nutr; 99:67-75.

Galisteo M, Sánchez M, Vera R, González M, Anguera A, Duarte J, Zarzuelo A, 2005, A diet supplemented with husks of *Plantago ovata* reduces the development of endothelial dysfunction, hypertension, and obesity by affecting adiponectin and TNF-alpha in obese Zucker rats. J Nutr; 135: 2399-404.

Hannan JM, Ali L, Khaleque J, Akhter M, Flatt PR, Abdel-Wahab YH, 2006, Aqueous extracts of husks of Plantago ovata reduce hyperglycemia in type 1 and type 2 diabetes by inhibition of intestinal glucose absorption. Br J Nutr; 96: 131-7.

Ozaslan M, Didem Karagöz I, Kalender ME, Kilic IH, Sari I, Karagöz A, 2007, *In vivo* antitumoral effect of *Plantago major* L. extract on Balb/C mouse with Ehrlich ascites tumor. Am J Chin Med; 35: 841-51.

Salas-Salvadó J, Farrés X, Luque X, Narejos S, Borrell M, Basora J, Anguera A, Torres F, Bulló M, Balanza R, 2007, Effect of two doses of a mixture of soluble fibres on body weight and metabolic variables in overweight or obese patients: a randomized trial. Br J Nutr; 99: 1380-7.

Plantago major L.

[From Latin *Plantago* = plantain and *major* = larger]

Local names:	Common Plantain, greater plantain, ekor anjing (Malaysia), ch'e ch'ien (China), plantain commun (France), llanten (Philippines)
Synonyms:	*Plantago borysthenica* (Rogow.) Wissjul., *Plantago dregeana* Decne., *Plantago latifolia* Salisb., *Plantago major* var. *borysthenica* Rogow., *Plantago major* var. *scopulorum* Fries, *Plantago officinarum* Crantz.
Description:	It is a perennial herb which grows in several temperate countries, in Europe, central Asia, Burma, Malaysia, India, Afghanistan, and China. The plant presents a rosette of simple leaves. The petioles form a sheath at the base, they are fibrous and grooved, and 3 - 5 cm long. The leaf blade is broadly elliptic, fleshy, 7 - 12 cm x 4.2 - 6 cm and shows several longitudinal secondary nerves which are flat above. The leaf blade is sparingly hairy on both sides. The flowers are grouped in compact spikes which are 9 - 14 cm long. The calyx presents 4 triangular lobes of about 1 mm long. The corolla is light pink to purple, urn-shaped, to 2 mm long and produces 4 tiny triangular lobes. The anthers protrude out of the corolla as well as a linear stigma. The fruit is a papery capsule, with an apical tip, and 2 mm x 1.5 cm (Figure 209).
Medicinal uses:	The plant is known for its healing properties in Europe where the leaves are applied to wounds. In India, the plant is used to treat rheumatism and intestinal discomfort. The seeds are taken for dysentery. In Vietnam, Cambodia, Laos and China the plant is used to check bleeding, to treat dysentery and pulmonary complaints. In the Philippines the plant is used to treat infected gums.

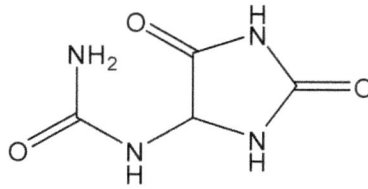

Allantoin

Pharmacology: The plant is know to contain allantoin which is a cell proliferant, hence the wound healing properties, and has been used in cosmetic and sunburn preparations. It also contains acubin. Several pharmacological activities have been observed from this plant (Samuelsen, 2000). The plant may have some protective effects against breast cancer since it reduces the frequency of tumour formation in female mice of the strain C3H Strong (Lithander, 1992). The inclusion of a polyphenolic complex from Plantago major-plantastine into animal feed inhibited the hepatocarcinogenic effect of nitrosodimethylamin (Karpilovskaia *et al.*, 1989). Ozaslan *et al.*, (2007) showed that an extract of *Plantago major* L. protected male Balb/C mice against Ehrlich ascites tumour in a dose dependent manner. The beneficial effect of the plant on the lungs has been clinically demonstrated. A rapid effect on subjective complaints and objective findings were observed on twenty five patients with chronic bronchitis receiving *Plantago major* L. (Matev *et al.*, 1982). The plant also has immunoenhancing (Gomez-Flores *et al.*, 2000), antibacterial (Hetland *et al.*, 2000), and antiviral (Chiang *et al.*, 2002) properties.

References: Chiang LC, Chiang W, Chang MY, Ng LT, Lin CC, 2002, Antiviral activity of *Plantago major* extracts and related compounds *in vitro*. Antiviral Res; 55: 53-62.

Gomez-Flores R, Calderon CL, Scheibel LW, Tamez-Guerra P, Rodriguez-Padilla C, Tamez-Guerra R, Weber RJ, 2000, Immunoenhancing properties of *Plantago major* leaf extract. Phytother Res; 14: 617-22.

Hetland G, Samuelsen AB, Løvik M, Paulsen BS, Aaberge IS, Groeng EC, Michaelsen TE, 2000, Protective effect of *Plantago major* L. Pectin polysaccharide against systemic *Streptococcus pneumoniae* infection in mice. Scand J Immunol; 52: 348-55.

Karpilovskaia ED, Gorban GP, Pliss MB, Zakharenko LN, Gulich MP, 1989, Inhibiting effect of the polyphenolic complex from *Plantago major* (plantastine) on the carcinogenic effect of endogenously synthesized nitrosodimethylamine Farmakol Toksikol; 52: 64-7.

Lithander A, 1992, Intracellular fluid of way bread (*Plantago major*) as a prophylactic for mammary cancer in mice. Tumor Biol; 13: 138-41.

Matev M, Angelova I, Koichev A, Leseva M, Stefanov G, 1982, Clinical trial of a *Plantago major* preparation in the treatment of chronic bronchitis. Vutr Boles; 21: 133-7.

Ozaslan M, Didem Karagöz I, Kalender ME, Kilic IH, Sari I, Karagöz A, 2007, *In vivo* antitumoral effect of *Plantago major* L. extract on Balb/C mouse with Ehrlich ascites tumor. Am J Chin Med; 35: 841-51.

Samuelsen AB, 2000, The traditional uses, chemical constituents and biological activities of *Plantago major* L. A review.. J Ethnopharmacol; 71: 1-21.

Figure 209: *Plantago major* L.

From: Flora of Malaya
Malaysia, Genting Highland, altitude 1550 m. Collection Sahadan Salim. Date of collection: 30 November 1980.

E. Order SCROFULARIALES Lindley 1833

The order Scrophulariales consists of 12 families and more than 11,000 species of herbs, shrubs and occasionally trees which are thought to have originated near to or in the Gentianales. Chemically speaking, Scrophulariales differ from the Solanales by producing iridoid glycosides and phenylethanoid glycosides. Notorious examples of Scrophulariales of pharmaceutical interest are *Digitalis purpurea* L. (purple foxglove) and *Digitalis lanata* Ehrh. (Grecian foxglove), the cardenolides of which, namely digitoxin and digoxin, are used to increase the force of myocardial contraction. Both these plants are members of the family Scrophulariaceae.

1.Family SCROPHULARIACEAE A. L. de Jussieu 1789 nom. Conserv., the Figwort Family

The family Scrophulariaceae consists of about 190 genera and 4000 species of flowering plants, mostly herbaceous, hairy, and of cosmopolitan distribution. Some of these are parasitic. The most common types of secondary metabolites isolated so far from this family are terpenes (triterpenoid saponins, phenylethanoid glycosides, cucurbitacin glycosides, iridoid glycosides, phytosterols) and hydroxyflavones. The leaves are simple, alternate or opposite, and without stipules. The flowers are organized in racemes or spikes The calyx comprises 5 sepals. The corolla tube is colorful, zygomorphic, tubular, bilobed, occasionally spurred and extraordinarily diverse in beauty. The androecium comprises 4 to 5 stamens attached to the corolla. The anthers are tetrasporangiate and dithecal. The gynoecium comprises a pair of carpels united to form a compound, superior, bilocular ovary. Each locule containing several ovules is attached to axile placentas. The fruits are capsular, dehiscent and contain several tiny angular seeds.

The Scrophulariaceae produces cohorts of ornamental plants such as *Antirrhinum majus* (snapdragon), *Castilleja sp.* (Indian paintbrush), *Linaria dalmatica* (dalmatian toadflax), *and Paulownia tomentosa (Thunb.)* Steud. (empress tree), *Penstemon barbatus* (common bearded tongue), *Verbascum* sp. (ornamental mullein), *Veronica spicata* (royal candle), and *Torenia fournieri* L. (wishbone flower).

This family has been neglected in terms of Pharmacologica Research. The dried corollas of *Verbascum thapsiforme*, *Verbascum phlomoides* or *Verbascum thapsus* (Verbascum Flowers, *French Pharmacopeia*, 1965) have been used in Europe in pulmonary complaints, usually as an infusion (1 in 20; dose.1 to 2 fl. oz.). Other official Scrofulariaceae are *Gratiola linifolia*, *Veronica officinalis* and *Veronica beccabunga* L. (Pharmacopoeia of Portugal). Of recent pharmacological interest in this family is the neuroprotective effect of catalpol, an iridoid glycoside isolated from the fresh *Rehmannia* roots, on the senescent mice induced by D-galactose (Zhang *et al.*, 2007). Biflorin from *Capraria biflora* increased the response elicited by 5-FU in mice which were inoculated sarcoma 180 and Ehrlich carcinoma cell lines (Vasconcellos *et al.*, 2007). Flavonoids isolated from *Linaria reflexa* Desf. were cytotoxic against several cancer cell lines (Tundis, 2005). *Bacopa monnieri* has been the subject of several studies for its CNS effects (Kumar V, 2006). The cytotoxic effects of the cucurbitacines elaborated by this plant are worthy of further study. In Southeast Asia about 50 species of Scrophulariaceae are medicinal.

References:

Kumar V, 2006, Potential medicinal plants for CNS disorders: an overview. Phytother Res; 20: 1023-1035.

Tundis R, Deguin B, Loizzo MR, Bonesi M, Statti GA, Tillequin F, Menichini F, 2005, Potential antitumor agents: Flavones and their derivatives from *Linaria reflexa* Desf. Bioorg Med Chem Letters; 15: 4757-60.

Vasconcellos MC, Bezerra DP, Fonseca AM, Pereira MR, Lemos TL, Pessoa OD, Pessoa C, Moraes MO, Alves AP, Costa-Lotufo LV, 2007, Antitumor activity of biflorin, an o-naphthoquinone isolated from *Capraria biflora*. Biol Pharm Bull; 30: 1416-1421.

Zhang XL, Jiang B, Li ZB, Hao S, An LJ, 2007, Catalpol ameliorates cognition deficits and attenuates oxidative damage in the brain of senescent mice induced by D-galactose, Pharmacol Biochem Behav; 88: 64-72.

Curanga fel-terrae Lour.

[From Latin *fel* = poison or gall and *terrae* = land]

Local names: Sagai-uak (Philippines), hempedu tanah (Malaysia)

Basionym: *Picria fel-terrae* Lour. *Flora Cochinchinensis* 2: 393. 1790

Synonyms: *Curanga amara* Vahl, *Curanga amara* Juss., *Curanga amara* R. & S., *Gratiola amara* Roxb., *Torenia cardiosepala* Benth.

Description: Annual, glabrous herb that grows up to 1 m long in sparse forests and fields; from 700 to 1400 m altitude in China, India, Indonesia, Laos, Malaysia, Burma, Philippines, Thailand, Vietnam, the Himalayas, and Indonesia. The stem is slender (1 mm diameter), quadrangular, glabrous, fibrous, divaricate, and rooting at nodes. The internodes are 1.6 - 1.7 cm long. The leaves are simple, opposite, sessile and without stipules. The leaf blade is broadly lanceolate, serrate with a very few hairs underneath. The midrib is sunken above and secondary nerves are not visible above. The inflorescence is a few flowered, about 2.5 cm long axillary raceme. The flower pedicel is about 1 cm long. The calyx is 0.6 cm long, the lobes are oblong-ovate and 1.4 x 1 cm in fruit. The corolla is red brown or white, 1.2 cm long; constricted at the middle; the lower lip 0.65 cm long; the upper lip erect 0.45 cm long, the base wide, apically narrowly sub-oblong, ethe marginated. The androecium shows 4 stamens. The capsule is ovoid, 0.5 cm long and compressed (Figure 210).

Medicinal Uses: The plant is used to break fever. Rumphius, writing in the Moluccas between 1653 and 1692, puts down its first use as for a vermifuge, and its second use for tertian fever, stimulating the liver and driving the bile into the intestines but not causing purging. Indonesians use it to treat skin diseases, coughs and to invigorate. Philippinos use the plant to stimulate appetite, to break fever, to promote urination, menses, to treat colic and lumbar pain. In Malaysia, the plant is used to assuage stomach pains, and to heal wounds.

Pharmacology: The first published data on the chemical constituents from this plant were in the Journal of the Chemical Society in 1900. The anti-inflammatory and febrifuge properties may involve some cucurbitacin and phenylpropanoids glycosides which abound in this herb. Cucurbitacin glycosides from the plant, including picfeltarraenin IA, picfeltarraenin IB, picfeltarraenin IV, showed complement-inhibiting activity (Huang *et al.*, 1998). 1-O-3,4-(dihydroxyphenyl)- ethyl-beta-D- apiofuranosyl-(1-->4)-alpha-L-rharmnopyranosyl- (1-->3)-4-O-caffeoyl-beta-D-glucopyranoside exhibited a remarkable inhibitory effect on lipid peroxidation initiated by either a free radical [AAPH; 2,2'-azobis-(2-amidinopropane)dihydrochloride] or by a generated hydroxyl radical (Fe2+/ascorbate) (Thuann *et al.*, 2007).

References: Huang Y, De Bruyne T, Apers S, Ma Y, Claeys M, Vanden Berghe D, Pieters L, Vlietinck A, 1998, Complement-inhibiting cucurbitacin glycosides from *Picria fel-terrae*. J Nat Prod; 26: 757-61.

Thuan ND, Ha T, Thuong PT, Na MK, Lee JP, Lee JH, Seo HW, Min BS, Kim JC, Bae K, 2007, A phenylpropanoid glycoside with antioxidant activity from *Picria tel-ferae*. Arch Pharm Res; 30: 1062-6.

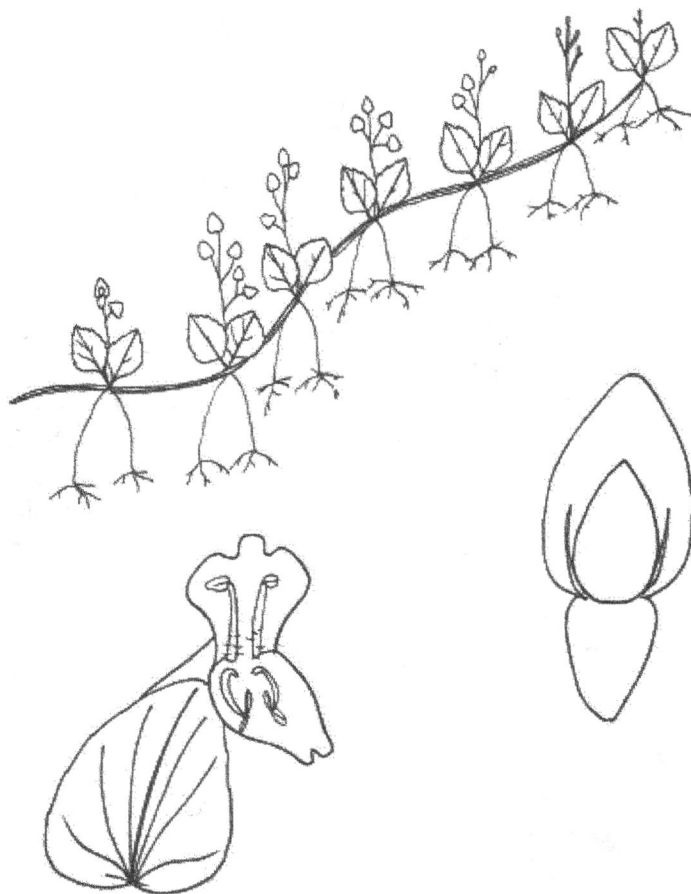

Figure 210: *Curanga fel-terrae* Lour.
Flora of Malaya, Herbarium of UKM
Malaysia, Pahang state, Jerantut, Sentul village near Sentul river. Growing on river bank. Altitude 40 m. Collection and identification: Razali Jaman, date of collection: 26 February 1985.

Cyrtandromoea acuminata Benth. & Hook.

[From Greek *kyrtos* = curved, and *andros* = male, and *homoios* = similar and from Latin *acuminata* = having a long tapering point]

Synonym: *Cyrtandromoea subsessilis* (Miq.). Radlk.

Description: It is a perennial erect herb which grows in shady and moist mossy rainforest understory to a height of about 30 cm. The stem is quadrangular, basally woody, glabrous with longitudinal striations and about 3 mm in diameter and hairy by the apex. The internodes are 1 to 5 cm long. The leaves are subsessile, opposite, simple and without stipules. The leaf-blade is elliptic lanceolate, membranaceous, serrate at the margin, hairy, 11 - 1.5 cm x 0.6 - 4 cm, tapering at the base and discretely acuminate at the apex. The inflorescence is axillary, cymose, and few flowered. The calyx is tubular, about 1 cm long and truncate at the apex. The corolla is bilabiate, whitish or purplish lower lip 3-lobed; upper lip 2-lobed; lobes orbicular and about 1.2 cm long. The androecium comprises 4 didynamous stamens confluent at the apex. The stigma is bifid. The fruit is a loculicidal capsule enclosed in calyx. The seeds are numerous, ellipsoid, and reticulate (Figure 211).

Medicinal Uses: The Malays use the plant to treat fever.

Pharmacology: Unknown.

Figure 211: *Cyrtandromoea acuminata* Benth. & Hook
From: Herbarium of University Kebangsaan Malaysia
Malaysia, Kelantan, Gua Musang, road to Kampong How from Kuala Betis.
Collector: Abdul Latiff and A. Zainuddin. Date of collection: 12 October 1985.

Herpestis monnieri (L.) Kunth.

[After French botanist Louis Guillaume Le Monnier (1717-1799)]

Local names:	Thyme leaved gratiola, herb of grace, water hyssop, pa chi t'ien (China), berimi (Malaysia), brahmi (Sanskrit), brami (India).
Basionym:	*Gratiola monnieri* L. *Die Natürlichen Pflanzenfamilien* 4(3b): 77. 1891.
Synonyms:	*Bacopa monnieri* (L.) Pennell, *Bramia indica* Lam., *Bramia monniera* (L.) Drake, *Bramia monnieri* (L.) Pennell, *Calytriplex obovata* Ruiz & Pav., *Gratiola monniera* L., *Habershamia cuneifolia* Michx., *Herpestis procumbens* Spreng., *Limosella calycina* Forsk., *Lymachia monnieri* L., *Monniera africana* Pers., *Monniera brownei* Pers., *Monniera pedunculosa* Pers., *Septa reptens* Lour.
Description:	It is a perennial herb which grows by water, in wet places, and on sandy beaches; below 1100 m in China, Taiwan, India, and most warm countries. The plant is an aquatic herb on stolon. The roots are fibrous. The stem is creeping, rooting at nodes, terete, somewhat swollen and articulate, glabrous, and 0.2 cm in diameter. The internodes are 1.7 - 1.9 cm long. The leaves are simple, sessile, opposite, without stipules and somewhat decussate. The leaf-blade is spathulate, 0.2 - 0.3 cm x 1.7 -1.8 cm, the margin entire or dentate, and rounded at the apex. The flower is solitary and axillary. The flower pedicel is 2 - 3 cm long and slender. The flower bud is 0.4 – 0.7 cm long. The calyx comprises 5 sepals which are 0.5 x 0.2 cm; lanceolate, overlapping to contortate. The corolla is white pinkish to pale bluish, 0.8 -1 cm long, obscurely 2-lipped with 5 lobes. The anthers are grayish – purple. The fruit is a capsule which is narrowly ovoid, enveloped in a persistent calyx, and acute at the apex. The seeds are yellow-brown, ellipsoid, truncate at one end, and longitudinally striated (Figure 212).
Medicinal uses:	*Herpestis monnieri* (L.) Kunth. is considered in India as one of the most important nervine herbs in Ayurvedic medicine. It is believed to give the knowledge of Brahman or supreme reality and to treat mental illnesses. It is also used to treat skin diseases, as a diuretic, tonic, aphrodisiac, and to treat epilepsy and hysteria. In Malaysia the plant is eaten as a salad and used to expel worms from the intestines. Philippinos use the plant to promote urination. Chinese use it as a tonic. In Vietnam, the plant is a tonic, diuretic, and antispasmodic.

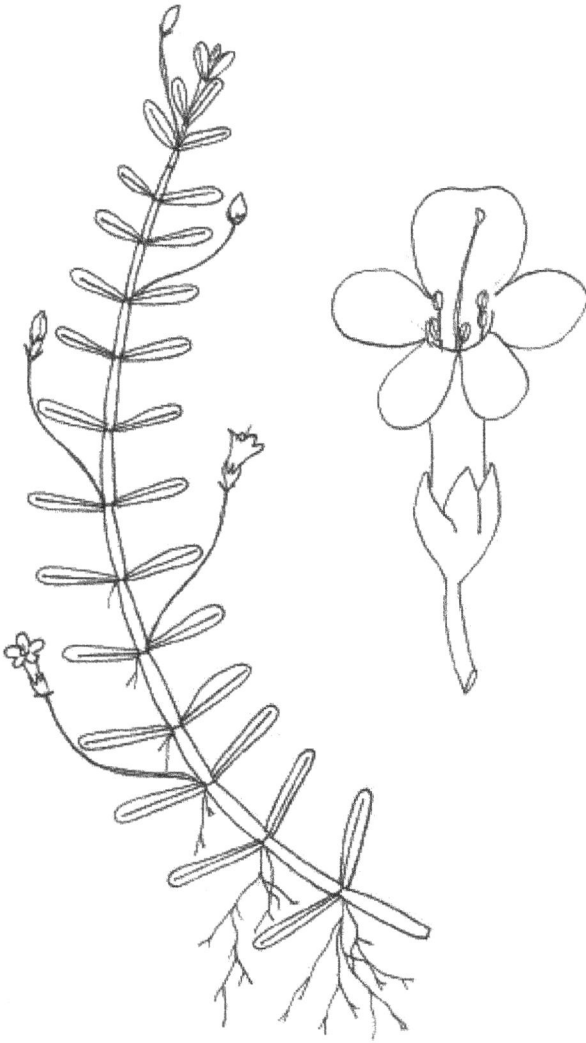

Figure 212: *Herpestis monnieri* **(L.) Kunth.**
From Herbarium of UKM
Malaysia, Kelantan state, Kota Bahru, Batu 6 1/2 Sabak, date of collection: 20 November 1984, Collection and Identification: Abdul Latiff, ALM 714.
From Botanical Inventory of Taiwan
Taiwan, Miaoli Hsien, Chunan Chen, sea side, date of collection: 30 September 1990.
Collection and identification: Chi-Hsien Lin *et al.*

Pharmacology:

Herpestis monnieri (L.) Kunth. has been the subject of several neuropharmacological studies, the outcome of which unambiguously demonstrated antidepressant, behavioral and neuroprotective effects. The plant also has anti-inflammatory effects (Channa *et al.*, 2006). Sairam *et al* (2002), showed that an extract of the plant when given to rodents in doses of 20 and 40 mg/kg orally once a day for 5 days, was found to have significant antidepressant activity in forced swim and learned helplessness models of depression and was comparable to imipramine.

The neuroprotective and anti-degenerative effects of the plant seem to involve some anti-oxidant properties. Dhanasekaran *et al.* (2007), demonstrated that the plant reduced divalent metals, dose-dependently scavenged reactive oxygen species, decreased the formation of lipid peroxides and inhibited lipoxygenase activity in the brain. Seventy-six adults aged between 40 and 65 years in a double-blind, randomized, placebo control study showed a significant effect of *Herpestis monnieri* (L.) Kunth. On the retention of new information by decreasing the rate of forgetting of newly acquired information, and anxiety levels were unaffected (Roodenrys *et al.*, 2002).

The plant abounds with dammarane-type or bacopasaponins, of which bacoside A, like in ginseng, might account for the medicinal properties described above (Garai *et al.*, 1996). Saponins from *Herpestis monnieri* (L.) Kunth. facilitate anterograde memory and attenuate anterograde experimental amnesia induced by scopolamine and sodium nitrite in mice (Kishore *et al.*, 2005). Note that bacoside A is hepatoprotective (Sumati *et al.*, 2008).

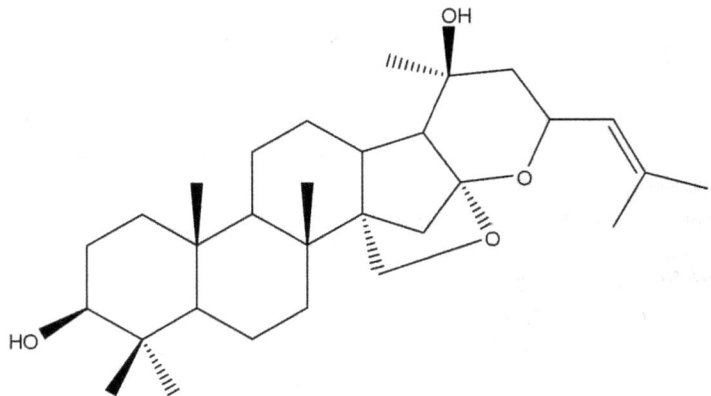

Bacopasaponin aglycone

References: Channa S, Dar A, Anjum S, Yaqoob M and Atta-ur-Rahman, 2006, Anti-inflammatory activity of *Bacopa monniera* in rodents, J Ethnopharmacol; 104: 286-89.

Dhanasekaran M, Tharakan B, Holcomb LA, Hitt AR, Young KA, Manyam BV, 2007, Neuroprotective mechanisms of ayurvedic antidementia botanical *Bacopa monniera*. Phytother Res; 21: 965-9.

Garai S, Mahato SB, Ohtani K, Yamasaki K, 1996, Dammarane-type triterpenoid saponins from *Bacopa monniera*. Phytochemistry; 42: 815-20.

Kishore K, Singh M, 2005, Effect of bacosides, alcoholic extract of *Bacopa monniera* Linn. (brahmi), on experimental amnesia in mice. Indian J Exp Biol; 43: 640-5.

Roodenrys S, Booth D, Bulzomi S, Phipps A, Micallef C, Smoker J, 2002, Chronic effects of Brahmi (*Bacopa monnieri*) on human memory. Neuropsychopharmacology; 27: 279-81.

Sairam K, Dorababu M, Goel RK, Bhattacharya SK, 2002, Antidepressant activity of standardized extract of *Bacopa monniera* in experimental models of depression in rats. Phytomedicine; 9: 207-11.

Sumathi T, Nongbri A, 2008, Hepatoprotective effect of Bacoside-A, a major constituent of *Bacopa monniera* Linn, Phytomedicine; 15: 901-5.

Limnophila villosa Bl.

[From Latin *limnophila* = swamp-loving and *villosa* = hairy]

Synonyms: *Limnophila javanica* A. DC., *Limnophila pulcherrima* Hook.f.

Description: It is an aquatic herb that grows in wet area and by water, in open muddy ditches, ponds and around the margin of the water. The roots are fibrous and immerged. The stem is aerial, erect, slender, angular, glabrous or with a few hairs, and 1 to 3 mm in diameter. The internodes are 1 cm long. The leaves are simple, sessile, without stipules and decussate. The leaf-blade is linear, serrate, 0.4 - 0.2 cm x 0.4 -1.2 cm and without visible innervations. The flowers are axillary. The calyx lobes are lanceolate, 5 mm long, hairy and dull maroon. The corolla is tubular, with 4 lobes, veined, membranaceous, about 0.8 cm, light yellowish with dull maroon vertical lines on the upper side, yellow green on the lower side, lobes blue and throat reddish (Figure 213).

Medicinal uses: The Malays pound the leaves and the paste obtained is applied to the skin to heal ulcers, inflamed parts and to break fever.

Pharmacology: To date nothing is known about the pharmacological properties of this herb. The anti-oxidant activity could account for the anti-inflammatory use mentioned previously, as strong antioxidant properties have been measured in *Limnophila aromatica*. Kukongviriyapan *et al.* (2007) demonstrated that *Limnophila aromatica* possessed high free radical scavenging and antioxidant activities both *in vitro* and *in vivo* and suggested that it may have potential roles in protection of vascular dysfunction. Highly oxygenated phenolic substances and flavonoids are known to occur in the closely related *Limnophila* species (Jang *et al.*, 2005). Other possible anti-inflammatory principles might be saponins which probably occur in the plant.

References: Jang DS, Su BN, Pawlus AD, Jones WP, Kleps RA, Bunyapraphatsara N, Fong HH, Pezzuto JM, Kinghorn AD, 2005, Limnophilaspiroketone, a highly oxygenated phenolic derivative from *Limnophila geoffrayi*. J Nat Prod; 68: 1134-6.

Kukongviriyapan U, Luangaram S, Leekhaosoong K, Kukongviriyapan V, Preeprame S, 2007, Antioxidant and vascular protective activities of *Cratoxylum formosum, Syzygium gratum* and *Limnophila aromatica*. Biol Pharm Bull; 30: 661-6

Reddy NP, Reddy BA, Gunasekar D, Blond A, Bodo B, Murthy MM, 2007, Flavonoids from *Limnophila indica*. Phytochemistry; 68: 636-9.

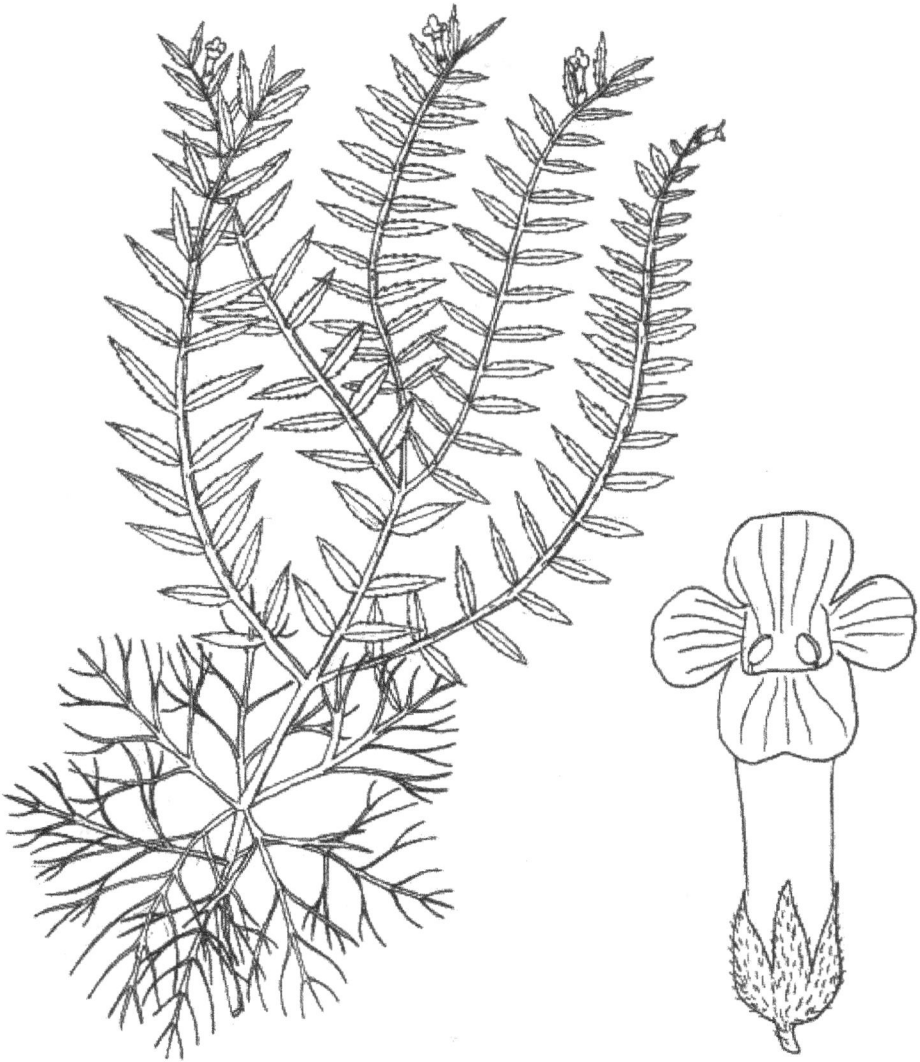

Figure 213: *Limnophila villosa* Bl.
From: Flora of Thailand, Prince of Songkla University
Thailand, Songkla province, Muang district, Chana border along the highway c. 2 Km
Northeast of Chana. Sea level. Date of collection: 17 January 1985. Collection and
identification: JF Maxwell No 85-73

Lindenbergia philippensis (Cham. & Schltdl.) Benth.

[After botanist Johann Bernhard Wilhelm Lindenberg (1781-1851) and Latin *philippinensis* = from the Philippines]

Local names:	Sap heng (Laos), zhong e cao (China)
Basionym:	*Stemodia philippensis* Cham. & Schltdl. *Linnaea* 3: 5-6. 1828.
Synonyms:	*Stemodia philippensis* Cham. & Schltdl; *Lindenbergia melvillei* S. Moore; *Lindenbergia. philippensis* var. *ramosissima* Bonati.
Description:	Perennial, erect, branching up to 2.5 m tall which grow on dry mountain sides, in rocky crevices, in mostly open, disturbed areas in primary evergreen forest on granite bedrock; from an altitude of 1200 - 2600 m in China, Cambodia, India, Laos, Burma, Philippines, Thailand, and Vietnam. The plant has a faint aromatic odor and is slightly bitter. The stem is stout, straight, much branched, glandular, hairy and terete. The internodes are 4.5 - 6 cm long. The leaves are simple, sessile, without stipules and opposite. The leaf-blade is dull-dark green above, dull light green underneath, membranaceous, hairy, lanceolate, 1.8 - 2.7 cm x 5 - 8 cm, serrate and shows 4 - 5 pairs of distinct secondary nerves underneath. The inflorescence is terminal, spicate-racemose, dense, 6 - 20 cm; with numerous bracts which are lanceolate. The flowers are subsessile. The calyx is 0.5 – 0.6 cm, light green, hairy; lobes triangular. The corolla is dull light green on both sides of the upper (narrow) lip and the outside of the lower (wider) lip. The inside of the lower lip is yellow with tiny dark red dots on the midlobe. The anthers are light green, the filaments whitish. The fruit is a narrowly ovoid, 5-6 mm, densely brown hirsute capsule apically containing several tiny yellowish seeds (Figure 214).
Medicinal uses:	In China the plant is boiled in water to make a drink used to dispel humors. In India, the plant is used to treat bronchitis and skin diseases.
Pharmacology:	The plant has not been studied for pharmacology. Saponins could account for the medicinal properties mentioned above.

Figure 214: *Lindenbergia philippensis* **(Cham. & Schltdl.) Benth.**
From Flora of Thailand
Thailand, Chiang Mai province, Muang district, Doi Sutep Pui National Park, West side of
Doi Sutep temple. Elevation: 1025 m. Date of collection: 10 February 1976. Collection and
identification: J.F. Maxwell, N° 96-194

Lindernia antipoda (L.) Alston

[After German botanist Franz Balthazar von Lindern (1682-1755) and Latin *antipoda* =
antipodes]

Local names:	Sparrow false pimpernel, ilemelakel (Palau)
Basionym:	*Ruellia antipoda* L. *Species Plantarum* 2: 635. 1753.
Synonyms:	*Bonnaya antipoda* (L.) Druce, *Bonnaya antipoda* (Retz.) Spreng., *Gratiola veronicifolia* Retz., *Ilysanthes antipoda* (L.) Merr., *Lindernia veronicifolia* (Retz.) F. Muell., *Vandellia antipoda* (L.) T. Yamaz., *Vandellia veronicifolia* (Retz.) Haines

Description:

It is a prostrate herb that grows in rice field and, wet grasslands of China, Taiwan, Bhutan, Cambodia, India, Japan, Laos, Malaysia, Burma, Nepal, Philippines, Sri Lanka, Thailand, Vietnam, Australia, and the Pacific Islands below 1700 m. The stem is angled, glabrous, rooting, branched, dull light greenish to dull light violet. The internodes are 1 - 4.5 cm long. The leaves are simple, dull dark green above, dull light green underneath, opposite and without stipules. The petiole is short. The leaf blade is oblong, 1.1 - 1.4 cm x 1.4 - 2.5 cm, glabrous, obscurely serrate and rounded at the apex, the midrib is sunken above, and 4 - 5 pairs of secondary nerves are visible underneath. The inflorescences are terminal racemes. The calyx is light green; with 1 cm long lanceolate sepals. The corolla is tubular, and zygomorphic, to 1.5 cm and bilobed. The corolla outside and both side of the upper lip is light lilac. The lower lip is 3 lobed and light blue. The corolla presents a pair of staminodes which are yellow. The fruit is a fusiform dehiscent capsule, green with purplish stripes and containing several angled seeds (Figure 215).

Medicinal Uses:

The plant is used to promote menses, to treat diarrhoea, and to expel worms from the intestines. Indonesians use it to treat vertigo.

Pharmacology:

To date, *Lindernia antipoda* (L.) Alston has not been tested for pharmacology.

Lindernia ciliata (Colm.) Penn.

[After German botanist Franz Balthazar von Lindern (1682-1755) and Latin *ciliata* = ciliate]

Local names:

Fringed false pimpernel, ci chi ni hua cao (China), oonmudia (Nepalese).

Basionym:

Gratiola ciliata Colsm. *Prodr. Desc. Grat.* 14. 1793.

Synonyms:

Bonnaya brachiata Link & Otto, *Bonnaya brachiata* (Colsm.) Spreng., *Gratiola ciliata* Roxb., *Gratiola serrata* Roxb., *Ilysanthes ciliata* (Colsm.) Kuntze, *Ilysanthes ciliata* (Roxb.) Urb., *Vandellia ciliata* (Colsm.) T. Yamaz.

Description:

It is a decumbent annual herb that grows up to 20 cm in moist places, rice fields, grassland, wastelands, trailsides, and open forests of the Himalayas, India, Burma, China, Taiwan, Malaysia, Australia, Cambodia, Japan, Philippines, and Vietnam. The stem

Figure 215: *Lindernia antipoda* **(L.) Alston**
Flora of Thailand, Chiang Mai University Herbarium, Thailand, Chiang Mai province, Chiang Dao district, Doi Chieng Dao animal Sanctuary, East of Huay Mae Gawk station. Elevation 1475 m. Date of collection: 13 September 1995. Shaded, disturbed area along narrow trail in mixed, seasonal evergreen hardwood and pine forest, granite bedrock in soil. Collector and identification: J.F. Maxwell.

Description (contd) is much branched, sometimes rooting at nodes. The internodes are 1.7 to 4.8 cm long. The leaves are simple, sessile; opposite, and without stipules. The leaf blade is oblong to lanceolate-oblong, dark green above, membranaceous, 0.3 - 0.6 cm x 1 -2cm, glabrous, slightly amplexicaul at the base, ciliate, and acute to obtuse at the apex. The raceme is terminal and delicate. The calyx is 0.5 cm long, green, the lobes narrowly lanceolate. The corolla is tubular, bilobed, 0.4 – 0.8 cm long, whitish; the lower lip with 2 blue vertical streaks inside below the midlobe.

Staminode with blue hue. The lower lip is almost as long as upper lip and often unequally 3-lobed. The androecium consists of 4 stamens, 2 of which being fertile. The fruit is a dehiscent capsule, which is fusiform, dark green, and 0.4 – 0.6 cm long. The seeds are minute and irregularly triangular (Figure 216).

Medicinal Uses: The plant is bitter.

Pharmacology: To date, *Lindernia ciliata* (Colm.) Penn. has not been being tested for pharmacology. Lan (1996), isolated beta-sitosterol, stigmasterol and lup-20(29)-en-3 beta-ol from a petroleum ether extract of the whole plant. The closely related *Vandellia cordifolia* had a diuretic effect on rats and rabbits by inhibiting Na+ and K+ reabsoprtion of renal tubules (Tsai, 1989). *Vandellia cordifolia* suppressed human mononuclear cells proliferation activated with phytohemagglutinin by blocking both interleukin-2 (IL-2) and interferon-gamma (IFN-gamma) production (Lin, 2000). Both activities might be due to oleananes, saponins or hydroxyflavone glycosides which are known to occur in the genus *Lindernia* (Miyase *et al.*, 1995; Tomás-Barberán *et al.*, 1988).

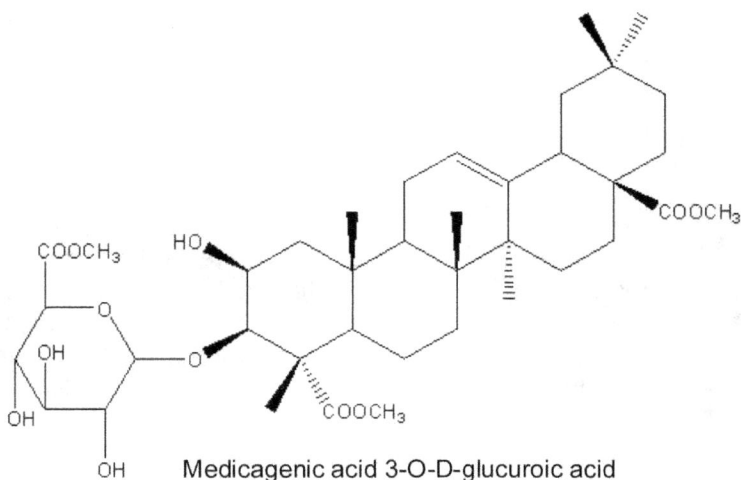

Medicagenic acid 3-O-D-glucuroic acid

References:
Lan S, 1996, Chemical components of *Lindernia ciliata* (Colsm) Pennell. Zhongguo Zhong Yao Za Zhi.; 21: 38-39, 64.

Lin AP, Tsai WJ, Fan CY, Lee MJ, Kuo YC, 2000, Vandellia cordifolia regulated cell proliferation and cytokines production in human mononuclear cells; Am J Chin Med; 28: 313-323.

Miyase T, Andoh T, Ueno A., 1995, Lindernioside A and B, oleanane saponins from *Lindernia pyxidaria*; Phytochemistry; 40: 1499-502.

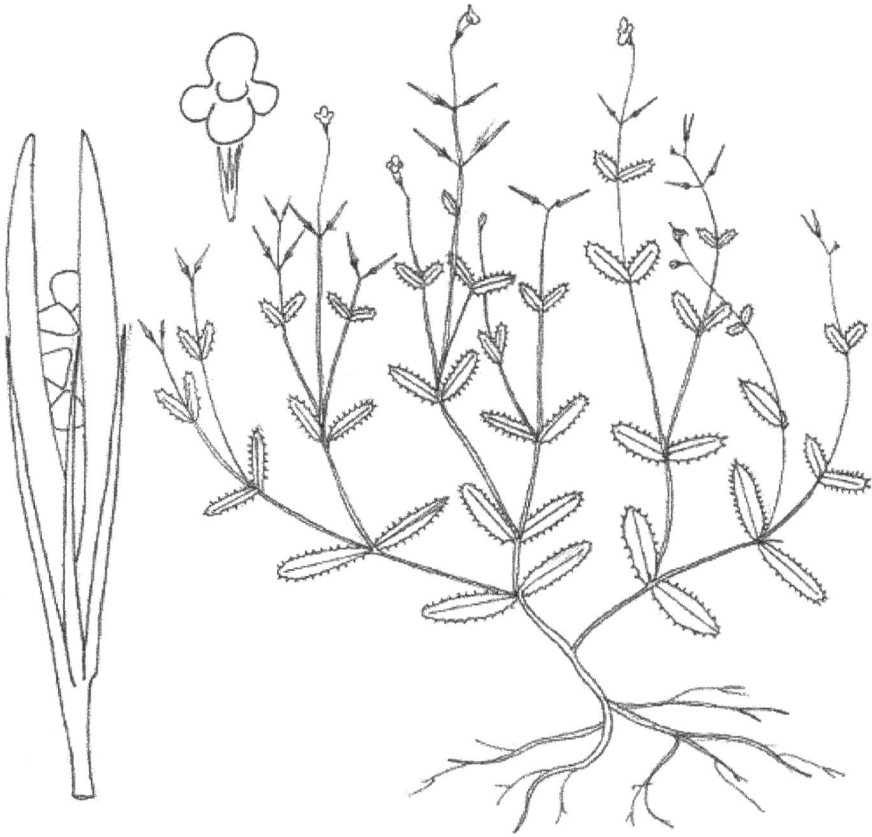

Figure 216 : *Lindernia ciliata* (Colm.) Penn.
Flora of Thailand, Chiang Mai University Herbarium.
Thailand, Lampang province, Hahng Chat district, Doi Kuhn Dahn National Park, Southeast side, Waw Gayo subdistrict, Mae Pry station area. Elevation 350 m, date of collection 29 July 1994. In open disturbed, fire-prone area in degraded, deciduous forest with much bamboos and secondary growth. Shale bedrock. Collection and identification by J.F. Maxwell. N° 94-826.

Tomás-Barberán FA, Grayer-Barkmeijer RJ, Gil MI, Harborne JB, 1988, Distribution of 6-hydroxy-, 6-methoxy- and 8-hydroxyflavone glycosides in the labiatae, the scrophulariaceae and related families; Phytochemistry; 27: 2631-2645.

Tsai HY, Chiang RT, Tan TW, Chen HC, 1989, The effects of *Vandellia cordifolia* on renal functions and arterial blood pressure. Am J Chin Med; 17: 203-10.

Lindernia crustacea (L.) F. Muell.

[After German botanist Franz Balthazar von Lindern (1682-1755) and Latin *crustacea* = having a shell or rind]

Local name: Malaysian false pimpernel

Basionym: *Capraria crustacea* L. *Mantissa Plantarum* 1: 87. 1767.

Synonyms: *Capraria crustacea* L., *Gratiola lucida* Vahl., *Pyxidaria crustacea* (L.) Kuntze, *Pyxidaria crustacea* (L.) Cham. & Schltdl., *Torenia flaccida* R. Br., *Torenia scabra* R. Br., *Vandellia alba* Benth., *Vandellia bodinieri* H. Lev, *Vandellia crustacea* (L.) Benth.

Description: Annual herb up to 10-20 cm tall which grows in moist areas, rice fields, grassland, trail sides and open disturbed forest, below 1300 m in tropics and subtropics. The stem is brownish red, glabrous, angular, with internodes of about 3 cm long. The leaves are simple, opposite, and without stipules. The petiole is 2 mm long. The leaf blade is triangular-ovate to broadly elliptic, 1.2 - 2 cm x 0.9 - 1.2 cm, crenate or serrate, and with a few hairs. The flower is axillary and solitary or in short apical racemes. The pedicel is slender, 0.5 -2.2 cm, subglabrous. The calyx is urn-like, 0.3 -0.5 cm, shallowly lobed; the lobes triangular-ovate. The corolla is purplish at the base, 0.5 – 0.8 cm long; the tube slightly longer than the calyx; the lower lip 3-lobed, the middle lobe larger and slightly longer than the upper lip; the upper lip ovate, and sometimes shallowly 2-lobed. The stamens are didynamous. The style is fugacious. The capsule is broadly ellipsoid, almost as long as the persistent calyx and contains several pale yellow-brown, subglobose, scrobiculate seeds (Figure 217).

Medicinal Uses: In Indonesia, the plant is used externally to treat ulcers, sores and boils. In the Philippines, the plant is used to promote menses and to treat dysentery.

Pharmacology: The pharmacological potential of this herb is yet unexplored. The healing property might involve saponins which are present in the genus.

Figure 217: *Lindernia crustacea* (L.) F. Muell.
From Flora of Thailand, CMU Herbarium, Faculty of Science, Chiang Mai University
Thailand, Lampang province, Hahng Chat district, Doi Kuhn Dahn National Park, Southeast
side, Waw Gayo subdistrict, Wae Pry station. Elevation 350 m. Date 29 July 1994. Collection
and identification: JF Maxwell N° 94-825.

Lindernia viscosa (Hornem.) Merr.

[After German botanist Franz Balthazar von Lindern (1682-1755) and Latin *viscosa* = sticky]

Local name: Nian mao mu cao (China)

Basionym: *Gratiola viscosa* Hornem. *Enumeratio Plantarum Horti Botanici Hafniensis* 19. 1807.

Synonyms: *Gratiola viscosa* Hornem., *Hornemannia viscosa* Willd., *Lindernia cruciformis* Hayata, *Tittmannia viscosa* (Hornem.) Rchb., *Vandellia viscosa* (Hornem.) Merr.

Description: It is a small annual herb which grows in open forests, next to rocks, from 900 to1300 m in China, Cambodia, India, Indonesia, Laos, Burma, New Guinea, Philippines, Thailand, and Vietnam. The stem is erect with few hairs and 1.2 to 3.5 cm long internodes. The leaves are simple, opposite, sessile and without stipules. The leaf blade is obovate, serrate, membranaceous, 0.7 - 2 cm x 1 - 4 cm, shows 1 or 2 pairs of secondary nerves, and presents a few hairs. The inflorescence is a 6-10-flowered lax raceme. The pedicels are slender and up to 1 cm long. The calyx is 3 mm long, with narrowly lanceolate lobes with are coarsely hairy outside. The corolla tube is whitish, the upper (entire) lip tan, the lower lip (3 lobed) lip is white. The throat of the corolla below the midlobe shows a yellow blot inside. The fruit is a greenish capsule which is 0.2 x 0.3 cm (Figure 218).

Medicinal Uses: The plant is used in the traditional Taiwanese system of medicine to assuage abdominal pains and to check hemoptysis.

Pharmacology: Unknown.

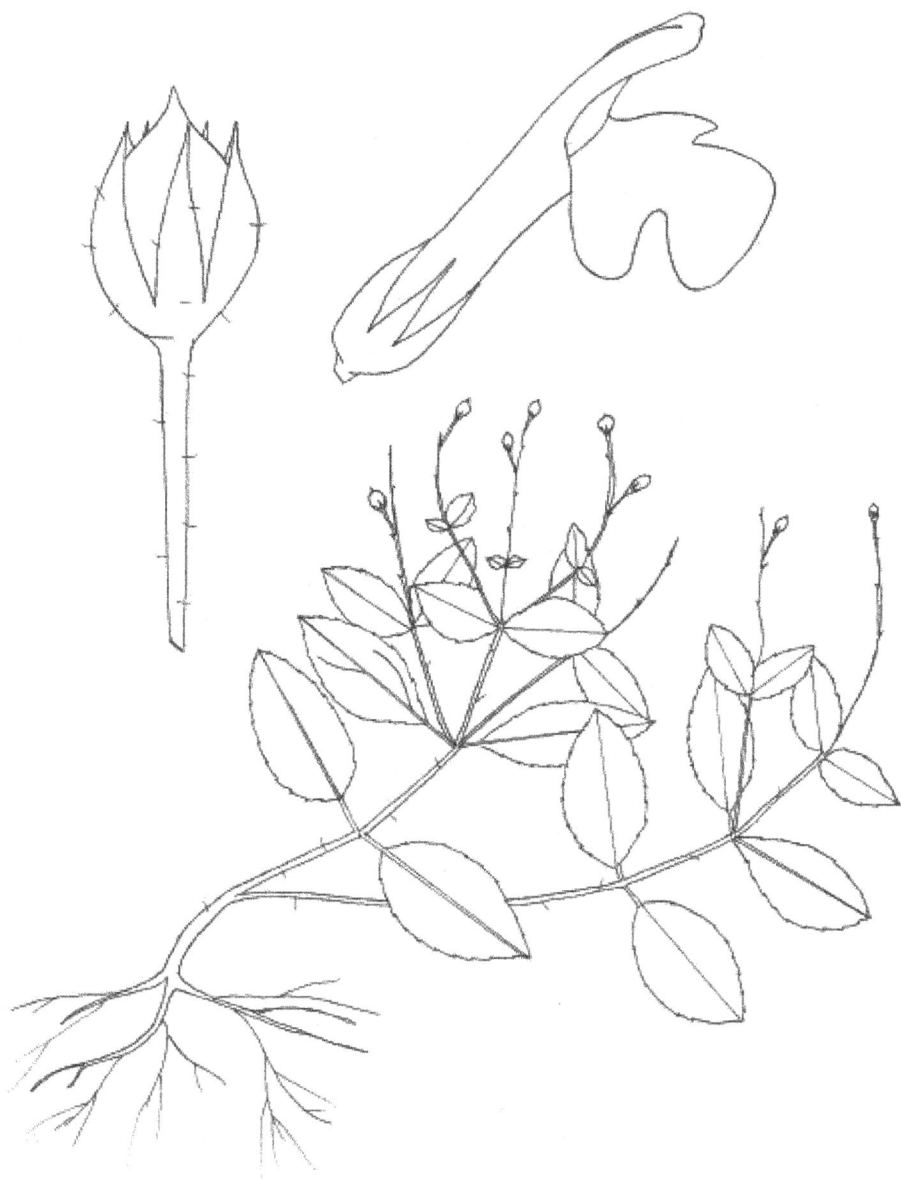

Figure 218: *Lindernia viscosa* **(Hornem.) Merr.**
From: Flora of Thailand, Chiang Mai University Herbarium
Thailand, Lampang province, Fae Sawn national park, northern part. Vahn
Nus district, Pahn Ngahm (Kahn Kaht) caves and limestone mountains, near
Haw Cave. Altitude 550 m. Date of Collection: 25 August 1996. Collection and
identification: JF Maxwell N° 96-1138

Striga asiatica (L.) O. Ktze

[From Latin *asiatica* = from Asia]

Local name: Asiatic witch weed, du jiao jin (China)

Basionym: *Buchnera asiatica* L. *Species Plantarum* 2: 630. 1753

Synonyms: *Buchnera asiatica* L; *Striga asiatica* var. *humilis* (Benth.) D. Y. Hong; *Striga hirsuta* Benth; *Striga. hirsuta* var. *humilis* Benth; *Striga lutea* Lour.

Description: It is a little annual parasitic weed which grows in crop fields, waste grasslands, open sandy glades and behind beaches, below 800 m. in China, Bhutan, Cambodia, India, Nepal, Philippines, Sri Lanka, Thailand, Vietnam and Africa. This herb is considered a pest by farmers since it alters crop production, hence the name witch weed. It reaches a height of 20 cm and is entirely hirsute. The stem is erect, with few branches, 0.1 cm in diameter and angular. The internodes are 0.4 - 1 cm long. The leaves are simple, linear, without stipules and sessile. The leaf blade is 1 x 0.8 cm and sometimes reduced to scales. The flowers are axillary, solitary or in a spike upward. The calyx is 0.4 -0.8 cm long, 10-ribbed with 5 linear lobes. The corolla is usually whitish yellow, 0.8 -1.5 cm long, apically strongly curved; the upper lip 3-lobed. The capsule is ovoid, and enveloped in a persistent ribbed calyx (Figure 219).

Medicinal Uses: In China, the plant is used to expel worms from intestines and to facilitate intestinal transit.

Pharmacology: The pharmacological property of this weed is unknown despite interesting results obtained with other species in the genus *Striga*. Note that parasiticidal effect have been observed in a methanol extracts of *Striga hermonthica,* which at a dose of 400mg/kg weight of mice, exhibited a high intrinsic antimalarial activity (68.5 % suppression) against *Plasmodium berghei* (Okpako *et al.*, 2004). Antioxidant, antifertility and anti-histaminic properties are probable with this weed since they have been observed in *Striga orobancoides* (Badami S. *et al.*, 2003; Hiremath *et al.*, 1997, 2000).

References: Badami S, Gupta MK, Suresh B, 2003,Antioxidant activity of the ethanolic extract of *Striga orobanchioides.* J Ethnopharmacol; 85: 227-30.

                   Harish MS, Nagur M, Badami S, 2001, Antihistaminic and mast cell stabilizing activity of *Striga orobanchioides.* J Ethnopharmacol; 76: 197-200.

Hiremath SP, Badami S, Hunasagatta SK, Patil SB, 2000,Antifertility and hormonal properties of flavones of *Striga orobanchioides*. Eur J Pharmacol; 391: 193-7.

Hiremath SP, Badami S, Swamy HK, Patil SB, Londonkar RL.,1997, Antiandrogenic effect of *Striga orobanchioides*. J Ethnopharmacol; 56: 55-60.

Okpako LC, Ajaiyeoba EO, 2004, In vitro and in vivo antimalarial studies of *Striga hermonthica* and *Tapinanthus sessilifolius* extracts. Afr J Med Sci; 33: 73-5.

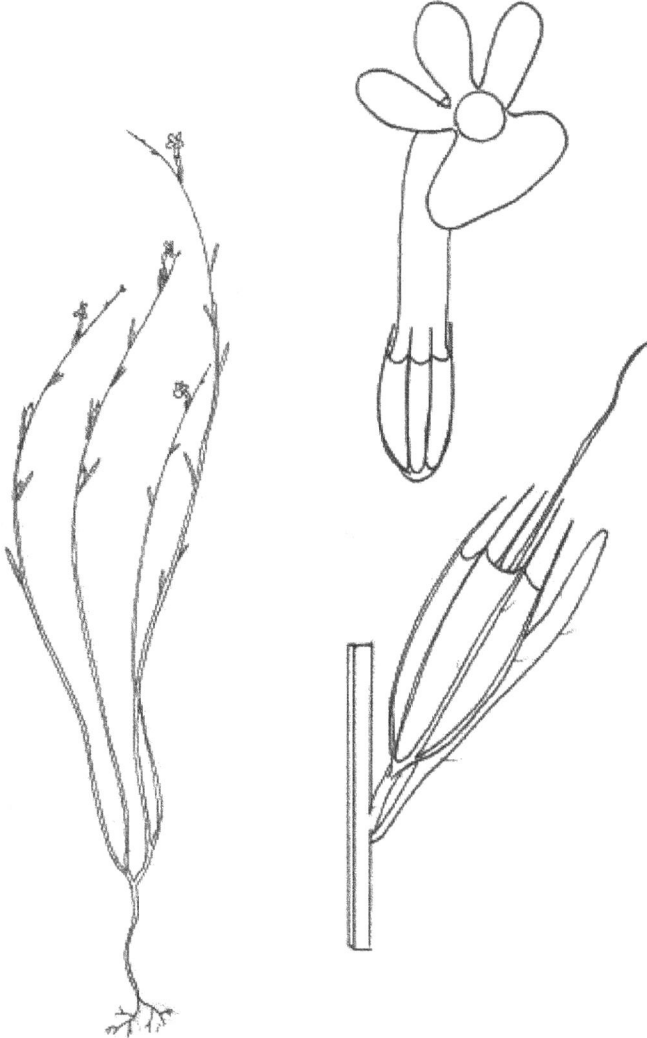

Figure 219: *Striga asiatica* **(L.) O. Ktze**
From Flora of Thailand, Prince of Songkla University.
Thailand, Songkla Province near Bak Bang village, sea level. Date of collection: 9 January 1986. Collection and identification: JF Maxwell

2, Family OROBANCHACEAE Vent. 1799 nom. Conserve., the Broom-rape family

The family Orobanchaceae consists of about 17 genera and 150 species of parasitic herbs which are believed to have evolved from some Scrophulariaceous ancestors. Orobanchaceae are best developed in temperate and subtropical countries. Most members of this family are part of the genus *Orobanche*. Members of this family do not produce chlorophyll and, like Scrophulariaceae, are know to produce iridoid glycosides and phenylpropanoid glycosides such as orobranchin, and some monoterpenoid alkaloids. This plant has much reduced leaves. The flowers are terminal, zygomorphic, and grouped in terminal racemes on top of hairy stems. The calyx is 5 lobed and hairy. The corolla is tubular, hairy, and bilabiate with 5 lobes; the lobes imbricate. The androecium comprises 4 stamens, with tetrasporangiate and dithecal anthers opening by longitudinal slits. The gynoecium consists of a pair of carpels united to form a unilocular and superior ovary containing several ovules attached to parietal placenta. The fruit is a loculicidal capsule containing numerous tiny seeds.

Some members of the family Orobanchaceae are invasive and considered a major threat to crops in some areas. They live on the roots of their host from which they get water and nutrients. Pharmacological evaluations of Orobanchaceae are rare. It could be of some interest to study this family further as a growing body of evidence tends to indicate that the phenylpropanoid glycosides of Orobanchaceae might have serious potential for the treatment of neurodegenerative diseases . Echinacoside, a phenylethanoid glycoside extracted from the medicinal Chinese herb *Cistanches salsa,* protected dopaminergic neurons against 1-methyl-4-phenyl-1,2,3,6-tetrahydropyridine and increased striatal dopamine and dopamine metabolite levels, limited cell death, and increased tyrosine hydroxylase expression. Therefore this compound and its analogues may be possible candidates for treatment of various neurodegenerative disorders, including Parkinson's disease. Another phenylpropanoids glycoside, Tubuloside B (Geng *et al.*, 2007) from *Cistanche salsa,* protected TNF-alpha-induced apoptosis in neuronal cells (Deng *et al.*, 2004). Antineuroapoptotic effects have also been reported (Tian *et al.*, 2005). Other pharmacological properties of interest are vasorelaxant (Yoshikawa *et al.*, 2006), immunostimulating (Wu *et al.*, 2005), anticancer and analgesic properties (Lin *et al.*, 2002). In Southeast Asia, *Boschniakia rossica* (Cham. & Schlecht.) B. Fedtsch. (*Boschniakia glabra* C.A. Mey.), *Cistanche ambigua* (Bge.) G. Beck., *Cistanche deserticola* Y.C. Ma, *Cistanche salsa* (C.A. Mey.), *Orobanche amnophila* C.A. Mey., *Orobanche coerulescens* and *Angenita indica* L. are medicinal and often used to invigorate.

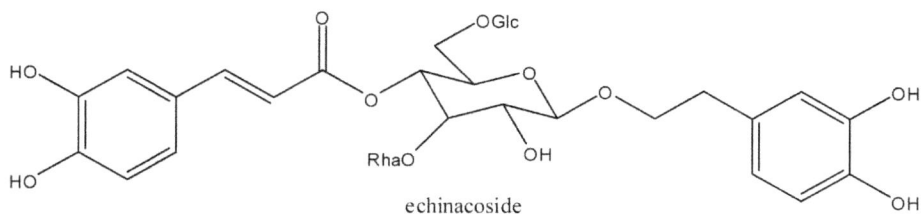

echinacoside

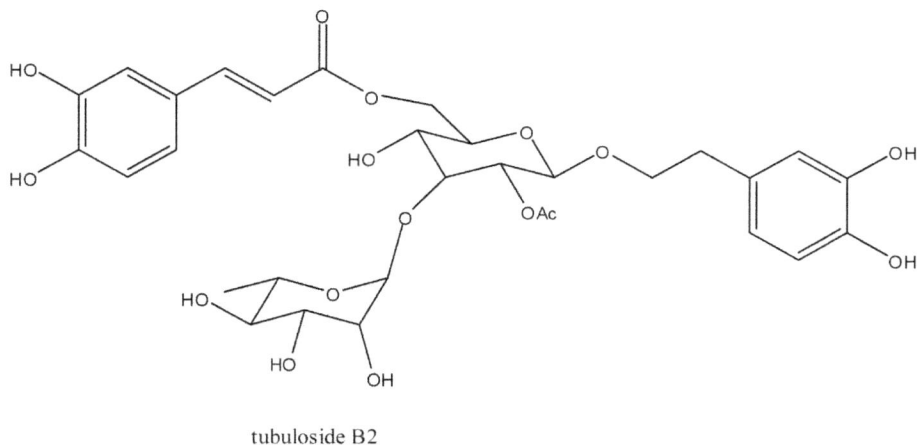

tubuloside B2

References:

Deng M, Zhao JY, Ju XD, Tu PF, Jiang Y, Li ZB, 2004, Protective effect of tubuloside B on TNFalpha-induced apoptosis in neuronal cells. Acta Pharmacol Sin; 25: 1276-84.

Geng X, Tian X, Tu P, Pu X, 2007, Neuroprotective effects of echinacoside in the mouse MPTP model of Parkinson's disease. Eur J Pharmacol; 564: 66-74.

Lin LW, Hsieh MT, Tsai FH, Wang WH, Wu CR, 2002, Antinociceptive and anti-inflammatory activity caused by *Cistanche deserticola* in rodents. J Ethnopharmacol; 83: 177-82.

Tian XF, Pu XP, 2004, Phenylethanoid glycosides from *Cistanches salsa* inhibit apoptosis induced by 1-methyl-4-phenylpyridinium ion in neurons. J Ethnopharmacol; 97: 59-63.

Wu XM, Gao XM, Tsim KW, Tu PF, 2005, An arabinogalactan isolated from the stems of *Cistanche deserticola* induces the proliferation of cultured lymphocytes. Int J Biol Macromol; 37: 278-82.

Yoshikawa M, Matsuda H, Morikawa T, Xiao H, Nakamura S, Muraoka O, 2006, Phenylethanoid oligoglycosides and acylated oligosugars with vasorelaxant activity from *Cistanche tubulosa*. Bioorg Med Chem; 14: 7468-75.

Aeginetia indica L.

[After Paulus Aegineta, Greek Surgeon (4 th century BC) and from Latin *indica* = from India]

Local names:	Dok din daeng (Thailand), ye gu (China),
Synonyms:	*Aeginetia japonica* Siebold & Zucc; *Orobanche aeginetia* L., *Phelipaea indica* (L.) Spreng. ex Steudel.
Description:	It is an annual herb which grows up to 20 cm tall on slopes and roadsides from an altitude of 200 to1800 m. in China, Bangladesh, Bhutan, Cambodia, India, Indonesia, Japan, Laos, Malaysia, Burma, Nepal, Philippines, Sri Lanka, Thailand, and Vietnam.
	It is parasitic on species of *Miscanthus* Anders. and *Saccharum* L. The stem is woody, straight, and somewhat reddish. The plant is leafless or presents some vestigial reddish bracts. The flowers are solitary in a sheath which is striated and about 2 cm long. The corolla is light pink with pale purple or reddish striations near its throat. The corolla tube is 2-4.5 cm, slightly curved; and produces 5 lobes which are sub-equal. The androecium consists of 4 stamens with purple filaments which are 7-9 mm long and glabrous. Anthers are yellow. The style 1-1.5 cm long; stigma light yellow. The fruit is an ovoid conical capsule which is 2-3 cm long and contains several tiny ellipsoid seeds (Figure 220).
Medicinal Uses:	In China, the roots and flowers are used to cool and detoxify. In India the plant is mixed with sugar and nutmeg and taken internally to treat scurvy. In Cambodia, Laos and Vietnam, the plant is used to heal sores. In the Philippines, the plant is used internally to treat diabetes and dropsy.
Pharmacology:	The plant has a strong potential for the development of immunostimulating agents for the treatment of cancer. An extract of seeds from *Aeginetia indica* L. protected BALB/c mice against ascitic form of tumour growth induced by Meth A tumour cells, via an immunostimulating effect involving CD4+ T cells immune activity (Chai *et al.*, 1992). This immunostimulating activity was further confirmed by the stimulation of the production of interleukin 2 (IL-2), interferon gamma (IFN gamma), tumor necrosis factor alpha (TNF-α) and interleukin 6 (IL-6) from T-enriched splenic lymphocytes and especially CD4 + cells exposed to this extract (Chai *et al.*, 1994). The active principle is a protein isolated by Okamoto *et*

al. (2000), the antitumour activity of which mediated by a Toll-like receptor 4 (Okamoto *et al.*, 2004). It could be interesting to conduct a clinical study to assess the effect of this protein as an anticancer agent. It might also have some potential in boosting the immune system of HIV positive patients.

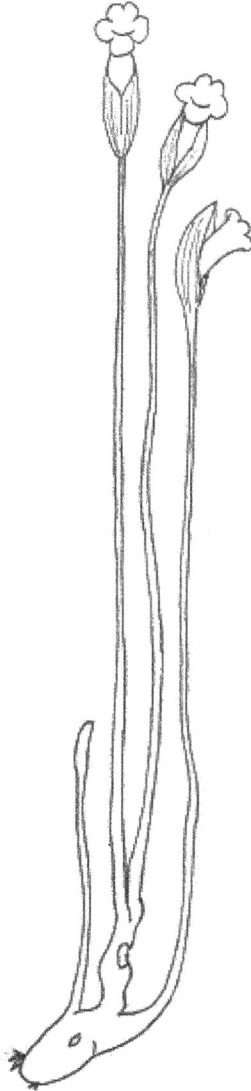

Figure 220: *Aeginetia indica* **L.**
From: Herbarium, Institute of Botany, Academia Sinica, Taipei (HAST). Botanical Inventory of Taiwan.
Location: Hsinchu Hsien, Chienshih Hsiang, Meihua Sechu along the river. Altitude 300 m - 400 m. Collection and identification: Chi-Hsien Lin 503. Date of collection: 12 August 1990.

References: Chai JG, Bando T, Nagasawa H, Himeno K, Sato M, Ohkubo S, 1994, Seed extract of *Aeginetia indica* L induces cytokine production and lymphocyte proliferation in vitro. Immunopharmacology; 27: 13-21.

Chai JG, Bando T, Kobashi S, Oka M, Nagasawa H, Nakai S, Maeda K, Himeno K, Sato M, Ohkubo S, 1992, An extract of seeds from *Aeginetia indica* L., a parasitic plant, induces potent antigen-specific antitumor immunity in Meth A-bearing BALB/c mice. Cancer Immunol Immunother; 35: 181-5.

Okamoto M, Oh EG, Oshikawa T, Furuichi S, Tano T, Ahmed SU, Akashi S, Miyake K, Takeuchi O, Akira S, Himeno K, Sato M, Ohkubo, S, 2004, Toll-like receptor 4 mediates the antitumor host response induced by a 55-kilodalton protein isolated from *Aeginetia indica* L., a parasitic plant. Clin Diagn Lab Immunol; 11: 483-95.

Okamoto M, Ohe G, Oshikawa T, Nishikawa H, Furuichi S, Bando T, Yoshida H, Sakai T, Himeno K, Sato M, Ohkubo S, 2000, Purification and characterization of cytokine-inducing protein of seed extract from *Aeginetia indica* L., a parasitic plant; Immunopharmacology; 49: 377-89.

3.Family GESNERIACEAE Dumortier 1822 nom. conserv., the Gesneriad Family

The family Gesneriaceae consists of about 120 genera and 2,500 species of tropical herbs or shrubs. Closely allied to the Scrophulariaceae, members of this family elaborate orobranchin, and phenylethanoid glycosides. The leaves are simple, opposite, often toothed, and without stipules. The flowers are zygomorphic, often colorful, solitary and axillary. The calyx consists of 5 sepals which are free or united into a lobed tube. The corolla is tubular, curved, and bilabiate. The androecium consists of 4 didynamous stamens, attached to the corolla tube and alternate with the lobes. The gynaecium consists of a pair of carpels merged into a compound, superior single - locular ovary, each locule containing several ovules attached to 2 parietal placentas. The stigma is bilobed. The fruits are loculicidal or a scepticidal capsules or berries containing several small seeds.

Members of the genera *Gloxinia*, *Achimenes*, *Sinningia* and *Streptocarpus* are ornamental. To date not much is actually known about the therapeutic potential of this large family. Phenylethanoid glycosides are common in the family (Damtoft and Jensen, 1994, Liu *et al.*, 1998) and flavones (Liu *et al.*, 1996, 1998; Rathore *et al.*, 1981) might have some antioxidant potential. An ethanolic extract of aerial parts of *Didymocarpus pedicellata* R. Br. exhibited significant antioxidant activity and protected rodents against ferric nitrilotriacetate (Fe-NTA) mediated renal oxidative stress, nephrotoxicity and tumour promotion response, probably on account of flavonoids which abound in the genus. About twenty plants classified within the family Gesneriaceae are used for medicinal purposes in Asia - Pacific. These are quite often used to counteract the putrefaction of the skin, to allay fever and to resolve inflammation.

References: Damtoft S, Jensen RS, 1994, Three phenylethanoid glucosides of unusual structure from *Chirita sinensis* (gesneriaceae) Phytochemistry; 37: 441-43.

Kaur G, Lone IA, Athar M, Alam MS, 2007, Protective effect of *Didymocarpus pedicellata* on ferric nitrilotriacetate (Fe-NTA) induced renal oxidative stress and hyperproliferative response. Chem Biol Interact; 165: 33-44.

Jensen SR, 1996, Caffeoyl phenylethanoid glycosides in *Sanango racemosum* and in the gesneriaceae. Phytochemistry; 43: 777-783.

Liu Y, Wagner H, Bauer R, 1996, Nevadensin glycosides from *Lysionotus pauciflorus*. Phytochemistry; 42: 1203-05.

Liu Y, Wagner H, Bauer R, 1998, Phenylpropanoids and flavonoid glycosides from *Lysionotus pauciflorus*. Phytochemistry; 48: 339-43.

Rathore JS, Garg SK, Nagar A, Sharma ND, Gupta SR, 1981, New Phenolic Components of *Didymocarpus pedicellata*. Planta Med; 43: 86-8.

Didymocarpus reptans Jack

[From Latin *didymocarpus* = with fruit in pairs and *repens* = having creeping and rooting stems]

Synonym:　　　　　*Henckelia reptans* (Jack) Spreng.

Description:　　　　It is a creeping herb which grows on moist, shady and mossy slopes of the rainforest of Malaysia and Borneo. The stem is about 0.5 cm in diameter, subglabrous, angled, woody, stoloniferous and transversally marked with a thin line at the nodes. The internodes are about 1 cm long. The leaves are simple, sub-opposite and without stipules. The petiole is 0.8 - 3 cm long, slightly winged, and clasping at the base. The leaf blade is spathulate, crenate at the margin, acuminate at the apex, 1.2 - 4.1 cm x 3.5 - 15 cm, cuneate at the base, recurved at the margin and marked with 6 - 9 pairs of secondary nerves visible underneath. The flowers are white (Figure 221).

Medicinal Uses:　　In Malaysia the plant is used to treat dysentery, colic and constipation.

Pharmacology:　　The plant has not yet been studied for pharmacology. Members of the genus *Didymocarpus* are known to produce flavonoids and it would be of some interest to investigate the chemical constituents of this plant and asses their pharmacological properties.

Reference:　　　　Adityachaudhury N, Asit K, Das AK, Choudhury A, Daskanungo PL, 1976, Aurentiacin, a new chalcone from *Didymocarpus aurentiaca*. Phytochemistry; 15: 229-230.

　　　　　　　　　Guha PK, Bhattacharyya A, 1992, 5, 8-Dihydroxy-7-methoxyflavone from the immature leaves of *Didymocarpus pedicellata*. Phytochemistry; 31: 1833-1834.

　　　　　　　　　Prakash C. Bose PC, Narayan Adityachaudhury N, 1978, Didymocarpin, a new flavanone from *Didymocarpus pedicellata*. Phytochemistry; 17: 587-588.

　　　　　　　　　Rathore JS, Garg SK, Gupta SR, 1981, A chalcone and flavanones from *Didymocarpus pedicellata*. Phytochemistry; 20: 1755-1756.

　　　　　　　　　Wollenweber E, Rehse C, Dietz VH, 1981, The occurrence of aurentiacin and flavokawin B on *Pityrogramma triangularis* var. pallida and Didymocarpus species. Phytochemistry; 20: 1167-1168.

Figure 221: *Didymocarpus reptans* Jack
From: Flora of Sabah.
Sabah, Pendalaman Reserve, Crocker range, bukit 4140, in rainforest.
Collector: A Zainuddin and Abdul Latiff, ALM 1964. Identification: A. Zainuddin. Date of identification: 4th November 1986.

4.Family ACANTHACEAE A. L. de Jussieu 1789 nom. conserv., the Acanthus Family

The family Acanthaceae consists of 300 genera and 2,500 species of herbs growing in tropical countries. Several kinds of secondary metabolites have been characterized from this family such as orobranchin, iridoid glycosides and phenylethanoid glycosides, diterpenes and aryl naphthalide lignans. The leaves are simple, opposite and without stipules. The calyx is tubular and 5 - lobed, the lobes are imbricate or valvate. The corolla is tubular, zygomorphic, and shows 5 lobes. The androecium consists of 2 or 4 stamens attached to the corolla tube and alternating with the corolla lobes. The anthers are tetrasporangiate, dithecal and open by longitudinal slits. The gynaecium consists of 2 median carpels fused in a 2 - locular and superior ovary, each locule containing numerous ovules. The fruits are upright, club - like explosively dehiscent capsules containing numerous seeds.

To this family belong cohorts of ornamental plants, especially from the genus *Acanthus*: *Alephandra, Barleria, Cossandra, Eranthemum, Fittonia, Justicia, Strobilanthes* and *Thunbergia* are ornamental. Examples of medicinal Acanthaceae are *Adhatoda vasica* (arusha, vasaka) and *Andrographis paniculata* Nees (Kalmegh, *Indian Pharmacopoeia*. 1955) . *Adhatoda vasica* is used to treat coughs. *Andrographis paniculata* Nees is incorporated in several health products but its side effects should be investigated. Asteracantha (*Indian Pharmaceutical Codex*, 1967) consists of *Hygrophila spinosa* (*Asteracantha longifolia*), a decoction of which (1 in 10, dose: 15 mL - 60 mL) has been used as a diuretic in Western medicine. Of particular pharmacological interest in this family are a series of arylnaphthalenes. Elenoside, from *Justicia hyssopifolia* which has central sedative effects and possible application in anxiety conditions (Navaro *et al.*, 2004). Justicidin A, an arylnaphthalene from *Justicia procumbens,* exhibited interesting antiviral activity against vesicular stomatitis virus. Perhaps one of the most pharmacologically studied Asian Acanthaceae is *Andrographis paniculata* Nees from which cohorts of activities have been demonstrated. *Andrographis paniculata* Nees is found in the market in the form of teas or capsules but one should ascertain its chronic toxic effects. Chakraborty *et al.* (2007), have reported encouraging anticancer properties from *Acanthus ilicifolius*. The possibility of isolating a molecule of chemotherapeutic value from this family over the next decades is quite high.

About 50 species of plants classified within the family Acanthaceae are used in Asia - Pacific for medicinal purposes. Note that these plants are often used to soothe inflammation, to allay fever, to promote urination, to heal boils and wounds occasioned by poisonous animals, to treat coughs, and liver discomfort.

References: Asano J, Chiba K, Tada M and Yoshii T, 1996, Antiviral activity of lignans and their glycosides from *Justicia procumbens* Phytochemistry; 42: 713-717.

Chakraborty T, Bunya D, Chatterjee M, Rahaman M, Singha D, Chatterjee BN, Datta S, Rana A, Samanta K, Srivastawa S, Maitra SK, Chatterjee M, 2007, *Acanthus ilicifolius* plant extract prevents DNA alterations in a transplantable Ehrlich ascites carcinoma-bearing murine model. World J Gastroenterol; 13: 6538-48.

Navarro E, Alonso SJ, Trujillo J, Jorge E, Pérez C, 2004, Central nervous activity of elenoside. Phytomedicine; 11: 498-503.

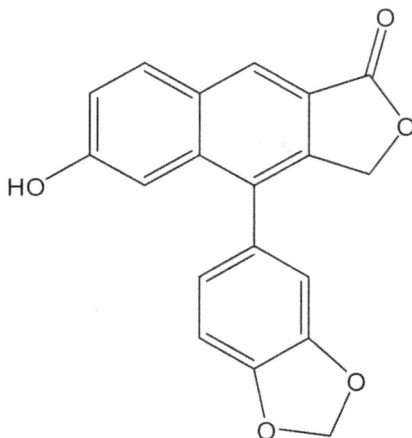

Elenoside

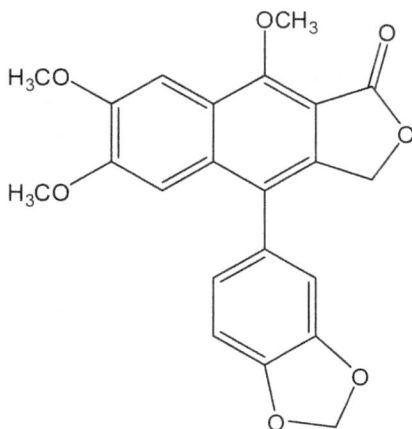

Justicidin A

Adhatoda vasica (L.) Nees

[Latinized form of Sinhalese *adatoda* = name of the plant and from [Latinized form of Sanskrit *vasaka* = protector of the dwelling place]

Local name:	Malabar Nut, Malabar Nut Tree, vasaka (Sanskrit), pavettia (India), noyer de Ceylan (France), mayagyi (Burma)
Synonym:	*Justicia adhatoda* L
Description:	It is a shrub which grows wild in plains, tea plantations and at roadsides, to a height of 2.5 m in India and Southeast Asia. The stem has a basal diameter of about 10 cm. The bark is thin, grey with fine brown pustular lenticels. The young stem is slightly swollen at the nodes, terete and glabrous. The internodes are 2 - 2.5 cm long. The leaves are simple, opposite, and without stipules. The petioles are 1.3 - 5 cm long and discretely channeled. The leaf blade is dark green above, glossy, membranaceous, slightly asymmetrical, 14.5 – 22cm x 4.4 - 10 cm, presents 10 to 12 pairs of secondary nerves, some tertiary nerves underneath, and wavy at the margin. The midrib is sunken above and light green. The inflorescence axis, bracts, and calyx are light to medium green. The flower is 3.5 x 1 cm and odorless. The corolla tube is 3 x 1 cm, light green, bilabiate, each lip white, the lip above bifid, the lip below trifid, with violet venations that look like blood capillaries. The anthers are cream, the connectives are green, and the filament, stigma and style are white (Figure 222).
Medicinal Uses:	In India, the plant is used to treat various ailments including bronchitis, fever, asthma, fever, vomiting, rheumatism, colds, gonorrhea, loss of memory and to expel worms. It is also used to abort. In Burma, the plant is used to heal wounds and to treat coughs, asthma, and tuberculosis

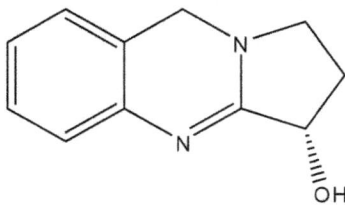

Vasicine

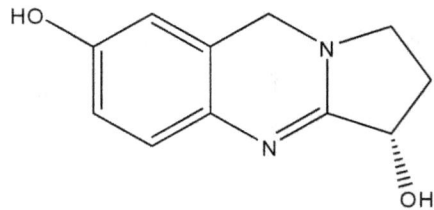

Vasicinol

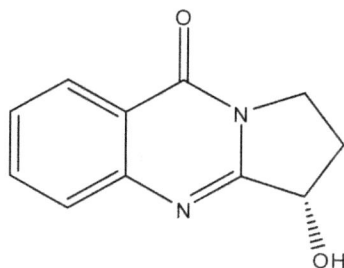

Vasicinone

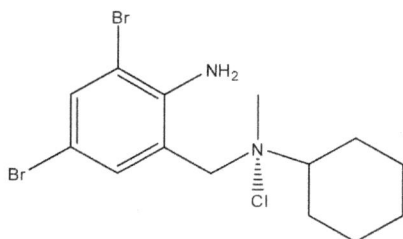

Bromhexine

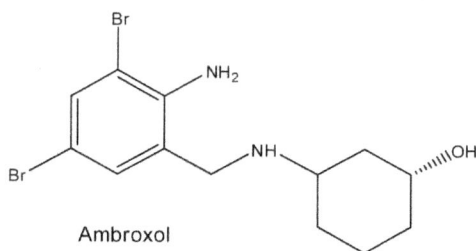

Ambroxol

Pharmacology:

Adhatoda vasica (L.) Nees has been the subject of several chemical and pharmacological studies since the nineteenth century (Claeson *et al.*, 2000), that led to the identification of a series of bioactive quinazoline alkaloids including vasicine, first isolated by Hooper in 1888 (Gosh *et al.*, 1925). Today, bromhexine, and its principal metabolite in man, ambroxol, are wildly-used mucolytic agents and could potentially be useful adjunctive agents in the therapy of tuberculosis (Grange *et al.*, 1996). Vasicine is uterotonic hence the abortifatient property of the plant (Gupta *et al.*, 1978). An other quinazoline alkaloid is vasicinione which is a bronchodilator (Amin *et al.*, 1959). In regards to the possible potential of the plant against tuberculosis, Gupta *et al.* (1954) demonstrated some *in* vitro, antimycobacterial effect of a distillate of leaves. This effect does not involve vasicine (Chopra *et al.*, 1925). Oral administration of an extract of the plant to guinea-pigs exposed to irritant aerosols. elicited antitussive effects comparable to that of codeine (Dhuley *et al.*, 1999). Alkaloids from the plant showed pronounced protection against allergen-induced bronchial obstruction in guinea pigs (10 mg/ml aerosol) (Dorsch *et al.*, 1991).

The alkaloid fraction showed potent anti-inflammatory activity (Chakraborty *et al.*, 2001). In addition, vasicine and vasicinol inhibited the activity of sucrase and alpha-glucosidase suggesting that these could have some potential for the treatment of diabetes (Gao *et al.*, 2008). The plant elicited a number of protective effects. Extract of leaves of *Adhatoda vasica* (L) Nees protected mice against 8 Gy radiations (Kumar *et al.*, 2006). A leaf extract showed a significant hepatoprotective effect on liver damage induced by d-galactosamine in rats (Bhattacharyya *et al.*, 2005), as well as antitumor (Jahangir *et al.*, 2007) and anti-ulcer effects (Shrivastava *et al.*, 2006).

References:

Amin AH, Mehta DR, 1959, A bronchodilator alkaloid (vasicinone) from *Adhatoda vasica* Nees. Nature; 184(Suppl 17):1317.

Barry VC, Conalty ML, Rylance HJ, Smith FR, 1955, Antitubercular effect of an extract of *Adhatoda vasica*. Nature; 176: 119-20.

Bhattacharyya D, Pandit S, Jana U, Sen S, Tapas K, Sur TK, 2005, Hepatoprotective activity of *Adhatoda vasica* aqueous leaf extract on d-galactosamine-induced liver damage in rats Fitoterapia; 76: 223-25.

Chakraborty A, Brantner AH, 2001, Study of alkaloids from *Adhatoda vasica* Nees on their anti-inflammatory activity Phytotherapy Res; 15: 532 -34.

Chopra R, Ghosh S, 1925, Some observations on the pharmacological actions and therapeutic properties of *Adhatoda vasica*. Indian J Med Res; 13: 205-212.

Claeson UP, Malmfors T, Wikman G, Bruhn JG, 2000, *Adhatoda vasica*: a critical review of ethnopharmacological and toxicological data. J Ethnopharmacol; 72: 1-20.

Dhuley JN, 1999, Antitussive effect of *Adhatoda vasica* extract on mechanical or chemical stimulation-induced coughing in animals. J Ethnopharmacol; 67: 361-365.

Dorsch W, Wagner, H, 1991, New antiasthmatic drugs from traditional medicine? Int Arch Allergy Appl Immunol; 94: 262-5.

Gao H, Huang YN, Gao B, Li P, Inagaki C, Kawabata J, 2008, Inhibitory effect on alpha-glucosidase by *Adhatoda vasica* Nees. Food Chemistry; 108: 965-972.

Ghosh TP, Sen J N, 1925, Vasicine - an alkaloid present in *Adhatoda vasica* Nees. Q. J. Ind. Chem. Soc; 1: 315-320.

Grange JM, Snell NJC, 1996, Activity of bromhexine and ambroxol, semi-synthetic derivatives of vasicine from the Indian shrub *Adhatoda vasica*, against *Mycobacterium tuberculosis in vitro*. J Ethnopharmacol; 50: 49-53.

Gupta KC, Chopra IC, 1954, Antitubercular effect of an extract of *Adhatoda vasica*. Nature; 173: 1194.

Gupta OP, Anand KK, Khattak BJ, Atap CK, 1978, Vasicine, alkaloid of *Adhatoda vasica*, a promising uterotonic abortifacient. Indian J Exp Biol; 16: 1075-7.

Jahangir T, Sultana, S, 2007, Tumor promotion and oxidative stress in ferric nitrilotriacetate-mediated renal carcinogenesis: protection by *Adhatoda vasica*. Toxicol Mech Methods; 17: 421-430.

Kumar M, Samarth R, Kumar M, Sylvan SR, Saharan B, Kumar A, 2006, Protective Effect of Adhatoda vasica Nees against radiation-induced damage at cellular, biochemical and chromosomal levels in Swiss Albino mice. Evidence-Based Compl Alt Med; 4: 343-350.

Shrivastava N, Srivastava A, Banerjee A, Nivsarkar M, 2006, Anti-ulcer activity of *Adhatoda vasica*. Nees. J Herb Pharmacother; 6: 43-9.

Figure 222: *Adhatoda vasica* (L.) Nees
From: Flora of Thailand, Chiang Mai University Herbarium,
Thailand, Chiang Mai province, Sahngahmpang district, Doi Lohn, West side, above Mas Gahm Bawn Village, Buay Gaye Subdistrict, in a tea plantation. Altitude: 1250 m. Date of collection: 7 January 1996.

Barleria cristata L.

[After 17th century French botanist, Jacques Barrelier and Latin *cristata* = comb-like]

Local name:	Crested Philippine violet, bluebell Barleria; kolintang-violeta (Philippines), bender kurro, katsaraiya (Nepal)
Synonym:	*Barleria ciliata* Roxb., *Barleria dichotoma* Roxb., *Barleria nepalensis* Nees
Description:	It is a perennial shrub-like herb which grows to a height of about 2 m. The plant is cultivated as a garden ornamental in several countries and originates from Southeast Asia. It is found wild from an altitude of 200 - 2000 m in the Himalayas, India, Burma, Cambodia, Laos, Vietnam, South China, and the Philippines. The stem is erect, smooth, 0.3 - 0.4 cm in diameter, hairy with 7 - 9 cm long internodes. The leaves are simple, dark green above, opposite, and without stipules. The leaf blade is 2.7 - 6.5 cm x 9 - 22 cm, oblong to elliptic, acuminate at the apex, and somewhat hairy underneath. The flower is violet and axillary and surrounded by light green, ovate-lanceolate, 2 cm long, persistent, and laciniately toothed, conspicuously nerved sepals which turn light brown. The corolla is 6 - 7 cm long, with a kneeled tube from which develop 5 lobes, 4 on top and a single one below. The fruit is a fusiform capsule which is smooth and about 2 cm long and opens to release a few seeds (Figure 223).
Medicinal uses:	In India, the seeds are antidotal for snake bite, and the roots and leaves are applied to skin to sooth inflamed parts. The plant is also used to treat coughs.
Pharmacology:	The pharmacological property of this plant is yet unexplored.

Barleria lupulina Lindl.

[After 17th century French botanist, Jacques Barrelier and Latin *lupulina* = hop-like]

Local names:	Madagascar acanthi, hophead, Philippines violet; salet pang, chong ra ar (Thailand).
Synonym:	*Barleria monostachya* Bojer ex Bouton
Description:	It is an erect shrub which grows by roadsides and in disturbed areas in India, Southeast Asia, the Pacific Islands and Australia. It is quite common in tropical gardens. The stem is glabrous and spiny at nodes. The internodes are 4.5 - 6.5 cm long. The spines

Figure 223: *Barleria cristata* L.
From: Flora of Thailand, Chiang Mai University Herbarium. Thailand, Lampoon, Mae The district, Doi Kuhn Dan national Park, summit ridge, and just below the summit of Doi Kuhn Dahn. Altitude 1325 m. Date of collection: 1ˢᵗ February 1994.

Description (contd)   are in pairs at axils with leaf petioles, straight, slender, hard, 1.2 x 0.1 mm. The leaves are simple, opposite and without stipules. The petiole is a few mm long. The blade is linear 1.5 - 7.5 cm x 0.6 - 1 cm. The midrib is broad and reddish underneath the leaf blade and secondary nerves are not visible. The inflorescence is about 12 cm x 2.5 cm terminal spike with overlapping bracts.

The bracts are broadly ovate, 1.5 cm long, shortly mucronate, spoon-like, and green with purplish-brown coloration at the apex. The calyx is 5 - lobed, the lobes lanceolate 0.8 - 1 cm long. The corolla is yellow, the tube 2 cm long and producing 4 lobes which are 1 cm long. The stamens are protruding (Figure 224).

Medicinal Uses:

In Malaysia, the plant is a snake bite antidote. In Thailand, it is used for insect bites, and herpes infection.

Pharmacology:

The antiviral property of this plant has been confirmed *in vitro*. An extract of *Barleria lupulina* Lindl. abrogated the survival of several strains of herpes simplex virus type 2 suggesting a therapeutic potential of this plant (Yoosook *et al.*, 1999). A methanol extract of the plant (at doses of 100, 200 and 300 mg/kg) reduced the spontaneous activity, alertness, awareness, pain response and touch response of rodents in a dose dependent manner as well as showing myorelaxing and hypnotic properties (Suba *et al.*, 2002). The methanol extract of aerial parts of *Barleria lupulina* orally tested at doses of 100, 200 and 300 mg/kg exerted a significant antihyperglycemic effect in streptozotocin-induced hyperglycemia in rats (Suba *et al.*, 2004). A methanol extract of aerial parts of the plant protected albino rats against experimentally induced gastric and duodenal ulcers (Suba *et al.*, 2004). An extract of induced powerful dose-dependent inhibitory effects in oedema models in rats and inhibited myeloperoxidase activity in inflamed tissue indicating that the anti-inflammatory effect of the extracts is associated with reduced neutrophil migration (Wakinat *et al.*, 2008). It would be of interest to study the chemical composition of this plant and elucidate the structure of the principle responsible for the pharmacological activities mentioned here. Arylnaphthalides are probably responsible for some of these effects.

References:

Suba V, Murugesan T, Rao RB, Pal M, Mandal SC, Saha BP, 2002, Neuropharmacological profile of *Barleria lupulina* Lindl. Extract in animal models. J Ethnopharmacol; 81: 251-5.

Suba V, Murugesan T, Rao RB, Ghosh L, Pal M, Mandal SC, Saha BP, 2004, Antidiabetic potential of *Barleria lupulina* extract in rats. Fitoterapia ; 75: 1-4. Erratum in: Fitoterapia; 75: 426.

Suba V, Murugesan T, Pal M, Mandal SC, Saha BP, 20042, Antiulcer activity of methanol fraction of *Barleria lupulina* Lindl. in animal models. Phytother Res; 18: 925-9.

Wanikiat P, Panthong A, Sujayanon P, Yoosook C, Rossi AG, Reutrakul V, 2008, The anti-inflammatory effects and the inhibition of neutrophil responsiveness by *Barleria lupulina* and *Clinacanthus nutans* extracts. J Ethnopharmacol; 116: 234-44.

Yoosook C, Panpisutchai Y, Chaichana S, Santisuk T, Reutrakul V, 1999, Evaluation of anti-HSV-2 activities of *Barleria lupulina* and *Clinacanthus nutans*. J Ethnopharmacol; 67: 179-87.

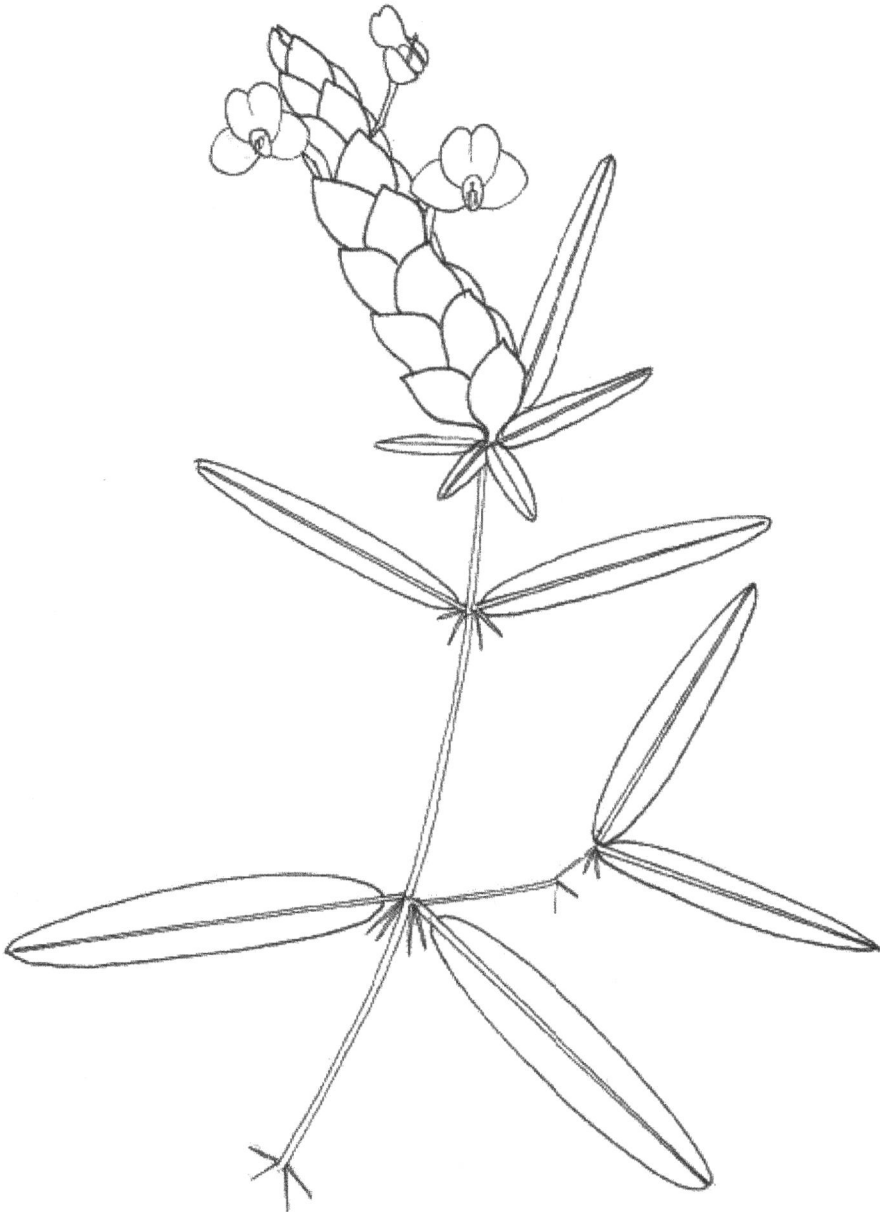

Figure 224: *Barleria lupulina* Lindl.

From Flora of Malaya
Singapore, Botanic Garden. Collector Mohd. Kassim.

Graptophyllum pictum (L.) Griffith

[From Greek *graptos* = painted and *phullon* = leaf and from Latin *pictum* = variegated]

Local names:	Caricature plant, benalu, pudding merah (Malaysia), daun ungu (Indonesia), bai tawng (Thailand), morado, kalpueng (Philippines).
Basionym:	*Justicia picta* L. *Species Plantarum, Editio Secunda* 1: 21. 1762
Synonyms:	*Graptophyllum hortensis* Nees, *Justicia ecbolium* Blco.
Description:	It is a shrub which grows to a height of 1.5 m. The plant is native to Papua New Guinea and grown as a garden and interior ornamental. The stem is quadrangular, longitudinally striated, with 1.5 - 4 cm long internodes. The leaves are simple, opposite, and without stipules. The petiole is about 7 mm long, channeled and grasping the stem. The leaf blade is membranaceous, 8 - 20 cm x 3 - 13 cm, oblong - lanceolate, cuneate at the base, glossy, variegated with whitish cream-pink patches and undulate. The margin of the leaf blade is recurved and displays 9 - 11 pairs of secondary nerves. The flowers are arranged in axillary panicles of 3 - 12 cm long. The flower pedicel is about 3 mm long. The calyx is 3 mm long with 1 mm long lobes. The corolla is tubular, glossy, dark red and 2 - 3.5 cm long (Figure 225).
Medicinal Uses:	In Malaysia, a decoction of the leaves is used as a laxative. It heals haemorrhoids, expels gallstones, and assuages liver discomfort. A paste of the leaves is applied to cuts, wounds, and ulcers, and to soothe swollen parts. The juice expressed from the plant is used as ear drops to assuage earache. In the Philippines, the leaves are applied to ulcers. In Indonesia, the plant is diuretic, anti -inflammatory on the skin, and the flowers are an emmenaguoge.
Pharmacology:	The anti-inflammatory property of the plant has been confirmed: an ethanol extract of leaves of *Graptophyllum pictum* (L.) Griffith given *per os* to rodent displays anti-inflammatory and analgesic properties (Ozaki *et al.*, 1989) in which flavonoids, iridoid glycosides or phenylethanoid glycosides might be involved.
Reference:	Ozaki Y, Sekita S, Soedigdo S, Harada M, 1989, Anti-inflammatory effect of *Graptophyllum pictum* (L.) Griff. Chem. Pharm. Bull. Tokyo; 37: 2799 - 2802.

Figure 225: *Graptophyllum pictum* (L.) Griffith
From: Flora of Malaya
Date of collection: 8 July 1972
Collection and identification: Mohd. Kassim

Justicia ventricosa Wall.

[After James Justice, 18th century Scottish botanist and Latin *ventricosa* = having a swelling on one side]

Synonyms: *Adhatoda ventricosa* Nees, *Gendarussa ventricosa* Nees

Description: It is a shrub which grows to a height of 2 m in open land and sandy alluvium in Southeast Asia. The stem is pitted, 0.3 - 0.5 cm in diameter, smooth minutely lenticelled, and striated longitudinally. The internodes are 2.5 - 10 cm long. The nodes are conspicuously marked with a deep ring which forms a constriction. The leaves are simple, opposite and without stipules. The petiole is slender, grooved and 2 - 5 cm long. The leaf blade is dull dark green above, papery, spathulate, tapering at the base, the apex shortly acuminate, the margin wavy, recurved, 3.4 - 6.2 cm x 8.7 - 22 cm and somewhat irregular in shape. The inflorescence is a terminal spike, of about 10 cm long, with numerous bracts which are dark green with a faint dark violet hue, 1.2 cm x 0.6 cm and broadly lanceolate. The flower is 1 - 1.5 cm long. The corolla tube is bilabiate, the lower lip trilobed. The corolla is whitish to very pale light greenish, the lips cream, the lower lip inside with oblique reddish lines. The anthers are light yellow. The fruit is a fusiform dehiscent capsule which is hairy and 1.2 x 0.4 cm (Figure 226).

Medicinal Uses: The plant is used as anti-inflammatory and febrifuge remedy in Southeast Asia.

Pharmacology: Unknown. It would be of some interest to characterize the pharmacologically active arylnaphthalenes which probably occur in the plant.

Polytrema vulgare C.B. Clarke

[From Latin *vulgare* = common]

Local name: Dac kim (Vietnam)

Description: It is a herb which grows along rivers to a height of about 25 cm in Southeast Asia. The stem is terete, articulated, subglabrous, 0.2 cm in diameter, and longitudinally striated. The internodes are 2 - 4 cm long and the nodes are slightly swollen. The leaves are simple, opposite, unequally sized per pair, and without stipules. The petiole is 0.3 - 0.6 cm long, channeled, and hairy.

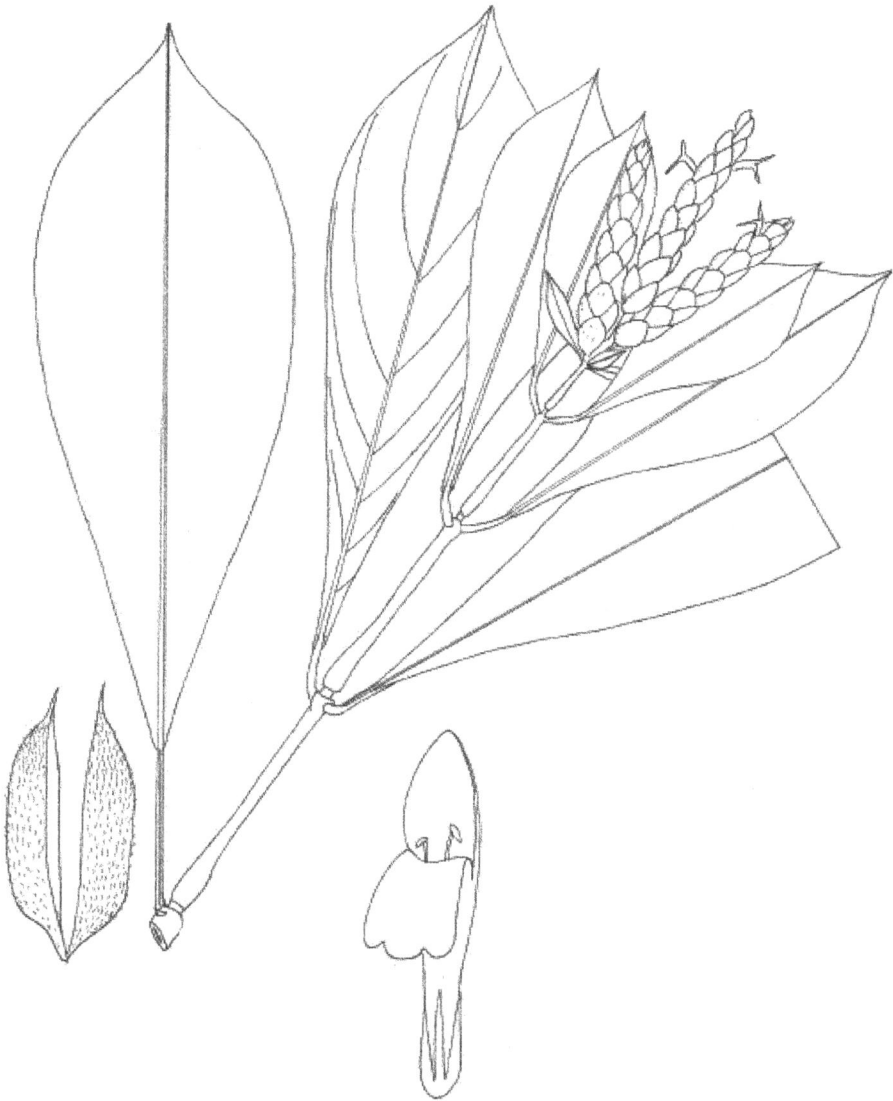

Figure 226: *Justicia ventricosa* Wall.

From: Flora of Thailand
Thailand, Chiang Mai province, Chiang Dao district, Doi Chiang Dao animal sanctuary, West side along Huay Kawng (stream) near Muang Kawn village, North of Bahn Yahng-Huay station. Altitude 700 m. Date of collection: 30arch 1995. Collection and identification JF Maxwell. N° 95-288 and N° 95-25.

The leaf blade is dark green above, light green underneath, lanceolate, papery, 2.8 - 3.5 cm x 4.5 -10 cm. The margin of the leaf blade is slightly wavy, the base is slightly asymmetrical and the apex is acute, and presents 5 - 6 pairs of secondary nerves. The inflorescence is an axillary few flowered cyme. The calyx is about 0.6 cm long with linear lobes. The corolla is white, inside of midlobe of lower lip light yellow. The anthers, filaments, stigma and style are white (Figure 227).

Medicinal uses: The plant is used to heal boils, ulcers and inflamed skin.

Pharmacology: Unknown.

Figure 227: *Polytrema vulgare* C.B. Clarke
From: Flora of Thailand, Prince of Songkla University
Thailand, Pattani province, Kok Po district, Sai Kow Falls. Altitude 200 m. Date of collection: 18 July 1985. Collection and identification: JF Maxwell.

Rungia parviflora (Retz.) Nees

[After Friedrich Ferdinand Runge (1795-1867), a German analytical chemist, and Latin *parviflora* = small-flowered]

Local names:	Pindi (Sanskrit), ukuchi jhar (Nepal)
Synonym:	*Rungia pectinata* (L.) Nees
Description:	It is an annual herb which grows in open forest, and on jungle paths from an altitude of 300 to 2000 m in India, Nepal, South China, Cambodia, Laos, Vietnam and Malaysia. The plant is covered with microscopic whitish and linear dots. The stem is branched, dull green, terete and pubescent with internodes 7.5 - 8.5 cm long. The leaves are simple, opposite, without stipules, and somehow fleshy. The petiole is slender, 1 - 1.4 cm long. The leaf blade is dark green above, pale light green underneath, thin, lanceolate, wavy, recurved, tapering at the base, 4.7 - 9 cm x 2.3 - 1.2 cm and shows 4-5 pairs of secondary nerves. The inflorescence is an axillary spike which is 0.6 - 2.5 cm long on 1 - 1.5 cm long pedicels. The bracts are 0.3 cm in diameter, hairy, orbicular, cuspidate, and greenish with reddish brown the apex. The calyx lobes are green with a red-brown tip. The corolla is blue to pale lilac, 0.5 cm long, with a few hairs outside, upper lip 0.15 cm long and ovate, lower lip 0.25 cm long and 3 - lobed. The anthers are brown. The fruits are ovoid capsules containing 2 - 4 seeds (Figure 228).
Medicinal uses:	In India, the juice expressed from the fresh leaves is given orally to children suffering from smallpox. The leaves are pounded and applied to inflamed skin. The roots are used to break fever.
Pharmacology:	The anti-inflammatory property of the plant has been confirmed. Zhao *et al.* (2008), demonstrated that an ethanol extract of *Rungia parviflora* (Retz.) Nees reduced, like dexamethasone, production of pro-inflammatory cytokines and mediators via blocking NF-kappaB activation but slightly stimulated the release of anti-inflammatory mediator HO-1 and suppressed IL-10 secretion. The principle involved here is unknown.
References:	Zhao L, Tao JY, Zhang SL, Jin F, Pang R, Dong JH, Guo YJ, Ye P, 2008, Anti-inflammatory mechanism of *Rungia pectinata* (Linn.) Nees. Immunopharmacol Immunotoxicol; 30: 135-51.

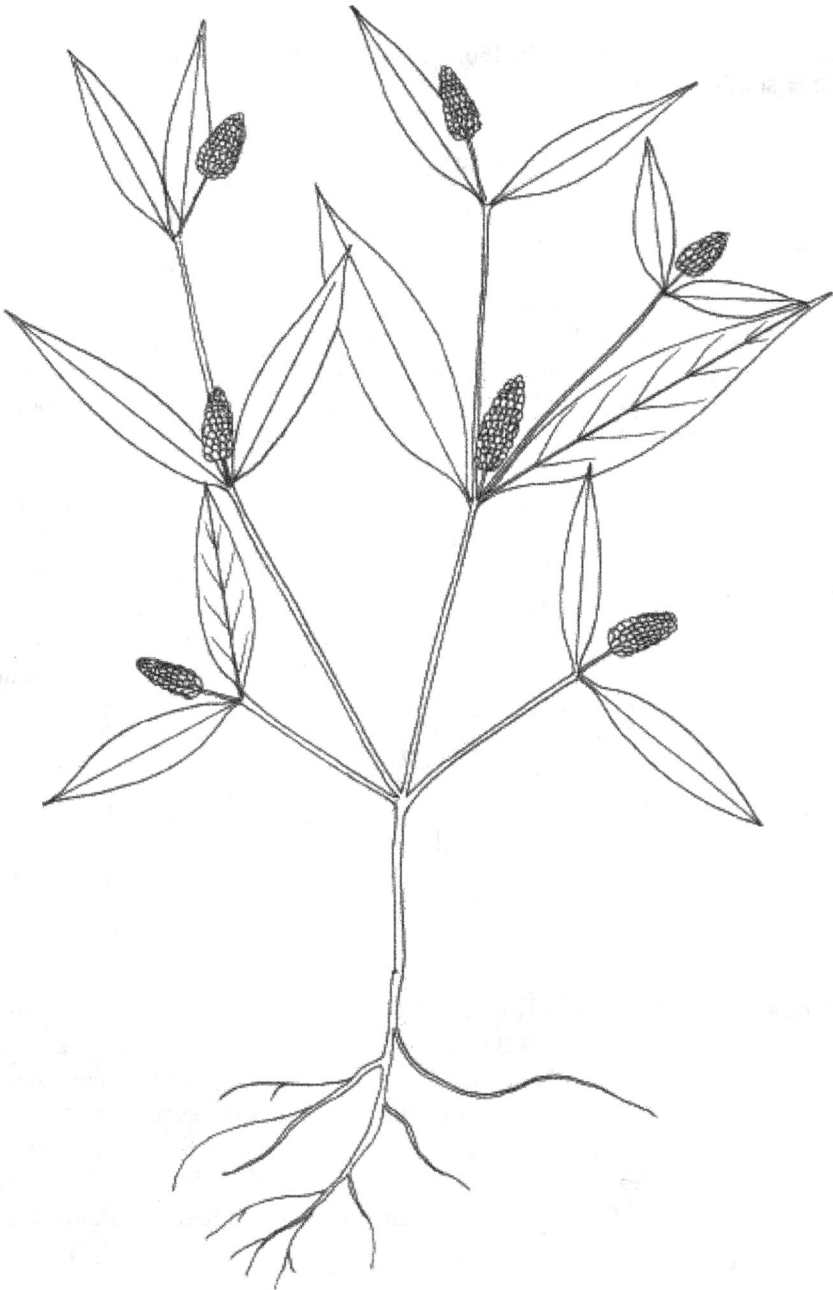

Figure 228: *Rungia parviflora* **(Retz.) Nees**
From: Flora of Thailand, Chiang Mai University Herbarium.
Thailand, Lampang province, Muang Bahn district, Jae Sawn National Park, headquarters area. Date of collection: 23 September 1995. Collection and identification: JF Maxwell.

5.Family BIGNONIACEAE A. L. de Jussieu 1789 nom. conserv., the Trumpet - creeper Family

The family Bignoniaceae consists of 100 genera and 800 species of soft wooded tropical trees, known to elaborate prenylated naphthoquinones, phenylpropanoid glycosides, and iridoid glycosides. The leaves are compound, without stipules, and opposite or occasionally whorled. The flowers are showy and zygomorphic. The inflorescences are cymose or racemose. The calyx is tubular, and 5 - lobed. The corolla is tubular, bilabiate, and develops a pair of upper lobes and 3 lower lobes. The androecium consists of 5 stamens which are attached to the corolla tube. A nectary disc is present. The gynaecium consist of 2 carpels united to form a superior and 2 - locular ovary, each locule containing several ovules attached to axile placentas. The style is long. The stigma is forked. The fruits are bivalved, septicidal or loculicidal capsules containing numerous seeds which are flat and winged, the wings being very thin and translucent.

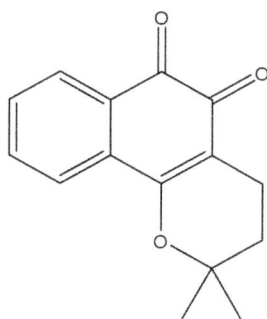

Lapachone

The Bignoniaceae includes several ornamental plants such as *Spathodea* species (flame - tree), *Jacaranda* species, *Catalpa* species, *Paulownia* species (empress - tree), *Campsis radicans* and *Bignonia* species (trumpet creeper). In terms of pharmacological interest, the quinones of Bignoniaceae might hold some potential as cytotoxic (Yamashita *et al.*, 2007), antimicrobial (Lenta *et al.*, 2007) or antiplasmodial agents. One example of such a principle is beta-lapachone from the bark of the lapacho tree (*Tabebuia avellanedae*). This naphthoquinone induces apoptosis in HepG2 hepatoma cell line through induction of Bax and activation of caspase (Woo *et al.*, 2006). It inhibits the growth of A549 human lung carcinoma cells by beta-visa induction of apoptosis and inhibition of telomerase activity (Woo *et al.*, 2005). Beta-lapachone induces growth inhibition and apoptosis in bladder cancer cells by modulation of Bcl-2 family and activation of caspases, (Lee *et al.*, 2006). Other molecules of interest in the Bignoniaceae are iridoid glycosides such as catalposide from *Catalpa ovata* G. Don, which inhibits the productions of tumour necrosis factor-α interleukin-1 β, and interleukin-6 as well as the activation of nuclear factor κB in RAW 264.7 macrophages activated with lipopolysaccharide (An *et al.*, 2002). This is an attractive candidate for adjunctive therapy in Gram-negative bacterial infections.

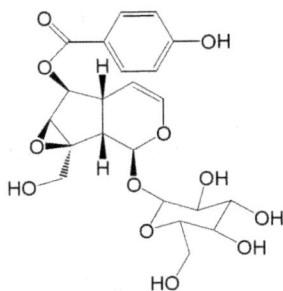

Catalposide

In Asia - Pacific, *Campsis grandiflora* (Thunb.) K. Schum., *Catalpa ovata* G. Don, *Crescentia alata* HBK., *Oroxylum indicum* (L.) Vent., *Pajanelia longifolia* (Willd.) K. Schum. (*Pajanelia multijuga* DC.), *Incarvillea sinensis* Lamk., *Markhamia stipulata* (Wall.)Seem., *Stereospermum chelonoides* DC., *Stereospermum fimbriatum* (Wall.) DC., *Spathodea campanulata* P. Beauv., *Millingtonia hortensis* L.f., and *Dolichandrone spathacea* (L. f.) K. Schum. are of medicinal value. The discovery of clinical agents from this family is highly likely.

References: An SJ, Pae HO, Oh GS, Choi BM, Jeong S, Jang SI, Oh H, Kwon TO, Song CE, Chung HT, 2002, Inhibition of TNF-alpha, IL-1beta, and IL-6 productions and NF-κB activation in lipopolysaccharide-activated RAW 264.7 macrophages by catalposide, an iridoid glycoside isolated from Catalpa ovata G. Don (Bignoniaceae) Int. Immunopharmacol; 2: 1173-81.

Lee JI, Choi DY, Chung HS, Seo HG, Woo HJ, Choi BT, Choi YH, 2006 , Beta-lapachone induces growth inhibition and apoptosis in bladder cancer cells by modulation of Bcl-2 family and activation of caspases. Exp Oncol; 28: 30-5.

Lenta BN, Weniger B, Antheaume C, Noungoue DT, Ngouela S, Assob JC, Vonthron-Sénécheau C, Fokou PA, Devkota KP, Tsamo E, Sewald N, 2007, Anthraquinones from the stem bark of Stereospermum zenkeri with antimicrobial activity. Phytochemistry; 68: 1595-9.

Woo HJ, Choi YH, 2005, Growth inhibition of A549 human lung carcinoma cells by beta-lapachone through induction of apoptosis and inhibition of telomerase activity. Int J Oncol; 26: 1017-23.

Woo HJ, Park KY, Rhu CH, Lee WH, Choi BT, Kim GY, Park YM, Choi YH, 2006, Beta-lapachone, a quinone isolated from Tabebuia avellanedae, induces apoptosis in HepG2 hepatoma cell line through induction of Bax and activation of caspase. J Med Food; 9: 161-8.

Yamashita M, Kaneko M, Iida A, Tokuda H, Nishimura K, 2007, Stereoselective synthesis and cytotoxicity of a cancer chemopreventive naphthoquinone from Tabebuia avellanedae. Bioorg Med Chem Lett ; 17: 6417-20.

Millingtonia hortensis L.f.

[After Lucy Bishop Millington, nineteenth-century botanist and from Latin *hortensis* = of or pertaining to gardens]

Local names:	Tree Jasmine, Indian cork tree, lao ya yan tong hua (China), egayit (Burma), gah chalong (Thailand).
Description:	It is a tree which grows to a height of about 25 m growing wild from an altitude of 500 - 1200 m in Cambodia, Laos, Burma, Thailand, and Vietnam. It is cultivated in India, Indonesia, and Malaysia. The bark is roughly corky, thickened and light brown. The leaves are compound, up to 100 cm long. The petiolule is about 1 cm long. The leaflets are broadly lanceolate, 5 - 7 cm x 1.5 - 4 cm, glabrous, the base rounded, oblique, the margin entire, the apex acuminate; secondary nerves 3 - 5. The inflorescences are cymose-paniculate. The flowers are large, white and pendulous. The calyx is 0.2 - 4 cm x 0.2 -0.4 cm. The corolla tube is 3 -7 cm x 0.2 - 0.3 cm and produces 5 lanceolate lobes. The fruit is a linear capsule which is 30 - 35 cm x 1 -1.5 cm and open to release several discoid-oblong, 1.5 - 3.5 cm x 1 -1.5 cm, compressed seeds, surrounded by membranous and transparent wings (Figure 229).
Medicinal Uses:	In Cambodia, Laos, Vietnam and Indonesia, various parts of the plant are used as a substitute for opium. In Southeast Asia it is used for the treatment of asthma, sinusitis and as a cholagogue and tonic.
Pharmacology:	The plant contains the flavonoids hispidulin and hortensin (3,4'-dihydroxy-6,7-dimethoxyflavone) (Bunyapraphatsara B *et al.*, 1989) which have antimutagenic properties against 2-aminoanthracene, aflatoxin B1, and dimethylnitrosamine (Chulasiri M *et al*, 1992). An aqueous extract of *Millingtonia hortensis* L.f. inhibited RKO human colon cancer cell growth and proliferation in a dose- and time-dependent manner via induction of apoptosis (Tansuwanwong *et al.*, 2006), an effect probably mediated by hispidulin (Yu *et al.*, 2007). Sharma *et al.* (2007), showed that an ethanol extract of the plant had stronger activity than fluconazole against *Candida krusei* and *Sacharomyces cerevisiae*. The opium-like effect of the plant is to date unexplored. Note however that hispidulin traverses the blood-brain barrier and exhibits anticonvulsive effects involving binding to benzodiazepine receptors (Kavvadias *et al.*, 2004).

Figure 229: *Millingtonia hortensis* L.f.

From Flora of Thailand

Thailand, Lampang province, Wahng Nus province, Jae Sawn National Park, northern part, Wahng Die Subdistrict, near the base of Maw Cave, Nahm Kaht limestone mountain. Altitude 500 m. Date of collection: 2 February 1997.Collection and identification: JF Maxwell № 97-114.

References: Bunyapraphatsara N, Blaskó G, Cordell GA, 1989, Hortensin, an unusual flavone from *Millingtonia hortensis*. Phytochemistry; 28: 1555-56 .

Chulasiri M, Bunyapraphatsara N, Moongkarndi P, 1992, Mutagenicity and antimutagenicity of hispidulin and hortensin, the flavonoids from *Millingtonia hortensis* L. Environ Mol Mutagen; 20: 307-12.

Kavvadias D, Sand P, Youdim KA, Qaiser MZ, Rice-Evans C, Baur R, Sigel E, Rausch WD, Riederer P, Schreier P, 2004, The flavone hispidulin, a benzodiazepine receptor ligand with positive allosteric properties, traverses the blood-brain barrier and exhibits anticonvulsive effects. Br J Pharmacol; 142: 811-20.

Sharma M, Puri S, Sharma PD, 2007, Antifungal activity of *Millingtonia hortensis*; 69: 599-601.

Tansuwanwong S, Hiroyuki Y, Kohzoh I, Vinitketkumnuen U, 2006, Induction of apoptosis in RKO colon cancer cell line by an aqueous extract of *Millingtonia hortensis*. Asian Pac J Cancer Prev; 7: 641-4.

Yu J, Liu H, Lei J, Tan W, Hu X, Zou G, 2007, Antitumor activity of chloroform fraction of *Scutellaria barbata* and its active constituents. Phytother Res; 21: 817-22.

6.Family LENTIBULARIACEAE L.C. Richard in Poiteau & Turpin 1808 nom. Conserv., the Bladderwort family

The Family Lentibulariaceae originates from the Scrophulariaceae. It consists of 5 genera and about 200 species of insectivorous cosmopolitan aquatic herbs known to elaborate iridoid and flavonoids glycosides. The leaves are simple, alternate and arranged into a basal rosette and without stipules. Root-like stems form a dense net in water. The flowers are solitary and terminal. The calyx is 4-5 lobed. The corolla is tubular bilabiate, with 5 imbricate lobes. The androecium is made of a pair of stamens with tetrasporangiate and unithecal anthers. The gynoecium consists of 2 carpels united to form a compound, unilocular ovary with several ovules attached to a free central placenta. The fruits are capsular, circumscissile with 1 to many little seeds.

Lentibulariaceae are botanical curiosities and some species are ornamental. Of interest are their carnivorous abilities and potential as removers of mosquito larvae. In Southeast Asia *Utricularia bifida* L., *Utricularia aurea* Lour. (*Utricularia flexuosa* Vahl) and *Utricularia uliginosa* (*Utricularia affinis* Wight) are medicinal. So far, the pharmacological potentials of Lentibulariaceae remain unknown.

Utricularia aurea Lour.

[From Latin *utriculus* = a small bag and *aurea* = golden]

Local names:	Golden bladderwort, gagan (Indonesia), saray andet (Cambodia), nae harng hern (Laos), inata (Philippines), sarai kao niew (Thailand), rong trung (Vietnam)
Synonyms:	*Utricularia blumei* (A. DC.) Miq., *Utricularia calumpitensis* Llanos, *Utricularia confervifolia* Jackson & D. Don, *Utricularia extensa* Hance, *Utricularia fasciculata* Roxb., *Utricularia flexuosa* Vahl, *Utricularia inaequalis* Benj., *Utricularia macrocarpa* Vahl, *Utricularia pilosa* (Makino) Makino, *Utricularia reclinata* Hassk
Description:	It is a perennial floating aquatic herb which grows in quiet muddy ponds, lakes and reservoirs in northern Australia, Southeast Asia, to Pakistan and Japan. The aerial part is a light green slender stem, about 20 cm long, with light brownish bracts. The underwater net consists of 1-8 cm long, multipinnate, dichotomous, light green tubular leaves with 3-5 primary segments with small light green bladders that trap little crustaceans. The bladders are obliquely ovoid, 0.1 -4 cm long and acuminate at the apex. The flowers are yellow, few, at the apex of the aerial stem. The calyx lobes are subequal, ovate, 0.2 -0.3 cm long, accrescent in fruit. The corolla is 1 -1.5 cm long, palate darker below, the upper lip with dull red lines inside. The

fruit is capsular, pale greenish-dull reddish, and 0.7 x 0.5 cm (Figure 230).

Medicinal Uses: In Cambodia, Laos and Vietnam, the plant is used externally to remove pustules from children.

Pharmacology: The plant contains a sulfated polysaccharide fucoidan, which inhibits the growth of KB cells via apoptosis (Choosawad *et al.*, 2005).

Reference: Choosawad D, Leggat U, Dechsukhum C, Phongdara A, Chotigeat W, 2005, Anti-tumor activities of fucoidan from the aquatic plant *Utricularia aurea* lour. Songklanakarin J Sci; 27(Suppl. 3): 799-807.

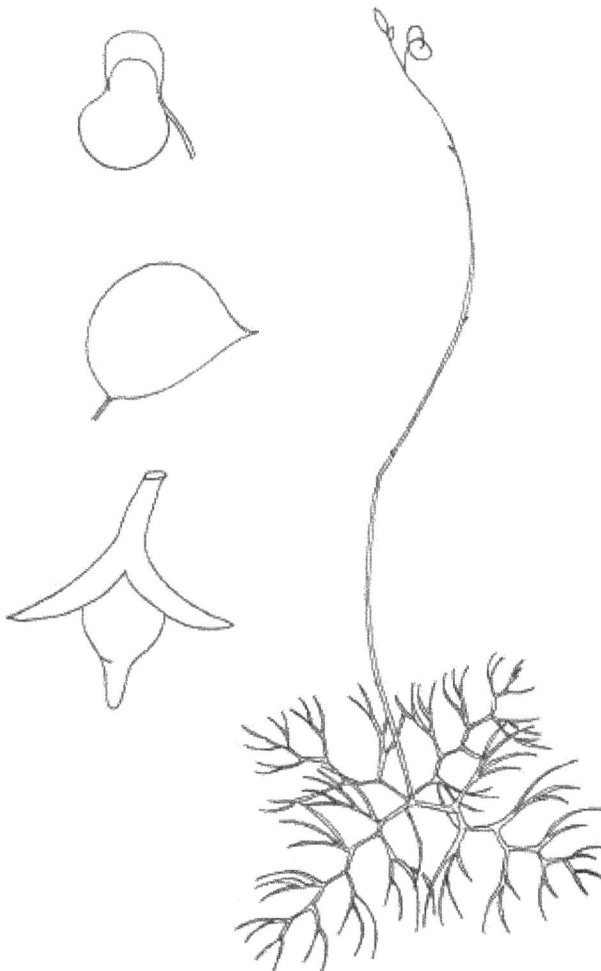

Figure 230: *Utricularia aurea* Lour.
From: Flora of Thailand, Chiang Mai University Herbarium, Faculty of Science, Chiang Mai, Thailand.
Thailand, Surattani province, Ban Takun district, Klong Seng wildlife sanctuary, Chiaw Lan Reservoir. Altitude 75 m. Date of collection: 16 February 1994.

Utricularia bifida L.

[From Latin *utriculus* = a small bag and *bifidum* = bifid]

Local names:	Bladderwort, mimikaki-gusa (Japan), arakjhawar (India)
Basionym:	*Nelipus bifida* (L.) Raf.
Synonyms:	*Askofake recurva* (Lour.) Raf., *Nelipus bifida* (L.) Raf., *Philydrum cavaleriei* M. Lev., *Utricularia alata* Benj., *Utricularia antirrhinoides* Wall., *Utricularia biflora* Hayata, *Utricularia brevicaulis* Benj., *Utricularia humilis* Vahl. *Utricularia ramosa* Vahl, *Utricularia recurva* Lour., *Utricularia sumatrana* Miq., *Utricularia wallichianum* Benj.
Description:	It is a small aquatic floating herb which grows in quiet muddy ponds and pools or moist mud in India, Southeast Asia, Australia, and Japan. The stem is whitish green, 1 mm in diameter, slender, creeping and much branched with little bladders that trap tiny aquatic insects. The flowering stem is aerial, to 15 cm long with a few bracts. The flowers are few, at the apex of the flowering stem on a short recurved pinkish green pedicel. The flower buds are 0.7 x 0.2 cm, pinkish to orange red. The calyx is yellowish with pinkish hue, and the sepals are ovate, and larger in fruits. The corolla is small, bright yellow, about 6 mm long, slightly curved and bilobed. The upper lip presents dark reddish vertical lines in the lower half inside. The fruit is capsular (Figure 231).
Medicinal Uses:	In Cambodia, Laos and Vietnam the plant is used to break fever and is applied to inflamed skin.
Pharmacology:	Unknown.

Figure 231: *Utricularia bifida* **L.**
From: UKM Herbarium, Malaysia, No 01511 identification: Mohd. Kassim. Collector: Siswa.
Date of collection: 13 February 1973.
and From: Flora of Thailand, Prince of Songkla University.
Thailand, Songkla province, Haad Yai province, Klong Hoi Kong, West of Toong Loong, sea
level. Date of collection: 12 June 1985. Collection and identification: JF Maxwell. N° 85-592.

E. Order CAMPANULALES Lindley 1833

The Order Campanulales consists of 7 families and about 2500 species of herbs, shrubs, or arborescent plants which might have originated from or near the Solanales. Members of this family produce some piperidine alkaloids, and accumulate inulin. A key botanical feature in this family is the corolla, the lobes of which are grouped on one side, and a particular mechanism of pollen presentation. Ornamental Campanulales are *Campanula medium* L. (Canterbury bell) and *Campanula rotundifolia* (bluebell of Scotland). Campanulales of pharmaceutical interest are few. The dried aerial part of *Lobelia inflata* (Lobelia *British Pharmaceutical Codex*, 1963) has been used for the treatment of bronchial asthma and bronchitis on account of the piperidine alkaloid lobelin. Lobelin has a peripheral action, close to nicotine; it excites nerve cells and paralyzes them. It stimulates the carotid sinus reflex, producing dilation of the bronchioles and increased respiration. Most species belong to the cosmopolitan family Campanulaceae which is closely related to the Pentaphragmaceae described next.

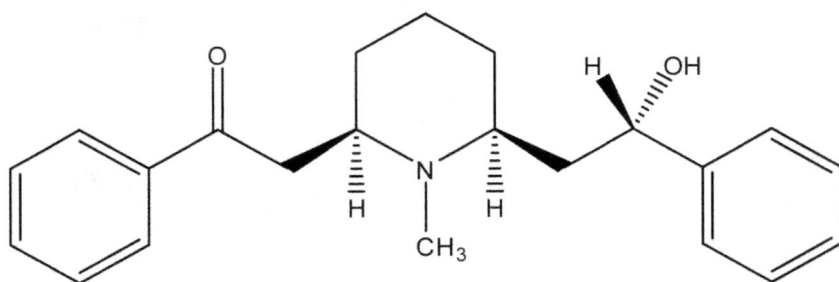

Lobeline

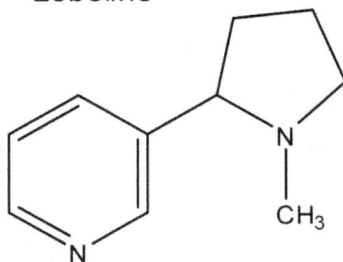

Nicotine

1.Family PENTAPHRAGMATACEAE J.G. Agardh 1858 nom. Conserv., the Pentaphragma Family

The family Pentaphragmaceae which consists of about 30 species in Southeast Asia, are perennial, fleshy, understorey jungle herbs. The leaves are simple, alternate, and without stipules. Leaf blades are large and often asymmetrical at the base. The inflorescence is cymose and comprises several little tubular flowers with 5 sepals and a 5 lobed corolla, the lobes valvate. The androecium consist of 5 stamens alternate with the corolla lobes. The gynaecium is made of 2 - 3 carpels united to form a 2 - 3 locular inferior ovary containing several ovules on axile placentas. The fruits are berries with tiny seeds.

This Family has not been the subject of any pharmacological study. *Pentaphragma ellipticum* Poulsen and *Pentaphragma begoniifolium* (Roxb. ex Jack) Wall. ex G. Don and are medicinal in Malaysia and Indonesia respectively.

Pentaphragma begoniifolium (Roxb. ex Jack) Wall. Ex G. Don

[From Greek *penta* = five, *phragma* = a wall and from Latin *begoniifolium* = with Begonia like leaves]

Description:	It is a perennial fleshy herb which grows in the rainforest of Malaysia. The stem is somewhat angled, hairy, and 0.3 - 0.4 cm in diameter. The leaves are simple, alternate and without stipules. The petiole is channeled, 2.5 - 4 cm long, flattish. The leaf-blade is membranaceous, 20 - 15 cm x 10 - 7.5 cm, hairy underneath, strongly asymmetrical at the base, acute at the apex, serrate at the margin and with 4 - 5 pairs of secondary nerves visible underneath. The inflorescence is terminal cyme of 0.7 cm long flowers which are white (Figure 232).
Medicinal uses:	Malays make a paste of the root, which they apply to swollen parts.
Pharmacology:	Unknown

Figure 232: *Pentaphragma begoniifolium* **(Roxb. ex Jack) Wall. Ex G. Don**
From: Herbarium of *University* Kebangsaan Malaysia
Flora of Malaya
Malaysia, Kelantan state, Gua Musang, Kuala Betis, 1 hour boat ride down river
Collector and Identification: Abdul Latiff , ALM 1030. Date of collection: 8 October 1985.

F. Order RUBIALES Bentham & Hooker 1873

This order consists of the family Rubiaceae.

1.Family RUBIACEAE A. L. de Jussieu 1789 nom conserv., the Madder Family

The family Rubiaceae consists of about 450 genera and 6,500 species of tropical and sub-tropical trees, herbs, shrubs and climbers, which are thought to have originated from the order Gentianales. This vast group of flowering plants elaborates a broad array of secondary metabolites but predominantly synthesies iridoid glycosides, monoterpenoid alkaloids, tannins, and anthraquinones. The leaves of Rubiaceae are simple, somewhat fleshy, decussate and with a pair of interpetiolar stipules. The flowers are tubular, actinomorphic, and cymose or packed in globose spikes. The calyx is small, and consists of 4 - 5 lobes. The corolla is tubular, regular, often white and consists of 3 - 5 connate, contorted, imbricate or valvate lobes. The androecium consists of 4 - 5 stamens attached to the edge of the corolla, and alternate with the corolla lobes. The anthers are 2 - celled and open lengthwise. The gynaecium consists of a pair of carpels merging into an inferior, 2 or plurilocular ovary, each locule containing a single or several ovules attached to axile placentas. The stigma is bifid, showy and protruding. The fruits are capsules, berries, or drupes often crowned on top by the calyx.

The family Rubiaceae is of economic importance as a source of ornamental plants and coffee. *Ixora coccinea* L. (Ixora), *Mussaenda elegans* Schum. & Thonn, *Gardenia jasminoides* Ellis. (Cape Jasmine), *Casasia clusiifolia* (Jacq.) Urban (Seven Year Apple) are examples of ornamental plants species in this family. The roasted kernel of the dried ripe seed of *Coffea arabica* (Arabica coffee), *Coffea liberica*, and *Coffea canephora* (robusta coffee) used by millions daily.

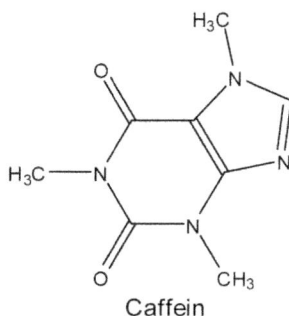

Caffein

Members of the genus *Cephaelis*, *Nauclea*, *Cinchona*, *Mitragyna*, *Corynanthe*, *Pausinystalia*, *Uncaria*, *Pogonopus* and *Remijia* species are of pharmacological interest because they have the ability to produce a series of monoterpenoid indole and quinoline alkaloids, some of which are used in clinical practice. Examples of such alkaloids are quinine, and emetine and mitragynine.

Quinine (*British Pharmaceutical Codex*, 1963) has been used for the treatment of malaria and as a bitter stomachic. It is extracted from *Cinchona ledgeriana* (ledger bark), *Cinchona officinalis* (pale cinchona bark, crown or Loxa bark), *Cinchona succirubra* (red cinchona bark) and *Cinchona calisaya* (yellow cinchona bark). Quinine suppresses the asexual cycle of development of *Plasmodium* in the erythrocytes and has been used as the sulphate, bisulphate, hydrochloride or dihydrochloride to prevent and control overt attacks of malaria, but parasites are becoming resistant to it. Quinidine (*British Pharmacopoeia*, 1963) has been given in prophylaxis of cardiac arrhythmia and for the treatment of cardiac fibrillation.

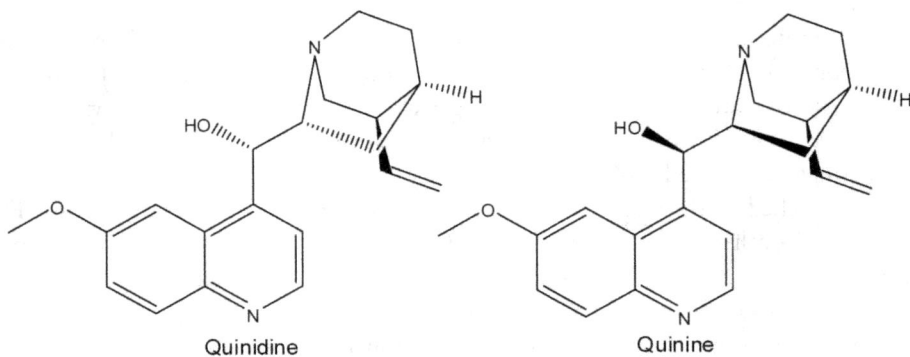

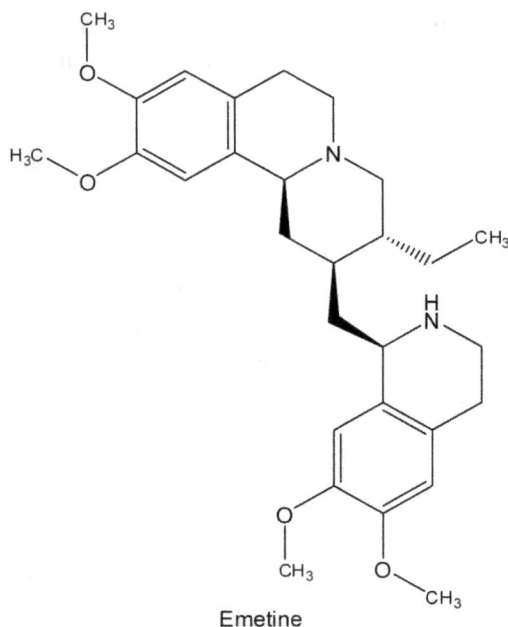

Quinidine   Quinine

Emetine

The dried root of *Cephaëlis ipecacuanha* (Brot.) A. Rich. (*uragoga* ipecacuanha, Brazilian ipecacuanha) or *Cephaëlis acuminata* Karsten (Cartagena ipecacuanha) (Ipecacuanha, *British Pharmacopeia*, 1963) which abounds with emetine, has been used in small doses as an expectorant in acute bronchitis and in larger doses to produce vomiting in the treatment of poisoning. Emetine has been used as the hydrochloride to treat amoebiasis.

The Rubiaceae family is of particular pharmacological interest and one can foresee with confidence the isolation of dozens of drugs of clinical value from it. Camptothecin, a monoterpene indole alkaloid produced by *Ophiorrhiza pumila* (Rubiaceae) has displayed strong cytotoxic effects and further studies have led to the synthesis of two derivatives: irinotecan and topotecan, which are used throughout the world for the treatment of various cancers. The market size of irinotecan/topotecan in 2002 was estimated at about $750 million and at $1 billion by 2003 (Lorence *et al.*, 2003) .

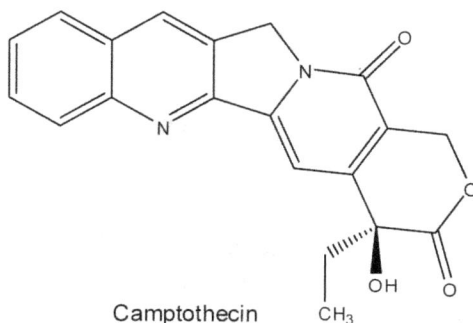

Camptothecin

Anti-HIV principles have been isolated from this family. Tuchinda et al. 2004 isolated series of cycloartane triterpenes with anti-HIV properties from *Gardenia thailandica*. The family elaborates series of cyclic polypeptides such as palicourein isolated from *Palicourea condensata* which inhibits the *in vitro* cytopathic effects of HIV against CEM-SS cells (Bockesh *et al.*, 2001). In regards to the neuropharmacological potentials of this family, Lee *et al.*, (2003), showed that the alkaloid fraction of *Uncaria rhynchophylla* protects against N-methyl-D-aspartate-induced apoptosis. Choi *et al.*, 2007 reported that an extract of *Gardenia jasminoides* mitigated the amyloid beta peptide-induced oxidative stress using PC12 cells, probably on account of geniposide which attenuates neuronal cell death in oxygen and glucose deprivation-exposed rat hippocampal slice culture (Lee *et al.*, 2006). Note that geniposide has Neurotrophic property as it induces the neuronal differentiation of PC12 cells (Liu *et al.*, 2006).

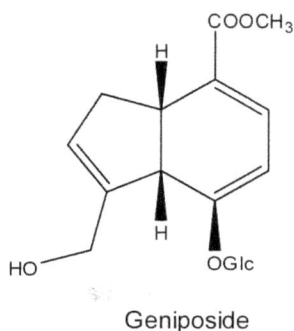

Geniposide

About 120 species of plants classified within the family Rubiaceae are used in Asia - Pacific for medicinal purposes.

References: Bokesch HR, Pannell LK, Cochran PK, Sowder RC, McKee
                    TC, Boyd MR, 2001, A novel anti-HIV macrocyclic peptide
                    from Palicourea condensata. J Nat Prod; 64: 249-50.

                    Choi SJ, Kim MJ, Heo HJ, Hong B, Cho HY, Kim YJ, Kim
                    HK, Lim ST, Jun WJ, Kim EK, Shin DH, 2007, Ameliorating
                    effect of Gardenia jasminoides extract on amyloid beta peptide-
                    induced neuronal cell deficit. Mol Cells; 24: 113-8.

                    Lee J, Son D, Lee P, Kim SY, Kim H, Kim CJ, Lim E, 2003,
                    Alkaloid fraction of Uncaria rhynchophylla protects against
                    N-methyl-D-aspartate-induced apoptosis in rat hippocampal
                    slices. Neurosci Lett. 2003 Sep 4;348(1):51-5.

                    Lee P, Lee J, Choi SY, Lee SE, Lee S, Son D., 2006,Geniposide
                    from *Gardenia jasminoides* attenuates neuronal cell death in
                    oxygen and glucose deprivation-exposed rat hippocampal slice
                    culture. Biol Pharm Bull; 29: 174-6.

                    Liu J, Zheng X, Yin F, Hu Y, Guo L, Deng X, Chen G, Jiajia
                    J, Zhang H, 2006, Neurotrophic property of geniposide for
                    inducing the neuronal differentiation of PC12 cells. International
                    Journal of Developmental Neuroscience; 24: 419-424.

                    Lorence A, Nessler CL, 2004, Camptothecin, over four decades
                    of surprising findings. Phytochemistry; 65: 2735-2749.

                    Tuchinda P, Saiai A, Pohmakotr M, Yoosook C, Kasisit J,
                    Napaswat C, Santisuk T, Reutrakul V, 2004, Anti-HIV-1
                    cycloartanes from leaves and twigs of *Gardenia thailandic*a.
                    Planta Med; 70: 366-70.

Anthocephalus cadamba (Roxb.) Miq.

[From Greek *anthos* = flower, *kephale* = head and from Sanskrit *kadamba* = name of the plant]

Local names: Common bur-flower; mau (Burma), gao (Cambodia, Laos and
                    Vietnam), kelempajan (Indonesia), kintab (Borneo), chinchona
                    brava (Portuguese), kadam (India), bagarilat (Philippines),
                    arattam (India),

Synonyms: *Anthocephalus chinensis* (Lam.) A. Rich. ex Walp., *Anthocephalus
                    indicus* A. Rich.,. Anthocephalus morindifolius Korth,
                    Cephalanthus chinensis Lam., Nauclea cadamba Roxb.,
                    Neolamarkia cadamba (Roxb.) Bosser, Samama cadamba
                    (Roxb.) Kuntze, Sarcocephalus cadamba (Roxb.) Kurz.

Description: It is a fast growing timber tree which grows in the forests of India, Sri Lanka, Burma, Laos, Cambodia, Vietnam, Thailand, Malaysia, the Philippines and Papua new Guinea. The plant can reach 20 m tall with a girth of 2 m. The bole is straight and buttressed. The bark is brownish, fissured, and rough. The stem is smooth, quadrangular, and glabrous. The leaves are simple, opposite and stipulate. The stipules are interpetiolar, and about 1.5 cm long. The petiole is stout, terete, and 2 - 5 cm long. The leaf-blade is, ovate to elliptic-oblong, 15 - 30 cm x 10 -17 cm, dark glossy green, glabrous, with 9 - 14 pairs of secondary nerves which are prominent underneath. The inflorescence is a globose head which is solitary, terminal, 2.5 - 4.5 cm in diameter, on a stout peduncle that can reach 6 cm long. The calyx is 0.2 cm long. The corolla is yellow, orange-yellow to orange, about 1 cm with 5 lobes which are imbricate and about 0.25 cm long. The stigma is white and much exerted. The fruit is globose pseudocarp which is 5 - 6.3 cm in diameter and yellow when ripe (Figure 233).

Medicinal Uses: In India the plant is used to break fever, to invigorate, to stimulate venereal appetite, to treat leprosy and dysentery. It is also used to treat inflammation of the eyes, aphthae and stomatitis and to boost milk production in young mothers. In Burma, the plant is used to break fever and to make a mouth wash. In Vietnam, the plant is used for coughs and fever and to invigorate. In Malaysia the plant is used to break fever. The fruits are eaten in India in case of famine.

Pharmacology: The plant produces an interesting series of indole alkaloids including cadamine and isocadamine as well as isoquinoline alkaloids (Brown et al., 1974, 1976) which could be of interest for their pharmacological potentials. The plant also produces 3'-O-caffeoylsweroside, kelampayosides A and B (Kitagawa et al., 1996) and quinovic acid glycosides (Sahu et al., 2000) and chlorogenic acid which is involved in hepatoprotective and antioxidant activity (Kapil et al., 1995; Umachigi et al., 2007). Extracts of the plant exhibited antimicrobial, wound healing (Umachigi et al., 2007), and antimalarial (Schwikkard et al., 2002) properties.

References: Brown RT, Fraser SB, 1974, *Anthocephalus* alkaloids: Cadambine and 3alpha-dihydrocadambine. Tetrahedron Lett; 15: 1957-59.

Brown RT, Stuart B, Fraser SB, Julie Banerji J, 1974, *Anthocephalus* alkaloids: Isodihydrocadambine. Tetrahedron Lett; 15: 3335-38.

Brown RT, C Lyn, Chapple CL, 1976, *Anthocephalus* alkaloids: 3beta-dihydrocadambine and 3beta-isodihydrocadambine. Tetrahedron Lett; 17: 2723-24.

Brown RT, C Lyn, Chapple CL, 1976, *Anthocephalus* alkaloids: cadamine and isocadamine. Tetrahedron Lett; 17: 1629-30.

Kapil A, Koul I, Suri OP, 1995, Antihepatotoxic effects of chlorogenic acid from *Anthocephalus cadamba*. Phytother Res; 9: 189-93.

Kitagawa I, Wei H, Nagao S, Mahmud T, Hori K, Kobayashi M, Uji T, Shibuya H, 1996, Indonesian Medicinal Plants. XIV. Characterization of 3'-O-Caffeoylsweroside, a new secoiridoid glucoside, and kelampayosides A and B, two new phenolic apioglucosides, from the bark of *Anthocephalus chinensis* (Rubiaceae). Chem Pharm Bull (Tokyo); 44: 1162-7.

Sahu NP, Koike K, Jia Z, Banerjee S, Mandal NB, Nikaido T, 2000, Triterpene glycosides from the bark of *Anthocephalus cadamba*. J Chem Res; 2000: 22-3.

Umachigi SP, Kumar GS, Jayaveera KN, Kishore Kumar DV, Ashok Kumar CK, Dhanapal R, 2007, Antimicrobial, wound healing and antioxidant activities of *Anthocephalus Cadamba*. Afr J Trad Comp Alt Med7; 4: 481-7.

Schwikkard S, van Heerden FR, 2002, Antimalarial activity of plant metabolite. Nat Prod Rep; 19: 675-92.

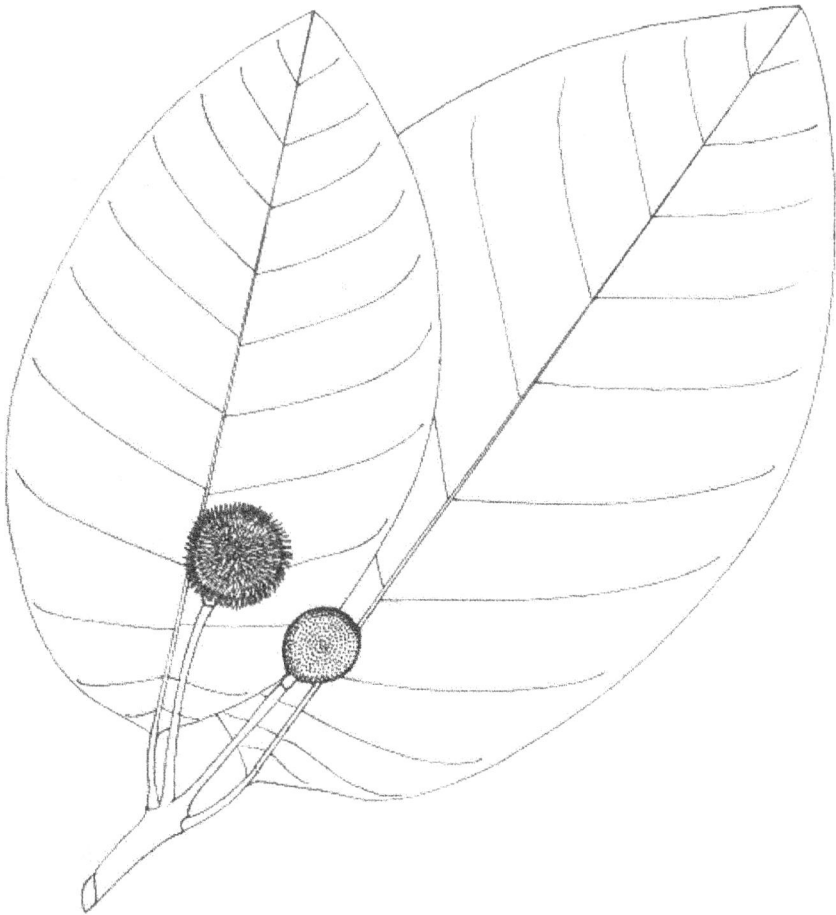

Figure 233: *Anthocephalus cadamba* **(Roxb.) Miq.**
From: Flora of Borneo
Malaysia, Sabah, Papan, Hulu Kumanis in open area. Collection and identification: Khairiah
Supangat KHS 0058. Date of collection: 13 September 1987.

Aphaenandra uniflora (Wall. ex Don) Bremek

[From Latin *uniflora* = with a single flower]

Synonyms:	*Mussaenda theifera* Pierre, *Mussaenda uniflora* Wall. ex G.Don
Description:	It is a deciduous perennial herb. The stem is terete, rooting at nodes, decumbent, light green, about 0.2 cm in diameter, hairy and slender. The internodes are about 9 cm long. The interpetiolar stipules are lanceolate, minute. The petiole is 0.2 -0.5 cm long and channeled. The leaf-blade is membranaceous, translucent, triangular, 1.2 - 2.5 cm x 3 - 5 cm, with about 5 pairs of secondary nerves, tapering and acute at the apex, wavy at the margin, hairy with 4 - 5 pairs of secondary nerves. The fruits are terminal, hairy, with 5 linear lobes. The calyx is green, hairy, about 0.3 cm long and has 5 linear lobes. The corolla is tubular, hairy outside, and produce 5 elliptic lobes which are about 3.5 x 0.8 cm. the fruits are capsular, hairy, with vestigial calyx lobes and about 1 cm long (Figure 234).
Medicinal Uses:	In Cambodia, Laos and Vietnam the plant is used for fever.
Pharmacology:	To date the pharmacological properties of this plant remain unexplored.

Canthium dicoccum (Gaertn.) Merr.

[From Malabar name *kanti* = a plant name and Latin *dicoccum* = with 2 seeds]

Local name:	Sri Lanka box wood; bertulang, merajah kayu (Malaysia), duk kang (Thailand), xuong ca (Vietnam)
Basionym:	*Psydrax dicoccos* Gaertn. De Fructibus et Seminibus Plantarum 1925.
Synonym:	*Canthium didymium* Gaertn. F, *Plectronia dicocca* (Gaertn.) Merr. *Plectronia didyma* Elm., *Psydrax dicoccos* Gaertn., *Vangueria dicocca* (Gaertn.) Miq.
Description:	It is a treelet which grows to a height of 4 m in the forests of India, Sri Lanka, Burma, Vietnam, Thailand, Malaysia, and the Philippines. The stem is terete, about 0.5 cm in diameter, fissured longitudinally, with a few elongated lenticels, peeling, and smoother at the apex. The internodes are 2 - 4.2 cm long. The leaves are simple, opposite and stipulate. The stipules are interpetiolar bifid, tiny, and scale-like. The petiole is flattish, about 0.5 cm long and glabrous. The leaf blade is dark green

Figure 234: *Aphaenandra uniflora* **(Wall. ex Don) Bremek**
From: Flora of Thailand, Chiang Mai University Herbarium
Thailand, Lampang province, Muang Bahn (Pan) district, Jae Sawn national park, hill West of park headquarters. By 18° North and 99° East. Elevation: 650 m. Date of collection: 20 July 1996. Collection and identification: JF Maxwell No 96-693.

Description (contd) above, broadly lanceolate, acuminate at the apex, coriaceous, glossy, 2.5 - 7 cm x 1 - 4 cm, leathery, the midrib flattish above, with 2 to 3 pairs of secondary nerves which are discrete. The inflorescence is a dull greenish axillary cyme, the base of the main peduncle of which is surrounded by a sheath-like formation. The inflorescence axis is about 2 cm long. The calyx is dull greenish conical with a few lobes and hairy at the apex and 0.2 x 0.15 cm. The corolla is white, about 0.5 cm long and 5 lobed. The fruit is globose, with few lenticels, marked at the apex with a vestigial calyx, lobes around a tiny opening, and 0.8 x 0.7 cm (Figure 235).

Medicinal Uses: The plant is used in Malaysia to treat diarrhoea. The plant is used for fever and dandruff in India.

Pharmacology: The plant is known to produce flavonoid glycosides (Gunasegaran *et al.*, 2001), quinovaic acid, acetylquinovaic acid and scopoletin (Herath *et al.*, 1979) and epi-betulin (Das, 1971). An extract of the plant exhibited some mild levels of inhibition against *Pseudomonas aeruginosa* and *Candida albicans* (Ram *et al.*, 2004) as well as *Bacillus subtilis*, *Bacillus cereus*, *Escherichia coli* and *Saccharomyces cerevisiae* (Jayasinghe *et al.*, 2002).

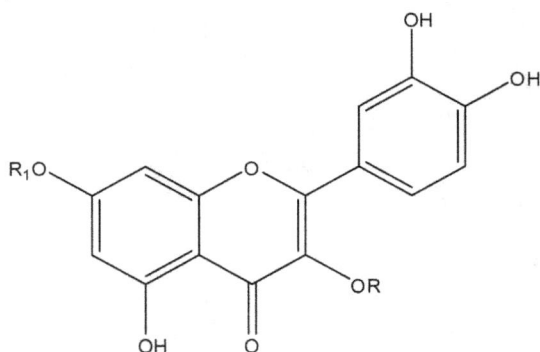

R = α -L-rhamnopyrano-(1-6)-glucopyranosyl
R$_1$= (6-O-benzoyl)-β-D-glucopyranosyl

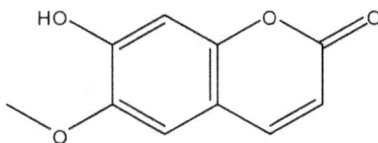

Scopoletin

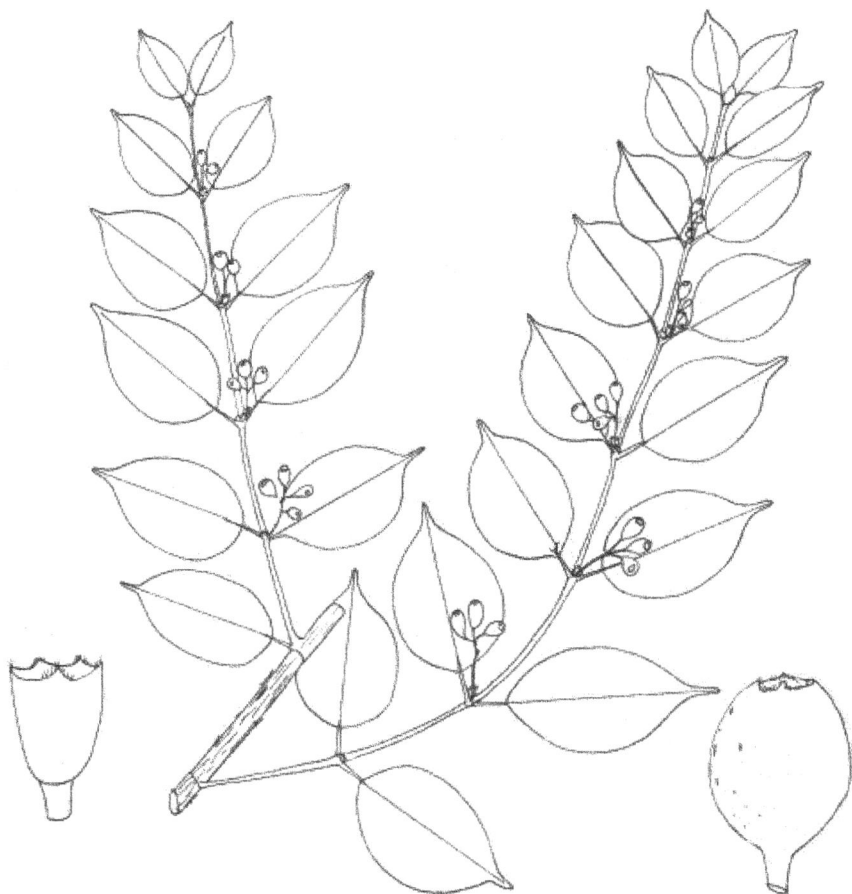

Figure 235: *Canthium dicoccum* (Gaertn.) Merr.
From: Flora of Thailand. Prince of Songkla University Herbarium.
Thailand, Songkla province, Sadao district, Kao Roop Chang , Padang Besar. By 8° North - 99° East. Altitude 125 m. Date of collection: 25 June 1986. Shaded slope near the summit of a limestone peak, primary evergreen forest. Collection and identification: JF Maxwell, N° 86-416.

Coffea arabica L.

[From Arabic *qahwa* = coffee and Latin *arabica* = Arabian]

Local name:	Arabian coffee, (Burmese) : ka-phi (Burma), kafe (Philippines), café d'Arabie (France), bergkaffee (German), café (Spain), kopi (Malaysia, Indonesia), kafae (Cambodia), gafae (Thailand), cà phê (Vietnam)
Description:	It is a small tree native to Ethiopia and Sudan, cultivated in several countries, including Asia, for the seeds which are used to make coffee. The plant grows up to 3 m tall. The stem is stout, somewhat articulated, smooth, lenticelled, glabrous, about 0.5 cm in diameter, somewhat squarish and with 1.5 - 8 cm long internodes. The nodes have conspicuous leaf-scars. The leaves are simple, opposite and stipulate. The stipules are scale - like, 0.3 x 0.5 cm, enclosing the stem. The petiole is 2 - 2.5 cm long, glabrous, non - channeled with a few transversal lenticels at the base and about 2.4 x 0.3 cm. The leaf-blade is coriaceous, leathery 12.5 - 20 cm x 6.8 - 10 cm, oblong, acuminate with 6 - 10 pairs of secondary nerves, midrib raised above. The inflorescence is an axillary cyme. The calyx is tubular, truncated and minute. The corolla is tubular, with 5 lobes which are linear and acute at the apex and longer than the corolla tube. The stigma is forked and much exerted. The fruit is a fleshy berry which is about 1 cm long, crimson, glossy, turning purple when ripe and marked at the apex with a little opening. Each berry contains 2 seeds, which are about 1 cm long, elliptic with a flattened surface that is marked by a sunken line (Figure 236).
Medicinal Uses:	In the Philippines, the berries are used as a remedy for headache and fever. In Indonesia, the seeds are used to treat urinary ailments. In Guiana, the seeds are used to treat fever and headache.
Pharmacology:	The seeds contain caffeine (British Pharmacopoeia, 1963), an alkaloid which stimulates the brain, heart and kidneys. Note that caffeine is toxic. Doses of 1 g or over produce alarming symptoms such as tachycardia, vomiting, muscle tremor, and diuresis. The fatal oral dose of caffeine is 10 g. Note that coffee also contains the diterpenes cafestol and kahweol which display a broad spectrum of pharmacological activity. These substances induce cancer chemopreventive enzymes (Higgins *et al.*, 2008) and exhibited hepatoprotective and antioxidant properties in rodents (Lee *et al.*, 2007a). Kahweol and cafestol are also known to inhibit cyclo-oxygenase expression in macrophages (Kim

et al., 2004) and exhibit protective effects against hydrogen peroxide-induced oxidative stress and DNA damage Lee *et al.*, 2007b).

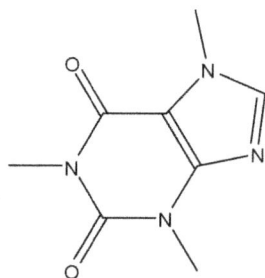

Caffein

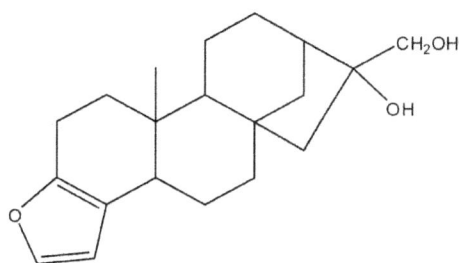

Cafestol

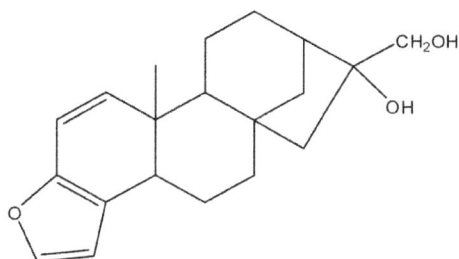

Kahweol

References:

Higgins LG, Cavin C, Itoh K, Yamamoto M, Hayes JD, 2008, Induction of cancer chemopreventive enzymes by coffee is mediated by transcription factor Nrf2. Evidence that the coffee-specific diterpenes cafestol and kahweol confer protection against acrolein. Toxicol Appl Pharmacol; 226: 328-37.

Kim JY, Jung KS, Jeong HG, 2004, Suppressive effects of the kahweol and cafestol on cyclooxygenase-2 expression in macrophages. FEBS Lett; 569: 321-6.

Lee KJ, Choi JH, Jeong HG, 2007a, Hepatoprotective and antioxidant effects of the coffee diterpenes kahweol and cafestol on carbon tetrachloride-induced liver damage in mice. Food Chem Toxicol; 45: 2118-25.

Lee KJ, Jeong HG, 2007b, Protective effects of kahweol and cafestol against hydrogen peroxide-induced oxidative stress and DNA damage. Toxicology Letters; 173: 80-87.

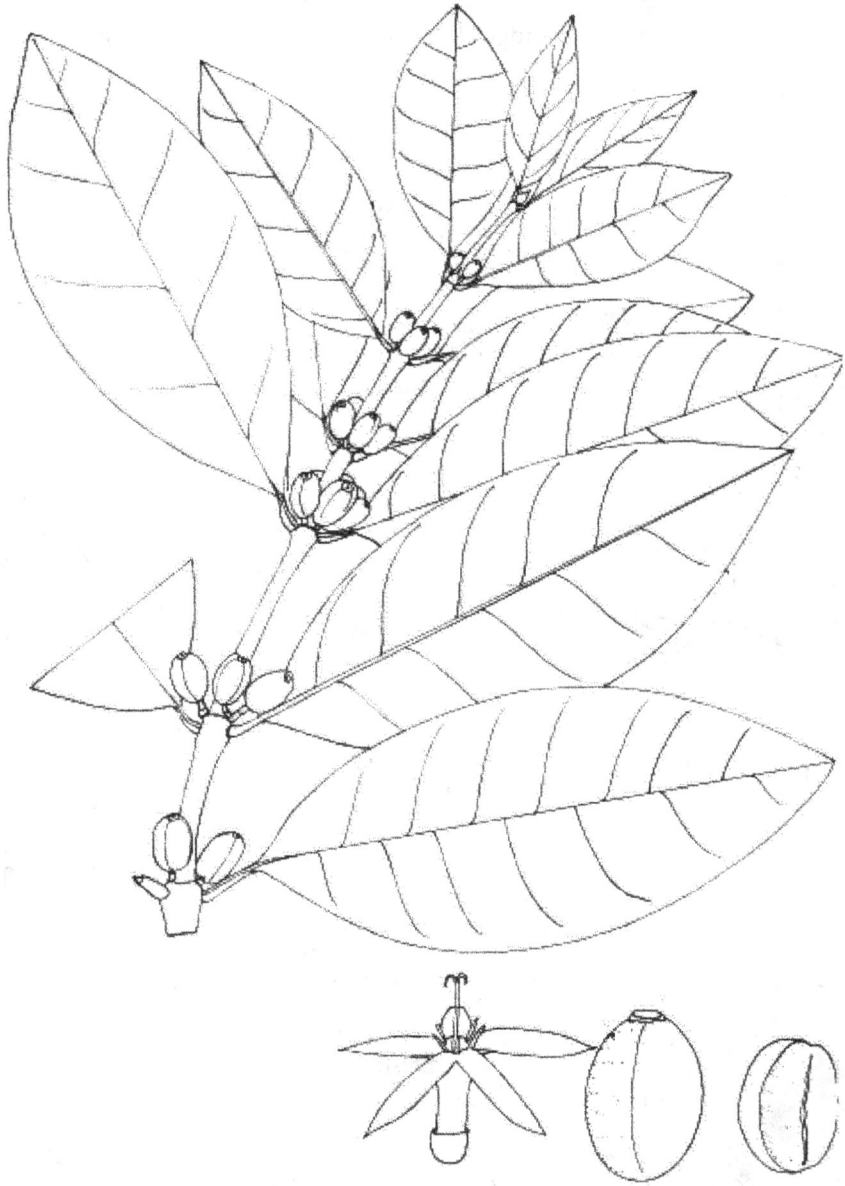

Figure 236: *Coffea arabica* L.
From: Flora of Malaya
Malaysia, Selangor state, Morib. Collection: Lee Poh Bee. Date of collection: 18 October 1982.

Gardenia jasminoides J. Ellis

[After American botanist and physician Alexander Garden (1730-1791), and Latin *jasminoides* = jasmine like]

Local names:	Common gardenia; kuchinashi (Japan), zhi zi (China)
Synonyms:	*Gardenia augusta* (L.) Merr., *Gardenia florida* L., *Gardenia grandiflora* Lour., *Gardenia radicans* Thunb., *Gardenia schlechteri* H. Lev.
Description:	It is a shrub native to China which is cultivated as an ornamental plant. The stem is terete, articulated, striated, fissured longitudinally, and hairy at the apex, with few lenticels. The nodes show prominent leaf-scar. The internodes are 1 - 5 cm long. The leaves are simple, opposite and stipulate. The stipules are lanceolate, deciduous, membranaceous, about 0.7 x 0.2 cm with discrete longitudinal nervations and rugose. The petiole is non-channeled, flattish, and hairy, about 1 cm long. The leaf blade is 8.4 - 15 cm x 3.2 - 5.4 cm, elliptic to elliptic spathulate, dark green, membranaceous, tapering at the base, acuminate to caudate at the apex, the margin wavy, with 11 - 13 pairs of secondary nerves looping at the margin, visible on both surfaces of the blade. The midrib is sharply raised below. The flower is pure white, fragrant with 6 lobes which are about 5 cm long. The fruit is a terminal, crimson red, about 3.5 x 1.5 cm. axillary capsule finely ringed, subglabrous, pear-shaped, with persistent calyx lobes which are about 2 cm long and linear (Figure 237).
Medicinal uses:	In China the plant is used for jaundice, wounds, rheumatism, bleeding, sores and abscesses. In Cambodia, Laos and Vietnam, the plant is used to treat infections of the eye and vagina. It is also used for fever and to treat dysentery, intestinal ills. In Malaysia, the plant is used to assuage headache, and to break fever.

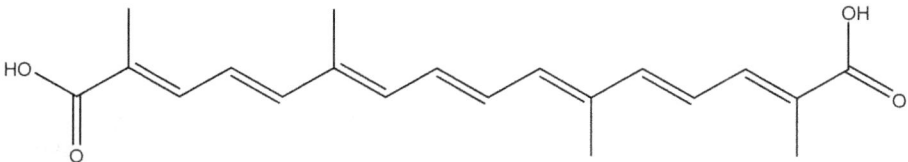

Crocetin

Pharmacology:	The plant has been subject of several pharmacological studies. It contains a dye, crocin which is hepatoprotective (Lin *et al.*, 1986) antitumoral (Wang *et al.*, 1996) antioxidant (Pham *et al.*, 2000)

and antihyperlipidemic (Lee IA *et al.*, 2005) via lipase inhibition (Sheng *et al.*, 2006). Miura *et al.* (1996), isolated a series of iridoid glycosides, including deacetylasperulosidic acid methyl ester that lowered the blood glucose level in normal mice. Other iridoid glycosides including A gardaloside, geniposide , 6alpha-hydroxygeniposide, ixoroside , and shanzhiside showed significant inhibition of IL-2 secretion by phorbol myristate acetate and anti-CD28 monoclonal antibody co-stimulated activation of human peripheral blood T cells (Chang *et al.*, 2005).

The fruit has antiangiogenic activity (Park *et al.*, 2003) on account of geniposide (Koo *et al.*, 2004).

References:

Chang WC, Lin YL, Lee MJ, Shiow SJ, Wang CJ, 1996, Inhibitory effect of crocetin on benzo(a)pyrene genotoxicity and neoplastic transformation in C3H10T1/2 cells. Anticancer Res; 16: 3603-8.

Chang WL, Wang HY, Shi LS, Lai JH, Lin HC, 2005,Immunosuppressive iridoids from the fruits of *Gardenia jasminoides*. J Nat Prod; 68: 1683-5.

Koo HJ, Lee S, Shin KH, Kim BC, Lim CJ, Park EH, 2004, Geniposide, an anti-angiogenic compound from the fruits of *Gardenia jasminoides*. Planta Med; 70: 467-9.

Lee IA, Lee JH, Baek NI, Kim DH, 2005, Antihyperlipidemic effect of crocin isolated from the fructus of *Gardenia jasminoides* and its metabolite Crocetin. Biol Pharm Bull; 28: 2106-10.

Lin JK, Wang CJ, 1986, Protection of crocin dyes on the acute hepatic damage induced by aflatoxin B1 and dimethylnitrosamine in rats. Carcinogenesis; 7: 595-9.

Miura T, Nishiyama Y, Ichimaru M, Moriyasu M, Kato A, 1996, Hypoglycemic activity and structure-activity relationship of iridoidal glycosides. Biol Pharm Bull; 19: 160-1.

Park EH, Joo MH, Kim SH, Lim CJ, 2003, Antiangiogenic activity of *Gardenia jasminoides* fruit. Phytother Res; 17: 961-2.

Pham TQ, Cormier F, Farnworth E, Tong VH, Van Calsteren MR, 2000, Antioxidant properties of crocin from *Gardenia jasminoides* Ellis and study of the reactions of crocin with linoleic acid and crocin with oxygen. J Agric Food Chem; 48: 1455-61.

Sheng L, Qian Z, Zheng S, Xi L, 2006, Mechanism of hypolipidemic effect of crocin in rats: crocin inhibits pancreatic lipase. Eur J Pharmacol; 543: 116-22.

Figure 237: *Gardenia jasminoides* J. Ellis
From: Ex Herbarium of University of the Ryukyus
Japan, Ryukyu, Shuri-Yamagawa, Naha, Okinawa -jima, half shaded fringe of thicket on limestone area. Date of collection: 25 August 1984. Collection and identification: Shimabuku K. 5666

Gardenia tubifera Wall.

[After American botanist and physician Alexander Garden (1730-1791), and Latin *tubifera* = having a tube]

Local name: Golden gardenia; jambu-jambu (Indonesia)

Synonyms: *Gardenia elata* Ridl., *Gardenia lobbii* Craib, *Gardenia resinifera* Korth., *Gardenia speciosa* (Hook.f.) Hook.f., *Randia speciosa* Hook.f.

Description: It is a tree, about 10 m tall, which grows in India, Malaysia, Thailand, and Indonesia. The plant has ornamental value. The bark is smooth, grey, the inner bark light brown, the sapwood brown. The stem is terete, fissured, articulated, about 0.2 - 0.4 cm in diameter with 1.5 cm internodes, and squarish at the apex. The leaves are simple, opposite and stipulate and gathered at the apex. The stipules are interpetiolar, tubular, and ciliate at the margin. The petiole is not channeled, about 1 cm long, flattish and hairy. The leaf-blade is spathulate, 6 - 15 cm x 2.5 - 5 cm, thinly coriaceous, tapering at the base, acuminate at the apex, the midrib flattish above with about 11 pairs of secondary nerves visible underneath. The flower is terminal, white turning yellow and fragrant. The calyx is membranaceous, cup-shaped and about 0.9 cm long. The corolla presents a 5 cm long tube with 6 lobes which are 1.8 - 2 cm x 0.5 - 1.2 cm. The fruit is globose, about 3 cm in diameter with conspicuous apical tube which is 0.3 cm long (Figure 238).

Medicinal Uses: The plant is medicinal in India.

Pharmacology: Reutrakul *et al.* (2004) isolated the triterpenes tubiferolide methyl ester and tubiferaoctanolide, together with the known coronalolide and coronalolide methyl ester and flavonoids from the plant. Coronalolide showed significant cytotoxic activities only in P-388 cell line. Tubiferolide methyl ester was cytotoxic against P-388, KB, Col-2 and Lu-1 cell lines. Coronalolide and coronalolide methyl ester displayed significant anti-HIV activities in the HIV-1RT assay.

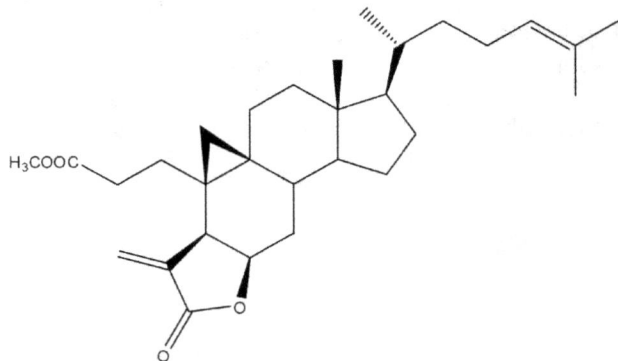

H$_3$COOC

Tubiferolide methyl ester

Figure 238: *Gardenia tubifera* Wall.

From: Flora of Malaya
Malaysia, Kedah state, road from Pedu to Belantik. Collection and identification: A. Zainuddin.
Date of collection: 14 October 1995.

References: Reutrakul V, Krachangchaeng C, Tuchinda P, Pohmakotra M, Jaipetch T, Yoosook C, Kasisit J, Sophasan S, Sujarit K, Santisuk T, 2003, Cytotoxic and anti-HIV-1 constituents from leaves and twigs of *Gardenia tubifera*. Tetrahedron; 60: 1517-1523.

Geophila herbacea (Jacq.) K. Schum.

[From Latin *geophila* = soil-loving and *herbacea* = herbaceous]

Local name:	Lafifi (Samoa)
Basionym:	*Psychotria herbacea* Jacq. *Enumeratio Systematica Plantarum* 16. 1760.
Synonyms:	*Carinta herbacea* Jacq. W.F. Wight, *Carinta repens* L. L.B. Smith & Downs, *Carinta uniflora* Hiern G. Taylor, *Geocardia herbacea* L. Stand., *Geocardia repens* L Bakh. f. *Geophila uniflora* Hiern, *Geophila reniformis* D., *Geophila repens* (L.) I. M. Johnst., *Mapouria herbacea* (Jacq.) Muell - Arg., *Psychotria herbacea* Jacq. *Rondeletia repens* L.
Description:	It is a pantropical forest understorey creeping herb which grows to a length of 35 cm. The stem is slender, 0.1 - 0.3 cm in diameter, rooting at nodes, 2 - 10 cm long internodes. The leaves are simple, opposite and stipulate. The stipules are truncate, and about 0.2 cm long. The petiole is slender, hairy, flattish, 1.5 - 7 cm long and inserts underneath the blade near its the base. The leaf-blade is dark green, pale light green and subglabrous underneath, *Centella*-like, broadly cordate, 2 - 4 cm - 2 x 1 - 3 cm, with 4 - 6 pairs of secondary nerves. The inflorescences are terminal pairs of flowers on a slender hairy 2 - 2.5 cm long pedicel. The calyx is green to brownish, the tube about 1.5 cm long with 4 linear to triangular lobes. The corolla is funnel-shaped white about 1 cm long with 4 lobes. The fruit is globose, juicy, bright red or orange, glossy, with a few lenticels, about 1 cm in diameter, crowned by the persistent calyx lobes which remain greenish and containing a few seeds which are 0.5 cm long and conical (Figure 239).
Medicinal Uses:	In Malaysia, the plant is used to heal sores. The plant in reputed, in India, to possess some properties similar to *Cephaelis ipecacuanha*. It is medicinal in numerous non Asian countries.
Pharmacology:	An extract of the plant exhibited a broad spectrum of antifungal activity *in vitro* (Portillo *et al.*, 2001). It would be interesting to investigate further the chemical constituents and pharmacological properties of *Geophila herbacea* (Jacq.) K. Schum.
Reference:	Portillo A, Vila R, Freixa B, Adzet T, Cañigueral S, 2001, Antifungal activity of Paraguayan plants used in traditional medicine. J Ethnopharmacol; 76: 93-8.

Figure 239: *Geophila herbacea* (Jacq.) K. Schum.
From: Flora of Thailand, Prince of Songkla University Herbarium
Thailand, Nakornsitammarat province, Lansagah district, Gahrome falls, Khao Luang National park. Altitude: 300 m. Date of collection: 19 May 1985. In shaded primary evergreen forest. Collection and identification: W. Ramsri N° 65.

Greenea corymbosa (Jack) Schum.

[After B.D. Green (1793-1862) an American botanist and from Latin *corymbosa* = corymbose]

Local names:	Tinjian belukan, ulai-ulai , sekam bulan (Malaysia)
Basionym:	*Rondeletia corymbosa* Jack *Malayan Miscellanies* 1(I): 4. 1820.
Synonym:	*Greenea jackii* W & A
Description:	It is a tree which grows to a height of 10 m in secondary forests and near streams in Burma, Thailand and Malaysia. The bark is smooth, dark brown. The stem is glabrous, stout, about 0.4 cm in diameter, marked with conspicuous leaf scars, hairy by the apex and with internodes which are 1 - 1.5 cm long. The leaves are simple, opposite and stipulate. The stipules are interpetiolar, 0.5 - 1.5 cm x 0.7 cm, fused at the edge, membranaceous, oblong, and glabrous. The petiole is 1- 3 cm long and non-channeled. The leaf blade is oblanceolate, membranaceous, 1 - 35 cm x 4 - 10 cm, hairy underneath, acuminate at the apex, tapering at the base, with 18 - 30 pairs of secondary nerves and scalariform tertiary nerves sunken above and raised underneath. The inflorescence is a terminal velvety panicle of a little comb-like formation, about 3 cm long. The peduncle of the inflorescence is about 6 cm long. The whole inflorescence is about 15 cm long. The flowers are arranged in 2 series on top of the peduncles. The calyx is cupular, hairy, 0.15 cm long with 4 glabrous lobes which are triangular and round at the apex. The corolla is green brownish turning white, to yellowish pink, about 0.6 cm long and conical in buds. The fruit is capsular about 0.3 cm in diameter, dehiscent, with few hairs and 4 vestigial calyx lobes and contains several tiny seeds (Figure 240).
Medicinal uses:	In Cambodia, Laos and Vietnam, the plant is used to break fever and to induce vomiting.
Pharmacology:	To date the plant has not been studied for pharmacology, although Koike *et al.* (1980) isolated cytotoxic diterpenes from *Rondetelia panamensis*. It would be of some interest to study the chemical constituents and pharmacological potential of *Greenea corymbosa* (Jack) Schum.
References:	Koike K, Cordell GA, Farnsworth NR, Freer AA, Gilmore CJ, Sim GA, 1980, New cytotoxic diterpenes from *rondeletia panamensis* (rubiaceae). Tetrahedron; 36: 1167-72.

Figure 240: *Greenea corymbosa* **(Jack) Schum.**
From: Flora of Malaya, Herbarium of University Kebangsaan Malaysia N° 02435, 02199,
23994 and 02435. Malaysia, Kedah state, Changloon, Sungai Badak forest reserve,
compartment 9. In over logged lowland dipterocarp forest. Collection and identification: A
Zainuddin. Date of collection: 7 June 1993.

Guettarda speciosa L.

[After J. Eugene Guettard (1715-1780), a French botanist and Latin *speciosa* = handsome]

Local names:	Beach gardenia, hinma (Sanskrit), utirpannir (India), bagaolan (Philippines), utilomar (Marshall), puopua (Tonga), bwa kasan bordmer (Seychelles)
Synonyms:	*Gardenia speciosa* A. Rich., *Guettarda vermicularis* Blco. *Nyctanthes hirsuta* L.
Description:	It is a soft wooded tree which grows up to 10 m tall on the sea shores in a geographical area ranging from East Africa to the Pacific Islands, and is common in islands and atolls. The bole is not straight. The bark is smooth grey brown. The stem is squarish, cracked, lenticelled, articulated, hairy at the apex, with 1 cm long internodes, and conspicuous leaf scars which are about 0.6 x 0.4 cm. The internodes are about 1 cm long. The leaves are simple, decussate and stipulate. The stipules are interpetiolar, hairy at the middle, 0.8 x 0.4 cm, broadly lanceolate and caducous. The petiole is 1.5 - 4 cm long, flattish, non-channeled, hairy at first, clasping the stem. The leaf-blade is broadly obovate, 9 - 24 cm x 6 - 20 cm, thinly coriaceous, glossy, and hairy underneath, with 6 - 11 pairs of stout yellowish secondary nerves sunken above and scalariform tertiary nerves prominent underneath, and recurved at the margin. The apex is acute to slightly acuminate, the base is cordate. The inflorescence is an axillary cyme on a 4 - 9 cm long velvety pedicel. The flower is fragrant and opens at dawn. The calyx is cupular, 0.4 cm long, hairy and without lobes. The corolla is tubular, white, 1.6 - 2.5 cm long, hairy, with 4 - 9 lobes which are imbricate and about 0.8 x 0.4 cm. The stigma is knob-like. The fruits are globose, depressed, marked at the apex with a tiny disc, pumpkin-like, pinkish, 1.5 - 2.5 cm in diameter, lobed, containing 4 - 6 pyrenes fused into a hard stone. The fruits are dispersed by the sea (Figure 241).
Medicinal Uses:	In Cambodia, Laos and Vietnam, the plant is used to heal wounds and in Indonesia it is part of a remedy for dysentery. In the Pacific Islands, the flowers are used to perfume the hair.
Pharmacology:	The pharmacological properties of this common tree are yet unexplored. The plant probably contains some quinovic triterpenoid saponins (Matos *et al.*, 1986) as well as some quinine-like alkaloids (Montagnac *et al.*, 1997). Note that quinovic acid (also spelled quinovaic) glycosides are not so common in flowering plants but are well represented in the Rubiaceae.

These pentacyclic triterpenoid saponins are known to elicit antileishmanial (Di Giorgio *et al.*, 2006), phosphodiesterase inhibition (Fatima *et al.*, 2002; Mostafa M *et al.* 2006), and antitumor properties (Raffauf *et al.*, 1978). *Guettarda speciosa* L. would be an interesting topic for pharmacological study.

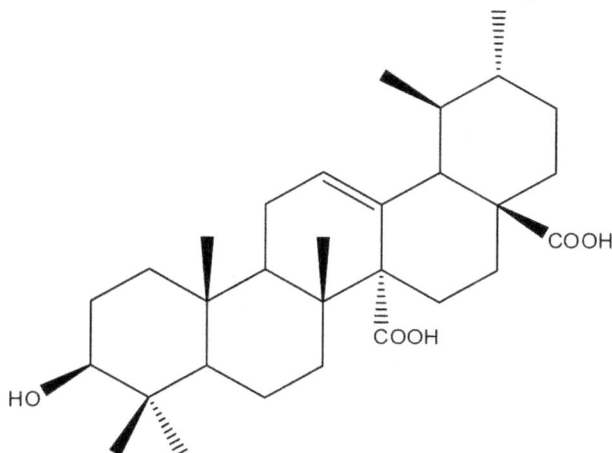

Quinovic acid

References:

Di Giorgio C, Lamidi M, Delmas F, Balansard G, Ollivier E, 2006, Antileishmanial activity of quinovic acid glycosides and cadambine acid isolated from *Nauclea diderrichii*. Planta Med; 2: 1396-402.

Fatima N, Tapondjou LA, Lontsi D, Sondengam BL, Atta-Ur-Rahman, Choudhary MI, 2002, Quinovic acid glycosides from *Mitragyna stipulosa*--first examples of natural inhibitors of snake venom phosphodiesterase I. Nat Prod Lett; 16: 389-93.

Matos MEO, Sousa MP, Machado MLL, Braz Filho R, 1986, Quinovic acid glycosides from *Guettarda angelica*. Phytochemistry; 25: 1419-1422.

Montagnac A, Litaudon M, País M, 1997, Quinine- and quinicine-derived alkaloids from *Guettarda noumeana*. Phytochemistry; 46: 973-975.

Mostafa M, Nahar N, Mosihuzzaman M, Sokeng SD, Fatima N, Atta-Ur-Rahman, Choudhary MI, 2006, Phosphodiesterase-I inhibitor quinovic acid glycosides from *Bridelia ndellensis*. Nat Prod Res; 20: 686-92.

Raffauf RF, Le Quesne PW, Ghosh PC, 1978, Antitumor Plants. V. Constituents of *Cinchona pubescens*. Lloydia; 41: 432-4.

Figure 241: *Guettarda speciosa* L.

From: University Kebangsaan Malaysia Herbarium.
Malaysia, Johor state, off Mersing at Pulau Tinggi. Collection and identification: A Zainuddin.
Date of collection: 30 January 1990.
& from: Flora of Malaya. Collection Zainall Mustaffa. Date of collection: 25 June 1988.
Identification: A Zainuddin.

Gynochthodes sublanceolata Miq.

[From Latin *sublanceolata* = sublanceolate]

Description: It is a climber which grows up to 10 long in the forests of
                 Malaysia, Thailand, and Indonesia. The stem is squarrish,
                 smooth to longitudinally striated, somewhat fleshy and, under
                 the microscope, show a "snake-like" pattern. The internodes are
                 1.3 to 8 cm long. The leaves are simple, opposite and stipulate.
                 The stipules are interpetiolar, deeply bifid, membranaceous, 0.2
                 x 0.4 cm and somewhat scale-like. The petiole is glabrous with
                 a few perpendicular lenticels, channeled, squarish and glabrous.
                 The leaf blade is elliptic lanceolate, 11 - 13 cm x 2 - 5 cm,
                 glabrous, recurved at the margin, leathery, elliptic, and glossy
                 above, the midrib sunken above and presents about 10 pairs
                 of secondary nerves visible underneath. The inflorescence is an
                 axillary tiny cyme on a 0.4 cm peduncle. The calyx is minute,
                 tubular and truncate. The corolla is white, about 0.5 cm long,
                 with 4 recurved lobes around a hairy throat. The fruit is globose,
                 to about 1 cm in diameter angled and smooth and shows a
                 tubular opening at the apex (Figure 242).

Medicinal Uses: In Malaysia the plant is used for stomachaches.

Pharmacology: Unknown

Figure 242: *Gynochthodes sublanceolata* Miq.
From: University Kebangsaan Malaysia Herbarium
Malaysia, Sabah, Lahad Datu, Pulau Baik. Collection and identification: Abdul Latiff, ALM
2884. Date of collection: 27 September 1988.

Hedyotis corymbosa (L.) Lamk.

[From the Greek *hedys* = sweet and *otos* = ears and from Latin *corymbosa* = corymbose]

Local names:	Corymbose Hedyotis; malaulasimanaso (Philippines), coc man (Vietnam), siku-siku (Malaysia), piriengo (Nepal), parpata (Sanskrit), valpatpaadagam (Sri Lanka).
Synonyms:	*Oldenlandia corymbosa* L., *Oldenlandia ramosa* Roxb.
Description:	It is an annual herb which grows on open land in a geographical area which covers East Africa, India, Sri Lanka, Thailand, Cambodia, Laos, Vietnam, Burma, Malaysia, Indonesia, Philippines, Australia and the Pacific islands. The plant grows to a height of 25 cm. The stem is branched, quadrangular, longitudinally striated and minutely lenticelled and about 0.2 cm in diameter. The internodes are 2 - 3 cm long. The leaves are simple, decussate, sessile and stipulate. The stipules are interpetiolar, membranaceous, incised and minute. The leaf blade is 1 - 3.3 cm x 0.2 - 0.7 cm, linear lanceolate, hairy below, the midrib sunken above, without visible secondary nerves, acute at the apex, and cuneate at the base. The inflorescence is an axillary cyme on a 1.8 cm long axis with 0.4 cm pedicels. The calyx is cup - shaped with 4 triangular lobes, and 0.1 cm long. The corolla is tubular, pure white, the lobes acute, 4 lobate, white and about 0.2 cm long. The fruit is a dehiscent capsule which is 0.2 cm long with 4 lobes at the apex. The seeds are muricate and about 0.1 cm in diameter (Figure 243).
Medicinal Uses:	In India, the plant is used to break fever, for jaundice, liver diseases, and to expel worms from the intestines. In Cambodia, Laos and Vietnam the plant is used to break fever and to expel worms from intestines. In Taiwan, the plant is used to break fever. In the Philippines it is used to promote digestion. In Malaysia it is used to heal wounds, boils, and sores. In China, the plant is used to treat hepatic disorders.
Pharmacology:	The hepatoprotective property has been validated by Sadasivan *et al.* (2006). An extract of the plant protected Wistar rats against the hepatotoxic effect of paracetamol evidenced by decreased serum enzyme activities, SGPT, SGOT, SAKP and serum bilirubin and an almost normal histological architecture of the liver. The active constituent is unknown. The plant is known to produce 6 alpha-hydroxygeniposide, scandoside methyl ester (6 beta-hydroxygeniposide), asperulosidic acid, deacetylasperuloside, asperuloside, 10-O-benzoylscandoside methyl ester, 10-O-p-hydroxybenzoylscandoside methyl ester, (+)-lyoniresinol-3 alpha-O-

beta-glucopyranoside, and rutin (Noiarsa *et al.*, 2008). Iridoids are known for their hepatoprotective effects (Dwivedi *et al.*, 1992) and therefore some of the iridoids present in the plant could account for the pharmacological effect.

Figure 243: *Hedyotis corymbosa* (L.) Lamk.
From: Flora of Thailand. Chiang Mai University Herbarium
Thailand, Lampang province, Nahng Chat district, Doi Kuhn Dalin National park, Southeast side . Mae Pry Station, Waw Graye subdistrict. Elevation: 350 m. Date of collection: 24 June 1994. In open, fire prone, degraded area in deciduous dipterocarp oak forest weedy area, granite bedrock.

References: Dwivedi Y, Rastogi R, Garg NK, Dhawan BN, 1992, Picroliv and its components kutkoside and picroside I protect liver against galactosamine-induced damage in rats. Pharmacol Toxicol; 71: 383-7.

Noiarsa P, Ruchirawat S, Otsuka H, Kanchanapoom T, 2008, Chemical constituents from *Oldenlandia corymbosa* L. of Thai origin. Nat Med (Tokyo); 62: 249-50.

Sadasivan S, Latha PG, Sasikumar JM, Rajashekaran S, Shyamal S, Shine VJ, 2006, Hepatoprotective studies on *Hedyotis corymbosa* (L.) Lam. J Ethnopharmacol; 106: 245-9.

Hedyotis glabra (Roxb.) R. Br.

[From the Greek *hedys* = sweet and *otos* = ears and from Latin *glabrum* = without hairs]

Synonyms:	*Exallage glabra* (R.Br. ex Wall.) Bremek. , *Hedyotis insularis* (Spreng.) Deb & R.M.Dutta, *Knoxia glabra* (R.Br. ex Wall.) DC., *Oldenlandia glabra* (Roxb.) Kuntze, *Spermacoce glabra* Roxb. *Spermacoce insularis* Spreng.
Description:	It is a decumbent herb which grows in disturbed areas, plantations, and at roadsides of Thailand and Malaysia. The stem is glabrous, terete, the nodes swollen and rooting. The internodes are 4 - 9 cm long. The leaves are simple, decussate and stipulate. The interpetiolar stipules are caudate. The petiole is minute to non-existent. The leaf blade is 7 - 7.5 cm x 1.1 - 1.5 cm, lanceolate, dark green above, light green underneath, with about 4 pairs of secondary nerves. The inflorescence is an axillary, slender minute cyme on a 0.5 cm long pedicel. The corolla, stamens and stigma are white. The fruit is capsular, about 0.1 cm in diameter, with 4 vestigial calyx lobes at the apex around a little disc (Figure 244).
Medicinal Uses:	The plant is used in Malaysia to clean the blood.
Pharmacology:	To date the pharmacological property of the plant remains unexplored. Ahmad *et al.* (2004) reported strong anti-oxidant properties from seven *Hedyotis* species as well as some levels of cytotoxicity against CEM-SS cell line and a spectrum of bacteria including MRSA. The cytotoxicity of *Hedyotis* species could be due to the beta-carboline alkaloids which are known to occur in the genus. One such alkaloid is chrysotricine from *Hedyotis chrysothrica* which exhibited inhibitory activity against the growth of HL-60 cell *in vitro* (Peng *et al.*, 1997).

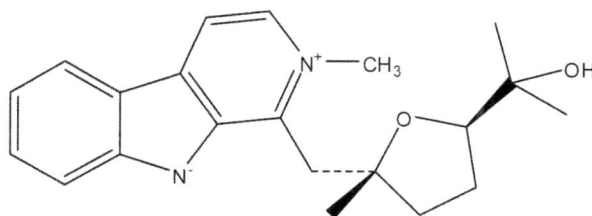

Chrysotricine

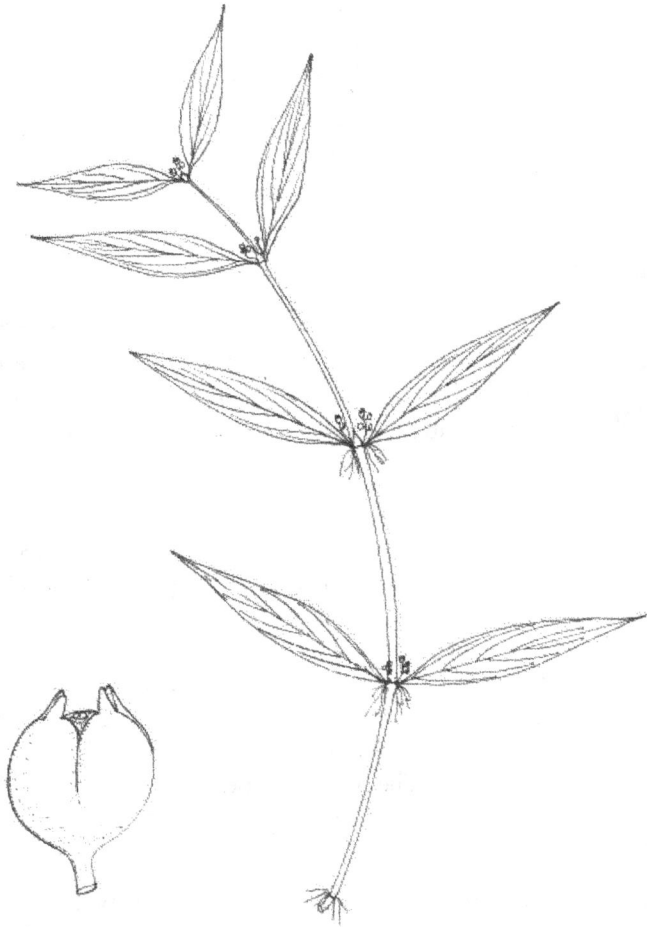

Figure 244: *Hedyotis glabra* **(Roxb.) R. Br.**
From: Flora of Thailand, prince of Songkla University.
Thailand, Songkla province, Haad Yai district, Ko Hong Hill, the base of West slope, by 8°
North - 99° East. Elevation: 50 m. Date of collection: 12 July 1986. In shaded, disturbed,
overgrown place in Hevea rubber estate, adjacent to a secondary forest. Collection and
identification: JF Maxwell N° 86-468

References: Ahmad R, Ali AM, Israf, DA, Ismail NH, h Shaari K, Lajis
                     NH, 2005, Antioxidant, radical-scavenging, anti-inflammatory,
                     cytotoxic and antibacterial activities of methanolic extracts of
                     some *Hedyotis* species. Life Sc; 76: 1953-1964.

                     Peng JN, Feng XZ, Zheng QT, Liang XT, 1997, A beta-
                     carboline alkaloid from *Hedyotis chrysotricha*. Phytochemistry;
                     46: 1119-1121.

Hedyotis philippinensis (Willd. ex Spreng.) Merr. ex C.B. Rob.

[From the Greek *hedys* = sweet and *otos* = ears and from Latin *philippinensis* = from the Philippines]

Local names:	Dilang-butiki (Philippines), bunga kakarang, lidah jin (Malaysia), saam nam (Thailand)
Basionym:	*Spermacoce philippensis* Willd. ex Spreng. *Systema Vegetabilium, editio decima sexta* 1: 401. 1825
Synonyms:	*Hedyotis congesta* R. Br., *Hedyotis laevigata* (DC) Miq., *Hedyotis prostrata* Korth., *Knoxia corymbosa* Elm., *Metabolus laevigatus* DC., *Metabolus prostrates* Bl., *Oldenlandia congesta* Kuntze, *Spermacoce philippensis* Willd. ex Spreng
Description:	It is a shrubby herb which grows to a height of 1 m in the forest of Thailand, Malaysia, Indonesia, the Philippines, Papua New Guinea and northern Australia. The stem is stout, prostrate, woody, 0.4 cm in diameter, conspicuously quadrangular, glabrous, and slightly swollen at the nodes with internodes which are about 4 cm long. The stems and leaves are purplish when young. The leaves are simple, decussate, and stipulate. The stipules are interpetiolar, triangular, deeply incised, and about 0.7 x 0.4 cm. The petiole is flattish and about 0.3 x 0.2 cm. The leaf blade is lanceolate, 6.5 - 15 cm x 2.5 - 4 cm with about 5 - 7 pairs of secondary nerves visible above the midrib which is sunken. The inflorescence is an axillary, many flowered head, which is about 1 cm in diameter. The calyx is 4-lobed, the lobes round. The flower is white. The fruit is green, smooth, somewhat rounded, and 0.15 - 0.2 cm in diameter (Figure 245).
Medicinal Uses:	In Malaysia, the plant is used to treat dysentery, gonorrhea, scalds and to assuage painful parts of the body. The plant is used after childbirth to invigorate young mothers.
Pharmacology:	The plant is known to produce a series of chromone glycosides, such as corymbosins K (Wang *et al.*, 2006). The pharmacological properties of this plant remain unexplored.
Reference:	Wang YB, Huang R, Zhang HB, Li L, 2006, Chromone glycosides from *Knoxia corymbosa*. J Asian Nat Prod Res; 8: 663-70.

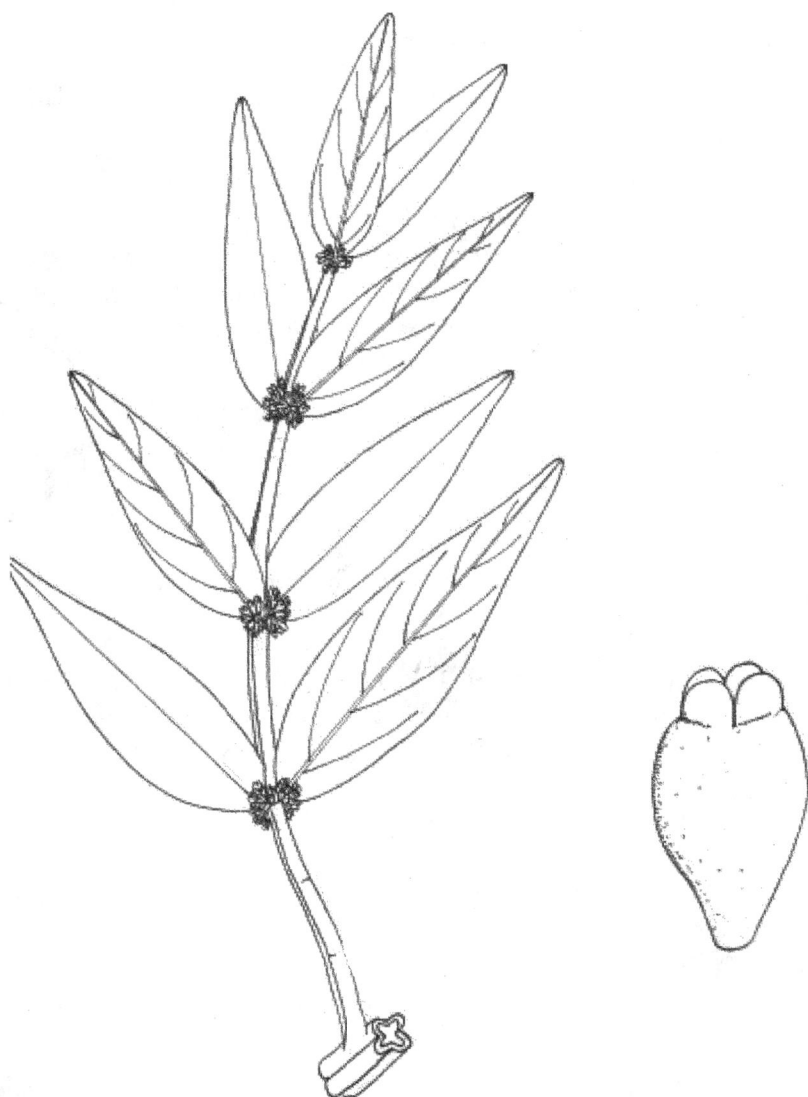

Figure 245: *Hedyotis philippinensis* **(Willd. ex Spreng.) Merr. ex C.B. Rob.**
From: University Kebangsaan Malaysia Herbarium No 01391
Malaysia, Terengganu state, near Dungun, Forest of Batu Bauk. Collection and identification:
Mohd. Kassim. Date of collection: 17 February 1973. Shrub on jungle trail.

Hymenodictyon excelsum Wall

[From Greek *hymen* = membrane and Latin = *dictyotum* = made in net fashion and *excelsum* = with a distinguished appearance]

Local names:	Lepar (Malaysia), kusan (Burma), ban muoc (Cambodia), chhalli (Sanskrit), Siva (India)
Synonym:	*Hymenodiction obovatum* Wight.
Description:	It is a tree which grows to a height of 7 to 12m in the rainforest of the Himalayas, Burma, Malaysia, Cambodia, Laos, Vietnam and the Philippines. The bark is grayish brown and smooth. The stem is striated longitudinally, pitted, somewhat articulated, stout, and marked by leaf scars. The leaves are simple, opposite and stipulate. The interpetiolar stipules are ovate with tiny teeth-like glands on the margin. The petiole is channeled, flattish, 1 - 6 cm x 0.2 cm. The leaf blade is membranaceous, wavy at the margin, obovate, 9 - 18 cm x 4 - 9 cm, with few hairs, 6 - 8 pairs of secondary nerves, hairy underneath. The inflorescence is terminal, paniculate, 7 - 30 cm long, and deflexed onward. The calyx is 0.25 cm, campanulate, pubescent with 5 lobes. The corolla is tubular, 0.5 cm long, with a narrow cylindrical tube with 5 lobes. The style is filiform and much exerted. The fruit is brown, rugose, lenticelled, 2-celled capsule, ellipsoid, and 0.8 -2 cm x 0.5 - 1 cm, with a conspicuous apical scar, splitting to release flat seeds which are winged and 0.3 - 0.35 cm x 0.2 cm (Figure 246).
Medicinal Uses:	In India, the plant is used to treat tumours and to cool fever. In Cambodia, Laos and Vietnam, the plant is used for herpes and as a tonic. In Burma the plant is a febrifuge. In the Philippines it is used for malarial fever and headaches.
Pharmacology:	An extract of the plant inhibited the growth of *Staphylococcus aureus* (Chea *et al.*, 2007).
	Jagdishprasad *et al.* (1988) have reported some anticoagulant, anti-inflammatory and sun screening effects from this plant. The plant is worthy of further study for pharmacology and especially for its antitumour activity.
References:	Chea A, Jonville MC, Bun SS, Laget M, Elias R, Duménil G, Balansard G, 2007, *In vitro* antimicrobial activity of plants used in Cambodian traditional medicine. Am J Chin Med; 35: 867-73.

Jagdishprasad P, Subba Rao N, 1988, Anticoagulant and anti-inflammatory and sunscreening effects of *Hymenodictyon excelsum*; 20: 221-222.

Figure 246: *Hymenodictyon excelsum* **Wall**
From Herbarium of University Kebangsaan Malaysia, Flora of Langkawi islands.
Malaysia, Langkawi, Tanjung Rhu, limestone hill. Collection and identification: A. Zainuddin.
Date of collection: 17 November 1992.

Ixora grandifolia Zoll. & Morr.

[Afer *Isvara* = a Hindu deity, and from Latin *grandifolia* = with large leaves]

Local names:	Pink river ixora; sikatan (Indonesia), jarum hutan (Malaysia), khem yai (Thailand).
Synonyms:	*Ixora crassifolia* Ridl., *Ixora ridleyi* Br.
Description:	It is a tree which grows to a height of 12 m and a girth of 20 cm in the forests of Sri Lanka, Burma, Cambodia, Laos, Vietnam, Thailand, Malaysia, and Indonesia, often by streams and swampy spots. The bark is smooth, grey-brown with few lenticels and fissures. The stem is terete, glabrous, fissured longitudinally with tiny tubercles and about 0.5 cm in diameter. The internodes are 3 - 6 cm long. The nodes show some vestiges of stipules. The leaves are simple, decussate and stipulate. The interpetiolar stipule is about 1 cm long and linear oblong. The petiole is woody, transversally fissured, channeled, glabrous, 1 - 1.3 cm x 0.2 cm and is constricted by the stem with a sort of sunken ring. The leaf-blade is membranaceous, elliptical, ovate or obovate, 15 - 25 cm x 6.5 - 14 cm and glabrous. The base is acute, the apex is acute, blunt or rounded, with 6-16 pairs of secondary veins plus a few tertiary nerves discrete above and raised underneath, especially the midrib which develops a sharp edge. The inflorescence is a light green terminal hairy cyme on a pedicel of about 4 cm and is about 5 cm in diameter. The calyx tube is light green, minute about 0.7 cm long with 4 triangular lobes. The corolla is whitish to pink with a slender tube 2 cm long with 4 lobes of about 0.2 cm long. The fruit is globose or 2-lobed, 0.3 cm long red ripening black with vestigial calyx tubes at the apex around an opening (Figure 247).
Medicinal Use:	In Malaysia the plant is used to assuage childbirth pain and stomach pains.
Pharmacology:	The analgesic properties mentioned above have not yet been validated. An extract of *Ixora coccinea* showed dose-dependent antinociceptive effects in hot plate and formalin tests involving a dopaminergic mechanism (Ratnasooriya *et al.*, 2005). An interesting topic of research would be to look for analgesic agents from *Ixora grandifolia* Zoll. & Morr. and *Ixora* species in general.
Reference:	Ratnasooriya WD, Deraniyagala SA, Bathige SD, Goonasekara CL, Jayakody JR, 2005, Antinociceptive action of aqueous extract of the leaves of *Ixora coccinea*. Acta Biol Hung; 56: 21-34.

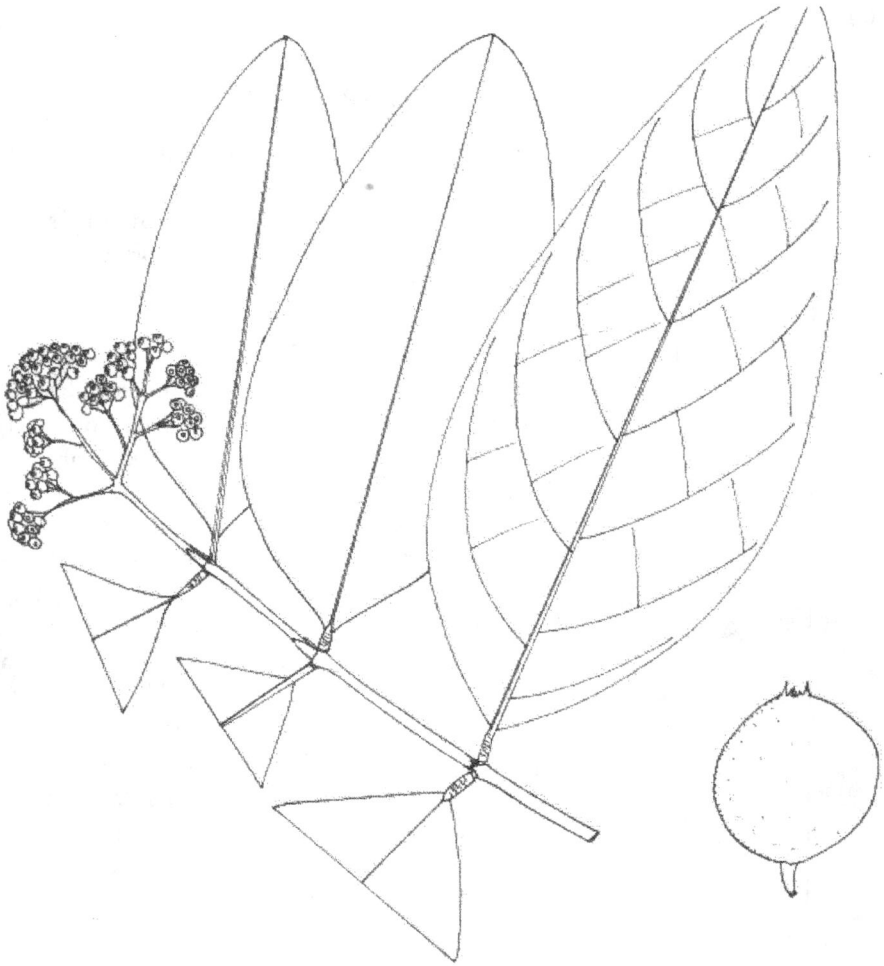

Figure 247: *Ixora grandifolia* **Zoll. & Morr.**
From: Flora of Thailand. Prince of Songkla University.
Thailand, Songkla province, Rattapoom district, Boripat Falls Park. Elevation: 50 m. Date of collection: 8 February 1985. In primary evergreen forest. Collection and identification: JF Maxwell, № 85-161

Ixora lobbii Loudon

[After Sanskrit *Isvara* = *a* Hindu deity, and after William Lobb (1809-1863), an English botanist]

Local name:	Glossy pink ixora; bunga selang (Malaysia), khem daeng (Thailand), petagar mangas (Indonesia).
Synonym:	*Pavetta lobbii* (Loudon) Teijsm. & Binn.
Description:	It is a shrub about 1.5 m tall which grows in the forests of Malaysia, Thailand and Indonesia. The stem is smooth, terete, and glabrous, 0.3 cm in diameter, with internodes which are about 4 cm long. The leaves are simple, decussate and stipulate. The interpetiolar stipule is triangular, acuminate at the apex, and about 0.5 cm long. The petiole is 0.5 cm long, woody, deeply constricted by stem. The leaf-blade is oblong to lanceolate, membranaceous, recurved and wavy at the margin, 12 -20 cm x 3 - 7 cm, caudate at the apex, with 15-26 pairs of secondary nerves visible underneath and a midrib raised on both surfaces. The inflorescence is corymbose on a pedicel which is about 2 cm long. The flower pedicels are red. The calyx is minute and campanulate. The corolla is pink and presents a 3 - 4 cm long tube which develops 4 lanceolate lobes which are 1 cm long. The fruit is black, globose or bilobed with vestigial calyx lobes at the apex and 0.8 x 0.7 cm (Figure 248).
Medicinal Uses:	In Malaysia the plant is used as a post-partum remedy and is used externally to assuage headache. In Brunei, the plant is used to invigorate.
Pharmacology:	Unknown

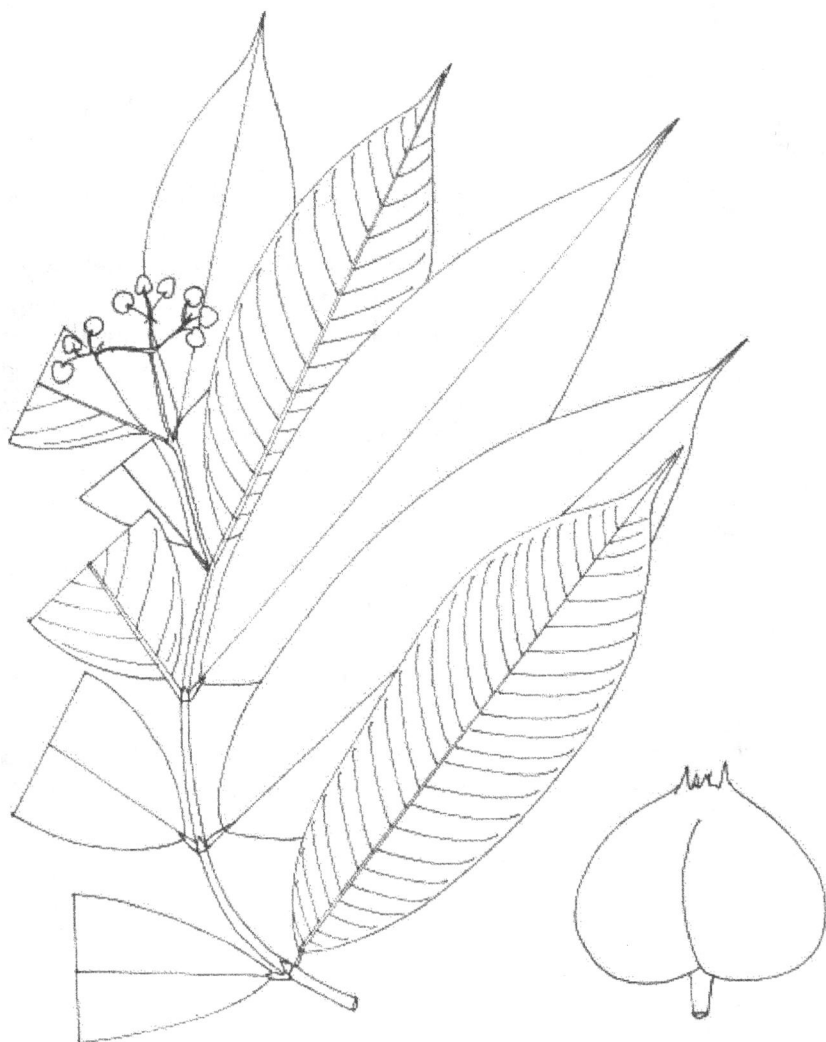

Figure 248: *Ixora lobbii* **Loudon**
From: University Kebangsaan Malaysia Herbarium No 21562
Malaysia, Pahang state, Taman Negara, track to Gua Telinga, virgin forest. Collection and identification: A. Zainuddin.

Ixora nigricans Wight & Arn.

[After *Isvara* = a Hindu deity, and from Latin *nigricans* = blackish]

Local name:	Sawkan (Burma), bong trang trang (Vietnam), udappu (India), khem tuut maa (Thailand).
Description:	It is a small tree which grows to a height of about 5 m in the forests of India, Burma, Vietnam, Thailand, Malaysia, and Indonesia. The stem is terete, peeling, fissured longitudinally and about 0.3 cm in diameter. The internodes are about 6 cm long. The leaves are simple, decussate and stipulate. The stipule is interpetiolar, cuspidate and about 0.4 cm long. The petiole is 0.3 cm long and terete. The leaf blade is thinly coriaceous, dark green above, broadly lanceolate, 5.7 - 9 cm x 3.2 - 4.2 cm, acute at the base, acuminate at the apex, the margin is recurved, with 7-9 secondary prominent below. The inflorescence is a light green terminal cyme which is many flowered to form a globose bunch. The flower pedicel is 0.15 cm long. The calyx is light green, turning dark maroon, 0.2 cm long, with 4 lobes which are oblong-triangular. The corolla tube is slender, 0.8 -1.2 cm long, glabrous, with 4 lobes which are 0.4 cm long, greenish - whitish turning cream and fragrant. The style is exerted. The fruit is globose or bilobed and contain a few plano-convex seeds which are rugose and black (Figure 249).
Medicinal Uses:	The plant is used to treat dysentery in Cambodia, Laos and Vietnam. It is also used there as post-partum remedy. Malays use the plant for influenza.

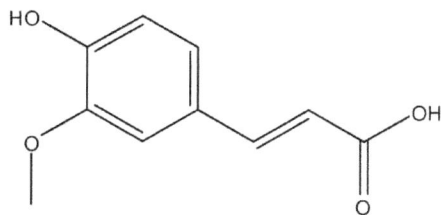

4-hydroxy-3-methoxy cinnamic acid   3-hydroxy-4-methoxy cinnamic acid

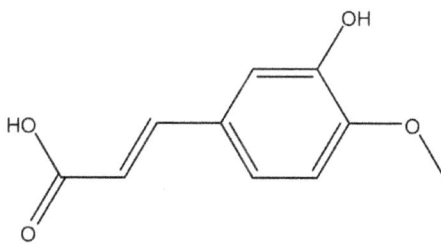

Pharmacology:	To date the pharmacological property of *Ixora nigricans* Wight & Arn. is unexplored. However, antitumour properties of *Ixora* species have been reported. A fraction obtained from an extract of flowers of *Ixora coccinea* L. increased the life-span of Dalton's lymphoma and Ehrlich ascites carcinoma in rodents (Latha *et al.*, 1998). Topical application of an extract of flowers of *Ixora javanica* inhibited the growth of intraperitoneally transplanted

sarcoma-180 and Ehrlich ascites carcinoma tumours in rodents possibly due to ferulic acid (4-hydroxy-3-methoxy cinnamic acid) and its isomer 3-hydroxy-4-methoxy cinnamic acid (Nair *et al.*, 1991).

Figure 249: *Ixora nigricans* **Wight & Arn.**
From: Flora of Thailand, Prince of Songkla University
Thailand, Rattapoom district, Boripat fall park. Elevation: 50 m. Date of collection: 4 July 1986. In partly open area, rocky stream bed, the margin of the evergreen forest. Collection and Identification: JF Maxwell, N⁰ 86-433

References: Latha PG, Panikkar KR, 1998, Cytotoxic and antitumor principles from *Ixora coccinea* flowers. Cancer Lett; 130: 197-202.

Nair SC, Panikkar B, Akamanchi KG, Panikkar KR, 1991, Inhibitory effects of *Ixora javanica* extract on skin chemical carcinogenesis in mice and its antitumor activity. Cancer Lett; 60: 253-8.

Mitragyna parvifolia (Roxb.) Korth

[From Latin *mitragyna* = mitriform female organ and from Latin *parvifolia* = small-leaved]

Local names:	Fake kratom; kaim; hteinthay, htaim-ping (Burma), vitanah (Sanskrit), sinnakkatampu (India)
Basionym;	*Nauclea parvifolia* Roxb.
Synonyms:	*Stephegyne parvifolia* Korth., *Nauclea parvifolia* Willd.
Description:	It is a large tree that grows in the rainforests of India, Bangladesh, Nepal, Sri Lanka, Burma, Thailand and Malaysia. The stem is quadrangular, with longitudinal lines and 5 - 6 cm long internodes. The leaves are simple, decussate and without stipules. The petiole is, stout, channeled above, 1 to 3 cm long. The leaf blade is 12 - 14 cm x 6 - 8 cm, elliptic, obovate, and coriaceous, with a sunken midrib above, cordate or acute at the base, acuminate at the apex, with 13 - 14 pairs of secondary nerves. A little tuft of hair is present at the axil of the secondary nerve and underneath the midrib. The stipule is 1.3 cm x 0.5 - 0.8 cm, oblong spathulate, pinkish and nerved. The inflorescence is a globose head which is about 2 - 2.5 cm. The calyx is tubular, funnel-shaped, truncate, and 0.2 cm long. The corolla is 0.6 - 0.8 cm long, infundibuliform, with 5 linear lobes which are 0.25 cm long and somewhat recurved. The anthers are visible at corolla lobe axils and the style protrudes slenderly out of the corolla. The head of the fruit is 1.3 - 1.6 cm in diameter. The fruit is a 0.3 cm long capsule which is ribbed (Figure 250).
Medicinal Uses:	The plant is used in India for fever, colic and muscular pain. In Cambodia, Laos and Vietnam the plant is used to promote appetite.
Pharmacology:	The plant produces a series of indolic and heteroyohimbine oxindolic alkaloids including 16,17 - dihydro-17 beta hydroxy isomitraphylline (Panday *et al.*, 2006; Shellard *et al.*, 1969, 1974). Some of these alkaloids may be cytotoxic (Stuppner et al., 1993). The plant might, like *Mitragyna speciosa* (Korth.) Havil. contain mitragynine which has been the subject of several neuropharmacological studies. Mitragynine binds to the μ - and δ - opioid receptors which are responsible for the control of morphine addiction and pain (Beckett *et al.*, 1966; Thongpradichote *et al.*, 1998; Watanabe *et al.*, 1997).

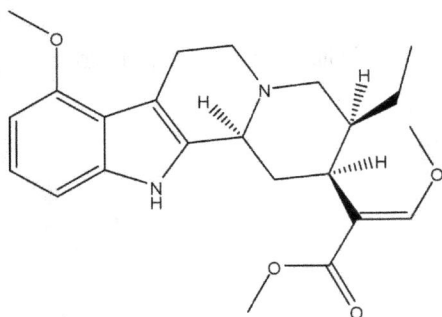

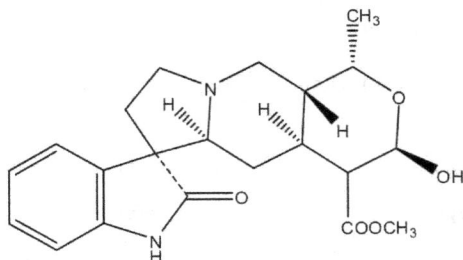

Mitragynine   16,17-dihydro-17β-hydroxyisomitraphyline

References:

Beckett AH, Shellard EJ, Phillipson JD, Lee CM, 1966, The *Mitragyna* species of Asia. VII. Indole alkaloids from the leaves of *Mitragyna speciosa* Korth. Planta Med; 14: 277-88.

Beckett AH, Shellard EJ, Phillipson JD, Lee CM., 1966, The *Mitragyna* species of Asia. VI. Oxindole alkaloids from the leaves of *Mitragyna speciosa* Korth. Planta Med; 14: 266-76.

Pandey R, Singh SC, Gupta MM, 2006, Heteroyohimbinoid type oxindole alkaloids from *Mitragyna parvifolia* .Phytochemistry; 67: 2164-2169.

Shellard EJ, Houghton PJ, 1974, The *Mitragyna* species of Asia. Part XXVII. The alkaloidal N-oxides in the leaves of *Mitragyna parvifolia* (Roxb.) Korth from Sri Lanka. Planta Med; 25: 172-174.

Shellard EJ, Houghton PJ, 1971, The *Mitragyna* species of Asia. Part XIX. The alkaloidal pattern in *Mitragyna parvifolia* (Roxb.) Korth. Planta Med; 20: 82-89.

Shellard EJ, Phillipson JD, Gupta D, 1969, The *Mitragyna* species of Asia. Part XIV. The alkaloids of the leaves of *Mitragyna parvifolia* obtained from Burma, Cambodia and Sri Lanka. Planta Med; 17: 51-58.

Shellard EJ, Phillipson JD, Gupta D, 1969, The *Mitragyna* species of Asia. Part XV. The alkaloids from the bark of *Mitragyna parvifolia* (Roxb.) Korth and a possible biogenetic route for the oxindole alkaloids. Planta Med; 17: 146-163.

Stuppner H, Sturm S, Geisen G, Zillian U, Konwalinka G, 1993, A differential sensitivity of oxindole alkaloids to normal and leukemic cell lines. Planta Med; 59: A583.

Thongpradichote S, Matsumoto K, Tohda M, Takayama H, Aimi N, Sakai S, Watanabe H, 1998, Identification of opioid receptor subtypes in antinociceptive actions of supraspinally-administered mitragynine in mice. Life Sci; 62: 1371-8.

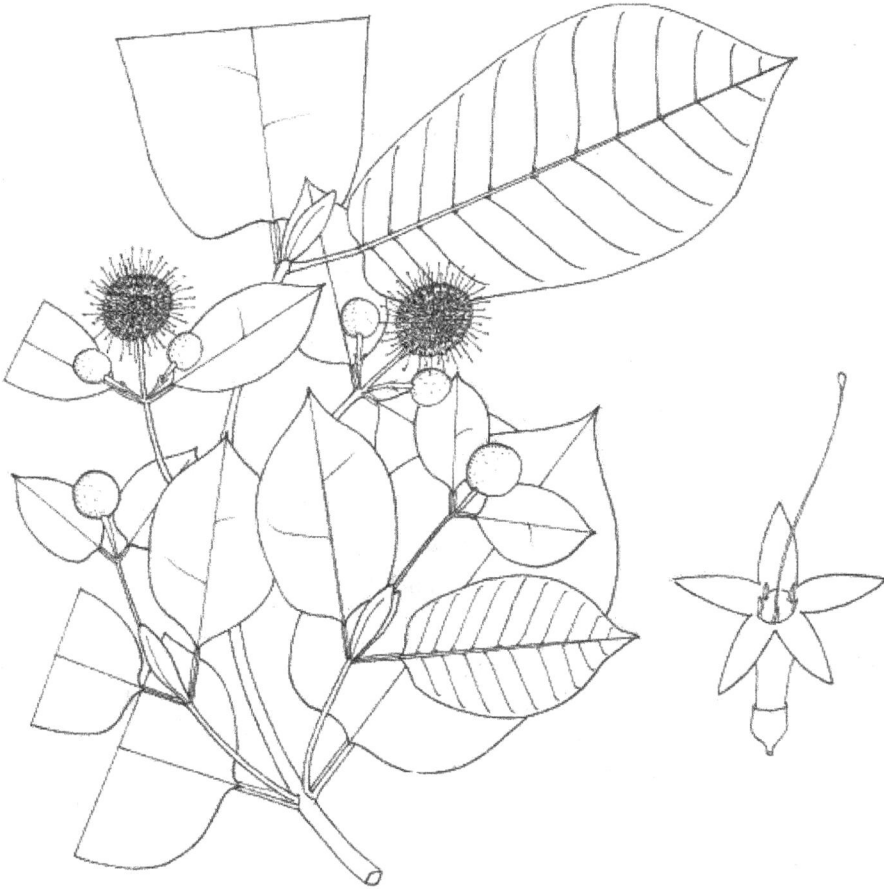

Figure 250: *Mitragyna parvifolia* (Roxb.) Korth
From: Herbarium of *University* Kebangsaan Malaysia
Malaysia: Jalan Bangi, Jendram. Date of Collection: 19 October 1972. Collection and Determination: Mohd. Kassim.

Morinda parvifolia Bartl.

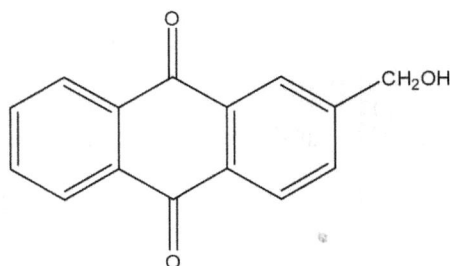

[From Latin *morus* = mulberry and *parvus* = small and *folia* = leaves]

Local names: Small-leaved Indian mulberry; little leaf Indian mulberry; bai yan teng, hong zhu (China)

Synonym: *Morinda rovoc* Lour.

Description: It is a climber which grows in South China, Taiwan, Cambodia, Laos, Vietnam and the Philippines. The stem is hairy at the apex, articulated, and quadrangular, fissured, lenticelled, glabrous, and with prominent leaf scars. The internodes are short, and about 0.6 cm long. The leaves are simple, mostly by the apex of the stem, decussate and stipulate. The interpetiolar stipule is membranaceous, covered with a few hairs, 0.2 cm long and forming a tube around the stem. The petiole is 0.2 - 0.5 cm, flattish, hairy and channeled. The leaf blade is 3.5 - 5.2 cm x 1.4 - 2 cm, dark green above and glossy spathulate, recurved at the margin, leathery, glabrous, with 4 - 5 pairs of secondary nerves underneath with minute tufts of hairs at axil with the midrib. The flower is greenish white, and 0.15 - 0.2 cm long. The calyx is truncate. The Corolla is 0.5 cm long, hairy at the throat, 4 - 5 lobed. The fruit is a red bright glossy 0.7 cm x 0.6 - 1.3 cm syncarp on a 1 cm long pedicel (Figure 251).

Medicinal Uses: In Cambodia, Laos and Vietnam the plant is used as a purgative.

Pharmacology: The plant abounds with anthraquinones, some of which are cytotoxic, such as morindaparvin-A and 2-hydroxy-methylanthraquinone.   2-hydroxy-methylanthraquinone displayed significant activity in the *in vivo* growth of P388 lymphocytic leukemia in mice (Chang *et al.*, 1982; 1984). These anthraquinones might account for the medicinal property of the plant.

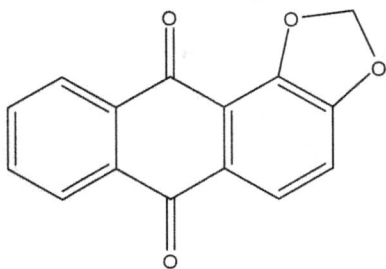

Morindaparvin-A   2-hydroxy-methylanthraquinone

References:

Chang P, Lee KH, Shingu T, Hirayama T, Hall IH, Huang HC, 1982, Antitumor agents 50. 1 Morindaparvin-A, a new antileukemic anthraquinone, and alizarin-1-methyl ether from *Morinda parvifolia*, and the antileukemic activity of the related derivatives. J Nat Prod; 45: 206-10.

Chang P, Lee KH, 1984, Cytotoxic antileukemic anthraquinones from *Morinda parvifolia*. Phytochemistry; 23: 1733-36.

Figure 251: *Morinda parvilofia* Bartl
From: Flora of Taiwan, Herbarium National Ping Tung Institute of Agriculture.
Taiwan, Heng chun Kenting. Date of collection: 5 may 1985. Collector: Ching-en Chang 16925

Morinda tomentosa Roth.

[From Latin *morus* = mulberry and parvus = small and *tomentosa* = densely covered with matted wool or short hair]

Local names:
: Indian mulberry; bakam (Arabic), morinda des teinturiers (France), nithe base (Burma), nuna (India)

Synonyms:
: *Morinda tinctoria* Roxb., *Morinda coreia* Buch.-Ham.

Description:
: It is a small deciduous tree which grows to a height of 7 m and a girth of 9 cm in India, Burma, and Thailand. The bark is spongy, deeply cracked, and grayish yellow. The flower stem is rough, stout, 0.6 cm in diameter, articulate, with many leaf scars and numerous nodes, glabrous, fissured, somewhat flaky and quadrangular. The internodes are 1 - 2 cm. The younger stems are terete and hairy. The leaves are simple, decussate, and stipulate. The stipules are interpetiolar, broadly lanceolate, bifid, and 0.3 x 0.2 cm. The petiole is 1.3 - 2.5 cm long, velvety and channeled. The leaf blade is about 4 - 6 cm x 9 - 13 cm, velvety underneath and elliptic-lanceolate. The base of the blade tapers down to the petiole, the apex is round with a minute tip, the margin is wavy and recurved. The leaf blade shows 6 - 7 pairs of secondary nerves and several scalariform tertiary nerves visible underneath. The midrib underneath is pimply. The inflorescence is solitary, and axillary at the end of stems. The peduncle is hairy, and varicose. The flower is scented. The corolla is tomentose outside, 1.3 - 2 cm long, with 5 linear lobes. The fruit is a syncarp which is 1.5 - 2 cm in diameter (Figure 252).

Medicinal uses:
: In India, the plant is used to heal boils and to stop diarrhoea. It is also the source of a yellowish - red dye named suranji which has been used since early times. In Cambodia, Laos and Vietnam, the plant is used to treat cholera. In Malaysia, the plant is used to treat fever.

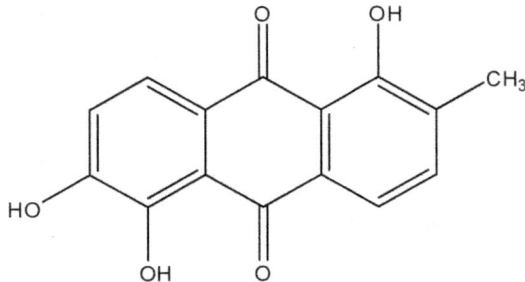

Morindone

References: Jayasinghe UL, Jayasooriya CP, Bandara BM, Ekanayake SP,
Merlini L, Assante G, 2002, Antimicrobial activity of some Sri
Lankan Rubiaceae and Meliaceae. Fitoterapia; 73: 424-7.

Vermes B, Wagner H, 1980, Synthesis and structure proof
of morindone 6-O-gentiobioside from *Morinda tinctoria*;
Phytochemistry; 19: 2493-2494.

Figure 252: *Morinda tomentosa* Roth
From: Flora of Thailand. Chiang Mai University Herbarium
Thailand, Chiang Mai province, Nuang district, Poi Suther-Pui National Park east side of Wat
Pahlat. Elevation: 540 m. By 18° North - 100° East, in a fire damaged deciduous dipterocarp-
oak forest on granite bedrock. Date of collection: 19 September 1996. Collection and
identification: Monyrak Meng.

Mussaenda dehiscens Craib

[From Sinhalese *mussenda* = *Mussaenda* species and Latin *dehiscens* = dehiscent]

Local name: Sui you (China)

Synonyms: *Schizomussaenda dehiscens* (Craib) Li, *Mussaenda elongata*
                Hutch., *Mussaenda henryi* Hutch., *Mussaenda glabra* Pierre,
                Schizophragma macrosepalum Hu, *Emmenopterys rehderi*
                Metcalf

Description: It is a tree which grows to a height of 7 m and a girth of 8 cm,
                in open forest, in a geographical area covering Burma, China,
                Laos, Vietnam and Thailand. The bark is thin, smooth, and
                grey. The stem is hairy, 0.5 cm in diameter, with 2 - 6.2 cm
                long internodes, lenticelled, the lenticels elongated. The nodes
                present a rind. The leaves are simple, decussate and stipulate.
                The interpetiolar stipule is deciduous, membranaceous, bifid,
                1.5 x 0.4 cm and hairy. The petiole is hairy, channelled and 0.7
                - 1 cm long. The leaf blade is dull dark green above, light green
                underneath, membranaceous, almost translucent, attenuate at
                the base, acute at the apex, wavy at the margin, 13 - 20 cm x 3.5
                - 7.5 cm, with 10 pairs of secondary nerves visible underneath.
                The midrib underneath the blade is hairy. The inflorescence is
                a 15 cm long cyme. The calyx presents 4 - 5 lobes which are
                linear, 0.1 - 0.3 cm x 0.1 cm. One of the lobes develops into a
                conspicuously leaf-like organ, 9 -12.5 cm x 3.3 -6.5 cm attached
                to the calyx by a 2.5 cm peduncle. The corolla tube is light green,
                hairy, about 2 cm long and developing 4-5 lobes which are
                trapezoid, pale light greenish outside, orange inside, and about
                0.4 cm long. The fruit is ovoid, about 0.8 x 0.5 cm, and crowned
                with vestigial calyx lobes around a disk (Figure 253).

Medicinal uses: In Cambodia, Laos and Vietnam the plant is used to treat
                smallpox. In China it is used for urethritis.

Pharmacology: Extracts of the flower displayed NO scavenging activity and
                inhibited lipid peroxidation, hydroxyl radical and ABTS radical
                scavenging property (Vidyalakshmi *et al.*, 2006). This antioxidant
                property may be a component of the medicinal use of the plant
                in China. *Mussaenda pubescens* exhibited antiviral activity against
                human respiratory syncytial virus *in vitro* (Li *et al.*, 2004).

References: Li Y, Ooi LS, Wang H, But PP, Ooi VE, 2004, Antiviral activities
                of medicinal herbs traditionally used in southern mainland
                China. Phytother Res; 18: 718-22.

                Vidyalakshmi KS, Dorni AIC, Vasanthi HR, Rajamanickam
                GV, Sukumar D, 2006, J Applied Sc; 6: 2251-56.

Figure 253: *Mussaenda dehiscens* Craib
From: Flora of Thailand. Chiang Mai University Herbarium
Thailand, central region of Doi Puh Kah national park, by 19° North - 100° East. Elevation:
1275 m. Date of collection: 23 July 1994. In open disturbed thicket with secondary growth
in very degraded primary evergreen hardwood forest on shale bedrock. Collection and
identification: JF Maxwell No 94801.

Mussaenda frondosa L.

[From Sinhalese *mussenda* = *Mussaenda* species and Latin *frondosa* = leafy]

Local name: Pink mussaenda, flag bush; aloalo vao (Samoa), dhobini (Nepal), vakep (India).

Synonyms: *Gardenia frondosa* (L.) Lam., *Mussaenda belilla* Buch.-Ham., *Mussaenda dovinia* Buch.-Ham., *Mussaenda flavescens* Buch.-Ham., *Mussaenda formosa* L. *Mussaenda fruticosa* L., *Mussaenda ingrata* Wall. ex Hook.f., *Mussaenda macrophylla* Kurz, *Mussaenda sumatrensis* B.Heyne ex Roth, *Mussaenda tomentosa* Wight ex Hook.f. *Mussaenda villosa* Schltdl. ex Hook.f

Description: It is a woody climber which grows to a height of 5 m in a geographical area which covers India, Malaysia, Indonesia, the Philippines and Taiwan. The plant is ornamental and cultivated in several subtropical and tropical regions of the globe. The stem is terete, hairy, 0.3 cm in diameter, lenticelled, the lenticels ovoid to 0.1 cm long, the internodes are 2.3 - 7 cm and the nodes are marked with a tiny rind. The leaves are simple, decussate and stipulate. The interpetiolar stipules are triangular, 0.4 x 0.1 cm, hairy, and deciduous. The petiole is slender, 1 - 3 cm, hairy, curved at the base, and channeled. The leaf blade is membranaceous, dark green, translucent, hairy, and cuneate at the base, shortly acuminate at the apex, broadly lanceolate, wavy at the margin and with 7 - 10 pairs of secondary nerves and scalariform tertiary nerves which are visible underneath. The inflorescence is a terminal cyme which is hairy. The calyx is about 0.7 cm long with 5 linear lobes, one of which develops into a strikingly pure white leaf-like organ on a 2.5 cm pedicel. It has an ovoid blade marked with longitudinal nervations and is about 8 x 6.5 cm long. The corolla tube is hairy, greenish, about 2 cm long and develops 5 triangular lobes merging into a bright red or orange star, the center of which is marked with a yellowish throat. The fruit is globose light green, 0.9 cm in diameter, lenticelled and marked with a light brown opening at the apex (Figure 254).

Medicinal uses: In India, the plant is used to heal sore mouths, sore throats, and to break fever to calm coughs, to heal ulcers and to counteract snake bites. In Cambodia, Laos and Vietnam, the plant is used to treat coughs, fever, asthma, cancer of the intestines and diseases of the skin.

Pharmacology: The plant accumulates a series of oleananes-type triterpenoid glycosides and aglycones which could account for the healing, antitussive and anti-inflammatory uses mentioned above. Note that some of these triterpenes abrogated the survival of a periodontopathic bacterium, *Porphyromonas gingivalis*. Such triterpenoid are 3-*O-alpha*-D-glucopyranosyl-28-*O*-R-L-rhamnopyranosyl-16R-hydroxyprotobassic acid, and 3-*O*-acetyloleanolic acid (Kim *et al.*, 1999). It would be of interest to search for cytotoxic agents from this plant which is traditionally used for the treatment of cancer of the intestines. Note that *Mussaenda pava* exhibited a moderate cytotoxic activity against human cervix carcinoma cell line (KB-3-1), (Tanamatayarat *et al.*, 2003). Oleanane derivatives are perhaps involved here; the antitumour, anti-inflammatory activity of oleanolic acid is well documented (Liu, 1995; Singh *et al.*, 1992).

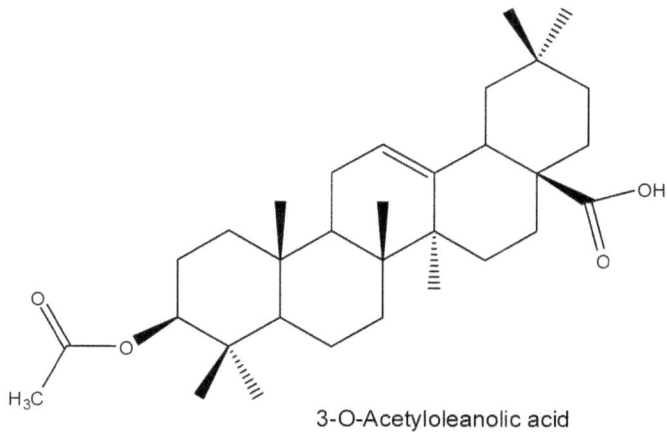

3-O-Acetyloleanolic acid

References: Kim NC, Desjardins AE, Wu CD, Kinghorn AD, 1999, Activity of triterpenoid glycosides from the root bark of *Mussaenda macrophylla* against two oral pathogens. J Nat Prod; 62: 1379-84.

Liu J, 1995, Pharmacology of oleanolic acid and ursolic acid. J Ethnopharmacol; 49: 57-68.

Singh GB, Singh S, Bani S, Gupta BD, Banerjee SK, 1992, Anti-inflammatory activity of oleanolic acid in rats and mice. J Pharm Pharmacol; 44: 456-458.

Tanamatayarat P, Limtrakul PN, Chunsakaow S, Duangrat C, 2003, Screening of some rubiaceous plants for cytotoxic activity against cervix carcinoma (KB-3-1) cell line. The ThaiJ Pharm Sci; 27: 167-172.

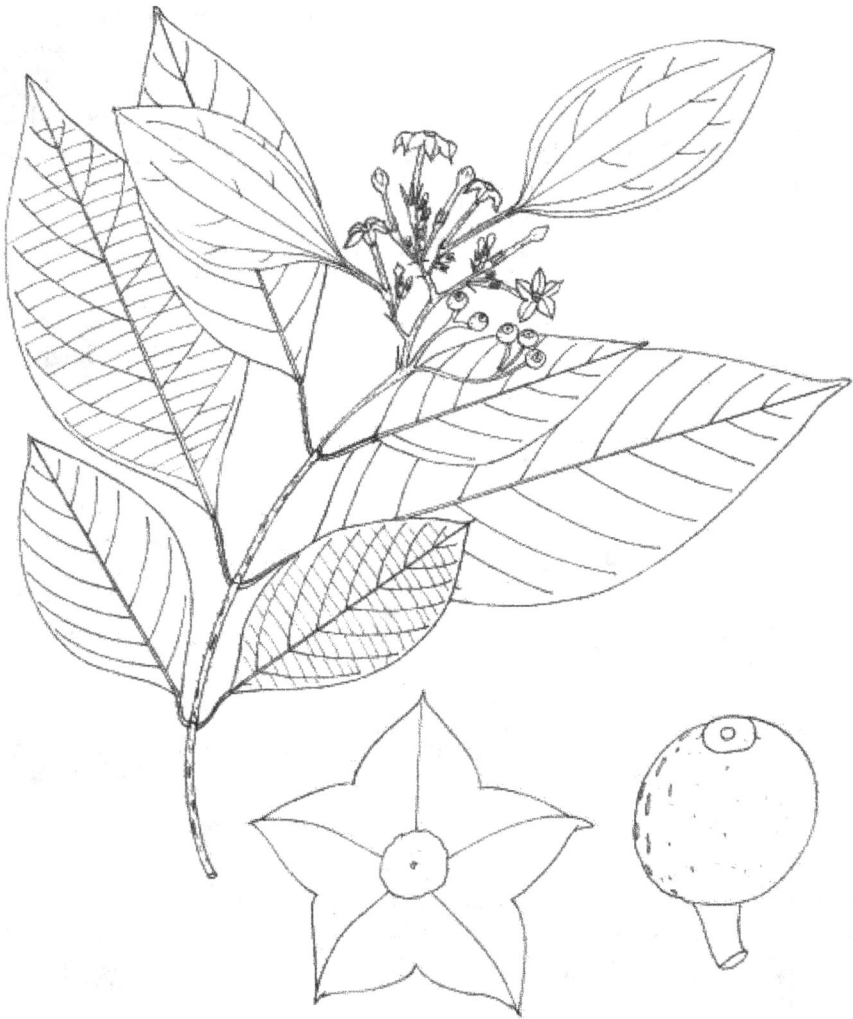

Figure 254: *Mussaenda frondosa* L.
From: Flora of Borneo. Michigan State University Herbarium
Malaysia, Sabah, Ranau district, poring hot spring at East the base of mount Kinabalu, 6°
03' North - 116° 42' East. Elevation: 550 m. Date of collection: 1987. In secondary forest.
Collection and identification: JH Beaman

Mussaenda glabra Vahl

[From Sinhalese *mussenda* = *Mussaenda* species and Latin *glabra* = glabrous]

Local name:	Dwarf yellow Mussaenda
Description:	It is a shrub found by roadsides and in open forest from India to Malaysia and cultivated in several tropical and subtropical countries as an ornamental. The stem is lenticelled, glabrous, angled to flattish at the apex. The leaves are simple, decussate and with pairs of interpetiolar stipules. The stipule is 0.7 x 0.4 cm, bifid at the apex, with a few hairs in the middle. The petiole is slender, 2 - 5.5 cm and glabrous. The leaf blade is 16 - 26 cm x 5.2 - 9.5 cm, broadly lanceolate, membranaceous, with 6 - 7 pairs of secondary nerves, wavy at the margin, attenuated at the base, acute at the apex with a minute thorn. The inflorescence is a terminal cyme. The flower is light yellow, tubular, about 2 - 3 cm long with 5 lobes. The fruit is a berry with 5 lobes, one of which accrescent and develops into a leaf on a 3 cm pedicel with a 7 x 4 cm almost white leaf blade-like organ (Figure 255).
Medicinal uses:	In Malaysia the plant is used for headaches, to treat coughs, fever, colic, and as a post-partum remedy,
Pharmacology:	The pharmacological property of this plant is unexplored. *Mussaenda macrophylla* contains some triterpenoid saponins and triterpenes including 3-O-acetyldaturadiol which inhibited the growth of periodontopathic bacteria, *Porphyromonas gingivalis* (Kim *et al.*, 1999). The triterpenoid saponins and their aglycones as well as iridoid glycosides (mussaenoside ?) probably present in *Mussaenda glabra* Vahl would be worth investigating.

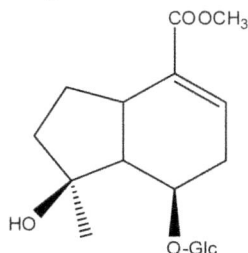

$COOCH_3$

Mussaenoside

References:	Inouye H, Takeda Y, Nishimura H, Kanomi A, Okuda, Puff C, 1988, Chemotaxonomic studies of rubiaceous plants containing iridoid Glycosides. Phytochemistry; 27: 2591-98.

Figure 255: *Mussaenda glabra* Vahl

From: Flora of Malaya
Malaysia, Genting Highland, Pahang state. Altitude: 1000 m. Date of collection: 13 February
1974. Collector: Mohd Kassim MK872

Mussaenda philippica A. Rich.

[From Sinhalese *mussenda* = *Mussaenda* species and Latin *philippica* = from the Philippines]

Local names:	Bangkok rose, tropical dogwood, Budda's lamp; kahoi-dalaga, tinga tinga (Philippines), janda kaya (Malaysia).
Synonyms:	*Calycophyllum grandiflorum* Meyen, *Mussaenda acutifolia* Bartl., *Mussaenda frondosa* Blco., *Mussaenda glabra* F.-Vill., *Mussaenda grandiflora* Rolfe, *Mussaenda philippica* forma aurorae (Sulit) Jayaw., *Mussaenda philippica* var. aurorae Sulit,
Description:	It is a shrub which grows up to 5 m, native to the Philippines and cultivated throughout Southeast Asia as an ornamental, and several varieties have been developed. Wild, it is common in thickets and secondary forests at low and medium altitude. The stem is terete, and hairy about 0.3 cm in diameter, with 2.5 - 4 cm internodes. The leaves are simple, decussate and stipulate. The stipules are interpetiolar, 1 x 0.4 cm, hairy outside, lanceolate and bifid. The petiole is about 0.5 cm long, channeled and hairy. The leaf blade is broadly lanceolate, 2 – 5cm x 4.5 - 11 cm, wedge-shaped at the base, acuminate at the apex, with 9 - 11 pairs of secondary nerves conspicuous underneath. The inflorescence is a terminal, few flowered, hairy cyme. The calyx is about 0.7 cm long, 5 lobed, one of the lobes forming a conspicuous leaf-like organ which is either pure white or light pink (when pink, the nervations are white), longitudinally nerved, hairy, ovoid, and about 4.5 - 5 cm x 5 - 7 cm. The corolla tube is hairy and about 2 cm long, and develops 5 triangular lobes that merge into a star which is orange or yellow. The fruit is 1 -1.5 cm long, oblong with conspicuous, somewhat varicose lenticels and displays an opening at the apex surrounded by vestigial calyx lobes (Figure 256).
Medicinal uses:	In the Philippines the plant is used for headaches, to treat ear infection, snake bite, dysentery, lung diseases, and jaundice.
Pharmacology:	A methanol extract of the flowers of the plant exhibited pronounced antioxidant activity in lipid peroxidation, hydroxyl scavenging assay (Vidyalakshmi *et al.*, 2006). The pharmacological property of this plant would be interesting to study as triterpenes, iridoids or anthocyanins may be involved here?
References:	Vidyalakshmi KS, Dorni AIC, Vasanthi HR, Rajamanickam GV, Sukumar D, 2006, J Applied Sc; 6: 2251-56.

Figure 256: *Mussaenda philippica* A. Rich.
From: Flora of Malaya, Herbarium of University Kebangsaan Malaysia
Malaysia. Date of collection: 15 January 1983. Collector: Rosinawah Abdul

Mussaenda villosa Wall ex G Don

[From Sinhalese *mussenda* = *Mussaenda* species and Latin *villosa* = villous]

Local name:	Balik adap (Malaysia)
Description:	It is a climber of Malaysia. The stem is terete, hairy, 0.4 cm in diameter, with few lenticels, the nodes swollen with a rind, and with 4.5 - 11 cm internodes. The leaves are simple, decussate, and without stipules. The interpetiolar stipule is 1 x 0.2 cm, linear, hairy, deeply bifid and deciduous. The petiole is 0.5 - 1.5 cm long and flattish. The leaf blade is dark green above, 13 - 15.5 cm x 5.5 - 8 cm, thinly coriaceous, acute and somewhat asymmetrical at the base, wavy at the margin, acute at the apex, with 8 - 11 pairs of secondary nerves visible underneath with some tertiary nerves which are scalariform. The midrib is hairy underneath. The inflorescence is a terminal cyme on a 4.5 - 5 cm axis, the pedicel 1.5 - 2.5 cm long. The calyx is green with large lobes which are white. Corolla lobes inside are orange, outside yellow, the corolla tube is cream yellowish. The fruit is a 1.2 - 1.3 cm x 0.5 - 0.8 cm globose berry marked at the apex with a conspicuous disk (Figure 257).
Medicinal uses:	In Malaysia, the plant is used to treat rheumatism.
Pharmacology:	Unknown.

Figure 257: *Mussaenda villosa* **Wall ex G Don**
From: Flora of Thailand. Prince of Songkla University.
Thailand, Nakornsitammarat province, Lansagah district, Gahrome Falls, Khao Luang
national park. Elevation: 200 m. Date of collection: 19 May 1985. In open margins of primary
evergreen forest, near the river.

Nauclea junghuhnii (Miq.) Merr.
[From Greek *nauclea* = a small ship]

Local names: Bangka l (Philippines), mengkal (Malaysia),

Synonyms: *Nauclea subedit* (Korth.) Steudel, *Platanocarpum subditum* Korth. *Sarcocephalus horsfieldii* Elm., *Sarcocephalus junghuhnii* Miq., *Sarcocephalus subditus* (Korth.) Miq.,

Description: It is a magnificent timber tree which grows to about 30 m in lowland swampy places, by streams in the primary forests of India, Cambodia, Laos, Vietnam, Malaysia, Indonesia and the Philippines, Australia, Papua New Guinea and Oceania. The bark is grayish brown, smooth, fissured or sometimes scaly. The inner bark is yellow to pale brown, laminated with reddish purple layer. The stem is squarish, smooth, glabrous, about 0.3 cm and hairy by the apex, with 3.5 - 5.7 cm long internodes. The nodes are swollen with a ring. The leaves are simple, decussate and stipulate. The stipules are interpetiolar ovate to elliptic, about 2 x 1 cm long with a central keel. The petiole is 0.3 - 2 cm long, fissured transversally, woody and channeled. The leaf blade is thin, ovate, 4 - 20 cm x 2 - 8 cm, elliptic, apiculate at the apex, wedge shaped at the base, with 6 - 13 pairs of secondary nerves flat above and raised and hairy underneath. The midrib is sunken above with few lenticels. The flowering head is solitary and axillary on a 1 - 5 cm long hairy pedicel, the head is 0.8 - 2 cm in diameter. The flower is yellow. The calyx tube is minute. The corolla is tubular, 0.3 cm long with 4 or 5 lobes which are imbricate and 0.1 cm long. The fruit is a dark green to brownish woody, rugose head which is about 2 cm in diameter (Figure 258).

Medicinal Uses: In the Philippines the plant is used to normalize menses.

Pharmacology: To date, the pharmacological property of this plant seems unexplored despite accumulating evidence of parasiticidal, cytotoxic and neurological potentials. An extract of *Sarcocephalus latifolium* abrogated the survival of *Leis mania major* (Aqua *et al.*, 2007). Sun *et al.*, (2008) isolated indole alkaloids, one of which is naucleidinal, had some levels of activity against *Plasmodium falciparum* and cytotoxic activity against SGC-7901, A-549, PC3, HL-60, and K562 human cancer cell lines cultured *in vitro*. Other antiplasmodial alkaloids were isolated by He *et al.* (2005) from *Nauclea orientalis*. An extract of *Nauclea latifolia* decreased the spontaneous motor activity and exploratory behaviour in mice and prolonged pentobarbital sleeping time in rats dose-dependently (Amos *et al.*, .2005). It would be of interest to study this tree for its chemical constituents and their pharmacological properties.

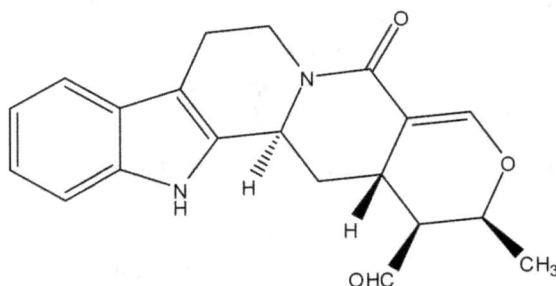

Naucleidinal

References:

Ahua KM, Ioset JR, Ioset KN, Diallo D, Mauël J, Hostettmann K, 2007, Antileishmanial activities associated with plants used in the Malian traditional medicine. J Ethnopharmacol; 110: 99-104.

Amos S, Abbah J, Chindo B, Edmond I, Binda L, Adzu B, Buhari S, Odutola AA, Wambebe C, Gamaniel K, 2005, Neuropharmacological effects of the aqueous extract of *Nauclea latifolia* root bark in rats and mice. J Ethnopharmacol; 97: 53-57.

He ZD, Ma CY, Zhang HJ, Tan GT,Tamez P, Sydara K, Bouamanivong S, Southavong B, Soejarto DD, Pezzuto JM, Fong HHS, 2005, Antimalarial Constituents from *Nauclea orientalis* (L.) L. Chem Biodivers; 2: 1378-86.

Sun J, Lou H, Dai S, Xu H, Zhao F, Liu K, 2008, Indole alkaloids from *Nauclea officinalis* with weak antimalarial activity. Phytochemistry; 69: 1405-10.

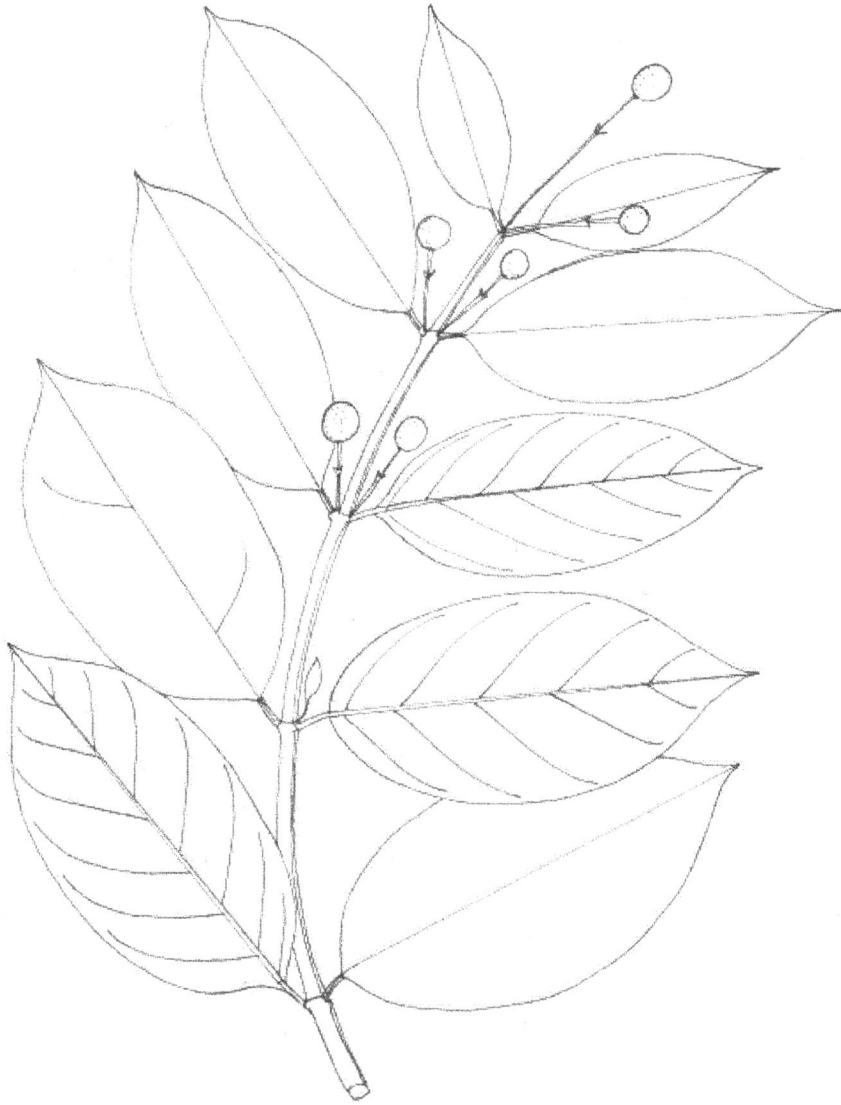

Figure 258: *Nauclea junghuhnii* (Miq.) Merr.
From Flora of The Philippines, Philippines National Herbarium, National Museum Manila.
PNH № 98352.
Philippines, Tungao Logging Camp, Agusan, Mindanao, in second growth forest. Altitude: 360
m - 390 m. Collection and identification: Dacalos, Jose B. Date of collection: 26 August 1967.

Oldenlandia herbacea (L.) DC.

[After Danish botanist and physician Henrik Bernard Oldenland (1663-1699) and Latin *herbacea* = herbaceous]

Synonyms:	*Hedyotis herbacea* L., *Oldenlandia hernia* G. Don
Description:	It is a delicate herb which grows in open sunny sandy places, and by roadsides, in a geographical area covering tropical and subtropical Africa and Asia, including the whole of Southeast Asia. The stem is squarish, branching dichotomously, minutely winged, at corners, somewhat articulated, 0.1 - 0.2 cm in diameter with internodes which are 1 cm long. The leaves are simple, decussate, sessile and without stipules. The leaf blade is 1 - 1.8 cm x 0.1 - 0.3 cm. The inflorescence is an axillary cyme. The flower pedicel is slender and 1 - 1.2 cm long. The corolla is 0.4 cm long with a slender tube and 4 lobes. The fruit is a globose membranaceous capsule which is dehiscent, about 0.25 cm in diameter with 4 vestigial calyx lobes and containing a few ellipsoid seeds (Figure 259).
Medicinal Uses:	In India, Cambodia, Laos and Vietnam the plant is used for fever. In Malaysia, the plant is sold as a tea.
Pharmacology:	The antipyretic property has not been validated yet. An extract of the plant exhibited mild cytotoxicity against CEM-SS cell-line as well as strong antioxidant properties Ahmad R *et al.*, (2005).

The plant elaborates series of anthraquinones including 2-hydroxymethyl-10-hydroxy-1,4-anthraquinone, 1,4-dihydroxy-2-hydroxymethylanthraquinone; 2, 3-dimethoxy-9-hydroxy-1,4-anthraquinone; and 1,4-dihydroxy-2, 3-dimethoxyanthraquinone (Permana *et al.*, 1999) as well as ursolic acid and flavonoid glycosides (Hamzah *et al.*, 1996). One could have some interest in evaluating the antiplasmodial properties of the anthraquinones so far isolated frpm this plant.

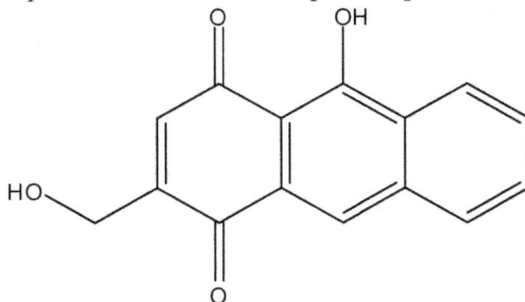

2-hydroxymethyl-10-hydroxy-1,4-anthraquinone

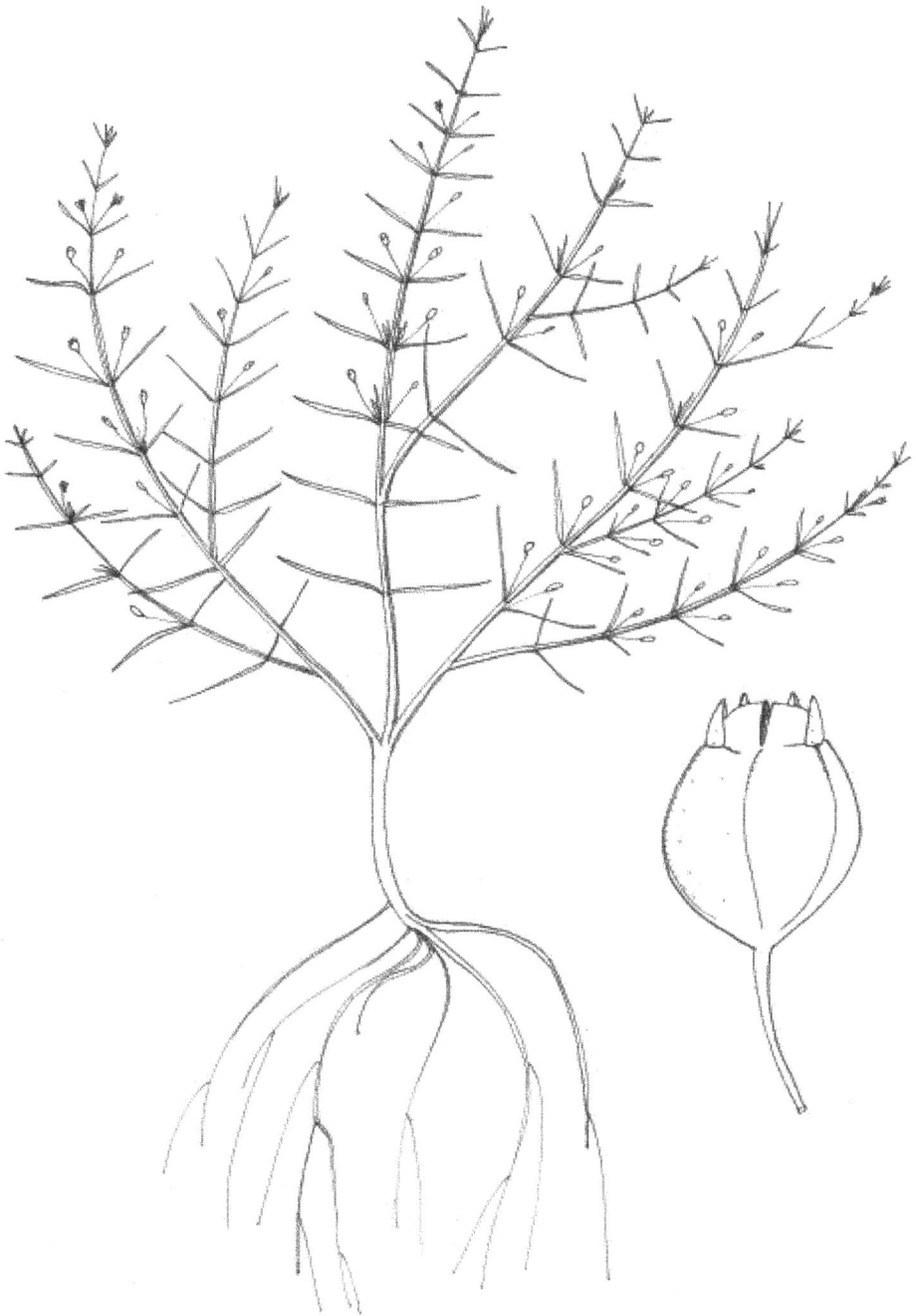

Figure 259: *Oldenlandia herbacea* (L.) DC.
From: University Kebangsaan Herbarium No 01148
Malaysia, Selangor state, Sungai Way. Collection and identification: Mohd. Kassim. Date of Collection: 11January 1973.

References: Ahmad R, Ali AM, Israf DA, Ismail NH, Shaari K, Lajis NHL,
                        2005, Antioxidant, radical-scavenging, anti-inflammatory,
                        cytotoxic and antibacterial activities of methanolic extracts of
                        some *Hedyotis* species. Life Sc; 76: 1953-1964.

                        Hamzah AS, Norio Aimi N, Nordin HJ, Lajis NHJ, 1996,
                        Constituents of *Hedyotis herbacea* (Rubiaceae). Biochem System
                        Ecol; 24: 273.

                        Permana D, Lajis NH, Othman AG, Ali AM, Aimi N, Kitajima
                        M, Takayama H, 1999, Anthraquinones from *hedyotis herbacea*.
                        J Nat Prod; 62: 1430-1.

Pavetta indica L.

[From India *pavattai* = *Pavetta indica* L. and Latin *indica* = from India]

Local names: Indian pellet shrub;. Pavette des Indes (France), soka (Sundanese).
                        pecha priok puteh (Malaysia), kangyaphul (Nepal), gusokan
                        (Philippines), kho som (Laos), khem paa. (Thailand), thanh,
                        khem khao, fa hai noi (Vietnam), hmitgyin (Burma), papata
                        (Sanskrit), pavattai (India).

Synonyms: *Ixora indica* (L.) Kuntze, *Pavetta tomentosa* Roxb. ex Smith,
                        Ixora pavetta Roxb.

Description: *Pavetta indica* is a small tree which grows up to 5 tall in primary
                        and secondary forests in a geographical area covering India, Sri
                        Lanka, the Andamans, China, Malaysia, and Australia. The stem
                        is terete, glabrous, and slender with internodes which are 0.5 - 3
                        cm long. The leaves are simple, decussate, mostly at the apex of
                        stems, and stipulate. The stipules are triangular. The petiole is 1
                        - 2.5 cm long, slender, glabrous, and channeled. The leaf blade
                        is elliptic lanceolate membranaceous, 9 - 15 cm x 3 - 4.2 cm,
                        acuminate at the apex, cuneate at the base, with 6 - 10 pairs of
                        secondary nerves arching at the margin. The inflorescences are
                        axillary and terminal cymes. The calyx is narrowly campanulate,
                        pubescent, and about 0.3 cm long. The corolla is white, about
                        1.3 cm long, with 4 lobes which are linear oblong. The style is
                        filiform, long-exerted and white. The fruit is a green globose
                        drupe ripening black, with a tiny tube at the apex , 0.6 cm - 1.4
                        cm in diameter on a somewhat conical peduncle (Figure 260).

Medicinal Uses: In India the plant is used as a laxative and as a treatment for
                        dropsy and painful piles. In Cambodia, Laos and Vietnam, the
                        plant is used for rheumatism. In Vietnam the plant is also used

as a post-partum remedy, it is a laxative and it is used for dropsy. In Burma, the plant is used to stimulate the appetite. Malays use the plant for boils, itching and as a post partum remedy. In the Philippines the plant is a laxative, and used to assuage the pain caused by piles.

Pharmacology:	Not much is known about the chemical constituents of this plants which might contain proanthocyanidins and alkaloids (Ganguly, 1994). Mandal *et al.* (2003) showed that a methanol extract of *Pavetta indica* L. exhibited an anti-inflammatory effect comparable with that of the standard drug indomethacin, a standard non-steroidal anti-inflammatory drug, validating thereby the anti-inflammatory use of the plant. An extract of *Pavetta* decreased CCl4- alterations in the liver histopathology as well as the serum enzyme levels of in albino rats (Thabrew *et al.*, 1987). Note that some antiplasmodial and antischistosomial activities have been reported from other members of the genus *Pavetta* (Baldé *et al.*, 1986; Sanon *et al.*, 2003). Amos *et al.* (2003), showed that an extract of *Pavetta crassipes* has behavioral effects acting centrally through the inhibition of dopaminergic pathway (Amos *et al.*, 2004).

References: Amos S, Aka PA N, Chindo BA, Hussaini IM, Wambebe C, Gamaniel K, 2004, Behavioural effect of *Pavetta crassipes* extract on rodents. Pharmacol Biochem Behavior; 77: 751-759.

Baldé AM, Van Marck E, Vanhaelen M, 1986, *In vivo* activity of an extract of *Pavetta owariensis* bark on experimental Schistosoma mansoni infection in mice. J Ethnopharmacol; 18: 187-92.

Ganguly SM, 1994, Constituents of *Pavetta indica* leaves. Fitoterapia; 65: 477.

Mandal SC, Mohana Lakshmi S, Ashok Kumar CK, Sur TK, Boominathan R, 2003, Evaluation of anti-inflammatory potential of *Pavetta indica* Linn. leaf extract (family: Rubiaceae) in rats. Phytother Res; 17: 817-20.

Sanon S, Azas N, Gasquet M, Ollivier E, Mahiou V, Barro N, Cuzin-Ouattara N, Traore AS, Esposito F, Balansard G, Timon-David P, 2003, Antiplasmodial activity of alkaloid extracts from *Pavetta crassipes* (K. Schum) and *Acanthospermum hispidum* (DC), two plants used in traditional medicine in Burkina Faso. Parasitol Res; 90: 314-7.

Thabrew MI, Joice PD, Rajatissa W, 1987, A comparative study of the efficacy of *Pavetta indica* and *Osbeckia octandra* in the treatment of liver dysfunction. Planta Med; 53: 239-41.

Figure 260: *Pavetta indica* L.

From: Flora of Malaya
Malaysia, Negeri Sembilan state, Pasoh Forest Reserve, compartment 14. Collection and Identification: A. Zainuddin AZ 2932.
Date of Collection: 20 July 1989.

Psychotria adenophylla Wall

[From Greek *psychotria* = vivifying and Latin *adenophylla* = having glandular leaves]

Synonyms:	*Grumilea adenophylla* (Wall.) Miq., *Psychotria connata* Kurz , *Psychotria siamensis* Ridl., *Uragoga adenophylla* (Wall.) Kuntze
Description:	It is a small tree widely distributed in India, Sri Lanka, Cambodia, Laos, Burma, Vietnam, Thailand, Malaysia, and Indonesia. The stem is glabrous, angled, somewhat articulated and flattish, with 2 - 2.5 cm long internodes. The leaves are simple, opposite and stipulate. The stipules are lanceolate, deciduous, about 1 cm long. The petiole is stumpy, up to 1 cm long. The leaf blade is glabrous, spathulate to elliptic, 25 - 17 cm x 5 - 7 cm, the base tapering near the stem, the apex acuminate, the margin wavy and recurved, with 12 - 15 pairs of secondary nerves looping by the margin, and with few internerves, both visible underneath. The inflorescence is cymose and terminal and about 3 cm long. The fruit is bullet shaped, ribbed, 1 x 0.6 cm and open at the apex (Figure 261).
Medicinal Uses:	In Cambodia, Laos and Vietnam the plant is used to treat chest diseases.
Pharmacology:	Unknown. Dan and Dan (1986) have performed a preliminary phytochemical study on the plant.
Reference:	Dan S, Dan SS, 1986, Phytochemical study of *Adansonia digitata*, *Coccolora exoriata*, *Psychotria adenophylla* and *Schleichera oleosa*. Fitoterapia; 62: 445-6.

Figure 261: *Psychotria adenophylla* **Wall**

From: Plant of Sabah. Herbarium of University Kebangsaan Malaysia, № 36391.
Malaysia, Sabah, Lamag district, Tawai Hill forest reserve, hill dipterocarp forest, ultrabasic.
Altitude 1310 m. Date of collection: 24 August -2 September 1991. Collection: Sukup Akim.
& from Flora of Thailand, Thailand, Kirimat district, altitude 750 m, date of collection: 30
January 1995. Collection and identification: JF Maxwell.

Psychotria griffithii Hook.f

[From Greek *psychotria* = vivifying and after Dr William Griffith (1810 - 1845) a medical doctor with the British East India Company and a dedicated botanist who collected widely in Burma, India and Afghanistan]

Description: It is a shrub of the Malaysian rainforest. The stem is glabrous, stout, 0.5 cm in diameter, terete becoming flattish by the apex, and longitudinally striated with pairs of lanceolate bracts which are hairy inside. The internodes are 9 - 10 cm long. The leaves are simple, decussate and stipulate. The stipules are interpetiolar, lanceolate and about 0.5 cm long. The petiole is glabrous, stout and 0.5 cm long. The leaf blade is 21 - 15.5 cm x 6 - 4.5 cm coriaceous, elliptic lanceolate, glabrous, cuneate at the base, acuminate at the apex, recurved at the margin. The midrib and secondary nerves are raised on both surfaces, the blade showing underneath some tiny bodies which are elongated and white. The inflorescence is a terminal cyme on a 5 - 7 cm long peduncle. The fruit is ovoid, 4 -ribbed, 1.2 x 0.7 cm, with a tiny tubular formation at the apex (Figure 262).

Medicinal Uses: In Malaysia, the plant is used to make an internal remedy taken to assuage pains in the bones.

Pharmacology: Unknown. It could be a source of analgesic properties as the plant may contain opioid analgesic pyrrolidinoindoline alkaloids (Leal *et al.*, 1996; Elisabetsky *et al.*, 1997).

References: Leal MB, Elisabetsky E, 1996, Opioid-like activity of *Psychotria brachypoda* Pharmaceut Biol; 34: 267-72.

Elisabetsky E, Amador TA, Leal MB, Nunes DS, Verotta L, 1997, Merging ethnopharmacology with chemotaxonomy: An approach to unveil bioactive natural products. The case of *Psychotria* alkaloids as potential analgesics. Cienc. Cult. (Sao Paulo); 49: 378-85.

Figure 262: *Psychotria griffithii* Hook.f

From Flora of Malaya
Malaysia, Selangor State, Gombak, Batu 13. Collection and identification: KM Wong. Date of Collection: 9 September 1987.

Psychotria luzoniensis (Cham. & Schlecht.) F. Vill.

[From Greek *psychotria* = vivifying and *luzoniensis* = from Luzon]

Local names:	Tagpong-gubat (Philippines), lolon jarum (Indonesia)
Synonyms:	*Coffea luconiensis* Cham. & Schltdl., *Psychotria luconiensis* (Cham. & Schlecht.) F. Vill., *Psychotria malayana* Fern.-Vill.
Description:	It is a small tree which grows up to a height of 5 m in open forests of the Philippine Islands and Indonesia. The stem is terete, glabrous, about 0.4 cm in diameter, lenticelled with 2 - 4 cm internodes. The leaves are simple, opposite, and stipulate. The stipules are interpetiolar, minute and triangular. The petiole is 2 - 2.2 cm long and channeled. The leaf blade is elliptical-oblong, 8-14 cm x 2.5 - 5.2 cm, acute at both ends, glossy and with about 10 pairs of secondary nerves visible underneath. The inflorescence is a 2 -3 cm long, few flowered cyme on an about 10 cm long axis. The calyx is minute and with 5 tiny linear lobes. The corolla is 0.4 – 0.45 cm long, white, hairy at throat, and 5 lobed, the lobes curved. The fruit is a reddish berry which is ovoid, 0.5 x 0.6 cm, laxly ribbed somewhat fleshy and hot air balloon-like (Figure 263).
Medicinal Uses:	The plant is used for headaches, dysentery, ulcers and wounds. Javanese use the plant for protecting skin from infection from open wounds and for other skin diseases.
Pharmacology:	The plant is known to contain polymeric tryptamine alkaloids hodgkinsine and chimonanthine (Hadi *et al.*, 2001.) Hodgkinsine produce *in vivo* a dose-dependent, naloxone reversible, analgesic effect in thermal models of nociception. In the capsaicin-induced pain test it shows a potent dose-dependent analgesic activity, indicating the participation of NMDA receptors (Amator *et al.*, 2000; Verotta *et al.*, 2002). Hodgkinsine showed some levels of cytotoxicity against cultured rat hepatoma cells (HTC line) derived from clone 7288 of a Morris rat hepatoma (Adjibadé *et al.*, 1990). The pharmacological properties of this plant and its alkaloidal constituents would be well worth further study.

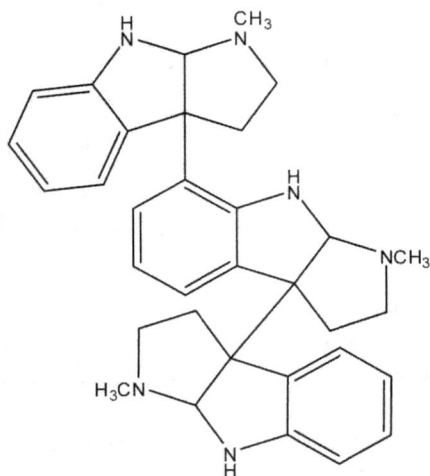

Hodgkinsine

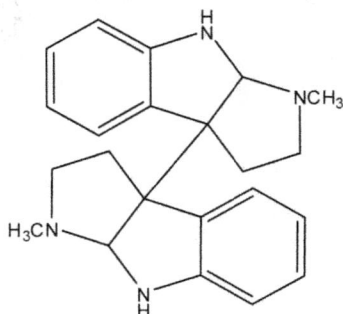

Chimonanthine

References:

Adjibadé Y, Saad H, Kuballa B, Beck JP, Sévenet T, Cabalion P, Anton R, 1990, *In vitro* cytotoxicity of polyindolenine alkaloids on rat hepatoma cell lines. Structure activity relationships. J Ethnopharmacol; 29: 127-36.

Amador TA, Verotta L, Nunes DS, Elisabetsky E, 2000, Antinociceptive profile of hodgkinsine. Planta Med; 66: 770-2.

Hadi S, Bremner JB, 2001, Initial studies on alkaloids from Lombok medicinal plants. Molecules; 6: 117-29.

Verotta L, Orsini F, Sbacchi M, Scheildler MA, Amador TA, Elisabetsky E, 2002, Synthesis and antinociceptive activity of chimonanthines and pyrrolidinoindoline-Type alkaloids. Bioorg Med Chem; 10: 2133-42.

Figure 263: *Psychotria luzoniensis* **(Cham. & Schlecht.) F. Vill.**
From: Flora of the Philippines. Distributed from the Philippine National Herbarium, National Museum Manila, PHN N° 79811. Philippines, San Vicente, Cagayan. Collection and identification E. Quisumbing and R. del Rosario. Date of Collection: 8 May 1961.

Psychotria manillensis Bartl. ex DC.

[From Greek *psychotria* = vivifying and from Latin *manillensis* = from Manila]

Synonyms:	*Psychotria liukfuensis* Hatusima, *Psychotria homalosperma auct. non* A. Gray
Description:	It is a shrub which grows in the forests of the Philippines, Taiwan and Ryukyus. The stem is terete glabrous, stout, longitudinally striated with lenticels, the apex of stems squarrish. Nodes are marked with a ring. The leaves are simple, decussate and stipulate. The stipules are linear, deciduous, 1.1 x 0.2 cm. The petiole is 0.5 - 3.6 cm long. The leaf blade is 13 - 9.5 cm x 2 -4 cm tapering at the base, acuminate at the apex, wavy at the margin, midrib stout and sunken above, 7 - 8 secondary nerves visible underneath. The inflorescence is a terminal or axillary, few flowered cyme. The calyx is cupular, 0.1 cm long with irregular lobes. The flower buds are 0.35 cm long. The corolla is white. The fruit are ellipsoid, ribbed, 0.8 - 1.3 cm x 0.5 - 0.6 cm, open at the apex and yellowish ripening red then dark purple (Figure 264).
Medicinal Uses:	In the Philippines the plant is used to regulate menses.
Pharmacology:	Unknown
Reference:	Sílvia Lopes S, Gilsane L, von Poser GL, Vitor A, Kerber VA, Fabiane M, Farias FM, Eduardo L, Konrath EL, Paulo Moreno P, Marcos E, Sobra MEl, José AS, Zuanazzi JAS, Henriques AT, 2004, Taxonomic significance of alkaloids and iridoid glucosides in the tribe Psychotrieae (Rubiaceae) Biochem System Ecol; 32: 1187-95.

Figure 264: *Psychotria manillensis* **Bartl. ex DC.**
From: Flora of Taiwan, Herbarium, National Pintung Institute of Agriculture. Botel Tobago.
Collection: Ching-en Chang. Date of Collection: 8 September 1984.

Psychotria montana Bl.

[From Greek *psychotria* = vivifying and from Latin *montana* = of the mountains]]

Local name:	Kayu semelit, selada. (Malaysia).
Synonyms:	*Psychotria expansa* Bl., *Chasalia montana* (Bl.) Miq., *Psychotria tabacifolia* Wall., *Psychotria viridissima* Kurz., *Uragoga montana* (Bl.) Kuntze
Description:	It is a small tree that occurs in forests, village groves, and also on limestone, on the rocky forest slopes of Burma, Thailand, and Vietnam to Peninsular Malaysia, and Sumatra and Indonesia. The stem is flattish and hairy. The leaves are simple, decussate and stipulate. The petiole is channeled, slender and hairy. The stipules are triangular, bifid at the apex, clasping the petiole as a conspicuous ring. The petiole is slender, channeled, hairy, and 1.5-3.5 cm long. The leaf blade is dark green, above, 24 - 20 cm x 6 - 8.5 cm, thinly coriaceous, cuneate at the apex, spathulate to elliptic lanceolate, the midrib and secondary nerves are sunken above and raised underneath, the nerves are hairy underneath with a few tertiary nerves. The leaf blade shows 9 - 12 pairs of secondary nerves. The inflorescence is a 2 - 6cm long, slender, terminal cyme of minute flowers, glabrous, attached to 4 cm long peduncles. The pedicels and calyx are green and hairy. The calyx is cup-shaped and obscurely 4 lobed and minute. The corolla tube is 0.2 - 0.3 cm long with 4 lobes which are linear, rounded at the apex, and 0.2 cm long and very pale light yellowish. The androecium is exerted out of the corolla tube and consists of 4 linear oblong anthers which have orange and white filaments. The fruit is a yellowish ripening orangish, red berry turning blackish, which is subglobose, about 1 cm in diameter, and slightly ribbed when dry (Figure 265).
Medicinal Uses:	In Peninsular Malaysia the plant is used to heal ulcers and swellings, to break fever and as a laxative. In Cambodia, Laos and Vietnam, the plant is used for sores and colic, swellings, rheumatism, stomach ache, and to wash wounds. The decoction is taken for bacillary dysentery. It is sometimes planted in gardens in Java.
Pharmacology:	The plant contains alkaloids of which dimethyltryptamine which is hallucinogenic (Arbain *et al.*, 1989).
Reference:	Arbain D, Cannon JR, Afriastini, Kartawinata K, Djamal R, Bustari A, Dharma A, Rosmawaty, Rivai H, Zaherman, Basir D, Sjafar M, Sjaiful, Nawfa R, Kosela S, 1989, Survey of some West Sumatran plants for alkaloids. Economic Botany; 43: 73-78.

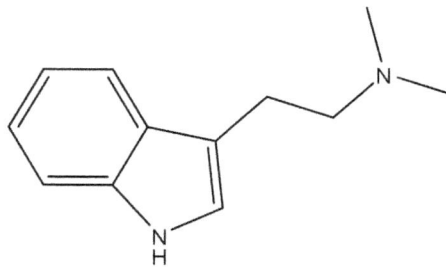

Dimethyltryptamine

Figure 265: *Psychotria montana* Bl.
From: Flora of Thailand, Prince of Songkla University
Thailand, Songkla province, Ratta Poo district. Elevation 150 m. Date of collection: 19
September 1984.. Collection and identification: JF Maxwell, Nº 84-217.

Psychotria rhinocerotis Reinw. ex Bl.

[From Greek *psychotria* = vivifying and from Latin *rhinocerotis* = rhinoceros]

Synonyms:	*Gaertnera lasianthoides* C.E.C.Fisch., *Psychotria curtisii* King & Gamb., *Psychotria subrufa* Miq., *Uragoga rhinocerotis* (Reinw. ex Bl.) Drake. *Uragoga rhinocerotis* (Reinw. ex Bl.) Kuntze, *Uragoga subrufa* (Miq.) Kuntze
Description:	it is a small tree about 1.5 m tall which grows in the rainforests of Malaysia, Burma and Thailand. The stem is terete, velvety, somewhat stout, almost articulated, and with internodes which are about 3 - 6 cm long. The leaves are simple, decussate and stipulate. The interpetiolar stipule is hairy, bifid, about 1 cm long with acuminate the apex. The petiole is velvety, to 1 cm long, stout, and channeled. The leaf blade is dark green and glabrous above, hairy underneath and velvety when young. It is lanceolate to elliptic, thinly coriaceous, acute at the base and the apex, with a recurved margin and is 15-10 cm x 5.9-7.5 cm. There are 12-15 pairs of secondary nerves and a few scalariform tertiary nerves with the midribs sunken above. The inflorescence is an axillary cyme with a 3 cm peduncle which is axillary. The calyx is about 0.6 cm long, hairy, ribbed and with 5 lobes, one of which ish prominent. The corolla tube is whitish, the lobes are whitish with a faint pinkish hue, and white hairs are present at the throat. The fruit is globose, black, 0.3 x 1 cm and enclosed in the persistent calyx with 0.3 cm long lobes (Figure 266).
Medicinal uses:	The plant is used by Malays as a post partum remedy.
Pharmacology:	Unknown.

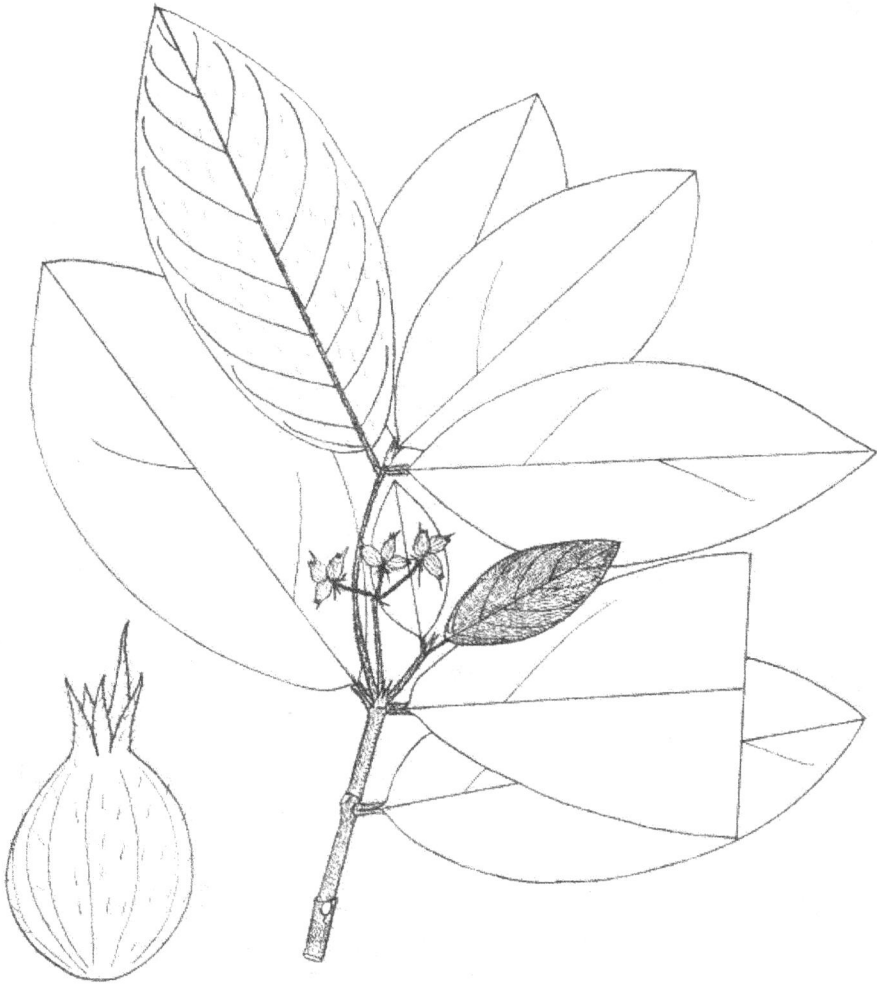

Figure 266: *Psychotria rhinocerotis* Reinw. ex Bl.
From: Flora of Thailand, Prince of Songkla University
Thailand, Trang province, Muang district, Altitude 250 m. By 98o East and 9o North. Date of collection: 1 February 1985.

Psychotria rostrata Bl.

[From Greek *psychotria* = vivifying and from Latin *rostrata* = beaked]

Local name:	Nyarum, sedoman, segerang (Malaysia).
Synonym:	*Chasalia rostrata* Miq.
Description:	It is a small tree which grows up to 3 m tall in lowland forests of Malaysia and Indonesia. The stem is terete and glabrous, with 6 - 8.5 cm long internodes. The leaves are simple, decussate and stipulate. The interpetiolar stipules are triangular, membranaceous and deciduous, soon caducous. The petiole is glabrous, 0.6 - 2 cm long, and channeled. The leaf blade is elliptic, spathulate, membranaceous, 12 - 20 cm x 4 - 7.2 cm, cuneate at the base, acuminate at the apex, recurved at the margin, glabrous. The midrib is raised on both surfaces, with 6 - 7 pairs of secondary nerves discrete above, with a few tertiary nerves visible underneath, wavy at the margin. The inflorescence is a terminal cyme which is 1.5 - 6 cm long, slender, glabrous, with 0.5 - 3 cm long peduncles. The calyx is campanulate, about 0.2 cm long. The corolla tube is 0.2 cm long with 4 lobes, 0.1 cm long. The fruit is globose, fleshy with a little disk at the apex. The stamens are slightly exerted. The fruit is a berry which is globose about 1 cm long, weakly 4-5-ribbed, and orange (Figure 267).
Medicinal Uses:	Malays use the plant for constipation.
Pharmacology:	The plant contains a series of indole alkaloids including trimeric indole alkaloids such as psychotrimine, and pentameric indole alkaloids such as psychopentamine (Lajis *et al.*, 1993; Takayama *et al.*, 2004). Extracts from *Psychotria rostrata* exhibited cytotoxic effects against RAW 264.7 cells (Saha *et al.*, 2004). Quadrigemine B, a major tetrameric indole alkaloid from this plant abrogated the survival of HEp-2 cells and normal human lymphocytes cultured *in vitro* and exhibited bactericidal activity against *Escherichia coli* and *Staphylococcus aureus* (Mahmud *et al.*, 1993).
References:	Lajis NH, Mahmud Z, Toia RF, 1993, The Alkaloids of *Psychotria rostrata*. Planta Med; 59: 383-4.
	Mahmud Z, Musa M, Ismail N, Lajis NH, 1993, Cytotoxic and bacteriocidal activities of *Psychotria rostrata*. Pharmaceut Biol; 31: 142-46.

Saha K, Lajis NH, Israf DA, Hamzah AS, Khozirah S, Khamis S, Syahida A, 2004, Evaluation of antioxidant and nitric oxide inhibitory activities of selected Malaysian medicinal plants. J Ethnopharmacol; 92: 263-7.

Takayama H, Mori I, Kitajima M, Aimi N, Lajis NH., 2004, New type of trimeric and pentameric indole alkaloids from *Psychotria rostrata*. Org Lett; 6(17):2945-8.

Figure 267: *Psychotria rostrata* Bl.
From Herbarium of *University* Kebangsaan Malaysia, No 05530
Malaysia, Johor State, Kampung Kenangan, Batu 6, Semangat. Collection: Hashim Mohamad. Date of Collection 25 December 1978. Identification: KM Wong 15 October 1987.

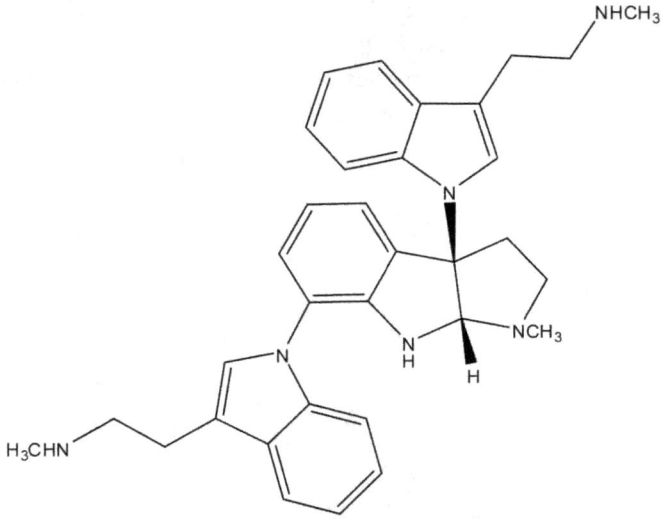

Psychotrimine

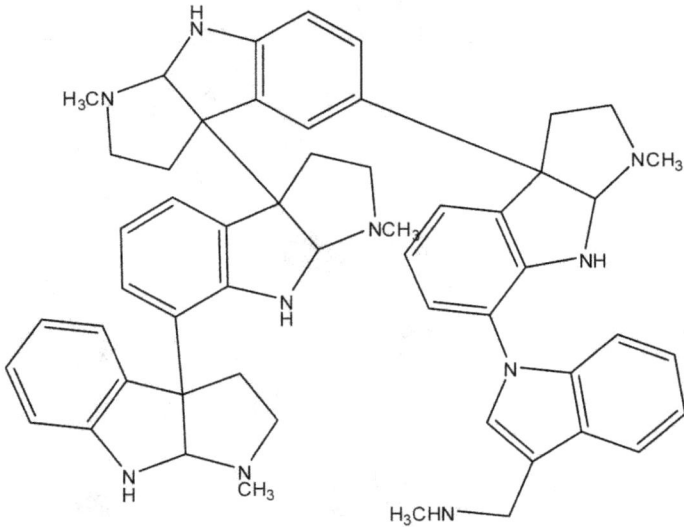

Psychopentamine

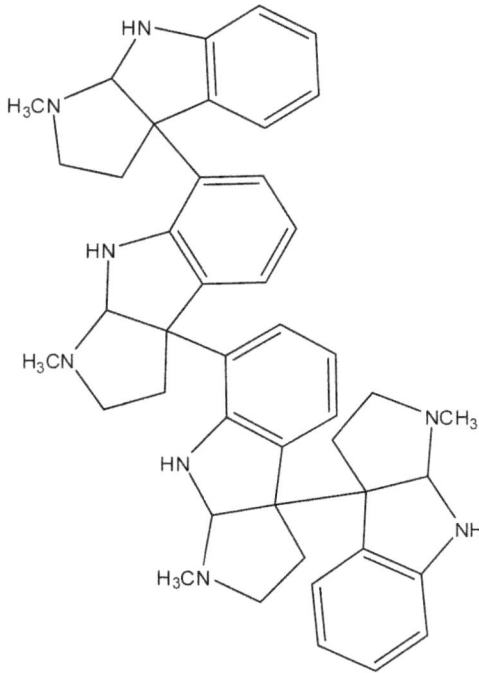

Quadrigemine B

Psychotria rubra (Lour.) Poir.

[From Greek *psychotria* = vivifying and from Latin *rubra* = red]

Basionym:	*Antherura rubra* Lour.
Synonyms:	*Antherura rubra* Lour., *Psychotria reevesi* Wall., *Psychotria elliptica* non Kerr.
Description:	It is a shrub which grows to 1 - 2 m tall in South China, Hainan Island, Ryukyus, Japan and Taiwan. The stem is terete, articulate, microscopically peeling, young parts smooth, squarish at the apex. The nodes are marked with a rind. The leaves are simple, decussate and stipulate. The interpetiolar stipules are triangular and 0.4 - 0.6 cm long. The petiole is lenticelled, curved at the base, glabrous and 0.7 - 2.2 cm long. The leaf blade is 12.5 - 17.6 cm x 3.6 - 5.1 cm, laurel-shaped, glabrous, recurved at the margin, slightly coriaceous, tapering at the base, acuminate at the apex. The apex has a tiny dot, and is wavy at the margin. The midrib and 4 - 5 secondary nerves are raised on both surfaces, and a minute tuft of hair can be seen at axils of secondary nerves and midrib underneath. The inflorescences are axillary cymes

which are lenticelled at the base. The corolla is white, 5 lobed pilose at the throat and 0.3 - 0.5 cm long. The fruits are globose, 0.4 - 0.7 cm x 0.4 - 0.8 cm and open at the apex (Figure 268).

Figure 268: *Psychotria rubra* **(Lour.) Poir.**
From: Botanical Inventory of Taiwan, Herbarium, Institute of Botany, Academia Sinica, Taipei
Taiwan, Neihu, on the mountain road from Chinlungshih (a Temple) to Vaishuanghsi in secondary broadleaf forest, 121° 34' 53" East 25° 06, 47", altitude 250 m. Determination: Wen-Pen Leu 22 February 1995. Collection: Yi Chung Chen *et al* 9 Septembre 1994

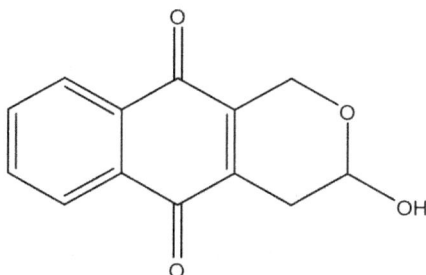

Psychorubrin

Medicinal uses:

In China, the plant is used for contusions and to assuage painful bruises. In Taiwan, the plant is used for swelling. In Cambodia, Laos and Vietnam, the plant is used to assuage the pain of ear and tooth aches and to treat malaria.

Pharmacology:

Hayashi *et al.* (1987), isolated a pyronaphthoquinone called psychorubrin from the plant which abrogated the survival of KB cell cultured *in vitro*. Naturally occurring pyranonaphthoquinones are of interest because they have been found to be antibacterial, antifungal, antimycobacterial, and cytotoxic, the latter mechanism of action resembling that of alkylating antibiotics such as the mitomycins (Kesteleyn *et al.*, 1999). It would be interesting to learn if psychorubin has antiplasmodial activity. The alkaloidal content of this plant could be a source of possible analgesic principles in view of the traditional use of the plant to assuage pain.

References:

Hayashi T, Smith FT, Lee KH, 1987, Antitumor agents. 89. Psychorubrin, a new cytotoxic naphthoquinone from *Psychotria rubra* and its structure-activity relationships. J Med Chem; 30: 2005-8.

Kesteleyn B, De Kimpe N, Van Puyvelde L, 1999, Total synthesis of two naphthoquinone antibiotics, psychorubrin and pentalongin, and their C(1)-substituted alkyl and aryl derivatives; J Org Chem; 64: 1173 -79.

Psychotria serpens L.

[From Greek *psychotria* = vivifying and from Latin *serpens* = snake-like

Local names:	Creeping psychotria; Chinese serpent vine; shiratamakazura (Japan).
Description:	It is an epiphytic climber of Taiwan, Japan, China, Cambodia, Laos, Thailand and Vietnam. The stem is rough, snake like at the apex, and 0.4 cm in diameter, somewhat articulated, deeply longitudinally striated, squarish by the apex, lenticelled and the nodes marked with a rind. The leaves are simple, decussate and stipulate and more abundant near the apex. The interpetiolar stipules are triangular, and 0.1 - 0.15 cm long. The petiole is 0.5 - 1 cm long. The leaf blade is light green, glaucous underneath, thick, spathulate, without visible secondary nerves, 2.7 - 4 cm x 1.2 - 2 cm, the margin recurved; the blade looks porous when dry. The inflorescence is a terminal cyme. The calyx is minute and 5 lobed. The corolla is greenish white, 5 lobed, the throat with yellowish hairs. The stamens are exerted. The fruit is like a coffee berry, fleshy, longitudinally ribbed, open at the apex, dirty white, marked with a brownish opening at the apex, 0.6 - 1.1 cm x 0.5 - 1 cm and contains a pair of dark seeds (Figure 269).
Medicinal uses:	The plant is found on Chinese medicinal markets and sold as remedy to improve the circulation of blood and to cure rheumatism and arthritis.

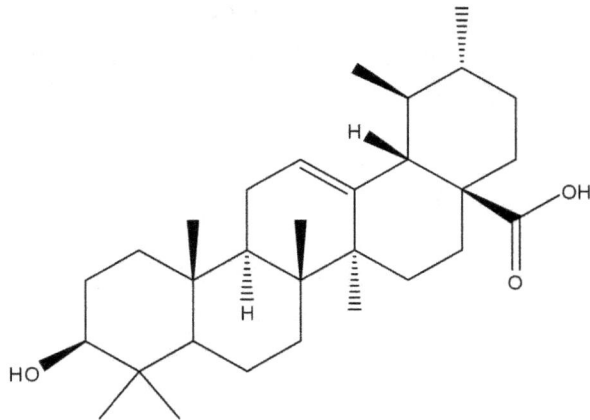

Ursolic acid

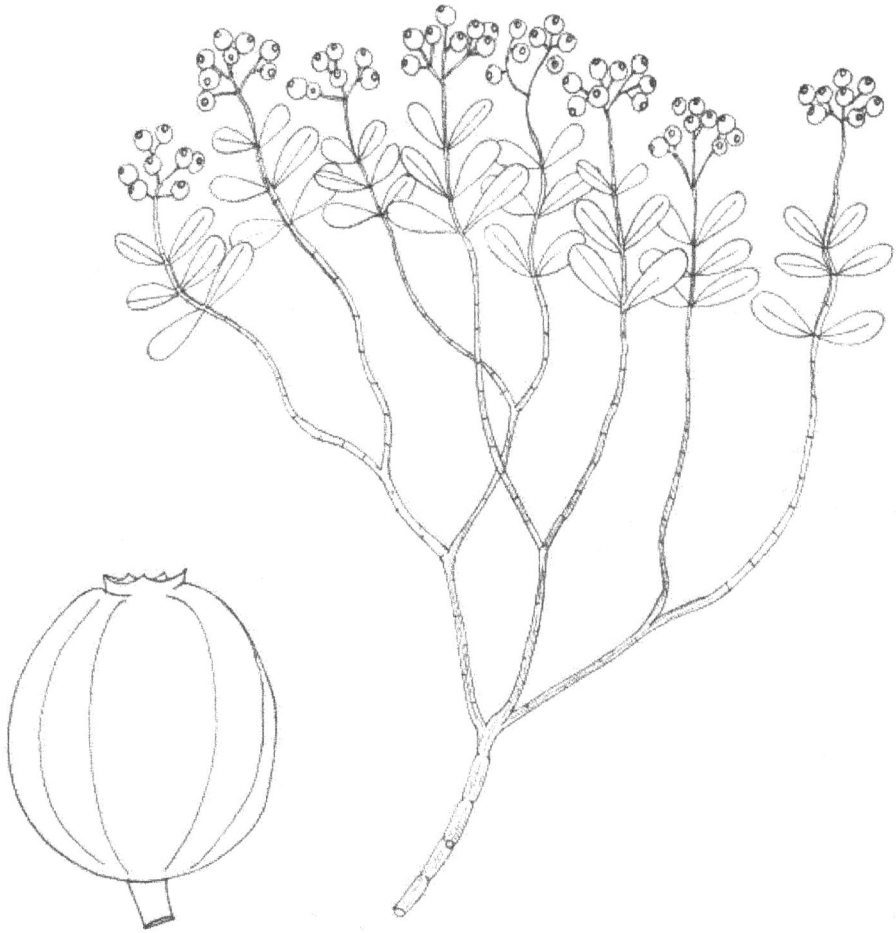

Figure 269: *Psychotria serpens* L.
From: Botanical Inventory of Taiwan, Herbarium, Institute of Botany, Academia Sinica , Taipei Taiwan, Neihu, on the mountain road from Chinlungshih (a Temple) to Vaishuanghsi in secondary broadleaf forest, 25° 06, 04" North -121° 34' 01" East altitude 260 m. Under semi shaded forest, creeping. Collection: Yi Chung Chen *et al* 9 September 1994

Pharmacology: Kuo *et al.* (2001) isolated a molecule called PS-A-6 from the plant. This substance suppressed HSV-1 multiplication in Vero cells through inhibition of early transcripts of HSV-1. The plant contains some triterpenes such as ursolic acid which is cytotoxic (Lee *et al.*, 1988). The medicinal uses mentioned above are not yet validated. However, extracts of *Psychotria serpens* showed strong scavenging activity against superoxide anion radical

(Ohsugi *et al.*, 1999), and therefore antioxidant activities might be important.

References: Kuo YC, Chen CC, Tsai WJ, Ho YH, 2001, Regulation of herpes simplex virus type 1 replication in Vero cells by *Psychotria serpens*: relationship to gene expression, DNA replication, and protein synthesis. Antiviral Res; 51: 95-109.

Lee KH, Lin YM, Wu TS, Zhang DC, Yamagishi T, Hayashi T, Hall IH, Chang JJ, Wu RY, Yang TH, 1988, The cytotoxic principles of *Prunella vulgaris*, *Psychotria serpens*, and *Hyptis capitata*: ursolic acid and related derivatives. Planta Med ; 54: 308-11.

Ohsugi M, Fan W, Hase K, Xiong Q, Tezuka Y, Komatsu K, Namba T, Saitoh T, Tazawa K, Kadota S, 1999, Active-oxygen scavenging activity of traditional nourishing-tonic herbal medicines and active constituents of *Rhodiola sacra*. J Ethnopharmacol; 67: 111-9.

Psychotria stipulacea Wall.

[From Greek *psychotria* = vivifying and from Latin *stipulacea* = having stipules]

Description: It is a shrub of the rainforest of Malaysia. The stem is smooth, glabrous, with a few lenticels and terete and with 2 - 4 cm long internodes. The leaves are simple, decussate and stipulate. The interpetiolar stipules are membranaceous, large, roundish and irregular at the apex and forming a sort of tube around the internode. The petiole is discrete, glabrous, and with few lenticels. The leaf blade is 12 - 15 cm (up to 23 cm long) x 3 - 4 cm. It is elliptic to somewhat spathulate, thinly coriaceous, attenuate at the base, along the petiole, the apex is acuminate and wavy at the margin. Nervations are inconspicuous above except for the midrib, vbut are isible underneath with few internerves. The inflorescences are heads on top of slender pedicels, 5 cm long, on 6 cm long axes. The fruits are globose, 0.7 cm in diameter, longitudinally ribbed with a 0.01 x 0.02 cm tube at the apex (Figure 270).

Medicinal Uses: In Malaysia, the plant is used externally to smooth swellings, to break fever, and to promote recovery from childbirth

Pharmacology: Unknown

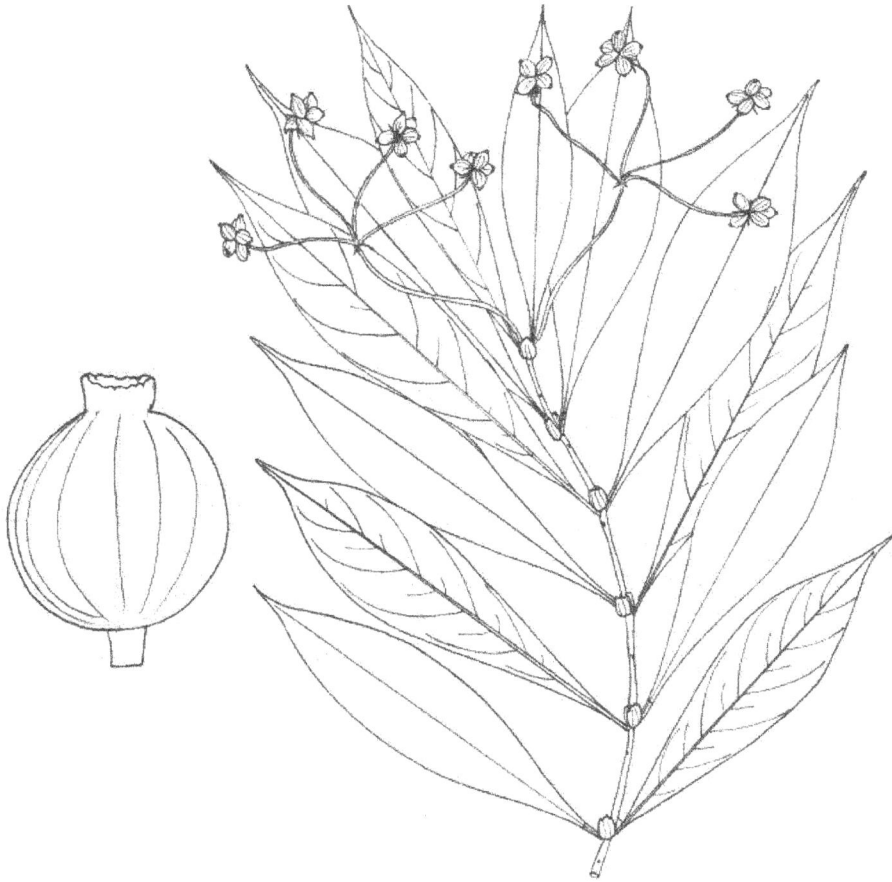

Figure 270: *Psychotria stipulacea* Wall.
From: Herbarium of *University* Kebangsaan Malaysia, No 41248, Plants of Sabah.
Malaysia, Sabah, Penampang, Crooker Range along the trail to Kampung Langagungan. Altitude 1550 m. 116° 22' East - 5° 59.7' North. Date of Collection: 11 September 1994.

Psychotria viridiflora Reinw. ex Bl.

[From Greek *psychotria* = vivifying and from Latin *viridiflora* = with green flowers]

Local names:	Java-Rauschkaffee (German), tenam betul (Indonesia), julong-julong bukit (Malaysia).
Synonyms:	*Psychotria sylvatica* Bl., *Psychotria jackiana* Hook.f.
Description:	It is a shrub which grows to a height of 1.5 m in secondary forest from sea-level up to 1200 m in India, Nepal, Burma, Thailand, Malaysia, and Indonesia. The stem is terete, glabrous, hairy at nodes; the internodes are 1.5 - 2 cm long. The leaves are simple, decussate and stipulate. The interpetiolar stipules are linear, 0.5 -1 cm long, toothed by the apex and deciduous. The petiole is slender, glabrous, channeled and about 2 cm long. The leaf blade is elliptic lanceolate, papery, attenuate at the base, the apex acute to slightly acuminate, 6 - 14 cm x 2 - 4 cm and showing 4 - 5 pairs of secondary nerves underneath, tertiary nerves are absent. The inflorescence is terminal, about 10 cm long on an axe which is about 4 cm long. The pedicel is hairy. The calyx is about 0.15 cm long, and hairy. The corolla is greenish-pink or white, 0.2 cm long, with 5 lobes around a densely hairy throat. The fruit is yellowish to red, ovoid, ribbed, 0.4 x 0.7 cm, glabrous, with a minute opening; berry very variable (Figure 271).
Medicinal Uses:	In Malaysia and Indonesia the plant is used to treat skin diseases and the bites of poisonous insects and snakes. The plant is used as a dye in Malaysia.
Pharmacology:	Unknown.

Figure 271: *Psychotria viridiflora* Reinw. ex Bl.
From: Herbarium of *University* Kebangsaan Malaysia, Nº 19106
Malaysia, Kelantan state, Jeli track to Kuala Yong off Sungai Pergau, near river bank.
Collection and identification: Abdul Latiff *et al*. Date of Collection: 22 September 1986.

Psychotria sarmentosa Bl.

[From Greek *psychotria* = vivifying and from Latin *viridiflora* = with green flowers]

Local names:	Gelang tikus jalir (Malaysia), yaa ruat (Thailand).
Synonyms:	*Psychotria sylvatica* Bl., *Psychotria jackiana* Hook.f.
Description:	It is a spreading climber occurring in forests, from sea-level up to 2300 m altitude in a geographical area covering India, Sri Lanka, Thailand, Malaysia, Vietnam and Indonesia. The stem is 0.3 cm in diameter by the apex, glabrous, rooting at nodes, longitudinally striated, climbing up tree trunks and crawling from one tree to another. The internodes are 4.5 - 5 cm long. The leaves are simple, decussate and stipulated. The interpetiolar stipules are hairy, triangular linear and about 0.3 cm long. The petiole is 0.4 cm long, hairy, stout, and discrete. The leaf blade is 4 -11 cm x 1 -1.5 cm, dark green above, tapering at the base, acute at the apex, elliptic lanceolate, with a few hairs and 6 - 7 pairs of secondary nerves visible underneath. The inflorescence is a terminal cyme on a 2 cm long axis, the pedicel strongly angled and1.5 - 5 cm long. The calyx is 0.2 cm long. The corolla is 0.2 cm long and hairy. The fruit is pulpy, soft, white, 0.3x 0.5 cm, ovoid, and crowned on top with vestigial calyx lobes, with black seeds (Figure 272).
Medicinal Uses:	In Malaysia the plant is used to heal sores, and precipitate parturition.
Pharmacology:	Note that the plant has analgesic property in rats (Ratnassoriya *et al.*, 1999). Indole alkaloids may be involved here.
References:	Ratnasooriya D, Dharmasiri MG, 1999, Water extract of leaf and stems of *Psychotria sarmentosa* has analgesic and antihyperalgesic activity in rats. Med Sci Res; 27: 715-18.

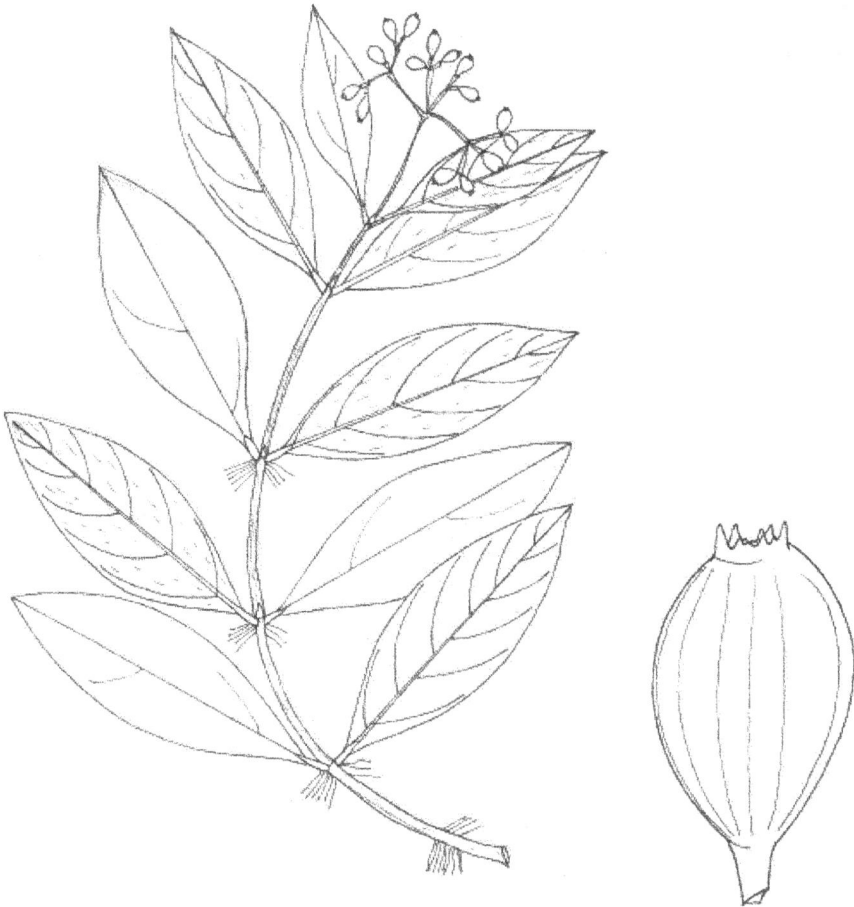

Figure 272: *Psychotria sarmentosa* Bl.
From: Flora of Thailand, Chiang Mai University Herbarium.
Thailand, Songkla province, Rattapoom district, Boripat Falls national park. Elevation 75m.
Date of collection: 20 August 1984. Elevation: 75m. Collection and identification: JF Maxwell
Nº 84-542

Saprosma glomerulatum King & Gamble

[From Greek *sapros* = rotten and from Latin *glomerulatum* = with glomerules]

Local name: Kentut (Malaysia)

Description: It is a smelly small tree which grows in Malaysia to a height of 6 m. The stem is terete, smooth, glabrous, dichotomous, 0.4 cm in diameter with 2.5 - 8.5 cm long internodes. The leaves are simple, decussate and stipulated. The interpetiolar stipules are broadly triangular with stiff bristles along the base on the inner side, persistent and exposed after the stipule falls away. The petiole is about 0.2 cm long. The leaf blade is fetid when bruised, elliptic lanceolate with 5 - 6 pairs of secondary nerves, and 6 - 9 cm x 1.9 - 3.5 cm. The inflorescence is a terminal cyme. The calyx is truncate with 4-5 linear lobes. The corolla tube is short, 4 lobed, the lobes broadly lanceolate, and valvate in buds. The stigma is 2 lobed and exerted. The fruit is olive-shaped, fetid, 1 x 0.7 cm, smooth, green ripening crimson black with a white waxy bloom, opened at the apex, and containing small 2 pyrenes (Figure 273).

Medicinal Uses: In Malaysia the plant is used to facilitate digestion.

Pharmacology: The pharmacological property of this plant is unknown. Singh *et al.* (2006), isolated 3,4-dihydroxy-1-methoxy anthraquinone-2-corboxaldehyde, and damnacanthal, which exhibited antifungal activity against *Candida albicans*, *Cryptococcus neoformans*, *Sporothrix schenckii* and *Trichophyton mentagrophytes*. The anthraquinone content of *Saprosma glomerulatum* King & Gamble could be of interest. Anthraquinones might be involved in medicinal use for their laxative effects.

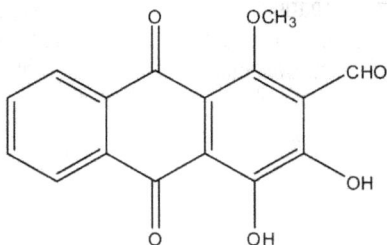

3,4-dihydroxy-1-methoxy anthraquinone-2-corboxaldehyde   Damnacanthal

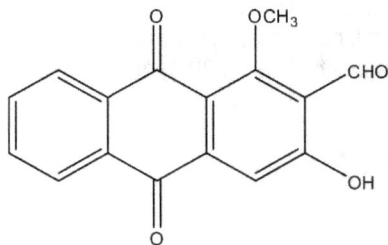

References: Singh DN, Verma N, Raghuwanshi S, Shukla PK, Kulshreshtha DK, 2006, Antifungal anthraquinones from *Saprosma fragrans*. Bioorg Med Chem Letters; 16: 4512-14.

Figure 273: *Saprosma glomerulatum* King & Gamble
From: Herbarium University Kebangsaan Malaysia, No 20620. Flora of Malaya.
Malaysia, Pahang state, Romping - Endau Expedition, Sungai Kincing, the base camp loop.
Collection and identification: A. Zainuddin *et al*.

Saprosma ternatum Hook.f.

[From Greek *sapros* = rotten and from Latin *ternatum* = with parts in groups of three]

Local name:	Kentut (Malaysia)
Synonym:	*Saprosma distans* Craib
Description:	It is a small tree which grows in the rainforest of Malaysia to a height of 3 m. The stem is terete, smooth, glabrous, 0.6 cm in diameter, with 2 - 3.5 cm internodes. The leaves are simple, decussate and stipulated. The interpetiolar stipules are broadly triangular with stiff bristles along the base on the inner side, persistent and exposed after the stipule falls away. The petiole is about 1 cm long with a tiny ring at the base, glabrous and channeled. The leaf blade is papery and fetid with bruised. It is broadly elliptic lanceolate and 13-18 cm x 7-10.7 cm, with 5-6 pairs of secondary nerves. The base is acute, the apex acuminate and the margin recurved. The inflorescences are terminal cymes with a few flowers on slender about 1 cm long pedicels from an axis which is slender and about 3 cm long. The calyx is 0.2 - 0.3 cm and produces 4-5 narrowly triangular lobes; the cup at the base is glabrous. The corolla tube is short, 4 lobed, the lobes broadly lanceolate, and valvate in buds. The stigma is 2 lobed and exerted. The fruit is olive-shaped, fetid, 0.9 x 0.7 cm, smooth, green, with an opening at the apex with vestigial sepals 0.3 cm in diameter, and contain 2 small pyrenes (Figure 274).
Medicinal Uses:	In Malaysia, the plant is used as a post partum remedy.
Pharmacology:	To date the pharmacological property of *Saprosma ternatum* Hook.f. is unexplored. Its medicinal use might, like *Saprosma glomerulatum* King & Gamble, involve antimicrobial and laxative anthraquinones. *Saprosma* species elaborate iridoids, the aglycones of which inhibit the enzymatic activity of lipoxygenase (Ling *et al.*, 2003).
Reference:	Ling SK, Tanaka T, Kouno I, 2003, Effects of Iridoids on lipoxygenase and hyaluronidase activities and their activation by beta-glucosidase in the presence of amino acids. Biol Pharm Bull; 26: 352.

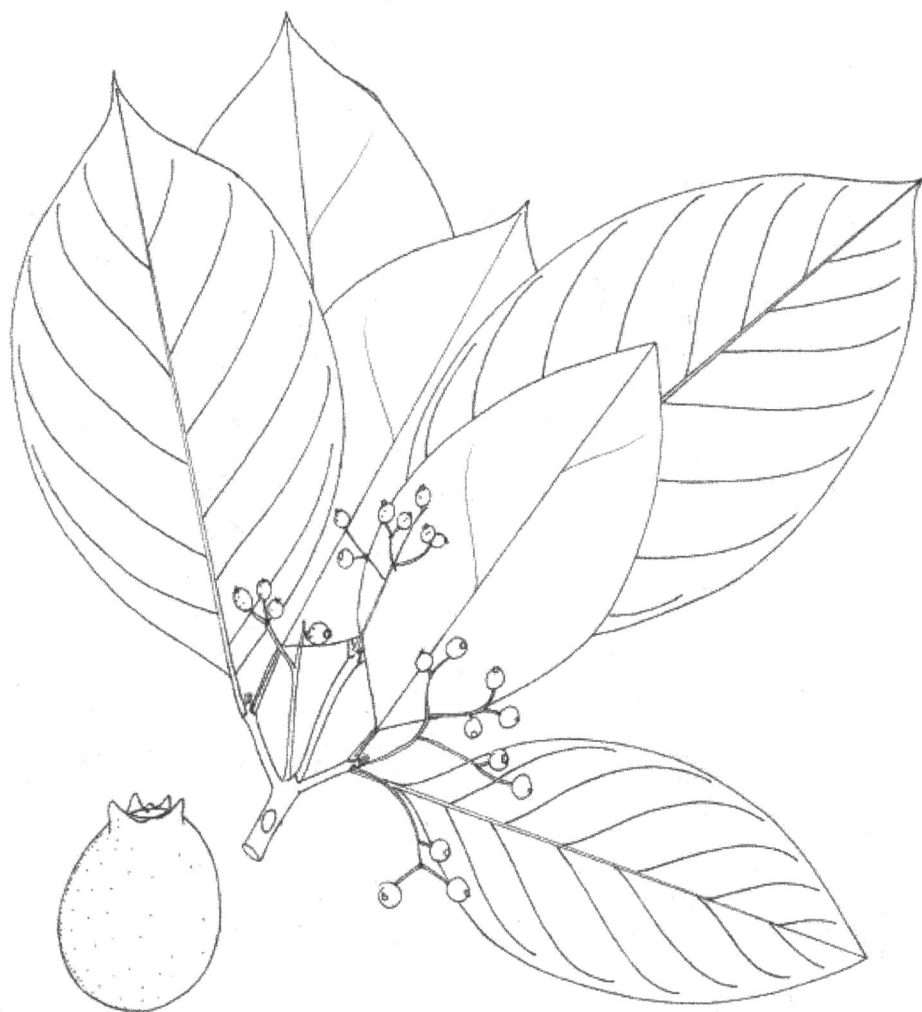

Figure 274: *Saprosma ternatum* **Hook.f.**
From: Herbarium University Kebangsaan Malaysia, N° 19081.
Malaysia, Kelantan state, Jeli, Sungai Yong off Sungai Pergau. Collection and identification:
Abdul Latiff. Date of Collection: 23 September 1986.

Tarenna stellulata (Hook.f.) Ridl.

[From Sri Lankan *tarana* = a plant name and from Latin *stellulata* = with small star-like markings] .

Synonyms:	*Ixora stellulata* (Hook.f.) Kuntze. *Pavetta aristata* Wall., *Webera stellulata* Hook.f.
Description:	It is a small tree that grows to a height of 4 m in the rainforests of Thailand and Malaysia. The plant has ornamental value and is sold as such. The stem is smooth, minutely peeling when older, somewhat flattish, triangular or terete to slightly angular, with internodes which are about 3 cm long. The leaves are simple, decussate and stipulate. The stipules are interpetiolar, broadly lanceolate, and about 0.6 cm long. The petiole is glabrous, channeled, and 0.5 - 1 cm long. The leaf blade is membranaceous, elliptic lanceolate, 7.5 - 15 cm x 3 - 5.5 cm, with 7 - 8 pairs of secondary nerves sunken above. It is slightly asymmetrical at the apex, wavy and recurved at the margin and hairy underneath. The inflorescence is cymose, erect, with green axes and about 7 cm long. The calyx lobes are broadly triangular. The corolla is yellowish green with 5 lobes with apiculate tips, ciliate the margin, and as long as the tube. The anthers are linear and exerted conspicuously from the throat. The fruit is globose, dark green, longitudinally ribbed, about 0.8 cm in diameter and crowned at the apex by vestigial calyx lobes (Figure 275).
Medicinal Uses:	In Malaysia the plant is used as a laxative.
Pharmacology:	To date the pharmacological property of *Tarenna stellulata* (Hook.f.) Ridl. is unexplored. The laxative use mentioned above could involve some anthraquinones and even some lignans. Note that lignans of *Tarenna attenuate* showed potent antioxidant activities against H_2O_2-induced impairment in PC12 cells (Yang XW *et al.*, 2007). The plant probably holds some iridoid glycosides (Yang XW *et al.*, 2006). One could have some interest in looking at the constituents and pharmacological activity of *Tarenna stellulata* (Hook.f.) Ridl.
References:	Djoudi R, Bertrand C, Fiasson K, Fiasson JL, Comte G, Fenet B, Rabesa ZA, 2007, Polyphenolics and iridoid glycosides from *Tarenna madagascariensis*. Biochem System Ecol; 35: 314-16.
	Yang XW, Ma YL, He HP, Wang YH, Di YT, Zhou H, Li L, Hao XJ, 2006, Iridoid constituents of *Tarenna attenuata*. J Nat Prod; 69: 971-4.

Yang XW, Zhao PJ, Ma,YL, Xiao HT, Zuo YQ, He HP, Li L, Hao XJ, 2007, Mixed lignan-neolignans from *Tarenna attenuata*. J Nat Prod; 70: 521 -25.

Figure 275: *Tarenna stellulata* (Hook.f.) Ridl.

From: Flora of Thailand. Prince of Songkla University Herbarium.

Thailand, Pattaling province, See Bahn Pohn district, Kae Boo national park, near Matcha Cave. Altitude 200 m, by 9° North - 98° 5' East, in shaded area, primary rain forest at the base of a limestone hill. Collection and identification: JF Maxwell N°86502.

Uncaria ferrea DC.

[From Latin *uncut* = hooks and Latin *ferrea* = belonging to iron]

Local names:	Kait kait (Dusun), ngop, naam chaochuu (Thailand), cantel wesi, kait beusi (Indonesia), bebokai (Papua New Guinea)
Synonyms:	*Uncaria lanosa* Wall., *Uncaria glabrata* DC., *Uncaria setiloba* Benth.
Description:	It is a woody climber about 3 m long which grows in the rainforests of Thailand, Malaysia, Indonesia, Papua New Guinea, Australia, and the Pacific Islands. It climbs on trees especially near rivers. The stem is hairy, slender, 0.3 cm in diameter, with 6 cm long internodes, rusty and with a pair of hooks which are about 1.5 cm long and with a few tufts of hairs at the apex. The leaves are simple, decussate and stipulate. The stipules are hairy, bifid, about 0.3 cm long, and hairy. The petiole is hairy, channeled, and about 0.2 - 0.4 cm long. The leave blade is 7 - 9 cm x 4 - 5 cm, broadly lanceolate, hairy underneath, with 4 - 7 pairs of secondary nerves and a few tertiary nerves visible underneath. It is rounded to acute at the base, acuminate at the apex. The leaf blade is glabrous above except at the sunken midrib. The inflorescence is a globose head at the axil of pairs of hooks. The peduncle is about 2 cm long. The head is about 1.5 cm long. The flower is minute, yellowish to pinkish, tubular, and 5 lobed. The calyx is about 0.5 cm long, hairy, thin, with linear lobes. The corolla is 1 - 2 cm long and produces 5 linear lobes. The fruit is oblong and 0.8 - 1.2 cm long (Figure 276).
Medicinal Use:	In Malaysia, the plant is used to heal wounds and ulcers and to treat diarrhoea. In Papua New Guinea, the plant is used to break fever and assuage stomachache. In Indonesia, the plant West Sumatra, and used as a remedy for food poisoning.
Pharmacology:	The plant abounds with tannins such as $(2R,3S)$-(+)-catechin (Arbain *et al.*, 1998) which most likely account for the medicinal uses mentioned above. Uncaria species, including *Uncaria ferrea* DC. Elaborate a series of indole alkaloids of pharmacological interest (Heitzman *et al.*, 2005). These are oxindole alkaloids, uncarine C (pteropodine), D (speciophylline), E (isopteropodine), (Beecham *et al.*, 1968), glabratine (Arbain *et al.*, 1992), uncarine E, C, D, and deoxycordifoline (Arbain *et al.*, 1993), 14alpha-hydroxyrauniticine, and rauniticine (Arbain *et al.*, 1998), akuammigine, harmane, mitraphylline, isomitraphylline, and isomitraphylline N Oxide (Phillipson *et al.*, 1978; Tanahashi, *et al.*, 1997). An extract of the plant inhibited the growth of

Streptococcus aureus and *Escherichia coli* as evaluated by the disk diffusion method (Arret *et al.*, 1971). Pteropodine inhibited the proliferation of human lymphoblastic leukemia T cells (CCRF-CEM-C7H2) cultured *in vitro* via apoptosis (Bacher *et al.*, 2006) and positively modulated the function of rat muscarinic M(1) and 5-HT(2) receptors (Kang *et al.*, 2002). Deoxycordifoline displayed moderate acetylcholinesterase inhibitor activity *in vitro* (Cardoso *et al.*, 2004). Mitraphylline inhibited the growth of both on glioma GAMG and neuroblastoma SKN-BE(2) cell lines (García Prado *et al.*, 2007).

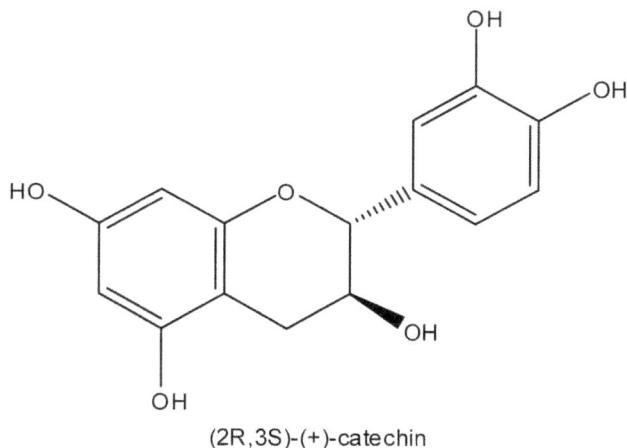

(2R,3S)-(+)-catechin

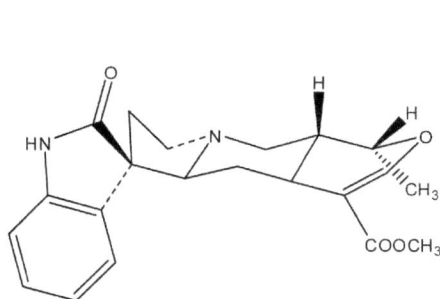

Mitraphylline

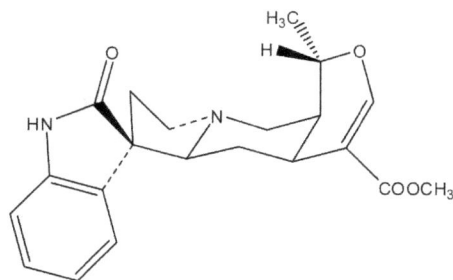

Pteropodine

References:

Arbain D, Byrne LT, Putra MM, Sargent MV, Syarif M, 1992, A new glucoalkaloid from *Uncaria glabrata*. J Chem Soc, Perkin Trans; 1: 665-666.

Arbain D, Putri MM, Sargent MV, Syarif M, 1993, The alkaloids of *Uncaria glabrata*. Austral J Chem; 46: 863-72.

Arbain D, Afrida X, Ibrahim S, Sargent MV, Skelton BW, White AH., 1998. The alkaloids of *Uncaria* cf. *glabrata*. Austral J Chem; 51: 961-64.

Arret B, Johnson DP, Kirshbaum A, 1971,Outline of details for microbiological assays of antibiotics. Second revision. J Pharm Sci; 60: 1689-94.

Bacher N, Tiefenthaler M, Sturm S, Stuppner H, Ausserlechner MJ, Kofler R, Konwalinka G., 2006, Oxindole alkaloids from *Uncaria tomentosa* induce apoptosis in proliferating, G0/G1-arrested and bcl-2-expressing acute lymphoblastic leukemia cells. Br J Haematol; 132: 615-22.

Beecham AF, Hart NK, Johns SR, Lamberton JA, 1968, Austral J Chem; 21: 491 - 504.

Cardoso CL, Castro-Gamboa I, Silva DH, Furlan M, Epifanio RA, Pinto AC, Moraes RC, Lima JA, Bolzani VS, 2004, Indole glucoalkaloids from *Chimarrhis turbinata* and their evaluation as antioxidant agents and acetylcholinesterase inhibitors. J Nat Prod; 67: 1882-5.

García Prado E, García Gimenez MD, De la Puerta Vázquez R, Espartero Sánchez JL, Sáenz Rodríguez MT, 2007, Antiproliferative effects of mitraphylline, a pentacyclic oxindole alkaloid of *Uncaria tomentosa* on human glioma and neuroblastoma cell lines.Phytomedicine; 14: 280-4.

Heitzman ME , Neto CC, Winiarz E, Vaisberg AJ, Hammond GB, 2005, Ethnobotany, phytochemistry and pharmacology of *Uncaria* (Rubiaceae). Phytochemistry; 66: 5-29.

Kang TH, Matsumoto K, Tohda M, Murakami Y, Takayama H, Kitajima M, Aimi N, Watanabe H, 2002, Pteropodine and isopteropodine positively modulate the function of rat muscarinic M(1) and 5-HT(2) receptors expressed in *Xenopus* oocyte. Eur J Pharmacol; 444: 39-45.

Phillipson JD, Hemingway SR, Ridsdale CE, 1978, Alkaloids of *Uncaria*. Part V. Their occurrence and chemotaxonomy. Lloydia; 41: 503-70.

Tanahashi T, Takenaka Y, Kobayashi C, Watsuji J, Nagakura N, Chen CC, 1997, Oxindole alkaloids from *Uncaria setiloba*. Nat Med; 51: 556.

Figure 276: *Uncaria ferrea* DC
From: Flora of Sabah, Herbarium of the Forest Department Sandakan, No SAN 101718.
Malaysia, Sabah, Sungai Mongkowogu Tongol, Kinabatangan district. Collector: Patrick *et al*.
Date of Collection: 21 September 1983, Side of logged area camp 1981.

Uncaria gambier Roxb.

[From Latin *uncus* = hooks and Malay *gambir* = gambier]

Local names:	Gambier; kancu, gambir (Malay, Indonesian), cachou cubique (France)
Synonym:	*Uncaria gambir* Roxb.
Description:	It is a climber crawling on trees in the rainforests of Malaysia, Borneo and Indonesia. The plant has commercial value as it is strongly tanniferous and many tons have been exported to Europe for tanning. The stem is glabrous, squarish, 0.8 mm in diameter, with few lenticels and the internodes are about 4 - 5 cm long. The leaves are simple, decussate with interpetiolar stipules. The stipules are about 0.5 cm long and broadly lanceolate. The petiole is flattish, 0.6 cm long and channeled. The leaf-blade is elliptic, 13 - 10 cm x 4 - 5.2 cm, thinly coriaceous, acuminate at the apex with a tail, acute at the base, with 4 - 5 pairs of secondary nerves, wavy at the margin, the midrib and secondary nerves sunken above, raised underneath. The tertiary nerves are numerous and scalariform underneath. Minute tufts of hairs are present at axils between midrib and secondary nerves. The inflorescence is an axillary globose head which is 4.5 cm in diameter on a 2.5 cm long peduncle. The calyx is hairy, 0.4 - 0.9 cm long with 5 minute round lobes. The corolla is tubular, 1.3 cm long, the tube slender, with 5 round lobes and light pinkish. The style protrudes out of the corolla tube and the anthers are visible between the lobes The fruit is a dehiscent capsule which is fusiform, striated, 1.3 - 1 cm x 0.4 cm on a 0.7 cm long pedicel. The fruit opens and exhibits a pair of membranaceous organs bifid at the apex (Figure 277).
Medicinal Uses:	A dried aqueous extract of the leaves and young shoots of *Uncaria gambier* (Hunt.) Roxb. (Catechu, *British Pharmaceutical Codex*, 1963), has been used in a mixture with chalk for the treatment of diarrhoea on account of its astringent property. Catechu Tincture (*British Pharmaceutical Codex*, 1963), has been used for the treatment of diarrhoea, as a styptic and an astringent gargle. It has also been used has lozenges and pastilles for the relief of relaxed conditions of the pharynx. In Malaysia, Gambier has been chewed with betel nut (*Areca catechu* L.), lime and the leaf of *Piper betle* L. for centuries as a social practice. It is used there medicinally for burns, to treat diarrhoea, and as a gargle for sore throat. In Indonesia, it is used as an astringent remedy.
Pharmacology:	The plant abounds with tannins of the proanthocyanidin type which account for the astringent property of the plant. Examples

of such tannins are dimeric proanthocyanidins, procyanidin B1, procyanidin B3, and gambiriin C (Taniguchi *et al.*, 2007). Tannins precipitate proteins and as such clean the intestine, heal wounds, check bleeding and assuage inflammation, but in the diet they are toxic above 5%. Proanthocyanidins are, on account of their polyphenolic nature strong antioxidants. They have antibacterial, antiviral and parasiticidal properties. They also inhibit the activity of countless enzymes and *in vivo* have been shown to lower blood pressure. A massive amount of publications on the bioactivity of proanthocyanidins are available and the topic is large enough to make a book on its own.

The plant contains also some alkaloids (Heitzman *et al.*, 2005) such as gambirdine and isogambirdine (Chan., 1968), gambirine, dihydrocorynantheine, rotundifoline, isorhynchophylline and rhynchophylline (Merlini *et al* 1972).

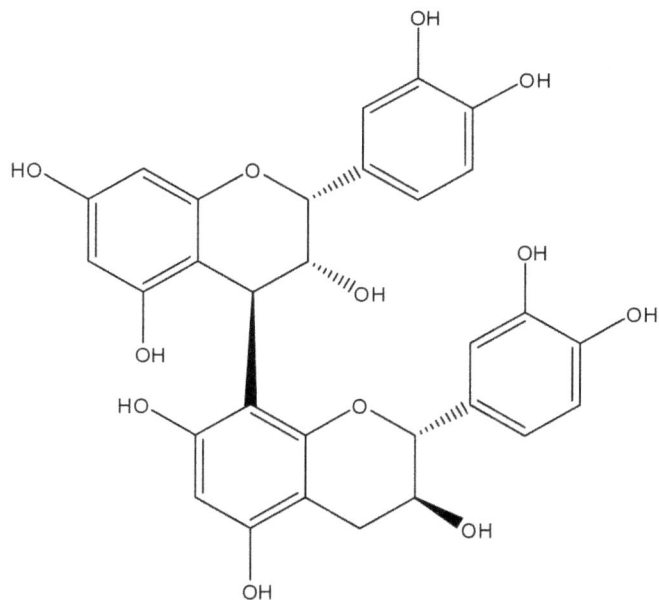

Procyanidin B1

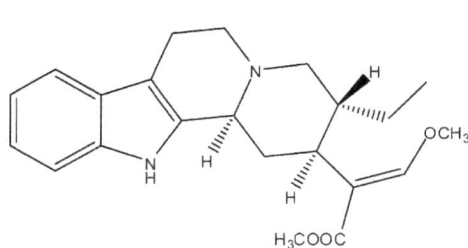

Dihydrocorynantheine

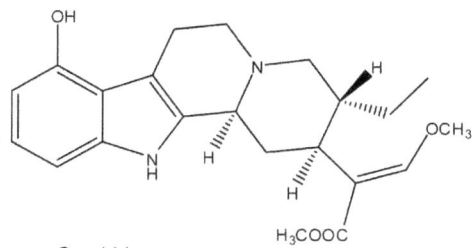

Gambirine

Gambirine injected into rodents caused a dose-related fall in both systolic and diastolic blood pressures as well as in heart rate (Mok *et al.*, 1992). Dihydrocorynantheine has cardiovascular effects on rodents (Chang *et al.*, 1989). Isorhynchophylline and rhynchophylline have interesting neurological effects as they both attenuated ischemia-induced neuronal damage in the hippocampus, and isorhynchophylline showed suppressive effects of on 5-HT2A receptor function in the brain (Kang *et al.*, 2004; Matsumoto *et al.*, 2005)

References:

Chan KC, 1968, Gambirdine and isogambirdine, the alkaloids from *Uncaria gambir* (Hunt) Roxb. Tetrahedron Lett; 30: 3403-6.

Chang P, Koh YK, Geh SL, Soepadmo E, Goh SH, Wong AK, 1989, Cardiovascular effects in the rat of dihydrocorynantheine isolated from *Uncaria callophylla*. J Ethnopharmacol; 25: 213-5.

Heitzman ME , Neto CC, Winiarz E, Vaisberg AJ, Hammond GB, 2005, Ethnobotany, phytochemistry and pharmacology of *Uncaria* (Rubiaceae). Phytochemistry; 66: 5-29.

Kang TH, Murakami Y, Takayama H, Kitajima M, Aimi N, Watanabe H, Matsumoto K, 2004,Protective effect of rhynchophylline and isorhynchophylline on *in vitro* ischemia-induced neuronal damage in the hippocampus: putative neurotransmitter receptors involved in their action. Life Sci; 76: 331-43.

Merlini L, Nasini G, Haddock RE, 1972, Indole alkaloids from *Uncaria gambir*. Phytochemistry; 11: 1525-26.

Matsumoto K, Morishige R, Murakami Y, Tohda M, Takayama H, Sakakibara I, Watanabe H, 2005, Suppressive effects of isorhynchophylline on 5-HT2A receptor function in the brain: behavioural and electrophysiological studies. Eur J Pharmacol; 517: 191-9.

Mok JSL, P. Chang P, Lee KH, Kam TS, Goh SH, 1992, Cardiovascular responses in the normotensive rat produced by intravenous injection of gambirine isolated from *Uncaria callophylla* Bl. ex Korth. J Ethnopharmacol; 36: 219-23.

Taniguchi S, Kuroda K, Doi K, Tanabe M, Shibata T, Yoshida T, Hatano T, 2007, Revised structures of gambiriins A1, A2, B1, and B2, chalcane-flavan dimers from gambir (*Uncaria gambir* extract). Chem Pharm Bull (Tokyo); 55: 268-72.

Figure 277: *Uncaria gambier* Roxb.
From: Flora of Sabah. Tree Flora Sabah-Sarawak Expedition.
Malaysia, Sabah, Sandakan, Telupid, Sungai Meilau off Sungai Karamuak, south trail. Elevation 100m in lowland dipterocarp forest.Collection and determination: A. Zainuddin. Date of Collection: 6 April 1994.

Urophyllum glabrum Wall.

[From Greek *oura* = tail and *phullon* = leaf and from Latin *glaber* = free from hair]

Local names:	Common urophyllum; pokok kekaran, merembong jantan, kopi-kopi. (Malaysia), ki chengkeh (Indonesia)
Synonym:	*Urophyllum arboreum* (Reinw. ex Bl.) Korth.
Description:	It is a small tree which grows to a height of 5 m in the lowland to lower hilly forests of Malaysia, Thailand, and Indonesia. The plant has a clove - like odour. The stem is terete, glabrous, and slender with internodes which are about 4 cm long. The leaves are simple, decussate and with interpetiolar stipules. The stipule is linear, oblong, lanceolate and velvety. The petiole is channeled and hairy and 1.25 cm long. The leaf-blade is 10 - 17 cm x 5 - 6 cm, thinly coriaceous, tapering at the base and acuminate at the apex, recurved at the margin, with 5 -11 pairs of secondary nerves. The midrib and secondary nerves are sunken above and raised underneath the leaf blade, the tertiary nerves are scalariform and visible underneath. The inflorescence is an axillary hairy cyme which is about 2 cm long with few flowers. The calyx is cup - shaped, 0.2 cm long. The corolla is yellowish-green and 5-lobed. The fruit is round, 0.4 - 0.7 cm in diameter, bright orange and opened at the apex (Figure 278).
Medicinal Uses:	In Malaysia, a maceration of the leaves is used to allay fever. In Indonesia, the leaves are used to flavour food and to treat a number of diseases.
Pharmacology:	Unknown.

Figure 278: *Urophyllum glabrum* Wall.
From: Herbarium of University Kebangsaan Malaysia N° 25298.
Malaysia, Negeri Sembilan state, Pasoh, main trail to tree tower. Date of collection: 20 July 1989. Collection and Identification: A Zainuddin AZ 2930.

Urophyllum hirsutum (Wight) Hk.f

[From Greek *oura* = a tail and *phullon*= leaf and from Latin *hirsutum* = hirsute]

Local names:	Kayau empau, kayuh bluti, kayuh uru uta (Malaysia)
Description:	It is a small tree which grows in the open forests of Malaysia, Indonesia and Singapore. The stem is squarrish, slender, 0.25 cm in diameter, and hirsute and with internodes which are about 3 cm long. The leaves are simple, decussate with interpetiolar stipules. The interpetiolar stipule is linear, up to 1 cm long, hirsute and deciduous. The petiole is hairy and 0.3 - 0.5 cm long. The leaf blade is 13 - 9 cm x 3 - 4.5 cm, membranaceous, elliptic lanceolate with 5 - 7 pairs of secondary nerves, acuminate at the apex, acute at the base, hairy underneath, the midrib sunken above with 6 - 10 pairs of secondary nerves and some scalariform tertiary nerves. The inflorescence is an axillary cyme with hairy pedicels. The fruits are globose berries which are about 0.5 cm in diameter on a 0.3 cm hirsute pedicel, with four obscure lobes at the apex around a tiny opening (Figure 279).
Medicinal Uses:	Malays make a drink from this plant which is taken after childbirth.
Pharmacology:	Unknown

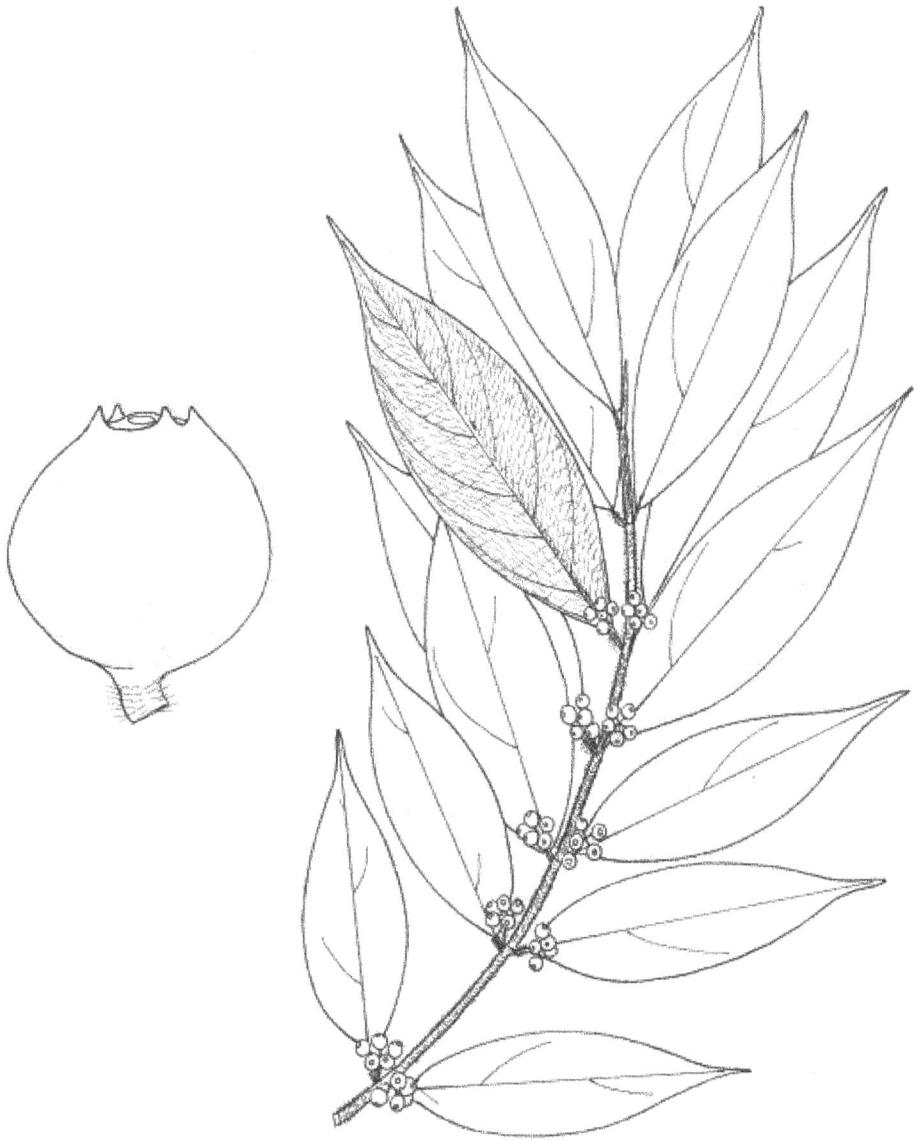

Figure 279: *Urophyllum hirsutum* (Wight) Hook.
From: Forest Research Institute of Malaysia (FRIM)
Malaysia, Kepong. Collection and identification: Date of Collection: 9 September 1987.
Identification: K. Wong.5 October 1983.
& from: Herbarium of University Kebangsaan Malaysia, Nº 01234.
Malaysia, Bangi. Date of collection17 May 1973. Collection: Mohd. Kassim

Conclusion

In this book I have managed to provide as much information as is possible on 290 medicinal plants growing in the East. Many more species await to be described. The number of plants which is yet awaiting full pharmacological investigation illustrates the fact that the medicinal plants of the East have to be seen as an "untapped chemical and pharmacological treasure". However, this treasure is being destroyed slowly and steadily. Therefore there is an urgent need to initiate further studies before the disappearance of plant species that could prove to be invaluable in the future as a source of drugs for cancer, AIDS and other fatal illnesses. We should therefore continue our research efforts into plants as a source of pharmaceutical compounds. Nature herself will continue to generate new diseases and render inactive our present drugs. It is a race against time and no one should have much confidence in the future health of Humanity unless something is done.

I firmly believe that somewhere, in the East, exist some plants containing substances that will put a definitive end to the inexorable route of fatal illnesses. I believe that one day Humanity will win the fight against cancer, microbial infections and other fatal conditions. Call me an utopist if you wish but the wonderful biodiversity of plants combined with the rapid growth of technologies will make that utopia a reality. In fact, it should have already happened. The number of pharmacological studies and the number of active principles isolated from plants since the sixties is enormous but yet in the end we have few molecules of clinical value. The last hundred years have been the theatre of tremendous engineering and technological progress but in terms of drug discovery it has been much slower. Of course antibiotics and other drugs have been found, but the number of diseases for which there is no cure is still unacceptably high. In the case of cancer, doctors are too often unable to treat their patients and are waiting for effective drugs. One can survive with HIV but the disease itself should be stopped instead of remaining. One can see the emergence of pandemic influenza virus infections within the coming decades and suitable drugs are not available. Neurodegenerative diseases are also often incurable and in some cases are synonyms for a death sentence. Bacterial and mycobacterial infections can be treated but the day will come when antibiotics will become ineffective due to increasing resistance. It is a disturbing thought that something is not quite right, and that we should have more drugs by now. Unfortunately, the major pharmaceutical companies are frequently not very attracted to drugs based on natural products.

I hope that this book will provide the reader with some information and concepts that will contribute to the discovery of drugs from plants. I wrote this book for those who have the will to find cures from plants and for those who are awaiting the commercialization of new drugs. The drugs are there, in the cloudy rainforest of the East, it is now up to you to find them.

Alphabetical list of plant names

www.ingramcontent.com/pod-product-compliance
Lightning Source LLC
Chambersburg PA
CBHW051945270326
41929CB00015B/2540